GROUP COUNSELING FOR SCHOOL COUNSELORS: A Practical Guide

Second Edition

Greg Brigman
and
Barbara Earley Goodman

J. WESTON

WALCH

PUBLISHER

Portland, Maine

User's Guide
to
Walch Reproducible Books

As part of our general effort to provide educational materials that are as practical and economical as possible, we have designated this publication a "reproducible book." The designation means that purchase of the book includes purchase of the right to limited reproduction of all pages on which this symbol appears:

Here is the basic Walch policy: We grant to individual purchasers of this book the right to make sufficient copies of reproducible pages for use by all students of a single teacher. This permission is limited to a single teacher and does not apply to entire schools or school systems, so institutions purchasing the book should pass the permission on to a single teacher. Copying of the book or its parts for resale is prohibited.

Any questions regarding this policy or requests to purchase further reproduction rights should be addressed to:

Permissions Editor
J. Weston Walch, Publisher
321 Valley Street • P.O. Box 658
Portland, Maine 04104-0658

1   2   3   4   5   6   7   8   9   10

ISBN 0-8251-4276-8

Contents

Part 4: Group Plans for All Levels

About the Authors

Barbara Earley Goodman, Ed.S., LPC, NCC, is a two-time national award-winning middle school counselor in Hall County, Georgia. Mrs. Goodman is an adjunct professor at Georgia State University in Atlanta, Georgia, and an education staff development trainer.

Greg Brigman, Ph.D., LPC, is a professor in the Department of Counselor Education at Florida Atlantic University in Boca Raton, Florida. Dr. Brigman is also a two-time national award-winning school counselor.

Contributing Authors

We want to thank the following authors who contributed chapters. We are very proud of the group plans these professionals designed for this book. It was a great learning experience to collaborate with this talented group of counselors. We know that school counselors will appreciate the practical and easy-to-use style of each group plan.

Lori Bednarek, M.Ed., is an elementary school counselor and teacher in Palm Beach County, Florida.

Doreen Cammarata, M.S., L.M.H.C., is an adjunct instructor at Florida Atlantic University for a graduate course focusing on educating professionals on grief counseling issues. She is also a school counselor for at-risk youth and is a grief and bereavement specialist working with adults and children at a local hospice program. She is the author of a book for children survivors of suicide, *When Someone You Love Commits Suicide*.

Chari Campbell, Ph.D., is an assistant professor in the Department of Counselor Education at Florida Atlantic University. Dr. Campbell is a former school counselor at all three levels and is the co-author of the *National Standards for School Counseling Programs*.

Michelle Feldman, M.Ed., is an elementary school counselor in Palm Beach County, Florida.

Maryanne Brannigan Grimes, Ed.S., is a high school counselor in Gwinnett County, Georgia.

Wes Hawkins, Ph.D., is a professor in the department of social work at Florida Atlantic University. Dr. Hawkins has developed curricula for group work with adolescents and has conducted numerous related research studies.

John Patrick Huerta, Ed.S., is a middle school counselor in Gwinnett County, Georgia.

Anya F. Koszas, M.Ed., is a high school counselor and director of guidance in Volusia County, Florida.

Mary Mills, M.Ed., is a high school counselor in Volusia County, Florida.

Donna Steinberg, M.Ed., is an elementary school counselor in Palm Beach County, Florida.

Introduction

The second edition of *Group Counseling for School Counselors* incorporates the growth in our understanding of how to effectively help children and adolescents deal with the most common issues they face. Since the first edition, there have been extensive reviews of research on successful youth, at-risk youth, resiliency, developing competence, social skills, learning skills interventions, and the efficacy of group counseling with children and adolescents.

Our goal has been to translate the research into practical, easy-to-use tools. Readers will find, in this edition, fourteen new groups with over 100 new group session plans. Based on the current research literature, the authors believe that the types of groups described in this second edition are the most effective interventions counselors have in helping youth with a wide variety of issues.

Group Counseling for School Counselors is a practical, step-by-step guide to leading effective groups for children and adolescents. It is designed for counselors, psychologists, and social workers interested in helping young people develop the skills, attitudes, and beliefs needed for success in school and in life.

The research-based topics, group format, and activities are field-tested, easy to use, and well received by young people. Some of the keys that have emerged from the research literature, which are embedded into the group plans, include:

- a structured, focused approach
- weekly goal setting
- progress monitoring
- modeling and coaching
- interactive application learning
- critical life skills

The group plans are divided into four sections: High School, Middle School, Elementary School, and All Levels. Each section has group plan categories that were carefully selected to address the issues most frequently encountered by students at this level. The group topics focus on the most critical learning, social, and self-management skills needed at the different levels for academic and social success. Also included at all three levels are group plans on dealing with loss/bereavement and parent divorce, two issues faced by a significant number of children and adolescents.

Group Counseling with Children and Adolescents: Why, What, and How

Group Counseling: Why?

There are many compelling reasons for school counselors to provide a solid group counseling program, including:

STRONG RESEARCH BASE—IT WORKS

Group counseling with children and adolescents works. Prout and Prout (1999) reviewed the research literature on counseling interventions with children and adolescents in schools over the last decade and found a distinct positive effect for group counseling. In well-controlled research studies, students receiving group counseling in schools were better off than 97 percent of comparison students. Borders and Drury (1992) reviewed 30 years of research on the effect of school counselors on student achievement, behavior, and attitudes. Group counseling was found to be effective in each of these three areas. In other reviews of the efficacy of counseling with children and adolescents, group counseling was as effective as, if not more effective than, individual counseling (Casey and Berman, 1985; Prout and DeMartino, 1986; Weisz et al., 1987; and Weisz et al., 1995).

NATURAL MEDIUM FOR LEARNING AND SUPPORT

Humans are social beings who live and work in groups. Groups provide a microcosm of a student's world in which students can practice new behaviors that are more constructive and adaptive.

ROLE MODELS FOR POSITIVE BEHAVIORS AND ATTITUDES

Modeling is one of the most effective learning tools. Groups provide multiple models. In groups there is more access to insights, confirming, and corrective messages than in individual counseling.

In addition, group counseling is considered a primary role of school counselors by the American School Counselor Association. Groups allow counselors to help more students. Without a solid group counseling program school counselors quickly become overwhelmed with individual counseling needs. School counselors are interested in providing the most effective and efficient services to help students. Therefore groups are a must for schools.

Group Counseling: What?

TYPES

Most school counselors offer groups on topics that represent the most frequent presenting problems or needs of children and adolescents. Group topics in schools also reflect the mission of the school: to help students learn the academic and social skills needed for success in living, working, and learning.

The most common types of groups offered by experienced school counselors include groups that focus on:

- social skills
- learning skills
- self-control/anger management
- divorce
- loss
- school adjustment/transition

The first three of these topics are in line with a recent review of research by Masten and Coatsworth (1998). They reviewed 25 years of research on developing competence and on successful and resilient children and adolescents and found three groups of skills that separated successful students from those who were not successful: Cognitive/learning skills, social skills, and self-regulation skills.

Another extensive review of research, covering 50 years, by Wang, Haertel, and Walberg (1994), focused on what helps students learn. They found similar skill areas, especially cognitive/learning skills and social skills, to be the most associated with school success. Group counseling involving these three skill areas are a must for any comprehensive school counseling program.

The encouraging news from these research reviews is that the skills students need to succeed academically and socially—and the model for teaching them these skills—are clear. The teaching model is based on Bandura's social learning model and involves a "tell, show, do, coach" approach. The group plans in this book follow this model, and many of the plans mirror the most critical skills found in these research reviews.

The last three group topics listed above—divorce, loss, and transition—represent areas of high need in most schools. Providing group counseling to address these needs is an effective and efficient way to help support students who are new to a school or school level or who have had a family change or loss.

Group Counseling: How?

Successful school counselors use both formal and informal needs assessments to determine which and how many groups to offer at what times. School counselors should be aware of the skills and information students need in order to be successful in the areas of learning, living, and working (see previous page under Types of Groups), and should base at least some counseling groups on these topics.

School counselors also make sure students, teachers, and parents are aware of the types of groups that are offered and know how to sign up to participate. School counselors provide information on group topics to students and teachers during classroom presentations and by posting flyers around the school. For parents, counselors make presentations during parent meetings and provide information through newsletters.

BUILD SUPPORT FOR GROUPS
- Tie group topics to the mission of the school and school improvement plan.
- Tie group topics to the most critical skills needed for student success.
- Tie group topics to providing the support students need to continue to learn.
- Tie group topics to increased achievement and prosocial behavior.
- Tie group topics to decreased antisocial behavior.
- Tie group topics to needs identified by teachers, parents, administrators, and students.

PLAN SESSIONS BASED ON RESEARCH AND SOUND THEORY
- 1–3 objectives for each session
- Strategies/activities for each objective
- Process questions and goal setting

Focused, structured, and goal-oriented group sessions have a better success rate and fit better with the mission of schools than those that are not. Effective counselors know the purpose of each group and have carefully developed group plans to facilitate teaching skills to children and adolescents. They are also careful to base each group on the research base rather than on activities that may be appealing but do not lead to positive student behavior change.

WHEN PLANNING GROUP LOGISTICS, "BEGIN WITH THE END IN MIND"

Remember that the purpose of group counseling is to help students improve in measurable ways. Set yourself and the group up for success by following the following logistical guidelines:

Length of group
- 8–12 sessions
- 30–60 minutes
- monthly follow-ups—booster sessions

Most effective groups have a minimum of eight sessions. Depending on age, the time per session varies from 30 minutes for primary students to 60 minutes for adolescents. Because the focus of most groups is on skill building and skill transfer, booster sessions have become prevalent. Wilson (1982) found the following success rates for various length groups for students at risk of academic failure:

- 8 or fewer sessions: success rate 1 of 5
- 9–12 sessions: success rate 5 of 9
- over 12 sessions: success rate 6 of 8

Based on experience and research such as Wilson's, many experienced school counselors provide booster sessions, usually spaced one month apart, after the regular eight-session group in order to achieve a high rate of success.

GROUP SIZE AND COMPOSITION

Group size is determined by the age of the students and the purpose of the group. Generally, the younger the students, the smaller the group. Most groups include 4–8 students. One or more "role models" (model students who are respected by their peers) are included in most groups. According to Myrick (1998), "experienced school counselors prefer to work with 5–6 and no more than 7–8. Having fewer members allows more participation by each person in the group."

Once you have developed a system for providing group counseling, it is important that you maintain its structure. Canceling or postponing sessions will impair the integrity of the program. If group counseling is to become one of the educational objectives of your school, students, teachers, parents, and administrators must understand what it is and know what to expect from it.

PRE-GROUP SCREENING
- Select only those students you feel reasonably certain can be helped in your group and who want to participate.

- Explain the purpose, benefits, logistics, expectations, and limits of the group.
- Use heterogeneous grouping. Select models when appropriate. Avoid loading a group with behavior problems.

Pre-group screening is essential. It is required by the code of ethics of the Association of Specialists in Group Work, the American School Counseling Association, and the American Counseling Association. Pre-group screening allows the student to understand the nature of the group and decide if he or she wants to participate. It also allows the counselor time to assess whether or not this particular group is appropriate at this time for this student.

Assuming that the counselor and student agree that the group is a good fit, a parent information letter describing the group should be given to the student to take home, have signed, and return. With older students some counselors prefer to send the letter home but not require that it be returned. This type of letter asks the parents to call the counselor if they have questions or concerns about the group. Each school district and school has a policy on informing parents about group participation. It is important for the counselor to know the prevailing policy.

FORMAT FOR SMALL GROUP COUNSELING PLANS

The following format is used for all plans in this book. It provides a simple and practical structure around which to build effective group plans. The format stresses self-monitoring, skill building through role-play and other active learning strategies, and transfer of skills to students' regular life.

Beginning

- Review last session.
- Check on student goals—applying lessons to their life.
- Check temperature of group, check on overall functioning—i.e., ask students to rate on a 1–10 scale how things are going on topics such as grades, homes, peers, teachers, fun, rest, exercise, diet.
- Preview today.

Middle

- Involve students in pair and whole group discussions.
- Ask before telling—related to today's topic.
- Provide some new information and ask students to personalize—which ideas would be most helpful/useful to you?
- Apply ideas in role-play and/or storytelling with multiple endings, provide feedback and coaching.
- Use a variety of mediums, e.g., art, music, games, bibliotherapy.

End

- Discuss what thoughts and feelings students had during the role-play/activity.
- Ask students to reflect on what the group did today, and what they learned or relearned.
- Ask them to commit to trying/applying some idea/skill from today's group meeting.

BUILDING SUCCESS INTO YOUR GROUPS

The last step in making your groups successful is to continuously monitor the impact on students.

What did you hope would happen when you designed the group? What are the goals for students who participate? How can you determine if the groups are working? Different groups require different measures of success.

Collecting simple data to show the positive impact of the group is essential to maintaining support for the group counseling program. This information will also tell the counselor when a group needs updating or changing.

Evaluate impact of group on stated objectives

- Pre/post student survey
- Pre/post teacher/parent survey
- Pre/post scores on grades or standardized achievement test already being administered by school

SUMMARY

- Conduct needs assessment.
- Develop written structured plan.
- Gain support/advertise group.
- Conduct pre-group screening.
- Implement research-based group plan.
- Evaluate impact of group and report findings.

Getting Started

1. Explain the group offerings to the students during the first two or three weeks of class when you are informing them of the different counseling services available. Leave sign-up forms in each class and have a box or basket at your office door where students can pick up or turn in their forms.

2. Develop or review lesson plans for groups you will offer. The groups offered should meet the needs of your school. The lesson plans in this book were developed based on: 1) needs assessments from teachers, students, parents, and administrators; 2) developmental theory; 3) counseling research; and 4) accepted practices endorsed by the American Association of School Counselors.

3. Around the end of September, send a referral sheet out to teachers. Let parents know about the groups through PTA presentations and newsletters.

4. By the time you get teacher referral forms and student and parent requests back, you will probably realize you have more students than you can handle. Keep a list of students who are not included in the first round of groups. Send them a note explaining that the group is filled and they will be placed on a list for the next group. It is important to plan several cycles of groups each year so that there are always groups available. Many experienced counselors offer the first series of groups in October, a second cycle in January, and a final cycle in March.

5. Conduct pre-group interviews or screening.

6. Send invitations/reminders on the morning of the first meeting.

Before the First Meeting: Pre-Group Screening

There are several reasons to meet individually with students who have been recommended by teachers and parents for group counseling:

1. To determine the appropriateness of the particular group for this student. It is your decision to determine who will be in the group. Certain students might be detrimental to the progress of the group. When teachers ask why a certain student isn't in your group, you can say, "It is not appropriate for him/her to be in this group. I am seeing him/her individually and I am working with his/her parents."

2. To give information about the nature of the group and your expectations regarding attendance, confidentiality, and so forth.

3. To gain commitment from the student regarding attendance, participation, and confidentiality. (Participation should be voluntary. If the student decides not to participate, advise the referring parent or teacher that when or if the student decides to voluntarily join the group, this service will be available, as soon as the next group begins.)

4. To help the student identify a goal(s) to work on in the group.

5. To clarify the student's expectations about the nature of the group.

6. To comply with ethical standards of the counseling profession (ACA, ASCA, AGSW).

This screening meeting usually takes approximately 10–15 minutes. Set aside a two-hour block per group for these interviews. If the student agrees to participate, the student is asked to take a group information or consent form home.

Here is an outline for a screening meeting:

Pre-Group Interview Outline

1. Introduction
   (a) General description of group (number of meetings, topics, and so forth)
   (b) Why the student is being asked to participate
   (c) Participation is voluntary.

2. What the student can gain from participating
   (a) Meet new people.
   (b) Work on goals.
   (c) Learn new skills.
3. Goal(s)
   (a) Help student select a general goal (goal more defined during group meetings).
   (b) Goals may change and are the business of the student.
4. Expectations
   (a) Attendance, participation, and confidentiality
   (b) Check student expectations.
5. Explain the parent and teacher forms and when they must be returned to the counselor.
6. Brief summary and emphasis on positive aspects of group

The screening process puts you in a better position to decide who is appropriate for the kind of groups you are offering. No one else can make this decision as skillfully as you. You know best your skills, the nature of the students participating, the content of the group, and the readiness of each individual screened.

What to Expect at Different Stages

It is helpful to be aware of the stages of group development as you prepare to lead your groups. We offer the following summary of three group stages to help you in your planning.

Stage 1: Trust—Orientation

In this stage, students get to know each other, establish trust, and decide how they fit into the group and how involved they will be. It usually takes 2–3 sessions for students to learn each others' names and to feel comfortable about being in the group. The leader provides more structured activities at this stage, and helps students identify goals.

Stage 2: Work—Productivity

The working stage is when the most insights and behavior changes occur. In an eight-session group, sessions 3–7 will contain most of the "work" of the group. This is the time when goals are acted on outside of the group and experimenting with behavior occurs inside the group. If the necessary conditions of trust, empathy, and hope have developed, students will gain from feedback, confrontation, and increased self-awareness and self-disclosure.

Stage 3: Closure—Consolidation

The consolidation stage begins by session 7 of an eight-session group. There is usually a feeling of community—sharing and caring—if sessions 1–6 have been successful. The need to summarize, solidify changes, carry learning over to the world outside the group, and attain closure characterize this stage. Session 8 might elicit responses like "I wish it wasn't over" and "Can we do this again?" It seems that just when you get a group going in the right direction, it's time to stop. Many experienced counselors decide to continue the group through booster sessions spaced a month apart to maintain gains. The benefits for some students will be wonderfully evident, and for others you will never know.

Process Questions for Each Stage

Here are some process questions for the different stages of group development.

STAGE 1: TRUST—ORIENTATION

Note: Most of the process questions for the Trust stage are used during pre-group screening and the first two sessions.

- What do you want to achieve by participating in this group?
- What are some concerns, doubts, and fears you have about being in this group?
- What would you most like to say you have learned at the end of this group?
- What do you need to give in order to get what you want from this group?
- What rules do we need to work out together in order to feel safe and enjoy ourselves?

STAGE 2: WORK—PRODUCTIVITY

Note: The process questions below for the Work stage should be used starting with the first session.

- How did you feel during this activity?
- What did you learn from this experience?
- How can you apply what you have learned today?

- What can you do this week to practice what you have learned?

STAGE 3: CLOSURE—CONSOLIDATION

- What are some of the most important things you have learned about yourself?
- How can you continue to practice what you have learned?

- What is one way you have changed during this group?
- What has been the most helpful part of this group for you?
- What is a goal you have set for yourself?
- How do you feel about the group ending?

Group Leadership Skills: Keys to Success

One of the most important ingredients for successful group counseling is the skill of the group leader. Take time to honestly evaluate your skill level, experience, and course-work background. There is no substitute for supervised practice. Developing your skills is an ongoing process. Jim Gumaer, in an article in *Journal for Specialists in Group Work* (1986), stated that "at a minimum level, graduating counselors should have passed successfully a group theory course, a group counseling practicum, and a supervised internship involving several counseling groups. . . ." If you do not have this background, we strongly recommend that you obtain it. In addition, it is very helpful to co-lead groups. If you are the only counselor in your school, try co-leading a group with another counselor or therapist in your area.

The group leadership skills that follow are basic and very effective. Listening to or watching a tape of your group session and identifying which skills you used or did not use can be a powerful way to recognize your strengths and weaknesses. Sharing your tape with a small group of trusted counselors in a peer coaching context or having a qualified counselor give you feedback can also be extremely beneficial.

Group Leadership Skills

PERSONALIZING

There are two important parts to this skill. The first is making sure that the group is sitting in a circle so that everyone can see everyone else's face without having to move. The second is making sure that you know the names of all group members and using their names frequently when responding to their comments. Encourage group members to use names when they respond to one another.

STRUCTURING

This skill is used to **explain the topic and time limit**. An important part of structuring is providing a rationale

for an activity. The rationale needs to be framed from a student's point of view. The rationale clarifies the benefits to students and creates interest and motivation. Structuring occurs at the beginning of a group session and whenever a new activity or topic is introduced.

This skill is also used to **redirect** or get the discussion back on the topic when it digresses.

Example: "For the next few minutes we'll be discussing friendship." When Maria starts getting off the topic, you might say, "I'd like to hear about that, Maria, but I'm concerned that we won't finish if we don't move on."

MODELING AND COACHING

In the most simple form modeling is going first and showing the group how you want them to respond.

Example: "This is what I want you to do. . . . (then demonstrate) Is everyone ready? Good, I'll go first."

Modeling is central to role-play and role-play is central to skills building. Students are able to learn faster and at a deeper level when they can see multiple models performing specific target behavior. Whether the topic is managing conflicts, refusal skills, or learning skills, using the "tell, show, do, coach" model is a powerful group skill. Effective group leaders not only provide a powerful model themselves but look for opportunities for students to become models.

Providing **supportive and corrective feedback** (coaching) is a very important part of skill teaching. Teaching group members to give coaching feedback is very useful. Before giving feedback we recommend asking the student doing the role-play to comment on what he or she liked and if there is anything that might be changed next time. After the role-player finishes, the leader and other group members give feedback.

The model we use is the **sandwich approach**. First, supportive feedback: strengths, positive, helpful behavior are pointed out: "I liked the way you . . .", "I thought the way you . . . was very helpful." This is the first slice of bread of the sandwich. Next, corrective feedback: non-helpful behaviors are pointed out in a respectful way and alternatives are suggested: "You may want to consider changing . . .", "Instead you may want to try . . .", "What are some other ideas the group has?" This is the sandwich filling.

Last is the second piece of bread—more supportive feedback. To finish the feedback process give a summary of the supportive feedback offered and some comment about your faith in the student using the feedback to continue to improve.

CONNECTING

Connecting helps to build a sense of belonging and acceptance by helping the participants to see that others share their ideas and concerns.

Examples:

"Who else has had that experience?"

"How many of you have ever felt that way?"

Another way to connect is to link the comments of the participants. "Juan, that sounds a lot like what Venetta was saying earlier." "Carl, I've noticed that you and Jim enjoy doing a lot of the same things. Can anyone else remember an idea some of us had in common?"

EMPATHIC RESPONDING

To encourage participants to discuss freely, it is important to reinforce their comments through empathic responses. The leader paraphrases the participant's comment and tries to reflect the underlying feeling. This is an important skill to teach all group members.

Examples:

"OK, Maria, thank you for sharing that. I could tell you were very angry about your friend setting you up."

"So, Carl, you like to be with people who share some of your interests and feel bored and on edge when you are around people who don't."

"Jenny, you seem to feel pretty excited about that."

This skill is especially important at the beginning of a group. It sets the tone. Making it safe to respond is critical.

INVOLVING EVERYONE

Several simple techniques can be used to get everyone involved.

The **go-round** lets everyone know you expect a response from each group member. When using the go-round, give some time before beginning. The leader usu-

ally goes first: "I'd like you to think of some qualities you look for in a friend. I'll give you a moment to think of two or three, then we will go around and hear the ideas from each of you." Or: "For the next few minutes I'd like us to think of things we enjoy doing for fun. I will give you a minute to think of three or four things, then we will go around the circle and hear from everyone."

If a group member does not have a response when the time comes, ask; "Would you like me to come back to you?" or "I'll check back with you in a minute." In addition, good eye contact and looking interested in each comment, nodding your head, and asking follow-up questions are important ways to keep participants involved.

The **hand-raise technique** simply involves asking participants to raise their hands if the statement applies. Often the request to raise your hand is given nonverbally when the leader models raising a hand. "How many of you have ever been in a group where one person tried to dominate?" (leader raises a hand).

Using **pair share** is a low threat way of getting high involvement. Ask students to share their ideas on a topic with a partner. Then ask pairs to report back to the group what they discussed.

In addition to the go-round, the "How many of you" hand-raise questions, and the pair share, remember to model the nonverbal behaviors of eye contact, leaning forward, and looking interested, and to ask follow-up, clarifying questions. Teach these important skills to the group and remind them to use them. Regularly provide feedback on your observations of their use of these skills.

SUMMARIZING AND GOAL SETTING

This skill can be used during the discussion or at the end. The leader can summarize or ask participants to summarize. The summary brings the focus back to the purpose of the discussion. An open-ended and personalized summary is often effective.

Example:

"We are almost out of time, and I would like for us to think about what we have talked about and have been doing. What can you remember?"

The leader fills in any gaps: "To end, I would like you to complete these two sentences: 'One thing I learned or relearned today was . . .' and 'One way I can use what I learned this week is . . .' I'll give you a minute to think, then ask you to share with a partner, and finally I'll ask for volunteers to share with the group."

In order for these skills to be effective, the group leader must communicate certain attitudes/qualities:

- acceptance
- caring
- being nonjudgmental
- warmth
- friendliness
- enthusiasm

Your caring and support, your leadership skills, the topics you choose to focus on, and the way you structure sessions will have a powerful impact on your groups. We believe that the group format is the most effective tool in a counselor's bag of interventions. We wish you the best in your work with student groups.

Reproducible
Sample Forms
for Groups

The following sample forms provide tools for the counselor, which may be modified to fit any of the group plans contained in this book and most of the types of groups offered by experienced counselors. The counselor leading each group should decide what changes (if any) need to be made to fit the sample form to the particular group.

Forms included in this section are:

- Referral for Group Counseling
- Group Membership Agreement
- Parent Permission Form
- Parent Permission Form for Participation in Anger Management Group
- Letter to Parents
- Group Attendance
- Feeling Faces
- Group Evaluation

Teacher _____ Date _____

Referral for Group Counseling

Please select, from the list below, the group that best fits each student you are referring.

Group counseling topics

- Student success skills (academic and social skills)
- Handling conflicts
- Self-control and anger management
- Bereavement
- Divorce

Student Name	Group Counseling Program	Reason for Referral (Be as specific as possible)

Group Membership Agreement

_____ has my permission to be in
(Student's name)

_____, which meets for _____ weeks
(Group name)

on _____ from _____ to _____ beginning _____.
(Day)   (Time)   (Time)   (Date)

_____
Teacher's Signature

_____

I _____ agree that it is my
(Student's name)

responsibility to get any assignments I miss while in the group.

   I also agree to let the counselor know if I am unable to attend any of the meetings due to tests, reports, and so forth.

_____
Student's Signature

*Teachers: After signing, please return to counselors.

Parent Permission Form

Dear _____
      (Parent's name)

_____ has been recommended for our _____ group by
      (Student's name)

_____. I have met with your son/daughter and explained the
      (Teacher's name)

content and nature of the group. The group consists of eight sessions, meeting once a week for 45 minutes. During these sessions we will be working on:

1. _____

2. _____

3. _____

4. _____

5. _____

6. _____

    If you have any questions or comments, please feel free to contact me. We want you to be informed of your child's activities. Thank you for your support in our mutual goals of raising competent, healthy, and successful children,

Sincerely,

Counselor

Return to counselor (check one).

_____ My child may participate in these counseling sessions.

_____ My child may not participate in these counseling sessions.

Parent's signature _____

Group Counseling for School Counselors: A Practical Guide

Parent Permission Form
for Participation in Anger Management Group

Dear _____:

_____ has been recommended to participate in an anger management counseling group that I will facilitate this year. I have met with your son/daughter and explained the content and nature of the group. This group will meet once a week. Your child is aware that he/she will miss a different class every week and he/she is responsible for obtaining make-up work from teachers. The group will be working on achieving these goals:

- Recognize the feeling of anger
- Understand the student's own anger style
- Identify what triggers the student's anger
- Learn to use constructive ways to deal with anger
- Prevent inappropriate ways of dealing with anger
- Practice effective ways to manage angry feelings

Since counseling is based on a trusting relationship between counselor and client, all information shared by group members is kept confidential except in certain situations in which there is an ethical responsibility to limit confidentiality. If a student reveals information about hurting himself/herself or another person, the parent will be notified.

Sincerely,

School Counselor

_____

By signing this form, I give my informed consent for my child to participate in small group counseling. I understand that:

1. The group will provide an opportunity for members to learn and practice interpersonal skills, discuss feelings, share ideas, practice new behaviors, and make new friends.

2. Anything group members share in group will be kept confidential by the group leader except in the above mentioned cases.

Parent's signature _____ Date: _____

Student's signature _____ Date: _____

Group Counseling for School Counselors: A Practical Guide

Letter to Parents

Dear Parents:

The counseling program at _____ is designed to
(Name of school)
be preventive and developmental. In addition to seeing students individually and in classroom guidance, we teach skills and information in small-group settings.

Your child, _____, has expressed an interest in participating in the _____ group. We emphasize to students that groups are for everyone, and participating does not indicate a problem. Groups are structured and goal focused. Students learn important life skills that enhance their ability to succeed academically and socially as well as cope with stressful situations.

Listed below are the types of groups we routinely offer.
• Student success skills: academic and social skills needed for school success
• Communication and conflict management
• You in control: self-control and anger management
• Changing family: dealing with divorce
• Loss: bereavement

Please check one of the two statements below, then return this letter to the counselor. If you have any questions about your child's participation in the group, please feel free to call at _____.

Sincerely,

School Counselor

Check one and return this letter to the counselor.
_____ My child may participate in this counseling group.
_____ My child may not participate in this counseling group.

Parent/guardian signature _____

Group _____ Date _____

Group Attendance

Student	Teacher	1	2	3	4	5	6	7	8

Session Topics
1.
2.
3.
4.
5.
6.
7.
8.

Group Counseling for School Counselors: A Practical Guide

Feeling Faces

Name of group _____ Date _____

Group Evaluation

Overall, being in this group was:

_____ very helpful

_____ helpful

_____ OK

_____ not helpful

In this group I felt _____

_____

because _____

_____

Some important things I learned were _____

_____

The most helpful part of this group was _____

_____

Something I have improved in is _____

_____

_____

A goal I have set for myself is _____

_____

_____

Some changes that would make this group better are _____

_____

_____

I would/would not recommend this group to my friends because _____

_____

_____

Other comments: _____

_____

_____

Part 1:
High School Group Plans

1.1
Academic and Social Support: Student Success Skills

| Grade Level: High School | Time Required: 8 Sessions | Author: Greg Brigman |

Purpose

The purpose of this group is to help students strengthen the academic, social, and self-management skills needed to succeed in school.

Background Information

A review of the research literature involving school counselor interventions with low-achieving and under-achieving high school students by Wilson (1982), confirmed by Prout and Prout (1998), included the following:

1. Group counseling seems to be more effective than individual counseling.
2. Structured group programs are more effective than unstructured programs.
3. Group programs lasting eight weeks or less had positive results in only one of five programs evaluated. Of nine programs lasting between nine and twelve weeks, five were effective; however, six of eight interventions lasting more than twelve weeks were successful.
4. Programs in which students volunteered for treatment were more successful than programs with nonvoluntary participants.
5. Programs that combined counseling and study skills were most effective.

Logistics

GROUP COMPOSITION

Students grades 9–12 mixed with regard to activity level and behavior control. Avoid loading group with only overactive behavior problem students. Students need multiple models of appropriate behavior. Groups with only behavior problem students usually do not show significant gains in prosocial behavior. Mixed groups are generally very effective.

GROUP SIZE

6–8 students

GROUP TIME PER SESSION

45–60 minutes

NUMBER OF SESSIONS

Eight, with booster sessions spaced approximately one month apart after regular group ends

Recommended Resources

Full bibliographic details for these publications are included in the Bibliography at the end of this book.

Brigman and Earley, 1991: *Group Counseling for School Counselors.*

Brown, 1999a: "Improving academic achievement."

Brown, 1999b: *Proven Strategies for Improving Learning and Academic Achievement.*

Goldstein and McGinnis, 1997: *Skillstreaming the Adolescent.*

Hattie, Biggs, and Purdie, 1996: "Effects of learning skills interventions on student learning."

Lee, Winfield, and Wilson, 1991: "Academic behaviors among high-achieving African-American students."

Masten and Coatsworth, 1998: "The development of competence in favorable and unfavorable environments."

McWhirter et al., 1998: *At Risk Youth.*

Moote, Smythe, and Wodarsky, 1999: *Social Skills Training with Youth in School Settings.*

O'Rourke and Worzybt, 1996: *Support Groups for Children.*

Wang, Haertel, and Walberg, 1994: *Educational Resilience in Inner City America.*

Session 1
Topic: Get acquainted, self-evaluation

Resources
- Student Success Skills Self-Evaluation handout

Beginning

INTRODUCTION

Review the purpose of the group (this has been covered individually during the screening): To identify existing strengths and develop new strengths related to the skills most needed to be successful in school and with people. Emphasize that the group is very active with a lot of role-play and should be fun and very helpful. It will give each person a chance to understand how to use his/her strengths to be successful in school, with friends, and handling stress. Go over number of meetings, time, and place.

GROUP RULES

Ask: "What rules do we need to work together, feel safe, and enjoy ourselves?" Be sure to include: Confidentiality (you own what you say and can share that with anyone, but what others say stays in the group), respect others' opinions (no put-downs); right to pass.

Secure group consensus on each group rule.

Middle

INTRODUCTIONS

Students break into pairs. Partners interview one another and then each student introduces his/her partner to the group.

Some interview questions:

- Do you have siblings? If so, what age?
- What do you like to do for fun?
- What is your favorite or best academic subject?
- What is the one subject in which you would most like to improve?

DISCUSSION OF SIMILARITIES AND DIFFERENCES

Get the students involved in looking for what group members have in common.

STUDENT SUCCESS SKILLS SELF-EVALUATION

1. Introduce the Student Success Skills Self-Evaluation handout. Let the group know that they will frequently go over these items and learn how to use problem solving to improve in any area where they are not doing as well as they would like.

2. As you go over the form, use each item as a discussion starter. These are the behaviors that successful students are able to do well and that struggling students have not yet mastered. Repeated exposure to concrete examples of how to perform these essential skills is the core of this group. If deficits in reading and/or math are present it is advisable to also involve the student with tutoring.

End

Ask students the purpose of the group, how many meetings, and so forth.

Ask them to share one thing they are looking forward to about the group.

Preview the second meeting.

Name_____ Date_____

Student Success Skills Self-Evaluation

Directions: Rate yourself on the following skills that are important for doing well in school. Rate each item on a 1–5 scale, where 5 is the highest/best and 1 is the lowest/worst.

Skill	Not so good————Great!				
I go to class and arrive on time with the materials I need.	1	2	3	4	5
I read and understand all assignments.	1	2	3	4	5
I have a folder or notebook for each class to help me stay organized.	1	2	3	4	5
I turn in all assignments on time—no zeros.	1	2	3	4	5
I keep track of my grades and know how my teacher determines the final grade.	1	2	3	4	5
I listen and focus during class and usually understand what is being taught.	1	2	3	4	5
I ask questions when I do not understand what is being taught. I know when and how to ask questions.	1	2	3	4	5
I know what to study for tests and what is expected for reports and I plan ahead for both to avoid last-minute cramming.	1	2	3	4	5
I have at least one dependable study buddy in each class.	1	2	3	4	5
I work well in pairs or small groups with others in class.	1	2	3	4	5

My top three strengths from the list above are:

    1. _____

    2. _____

    3. _____

The areas I most want to improve in are:

    1. _____

    2. _____

      14   *Group Counseling for School Counselors: A Practical Guide*

Session 2
Topic: Life management scale, role-play

Resources

- Life Management Scale handout
- Progress Monitoring handout
- Folder for each student
- Index card with role-play questions

Beginning

1. Ask students to tell you some things they remember from last meeting. Get their summary of group rules and purpose of group.
2. Distribute the Life Management Scale handout, and ask students to rate themselves from 1–5 on the scale. Have a folder for each student with a blank rating form inside each folder.
3. Discuss the connection between performance in school and friends and the other seven items on the list. Discuss how energy and mood are affected by exercise, sleep, diet, social support, and doing well in school. Discuss the connection between stress and the same items.
4. Introduce the notion of monitoring these items as a way to see connections and gain knowledge about how students' bodies and minds interact to affect how they feel and act.

Middle

1. Ask the group members to pick one situation, either about school this past week or peers/social life this past week, to explore through role-play.
2. After a go-round of hearing a brief description of a situation from each member, have the group vote on a topic to role-play that has the most common ground among group members.
3. Ask the person with the chosen situation to become the director and choose 1–3 group members to help act out the story. The director plays herself or himself and shows/tells the other actors what to do/say. General guidelines for setting the scene and directing the story include answering the following questions. Give the director an index card with the following questions:

ROLE-PLAY QUESTIONS

- What is the setting (where and when)?
- Who are the main characters and how are they feeling at the beginning of the story?

- What is the problem?
- What happens first?
- What are the feelings and reactions of the other characters?
- What do the characters do to try and solve the problem?
- How does the story end and how are the characters feeling?

Limit role-play prep to 2–3 minutes and role-play to 2–3 minutes.

4. After the role-play, have group discuss the pros and cons of how the director handled the situation and explore alternative ways to handle the situation. Have group members act out alternative ways of handling the situation, and get group feedback as to strengths and things that may need changing.

   Note: Discuss giving feedback/coaching. Both supportive and corrective feedback/coaching are needed to help people improve. Model the sandwich approach: Give supportive feedback (bread), then corrective feedback (the meat), then finish with supportive feedback (the bread).

   Example: "John, I liked the way you stood up for yourself and did not get pushed around. One thing you may want to consider changing is saying what you have to say in a calmer voice, without yelling, but still getting your message across. With your self-confidence I think you will develop the assertiveness skills very quickly."

5. Ask students to use a go-round to share positives about the role-play—"I liked the way you . . .". Then have another go-round for coaching feedback—"You may want to consider . . .".

End

Distribute the Progress Monitoring handout. Ask the students to complete the handout for one subject and provide sheets for other subjects. Keep the completed sheet in each student's folder. Discuss the importance of knowing how you are doing at any given time in the grading period.

Ask group participants to share something they learned or relearned today and something about how they can use it this week.

Preview the next meeting.

Name_____ Date _____

Life Management Scale

Directions: Rate yourself on the nine items below on a scale from 1–5, where 5 is the highest or best rating and 1 is the lowest or worst rating.

	Not so good———————Great!				
How school was for me this past week	1	2	3	4	5
How my social life was this past week	1	2	3	4	5
How I got along with teachers this past week	1	2	3	4	5
Amount of stress I felt this past week	1	2	3	4	5
Amount of exercise I got this past week	1	2	3	4	5
Amount of sleep I averaged this past week	# of hours: _____				
Quality of my diet this past week	1	2	3	4	5
Amount of energy I had on average this past week	1	2	3	4	5
My mood on average this past week	1	2	3	4	5

1. What do you think is the connection between performance in school and with friends and the other seven items on the list?

   _____

   _____

2. How much are your energy level and mood affected by exercise, sleep, diet, social support, and doing well in school?

   _____

   _____

3. What is the connection between stress and exercise, sleep, diet, social support, and doing well in school?

   _____

   _____

Name_____ Date_____

Progress Monitoring

Subject: _____

Last report period grade	Goal for this report period	Midterm grade for this report period	Final grade

Date	Homework	Quiz	Test	Project/Report

Strategies to help reach goal:

1. Study for tests ahead of time.
2. Get high grades on homework.
3. Have a study buddy.
4. Turn in extra credit.
5. Use note cards/outline/concept map for key concepts.

Session 3
Topic: Progress monitoring

Resources

- Student folders
- Progress Monitoring handouts
- Student Success Skills Self-Evaluation handout
- Index card with role-play questions

Beginning

1. Ask students to tell you some things they remember from last meeting. Ask, "Who used something we talked about last week during the week? How did it go?"

2. Have students rate themselves on the Student Success Skills Self-Evaluation scale. Go through each item one at a time with the group. Ask, "How many had a 4–5 on item one? How about a 2–3? A 1?" Ask for events tied to ratings. "What happened that led to your rating?" This process usually takes 10–15 minutes and can take longer if some events are highly charged with emotion and need more time. You and the group are scanning these mini stories for 1–3 events to role-play for the next part, the group session.

Middle

1. Ask group members to help decide on 1–3 events for the group to role-play. Look for events with the most common ground among group members.

2. Ask the person with the chosen situation to become the director and choose 1–3 group members to help act out the story. The director plays herself/himself and shows/tells the other actors what to do/say. General guidelines for setting the scene and directing the story include answering the following questions. Give these questions on a card to the person who is acting as director.

ROLE-PLAY QUESTIONS

- What is the setting (where and when)?
- Who are the main characters and how do they feel at the beginning of the story?
- What is the problem?
- What happens first?
- What are the feelings and reactions of the other characters?
- What do the characters do to try and solve the problem?
- How does the story end and how are the characters feeling?

Limit role-play prep to 2–3 minutes and role-play to 2–3 minutes.

3. After the role-play, have the group discuss the pros and cons of how the director handled the situation and explore alternative ways to handle the situation.

4. Both supportive and corrective feedback/coaching are needed to help people improve. Model the sandwich approach: give supportive feedback (bread), then corrective feedback (the meat), then finish with supportive feedback (the bread).

5. Ask students to use a go-round to share positives about the role-play—"I liked the way you . . .". Then do another go-round for coaching feedback—"You may want to consider . . .".

6. Have group members act out alternative ways of handling the situation, and get group feedback as to strengths and things that may need changing.

End

Ask students to complete the Progress Monitoring sheet for math and English/language arts. Keep the completed sheets in each student's folder.

Ask group participants to share something they learned or relearned today and something about how they can use it this week.

Preview the next meeting.

Session 4
Topic: Handling conflicts

Resources

- Student folders
- Progress Monitoring handouts
- Flip chart
- Life Management Scale handout

Beginning

1. Ask students to tell you some things they remember from last meeting. Ask, "Who used something we talked about last week during the week? How did it go?"

2. Ask students to rate themselves from 1–5 on the Life Management Scale. Have a folder for each student with a blank rating form and their last rating. After completing the scale for this week ask them to compare it with their rating from Session 2. What differences and similarities do they notice?

3. Discuss the connection between performance in school and with friends and the other seven items on the list. Discuss how energy and mood are affected by exercise, sleep, diet, social support, and doing well in school. Discuss the connection between stress and the same items.

4. Introduce the notion of monitoring these items as a way to see connections and to gain knowledge about how their bodies and minds interact to affect how they feel and act. Plan to use these items each week or every other week for rating and reflection.

Middle

HANDLING CONFLICTS

1. Ask students to write down typical problems either that they have had with other students at school or that they notice lots of other students have with each other at school. Ask them not to put their names on the list. Tell them you will collect everyone's ideas in a moment and the group will discuss:

(a) if they agree that the problem is typical and (b) some possible solutions.

2. Collect list of problems. Read each one and ask if it is a typical problem for this age group. List on a flip chart all the agreed-upon typical problems. Ask the group members to rank the top three problems in terms of how interested they would be in having the group discuss possible solutions.

3. Lead a discussion on possible solutions for the top three problems selected. Use a brainstorming technique. List all offered solutions first. Then go back and have the group code each one as "H" helpful or "HA" harmful to self or others. *Note:* Some will be rated as both. Have the group decide if the helpful side outweighs the harmful side.

4. Ask group to divide into pairs and plan a role-play for one of the three problems. The role-play should include one of the helpful solutions. Allow approximately five minutes for planning.

5. Ask each pair to present their role-play. Ask the rest of the group to discuss how realistically the problem and solution were portrayed, and to demonstrate additional suggestions for handling the problem. The leader can also demonstrate various positive alternative ways to handle the situation or coach students in different ways to act. *Note:* It is the role-play and coaching that make this a powerful learning activity.

End

1. Ask students to complete the Progress Monitoring sheet for math and English/language arts. Keep the completed sheet in each student's folder. Ask students to share with a partner how they are doing in these two classes and share a goal for continued improvement.

2. Ask group participants to share something they learned or relearned today and something about how they can use it this week.

3. Preview the next meeting.

Session 5
Topic: Rating, monitoring, role-play

Resources

- Student folders
- Progress Monitoring handouts
- Student Success Skills Self-Evaluation handout
- Index card with role-play questions

Beginning

1. Ask students to tell you some things they remember from last meeting.

2. Ask, "Who used something we talked about last week during the week? How did it go?"

3. Have students rate themselves on the Student Success Skills Self-Evaluation scale. Go through each item one at a time with the group. Ask, "How many had a 4–5 on item one? How about a 2–3? A 1?" Ask for events tied to ratings. "What happened that led to your rating?" This process usually takes 10–15 minutes and can take longer if some events are highly charged with emotion and need more time. You and the group are scanning these mini stories for 1–3 events to role-play for the next part, the group session.

Middle

1. Ask group members to help decide on 1–3 events for the group to role-play. Look for events with the most common ground among group members.

2. Ask the person with the chosen situation to become the director and choose 1–3 group members to help act out the story. The director plays herself or himself and shows/tells the other actors what to do/say. General guidelines for setting the scene and directing the story include answering the following questions. Give these questions on a card to the person who is acting as director.

ROLE-PLAY QUESTIONS

- What is the setting (where and when)?
- Who are the main characters and how do they feel at the beginning of the story?
- What is the problem?
- What happens first?
- What are the feelings and reactions of the other characters?
- What do the characters do to try and solve the problem?
- How does the story end and how are the characters feeling?

Limit role-play prep to 2–3 minutes and role-play to 2–3 minutes.

3. After the role-play, have the group discuss the pros and cons of how the director handled the situation and explore alternative ways to handle the situation.

4. Both supportive and corrective feedback/coaching are needed to help people improve. Model the sandwich approach: give supportive feedback (bread), then corrective feedback (the meat), then finish with supportive feedback (the bread).

5. Ask students to use a go-round to share positives about the role-play—"I liked the way you . . .". Then do another go-round for coaching feedback—"You may want to consider . . .".

6. Have group members act out alternative ways of handling the situation, and get group feedback as to strengths and things that may need changing.

End

Ask the students to complete the Progress Monitoring sheet for math and English/language arts. Keep the completed sheets in each student's folder. Ask students to share in pairs how they are doing in these two classes and set a goal for continued improvement.

Ask group participants to share something they learned or relearned today and something about how they can use it this week.

Preview the next meeting.

Session 6
Topic: How taking care of yourself affects school performance

Resources

- Student folders
- Life Management Scale handouts
- Progress Monitoring handouts
- Index card with role-play questions

Beginning

1. Ask students to tell you some things they remember from last meeting. Ask, "Who used something we talked about last week during the week? How did it go?"

2. Ask students to rate themselves from 1–5 on the Life Management Scale. Have a folder for each student with a blank Life Management Scale and the completed forms from Session 2 and Session 4. After completing the form ask students to share in pairs similarities and differences they noticed between today's rating and the ratings several weeks ago.

3. Discuss the connection between performance in school and with friends and the other seven items on the list. Discuss how energy and mood are affected by exercise, sleep, diet, social support, and doing well in school. Discuss the connection between stress and the same items.

4. Discuss the notion of monitoring these items as a way to see connections and to gain knowledge about how their bodies and minds interact to affect how they feel and act.

Middle

1. Ask group members to pick one situation either about school this past week or peers/social life this past week to explore through role-play.

2. After a go-round of hearing a brief description of a situation from each member, have the group vote on a topic to role-play that has the most common ground among group members.

3. Ask the person with the chosen situation to become the director and choose 1–3 group members to help act out the story. The director plays herself or himself and shows/tells the other actors what to do/say. General guidelines for setting the scene and directing the story include

answering the following questions. Give these questions on a card to the person who is acting as director.

ROLE-PLAY QUESTIONS

- What is the setting (where and when)?
- Who are the main characters and how do they feel at the beginning of the story?
- What is the problem?
- What happens first?
- What are the feelings and reactions of the other characters?
- What do the characters do to try and solve the problem?
- How does the story end and how are the characters feeling?

Limit role-play prep to 2–3 minutes and role-play to 2–3 minutes.

4. After the role-play, have the group discuss the pros and cons of how the director handled the situation and explore alternative ways to handle the situation. Have group members act out alternative ways of handling the situation and get group feedback as to strengths and things that may need changing. Both supportive and corrective feedback/coaching are needed to help people improve. Model the sandwich approach: Give supportive feedback (bread), then corrective feedback (the meat), then finish with supportive feedback (the bread).

5. Ask students to use a go-round to share positives about the role-play—"I liked the way you . . .". Then do another go-round for coaching feedback—"You may want to consider . . .".

End

Ask the students to complete the Progress Monitoring sheet for math and English/language arts. Keep the completed sheet in each student's folder.

Ask group participants to share something they learned or relearned today and something about how they can use it this week.

Preview the next meeting.

Session 7

Topic: Transferring what you learn to daily life

Resources

- Student folders
- Student Success Skills Self-Evaluation handouts
- Progress Monitoring handouts
- Index card with role-play questions

Beginning

1. Ask students to tell you some things they remember from last meeting. Ask, "Who used something we talked about last week during the week? How did it go?"

2. Ask students to rate themselves on the Student Success Skills Self-Evaluation scale. Go through each item one at a time with the group. Ask, "How many had a 4–5 on item one? How about a 2–3? A 1?" Ask for events tied to ratings. "What happened that led to your rating?" This process usually takes 10–15 minutes and can take longer if some events are highly charged with emotion and need more time. You and the group are scanning these mini stories for 1–3 events to role-play for the next part of the group session.

Middle

1. Ask group members to help decide on 1–3 events for the group to role-play. Look for events with the most common ground among group members.

2. Ask the person with the chosen situation to become the director and choose 1–3 group members to help act out the story. The director plays himself or herself and shows/tells the other actors what to do/say. General guidelines for setting the scene and directing the story include answering the following questions. Give these questions on a card to the person who is acting as director.

ROLE-PLAY QUESTIONS

- What is the setting (where and when)?
- Who are the main characters and how do they feel at the beginning of the story?
- What is the problem?
- What happens first?
- What are the feelings and reactions of the other characters?
- What do the characters do to try and solve the problem?
- How does the story end and how are the characters feeling?

Limit role-play prep to 2–3 minutes and role-play to 2–3 minutes.

3. After the role-play, have the group discuss the pros and cons of how the director handled the situation and explore alternative ways to handle the situation.

4. Both supportive and corrective feedback/coaching are needed to help people improve. Model the sandwich approach: Give supportive feedback (bread), then corrective feedback (the meat), then finish with supportive feedback (the bread).

5. Ask students to use a go-round to share positives about the role-play—"I liked the way you . . .". Then do another go-round for coaching feedback—"You may want to consider . . .".

6. Have group members act out alternative ways of handling the situation, and get group feedback as to strengths and things that may need changing.

End

Ask the students to complete the Progress Monitoring sheet for math and English/language arts. Keep the completed sheet in each student's folder. Ask students to share in pairs how they are doing in these two classes and set a goal for continued improvement.

Ask group participants to share something they learned or relearned today and something about how they can use it this week.

Preview the next meeting.

Session 8
Topic: Spotlighting, evaluation

Resources
- Index cards or sheets of paper
- Group Evaluation form (page 10)

Beginning

Ask, "Who used something we talked about last week during the week? How did it go?"

REVIEW LIFE OF GROUP

1. Briefly go over each topic you've covered during the last seven weeks, asking for what students remember.
2. Then ask the following questions:
   - What are some of the most important things you have learned about yourself?
   - What has been the most helpful part of this group for you?
   - What is a goal you have set for yourself?

Middle

ACCEPTING AND GIVING COMPLIMENTS

1. Hand out index cards or sheets of paper. Each person is to write down at least one thing he or she admires, likes, or appreciates about each of the other group members.
2. Spotlight: Ask each group member to say directly to the "spotlighted" person, with eye contact: "[person's name] one thing I admire, like, or appreciate about you is . . .". Explain and give examples of the types of qualities you are asking the students to think of and how to say and receive them. Ask students not to use appearance compliments such as "I like your shirt, shoes, hair," etc., but rather qualities or actions.
3. After each comment, the spotlighted person says "thank you," nothing else. (Be sure you get in on this—it feels good.)

End

1. Process the spotlighting activity. How did it feel receiving compliments? Giving compliments?
2. Students complete anonymous evaluation.
3. Concluding remarks. Invite students to make individual appointments if they want. Remind them of the monthly follow-up sessions.

1.2
Refusal Skills

Grade Level: High School	Time Required: 8 Sessions	Author: John P. Huerta

Purpose

The purpose of this group is to help students develop or strengthen the social and self-management skills needed to resist requests that involve possible harm, danger, or negative consequences. The group is designed to provide students with a practical model for saying no to negative peer pressure. The five-step model leads students through a logical decision-making process and provides practice and coaching feedback through role-play.

Logistics

GROUP COMPOSITION

Students grades 9–12 mixed with regard to activity level and behavior control. Avoid loading group with only overactive behavior problem students. Students need multiple models of appropriate behavior. Groups with only behavior problem students usually do not show significant gains in prosocial behavior. Mixed groups are generally very effective.

GROUP SIZE

6–8 students

GROUP TIME PER SESSION

45–60 minutes

NUMBER OF SESSIONS

Eight, with optional booster sessions spaced approximately one month apart after regular group ends; sessions 5, 6, 7 follow the same format.

Recommended Resources

Full bibliographic details for these publications are included in the Bibliography at the end of this book.

Brigman and Earley, 1991: *Group Counseling for School Counselors.*

Goldstein and McGinnis, 1997: *Skillstreaming the Adolescent.*

McWhirter et al., 1998: *At Risk Youth: A Comprehensive Response.*

Moote, Smythe, and Wodarsky, 1999: *Social Skills Training with Youth in School Settings.*

O'Rourke and Worzybt, 1996: *Support Groups for Children.*

Weisz et al., 1995: "Effects of psychotherapy with children and adolescents revisited."

Session 1
Topic: Situations involving peer pressure

Resources

• Paper and pencils/pens

Beginning

Review the purpose of the group (this has been covered individually during the screening). The three goals of Refusal Skills are:

• to keep your friends

• to stay out of trouble

• to have fun

The refusal-skills group is designed to give students a practical model for saying no to negative peer pressure. The five-step model leads the student through the process of logical decision making, thereby generating positive alternatives to peer pressure. The teaching process involves role-playing and modeling each step of the skill to students, helping them practice, and coaching them throughout the learning experience.

Go over number of meetings, time, and place.

INTRODUCTIONS

Ask students to interview a partner and find out the following: name, two things they do for fun, birth order (oldest, youngest, middle, only) and one thing they are looking forward to this year. "Be prepared to introduce your partner to the group in one minute." Ask students to introduce partners. Ask other students to listen for similarities and differences and to point these out as the introductions progress.

GROUP RULES

Ask, "What rules do we need to work together, feel safe, and enjoy ourselves?" Be sure rules include: confidentiality (you own what you say and can share that with anyone, but what others say stays in the group); respect for others' opinions (no put-downs); the right to pass. Secure group consensus on each group rule.

Middle

1. Ask students to describe a situation in which teenagers have a hard time saying no. As this is the first meeting, students should write a situation on a sheet of paper without their name on it. The group leader can then read the situations and lead into discussion.

2. Ask students to discuss the personal effects that peer pressure has on them. Introduce the concept of inclusion, the need to belong, as a basic need of teens, and the power that the need to belong has over their choices and behavior.

3. Ask, "Is it possible to say no and still meet the three goals of the Refusal Skills model?" Solicit from group experiences of resisting peer pressure, and discuss whether or not they also achieved the three goals.

   Note: This is an important time for the group leader to model respect for opinions, and use facilitation skills to involve everyone, connect ideas, and create a safe climate for sharing thoughts and feelings.

End

1. Ask the group to summarize the purpose of the group and meeting times and places.

2. Ask each student to complete the sentence, "One thing I am looking forward to in this group is . . .", and share with a partner. After partner sharing, ask for volunteers to share with the whole group.

3. Preview next meeting.

Session 2
Topic: Refusal-skills model

Resources
- Refusal Skills: Steps to Take handout

Beginning

NAME GAME

Use the name game to validate each person as a member of the group. Go around and have each member share his/her name and an animal that has qualities that the student admires. Ask each student to briefly state which qualities the animal has that they admire. Use linking and connecting skills to show the universality of many of the qualities. Each person repeats the names of previous students and their animals before sharing their own. Group leader goes first. Ask for volunteers at the end to say everyone's name and animal.

REVIEW

Review the three goals of Refusal Skills.

Middle

1. Introduce the Refusal Skills model by passing out the Refusal Skills: Steps to Take handout and explaining the steps. The five steps are:
   1. Ask questions.
   2. Name the trouble.
   3. Identify the consequence.
   4. Suggest an alternative, then start to leave.
   5. Keep the door open.

2. Describe a personal situation to illustrate the five-step model, reviewing each step and explaining how each step was helpful. Each step of the model assists in decision making and consequently may influence friends positively by giving them more information. Specifically:

   I. **Ask questions.** Determine if it is a situation that will involve trouble. Encourage students not to be afraid to ask "dumb" questions. Too many times we get in trouble or make poor decisions because we don't think—we just do. Step 1 ensures that at least one person in the group will encourage others to think about the situation.

   II. **Name the trouble.** Too many kids base decisions on faulty information, e.g., "It's not burglary if the window is open." (A worksheet is provided for Session 3 primarily to gather information and to discuss what is right and wrong.)

   III. **Identify the consequences.** Decide what you will be risking and express your thoughts. Again, many students do not consider all of the consequences of a decision. Step 3 encourages them to consider not only the legal but also the social, personal, and health consequences of a decision. Many groups may be influenced positively by Step 3; in that case, the student has effectively resisted peer pressure just by getting his or her friends to think.

   IV. **Suggest an alternative, then start to leave.** If a person still finds himself/herself being pressured after the first three steps, then he or she needs to suggest an alternative and leave. This step is the key to saying no and still achieving the three goals. It is very important to teach that one should not engage in an argument or discussion over the merits of the negative or positive alternative. The good guys do not always win these arguments, so don't even start. Suggest something positive and then leave. Many kids are looking for a way out, and while a positive alternative may not sway the whole group, there are many who are looking for something that will not involve trouble. (The worksheet for Session 4 is designed to generate alternatives.)

   V. **Keep the door open.** Encourage students not to put down or threaten the group that they are leaving if they want to achieve the three goals. However, many may choose to end a friendship if the stakes are too high.

3. Choose a low-level peer-pressure situation suggested by the group and role-play. The group leader should take the roles of the "good guy" and the "bad guy" in order to ensure proper modeling at the start of the learning process. In subsequent role-plays, the counselor plays the bad guy and the students play the good guy. The counselor offers corrective feedback (coaching) after each role-play, first asking other group members for their evaluation. After the role-play, discuss whether the five steps were followed and whether or not the "good guy" achieved the three goals.

End

1. Ask the students to recite the five steps of the Refusal Skills model.

2. Ask them to complete the sentences, "One thing I learned today was . . ." and "One way I can use what I learned this week is . . .".

3. Ask students to share answers with a partner. Then ask for volunteers to share with the whole group.

4. Preview next meeting.

Name_____ Date _____

Refusal Skills: Steps to Take

1. **Ask questions**—"*Why . . . where . . . ?*" Determine if it is a situation that will involve trouble.

2. **Name the trouble**—"*That's . . . .*" Tell your friend the real or legal name of the trouble.

3. **Identify the consequences**—"*If I get caught . . . .*" Tell your friend what you will be risking: legal, family, school, self-image, job, and health.

4. **Suggest an alternative, then start to leave**—"*Why don't we . . . ?*" Suggest something else that is fun.

5. **Keep the door open**—"*If you change your mind . . . .*" Leave, and invite your friend to join you if he/she decides to come later.

Group Counseling for School Counselors: A Practical Guide

Session 3
Topic: Consequences, role-play

Resources

- Consequences—What Might Happen handout

Beginning

1. Review the five steps of the refusal skills model.
2. Ask who has had a chance to use the model. After each example, ask students to provide positive feedback and suggestions for alternative ways to use model.

Middle

1. Ask students to work in pairs to complete the Consequences—What Might Happen handout.
2. After pairs have finished, have the whole group go over each situation and reach consensus on the answers to ensure that everyone has correct information.
3. Ask for student volunteers to role-play the "good guys," and the counselor plays the "bad guy" in peer situations that the group has suggested. (The National PTA has gone on record as being opposed to students role-playing the "bad guys," since this provides practice in negative behavior. We strongly recommend that you have students role-play only the "good guys" when the role-play involves controversial issues or illegal activities. It is important to choose relatively easy situations at first to ensure initial student success. Situations that have attractive alternatives are usually the best. If necessary, the group leader can "freeze" the action if a student gets stuck. Freeze the action, solicit help or suggestions from the group, and then continue. The group leader can take the role of a coach during the role-play to help the "good guy" effectively resist peer pressure.
4. After the role-play, ask other group members to provide positive and corrective feedback to the volunteer. Include in the feedback whether the five steps were followed and whether or not the "good guy" achieved the three goals.

End

1. Ask students to share in pairs their endings to the statements, "One thing I learned today was . . ." and "One way I can use it this week is by . . .".
2. After pair sharing, ask for volunteers to share with the group.
3. Preview next meeting.

Name_____ Date_____

Consequences—What Might Happen?

Directions: For each of the troubles below, list the consequences. Also, fill in the legal name for that trouble, if any. In the last row of the Trouble column, write a situation of your own. Complete the consequences for that situation, too.

TROUBLE	CONSEQUENCES				
Situation	Legal	School	Family	You	Others
Taking a CD from a store without paying					
Smoking pot					
Skipping school					
Getting drunk with friends					
Cheating on a test					
Painting words on a public building					

     Group Counseling for School Counselors: A Practical Guide

Session 4
Topic: Alternatives to giving in

Resources
- Alternatives handout

Beginning

REVIEW

1. Ask student to share what they remember from the last meeting.
2. Review the five steps in the Refusal Skills model.
3. Ask student to share examples of them using refusal skills during the week.

Middle

1. Ask students to work in pairs to complete the Alternatives handout.
2. When all group members have completed the worksheet, the group goes over each item to generate multiple alternatives for each situation.
3. Students volunteer to role-play the "good guys," and the counselor plays the "bad guy" in peer situations that the group has suggested. It is important to choose relatively easy situations at first to ensure initial student success. Situations that have attrac-tive alternatives are usually the best. If necessary, the group leader can "freeze" the action if a student gets stuck. Freeze the action, solicit help or suggestions from the group, and then continue. The group leader can take the role of a coach to assist the "good guy" to effectively resist peer pressure.
4. After the role-play, ask group members to provide positive and corrective feedback to the volunteer. Include whether the role-play included the five refusal skills steps and met the three goals of the Refusal Skills model.
5. The group leader can guide other group members to demonstrate alternative ways of handling the role-play situation and receive feedback from the leader and the group. These multiple models situations are the best learning experience for the development of new skills.

End

1. Ask students to share with a partner their completion of the statements, "Today I learned . . ." and "One way I can use what I learned is . . .".
2. Preview next meeting.

Name_____ Date_____

Alternatives

Directions: Work with a partner to complete this sheet. For each place listed in the first column, suggest an alternative course of action, and a way to say this to your friend without damaging your friendship. There are also blank lines in each "Your friend wants to . . ." column. Use these to write other risky choices a friend might want to make. Suggest alternatives for these choices, too.

Place	Your friend wants to . . .	"Why don't we . . ."	How do you say it and still keep your friend?
Class	1. cheat on a test. 2. copy someone's homework. 3. pass notes. 4. _____	_____ _____ _____ _____	
Cafeteria	1. have a food fight. 2. steal lunch money. 3. _____ 4. _____	_____ _____ _____ _____	
On the weekend	1. sneak out of your house late at night. 2. have a party when your parents are out of town. 3. go to a keg party. 4. _____	_____ _____ _____ _____	
Parking lot	1. get high. 2. steal tapes from someone's car. 3. _____ 4. _____	_____ _____ _____ _____	
After school	1. smoke cigarettes. 2. leave without paying the bill at a restaurant. 3. _____ 4. _____	_____ _____ _____ _____	

     Group Counseling for School Counselors: A Practical Guide

Sessions 5, 6, 7
Topic: Role-play using new refusal skills

Resources
- Alternatives handout from Session 4
- Refusal Skills Practice Sheet handout

Beginning

REVIEW
1. Ask students to review the five steps of the Refusal Skills model and the three goals.
2. Ask for volunteers to share their use of the model during the week.
3. Temperature check: Ask each student to rate how he or she is feeling and his/her energy level on a scale of 1–10, where 1 is low and 10 is high. Using the same scale, have students rate the past week. Give each student about one minute to elaborate on his or her rating.

Middle

Note: Building new skills takes time and repetition. In these three sessions, make sure all group members have opportunities to role-play and receive feedback.

1. Have students suggest peer situations for role-playing; students volunteer to role-play the "good guys," and the counselor plays the "bad guy." Situa-

tions that have attractive alternatives are usually the best. If necessary, the group leader can "freeze" the action if a student gets stuck. Stop the action, solicit help or suggestions from the group, and then continue. The group leader can take the role of a coach to assist the "good guy" in effectively resisting peer pressure.

2. After the role-play, ask group members to provide positive and corrective feedback to the volunteer. Include whether the role-play followed the five refusal skills steps and met the three goals of the Refusal Skills model.

3. The group leader can guide other group members to demonstrate alternative ways of handling the role-play situation and receive feedback from the leader and the group. These multiple models situations are the best learning experience for the development of new skills.

End

1. Ask students to share with a partner their completion of the statements, "Today I learned . . ." and "One way I can use what I learned is . . .".
2. Preview next meeting.

Name_____ Date_____

Refusal Skills Practice Sheet

Directions: Work with a partner to choose one place and one situation that might call for refusal skills. Use what you have learned about refusal skills to complete all the columns.

Place	Your friend wants you to . . .	Ask questions: Why? Where? etc.	Name the trouble.	Identify consequences.	Suggest an alternative and start to leave.	Keep the door open.

Session 8
Topic: Spotlighting, evaluation, closure

Resources
- Index cards or sheet of paper
- Group Evaluation form (page 10)

Beginning
Ask, "Who used something we talked about last week during the week? How did it go?"

REVIEW LIFE OF GROUP
Briefly go over each topic you've covered during the last seven weeks, asking for what students remember.

Then ask the following questions:
1. What are some of the most important things you have learned about yourself?
2. What has been the most helpful part of this group for you?
3. What is a goal you have set for yourself?

Middle

ACCEPTING AND GIVING COMPLIMENTS
1. Hand out index cards or sheets of paper. Each person is to write down at least one thing he or she admires, likes, or appreciates about each of the other group members.
2. Spotlight: Ask each group member to say directly to the "spotlighted" person, with eye contact: "[person's name], one thing I admire, like, or appreciate about you is . . ."

   Explain and give examples of the types of qualities you are asking the students to think of and how to say and receive them. Ask students not to use appearance compliments such as "I like your shirt, shoes, hair," etc., but rather qualities or actions.
3. After each comment, the spotlighted person says "thank you," nothing else. (Be sure you get in on this—it feels good.)

End
1. Process the spotlighting activity. How did it feel receiving compliments? Giving compliments?
2. Students complete anonymous evaluation.
3. Concluding remarks. Invite students to make individual appointments if they want. Remind them of the monthly follow-up sessions if any are planned.

1.3
Anger Management/Taking Control

Grade Level: High School	Time Required: 8 Sessions	Author: Anya F. Koszas

Purpose

To help students develop coping strategies to manage stress and anger appropriately. Students learn to

- Recognize the feelings and physical signs of anger.
- Understand their anger management style.
- Identify what triggers their anger.
- Deal with their anger in constructive ways.
- Prevent inappropriate ways of dealing with anger.
- Practice effective ways of dealing with anger.

Logistics

GROUP COMPOSITION

Students grades 9–12 mixed with regard to activity level and behavior control. Avoid loading group with only overactive behavior problem students. Students need multiple models of appropriate behavior. Groups with only behavior problem students usually do not show significant gains in prosocial behavior. Mixed groups are generally very effective.

GROUP SIZE

6–8 students

GROUP TIME PER SESSION

45–60 minutes

NUMBER OF SESSIONS

Eight, with optional booster sessions spaced approximately one month apart after regular group ends

Recommended Resources

Full bibliographic details for these publications are included in the Bibliography at the end of this book.

Brigman and Earley, 1991: *Group Counseling for School Counselors.*

Bete, 1997: *When Anger Heats Up.*

Eggert, 1994: *Anger Management for Youth.*

Guidance Club for Teens, 1993: *Anger, Temper Tantrums and Violent Emotions* (videocassette).

Korb-Khalsa, Azok, and Leutenberg, 1991: *Life Management Skills II.*

Kramer, 1994: *The Dynamics of Relationships.*

Peterson, 1995: *Talk With Teens About Feelings, Family, Relationships, and the Future.*

Rizzon-Toner, 1993: *Stress Management and Self-Esteem Activities.*

Schilling and Dunne, 1992: *Understanding Me.*

Taylor, 1994: *Anger Control Training for Children and Teens.*

Vernon, 1989: *Thinking, Feeling, Behaving.*

Session 1
Topic: Getting acquainted

Resources
- Index cards
- Box, bowl, or bag to hold cards

Beginning

WELCOME MEMBERS TO GROUP

Emphasize the meaning of "Don't be controlled" (name of group). Introduce yourself and explain the purpose of the group. *Example:* "All of us get angry, and it's how we respond to our anger that matters. We will learn what causes our own anger and we will learn and practice with group members good ways to respond to anger. We will ask you to give your own real-life examples of how you have responded to anger recently and—with the help of group members—we will help you figure out better ways to respond to anger.

"The group meets eight times, same place, same time, every week. As I mentioned when I met with each of you individually, there are three ways people get to participate in this group: 1) you heard about the group and thought it sounded good and signed up; 2) your parent heard or read about it and wanted you to check it out; 3) your teacher thought you'd enjoy it and that you'd be able to benefit from being in the group.

"As you probably know, this group is open to everyone. You don't have to have a problem with your anger to be here. We are here to learn about ourselves and to help others in dealing with life's problems that make us angry."

INTRODUCTIONS

Have students pair up and have them interview their partners to learn their names, what they like to do, and what they hope to get out of the group. Then have each student introduce his/her partner, based on the interview.

Middle

GROUP RULES

Ask, "What are some rules you think would help our group run better? I've found it's helpful to have a few rules to make our group run smoothly." Make sure to include the following:

1. Anything we talk about here is confidential—you own what you say but we do not talk about what anyone else says outside the group.

2. We do not want to make anyone uncomfortable. You have the right to say "pass" if you do not want to share your opinion on something.

3. One person talks at a time—the rest of us listen.

4. We respect each other's right to have different opinions even if we do not agree—no put-downs.

5. Share the time—no monopolizing "talk time."

   Ask for additional suggestions—get a group consensus on all rules.

GET ACQUAINTED

Say to students, "One of the most important parts of working in a group is getting to know one another and feeling comfortable and psychologically safe. We can begin that process by using these questions as discussion starters. Take a card from the bowl as it is passed around, read it to the group, and respond. Then we can hear what others think about the same question. I'll start."

Put the following questions on 3 × 5 cards and place in a bowl or box to pass around the circle.

- I trust people who . . .
- I can tell someone cares about what I am saying by the way they . . .
- Some feelings I have about starting this group are . . .
- I hope the group . . .
- When I first meet someone I usually . . .
- When I get angry I usually . . .
- Learning to control anger is important because . . .
- Taking good risks like being willing to share how you think and feel helps build good relationships because . . .
- I admire people who . . .

End

1. Ask students to share in pairs what they learned about the group and each other today and what they are looking forward to doing/learning in the group. Ask volunteers to share with whole group.

2. Ask students to review what the purpose of the group is, how many meetings, and so forth.

3. Preview the second meeting.

Session 2

Topic: Understanding what anger is: self-assessment

Resources

- Anger Management Self-Assessment handout

Beginning

REVIEW

Ask students to complete the sentence, "Something I remember from last meeting is . . .".

Briefly discuss anger triggers. Include the importance of knowing what your main triggers are so that you can prepare to handle them constructively.

Ask students to complete the sentence: "One of my top anger triggers is . . .".

Middle

1. Have students complete the Anger Management Self-Assessment handout. Encourage them to be honest. This is confidential information. They will do another self-assessment at the end of group and compare results for themselves.

2. Ask students to share their answers in pairs.

3. Lead the whole group in a discussion of the five items. Ask questions to help students clarify specifics related to each item, such as for 1, "How do you know when you are angry—what are the physical, mental signals?" And for 2, "What is your style—your predictable pattern?"

4. As the group discusses each item, ask participants to look for similarities and differences. Ask connecting questions such as, "Who noticed some similarities or differences in Jim's answers to what we have heard so far?" and "How many of you have had that experience or feel that way?" Especially have students explore why each of the questions is important to understand—the benefits to them—and get them to start sharing constructive anger management styles.

End

1. Ask students to share, in pairs, their responses to the statement, "One thing I learned or relearned that I can use right away is . . .".

2. Ask students to notice their anger triggers and anger response styles this week and be ready to share these with the group next week.

Name_____ Date _____

Anger Management Self-Assessment

Directions: Please rate yourself according to the following scale:

1 never	2 once in a while	3 often	4 most of the time	5 always

1. I know when I am angry.	1	2	3	4	5
2. I am aware of my own anger style.	1	2	3	4	5
3. I know what triggers my anger.	1	2	3	4	5
4. I feel I deal with my anger in constructive ways.	1	2	3	4	5
5. My anger gets me in trouble.	1	2	3	4	5

Session 3
Topic: Understanding anger styles

Resources

- Anger Styles handouts—Stuffers, Escalators, Problem Solvers
- Anger Diary handout

Beginning

REVIEW

1. Ask the group, "What were some things we did last week in here?"

2. Share in pairs examples from the week of anger triggers and anger responses. Ask for volunteers to share with whole group.

Middle

1. Discuss what "stuffing" is. Encourage members to share a situation in which she/he "stuffed" anger, why, and the consequences. Distribute the Anger Styles: Stuffers handout.

2. Discuss "escalating." Share a situation in which a member or someone they know "escalated" to anger, why, and the consequences. Distribute Anger Styles: Escalators handout.

3. Discuss the "problem solver" approach—an assertive approach. Distribute the Anger Styles: Problem Solvers handout.

End

1. Ask students to share in pairs, "One thing I learned or relearned that I can use right away is . . .".

2. Ask students to notice their anger response styles this week. Give each student a copy of the Anger Diary and ask them to use it this week and to be prepared to share examples next week.

Name_____ Date _____

Anger Styles: Stuffers

Stuffing—Passive	Escalating—Aggressive	Problem Solving—Assertive

Stuffers tend to avoid direct confrontation.

> Stuffers tend to deny anger. They may not admit to themselves or to others that they are angry. Stuffers may not be aware that they have the *right* to be angry.

A. Which of the following reasons for stuffing apply to you?

_____ 1. Fear of hurting/offending someone

_____ 2. Fear of being disliked or rejected

_____ 3. Fear of losing control

_____ 4. Feeling it's inappropriate (not OK) to be angry

_____ 5. Feeling unable to cope with such a strong, intense emotion

_____ 6. Fear of damaging/losing a relationship

_____ 7. It's a learned behavior (but, it can be unlearned!)

_____ 8. Trying to use a different style than the one I was raised with

B. What are some other reasons people stuff anger?

9. _____

10. _____

C. Consequences/problems associated with stuffing:

1. The anger comes out regardless.

2. Stuffing impairs relationships.

3. Stuffing compromises physical and mental health.

4. _____

5. _____

D. When would it be appropriate to take a passive approach and temporarily stuff anger?

_____

_____

_____

Name_____ Date _____

Anger Styles: Escalators

Stuffing—Passive	Escalating—Aggressive	Problem Solving—Assertive

Escalators try to control with anger and rage.

> Escalators tend to blame and shame the provoker.
> Escalating often leads to abusive situations.

A. Which of the following reasons for escalating apply to you?

___ 1. Feeling "I have no other choice"

___ 2. To demonstrate an image of strength/power

___ 3. To avoid expressing underlying emotions

___ 4. Fear of getting close to someone

___ 5. It's a learned behavior (but, it can be unlearned!)

___ 6. Lack of communication skills

B. What are some other reasons for escalating?

7. _____

8. _____

C. Consequences/problems associated with escalating:

1. The desired results may be short-term.

2. It may lead to physical destruction.

3. Escalating impairs relationships.

4. Escalating compromises physical and mental health.

5. Escalating can have legal ramifications.

6. _____

7. _____

D. Are there times when escalating would be appropriate? _____

_____

_____

_____

Name_____ Date_____

Anger Styles: Problem Solvers

Stuffing—Passive	Escalating—Aggressive	Problem Solving—Assertive

Problem solvers try to find a win-win solution.

> Problem solvers tend to try negotiation to right a wrong.
>
> Problem solvers tend to confront the situation/person respectfully but directly.

A. Which of the following reasons for problem solving apply to you?

___ 1. Feeling "I have a choice and I choose to show strength/power in a positive way"

___ 2. To demonstrate self-respect and respect for others

___ 3. To avoid the negative consequences from stuffing or escalating

___ 4. Knowing that sharing of feelings is essential to getting close to someone

___ 5. Problem solving is a style of handling anger that can be learned.

___ 6. The communication skills needed to be a problem solver are helpful in many other areas of life.

B. What are some other reasons for the problem-solving style of handling anger?

7. _____

8. _____

C. Consequences/problems associated with problem solving:

1. Results tend to be long-term.

2. Problem solving promotes positive physical and mental health.

3. Problem solving improves relationships.

4. _____

5. _____

6. _____

D. Are there times when problem solving would not be appropriate? _____

_____

_____

_____

Name_____ Date _____

Anger Diary

Directions: For the next week, use this Anger Diary every day to keep track of what causes you to become angry, and the way you respond. Make extra copies of the diary as needed, or use the categories to make your own diary pages. At the next group meeting, bring at least three situations that caused you anger, and your responses to them. Be prepared to share excerpts from your diary with the group.

Date _____ Time _____

First symptom(s): _____

_____

_____

What triggered your anger response? _____

_____

_____

_____

Your response: _____

_____

_____

_____

+/– Generally, do you think you did well or not so well? _____

_____

_____

_____

What was something you did well in this situation? _____

_____

_____

Is there something you can do in the future to better manage your anger? What? _____

_____

_____

_____

Session 4
Topic: Understanding uncontrolled anger sequence

Resources
- Completed Anger Diaries from Session 3
- Uncontrolled Anger Sequence handout
- Index cards with role-play questions
- Anger Diary handout

Beginning
1. Review anger styles discussed at last session.
2. Ask for volunteers to share a situation from their anger diaries when they felt angry and discuss briefly how they handled the situation, how they felt about how it ended, and any ideas for improvement for the future.

Middle
1. Using student examples of anger situations, teach the Uncontrolled Anger Sequence: triggers, thoughts, feelings, behavior, and consequences. Use the handout to help students gain a better understanding of the sequence of events when anger is experienced.
2. Ask volunteers to share personalized answers from each area. Ask students to listen for similarities and differences and use your connecting and linking skills to facilitate the discussion. The focus should be on building the ability to judge constructive vs. destructive ways of handling anger.
3. Ask the group members to pick one situation either about school this past week or peers/social life this past week to explore through role-play. Look for a situation that many group members can identify with.
4. Ask the person with the chosen situation to become the director and choose 1–2 group members to help act out the story. The director plays herself/himself and shows/tells the other actors what to do/say. General guidelines for setting the scene and directing the story include answering the following questions. Write these questions on an index card, then give the card to the person who is acting as the director.

ROLE-PLAY QUESTIONS
- What is the setting (where and when)?
- Who are the main characters and how are they feeling at the beginning of the story?
- What is the problem?
- What happens first?
- What are the feelings and reactions of the other characters?
- What do the characters do to try and solve the problem?
- How does the story end and how are the characters feeling?

Limit role-play prep to 2–3 minutes and role-play to 2–3 minutes.

5. After the role-play, have the group discuss the pros and cons of the way the director handled the situation and explore alternative ways to handle it. Have group members act out alternative ways of handling the situation and get group feedback as to strengths and things that may need changing.

Note: Discuss giving feedback/coaching. Both supportive and corrective feedback/coaching are needed to help people improve. Model the sandwich approach: Give supportive feedback (bread), then corrective feedback (the meat), then finish with supportive feedback (the bread).

Example: "John, I liked the way you stood up for yourself and did not get pushed around. One thing you may want to consider changing is saying what you have to say in a calmer voice, without yelling, but still getting your message across. With your self-confidence I think you will develop the assertiveness skills very quickly."

Ask students to use a go-round to share positives about the role-play—"I liked the way you . . .".

Then do another go-round for coaching feedback—"You may want to consider . . .".

End
1. Ask students to think of what they discovered or learned today and how they can use it this next week. Share with partner first, then share with group.
2. Give each member another copy of the Anger Diary and ask them to record at least one example this week and bring it to group next time for discussion.

Name_____ Date_____

Uncontrolled Anger Sequence

1. **Triggers:**

> Something happens, like you get criticized, and you get angry.

What are some things that push your button? What causes you to get upset? To lose it? (For example, bossing, yelling, "jumping on your back" when you haven't done anything, getting rejected.)

_____

_____

_____

_____

What are some things you've observed that make others mad?

_____

_____

_____

_____

2. **Thoughts:**

> We evaluate when our buttons get pushed; we think certain things, like "What a jerk!" or "How could I be so stupid?" or "He shouldn't act like that!" or "I can't take it anymore!" or "Jerk! Unfair! Terrible! Awful! Shouldn't be! They'll pay!"
>
> These thoughts are triggered by our attitudes, our beliefs, our biases!

What thoughts or ideas usually come to your mind when the triggers we identified happen to you?

_____

_____

_____

_____

Write down some things you usually tell yourself—your self-talk (for example, "I'm going to show him" or "_____!") _____

_____

_____

_____

(continued)

Name_____ Date _____

Uncontrolled Anger Sequence *(continued)*

3. **Feelings:**

> Our thinking produces feelings! We feel the way we think.

So, how do you usually feel in the situations we identified?

Emotionally? (For example, anger is a secondary feeling that is aroused by other feelings, such as hurt, scared, attacked, mad, and frustrated.)

_____

_____

_____

Physically? (For example, what happens in parts of your body when you get really upset emotionally?)

_____

_____

_____

4. **Behaviors:**

> Upset feelings generate actions!

What do you do? How do you usually respond behaviorally? For example: Run! Fight! Attack! Cry! Withdraw!

_____

_____

_____

5. **Consequences:**

> Negative behaviors usually result in negative consequences.

What are some consequences you often experience for getting out of control?

_____

_____

_____

_____

Session 5

Topic: Building skills—assertiveness and managing your anger

Resources

- Completed Anger Diaries from Session 4
- Index cards from Session 4
- Assertiveness handout
- Be Assertive handout
- Anger Diary handout

Beginning

REVIEW

Ask students what they remember from last meeting.

REPORT ON ANGER DIARY

Ask for examples from students' anger diaries. Focus on how they managed each situation and how they felt about the way it ended. Get feedback from group members and brainstorm alternative ways of managing similar situations in the future.

Middle

1. Discuss the handout on assertiveness. The beliefs that underlie each style—passive, aggressive, and assertive—are the keys to maintaining these styles. Since assertiveness is the most appropriate and healthy style for managing anger in most situations, it is important to spend time on clarifying the unintentional or intentional negative effects of the underlying beliefs of the other two styles. As usual, getting examples from the group of real-life situations of each style helps bring this discussion energy and interest.

2. Next, use the three situations from the Be Assertive handout to check for understanding of these three styles of managing anger.

3. Last, choose an example from the group to role-play each of the three ways—passive, aggressive, and assertive. Get as many group members involved in the role-plays as possible and ask the group to give feedback to the role-players on their performance. Use the setting cards from last week to help the director give background information about the situation.

End

1. Ask students to think of what they discovered or learned today and how they can use it this next week. Share with partner first, then share with group.

2. Give each member another copy of the Anger Diary. Ask them to record at least one example this week and bring it to group next time for discussion.

Name_____ Date _____

Assertiveness

Aggressive people:

- intentionally attack, take advantage of, humiliate, hurt, put down, or depreciate other people.
- act on the belief that others are not as important as they are.

The aggressive person's mottos are:

"Get them before they get you."
"How you play doesn't count, only that you win."
"Never give a sucker an even break."

Example:
As you leave a store after purchasing something, you realize that you have been shortchanged 65 cents. You hurry back into the store and loudly demand 65 cents, adding a derogatory comment about cashiers who can't add.

Passive people:

- permit others to take advantage of them.
- discount themselves and act as if others are more important than they are.

The passive person's mottos are:

"I should never make anyone feel uncomfortable, resentful, or displeased, except myself."
"I should never disappoint anyone or cause anyone to disapprove of me."

Example:
As you leave a store after purchasing something, you realize that you have been shortchanged 65 cents. You pause to decide if 65 cents is worth the effort. After a few moments of indecision, you decide not to cause a hassle, and leave.

Assertive people:

- express themselves openly and honestly to communicate their needs, wants, or feelings, without discounting the wants, needs, or feelings of others.

The assertive person's mottos are:

"We all have the right to ask for what we want."
"We all have the right to refuse a request."

Example:
As you leave a store after purchasing something, you realize that you have been shortchanged 65 cents. You go back, get the attention of the clerk, display the change you received, and state that you were shortchanged 65 cents.

Name_____ Date _____

Be Assertive

Directions: Decide which responses are assertive (AST), aggressive (AGG), or passive (PAS). Label them accordingly.

> *Situation:* Your parents tell you they don't want you to stay out past 1 A.M. on weekends, and you aren't pleased with the decision.

_____Response 1: You say nothing but are really angry and consider staying out later anyway.

_____Response 2: You confront your parents, saying that everyone else gets to stay out later and that they are just mean and old-fashioned. You say you hate living in their prison and you don't see why they have to make life so miserable for you.

_____Response 3: You tell your parents you think that, because you are 16, you should be able to stay out later at least once in a while. You ask them nicely if they will consider letting you do it sometimes.

> *Situation:* Your boyfriend or girlfriend stands you up.

_____Response 1: You call him/her and say firmly, but not in an angry tone, that you are upset that he/she didn't call and don't like to be treated like that. You tell him/her that, if there is a problem in the relationship, you'd like to discuss it but that you don't want to be treated so disrespectfully.

_____Response 2: You call him/her and, in an angry tone of voice, say that he/she is the most inconsiderate person you have ever dated, that you never want to see him/ her again, and that you think he/she is a real jerk.

_____Response 3: You don't say anything, but you are upset and act very cool and aloof the next time you see him/her. When he/she asks you what the matter is, you say nothing is wrong.

> *Situation:* You get a bad grade on a test, and you think that the teacher was unfair in grading it.

_____Response 1: You do nothing about it.

_____Response 2: You ask the teacher nicely if you could discuss the test. You indicate that you think your answer to the first question is right and request politely that he or she reconsider the response and the grade.

_____Response 3: You push your paper in front of the teacher and angrily accuse him or her of being unfair. You tell the teacher that you want your answer looked at again because you know you are right.

   Group Counseling for School Counselors: A Practical Guide

Session 6
Topic: Building skills—practicing managing your anger

Resources

- Completed Anger Diaries from Session 5
- Coping with Anger handout
- Anger Diary handout
- Index cards with setting questions from Session 4

Beginning

REVIEW

Ask students what they remember from last meeting.

REPORT ON ANGER DIARY

Ask for examples from students' anger diaries. Focus on how they managed each situation and how they felt about the way it ended. Get feedback from group members and brainstorm alternative ways of managing similar situations in the future.

Middle

1. Use the Coping with Anger handout to teach a model for effective anger management that includes positive self-talk. Go through the six steps one at a time, reading each out loud and brainstorming other self-talk possibilities.

2. Role-play scenarios. Ask students to write an anger-provoking situation on a piece of paper. Place it in a hat. Choose one situation. Use the setting cards to help the director give background information. After the role-play, ask group members to identify other effective techniques that would help the individual manage his/her anger constructively in the future.

End

1. Ask students to think of what they discovered or learned today and how they can use it this next week. Share with partner first, then share with group.

2. Give each member another copy of the Anger Diary. Ask them to record at least one example this week and bring it to group next time for discussion.

Name_____ Date_____

Coping with Anger

C **Calm down**

Say "Calm down, I can handle this. It won't help to blow up."

Other positive self-talk statements:

_____

_____

_____

_____

O **Overcome**

Say "I can overcome my automatic thinking—this isn't awful, dreadful, terrible, or catastrophic. I can handle this."

Other positive self-talk statements:

_____

_____

_____

_____

P **Problem solve**

Say "What are my best alternatives? What is my plan for this type of situation? Stop and think—there are always alternatives."

Other positive self-talk statements:

_____

_____

_____

_____

_____

(continued)

       Group Counseling for School Counselors: A Practical Guide

Name_____ Date_____

Coping with Anger *(continued)*

I Invite

Say "Invite creative thinking. Invite respect. Don't insult."

Other positive self-talk statements:

_____

_____

_____

_____

N Negotiate

Say "When I am angry it is important to think win-win—to negotiate. Don't get into the negatives, the blaming, the put-downs—they lead nowhere."

Other positive self-talk statements:

_____

_____

_____

_____

G Go for it!

Say "Good job. Way to go! You are getting better and better at this anger management stuff."

Other positive self-talk statements:

_____

_____

_____

_____

         Group Counseling for School Counselors: A Practical Guide

Session 7
Topic: Steps to coping with anger

Resources

- Completed Anger Diaries from Session 6
- Coping with Anger handout from Session 6
- Index card with setting questions

Beginning

REVIEW

Ask students what they remember from last meeting.

REPORT ON ANGER DIARY

Ask for examples from students' anger diaries. Focus on how they managed each situation and how they felt about the way it ended. Get feedback from group members and brainstorm alternative ways of managing similar situations in the future.

Middle

1. Review the Coping with Anger handout from last week to prepare for a role-play. Choose a situation from examples provided by students when they shared situations from their anger diaries.

2. Ask the person with the chosen situation to become the director and choose 1–2 group members to help act out the story. The director plays himself/herself and shows/tells the other actors what to do/say. General guidelines for setting the scene and directing the story include answering the following questions. Give these questions on a card to the person who is acting as the director.

ROLE-PLAY QUESTIONS

- What is the setting (where and when)?
- Who are the main characters and how are they feeling at the beginning of the story?
- What is the problem?
- What happens first?
- What are the feelings and reactions of the other characters?
- What do the characters do to try and solve the problem?
- How does the story end and how are the characters feeling?

Limit role-play prep to 2–3 minutes and role-play to 2–3 minutes.

3. After the role-play, have the group discuss the pros and cons of how the director handled the situation and explore alternative ways to handle it.

4. Let different group members take the lead role to provide multiple models of effective anger management. Be sure to ask about their self-talk. Have the group give feedback on the various ways of managing the situations.

End

Ask students to think of what they discovered or learned today and how they can use it this next week. Share with partner first, then share with group.

Session 8
Topic: Closing/evaluation

Resources

- Anger Management Self-Assessment handout (page 39)
- Group Evaluation form (page 10)
- Refreshments

Beginning

REVIEW

Ask students what they remember from last meeting.

SELF-ASSESSMENT

1. Distribute self-assessment sheets. Students complete a new one.
2. Return to students the self-assessment they completed at the beginning of the group. Ask students to compare both.

Middle

1. Ask them to share their conclusions from the pre-group and post-group inventory with a partner. Ask them to share positive gains and areas they would like to continue to work on.
2. With the whole group, ask students to complete the statements "The most important thing I have learned about managing my anger is . . ." and "One way that I have improved in managing my anger is . . .".
3. As students share their answers to these two questions, ask the group if anyone wants to give some positive feedback to the person.

End

1. Complete group evaluation form. Stress confidentiality of information, and the fact that it will help you with your next anger management group.
2. Let students know that you are available to meet with them and that you will get the group together again in one month to check on their progress.
3. Share refreshments as a group.

1.4
Loss/Bereavement

Grade Level: High School	Time Required: 8 Sessions	Author: Doreen Cammarata

Purpose

Typically, adolescents repress their feelings or express them behaviorally; consequently, school work and participation in school activities are often affected. Therefore, the primary goal of the support group is identifying, validating, and encouraging expression in constructive ways. Another goal is to commemorate the life of the departed and to inspire the bereaved individual to continue to live, love, and learn, knowing that time will bring healing.

Logistics

GROUP COMPOSITION

Students in grades 9–12 who have recently (within the past year) experienced the death of an immediate family member. Students within 1–2 grade levels of one another may be grouped together.

GROUP SIZE

6–8 students

NUMBER OF SESSIONS

Eight

Background Information for the Grief Group Facilitator

Grief support groups address the significance of loss experienced by adolescents upon the death of someone close to them. The complexity of issues brought upon specifically by the impact of a death loss is quite unique. Although this grief shares similarities with the grief associated with other kinds of loss or separation (e.g., divorce), it is imperative to note that grief support groups are designed for those individuals who have experienced death loss. Careful screening of members and consents for minors must be done. Individuals experiencing other kinds of loss or separation should be referred to appropriate groups.

Before beginning a support group, the facilitator must acknowledge his or her own death issues. Any self-disclosure should be limited to promoting group rapport and group cohesion. Be aware that a variety of feelings may arise for the facilitator throughout the sessions; the facilitator's knowledge of his or her own limits and the perception that sharing must be for the betterment of the group are critical. Creating a safe and loving atmosphere is paramount. Collegial consultation along with continued education is always encouraged.

Encouraging grieving teens to externalize their grief is vitally important. It is crucial that professionals working with these groups are cognizant of the very specific and complex needs of grieving adolescents. Therefore, it is recommended that the facilitator of these groups have grief training, counseling experience, and group skills training.

A portion of this chapter is derived from the work and research that my colleague, Jeri Williams, and I completed while working for The Hospice of Martin and St. Lucie Inc.

Recommended Resources

Full bibliographic details for these publications are included in the Bibliography at the end of this book.

Buscaglia, 1982: *The Fall of Freddie the Leaf.*

Gootman, 1994: *When a Friend Dies.*

Grollman, 1993: *Straight Talk About Death for Teenagers.*

Grollman, 1995: *Bereaved Children and Teens.*

Hipp, 1995: *Help for the Hard Times.*

Kübler-Ross, 1974: *On Death and Dying.*

Oates, 1993: *Death in the School Community.*

O'Rourke and Worzybt, 1996: *Support Groups for Children.*

Traisman, 1992: *Fire in My Heart Ice in My Veins.*

Session 1
Topic: Getting acquainted, explanation of journaling

Resources
- Folders for use as student journals

Beginning

INTRODUCTION

Introduce yourself, discuss the purpose of the support group, allow the group members an opportunity to get to know one another, and establish informed consent.

"Welcome to this loss group. Each of you has experienced the death of someone close to you. It is my hope that throughout our sessions you will come to find this environment a safe place to share your feelings. We will be learning about the grief process along with constructive ways in which to cope with grief. I will stress in here that there is no right or wrong way to grieve but healthy and unhealthy ways to cope with our individual grief. Together we will try to uncover what works for each of you and how you may implement that in your life."

"Today, I'd like to start off by breaking into pairs and interviewing one another. Find out the following five things about your partner, then introduce him or her to the large group. Find out your partner's name, where he or she is from, whom he or she lives with, something that makes your partner sad, and something that makes your partner happy."

Having members introduce one another is likely to promote a level of trust in the group. The early phase of a group is critical to create a trustworthy and safe environment for the members.

Middle

1. Discuss the important ground rules set for the group. Explain confidentiality and its limits.

Encourage each member to share as he or she feels comfortable, and stress that no one is ever forced to share. Accentuate the significance of respecting fellow group members by actively listening and using nonjudgmental statements toward one another.

"You own what you say but not what others say. Anything others share in here should be kept among the group members and expressed only during group time. You may share what you say with whomever you choose. I will keep confidential everything any of you say. The most important exceptions to confidentiality occur if you pose a threat to yourself or to anyone else. In all other instances confidentiality is accepted and maintained."

2. Introduce the concept of journaling thoughts and feelings.

Hand out folders to be used as journals and have students write their names on them. Explain that at the end of each session you will collect these and that members are welcome to keep an additional journal at home which may be added to this at any time.

End

First through their journals and then through sharing in the large group, have students respond to the following statements:

"I feel . . . about coming to this group."

"Something I hope to get out of this group is . . ."

"Today I learned . . ."

Session 2
Topic: Trust, sharing losses

Beginning

Have students complete the statement, "My week was . . . and I'd like to share . . .".

Middle

1. Begin discussion on trust. Have members define trust and its importance in this group in comparison to other environments. An optional activity is a trust walk. Have the members pair up. One is blindfolded while the other leads him or her on a short walk. Then have the pairs alternate roles.

    "At various times in our lives we place trust in other people. Share how it feels to have someone place trust in you and/or to be the one putting trust in another."

2. Allow members to brainstorm the meaning of loss. Have them identify the losses they have endured in their lives, including the current death. At this time give each member an opportunity to talk about who died, when, how, and the way in which the group member found out about the death. If there is a strong level of comfort, members can also share what has been most difficult for them since the death.

    "Let's brainstorm what loss is and list all the types of losses that we can think of. After this we will take a closer look at the loss that has brought each of you to this group."

After the discussion the facilitator could say the following:

"Loss is when we no longer have something or someone that is meaningful to us. We will be discussing our reactions to loss in the coming weeks, but for today, let us take some time to speak about the death of our loved ones. Let's go around the room and share who died, when, how, and the way in which you found out about the death. If you would like, you can also share with the group what has been most difficult for you since the death."

Provide each member a chance to speak. Not everyone will feel comfortable talking. Try to encourage participation but allow for the members to share at their own comfort level. It may be wise to start by asking for a volunteer and then go around the room. Empathy and caring skills should be utilized at this time.

End

First through their journals and then through sharing in the large group, have students respond to the following statements:

"I learned . . ."

"I can see that I need to . . ."

Session 3
Topic: Stages of grief

Resources
• Chart paper

Beginning
Have students respond to the statement, "Today I feel . . .".

REVIEW
Ask members to recall the definition of loss. Give members an opportunity to discuss if they have been utilizing a journal outside the group. Have them share whether the journal has been a helpful tool for them.

Middle
"Today we are going to learn about grief. Grief is a normal reaction to loss. Theorists have created various labels and tools to help educate people about grief. I'd like to show you one model and get your feedback about it."

List on a chart Dr. Elisabeth Kübler-Ross's stages of grief: denial, anger, bargaining, depression, and acceptance. Explain to the members that not everyone experiences each of these stages, and a person may not gradually move through these stages, starting at denial and ending at acceptance. Rather, this was designed as a guide to understanding some of the most common symptoms experienced in grieving individuals. It is just as common for people to revisit a stage once they have moved through that stage as it is for some to skip over various stages. People vacillate between stages, and the length of the stages will vary according to the individual. Accentuate to your group that everyone grieves differently and that there is no right or wrong way to grieve.

Have students share their reactions: "Which of these stages can you identify with?"

Linking members by looking for and pursuing common themes within the group will strengthen group cohesion. Through empathizing and reflecting, the facilitator can encourage members to explore their feelings. Be prepared for and sensitive to group members expressing intense emotional reactions. It is likely that your members will be in very different places with their grief so you may ask them to recall how they felt right after the death occurred as opposed to their current feelings.

End
First through their journals and then through sharing in the large group, have students respond to the following statements:
"I learned . . ."
"I see that I need to . . ."

Session 4
Topic: Reactions to grief

Resources
- Blackboard/Whiteboard or chart paper
- Video on teen grief (recommended: *Teen Grief: Climbing Back*)

Beginning
Have students respond to the statement, "This week I felt . . .".

REVIEW
Ask members to recall the stages of grief.

Middle

1. "Let's create a list of grief reactions and emotions that each of us has experienced. Break into small groups and come up with as many as you can think of; then we will share your responses in a large group."

   Allow small groups time to complete the activity. Then, on a blackboard or chart, list the groups' responses, along with the following symptoms of grief in older children and teens:

difficulty concentrating	truancy
forgetfulness	accident proneness
poor schoolwork	overeating/under-
lowered grades/	eating
performance/effort	experimentation with
insomnia or sleeping	drugs/alcohol
too much	seeming depressed
reclusiveness or social	sexual promiscuity
withdrawal	staying away/running
antisocial/destructive	away from home
behavior	talk of or attempted
negative risk-taking	suicide
resentment of authority	nightmares/symbolic
overdependence	dreams
regression	drastic change in
frequent sickness	interests/friends

"When we look at the behaviors listed, we can immediately identify the majority of them as being negative. In the weeks to come I will point out positive gains we can experience from grief. However, I feel it is important that each of you is aware of all the ways in which one may react to grief."

Disclosing a personal experience can assist your members by validating their reactions. An example I have utilized from my own personal losses is as follows:

"I recall when I was thirteen and a very close cousin of mine died of leukemia. I had many strong reactions like those we've listed. I felt so alone and misunderstood. It wasn't until someone explained to me that I was experiencing grief that I began to feel some relief."

2. Show a video on teen grief. I recommend *Teen Grief: Climbing Back*.

   "Let's take a look at a video and see how some others who have experienced loss are reacting."

3. After the video, have members discuss their reactions. Stress how this group, like the group viewed on the video, can help members to grow in a positive direction. Accentuate the healthy coping mechanisms displayed by the group members on the video. Ask group members to take notice throughout the next week of all the ways in which each of them is dealing with their grief.

End

First through their journals and then through sharing in the large group, have members respond to the following statements:
   "I learned . . ."
   "I relearned . . ."
   "I need to . . ."

Session 5
Topic: Dealing with grief, memory boxes

Resources
- Student folders
- Magazines
- Scissors
- Paper clips

Beginning

Have students respond to the statement, "This past week something I noticed about the way I'm coping with my grief is . . .".

REVIEW

Briefly review the symptoms of grief discussed in the prior meeting.

Middle

1. "Today in large group let's identify some constructive ways to deal with our grief. Specifically, refer to what kinds of things you can do that may be healthy."

   Have members disclose their reactions. Add to the group's responses by suggesting the following: Make a scrapbook or collage, write poetry or stories about your loved one, write a letter to your loved one, plant flowers or a memory tree, have friends and family write or tell you about special memories, keep something that reminds you of your loved one in a special place, pray, visit the grave, cry to release your tears, play sports or do something physical to release your anger, seek individual grief counseling.

2. "We keep referring to the importance of memories. It is obvious that after someone we love dies we tend to value time spent with them before the death. Things that may trigger our memories include pictures, songs, smells, being at a specific place, objects, etc. The activity we are about to do is making a memory box. This will take us until next session to complete. While we work on this, I would like you to spend time talking with those around you about some of your memories. For next week please bring in a picture or a written memory of your loved one, along with some music that reminds you of him/her."

   Members can begin their memory boxes by cutting out pictures and/or words from magazines that remind them of the deceased. Have students paperclip them and leave in their folders until next week.

End

First through their journals and then through sharing with the large group, have students respond to the following statements:

"I learned . . ."

"One way I can use what I learned is . . ."

Session 6
Topic: Rituals

Resources

- Small boxes
- Collage materials
- Glue sticks
- Tape and/or CD player

Beginning

Have students respond to the statement, "I feel happy when . . .".

REVIEW

Allow students time to express their reactions to last week's session.

Middle

1. While playing music that members brought to session, allow time to complete memory boxes. Instruct members to decoupage all the magazine pictures and words from last week onto their boxes.

2. Go around the group and have members share either about the memory object that they brought in or the pictures and words they chose for their boxes.

3. "Our society utilizes various services for memory rituals. Funeral services, memorial services, and services of remembrance are all types of ritual services that help grieving individuals obtain closure or reach acceptance after the death of a loved one. If you attended any service for your loved one, please share what it was like, how you felt about going, and anything you would have changed about it."

Encouraging group members to share about these experiences may evoke intense emotions. Responding genuinely with warmth and caring will create an atmosphere that encourages members in releasing their grief, and will ultimately assist them in healing from their loss.

End

First through their journals and then through sharing in the large group, have students respond to the following statements:

"I learned . . ."
"I relearned . . ."
"I need to . . ."

Session 7

Topic: Bibliotherapy, preparing for termination

Resources

- Book about death (recommended: *The Fall of Freddie the Leaf,* by Leo Buscaglia)
- List of grief-related resources available for students
- Gains from Loss handout

Beginning

Have students respond to the statement, "Over the past sessions I have felt that . . .".

REVIEW

Allow members time to process some of the previous material discussed in the group.

Middle

1. Read a book to the members about death. Recommended is *The Fall of Freddie the Leaf,* written by Leo Buscaglia.

2. Have group members share their individual interpretations of the meaning of the story. In addition, encourage them to discuss any other books on the topic of death that they have read. Provide members with a bibliotherapy list of appropriate grief books from the resource list at the beginning of this chapter, along with any others gathered from your local library or bookstores.

3. "As we approach our last meeting, I would like you to think about how you feel about the work you have done in these sessions and if you wish you had done anything differently. In addition, I would also like you to reflect upon how you feel about the group coming to an end and identify individuals outside the group from whom you can receive support."

Preparing group members for termination will help them make a sustained effort to review and think through the specifics of the work they have done. The facilitator can explore the issue of separation and encourage members to look for support in their relationships outside the group. Specific plans for follow-up work and evaluation should be made and confirmed during the last session.

4. "Before closing today's session I would like to highlight some of the long-term gains that you may experience from working through your loss. The following list is taken from research done by an unknown author; it is titled 'Gains from Loss.'" Distribute the Gains from Loss handout.

End

First through their journals and then through sharing in the large group, have students respond to the following statements:

"I learned . . ."

"One way I can use what I learned this week is . . ."

Name_____ Date _____

Gains from Loss

1. There is generally a strengthening effect on children/adolescents who have experienced a serious loss and worked through it.

2. They see themselves as "survivors," despite adverse situations.

3. They recognize the importance of family, friends, and life as gifts to be cherished, not taken for granted.

4. They are generally more sensitive and compassionate than most other children/adolescents.

5. They have faced grown-up issues early and tend to mature faster.

6. They often have a broader, more developed perspective on life.

7. They are generally more aware of pain and suffering in others.

8. They are the best examples for other kids/adolescents who are hurting and feel hopeless. Many of them become peer counselors or go into helping professions.

9. Many develop a stronger, deeper faith.

10. The healing usually draws siblings closer together.

11. These children/adolescents have learned successful coping skills that can be used to get them through any future losses.

 Group Counseling for School Counselors: A Practical Guide

Session 8
Topic: Review, share, close

Resources
- Group Evaluation form (page 10)

Beginning
Have students respond to the statement, "I hope . . .".

Middle
1. "Today will be our last consecutive session. I would like to confirm a follow-up date exactly one month from now. If anyone feels that he or she would like to schedule an individual appointment with me prior to that meeting, please feel free to do so at the end of our session today or as needed."

   One way of maximizing the chance that members will receive lasting benefits from the group is to arrange a follow-up session. This is especially true for grieving adolescents. As the adolescent progresses through developmental phases, he or she will experience the grief in a new way. Providing ongoing support is highly beneficial for these individuals.

2. "As a closing activity, I would like each of you to close your eyes and imagine all the events during the time we've been together. Play back the most significant events in your mind as if watching them on a videotape. What impressions are the strongest for you? What do you recall most clearly? What had the most meaning for you? Take a few moments. When you are ready, open your eyes and allow yourself to share with the rest of the group what you are recalling."

   Allow each member ample time to share responses.

3. Written evaluation (see Group Evaluation form).

End
Return folders that were used as journals to the members and have them share the following in the large group:

"Something I learned from being in this group is . . ."

1.5
Divorce/Changing Families

Grade Level: High School	Time Required: 6 Sessions	Author: Mary Mills

Purpose

To help students find healthy ways to manage the stress and turmoil that usually accompany parent divorce.

Students learn about the typical thoughts, feelings, and issues adolescents experience when their parents divorce. The focus is on building communication and coping skills to help students deal effectively with this serious life stressor.

Logistics

GROUP COMPOSITION

Students in grades 9–12 who have recently experienced the divorce of their parents

Students who are within 1–2 grade levels may be grouped.

GROUP SIZE

6–8 students

GROUP TIME PER SESSION

45–60 minutes

NUMBER OF SESSIONS

Six, with optional booster sessions spaced approximately one month apart after regular group ends

Recommended Resources

Full bibliographic details for these publications are included in the Bibliography at the end of this book.

Admunson-Beckman and Lucas, 1989: "Gaining a foothold in the aftermath of divorce."

Alpert-Gillis, Pedro-Carroll, and Cowen, 1989: "The Children of Divorce Intervention Program."

Cordell and Bergman-Meador, 1991: "The use of drawings in group intervention for children of divorce."

Crosbie-Burnett and Newcomer, 1990: "Group counseling children of divorce."

Garvin, Leber, and Kalter, 1991: "Children of divorce."

Grych and Fincham, 1992: "Interventions for children of divorce."

Jackson, 1998: *When Your Parents Split Up.*

Marta and Laz, 1997: *Rainbows: Facilitator Component Module.*

O'Rourke and Worzybt, 1996: *Support Groups for Children.*

Rose, 1998: *Group Work with Children and Adolescents.*

Session 1
Topic: Sharing family situations

Resources

- Sentence Completion 1 handout

Beginning

1. Review the purpose of the group. (Purpose was covered in pre-group screening, and permission letter was given at that time.)

2. Explain that students who have experienced the divorce or separation of their parents have found group sessions such as this helpful because they can share their feelings with students who have similar experiences; and that feeling alone, confused, angry, ashamed are all normal feelings and represent the different stages that we go through when we have a breakup in our family. The purpose of this group is to help students find healthy ways to manage the stress and turmoil that usually accompany parent divorce or separation.

INTRODUCTIONS

Ask students to interview a partner and then introduce the partner to the group. Find out: name, grade, birth order (oldest, youngest, middle, only), and one thing the partner does to cope with stress. After interviews are complete ask students to introduce their partners.

GROUP RULES

Ask students to develop rules for group to ensure that everyone feels safe sharing ideas and feelings.

Be sure to include: Right to pass, no put-downs, and confidentiality (you own what you say and can share with whom you like, but you do not own what others say and should keep everyone else's comments in the group).

Middle

1. After introductions, use a go-round to hear from each student a brief summary of family situation (how long parents separated or divorced, with whom students are living, and their biggest family concerns at this time). This is an important time for the leader to use facilitation skills to link/connect/universalize similar ideas, feelings, and situations and to model effective listening and respect/caring.

2. Distribute Sentence Completion 1 handout. Have students discuss these three questions in pairs.

3. Then have pairs share with the group what it was like to discuss the sentences with their partner. Next, go through each sentence and ask volunteers to share their ideas/feelings.

End

1. Use a go-round and have each group member complete the following statement: "Today in group, I learned . . .".

2. Preview next meeting.

Name_____ Date_____

Sentence Completion 1

Directions: Complete each of the following statements.

1. When I first found out that my parents were getting a divorce, I felt _____

   _____

   _____

   _____

   _____

   _____

   _____

   _____

2. One thing that has improved since the divorce/separation is _____

   _____

   _____

   _____

   _____

   _____

   _____

3. One thing that I miss is _____

   _____

   _____

   _____

   _____

   _____

   _____

Session 2
Topic: Coping with stress

Resources

- Stress Coping Self-Monitoring handout
- Folders for students
- Sentence Completion 2 handout

Beginning

1. Introduce the Stress Coping Self-Monitoring sheet.

   "When a family goes through a divorce or separation it is usually a very stressful time for all family members.

   "Our feelings and energy are indicators of how we are coping with the stress. The self-monitoring sheet can help you keep track of your stress level and improve your stress coping skills."

2. Go over the seven items with the group and have them fill out the form as you go. Next have them share their responses with a partner.

3. Last, have volunteers share what it was like for them to share these answers with their partner.

PROCESS FOR USING THE STRESS COPING HANDOUT

1. Provide a folder for each student. Throughout the course of this group, you should have students complete the Stress Coping handout each week and compare it with previous weeks to look for patterns.

2. When students have completed the Stress Coping handout, have them pair-share two or three of the most significant items from the Stress Coping sheet.

3. Use "How many of you" questions for each item, asking for raise of hand or thumbs-up. *Example:* "How many rated mood/feelings for the week at 7 or more or at 4 or below?"

   "How many rated mood higher this week than last?"

4. Discuss the connection between mood and energy and the other items. Note that we have a lot of control over items 3–7. These in turn have a lot of control over items 1–2.

   Spend 5–10 minutes per session on this very important activity.

Middle

1. Ask group members to discuss in pairs Sentence Completion 2 handout.

2. Ask pairs to share answers with group.

3. Next, ask individuals to write anonymous "Dear Abby" letters to be turned in and discussed at the next session. The letter should reflect a current problem the student is experiencing because of the changes in the family. Collect the letters in a box and keep for next time.

End

1. Ask students to share with partner their response to these two sentence stems: "Today in group, I learned . . ." and "One way I can use what I learned is . . .". Ask for volunteers to share answers with entire group.

2. Preview next meeting.

Name_____ Date_____

Stress Coping Self-Monitoring

Directions: Rate each of the following on a 1–10 scale, where 1 is the lowest/negative and 10 is the highest/positive.

1. Feelings and moods My most positive feelings were _____ and were connected to high points: _____ (experience events)	1 2 3 4 5 6 7 8 9 10
My most negative feelings were _____ and were connected to low points: _____ (experience events)	1 2 3 4 5 6 7 8 9 10
2. Energy My average energy level for the last week: My energy level for today/right now:	1 2 3 4 5 6 7 8 9 10 1 2 3 4 5 6 7 8 9 10
3. Food/Nutrition _____ I ate better/more healthily this week compared to my usual. _____ I ate worse/less healthily this week than usual.	1 2 3 4 5 6 7 8 9 10 1 2 3 4 5 6 7 8 9 10
4. Exercise _____ I exercised at least 3 times this week for at least 30 minutes each time.	1 2 3 4 5 6 7 8 9 10

(continued)

Name_____ Date _____

Stress Coping Self-Monitoring *(continued)*

5. Sleep Check all that apply: _____ I got 7–10 hours of sleep most nights. _____ I have trouble going to sleep. _____ I wake up and can't go back to sleep. _____ I sleep 10 or more hours regularly.	1 2 3 4 5 6 7 8 9 10
6. Fun How much fun I had this week:	1 2 3 4 5 6 7 8 9 10
7. Social support My level of social support this week with friends: with family:	1 2 3 4 5 6 7 8 9 10 1 2 3 4 5 6 7 8 9 10

Name_____ Date _____

Sentence Completion 2

Directions: Complete each of the following statements.

1. One way I have changed since the divorce/separation is _____

   _____

   _____

   _____

   _____

   _____

   _____

   _____

2. The biggest change since the divorce/separation has been _____

   _____

   _____

   _____

   _____

   _____

   _____

3. Something I still do not understand is _____

   _____

   _____

   _____

   _____

   _____

   _____

   _____

Session 3
Topic: Dear Abby (problem solving)

Resources
- Student folders
- Stress Coping Self-Monitoring handout (page 70)
- "Dear Abby" letters written during Session 2

Beginning
1. Go over the seven-item Stress Coping Self-Monitoring handout with the group and have them fill out the form as you go.
2. Have students share their responses with a partner.
3. Last, have volunteers share any patterns they discovered from looking at this week's and last week's stress coping handout.

Middle
1. Discuss the "Dear Abby" letters. This is a chance to introduce problem solving and to reinforce healthy alternative ways to manage difficult situations.

   Sample questions for discussion include: What would you do in that situation? How would that alternative affect you, others? What else could you do? Who agrees that this alternative would be a good one? Who thinks there are some problems with this alternative? What are they?
2. Choose a situation that has a lot of common ground and set up a role-play to demonstrate positive ways to handle it.
3. Ask for a volunteer to take the lead role. The lead role person then selects students to play the other role(s).
4. Ask students to evaluate the role-play, sharing positives first, then ideas for improving how the situation was handled.
5. Have students with the best alternatives role-play how it would go.
6. Again, have the group give feedback.

End
1. Ask students to share with partners their responses to these two sentence stems: "Today in group, I learned . . ." and "One way I can use what I learned is . . .". Ask for volunteers to share answers with entire group.
2. Preview next meeting.

Session 4
Topic: Communicating with parents

Resources

- Student folders
- Stress Coping Self-Monitoring handout (page 70)

Beginning

1. Go over the Stress Coping Self-Monitoring hand-out with the group and have them fill out the form as you go.

2. Next have them share their responses with a partner.

3. Last, have volunteers share any patterns they discovered from looking at this week's and the last two weeks' stress coping questions.

Middle

1. Ask the group to discuss the following statements.

   "I can tell if Mom/Dad is really listening to me when . . ."

   "When I have something bothering me, I let them know by . . ."

   "When they start giving advice, I feel . . ."

   "I am willing to listen to them if . . ."

   "The best time to talk with Mom/Dad is . . ."

   "When the parent I am visiting makes negative comments about my other parent, . . ."

2. Discuss with students appropriate times to talk with parents. Talk about adult moods and the best way to introduce a topic.

ROLE-PLAY

1. Ask students to choose a situation to role-play based on today's discussion.

2. Choose a situation that has a lot of common ground and set up a role-play to demonstrate positive ways to handle it.

3. Ask for a volunteer to take the lead role. The lead role person then selects students to play the other role(s).

4. Ask students to evaluate the role-play, sharing positives first, then ideas for improving how the situation was handled.

5. Have students with the best alternatives role-play how it would go.

6. Again, have the group give feedback.

End

1. Ask students to share with partner their responses to these two sentence stems: "Today in group, I learned . . ." and "One way I can use what I learned is . . .". Ask for volunteers to share answers with the entire group.

2. Preview next session.

Session 5
Topic: True-false questionnaire

Resources

- Student folders
- Stress Coping Self-Monitoring handout (page 70)
- True-False Questionnaire

Beginning

1. Go over the Stress Coping Self-Monitoring hand-out with the group and have them fill out the form as you go.
2. Next have them share their responses with a partner.
3. Last, have volunteers share any patterns they discovered from looking at this week's and the last three weeks' stress coping questions.

Middle

1. Introduce the True-False Questionnaire. Ask pairs to discuss and reach consensus on each item.
2. Next, ask pairs to report their conclusions to the group. Invite the group to discuss possible positive and negative consequences to various answers given.

ROLE-PLAY

1. Choose a situation that has a lot of common ground and set up a role-play to demonstrate positive ways to handle it.
2. Ask for a volunteer to take the lead role. The lead role person then selects students to play the other role(s).
3. Ask students to evaluate the role-play, sharing positives first, then ideas for improving how the situation was handled.
4. Have the students with the best alternatives role-play how they would go.
5. Again, have the group give feedback.

End

1. Ask students to share with partner their response to these two sentence stems: "Today in group, I learned . . ." and "One way I can use what I learned is . . .". Ask for volunteers to share answers with the entire group.
2. Preview next meeting.

Name_____ Date _____

True-False Questionnaire

Directions: Decide whether each statement below is true or false. Mark statements "T" for true or "F" for false.

1. _____ Parents who don't love each other should stay together for the sake of the children.

2. _____ Parents should tell their children why they are getting a divorce.

3. _____ If your parents are divorced, it is likely that when you grow up, you will get a divorce.

4. _____ The parent that you visit should not have rules or make you work.

5. _____ One parent should not make negative comments about the other parent.

6. _____ Your stepparent has no right to discipline you.

7. _____ Children should be included in the decision of whom the parent remarries.

8. _____ Children should not let their parents know how they feel about the divorce.

9. _____ A child should try to make up for the parent who has left by taking on extra responsibilities and being an emotional support to the parent he or she is living with.

10. _____ Children should be able to decide which parent they want to live with.

Group Counseling for School Counselors: A Practical Guide

Session 6
Topic: Review, spotlighting, closure

Resources

- Student folders
- Stress Coping Self-Monitoring handout
- Index cards or sheets of paper
- Group Evaluation form (page 10)

Beginning

1. Go over the Stress Coping Self-Monitoring handout with the group and have them fill out the form as you go.
2. Next, have them share their responses with a partner.
3. Last, have volunteers share any patterns they discovered from looking at this week's and the last four weeks' stress coping questions.
4. Review the previous five small group sessions. Then ask the following questions:
   - What are some the most important things you have learned about yourself?
   - What has been the most helpful part of this group for you?
   - What is a goal you have set for yourself?

Middle

ACCEPTING AND GIVING COMPLIMENTS

1. Hand out index cards or sheets of paper. Each person is to write down at least one thing he or she admires, likes, or appreciates about each of the other group members.
2. Spotlight: Ask each group member to say directly to the spotlighted person, with eye contact: "[Person's name], one thing I admire, like, or appreciate about you is . . .".

   Explain and give examples of the types of qualities you are asking the students to think of and how to say and receive them. Ask students not to use appearance compliments such as "I like your shirt, shoes, hair," etc., but rather qualities or actions.
3. After each comment, the spotlighted person says "thank you," nothing else. (Be sure you get in on this—it feels good.)

End

1. Process the spotlighting activity. How did it feel receiving compliments? Giving compliments?
2. Students complete anonymous evaluation.
3. Concluding remarks. Invite students to make individual appointments if they want. Remind them of the monthly follow-up sessions if any are planned.

1.6
Pregnancy Education

Grade Level: High School	Time Required: 6 Sessions	Author: Maryanne Brannigan Grimes

Purpose

To provide factual information on the birthing process to pregnant teens

To educate students about options and alternatives available to pregnant teens

To provide a safe atmosphere for pregnant teens to explore their feelings concerning their pregnancy

Logistics

GROUP COMPOSITION

Pregnant girls. Also, statistics show that 50 percent of all pregnant teens drop out of school. I have found this to be true. For this reason, teen mothers might be invited to join.

GROUP SIZE

7–8 students

GROUP TIME PER SESSION

45–60 minutes

NUMBER OF SESSIONS

Six, with optional follow-up sessions

GROUP RULES

1. Everything that is said is confidential.
2. No question is stupid.
3. Don't press your values/beliefs on other group members.

Recommended Resources

Full bibliographic details for these publications are included in the Bibliography at the end of this book.

DiClemente, 1992: *Adolescents and AIDS.*

Hechinger, 1992: *Fateful Choices.*

McWhirter et al., 1998: *At Risk Youth.*

Miller et al., 1992: *Preventing Adolescent Pregnancy.*

Musick, 1993: *Young, Poor, and Pregnant.*

Session 1
Topic: Get acquainted

Resources

- Get Acquainted handout
- 3 × 5 index cards
- Pencils
- Grapes, bowl

Beginning

GRAPE ACTIVITY

Give each student a grape. Have students examine their grapes and get to know them. Then have them put the grapes back in a bowl. Shake them up and ask the students to find "their" grape. Usually they aren't sure if they're finding the right grape. It's difficult to know someone unless you learn about him or her—looking at the surface isn't always enough.

Middle

1. Distribute the Get Acquainted handout.
2. Allow students five minutes to complete the sheets.

3. Have students form pairs and discuss their answers with their partners.
4. After sufficient time has passed, have students form a circle and introduce their partners to the group.
5. Talk about group rules. If students would like to add another one or two, allow them to do so. Keep the rules simple.
6. Going around the circle, have students complete the statement, "I hope to get/gain/learn _____ from this group . . .".
7. Give students index cards to write down any questions they might be too embarrassed to verbalize. (Using index-card questions, modify future lesson plans as needed. You may want to address a few of these questions during each session, and allow several more opportunities for students to write anonymous questions.)

End

Each student completes the following sentence: "Today I learned . . .".

Parent Letter

Dear Parent:

Your daughter, _____, has expressed an interest in being involved in a pregnancy education/support group.

The group will meet once a week and will allow your child to meet with other pregnant teens. The group will be led by a trained counselor who is skilled in promoting a safe atmosphere for communication. The basic ground rule is strict confidentiality.

Students involved in the group will miss class once a week (during a different class period each week) and have agreed to make arrangements in advance to remain current in their class work.

If you would like further information on this group please feel free to contact me at

_____.

Counselor

_____

Please sign below if you agree to allow your child to participate in this group.

_____

Name_____ Date_____

Get Acquainted

Directions: Answer the following questions and then share the information with your partner.

1. What is your name? Are you the oldest, middle, youngest, or only child in your family? _____

   _____

2. Who are you most like in your family? Why? _____

   _____

3. Who do you think loves you most in the world? (can be more than one person)

   _____

   _____

4. What do you enjoy doing in your spare time? _____

   _____

5. What do you like best about yourself? _____

   _____

6. If you could change one thing about yourself, what would it be, and why?

   _____

   _____

7. Where do you think you'll be in five years, and what do you think you'll be doing?

   _____

   _____

8. Whom are you depending on most right now? _____

   _____

Session 2
Topic: Pregnancy quiz, egg babies

Resources

- Hard-boiled eggs—half marked with pink dots, half with blue
- Small wicker baskets to carry eggs in
- Pregnancy Quiz handout

Beginning

REVIEW

In the last session students learned each other's names and a little about each other. Have each student recall something she remembers about a member of the group.

Middle

1. Students will each reach into a bag and select a hard-boiled "egg baby." If it has a blue dot, it's a boy; if it has a pink dot, it's a girl. Allow students to draw faces on their babies and ask them to talk about what they think their real baby will look like. Evaluate students' reality level by listening to how they describe what their babies will look like in the future.

2. After students have finished decorating their egg babies, explain the rules for the egg-baby assignments.

   (a) Students must keep their eggs with them at all times, or they must hire a responsible babysitter.

   (b) Students must keep a realistic diary of feedings, diaper changes, and hours of sleep.

   (c) They will report back to the group in a week.

3. Hand out the pregnancy quiz and allow time for students to complete it.

4. Discuss correct/incorrect answers and clear up any misconceptions.

5. Ask if there is anything else students would like to discuss.

6. End with the open-ended statement, "What I liked most/least about this session was . . .".

PREGNANCY QUIZ ANSWERS

1. T
2. F Pregnancy is not a time to diet. The developing baby needs nutrients to grow.
3. T
4. F Anything you feel the effects of, the baby can feel the effects of. It is dangerous to use drugs or alcohol.
5. F You should consult your doctor before continuing your regular exercise program, but exercise is a good habit that usually can be continued during pregnancy.
6. F In many ways the first three months are the most important. Bad habits should be corrected.
7. F Most women report that they feel tired more during the first three months than they do during the rest of the pregnancy.
8. T
9. F Do not feel intimidated by doctors or nurses. Ask.
10. F Smoking during pregnancy can reduce oxygen to the developing fetus and can result in low birth weight.

End

Students complete the following: "Today I was surprised that . . .".

Name_____ Date _____

Pregnancy Quiz

Directions: Put a T on the line if the statement is true, an F if the statement is false.

_____ 1. A woman must eat carefully to supply adequate protein, carbohydrates, and fat to the fetus.

_____ 2. A woman can safely diet during pregnancy.

_____ 3. Common discomforts of pregnancy include nausea, constipation, heartburn.

_____ 4. It is okay to use drugs or alcohol during pregnancy as long as it is in moderation.

_____ 5. You should stop exercising when you find out you are pregnant.

_____ 6. The first three months of pregnancy are the least important, so you may continue old habits without care.

_____ 7. During the first three months of pregnancy the mother will probably have extra energy.

_____ 8. Prenatal vitamins guarantee that the mother receives needed nutrients.

_____ 9. Because you are a teen, you have no rights concerning your health care.

_____ 10. Smoking is not harmful to the developing baby.

Session 3
Topic: Personal issues

Resources

- Personal Issues handout
- Pencils

Beginning

Each student in the circle will briefly tell the group about her last doctor's appointment and what she learned.

Middle

1. Moving around the circle, have each student report on her egg-baby experience.
2. Discuss with students the differences between this activity and real life. (Pregnant teens are often unaware of the realities of having a baby. They imagine a dream-like existence after the baby is born. Your goal as group leader is to help them understand the reality of having a baby.)
3. Using the Personal Issues handout, ask the questions one at a time and allow students time to answer.
4. End with a summary of the discussion and, if necessary, what question the group will begin with next week.
5. This lesson plan may be used for two sessions if trust level is high and students do not get through all the questions. Modify future lesson plans accordingly.

End

Students complete the sentence, "Today I learned . . .".

Name_____ Date _____

Personal Issues

Be prepared to discuss the following questions with the group.

1. Do you have any definite plans for after the birth of the baby?

2. How has your relationship with the father of the baby changed since you found out you were pregnant?

3. How did your parents react when you told them you were pregnant, and how has your relationship with them changed since you told them?

4. Have you lost any friends because you are pregnant? Have your friends supported your decisions concerning this pregnancy?

5. Do you see yourself any differently than before you became pregnant?

6. Are you planning on staying in school? If yes, how will you manage school and your baby? If no, what will you be doing instead?

7. Are you receiving regular prenatal care, and with whom?

8. What are you most afraid of concerning this pregnancy?

9. How do you think having a baby will change your life?

10. If you could change one thing in your life right now, other than being pregnant, what would it be?

Session 4
Topic: Relaxation, labor and delivery

Resources

- Relaxation tape or exercise
- Guest speaker from hospital, clinic, birthing center, Lamaze, or Better Birth Foundation

Beginning

Using any relaxation tape or relaxation exercise, have students learn the value of relaxation. Remind them that this will be useful when they go into labor.

REVIEW

Have students talk about something they learned from the last session.

Middle

1. Have a guest speaker from a hospital, clinic, or birthing center show pictures of the fetus and the stages of labor and delivery, and explain them. The speaker should also tell students about the kinds of painkillers that are available and their effects.

2. Students will ask the speaker questions. (Students may have so many questions that you may want to lengthen the session or have one speaker to discuss the developing fetus and one to discuss the labor process.)

End

Each student completes the following: "Today I was surprised about . . ."

Session 5
Topic: Teen mother presentations

Resources

- Two or three teen mothers (don't get them all from your school), including:
    A teen mother who dropped out of school
    A teen who gave her baby up for adoption

Beginning

REVIEW

Have students talk about something they learned from the last session.

Play a round of "telephone." Make up a story about yourself and include details. Have students whisper the message from one to another, and have the last student tell the message to the group. The message has usually been altered. Explain to the students that listening to "others" rather than to the actual source of information is usually the reason for misconceptions. That is why you are providing them with the source of information: teen mothers who will tell them about their experiences.

Middle

1. Remind students of the values rule and confidentiality rule.

2. Ask each mother to tell her story, including the decision-making processes that she went through. Ask that each include how she feels about those decisions now. Also ask those who kept their babies to talk about their responsibilities and how they manage school, or to share their feelings about dropping out if that was their choice.

3. Allow students time to ask questions. If students don't have enough time to answer/ask all the questions that they need to, you may ask the mothers if they feel comfortable giving out their phone numbers so that students can call with further questions.

End

Students complete the statement, "Today I learned . . .".

Session 6
Topic: Closure, evaluation

Resources

- Envelopes
- Strips of paper with group members' names on them. Make enough so that each student has a strip with every other group member's name on it.
- Pregnancy Group Evaluation form

Beginning

Hand each student strips of paper with group members' names on them. Have each write a positive message or wish to each girl. Collect all the messages and sort them by name, then give each group member an envelope of wishes.

Middle

1. Remind students that because this is the last session, they can deal with new material on an individual basis with the counselor.
2. Ask if there are any unresolved issues that should be dealt with before the group ends.

End

1. Allow students to share feelings about the group's end.
2. Have students complete group evaluation.
3. Make arrangements with individuals to meet their specific needs.

Note: Use the results of the evaluations to modify future groups.

Name_____ Date_____

Pregnancy Group Evaluation

Directions: Please answer these questions as honestly as possible. Your answers will help us to modify future groups.

1. Was the group what you expected it to be? _____
   _____

2. Did you receive all the information you needed from group sessions? If not, what should be added?
   _____
   _____

3. Would you prefer to meet individually with your counselor to discuss your situation, or do you prefer group sessions?
   _____
   _____

4. Which group sessions were most helpful? _____
   _____

5. Which sessions were least helpful, and why? _____
   _____
   _____

6. What can you suggest that would improve the group experience? _____
   _____
   _____

7. Do you feel that pregnancy support/education groups should be offered to pregnant teens in the future?
   _____
   _____

8. On a scale of 1 to 10, 10 being the best, how would you rate the overall group experience?

   1   2   3   4   5   6   7   8   9   10

1.7
Transition—The Buddy System

Grade Level: Freshmen and Seniors in High School	Time Required: 7 Sessions	Author: Gayle Kelley

Note: For an additional plan for students who are transitioning into new schools, see Part 4 in this volume, Group Plans for All Levels (page 289).

Purpose

The purpose of this group is to team a senior who previously had difficulties in school—such as academic failure, attendance, and/or peer relationships—with a freshman having similar difficulties.

GOALS AND OBJECTIVES

- To aid freshmen/seniors in enhancing self-empowering beliefs
- To improve peer relationships
- To give students a better understanding of the skills necessary for a successful high school career
- To improve communication skills
- To improve academic performance
- To facilitate students' ability to request help when needed
- To help students recognize problem areas and seek appropriate help
- To encourage student participation in extracurricular/community activities
- To help students access and better understand their feelings
- To help students recognize how the need for approval shapes behavior, thoughts, feelings, and actions
- To facilitate sharing ideas for success

Logistics

GROUP COMPOSITION

Freshmen having some difficulty in school (academic, social, etc.) and seniors who coped with similar problems

GROUP SIZE

8–12 freshmen plus 8–12 seniors

GROUP TIME PER SESSION

45 minutes

NUMBER OF SESSIONS

Seven

Method

- Request names of freshmen and seniors from teachers, administrators, and counselors.
- Ask seniors if they would like to be a buddy. Ask freshmen who need support if they would like to have a buddy. (Seniors participating in the Buddy System frequently have had previous training as peer helpers. In addition, they will have 2–5 training sessions according to their need. Ongoing training as the program progresses is tailored to the specific needs of the buddies, i.e., tutoring skills, encouragement skills, and listening/problem-solving skills. For a listing of specific peer-training materials, see the Resources listed at the end of this section.)
- Team the senior and the freshman based on the information available (sex, same number of courses failed, attendance problems, similar home situations, etc.) so that a common bond can be more readily formed.
- Give a permission slip to both seniors and freshmen, and relate details and purpose of the program.
- After permission slips have been returned, issue a group pass to each student.

Sample Pass to Buddy Group

Dear _____

    This is your pass to the group meetings on the below listed dates. Please check in with your teacher and then come directly to the counselor's office. We will start right after the bell. Please have your teacher initial this pass before coming to group.

Session #	1	Wednesday, (month, day)	1st period
	2	_____	2nd period
	3	_____	3rd period
	4	_____	4th period
	5	_____	5th period
	6	_____	6th period
	7	_____	TBA

See you Wednesday.

Note: Many teachers find it very helpful to know the exact day the students will be absent from their class. They record it on their attendance register and find that on some days, due to various school functions, activities, group meetings, prearranged absences, etc., they would be wise to plan an alternate lesson rather than have a majority of students miss an important lecture or test. This is helpful in creating a cooperative atmosphere between teachers and the counseling department.

Scheduling

Sessions 1 and 2 should take place in the same month. Sessions 3, 4, and 5 should take place once a month. Sessions 6 and 7 should take place in the same month. All group sessions after Session 1 include seniors and their freshman buddies.

The primary activity will occur between seniors and freshmen outside of group sessions. The basic assumption is that the freshmen will listen, relate to, and incorporate information from the seniors more readily than from "just one more adult." The meetings may occur in any number of locations, such as the peer counselor/leader room, media center, classroom after school, the individuals' homes, or perhaps a local favorite such as McDonald's or Burger King.

The purpose of the group sessions is to bring together these individuals and introduce activities that will stimulate ideas that they can use for themselves or with their buddy. The activities are experiential and designed to have the students use various methods of identifying and solving problems.

The counselor may wish to have both freshmen and seniors meet together for all sessions. If this is done, the counselor needs to schedule separate meetings for the freshmen and seniors at least every other month.

The purpose of having freshmen and seniors meeting separately is to have time to process the buddy meetings without the buddy being present. It has been found that problems may be occurring and the buddy does not address the issue because the other buddy is present. Also, buddies may simply feel that it is not a problem of any major concern that needs to be addressed to the group. However, if a session is limited to just freshmen or just seniors, these problems can be addressed. The counselor must ask for concerns of the group members: Does their buddy seem to be giving too much advice, or is he/she not keeping appointments with them? Once the conversation begins, both positive and negative comments are expressed concerning the buddies. The group process begins so that the others can offer what has worked for them or say that the problem also exists for them.

The counselor may wish to have every other session one in which freshmen and seniors meet separately. Any number of arrangements can be used so that not only is the cohesiveness of the group members considered, but so also is the need for discussion of their buddies without hesitation or embarrassment.

Seniors will be required to keep a log or calendar to record contacts with the buddy. Seniors may contact the counselor at any time to discuss a buddy or to ask for additional study information.

Evaluation

The Buddy System is designed to start a few weeks after the beginning of a semester and to conclude a few weeks before the end of that same semester. Therefore, all pre-assessments of attendance and grades are based on the previous semester. All post-assessments are based on the final grades and attendance of the current semester.

A pre-behavior rating scale and self-esteem inventory, such as the Cooper-Smith Self-Esteem Inventory, should be distributed/administered at the beginning of the group (preferably before Session 1). The post-assessments of the same should be distributed/administered at the conclusion of the group sessions.

Seniors	Freshmen
Pre- and Post-Assessments	Pre- and Post-Assessments
Grades	Grades
Self-esteem	Self-esteem
	Attendance
	Behavior Rating Scale

Data on the freshmen are necessary for the accountability of the group. The additional data on the seniors are optional, but may provide pertinent information concerning the effectiveness of the program for seniors as well as freshmen.

Recommended Resources

Full bibliographic details for these publications are included in the Bibliography at the end of this book.

Brigman and Earley, 1990: *Peer Helping*.

Myrick, 1998: *Development Guidance and Counseling*.

National Peer Helpers Association.

Tindall, 1995: *Peer Counseling*

Parent Letter

Dear Parent:

    At _____ High School we are constantly trying to improve our services to students and parents. Your son or daughter has been selected for a Support for Freshman Transition project called The Buddy System. This project pairs seniors with freshmen to provide mentoring. Seven small-group sessions are conducted by the school counselor. Additional mentoring time is encouraged for each pair. We will be monitoring grades, attendance, and behavior to determine the success of the project.

    If you have any questions, or do not want your child involved in this project, please inform me by calling _____.

Sincerely,

Counselor

My son or daughter, _____, has my permission to attend the pilot Buddy System project. I understand that my student will miss no more than one class period of each subject (the group will rotate the meeting through the six class periods). The student is responsible for obtaining work that he/she will miss due to the group meeting.

_____   _____
          signature   date

Session 1
Topic: Introduction, ground rules, and guidelines

Resources

- Paper and pencils
- For seniors—Buddy System Criteria
- Poster board or chart paper
- Buddy System contract

For the first session, meet with seniors separately and then meet with freshmen.

Beginning

INTRODUCTION

Begin by explaining the purpose of the Buddy System and the group rules (confidentiality, attendance, no put-downs, and one person talking at a time). Also explain that whether in large-group session or in buddy session, the peer must report to the counselor and the counselor must report any information that might be viewed as a threat or potential threat to the life of the individual or another (this includes but is not limited to suicide; drug abuse; physical, emotional, or sexual abuse; or threats on the life of another) according to the policy set forth by the school.

Middle

Use the following activity to introduce group members to one another and to facilitate group cohesiveness.

THE INTERVIEW

1. Have students get into pairs. Supply each person with a sheet of paper and pencil. The first person interviews the second person so that the first person can introduce the second person to the group. (Allow three to four minutes.) Then the second person interviews the first person.

   When interviews are complete, begin with a volunteer to introduce his/her partner to the group. Continue around the circle. (Leader may preface activity by stating that we probably all feel uncomfortable introducing ourselves, so we will allow someone else to help us.)

2. From information gleaned from introductions, discuss similarities among group members. Continue discussion with the following questions:

- How do you feel about being chosen for the program?
- How do you feel about the nature of the program?

   Seniors: What do you think you can contribute to this freshman?

   Freshmen: What information or help do you want from this senior?

3. **Seniors:** Go over some of the techniques of information giving. Remind them not to give advice. Review use of I-messages, as opposed to you-messages; listening skills; use of feeling words. Supply seniors with a list of feeling words as well as a packet of study skills/test-taking information, log, and any other materials suitable for use.

   Freshmen: Have students make a list of the problems they encountered last semester that interfered with their academic/social success. What problems are they now encountering? Process their responses as a group and encourage them to share their responses with their senior buddies. (Leader writes problems on poster board to use in Session 6.)

End

Review similarities from introductions. Briefly restate ground rules. **Freshmen:** Have them review the kind of help they hope to receive from buddy. **Seniors:** Have them review the kind of help they hope to give buddy.

Double-check on names with "Good-bye _____" activity. Ask each student to turn to the person on the right and say "good-bye" and then that person's name. Repeat the process with the person on the left.

HOMEWORK

Seniors: Give students a copy of the Buddy System Criteria. Have them keep a record of sessions with buddy; include weekly grades, attendance, and goal. Remember the criteria established for the recording of sessions.

Freshmen: Keep a record of weekly grades and attendance. Distribute the Buddy System contract to students. Have them complete it and keep in their folders.

Name_____ Date _____

Buddy System Contract

I understand:

_____ that I have made a commitment to attend the group for consecutive sessions.

_____ that attendance will be taken in group and it is my responsibility to report to the group room and be ready to begin on time.

_____ that it is my responsibility to make arrangements in advance with classroom teachers for any work that I may miss by being in group.

_____ that it is my responsibility to keep what others say and do in group confidential.

_____ that the group leaders will also keep confidential what I say and do in group, involving other people only when they become concerned for my health, safety, or welfare.

_____ that all school policies regarding acceptable behavior apply to the group.

_____ that I am responsible for completing all assignments that are part of the group.

Signed: _____

(Student)

Name_____ Date _____

Buddy System Criteria

These are the requirements for a senior meeting with a freshman buddy.

1. There should be a meeting twice a week, preferably at the beginning of the week and near the end of the week. Occasionally, the meeting time may be limited to only once a week due to schedules and other difficulties. This should not occur more than twice for the entire length of the group session.

2. Seniors may use their scheduled meeting time for peer counseling, tutoring, support, or just building a rapport. Any problems such as abuse (within the family, or the individual abusing self or substances), suicide, or other major areas of concern should always be reported to the counselor immediately.

3. Seniors should feel free to consult with the counselor, teacher, or other professional support staff to obtain material, information, or support for helping their buddy. (They may ask the counselor for material for test-taking skills, a teacher for information regarding problem-solving techniques for a particular subject area, the media specialist for tutoring materials.)

4. Seniors will keep a record of their sessions with their buddy, using the Buddy Session Record form.

5. Seniors will give the record of these sessions to the Buddy System counselor at scheduled meetings or as directed by the counselor at times other than scheduled meetings. The counselor may wish to keep the record or simply review and return it to the senior.

Buddy Session Record

Name of Senior Buddy _____

Name of Freshman Buddy _____

Date and time	Location	Focus of session*	Attendance during last week	Weekly grades in core subjects	Behavior for last week	Next scheduled session's date, time, and location	Anticipated topic of next session

*Main focus of session—tutoring in math, peer counseling related to school, friends, etc.

Session 2
Topic: Commonalities, introducing buddy pairs

Resources
- Refreshments
- List of senior/freshmen buddy pairs

Preparation
Before beginning this session, you need to match senior and freshman buddies. Use information such as gender, similarity of home situations, similarity of school changes—e.g., attendance, similarity in number/type of courses failed, to make the best possible buddy pair matches.

Beginning

INTRODUCTION
Welcome both freshmen and seniors. Begin by stating the purpose and ground rules of the group. Preface the activity by stating that the activity will help us relax with one another and learn some interesting things about one another.

Middle

DOUBLE LINE
1. Begin by forming a double line with an equal number of students on both sides. Each line alternates seniors and freshmen. Each set of partners has 14 seconds to answer a question, 7 seconds each. ("Stop" will be called after 7 seconds as a signal to switch. Then "Move one person" will be called and the line on the right of the leader moves ahead one person (end person comes around to other end). Here are possible questions:
   - If you could spend an hour with a famous person, who would it be, and why?
   - If you had to live somewhere else for a year, where would it be?
   - Who is your hero/heroine, and why?
   - If you had to change your first name, what would the new one be, and why?
   - What is one thing about school you like and one thing you dislike?

- What subject in school are you best at, and why?
- What is one thing that makes you happy, and why?
- What is your favorite (TV program, food, musical group, pastime, color, season, etc.), and why?
- If you had to move to Pakistan next year, what would you miss most about the place where you now live?
- What one change would you most like to see in our society?

Allow the line to move completely through at least one time (more if you have time and see that the group is really enjoying the activity).

2. Discuss any similarities among students. Ask them to raise hands if their partner started a topic they would like to go back and discuss some more, or that they found interesting or funny. Remind them that making new friends is often very easy once you have something to talk about or share. The buddy system will give them an opportunity to share with one another.

End

EXCHANGE OF NAMES
Call names of buddy pairs. Ask students to write down their buddy's full name, address, phone number, schedule of classes and teachers (room numbers if possible), and list of after-school events in which they are participating (include days and practice times).

SUMMARY
After giving the buddy pairs ample time to exchange information, ask the group to remember that confidentiality extends into the buddy sessions with one another. Encourage them to continue with fellowship. Give homework assignment. Enjoy snacks and mingle.

HOMEWORK
Same as assignment from Session 1. Tell groups to wear slacks or shorts to next meeting.

Session 3

Topic: Cooperative skills, problem-solving skills

Beginning

Ask students to state their name and the problem areas in which they are working with their buddies. Allow for questions and any information-giving, as necessary.

Middle

ENTANGLEMENT

1. Students form a circle, arms crossed and outstretched in front of them. Each student reaches into center of the circle and grasps the hands of two people. (Make sure they are holding the hands of people other than those standing next to them.) Without releasing their grip, they must untangle the knot formed by the group. They should end up in a circle; however, some may be facing inward and some outward.

2. Ask the following questions: How did you feel at different times when untangling the knot? Use feeling words (e.g., confused, no direction, confident, excited when accomplished). What were some of the qualities of the people that helped untangle the group? Use feeling words (e.g., cooperation, leadership, acceptance, willingness to try). Relate these qualities to the buddy system.

End

Ask each person to state a feeling that came to them while tangling/untangling that might be a benefit in the process of helping/being helped by their buddy. *Example:* I need to be more accepting; buddy needs to be more excited about learning; etc.

Session 4
Topic: Feelings and our need for approval

Beginning

Have students share with the group successes with or concerns about buddy. Ask them to share how they or their buddy used what was learned in the last session.

Middle

"I AM"

1. This exercise is a series of unfinished statements. With the group in a circle, go around the room, having each member complete a different sentence with whatever comes to mind. Allow for a second or third round if participants are interested. Another alternative is to throw out several of the statements to the group as a whole. A discussion or elaboration may follow.

   I'm happiest when . . .

   In a group, I am . . .

   When I'm alone at home, I . . .

   Most people I know . . .

   I get angry when . . .

   What I want most in my life is . . .

   I often find myself . . .

   People who know me well think I am . . .

   I used to be . . .

   It makes me uncomfortable when . . .

   When people first meet me, they . . .

   When someone tries to bully me, I feel . . .

   When I'm on cloud nine, I feel . . .

   When someone praises my work, I feel . . .

   When I'm on a blind date, I feel . . .

   When people don't appreciate what I have done, I feel . . .

   When everyone is telling me what to do, I feel . . .

   When I'm loved, I feel . . .

   I have never liked . . .

   I trust those who . . .

   In a group, I am most afraid of . . .

   I respect . . .

   I feel irritated when . . .

   From past experiences, I believe teachers think I am . . .

   My family thinks that I am . . .

   What I like best at school is . . .

   Usually when the teacher calls on me, I feel . . .

   I would consider it risky to . . .

   I need to improve most in . . .

   It makes me proud . . .

   A good thing that happened recently was . . .

   Since last year, I have changed most in . . .

   Usually I don't like to talk about . . .

   People seem to like my . . .

2. Ask, "Did any of you not say your first thought because you were concerned about what others might think—that they might not approve of you or what you thought? Discuss how you felt when you realized that your first reaction might not be approved of by others. We all want the approval of others. How does this affect our conduct in class, study habits, projects, participation in class discussions, etc.? Do we always seek approval in positive ways? How so?

   "How does this discussion help you see yourself and help you relate to your buddy?"

End

Review the session, using students' statements about approval. Ask them to keep this session's discussion in mind while they silently respond to the following statement:

"Approval from others is more important to me than my own self-approval." (Respond with *strongly agree; agree, neutral, disagree;* or *strongly disagree.*)

Ask students to consider how their response relates to the way they approach academic/social activities (positive or negative). Ask them to keep their response in mind the next time a situation arises in which they withhold their first response or reaction (either positive or negative).

HOMEWORK

Write on paper an incident in which you changed your answer or behavior because of what others might think.

Session 5
Topic: Problem-solving skills, communication skills

Beginning

1. Ask for any questions or concerns.
2. Share homework assignment (how we changed an answer or action because of what others might think).
3. Have group discuss any common feelings or incidents.

Middle

BODY SCULPTURES

1. Introduce the concept of body sculptures. Using group members, sculpt a problem. (*Example:* A student talks to friend on phone while doing homework in the living room, where his little brother is playing a video game.) Place group members to show this scene. Discuss how you can actually see how this arrangement of people interferes with learning/studying. Resculpt with the friend waiting until the student finishes homework, the student in another room at a comfortable studying area/position, and the brother playing his video game in the living room. (This is a suggestion. Try to elicit a real problem from the group and sculpt it.)
2. Encourage other group members to discuss what is going on. *Example:* "Can you see anything that interferes with the student's studying? Can you see why his study efforts are being defeated? How can this be changed? Do it!"

3. Some problems may not lend themselves readily to sculpting, but an effort can be made. The idea is to visualize a problem and then change its direction. Others can learn from how a person changes his or her own personal situation.
4. "How did it feel to share the success of a problem conquered? How did it feel to 'look' at the problem? Could you 'see' why a situation might be difficult? When the situation changed, could you see as well as feel that the change was positive?"

End

Review what was learned in today's activity. Encourage group to visualize problems so that they can better work solutions. Suggest a problem area that they might work on next.

HOMEWORK

Ask the group to mentally sculpt a problem and then sculpt a solution. Ask them to write down the problem, the parts that contribute to the problem, and the solutions taken. *Example:*

Problem: Poor grades on homework

Parts that contribute: Friend on phone, brother playing game in same room, etc.

Solution: Have friend call later, study in own room or when brother is finished with game.

Suggest that visualizing a problem by sculpting with people or visualizing it on paper helps facilitate better solutions.

Session 6
Topic: Feelings, self-esteem, skills required for high school success

Beginning

Begin by sharing successes great and small.
Freshmen: How has your buddy helped you the most?
Seniors: How has your buddy improved? Do you think this is a worthwhile project? Why or why not? Any suggestions for the next group of buddies?

Middle

1. **Freshmen:** Bring out the list of problem areas from Session 1; cross off the successes. Ask students: "How does it feel to cross off some of the areas? How does it feel if some areas are still left?" (Words such as hopeful, small obstacles, inconvenient but obtainable, etc., will probably be used in discussing areas still left.)

   Seniors: Go over some of the communication skills taught in Session 1. Ask each senior how he/she used these skills with buddy.

2. Discuss: "How does it feel to have the group sessions over, as well as the buddy system? How can you use what you have learned now that the program is over?" (Encourage lots of feeling words.)

End

Each person takes a turn at completing the sentence stem, "At the beginning of the Buddy System I . . . but now I . . .". Process the feelings from the stem. Give an invitation to the total group get-together (Session 7).

HOMEWORK

Bring a goodie to share for the get-together.

Session 7
Topic: Peer relationships, group termination

Beginning

1. Both freshmen and seniors attend this meeting. Arrange the chairs in a large circle, and have buddy sit next to buddy.
2. Begin by stating that this is the final session of the Buddy System. Ask each buddy to say his/her own name and how he/she feels about helping or having been helped. Encourage open discussion. Point out similar problems and successes among buddy pairs.

Middle

1. Give each person a pen or pencil and a piece of paper. Ask buddies to write each other a thank-you note, mentioning specific instances that helped them or that they enjoyed. After notes are written, ask them to hold the notes until the conclusion of the session.
2. Discuss: "How did you feel as you wrote the note?" (Awkward, too much to say and not enough paper, embarrassed, nothing to say, etc.)
3. Would you recommend that the Buddy System be used again? Why or why not? List on paper the pros and cons.

4. Read pros and cons aloud after all the contributions have been made. Ask if the group agrees. Discuss with the group whether the Buddy System should be used again.

End

Ask each student to finish with a word or two of praise for his/her buddy (helpful, energetic, cooperative, knowledgeable, tries, works hard, creative, responsible, loads of patience, etc.). After all have had a chance to praise their buddy, the thank-you notes are exchanged. As students exchange notes, encourage them to share successes as they snack on refreshments and enjoy the fellowship of all the buddies.

HOMEWORK

Ask the group members to remember the lessons presented and to continue working on more successes. Since most of them have enjoyed the group, encourage them to become active in extracurricular/community activities. These activities will provide continued enjoyment, friendship, and success.

Part 2:
Middle School Group Plans

2.1
Academic and Social Support: Student Success Skills

Grade Level: Middle School and High School	Time Required: 8 Sessions	Authors: Greg Brigman and Barbara Earley Goodman

Purpose

To provide support for underachieving students with the aim of improving academic performance

Logistics

Ten weekly group meetings, each lasting approximately 40 minutes, followed by monthly booster sessions
Six–eight students per group

Background Information

Every school has students who are performing below their ability. These students may exhibit any or all of the following characteristics and behaviors: apathy, discouragement, disruptive behavior, slow learning, attendance problems, home problems, low motivation, or learning skills deficits.

This field-tested group plan has worked successfully with many students who fit one or more of these profiles.

The following steps are helpful for building success into your group program:

1. Ask teachers to identify students who are underperforming and not already receiving support services.

2. Invite students in for a pre-group screening. During the pre-group screening, explain the benefits of participating, discuss expectations for participation, help students begin to set goals, and answer any questions students may have. Use the Student Contract that follows to clarify the level of commitment you are asking of students.

3. Make sure the program is voluntary.

4. Inform parents about the benefits of the academic support group and ask them to sign a permission and commitment form, like the one on page 110.

5. It is very helpful to have parent-teacher conferences, telephone contact, and conferences with students individually as adjuncts to the group.

When these steps are followed, it is likely that students will rate this group experience as positive and helpful—and that their report cards will show marked improvement. This has been the case for the authors when conducting these groups.

Finally, some background information is important to keep in mind as you plan your academic support group:

A review of the research literature involving school counselor interventions with low-achieving and underachieving elementary-, middle-, and high-school students by Wilson (1982) and confirmed by Prout and Prout (1998) included the following:

1. Group counseling seems to be more effective than individual counseling.

2. Structured group programs are more effective than unstructured programs.

3. Group programs lasting eight weeks or less had positive results in only one of five programs evaluated. Of nine programs lasting between nine and twelve weeks, five were effective; however, six of eight interventions lasting more than twelve weeks were successful.

4. Programs in which children volunteered for treatment were more successful than programs with nonvoluntary participants.

5. Programs that combined counseling and study skills were most effective.

Recommended Resources

Full bibliographic details for these publications are included in the Bibliography at the end of this book.

Brigman and Earley, 1991: *Group Counseling for School Counselors.*

Brown, 1999a: "Improving academic achievement."

Brown, 1999b: *Proven Strategies for Improving Learning and Academic Achievement.*

Goldstein and McGinnis, 1997: *Skillstreaming the Adolescent.*

Hattie, Biggs, and Purdie, 1996: "Effects of learning skills interventions on student learning."

Lee, Winfield, and Wilson, 1991: "Academic behaviors among high-achieving African-American students."

McWhirter et al., 1998: *At Risk Youth.*

Masten and Coatsworth, 1998: "The development of competence in favorable and unfavorable environments."

Moote, Smythe, and Wodarsky, 1999: *Social Skills Training with Youth in School Settings: A Review.*

O'Rourke and Worzybt, 1996: *Support Groups for Children.*

Wang, Haertel, and Walberg, 1994: *Educational Resilience in Inner City America.*

Student Contract

I, _____, have agreed to join this group because

_____

_____

_____

I agree that:

_____ I will attend the group each week.

_____ I will share my ideas and feelings in group. I also have the right to pass.

_____ I will set reasonable grade goals for myself and work to achieve them.

_____ I will be present at school every day unless I am sick.

_____ I will do my homework each night.

_____ I will use an assignment notebook daily.

_____ I will turn all assignments in on time to avoid any zeros.

_____ I will use a folder or notebook for each subject.

Name: _____

Date: _____

Parent Letter—Student Success Skills

Dear Parent:

Your child, _____, has indicated an interest in participating in our Student Success Skills group. The purpose of the group, which meets once per week for 10 weeks, is to help students strengthen the skills needed to be successful academically. This is a voluntary program that has been helpful to students who have participated in the past. We hope you will support your child's decision to participate.

Attached is a copy of a contract your child has signed indicating his/her commitment to follow through on eight specific behaviors. We are also asking each parent to commit to the six specific behaviors on the attached sheet (although we realize that you may already be using these behaviors). Please complete the Suggestions for Parents form and return it to the counselor.

We are available to talk with you about your child's progress, and we appreciate your willingness to work with us to make this a good year for your child. Please let us know if you have questions about this program or anything else.

Sincerely,

School Counselor

Suggestions for Parents

_____ I will talk with my child in an encouraging manner about the Student Success Skills group and I support my child's commitment to the Student Contract.

_____ Together my child and I will decide on a specific study time and location that is free from distractions.

_____ I will sit down with my child for 10 minutes at the beginning or ending of the study time to review what was learned in each class that day and to find out if homework was assigned.

_____ I realize that school assignments are my child's responsibility and that I am not expected to do my child's homework or projects.

_____ I will arrange a conference with my child's teachers or counselor for suggestions on what to do at home to support my child's academic success.

_____ I will meet with my child at least once a week to discuss his/her progress.

I support my child's decision to participate in the Student Success Skills group and I commit to doing the six suggestions listed above.

Student Name: _____

Parent Signature: _____

Session 1
Topic: Self-evaluation, getting acquainted

Resources
- Student Self-Evaluation handout

Beginning

INTRODUCTION

1. Ask students to form pairs and interview each other in preparation for introducing their partner to the group. Pairs ask each other name, birth order (oldest, youngest, middle, only), and two things they do for fun.

2. Pairs introduce partners to group and group listens for similarities and differences.

3. Explain group purpose to students. *Example:* "We wanted to support you in being successful in school. We have a plan that has worked for students your age. For the next 10 weeks we are offering a group that will include activities on:
   - goal setting
   - tips to make learning faster and easier
   - communicating with your teacher
   - organization
   - motivation

   We will also be sending a letter to your parents explaining the group and asking them to encourage your efforts to improve."

GROUP RULES

Ask students to suggest rules for the group to work together well. Get consensus on any that you adopt. Ask a student to write these down. Make sure you include the following:
- Respect other's opinions—no put-downs.
- We encourage sharing ideas but you have the right to pass.

- Confidentiality—You own what you say and can tell who you want. You do not own what others say; what others say stays within the group.

Middle

1. Distribute the Student Self-Evaluation handout. Let the group know that each week they will go over these items and learn how to use problem solving to improve in any area where they are not doing as well as they would like.

2. Ask students to rate each of the 11 statements on a scale of 1–4. These are behaviors associated with students who are successful in school and who get along well with others. If students are willing to improve in these behaviors they will be more successful academically and socially.

3. Go through the statements, asking for ratings from each student. This usually generates discussion. You will need to keep the focus on accepting responsibility instead of blaming a teacher or others.

4. Let students know that the group meetings will address areas they feel need improvement.

Note: Repeated exposure to concrete examples of how to perform these essential skills is the core of this group. If deficits in reading and/or math are present it is advisable to also involve the student with tutoring.

End

1. Ask students to summarize purpose of group.

2. Ask students to write a specific goal based on one of the 11 areas from the Student Self-Evaluation form for this week.

3. Students share their goals with the group. After each goal is shared, have the entire group say in unison, "You can do it [name of student], go for it!"

4. Preview some of the areas of focus in the coming meetings.

Name_____ Date_____

Student Self-Evaluation

Directions: Rate yourself on a scale of 1–4 on each item below. Follow the rating system listed here.

1. outstanding   2. above average   3. satisfactory   4. needs improvement

I listen carefully and follow directions.	1	2	3	4
I participate in class discussion.	1	2	3	4
I know when and how to ask questions when I'm unsure or don't know.	1	2	3	4
I work well in small groups.	1	2	3	4
I get along well with others in class.	1	2	3	4
I read all assignments and understand what I read.	1	2	3	4
I complete work assigned on time; I do not get zeros.	1	2	3	4
I have at least one dependable study buddy in each class whom I can call at home for help.	1	2	3	4
I have a system to help me remember important facts and concepts, such as making an outline, putting key information on note cards, or concept mapping.	1	2	3	4
I know what to expect on tests and have a study plan that begins several days in advance, instead of cramming the night before.	1	2	3	4
I keep a list of test grades and other grades for each course in my course folder and I know how my teacher calculates my final grade.	1	2	3	4

Session 2

Topic: Goal setting, grade monitoring, student success training

Resources

- Student Success Training Goal handout
- Student folders
- Grade Monitoring Form
- Optional: tape recorder and blank tapes

Beginning

1. Ask students to record grades for the week on the Grade Monitoring Forms in their folders.
2. Ask students to respond in a go-round to the statements: "My name is . . . and one thing that is going better is . . ." and "I could make better grades if . . .".

REVIEW

1. Ask students to share what they remember about last meeting.
2. Ask students to report on last week's goals.

Middle

GOAL SETTING

1. Introduce Student Success Training. You can read aloud the script located at the end of this plan or tape record it beforehand.

   Tell students, "This script presents techniques used by high achievers in sports, school, and business. Three techniques you should pay attention to: relaxation training, goal setting, and picturing success. Following the script, you will be asked to write a specific goal and a plan to reach it."
2. Ask students to sit comfortably with eyes closed. Then play the tape or read the script.
3. After presenting the script, ask students to write a goal and plan as directed on the tape, using the Student Success Training Goal handout.
4. Have students share their goals and plans. They can divide into groups of 2–4, or share with the whole group. You should critique the goals and plans as to how clear, definite, and specific they are.

End

1. Ask students to write an ending to the following statements. Ask them to share their answers with a partner. Then ask for volunteers to share what they wrote.

   "Today I learned . . ."

   "My goal for next week is . . ."
2. Students share their goals with the group. After each goal is shared the entire group says in unison, "You can do it, [name of student], go for it!"
3. Preview next meeting.
4. Remind students to bring the signed parent commitment form to the next session.

Student Success Training Script

Hello, this is your Student Success Training material. Student Success Training has many similarities to the training used by top athletes around the world. Many U.S. Olympic and professional athletes use the skills that you will be learning about in Student Success Training. Learning how to set clear, definite, and possible goals, learning how to design programs that help you achieve those goals, and learning how to keep your motivation up are the keys to Student Success Training.

Succeeding in school is one of the main ways young people learn that they are capable and can compete successfully in the world. We all want to be successful. Students who have given up on being successful in school sometimes offer phony reasons for not trying. They say, "Oh, I don't care if I get bad grades," or "School's not important to me." Don't fall for these lines. Remember, everyone wants to be successful. Students who don't try in school usually have given up because they are scared—scared they won't do well even if they try their best. They have bought the idea that they can't learn. What they need is a new plan and the courage to try again.

Listen closely: Each of you can be successful in school. Each of you can learn the key facts of any course. It may take you a shorter or longer time than someone else, but each of you can learn. You own the most fantastic computer ever made: your brain. We are made to be lifetime learners.

We have built-in curiosity to make learning fun. Do you know that boredom is an unnatural state? Boredom is the lack of curiosity. If you often find yourself bored, it simply means you haven't yet learned to use that incredible learning machine, the brain. The good news is that you can learn to use it well. Today you will learn, or relearn, several skills that will help you get more out of your incredibly sophisticated brain. You will learn a process for setting clear, definite, and possible goals, and you will learn the steps in relaxation training that will help you use your creativity.

To begin, I would like you to follow my instructions for a relaxation-training exercise. Evidence suggests that we can speed up our learning when our body and mind are relaxed and calm. Therefore, anyone wanting to make learning easier and faster will want to master these simple steps in relaxation training and use them regularly. The exercise will last about 12 minutes. At the end of that time, I will ask you to do two things: First, rate how deeply you allowed yourself to relax; and second, write out a specific goal that is important to you.

Let's begin. Get into a comfortable position, close your eyes, uncross your arms and legs, and take several slow, deep breaths. These should be gentle and noiseless; the person next to you should not be able to hear you breathe. Now you are going to go through the main muscles in your body and tell them to relax. The key is to put your attention where you want to relax and imagine the muscles relaxing.

I want you to start with the muscles in your forehead and eyes. Name the part and tell it to relax. For example, say "Forehead and eyes, relax," then imagine them letting go. Feel the release. Next, tell your jaw and neck to relax. Feel them relaxing and letting go.

When you learn to relax the muscles in your face and neck, the rest of your body follows. Now, tell your shoulders and arms to relax. If you don't feel them relaxing immediately, then imagine that they are deeply relaxing. Your body will follow your thoughts.

Now, tell the muscles in your upper back and chest to relax and let go.

Now, tell your stomach and lower back to relax and let go.

Now, tell your thighs and knees to relax and let go.

Now, tell your calves, ankles, and feet to relax and let go.

Now, continue to breathe slowly, deeply, and gently as I tell you how to train your mind to relax. To relax your mind, you use your imagination. First, I would like you to picture yourself in a very relaxing, soothing, comfortable, and safe place. This place may be familiar to you, like your room at home, a treehouse in the woods, or a favorite spot at the beach. Or it can be a place you create. As you picture yourself in this resting place, pay attention to what you can see and hear around you. Also notice what you can feel and smell. Let all of your senses be aware of this pleasant and peaceful place.

Now that your body and mind are relaxed, I'd like to guide you through creating a clear, definite, and possible goal for yourself. Setting specific goals and picturing yourself achieving those goals gives your brain a map for success. Right now, I want you to pick one school subject in which you have a test coming up between four and seven days from today. Pick a subject that you would like to do well in. Remember, the test must be between four and seven days from now. This short-term time frame will give you a chance to practice your success plan right away.

After you choose the subject, decide the letter grade that you would like. This letter grade should be no more than one letter above your average test grade in this subject. For example, let's say you choose science as the subject that has a test coming up in five days, and your average test grade so far has been C. Set your goal as a B for this test. I will give you a few moments to decide on a subject and letter-grade goal.

Now that you have a clear goal, the next step is to develop a plan that will allow you to reach your goal. A good plan will include where you will study, what you will study, when you will study, and how long you will study. It is also useful to identify people or resources that can be helpful to you while you are learning the material.

Learning for most people is faster and easier when you have few or no distractions, so choose a place that is quiet. If you prefer music playing in the background, it should be instrumental—that is, without lyrics. Picture yourself sitting in a place after school that would be the best place to study.

Knowing what to study makes all the difference. You should know the type of test and the pages in the text that the test covers, and you should be sure to have an accurate set of notes and teacher handouts. Picture yourself starting today at the study place you have chosen, reviewing your notes and readings for the upcoming test. Write down any questions you have about any of the material you don't understand. See yourself asking your teacher about any questions from your studying, before class or after class or when the teacher asks if there are any questions.

The key to doing well on tests lies in reviewing notes and readings each day. It only takes a few minutes to go over the key points. Picture yourself reviewing the key points from your notes and reading at your study place for a few minutes, starting today and including each day between today and the test day.

Now, finally, I want you to picture yourself feeling confident as you sit down to take the test, knowing that you have stuck to your plan and are prepared. Picture yourself handing in your test, feeling sure that you did well. Picture yourself getting your test paper back with the grade you chose as your goal. See yourself smile, feeling good about achieving your goal.

Picturing successful completion of a goal is a key skill. Many top athletes, businesspeople, and students use this skill regularly. It can help you reach your goals.

In just a moment, I will ask you to open your eyes. After going through a relaxation-training exercise, as you just have, you can expect to feel relaxed, alert, and energized. The more you practice, the better the results. After I ask you to open your eyes, I will ask you to do three things. Now, open your eyes, feeling alert and awake.

First, rate how relaxed you were during the exercise on a 1–10 scale, 10 being the most relaxed. Write this number down. Second, write down the goal you chose, the subject, the letter grade, and the place and amount of time per day you plan to study. And third, now that you have a clear, definite, and possible goal, go achieve it and experience the good feelings that come when you succeed.

Name_____ Date_____

Grade Monitoring Form

Subject _____

Last report period grade	Goal for this report period	Midterm grade for this report period	Final grade

Date	Homework	Quiz	Test	Project/Report

Strategies to help reach goal:

1. Study for tests ahead of time.
2. Get high grades on homework.
3. Have a study buddy.
4. Turn in extra credit.
5. Use note cards/outline/concept map for key concepts.

Name_____ Date _____

Student Success Training Goal

Course: _____

1. Set a goal.

    Goals that are:

    1. clear

    2. have a definite time limit; and

    3. are reasonable

    have the best chance of being achieved.

    > My Grade Goal for this course this six weeks is _____ (A, B, C).

2. Develop a study plan.

    Be sure to include:

    - amount of time
    - study place
    - starting time
    - how many days per week

    > *Example:* To study 20 minutes per day beginning at 4 P.M. in my room at least three days per week.

    > My study plan to achieve this goal:
    >
    > _____
    >
    > _____
    >
    > _____
    >
    > _____

Good luck on reaching your goal!

Session 3
Topic: Student success skills

Resources

- Student Success Skills Guide to Scoring in the Game of Academics handout
- Student Self-Evaluation handout (page 112)

Beginning

1. In a go-round ask students to complete the sentences, "My name is... and the way I feel about school this week is . . ." (give a number between 1 and 10, where 1 is awful and 10 is wonderful). "I feel this way because . . ."

2. Students share progress they made on the goals they set last meeting.

Middle

STUDENT SUCCESS SKILLS GUIDE TO SCORING IN ACADEMICS AND SELF-EVALUATION

1. Briefly go over the Student Success Skills Guide to Scoring in the Game of Academics. (This is an awareness activity rather than a time for skill teaching.) Ask students to evaluate their strengths and areas of weakness as you go through the various sections.

2. Next, ask students to discuss in pairs the following three statements:

    "One of my academic strengths (strong points for doing well in school) is . . ."

    "One reason I sometimes make bad grades is . . ."

    "The most important thing I can do to take responsibility for making good grades is . . ."

3. Ask pairs to share answers with the group. Ask group for feedback on answers.

4. Ask for a show of hands after each strength and each reason for making bad grades is given.

Those who share the strength or reason should raise their hands. Which answers show "taking responsibility"?

5. Discuss the positive power of taking responsibility. It is important to show the benefits to students of their taking responsibility, i.e., academic improvement, stress reduction, social gains, parent relations, and so forth.

6. Go through the Student Self-Evaluation form item by item, asking students to rate each on a 1–4 scale. Ask for show of hands on each item. How many had 3–4? Discuss how the first three items (listening, participating, asking questions) are connected.

7. Discuss the fact that if you are doing well on the first three, you can have more fun with the next two (working in small groups and getting along with others).

8. Ask students to write a goal for the week based on one of the 11 areas discussed.

9. Collect parent letter. Ask students how their parents reacted and if they sat down and discussed the checklist.

End

1. Ask students to discuss in pairs the following two sentences:

    "Today I learned . . ."

    "My goal for next week is . . ."

2. Students share their goal with group. After each goal is shared, the entire group says in unison, "You can do it [name of student], go for it!"

3. Preview next meeting.

Name_____ Date _____

The Student Success Skills Guide
to Scoring in the Game of Academics

1. **How to improve concentration and memory**

   (a) Space out review, rather than cramming.

   (b) Use graphic organizers: Outlines, concept maps.

   (c) Use the index card method: Put one key term/concept per card. Use cards several days in advance for repeated review.

   (d) Use memory techniques for key terms, i.e., acronyms, memory location techniques, associations.

   (e) Make information meaningful.

      1. Ask questions.

      2. Find something interesting.

      3. Anticipate questions teacher will ask.

   (f) Use several types of learning.

      1. Reading

      2. Writing

      3. Listening

      4. Speaking

2. **Preparing for tests**

   (a) Read material and take notes.

   (b) Answer review questions; put key terms in notes.

   (c) Reduce class and reading notes to 1–2 pages, then to note cards.

   (d) Go over these 1–2 pages/note cards 5–10 times, spaced over 2–3 days.

(continued)

Name_____ Date _____

The Student Success Skills Guide
to Scoring in the Game of Academics *(continued)*

(e) Find out all you can about the test.

1. What kind—i.e., short answer, multiple-choice, essay, matching, etc.

2. Make up a practice test.

3. Ask your teacher about the test.

(f) No new reading within 24 hours of test, if possible. Instead, have notes organized by the night before and only review.

(g) Picture yourself doing well.

3. Taking tests

(a) Use slow breathing to relax.

(b) Look over the test; answer easy questions first.

(c) Go back to hard items; look for clues; eliminate wrong answers; take educated guesses.

(d) Go for items with the most points first.

(e) Budget your time.

4. How to avoid test anxiety

(a) Overlearn the details, facts.

(b) Know all you can about the test—see #2(e).

(c) Use a practice test—make up your own or ask teacher.

(d) Have a test-taking strategy and follow it—see #3 above.

(e) Imagine yourself taking the test and doing well.

(f) During the test, use nickel-breathing technique: breathe in slowly to a count of five; hold for five counts; exhale slowly to five counts; repeat five times. (Practice before test day.)

Session 4
Topic: Handling conflicts, role-play

Resources

- Student Self-Evaluation handout (page 112)
- Grade Monitoring handout (page 116)
- Student folders
- Paper and pencils
- Chart paper

Beginning

1. Ask students to record grades for the week on the grade monitoring forms in their folders.
2. Ask students to respond in a go-round to the statements:

   "My name is . . ."

   "One thing that is going better is . . ."

   "What I have the most trouble with is . . ."

REVIEW

1. Ask students to share what they remember about last meeting.
2. Ask students to report on last week's goals.

Middle

HANDLING CONFLICTS

1. Ask students to write down typical problems either that they have had with other students at school or that they notice lots of other students have with each other at school. Ask them not to put their names on the list. Tell them you will collect everyone's ideas in a moment and the group will discuss: (a) if they agree that the problem is typical and (b) some possible solutions.
2. Collect lists of problems. Read each one and ask if it is a typical problem for this age group. List on a flip chart all the agreed-upon typical problems. Ask the group members to rank the top three problems in terms of how interested they would be in having the group discuss possible solutions.
3. Lead a discussion on possible solutions for the top three problems selected. Use a brainstorming technique. List all offered solutions on chart paper or blackboard/white board. Then go back and have

the group code each one as "H," helpful, or "HA," harmful to self or others. *Note:* Some will be rated as both. Have the group decide if the helpful side outweighs the harmful side.

4. Ask group to divide into pairs and plan a role-play for one of the three problems. The role-play should include one of the helpful solutions. Allow approximately five minutes for planning.
5. Ask each pair to present their role-play. Ask the rest of the group to discuss how realistically the problem and solution were portrayed and to demonstrate additional suggestions for handling the problem. The leader can also demonstrate various positive alternative ways to handle the situation or coach students in different ways to act. *Note:* It is the role-play and coaching that make this a powerful learning activity.

STUDENT SELF-EVALUATION

1. Go through each of the seven items, reading them aloud and asking students to rate how they did that week. Ask, "Who rated that item 'Good,' who rated it 'OK,' who rated it 'Needs to improve'?"
2. Use the items to stimulate discussion and to clarify problem areas that need to be addressed.
3. Use group problem solving by asking students to brainstorm solutions to problems students bring up as you move down the list. Role-playing solutions to problems is a valuable way to help students learn alternative strategies for handling difficult situations. The problem solving can also include how to handle the social problems that come up during the group meetings.

End

1. Ask students to write an ending to the following two statements. Ask them to share their answers with a partner. Then ask for volunteers to share what they wrote.

   "One thing I learned today was . . ."

   "One way I can use what I learned today is . . ."

2. Preview next session.

Session 5
Topic: Asking questions, role-play

Resources

- Student Self-Evaluation (page 112)
- Grade Monitoring form (page 116)
- Student folders
- List of web sites for study help, references

Beginning

1. Ask students to record grades for the week on the grade monitoring forms in their folders.

2. Ask students to respond in a go-round to the statement:

   "My name is . . . and one thing that is going better is . . ."

REVIEW

1. Ask students to share what they remember about last meeting.

2. Ask students to report on last week's goals.

Middle

ASKING QUESTIONS

1. Students sometimes don't ask questions in class when they don't understand something because they're afraid they'll look dumb. If you know when and how to ask questions, you can look smart even when you don't understand something.

   When Ask: "When are the best times to ask your teacher questions about assignments?" Some recommended times are:

   - before class;
   - when the teacher asks, "Are there any questions";
   - right after you miss a key point, assuming you have been listening and know how to look smart when you ask a question.
   - at the end of class.

   How The do's and don'ts of asking questions. Ask: "What are some ways to ask questions that might make you look dumb?"

   - Say "Huh?"
   - Say "What did you say?"
   - Ask "What are we supposed to do?" right after teacher gives instructions.

2. Go over with students the basics of looking good when asking questions:

- When asking a question, let the teacher know you heard part of what was said. "Ms. Jones, I understand about . . . and I heard you say . . ., but where I lost you was . . . . Could you say a little more about that?"
- Let the teacher know you care. "Mr. Smith, I want to understand this point, but I'm really having a hard time. Could you explain it once more, please?"

Both examples include nonverbal messages—tone of voice, facial expressions, and body language—that must match the verbal message of sincerity in order for questions to be received positively.

ROLE-PLAY

1. Have students set the scene—teacher, class, subject. One student plays the teacher and begins lecturing or giving directions. Another student models looking smart when asking a question.

2. Try several variations—Beginning of class, after teacher asks "Are there any questions," as soon as student misses a key point, and end of class.

3. Brainstorm other ways to be sure students know what to do on an assignment or what to study for a test, e.g., check with a friend, call a study buddy.

4. Brainstorm and create a list of web sites that provide tutoring help or easy references. Check with your school media center or public library ahead of time for examples.

STUDENT SELF-EVALUATION

1. Go through each of the seven items, reading them aloud and asking students to rate how they did that week. Ask, "Who rated that item 'Good', who rated it 'OK', who rated it 'Needs to improve'?"

2. Use the items to stimulate discussion and to identify problem areas that need to be addressed.

3. Use group problem solving by asking students to brainstorm solutions to problems raised by group members as you move down the list.

4. Role-playing solutions to problems is a valuable way to help students learn alternative strategies for handling difficult situations. The problem solving can also include how to handle the social problems that come up during the group meetings. The idea is for all participants to move to 3–4 range on all 11 topics.

End

1. Ask students to write an ending to the following two statements. Ask them to share their answers with a partner. Then ask for volunteers to share what they wrote.

   "One thing I learned today was . . ."

   "One way I can use what I learned today is . . ."

2. Preview next session. Direct students to bring their social studies text to the session.

Session 6
Topic: How to approach any reading assignment

Resources

- How to Approach Any Reading Assignment handout
- Student Self-Evaluation handout (page 112)
- Grade Monitoring form (page 116)
- Student folders
- Student social studies text

Beginning

1. Ask students to record grades for the week on the grade monitoring forms in their folders.
2. Ask students to complete the following statements:
   "When people talk to me, I like for them to . . ."
   "A person who talks all the time makes me feel . . ."
   "When people give me unwanted advice, I feel . . ."
   "I trust people who . . ."
   "I am willing to listen to others if . . ."

REVIEW

1. Ask students to share what they remember about last meeting.
2. Ask students to report on last week's goals.

Middle

READING STRATEGIES

1. Go over the How to Approach Any Reading Assignment handout with students.
2. Guide students through an upcoming chapter in their social studies book, using the reading handout.

Note: It is essential to use student text and current chapter with the reading strategies. Students need to practice the strategies in context; simply going over these strategies without a proper context is not effective. It would be ideal if you could work with the teachers and have them reinforce these or similar strategies with their entire class.

STUDENT SELF-EVALUATION

1. Go through each of the seven items, reading them aloud and asking students to rate how they did that week. Ask, "Who rated that item 'Good', who rated it 'OK', who rated it 'Needs to improve'?"
2. Use the items to stimulate discussion and to clarify problem areas that need to be addressed.
3. Use group problem solving by asking students to brainstorm solutions to problems students bring up as you move down the list.
4. Role-playing solutions to problems is a valuable way to help students learn alternative strategies for handling difficult situations.
5. The problem solving can also include how to handle the social problems that come up during the group meetings. The idea is for all participants to move to 3–4 range on all 11 topics.

End

1. Ask students to write an ending to the following two statements. Ask them to share their answers with a partner. Then ask for volunteers to share what they wrote.
   "One thing I learned today was . . ."
   "One way I can use what I learned today is . . ."
2. Preview next session. Direct students to bring their math text to the next session.

Name_____ Date _____

How to Approach Any Reading Assignment

There are many ways you can improve your understanding of what you read. We recommend that you have a clear step-by-step approach that can be easily followed.

1. **Develop an overview** of the reading. Ask yourself, "What are this section's key points?" To begin to get the "big picture" of what the section is about:

   - Look at any pictures, graphs; read captions.
   - Read introduction paragraph and summary paragraph.
   - Read questions, if any, at the end of the section.
   - Look over the vocabulary list.
   - Look at boldface headings. Turn each heading into a question you will answer when you read the section.

2. **Read the section.** As you read, mentally answer the questions you made up from each heading. Make a list of any terms you don't understand. As you finish each subsection, mentally summarize the main ideas.

3. **Review what you have read.** Look over questions and key terms at the end of the section. If you cannot answer them, return to the section where they are covered and reread. Before leaving the section, be sure you can answer the *W* and *H* questions:
   who, what, when, where, why, and how.

(continued)

Name_____ Date_____

How to Approach Any Reading Assignment *(continued)*

The chart below summarizes these steps and indicates the percentage of comprehension we gain as we progress through each step.

How to Make Remembering What You Read Easier		
Preview 10–20% comprehension	**Read** 50–80% comprehension	**Review** 85–98% comprehension
1. Look at pictures, graphs, charts, read captions.	1. Read to answer questions.	1. Go back to questions and try to answer them mentally.
2. Read summary and questions.	2. Write down any boldface words or terms you don't understand.	2. For those you can't answer, refer to the text.
3. Read the headings, turning them into questions.	3. After reading each subsection, mentally summarize.	3. Make sure you answer all the *W* and *H* questions.

Session 7
Topic: Math checklist

Resources
- Grade Monitoring form (page 116)
- Student folders
- Math checklist handout
- Student Self-Evaluation handout (page 112)
- Student math text

Beginning
1. Ask students to record grades for the week on the grade monitoring forms in their folders.
2. Ask students to complete the following statements:
   "One reading tip I used this week was . . ."
   "One subject I am improving in is . . ."

REVIEW
1. Ask students to share what they remember about last meeting.
2. Ask students to report on last week's goals.

Middle
1. Present the Math Checklist by asking volunteers to read each point or paragraph aloud to the group. Stop after each section to discuss, asking for student opinions and experiences.
2. This is a good time to ask about who is being tutored or who may want a tutor. It is important to provide coordinating tutoring services when needed. This academic support group is not a substitute for skill training in reading or math. Specialists in each of these areas need to be involved if a deficit exists. Coordination with classroom teachers is an important part of the success of the Student Success Skills group program.

3. Ask students to generate any current problems in math. Process the handout, using the particular problems they bring up in the math book.
4. Have students get into pairs, going through math problems that are causing difficulty while using the strategies on the handout.

Note: The handout can also be used by a peer tutor or adult tutor.

STUDENT SELF-EVALUATION FORM
1. Go through each of the 11 items, reading them aloud and asking students to rate how they did that week. Ask, "Who rated that item 'Good,' who rated it 'OK,' who rated it 'Needs to improve'?"
2. Use the items to stimulate discussion and to clarify problem areas that need to be addressed.
3. Use group problem solving by asking students to brainstorm solutions to problems students bring up as you move down the list.
4. Role-playing solutions to problems is a valuable way to help students learn alternative strategies for handling difficult situations. The problem solving can also include how to handle the social problems that come up during the group meetings. The idea is for all participants to move to 3–4 range on all 11 topics.

End
1. Ask students to write an ending to the following two sentences. Ask them to share their answers with a partner. Then ask for volunteers to share what they wrote.
   "One thing I learned today was . . ."
   "One way I can use what I learned today is . . ."
2. Preview next session.

Name_____ Date _____

Math Checklist

You can master the needed steps for any math problem. Use this problem-solving approach.

> 1. Pinpoint the type of math problems on which you are having difficulty.
>
> 2. Choose a problem. As you begin working, say out loud each step you are using.
>
> 3. When you cannot specify what you should do next or when you give the wrong step, stop. Find an example with an explanation in the text. Read this example aloud, step by step.
>
> 4. If no clear example is available, ask for help. Ask him or her to write out the necessary steps. Then try the problem again, using the steps presented.
>
> Working math problems involves applying a series of steps in a set order. It makes it easier if you follow this simple two-step process.
>
> (a) Write out the steps.
>
> (b) Say the steps as you perform each operation, checking them off as you go.

Many difficulties in math occur because students have not mastered the basic four operations—adding, subtracting, multiplying, and dividing.

These four operations are like any skill. Mastering them requires repetition.

The sooner you master the four operations, the sooner math will become easier.

It is helpful to have someone check these basic operations when you notice errors. When you have trouble with computational skills, flash cards and sample problems can help you to master the skill.

Think of some of your favorite athletes, musicians, dancers, or artists. They have all put in a lot of time to master the basics. When you master the basics, in any area of life, then you have more control and freedom.

The first step is to determine where you need to strengthen your skills. The next step is to set a plan to work on building these skills to a mastery level. Then you get to enjoy using these skills and appreciating the good feeling that comes from being successful.

Session 8
Topic: Review, spotlight, evaluation

Resources
- Index cards or sheets of paper
- Group Evaluation form (page 10)

Beginning

Ask, "Who used something we talked about last week during the week? How did it go?"

REVIEW LIFE OF GROUP

1. Briefly go over each topic you've covered during the last seven weeks, asking students what they remember.
2. Then ask the following questions:
   - What are some of the most important things you have learned about yourself?
   - What has been the most helpful part of this group for you?
   - What is a goal you have set for yourself?

Middle

ACCEPTING AND GIVING COMPLIMENTS

1. Hand out index cards or sheets of paper. Each person is to write down at least one thing he or she admires, likes, or appreciates about each of the other group members.
2. Spotlight: Ask each group member to say directly to the "spotlighted" person, with eye contact: "[person's name], one thing I admire, like, or appreciate about you is . . .".
3. Explain and give examples of the types of qualities you are asking students to think of and how to say and receive them. Ask students not to use appearance compliments such as "I like your shirt, shoes, hair," etc., but to use qualities or actions.
4. After each comment, the spotlighted person says "thank you," nothing else. (Be sure you get in on this—it feels good.)

End

1. Process the spotlighting activity. How did it feel receiving compliments? Giving compliments?
2. Students complete anonymous Group Evaluation.
3. Concluding remarks. Invite students to make individual appointments if they want. Remind them of the monthly follow-up sessions.

Booster Session Generic Plan

Meeting once a month with the group after the weekly sessions end is a good way to maintain the gains the students have made and provides additional support for their continued growth. It also provides a way to monitor the long-term effect of participating in your groups.

Resources

- Grade Monitoring Form (page 116)
- Student Self-Evaluation handout (page 112)

Beginning

MOVEMENT, GROUP TEMPERATURE, REVIEW, AND GOAL REPORT

1. In a go-round ask students to rate how they are feeling on the "great, pretty good, not so good, really bad" scale. Be sure to check with any not so good or really bad to determine if follow-up is needed.

2. Ask students to fill out grade forms for the core subjects using grades from the last report card or midterm progress report. Turn in grade forms to you.

3. Ask students to share in a go-round their rating of how their grades are doing on a scale of 1–10, where 10 is great and 1 is poor.

Middle

STUDENT SELF-EVALUATION

1. Go through each of the 11 items, reading them aloud and asking students to rate how they did the past month. Ask, "Who rated that item 'Good,' who rated it 'OK,' who rated it 'Needs to improve'?"

2. Use the items to stimulate discussion and to clarify problem areas that need to be addressed.

3. Use group problem solving by asking students to brainstorm solutions to problems students bring up as you move down the list.

4. Role-playing solutions to problems is a valuable way to help students learn alternative strategies for handling difficult situations.

SOCIAL PROBLEM SOLVING

1. Ask students about problems that they have had with other students/teachers at school. Make a list.

2. Ask the group members to rank the top three problems in terms of interest to them for group to discuss possible solutions.

3. Lead a discussion on possible solutions for the selected top three problems. Use a brainstorming technique. List all offered solutions first. Then go back and have the group code each one as "H," helpful, or "HA," harmful to self or others. *Note:* Some will be rated as both. Have group decide if the helpful side outweighs the harmful side.

4. Ask group to divide into pairs and plan a role-play for one of the three problems. The role-play should include one of the helpful solutions. Allow approximately five minutes for planning.

5. Ask each pair to present their role-play. Ask the rest of the group to discuss how realistically the problem and solution were portrayed. Ask students to demonstrate additional suggestions for handling the problem. You can also demonstrate various positive alternative ways to handle the situation or coach students in different ways to act. *Note:* It is the role play and coaching that make this a powerful learning activity.

End

1. Ask students to write an ending to the following two sentences. Ask them to share their answers with a partner. Then ask for volunteers to share what they wrote.

    "One thing I learned today was . . ."

    "One way I can use what I learned today is . . ."

2. Preview next month's session.

Student Success Skills:
Positive Student Impact Frequency Table

It is useful to tally how many students brought their grades up and to share this with teachers and parents. A frequency table is helpful. A sample is shown below.

Many counselors also include a behavior rating by teachers as a measure of positive impact on student performance. One example of a K–12 nationally normed scale that closely mirrors the training of this group is the *School Social Behavior Scales* (Merrill, 1992). This instrument has subscales that measure academic competence and social competence.

Counselors are increasingly including pre/post nationally standardized achievement scores as indicators of positive impact.

Total number of students in Student Success Skills group: _____

Criteria for selection: _____

_____

_____

Number who brought at least one core academic subject up
at least one letter grade: _____

                 percent of total: _____

Number who brought two or more core academic subjects up
at least one letter grade: _____

                 percent of total: _____

2.2
Coping with Stress and Anger

Grade Level: Middle School and High School	Time Required: 8 Sessions	Authors: Wes Hawkins and Greg Brigman

Purpose

To help students develop coping strategies to manage stress and anger appropriately. Students learn:

- causes and personal triggers of anger
- appropriate ways to respond to anger
- an easy-to-use anger/conflict self-monitoring system
- a helpful social problem-solving model

Real-life situations are used to role-play various situations and practice new ways of responding to anger and stress.

Logistics

GROUP COMPOSITION

Students grades 6–8 mixed with regard to activity level and behavior control. Avoid loading group with only overactive behavior problem students. Students need multiple models of appropriate behavior. Groups with only behavior problem students usually do not show significant gains in prosocial behavior. Mixed groups are generally very effective.

GROUP SIZE

6–8 students

GROUP TIME PER SESSION

45 minutes

NUMBER OF SESSIONS

Eight, with optional booster sessions spaced approximately one month apart after regular group ends.

Recommended Resources

Full bibliographic details for these publications are included in the Bibliography at the end of this book.

Begun and Huml, eds, 1999: *Violence Prevention Skills: Lessons and Activities.*

Bloom, 1984: *Community Mental Health.*

Bowman et al., 1998: *Aggressive and Violent Students.*

Goldstein and Conoley, eds, 1997: *School Violence Intervention.*

Hawkins, 1986: *Circle of Friends Project.*

Kivel et al., 1997: *Making the Peace.*

Sunburst Communications: *When Anger Turns to Rage.* (videocassette)

Sunburst Communications: *When You're Mad! Mad! Mad!* (videocassette)

Sunburst Communications: *Handling Your Anger.* (videocassette)

Sunburst Communications: *Anger: You Can Handle It.* (videocassette)

Sunburst Communications: *Anger Management Skills.* (videocassette)

Taylor, 1994: *Anger Control Training for Children and Teens.*

Whitehouse et al., 1996: *A Volcano in My Tummy: Helping Children to Handle Anger.*

Wilde, 1995: *Anger Management in Schools.*

Wilde, 1994: *Hot Stuff to Help Kids Chill Out.*

Session 1

Topic: What's this group about; getting to know each other

Resources

- Chart paper/blackboard/whiteboard

Beginning

1. Introduce yourself and explain the purpose of the group.

   Example: "All of us get angry, and it's how we respond to our anger that matters. We will learn what causes our own anger and we will learn and practice with group members good ways to respond to anger. We will ask you to give your own real-life examples of how you have responded to anger recently and—with the help of group members—we will help you figure out better ways to respond to anger.

   "The group meets eight times, same place, same time, every week. As I mentioned when I met with each of you individually, there are three ways people get to participate in this group: 1) you heard about the group, thought it sounded good, and signed up; 2) your parent heard or read about it and wanted you to check it out; 3) your teacher thought you'd enjoy it and that you'd be able to benefit from being in the group.

   "As you probably know, this group is open to everyone. You don't have to have a problem with your anger to be here. We are here to learn about ourselves and to help others in dealing with life's problems that make us angry. Think of the group as 'keeping a cool head with a little help from your friends.'"

INTRODUCTIONS

Have students pair up and have them interview their partners in terms of their names, what they like to do, and what they hope to get out of the group. Then have each student introduce his/her partner, based on the interview.

Middle

GROUP RULES

1. Ask, "What are some rules you think would help our group run better? I've found it's helpful to have a few rules to make our group run smoothly." Make sure to include the following:

   - Anything we talk about here is confidential— you own what you say but we do not talk about what anyone else says outside the group.
   - You have the right to say "pass" if you do not want to share your opinion on something. We do not want to make anyone uncomfortable.
   - One person talks at a time—the rest of us listen.
   - We respect each other's right to have different opinions even if we do not agree—no put-downs.
   - Share the time—no monopolizing "talk time."

2. Ask for additional suggestions—get a group consensus on all rules.

ANGER STRATEGIES

1. Have students work in pairs to generate strategies that people their age use for dealing with anger. We are trying to generate typical strategies for handling anger. The strategies could be healthy and helpful or could be unhealthy and harmful.

2. Next have pairs report and list their strategies on a flip chart or board.

3. Have the group code each idea as "H" for helpful or "HA" for harmful.

4. Then ask group to choose the top 2–3 that represent how most people their age deal with anger.

End

1. Ask students to share in pairs what they learned about the group and each other today and what they are looking forward to doing/learning in the group. Ask volunteers to share with whole group.

2. Ask students to review what the purpose of the group is, how many meetings, and so forth.

3. Preview the second meeting.

Session 2
Topic: It's how you respond to anger that counts

Resources

- Prince Llewelyn and his Dog Gelert handout
- Life Problem Solver handout
- Monitor Your Anger handout
- Blackboard/whiteboard/chart paper

Beginning

1. Have students read the story of Prince Llewelyn of Wales and his beloved dog, Gelert. If they wish, they can use the lines at the bottom of the page to make notes about their reactions. Have them respond to the story and discuss if they have ever acted out of anger when they wished they hadn't.

2. Begin discussion by noting that we all become angry at times but it is how we respond that counts. Note that anger is like stress. We will always have it; what is important is how we **respond** to it. For example, Prince Llewelyn suffered the rest of his life because he acted in anger and killed his dog. Many past presidents (Carter, Clinton, Kennedy, Nixon) advise you not to act when you are mad or you are likely to make mistakes.

3. Note that the purpose of this group is to identify the ways we have responded to anger and, with group input, to identify other possible ways of responding to anger and discuss the outcomes.

Middle

1. Explain the Life Problem Solver handout. Model the use of the chart. Have students fill out how they responded when they last became angry.

2. After students have filled out the form, use the board and ask for volunteers to share how they responded to anger. Then identify other possible ways they could have responded.

3. Compare outcomes on the form to demonstrate that our responses to anger do affect outcomes.

4. List the different types of responses to anger and discuss with the group. Write the list on chart paper and post it on the wall for future sessions.

End

1. Have students complete the statement: "What I learned from group today was . . ."

2. Emphasize that responses to anger do affect the outcome—as with Prince Llewelyn.

LIFE GOAL* FOR NEXT WEEK:

Demonstrate how to use the Monitor Your Anger handout. For this week, students need only complete Step 1, keeping track of how many times they get angry each day. Ask students to use the handout to chart the number of times they become angry during the ensuing week.

*We chose to call this exercise a "Life Goal" instead of homework because the skills learned here are to be generalized in the student's environment as life skills.

Name_____ Date _____

Prince Llewelyn and his Dog Gelert

In the 13th century, the Prince of North Wales, Llewelyn, went hunting one day without his faithful hound, Gelert. Gelert usually accompanied his master, but for some unknown reason he stayed at the prince's castle this day. On the prince's return, he found Gelert stained and smeared with blood. Gelert joyfully sprang to meet his master. The prince started to greet Gelert, but then saw that the cot of his infant son was empty and smeared with blood. Swelling with anger, the prince plunged his sword into the faithful hound's side, thinking the dog had killed his son. Gelert yelped in extreme pain and, looking into his master's eyes, fell to the floor and died. The dog's dying cry was answered by a child's cry. Prince Llewelyn searched and discovered his son unharmed. Nearby lay the body of a mighty wolf, which Gelert had slain to protect the prince's son. The prince, filled with remorse and sadness, was said never to have smiled again. Gelert is buried in Beddgelert, Wales. This story is a memorial to the life of Gelert, the faithful hound.

_____

_____

_____

_____

_____

_____

Name_____ Date_____

Life Problem Solver

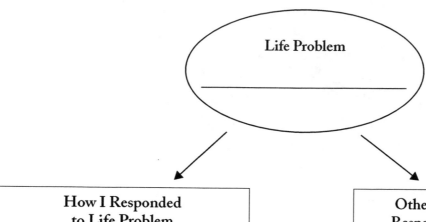

How I Responded to Life Problem	Other Ways I Could Have Responded to Life Problem

Outcome of Response to Life Problem	Probable Outcomes of Other Responses to Life Problem

Name _____ Date _____

Monitor Your Anger

Directions:

1. Look at the chart below. Each time you become angry in a given day, put a dot in the row that corresponds to that day of the week. If it is the first time you got angry that day, put a dot in the "1" box for the day. If you get angry again on the same day, put a dot in the "2" box, and so forth.

2. Each time you get angry, write a brief description of the event/s that preceded your anger on the lines below. If you need more space, use the back of this sheet.

_____

_____

_____

_____

_____

_____

_____

3. At the end of the week, circle the highest dot you recorded for each day. Then draw a line to connect the circles.

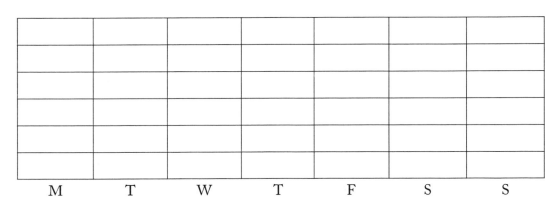

Session 3
Topic: What is my kind of anger?

Resources

- Blackboard/whiteboard/chart paper
- Completed Monitor Your Anger handouts from Session 2
- My Kind of Anger handout
- Monitor Your Anger handout (page 137)

Beginning

1. Have students complete the statement, "What I get mad about the most is . . .".
2. Review the Monitoring Your Anger results for the last week.

Middle

1. Begin discussion by noting that this time we want to identify our own anger and, specifically, what **causes** or **triggers** our anger. The emotion of anger often arises when we perceive that our rights have been violated or threatened. Fear of rejection and stress are two other leading causes of anger. Sometimes anger is a secondary feeling that follows a primary feeling. For example, if we are rejected and feel hurt we sometimes change from the primary feeling—hurt—to the secondary feeling—anger. It is important to understand where the anger is coming from. Another example of primary/secondary feelings connected to anger is depres-

sion. Sometimes people express their depression in the form of lashing out at others in anger. The purpose of today's group is to identify which types of events or stressors cause us to feel angry (e.g., disrespect for others, teasing, time pressure, loss, stress, etc.) and to practice good ways to respond so that we have the outcome we want.

2. Have students complete the My Kind of Anger handout.
3. When students have completed the handout, have them discuss their specific anger triggers.

End

1. Have students complete the statement, "What I learned from group today was . . .".
2. Using student responses, emphasize that each person has his/her own type of anger, in that each person usually has **predictable** types of triggers/stressors/events that produce anger. Note again that a first step in responding to and controlling one's anger is to identify the triggers that are specific to oneself.

LIFE GOAL FOR NEXT WEEK

List the times you became angry each day, as you did last week. This time also list **why** or **what event** made you angry on the Monitor Your Anger handout.

Name_____ Date _____

My Kind of Anger

Part I

Directions: Think back to times you have become angry. Place a check mark beside any situation in which you have felt angry.

_____ Grades or academic
       problems

_____ Interaction with friends

_____ Interaction with parents or
       family members

_____ Interaction with teachers

_____ Interaction with principal

_____ Teasing/bullying

_____ Put-downs by peers

_____ Time issue

_____ Test

_____ Others—Please list:

_____

_____

_____

Summarize your responses: _____

_____

_____

_____

Part II

What events/triggers/stressors happened to cause your anger?

_____

_____

_____

Part III

Is there a pattern in your anger responses?

_____

_____

_____

Session 4
Topic: Strategy for responding to anger

Resources

- The Coconut Grove Fire handout
- Completed Monitor Your Anger handouts from Session 3
- Life Problem Solver handout (page 136)
- Poster board/chart paper
- Monitor Your Anger handout (page 137)

Beginning

1. Have students read the Coconut Grove Fire handout.

2. Have them respond to the story and to the statement, "Talking about my problems when I am angry makes me feel . . .".

3. Review the Monitor Your Anger results for the last week.

4. Note that there are many ways to deal with anger, but ignoring anger is seldom effective. Learning to deal with our anger is a very important life skill. Not learning to deal with our anger can seriously affect our relationships and career in negative ways.

Middle

1. Using the Life Problem Solver, have a pair of students role-play responding to a past situation in which they wished they had managed their anger differently.

2. Brainstorm other strategies for effectively dealing with anger in this situation, then redo the role-play.

3. Use the role-play as a springboard for a discussion of effective ways to deal with the types of situations students identified last week using the My Kind of Anger form.

4. Put responses on posters and place on the wall for future sessions. This is an important session in which positive alternatives need to be identified. Some possible ideas for positively handling anger include:

   - take a "time-out" to cool down
   - think through how you want to respond
   - talk it over with a trusted friend, family member, teacher, counselor
   - check out your self-talk and change any non-helpful messages to healthy ones
   - talk it over with the person with whom you are angry after calming down
   - humor
   - physical activity
   - rest, relaxation

End

Have students complete the statement, "What I learned from group today was . . .".

LIFE GOAL FOR NEXT WEEK

Use or practice a strategy we have discussed today to deal with anger this week. Be ready to discuss it next group session in the Life Problem Solver strategy time.

Name_____ Date _____

The Coconut Grove Fire

In 1942, the Coconut Grove was a popular nightclub in Boston, Massachusetts, where crowds gathered to dance the night away. One fateful night, a large fire broke out in the nightclub. Hundreds of people died. Many of them died because the doors opened inwards. So many people were pressed against the doors that they couldn't be opened.

Many of those who survived the fire were in much emotional stress and grief. At the time, we didn't know how to help people who were exposed to a crisis such as this. A psychiatrist from Harvard was asked to study how to help these survivors. He found out that those survivors who could **talk about their feelings** felt less stress and suffered less psychological distress and illness than those who did not talk about their feelings.

This was a landmark study in mental health. It provided evidence that talking about problems is very important for mental health.

This study also served as the origin of the intervention teams that come to a school or community after a major crisis such as school violence, a hurricane, or a bus accident.

Session 5
Topic: Anger response strategy—keep-cool rules

Resources

- Completed Monitor Your Anger handouts from Session 4
- Keep-Cool Rules handout
- Posters from Session 4
- Monitor Your Anger handout (page 137)

Beginning

1. Have students respond to the statement, "There are times one has to deal with anger head-on. Those times are . . .".
2. Review the Monitor Your Anger results for the last week.

Middle

1. Review the fact that there are many ways to deal with anger, as indicated on the posters from last week.
2. Introduce the notion of **assertiveness**, respecting yourself and the other person, as one effective way to resolve conflicts.
3. Discuss the two extremes on either side of assertiveness: **passivity** and **aggression**. Being too passive means always avoiding conflict, not showing respect for yourself, and treating yourself like a doormat. Being aggressive means being too pushy, acting like a bully, and respecting only yourself and not the other person.

4. Draw an assertiveness continuum on the board to make this point and distinguish among passive, assertive, and aggressive. Ask group members to stand at the point along the continuum that represents how they usually handle conflict.
5. Next, brainstorm what each style looks like and sounds like: body language, voice, tone.
6. Last, discuss the social consequences of each style.

KEEP-COOL RULES

1. Explain how to use the Keep-Cool Rules.
2. Model the use of these rules to students using the Life Problem Solver (page 136) on a simulated problem.
3. Then, using the Life Problem Solver, have students role-play responding to a past anger situation or a simulated situation using the Keep-Cool Rules.

End

1. Have students complete the statement, "What I learned from group today was . . .".
2. Distribute Monitor Your Anger handout and ask students to complete it for the ensuing week.

LIFE GOAL FOR NEXT WEEK

Use or practice the Keep-Cool Rules to deal with your anger strategy with friends or family. Be ready to discuss during the next group session, using the Life Problem Solver.

Keep-Cool Rules

When you get angry, follow the four rules below:

1. **Stop! Cool down.**

   Do not respond if you are at an 8, 9, or 10 on the 1–10 anger scale. Take a time-out. Get out of the situation. Find a place to think.

2. **Think!**

   Review the situation and figure out why you are angry and what you can say/do that will lead to the outcome you want.

3. **Act!**

   Schedule a time to talk to the other person, or to a neutral person, if you need to vent first. If you need the help of another person, talk to the school counselor or peer mediation leader to set up a peer mediation meeting.

4. **Resolve!**

   Follow the steps below to resolve anger with another person:

   Step 1: Person who is angry (Person 1) expresses feelings and behavior to other person (Person 2): "I felt angry when you (state exact behavior) . . ."

   Step 2: Person 1 asks Person 2: "What did you think happened?"

   Discuss how each person perceived the situation and how each felt about it.

   Both persons should be able to restate the other's point of view and feeling.

   Step 3: Person 1 asks Person 2: "In the future, I would like for you to . . . . How does that sound to you?"

   Step 4: Person 2 responds. Repeat steps 1–4 until a resolution is reached that is satisfactory to both persons. Shake hands and say one positive comment to each other in dealing with this issue.

Session 6
Topic: Practice makes for cool heads

Resources

- Completed Monitor Your Anger handouts from Session 5
- Life Problem Solver handout (page 136)
- Poster board/chart paper
- Optional: video camera and TV/VCR
- Monitor Your Anger handout (page 137)

Beginning

1. Have students respond to the statement, "I used or practiced the Keep-Cool Rules last week to deal with anger involving . . . and found the Keep-Cool Rules to . . .".
2. Review the Monitor Your Anger results for the last week.
3. Tell students, "The purpose of today's group is to practice and figure out ways to use the Keep-Cool Rules at school, at home, and in our personal lives (romantic and platonic relationships). We will figure out ways to reduce barriers to use, etc."

Middle

1. Using the Life Problem Solver, have students fill out how they responded when they last became angry and how they can use the Keep-Cool Rules.

2. Discuss combining the direct approach of talking to the person with whom you are angry with other anger management strategies.
3. Have students brainstorm ways to make sure they use the Keep-Cool Rules (e.g., establish buddy system, call someone). Put responses on a poster and put on the wall for visual clues.
4. Role-play a few examples of group members' use of the Keep-Cool Rules, or situations they want to practice that are likely to come up this week.
5. Have group give feedback on steps.
6. Videotaping the role-plays and using the tape to give feedback is a very powerful way to teach these skills.

End

1. Have students complete the statement, "What I learned from group today was . . .".
2. Distribute Monitor Your Anger handouts for students to complete over the coming week.

LIFE GOAL FOR NEXT WEEK

Use or practice the Keep-Cool Rules to deal with your anger strategy with friends or family. Be ready to discuss during the next group session, using the Life Problem Solver.

Session 7
Topic: Making anger management part of your life

Resources

- Completed Monitor Your Anger handouts from Session 6
- Poster board/chart paper

Beginning

1. Ask students to respond to the statement, "People have control over how they respond to anger."
2. Review the Monitor Your Anger results for the last week.
3. Say to students, "People do have control over how they respond to anger. The strategies we have learned in this group are life skills, and the real importance of these skills is to use them long after this group is over, with friends, peers, parents, teachers, etc.

   "Family and friends and peers will be with us long after this group is finished. The purpose of today's group is to develop and put in place a plan for establishing conflict resolution areas at school, at home, and within the family. Note that this is much like a designated driver program—we will find a designated place in our school, home, or place with peers to resolve conflict in a positive way.

   "This may not seem cool to do, but how we solve problems in today's world is important. We see many adults, for example, yelling at each other, hitting each other, and even killing others. Sometimes even multi-million-dollar baseball players solve their problems on the baseball field by having a group punch-out, making ridiculous role models for our youth."

Middle

1. Have the group develop a plan to designate places at school (coordinated with school counselor), home, and with peers as a "designated conflict resolution areas." Have copies or large blown-up copies of the Keep-Cool Rules made for posting on the walls of the designated conflict resolution places.
2. Note that there are many ways to make sure we use the Keep-Cool Rules (e.g., put printed cards in wallet or purse, establish buddy system, call someone). Brainstorm plans for how group members can use the designated conflict management areas when needed.
3. Brainstorm other ideas from the group about managing anger and stress. Write these ideas on a poster, and post it on the wall for last session review.

End

Have students complete the statement, "What I learned from group today was . . .".

LIFE GOAL

As a group, put in place the designated conflict management area in your school. Individually, put it in place with your family. Use them—don't lose them.

Session 8

Topic: What we learned, how to use it

Resources

- Blackboard/writing board
- Index cards/paper

Beginning

Report on Life Goal from last week, which was: As a group, put in place the designated conflict management area in your school. Individually, put it in place with your family.

Middle

1. Hand out index cards or sheets of paper. Each person is to write down at least one thing they liked or appreciated about each of the other group members in helping him/her deal with anger.

2. Have each group member share those positive statements by spotlighting each group member.

3. When receiving compliments, the student must not negate the compliment but simply say "thank-you" or another positive response.

End

1. Have students singly respond to the statements, "What I have learned about responding to anger in this group is . . ."

   "I will use the strategies to respond to anger in the future because . . ."

2. Say good-bye, shake hands, and compliment each other for attending this group and trying to make the world a better place to live for others.

3. Remind group that you are available and that the group will meet in one month to review each person's progress in managing his or her anger.

2.3
Loss/Bereavement

Grade Level: Middle School	Time Required: 7 Sessions	Authors: Barbara Earley Goodman and Greg Brigman

Purpose

A loss group provides a support system for students who have experienced the death of a parent or other family member. These students may have difficulty accepting the death and expressing their feelings. They often act brave and believe the feelings will go away. They think no one understands. Frequently there are unresolved conflicts, feelings of abandonment, anger, and guilt. They may be in a stage of limbo, not able to move ahead because they feel as if their life is over.

Before the group begins, talk with each child in an individual session to let him or her know what the group is about and to learn what his or her particular situation is. Give students a parent letter to take home that explains the group and asks for a parent signature; see page 148 for a sample letter.

It is important that you feel comfortable with the topic of death before leading a group. There are many good books and journal articles on helping kids deal with loss. Since this topic involves deep feelings, we could not encourage anyone to attempt this group without doing background reading and having some experience leading other types of groups.

Know your own feelings about death. Tune in to your philosophy and beliefs, but be careful about discussing your religious beliefs with students. Look at the losses in your life and how you have dealt with them. Some introspection is helpful before you start leading group sessions. During the group, maintain an attitude of acceptance, concern, and caring. This environment of support allows the expression of sadness and promotes movement through the various stages of loss, which lead to healing.

If this group is meeting because of the death of a fellow student or a teacher, the leader could still use some of these lessons with a small group or a classroom but should perhaps modify the amount of time.

If there is a school crisis, assistance support groups could come from community therapists, hospital chaplains, mental health social workers, or other school counselors in the system.

Logistics

GROUP COMPOSITION

Students in grades 6–8 who have recently experienced the death of a loved one. Students who are within 1–2 grade levels may be grouped.

GROUP SIZE

6–8 students

GROUP TIME PER SESSION

45 minutes

NUMBER OF SESSIONS

Seven

Recommended Resources

Full bibliographic details for these publications are included in the Bibliography at the end of this book.

Buscaglia, 1982: *The Fall of Freddie the Leaf.*

Elkind, 1988: *The Hurried Child: Growing Up Too Fast Too Soon.*

Gootman, 1994: *When a Friend Dies: A Book for Teens About Grieving and Healing.*

Grollman, 1995: *Bereaved Children and Teens: A Support Guide for Parents and Professionals.*

Hipp, 1995: *Help for the Hard Times: Getting Through Loss.*

Kroen, 1996: *Helping Children Cope with the Loss of a Loved One.*

Kübler-Ross, 1974: *On Death and Dying.*

Le Shan, 1976: *Learning to Say Good-Bye: When a Parent Dies.*

Oates, 1993: *Death in the School Community.*

Romain, 1999: *What on Earth Do You Do When Someone Dies?*

Traisman, 1992: *Fire in My Heart Ice in My Veins.*

Parent Letter

Dear Parent:

Your child, _____, has chosen to participate in a group dealing with loss and grief. Often students experience a loss and are not prepared to cope with it. Children may suffer the loss of a parent, a sibling, a friend, or a classmate.

Loss is an issue that has deep impact on people. I hope that our discussions in school will be the beginnings of family discussions in the home.

If you have questions or anything you would like to share with me concerning your child or the counseling program, please call me at _____.

Counselor

Student's Signature _____

Parent's Signature _____

Session 1

Topic: Responses to death, bibliotherapy, journaling

Resources

- Optional: books on death, such as *What on Earth Do You Do When Someone Dies?* (Romain), *When a Friend Dies: A Book for Teens About Grieving and Healing* (Gootman), *Learning to Say Good-Bye*, or *Fire in My Heart Ice in My Veins*

Beginning

INTRODUCTION

Introduce yourself and explain the purpose of the group:

"This is a loss group, and I know that you have experienced a loss in your family. We'll be meeting each week at this time to share with each other how things are going and how you are feeling. This group will be a place where you can talk openly about how you are feeling.

"Sometimes your friends may not understand what you are going through and you may not have anyone to talk to. I have found in leading groups like this that students feel more comfortable talking about death when they realize others have had similar experiences."

SHARING THE SITUATION

"I'd like to begin by going around the group and having each of you state your name and what your particular situation is. Tell us who has died in your family, when it happened, and any details you would like to share with the group."

Talking about their situations in front of the group could stir deep feelings and emotions for some students. Be prepared to use your skills of reflective listening and group leadership.

Middle

1. Discuss with students how friends sometimes don't know what to say. "What are some of the responses you have received when your friends found out about the death?" (Students report that friends sometimes don't say anything, make inappropriate remarks, or ask questions about specific details of the death.)

   "Adults often offer platitudes: 'He's better off because he doesn't have to suffer,' or 'It was his time to go.' None of these exchanges helps us in our grief. Our friends want to help, but because they feel awkward and uncomfortable, they may say the wrong things. What would you like for your friends to say? What would be helpful? If someone you knew were to experience a death of someone close to him or her, what would you do or say?"

2. You may read aloud to the group some selections from books such as *What on Earth Do You Do When Someone Dies?* or *When a Friend Dies: A Book for Teens About Grieving and Healing.*

   Show students some books on death from your guidance library or the school library. Briefly explain each one, and let them check out the books to take home. You may read some passages aloud to the group. *Learning to Say Good-Bye* by Eda Le Shan is a helpful book to read to upper elementary, middle, or high school students.

3. Encourage students to keep a journal during the weeks that the loss group meets. The leader can provide the paper or notebook and allow time to begin writing while in the group. You may give a sentence stem or give an idea each time. *Fire in My Heart Ice in My Veins* is a journaling book for teens. Each participant could have his or her own copy and could continue the writing assignments after the group is over. Some examples of sentence stems are:

   - Our funniest time together . . .
   - Some things I remember you saying . . .
   - What it felt line going back to school after you died . . .
   - Helpful things that others have said or done . . .

End

JOURNAL WRITING

Ask students to think and write their endings to the following sentence stems. Then ask students to share what they would like with a partner. Last, ask volunteers to share with the whole group.

"Today I learned . . ."
"I relearned . . ."
"I was surprised that . . ."
"I can use what I learned this week by . . ."
Preview next session.

Session 2
Topic: Stages of grief

Resources

- Chart paper
- Student journals

Beginning

1. Ask students to share in a go-round their endings for the following statements:

   "My name is . . . and I wish . . ."

   "Some thoughts I have had this week are . . ."

   "A journal writing I would like to share with the group is . . ."

2. Ask students to review what they remember from the last session.

3. Ask if anyone used anything they got from the last session.

Middle

1. Begin discussion with the following. "In our lives we experience many kinds of losses, not just death. What are some other losses you have had?" Students often mention loss of friendships, moving, losing a favorite possession, losing a favorite teacher, having something stolen from them, or losing a pet. Allow students to discuss their particular situation and how they felt when it happened. "What were the feelings you experienced in the beginning, a little later, and when did you finally accept what happened?"

2. Let students know that people experience any kind of loss in stages. According to Dr. Kübler-Ross, in her book *On Death and Dying*, the stages of grief are:

- denial
- anger
- bargaining
- depression
- acceptance

List these stages on a chart and have the group members personalize their situations and discuss how they went through or are going through the various stages, and in what order. A person in grief can move back and forth between stages, or can remain stuck in a stage before finally reaching the acceptance stage.

Ask each student: Which stage are you in now?

For those students who may not be in the acceptance stage, use your best empathy and caring skills to help them explore their feelings. Your goal is not to move them to the acceptance stage, but to allow them to state their feelings while you listen and remain there for them.

End

JOURNAL WRITING

Ask students to write in their journals their answers to these sentence stems. When they are done, ask them to share what they choose with the whole group.

"Today I learned or relearned . . ."

"I can see that I need to . . ."

Preview next session.

Session 3
Topic: Changes due to loss

Beginning

Ask students to share their responses to the statement, "My name is . . . and today I feel . . ."

REVIEW

1. Ask students to remember the five stages of grief.
2. Ask them what else they remember about the last meeting.
3. Ask them to share anything they have used from the group this past week.

Middle

THREE QUESTIONS

1. Say to students, "Today I would like to give each of you some time to share with us what is going on with you. As I talk with each person, the rest of you think about how your feelings and experiences are similar or different. Here are some questions I would like you to think about:
   - Since the loss occurred in your family, how has your life changed?
   - What is difficult for you right now?
   - What needs working on or needs to be improved?

2. Say, "Let me give you a minute to think about those questions and we'll begin when you're ready." Give thinking time. "Would someone volunteer to begin our discussion? Maria, you look like you're ready to begin. How has your life changed?"

3. Gently move through the questions, allowing enough time so every group member will have a chance to participate before the period is over.

4. Leave some time at the end of the session to explore similar experiences of other group members. Pull together the idea that everyone has situations that need to be improved, and perhaps some of these situations are normal in any family, not just grieving families.

End

1. Journal writing and sharing:
   "I learned . . ."
   "I relearned . . ."
   "I see that I need to . . ."
2. Preview next meeting.

Session 4
Topic: Memories

Beginning

"The high point of my week was when . . ."
"The low point was when . . ."

REVIEW

1. Spend time summarizing similar experiences that the group shared from last week's activity.

2. Ask for volunteers to share what they have used from the group this past week.

Middle

1. "Focus on a happy memory that you have of the person you have lost. Perhaps there was a vacation you shared, a funny experience, or an especially happy event. I'll give you some thinking time, and then we'll go around the circle and let each person share a happy memory." Have each group member share his or her happy memory. Process the activity by pointing out similarities, differences, and giving affirmation for sharing their personal experiences.

2. "If you could write a letter to that person right now, what would you like to say? Would you like to tell the person how you are doing, about a happy memory, or what you would like him/her to know?

   "What qualities did that person have that you want to have in your life? What messages about living did he or she give you, either with words or by how he/she lived?

"I'll give you some paper and time to think. When you're ready, begin your letter with 'Dear . . .' and write whatever you're feeling. This letter is private, so you won't have to share it with group unless you feel like it."

3. Allow time for everyone to finish the letter. Allow them to discuss the feelings they had while writing the letter. Permit those students who want to read their letter to the group to do so.

4. Sharing these memories often elicits tears and sadness. Sometimes students tune in to the loss of future happy times together. It's important for the counselor not to shut off the expression of sadness. This expression is one key to the healing process. Most people in the student's life are probably uncomfortable with these feelings and don't allow their expression.

End

1. Journal Writing:
   "I learned . . ."
   "I relearned . . ."
   "One thing I can use this week is . . ."

2. Ask students to talk to friends or family about their thoughts or experiences while attending this group.

3. Preview next meeting.

Session 5
Topic: Loss-related art activity

Resources

- Art supplies

Beginning

Ask students to finish the sentence stems:
"I feel happy when . . ."
"I feel sad when . . ."

REVIEW

1. Allow time for students to express how they felt during last week's activity.
2. Ask students to share their experience talking to friends or family about their thoughts or experiences while attending this group.

Middle

1. Provide art supplies and have students draw a picture of the pain associated with their loss. Explain, "The picture does not need to be realistic. You may use symbols, or colors, or simple shapes to express the pain you feel. No one else needs to be able to tell what the picture is about. You will know, and that is all that matters." Students and leaders who insist they have no artistic ability and are reticent about beginning this activity will get deeply involved once you are able to convince them to begin. They may also want to write a poem or short story to accompany their picture.

2. Have each person share his or her drawing with the group, and explain what it means and how he/she is feeling. Students may wish to display their drawings on a wall of the group room.

3. Discuss any books on death the students have read while participating in the group. Encourage them to share their readings and the group discussions with siblings and family members.

End

1. Ask students to discuss what it was like to draw their pain and to share their pictures.
2. Ask students to complete the following sentence stems:
   "Today I learned or relearned . . ."
   "I can see I need to . . ."
3. Preview next meeting.

Session 6
Topic: Rituals

Resources

- Small, soft ball
- Drawing supplies

Beginning

Hold a soft ball in your hand and complete this statement, "A way that I could help someone who is going through loss is . . .".

Throw the ball to a group member who repeats the sentence. Continue until each person has had a turn.

REVIEW

Allow time for students to talk about last week's art activity.

Middle

1. Have students discuss rituals of death: funerals, cremations, wakes, customs of sending flowers and bringing food to the home. Some cultures may have customs that are not familiar to other cultures. What is the importance of the rituals?

Be careful that students are respectful of each others' religions, beliefs, and customs. This discussion can help students understand and appreciate differences.

2. Ask students to draw three pictures using symbols and colors:

   (a) Their life before the loss

   (b) Their life now

   (c) Their life as they hope it will be in the future

3. Ask students to share their pictures with the group.

End

1. Ask students to share what it was like to draw and share today's pictures.

2. Journal writing: "One thing I can start doing now that will help me have the kind of future I want . . ."

3. Ask students to share journal writing.

4. Preview last session.

Session 7

Topic: Handling stress, evaluation, closure

Resources

- Optional: the Children's Stress Scale, in David Elkind, *The Hurried Child*
- Group Evaluation form (page 10)

Beginning

1. Have students complete the sentence, "I hope . . ."
2. Review last session.
3. Share how students are using what they are learning in group.

Middle

1. Losses and changes can create stress. Discuss with the group ways to handle stress. Encourage members to:
   - Get involved in physical activities
   - Develop solid social support networks with family and friends
   - Have a list of positive fun activities they can do in various time limits and at limited or no costs
   - Get enough sleep
   - Eat a healthy diet
2. You may want to look at the Children's Stress Scale, an adaptation of the Holmes Stress Inventory, which is found in David Elkind's book, *The Hurried Child*. Be careful in using this or any

survey. You don't want to cause alarm if a student scores high on the number of losses experienced in the past year. Rather, focus on positive activities—hobbies, physical exercise. Use the scale as an awareness technique, pointing out the importance of taking care of yourself to prevent stressful situations.

Some students remain in the shock stage for months. Often teachers expect these students to be back to normal after several weeks. It may take a year or longer for students to move to acceptance. The most important part of the healing process is to allow the person to express sadness. If someone cannot express sadness, long-term problems often result.

End

1. Ask students to complete written evaluation.
2. Have students respond to the statement, "Something I learned from being in this group is . . .".
3. Let students know that after the group is over, you plan to see each member individually in the next few weeks.
4. If some group members are in need of additional resources, have a conference with a family member and talk to him or her about counseling from a private therapist or community agency.

2.4
Divorce/Changing Families

| Grade Level: Middle School | Time Required: 10 Sessions | Author: Barbara Earley Goodman |

Purpose

To help students cope with the stress of parent divorce. Students are taught coping skills, and learn about how to constructively deal with typical issues associated with divorce. Bibliotherapy is used to stimulate sharing of thoughts, feelings, and positive coping strategies.

Parent divorce is a significant and growing issue effecting children's social and academic development. Parent divorce is one of the most stressful events that can happen to a child. Support groups have been found to be effective in helping students deal constructively with parent divorce and to be able to return their attention to academic performance and positive peer relations.

Before the group begins, talk with each child in an individual session to let him or her know what the group is about and to learn what his or her particular situation is.

The group leader should be comfortable with his or her own issues about divorce. Self-disclosure should be limited to promoting group rapport and cohesion.

Logistics

GROUP COMPOSITION

Students in grades 6–8 who have recently experienced the divorce of their parents. Students who are within 1–2 grade levels may be grouped.

GROUP SIZE

6–8 students

GROUP TIME PER SESSION

45 minutes

NUMBER OF SESSIONS

Ten

Recommended Resources

Full bibliographic details for these publications are included in the Bibliography at the end of this book.

Brown and Brown, 1986: *The Dinosaurs Divorce.*

Clark, 1998: *When Your Parents Divorce.*

Curran, 1983: *Traits of a Healthy Family.*

Gardner, 1971: *The Boys and Girls Book About Divorce.*

Heegaard, 1990: *When Mom and Dad Separate.*

Heegaard, 1993: *When a Parent Marries Again.*

Jackson, 1998: *When Your Parents Split Up.*

Margolin, 1996: *Complete Group Counseling Program for Children of Divorce.*

Schneider and Zuckerberg, 1996: *Difficult Questions Kids Ask and Are Too Afraid to Ask About Divorce.*

Stern and Stern, 1997: *Divorce Is Not the End of the World.*

Sunburst Communications, 1991: *If Your Parents Break Up* (videocassette).

Session 1
Topic: Sharing family situations

Resources
- Parent Letter handout

Beginning

INTRODUCTION

You may want to begin this way:

"Some of you may have parents who have recently separated, are divorced, or who have divorced and remarried, giving you additional parents and families. Students have found this group to be very helpful because they can share their feelings with other students who have similar experiences. You may remember times when you felt alone and thought no one else could possibly understand what you were feeling. Or you may have felt embarrassed, ashamed, guilty, angry, or hurt. These feelings are all normal, and represent the different stages we go through when we have a breakup in our family.

"At the end of these ten weeks, I hope you will have learned some new skills to help you adjust to your situation, to understand what has happened, and to improve the communication within your family."

SHARING THE CURRENT SITUATION

1. Ask students to tell their name, grade, and a brief summary of their family situation (how long their parents have been divorced or separated, whom they are living with, and what their biggest family concerns are at this time). Give them 30 seconds to think about what they want to say. The counselor may introduce himself/ herself first to get the group started.

2. After the introductions, ask the following questions:

   "What are some things you noticed we had in common with each other?"

   "Sometimes it's helpful to remember that others have problems similar to ours. How many of you have ever felt that you were the only one who had divorced parents, or felt that no one else understood?"

Middle

RULES AND HOUSEKEEPING

1. Let students come up with the rules, but be sure they include:
   - What is said in group is confidential. You own what you say and can share what you say with others if you choose. You do not own what others say and it is important to keep what others say within this group.
   - Don't put each other down.

2. Distribute and explain the parent letter. Remind students that the group meets once per week for ten weeks. They are expected to make up the work they miss while in the group. (You may want to go around and ask each person what class is being missed and how the work will be made up.)

3. Address any comments or questions.

   Ask students to think about the statement, "One thing that has improved since the divorce/separation is . . .". Give them a minute, then go around the circle and ask students to respond.

End

1. Ask students to summarize the purpose of group and the number of sessions.
2. Ask students to complete the statement, "One thing I learned today was . . .".
3. Preview next meeting.
4. Remind students to return the letter in order to attend group next time.
5. Remind students that you are available to them on an individual basis as well as in the group.

Parent Letter

Dear Parents:

We would like to acquaint you with the counseling services at our school. In addition to individual counseling, classroom guidance, and parent-teacher conferences, we offer group sessions that deal with specific concerns. Topics such as getting along with others and managing conflicts, making friends, academic support, changing family group (divorce), dealing with loss, handling peer pressure, and coping with stress and anger are offered to students.

We have invited your child to join a group that emphasizes coping with parent divorce, separation, or remarriage. Many students think of themselves as having problems that no one else has. In the group they discover that other students have similar kinds of issues and problems. For students who have been through a divorce, a separation, or a remarriage, it is frequently a comfort to learn how to accept the situation, build better communication in the family, and then go on with life.

Your son/daughter, _____, has expressed an interest
(student name)
in this group. If you would like to know more about the group, please call. Also, please sign and return this letter to our office.

Sincerely yours,

Counselor

_____
Parent Signature

Session 2

Topic: Video discussion, bibliotherapy

Resources

- Video: *If Your Parents Break Up* (Sunburst)
- Library, other books on divorce

Beginning

1. Ask students to complete this statement: "My name is . . . and today I'm feeling . . ." (on a scale of 1 to 10, where 1 is rotten and 10 is the top of the world). After everyone has responded, ask who can name everyone in the group.
2. Ask students to briefly share with a partner how the past week has gone.
3. Ask volunteers to share past week with group.
4. Collect parent permission letters and discuss parent reaction to student being in group.

Middle

1. Introduce video *If Your Parents Break Up* (Sunburst). Ask students to write down any ideas that occur to them during the video—something they agree or disagree with, or something they hadn't thought of before. Ask them about those ideas when the video is over.
2. Discuss ideas from the video. "What was similar to your situation? What was different? What things did you agree with/disagree with?"
3. Show students library books on divorce. Encourage them to read one during the next ten weeks. (See the list of Recommended Resources on page 156.) You may wish to collect magazine articles on divorce. Ask your media specialist for the Book-Finder, a book that lists children/adolescent books by special topics.)
4. Discuss some positive ways that families can help each other in adjusting to divorce.

End

1. Ask students to think and write their answers to the following:

   "Today I learned . . ."

   "Today I relearned . . ."

   "Today I was surprised that . . ."

   "One thing I learned that I can use this week is . . ."
2. Ask students to share their answers with a partner first, then ask for volunteers to share what they choose with group.
3. Preview next meeting.

Session 3
Topic: Art activity

Resources

- Art supplies

Beginning

Ask students to complete the following statements with a partner:

"I wish my mother would . . ."

"I wish my father would . . ."

"This week has been . . ."

Middle

ART ACTIVITY

1. Provide students with art supplies and have them draw their family. (Long construction paper, magic markers, pieces of fabric, glitter, and glue are useful to have on hand.)

2. Some suggested directions for the family picture: Where in the house are the family members, and what are they doing?

3. When they finish, ask each student to tell group about his/her picture, and then hang the picture on the wall.

4. As the sharing progresses, ask students to comment on similarities they notice.

BOOKS

Discuss books the students have been reading.

End

1. Ask students to think and write their answers to the following:

   "Today I learned or relearned . . ."

   "Today I was surprised that . . ."

   "One thing I learned that I can use this week is . . ."

2. Ask students to share their answers with a partner first, then ask for volunteers to share what they choose with the group.

3. Preview next meeting.

Session 4
Topic: True-False Questionnaire

Resources

- True-False Questionnaire handout
- Optional: Curran, *Traits of a Healthy Family*

Beginning

Ask students, "What are three things that you will do as a parent if you have children one day? They can be things that your parents do that you like, or things you wish they would do. Write them down." Give students time, then ask them to discuss responses in pairs. Ask volunteers to share with group.

Ask students to rate on a scale of 1–10 how things are going at home this week.

Ask who has been trying something they learned in group and how it went.

Give students time to discuss their weekend visitation with a parent or problems at home.

Middle

1. Distribute the True-False Questionnaire, and ask students to fill it out. Discuss each item. Remember to be nonjudgmental!

2. You may want to discuss their future relationships and how their marriages will not necessarily end in divorce.

3. Sometimes students have already decided that they won't get married. It would be a good time to discuss what kinds of things make a good marriage. (*Traits of a Healthy Family* is an excellent book for the purposes of this discussion.)

End

1. Ask students to think and write their answers to the following:

   "Today I learned . . ."

   "Today I was surprised that . . ."

   "One thing I learned that I can use this week is . . ."

2. Ask students to share their answers with a partner first, then ask for volunteers to share what they choose with the group.

3. Preview next meeting.

Name_____ Date_____

True-False Questionnaire

Directions: Write either **T** for true or **F** for false.

1. _____ Parents who don't love each other should stay together for the sake of the children.

2. _____ Parents should tell their children why they are getting a divorce.

3. _____ If your parents are divorced, it is likely that when you grow up you will get a divorce.

4. _____ The parent that you visit should not have rules or make you do work.

5. _____ One parent should not make negative comments about the other parent.

6. _____ Your stepparent has no right to discipline you.

7. _____ Children should be included in the decision of whom the parent remarries.

8. _____ Children should not let their parents know how they feel about the divorce.

9. _____ A child should try to make up for the parent who has left by taking on extra responsibilities and being an emotional support to the parent he or she is living with.

10. _____ Children should be able to decide which parent they want to live with.

Session 5
Topic: Sentence completion

Resources

- Sentence Completion handout
- Pencils and paper

Beginning

1. Ask students to complete the following sentences with a partner. Then ask volunteers to share with group.

    "I feel lonely when . . ."

    "I am happy when . . ."

    "I wish . . ."

2. Ask students to review the previous session, anything they tried from group, and how it went.

3. Last, ask students to rate their mood and energy today, each on a 1–10 scale. Discuss briefly how exercise, social support, and fun activities can help increase mood and energy.

Middle

SENTENCE COMPLETION HANDOUT

1. Students fill out two sentences at a time and discuss with a partner. Then volunteers share answers with the group.

2. Have students change partners and answer the next two questions, share answers with partner, then share with group.

3. Continue in this way until all sentences have been completed.

FURTHER DISCUSSION

Rate how things are going at home and discuss reasons for rating.

READING

Discuss books that the students have been reading on the topic of divorce.

End

1. Have students write anonymous "Dear Abby" letters, to be turned in to you and discussed the following week. The letters should be written about a current problem that the student is experiencing because of the family situation. They can make up names to sign the letters (like "Worried and Confused") so that when they're read aloud the letters will be anonymous.

2. Ask students to think and write their answers to the following:

    "Today I learned or relearned . . ."

    "Today I was surprised that . . ."

    "One thing I learned that I can use this week is . . ."

    Ask students to share their answers with a partner first, then ask for volunteers to share what they choose with group.

3. Preview next meeting.

Name_____ Date _____

Sentence Completion

Directions: Complete the following sentences.

1. When I first found out that my parents were getting a divorce, I felt

   _____

   _____

   _____

2. Something I still don't understand about divorce is _____

   _____

   _____

3. One thing that I miss is _____

   _____

   _____

4. A way that I have changed is _____

   _____

   _____

5. I appreciate my mom for _____

   _____

   _____

   but I wish she would _____

   _____

   _____

6. I appreciate my dad for _____

   _____

   _____

   but I wish he would _____

   _____

   _____

(continued)

             Group Counseling for School Counselors: A Practical Guide

Name_____ Date_____

Sentence Completion *(continued)*

7. When my friends learn that my parents are divorced, they _____

_____

_____

8. The way I feel about divorce is _____

_____

_____

9. I can help other students whose parents are divorced by _____

_____

_____

10. If I could change one thing about myself now, it would be _____

_____

_____

11. Negative effects of the divorce are _____

_____

_____

12. Positive things that have happened because of the divorce are

_____

_____

_____

13. Marriage is _____

_____

_____

Session 6
Topic: Dear Abby, role-play

Resources

• "Dear Abby" letters from Session 5

Beginning

Ask students to share their answers to these sentence stems with a partner. Then ask volunteers to share with the group.

"One strength I have . . ."

"One way I am getting better at handling the divorce is . . ."

"One thing I am doing to take good care of myself is . . ."

REVIEW

1. Ask students to state one thing they learned in last week's session, then share something they tried that they learned from group and how it went.

2. Have a quick go-round to share where students are today, on a scale of 1–10, in terms of mood and energy.

Middle

1. Read "Dear Abby" letters and discuss solutions to problems. The students give advice to each other about what to do in each situation. These are usually significant situations and deserve time and attention.

2. After sharing situations and brainstorming solutions, ask students to pick several situations that have the most common ground and then, one at a time, role-play solutions from the group. Multiple students can play the child role in each situation to provide multiple models. The leader may also decide to role-play the student handling a situation.

Note: This session and the previous session with the open sentences provide much material to explore. These could be extended into several sessions. Decide what seems to be most helpful to the students in your group.

End

1. Ask students to think and write their responses to the statements,

"Today I learned or relearned . . ."

"Today I was surprised that . . ."

"One thing I learned that I can use this week is . . ."

2. Ask students to share their answers with a partner first, then ask for volunteers to share what they choose with group.

3. Preview next meeting.

Session 7
Topic: Communicating with body language

Resources

- Body Language in Communication handout

Beginning

1. Ask students to rate their mood and energy on a 1–10 scale and share with group in a go-round.

2. Ask students to share with partner their responses to the statements, "One thing that is going better is . . ." and "One thing I need to work on is . . .".

3. Ask for volunteers to share with group their pair-share discussion.

REVIEW

Ask students to review last meeting, then share what they tried from group this past week and how it went.

Middle

NON-LISTENING EXERCISE

1. Have students get into pairs. One student talks for one minute about any topic: favorite movies, pet, hobby, or vacation spot. The other student demonstrates not paying attention, interrupting, and any other non-listening practices.

2. Switch roles, but this time have the other person demonstrate what he or she considers to be good listening practices.

3. Have the group discuss the behaviors that they noticed with not listening and listening. Have a recorder write down the group's lists of behaviors for both.

BODY LANGUAGE IN COMMUNICATION

1. Distribute the Body Language in Communication handout and go over it with students. Stress the importance of good listening during conflicts and discussions with high emotional levels.

2. Explain the importance of nonverbal communication by using the information on the handout. As you go over each item, ask group to demonstrate do's and don'ts.

3. Use the body language and listening information to role-play some of the situations from the Dear Abby letters from last week. Have group members give feedback on listening and body language after each role-play.

End

1. Ask students to summarize the session.

2. Ask students to share with a partner their responses to the statement, "One thing I learned that I can use this week is . . .".

3. Preview next meeting.

Name_____ Date_____

Body Language in Communication

The communication process is always nonverbal as well as verbal. Behavior expresses meaning, sometimes more clearly than words. To be an effective communicator, one must tune in to body language and tone of voice. Consider the following:

70 percent of what we communicate is through body language.

23 percent of what we communicate is through tone of voice.

7 percent of what we communicate is through words.

How we say something is frequently more important than *what* we say.

	Dos	Don'ts
Eyes	good eye contact	stare, glare, jittery, no eye contact
Voice (volume)	loud enough to be heard clearly	too soft or too loud
Voice (tone)	tone communicates understanding	disinterested, gruff tone, sarcastic
Facial expressions	matches your own or other's feeling; smile	frown, yawn, sigh, scowl, blank look
Posture	leaning forward slightly, relaxed	leaning away, rigid, slouching, crossing arms
Movement	toward	away
Distance	arm's length	too close (less than two feet); too far (more than five feet)

Session 8
Topic: Communication skills

Resources
- Communication Skills handout

Beginning
1. Ask students to rate how they are feeling and their energy level today on a scale of 1–10.
2. Ask them to share with a partner something positive that's happened to them this past week and something they want to change or improve on.

REVIEW
Ask students if, during the last week, they paid attention to body language. What did they notice?

Middle

COMMUNICATION SKILLS
1. To introduce communication skills, have the group members complete the sentence stems on the Communication Skills handout.
2. Discuss with students appropriate times to talk with parents or teachers. Talk about being aware of adult moods, and how to best introduce a topic. Suggest that they make an appointment with the parent. *Example:* "Mom, after we've finished with the dishes tonight, there's some stuff going on at school that I would like to talk with you about. Would you have some time around 8:00?"
3. Have students brainstorm topics they would like to discuss with their parents.
4. Then ask volunteers to role-play the situations. Have the group give feedback on the use of good listening, body language, and communication skills.

End
1. Ask students to share with a partner their responses to the following statements, then ask for volunteers to share with group.

   "Today I learned . . ."

   "One thing I need to do when communicating with my parents is . . ."
2. Preview next week's session.

Name_____ Date_____

Communication Skills

Directions: Complete each of the following statements.

I can tell if Mom or Dad is really listening to me when _____

_____

_____

_____

When something is bothering me, I let them _____

_____

_____

_____

When they start giving advice, I feel _____

_____

_____

_____

I am willing to listen to them if _____

_____

_____

_____

The best time to talk to Mom/Dad is _____

_____

_____

_____

When the parent I am visiting makes negative comments about my other

parent, I _____

_____

_____

Session 9
Topic: I-messages

Resources

- I-Message Model handout
- "Dear Abby" letters from Session 5

Beginning

"A time someone listened to me this week was . . . and I could tell they were listening because . . ."

REVIEW

1. Ask students to recall what the group did last meeting.
2. Ask students to give examples of communication skills—body language, listening, and timing—that they used this past week.

Middle

1. Distribute the I-Message Model handout, and go over it with students.
2. Take a situation from the "Dear Abby" letters or have students describe briefly on paper a problem they are having with a parent right now. Allow 2–3 minutes. In pairs, students take turns being the person who has the problem and giving an I-message to the other person. The person receiving the message checks its accuracy using the checklist on the I-Message Model handout.
3. Save time for some participants, who you can see have the right idea, to role-play their situations in front of the group.

End

1. Ask students to complete the following statements in pairs:

   "Today I learned or relearned . . ."

   "One way I can use what I learned is . . ."
2. Preview the next and last meeting.

ASSIGNMENT

Find a time this week to use an I-message with your parent.

Name_____ Date _____

I-Message Model

When your goals, rights, or safety are being interfered with, **I-messages** are one of the most appropriate ways to communicate what the conflict is to the other person.

I-messages show your concern in a calm and respectful way.

We commonly use **you-messages** instead, which accuse and blame the other person and are usually said with anger or sarcasm.

These are the messages we send with I-messages and you-messages.

I-Messages	You-Messages
I respect you.	do not show respect
This is how I feel.	blame, cause hurt, anger
This is what I want to happen.	accuse, ridicule, criticize

A typical I-message has three parts, which can come in any order: (a) what the speaker feels, (b) the cause of the speaker's feelings, and (c) the reason the speaker feels that way.

"I feel (state feeling) when you (describe specific behavior) because (state how it affects you)."

(continued)

Name_____ Date_____

I-Message Model *(continued)*

Examples of I-Messages and You-Messages

- **I-message:** *I feel* angry *when you* tell something I told you in secret *because* I didn't want anyone else to know.
  You-message: You can't ever keep a secret. You are a pig. I'm never going to speak to you again.

- **I-message:** *I feel* irritated *when you* back out of going at the last minute *because* it leaves me stuck with no one to go with.
  You-message: You're always messing up my plans. I can never count on you. You are such a loser.

- **I-message:** *I feel* upset *when you* tell me to tell Dad stuff about the child support *because* it makes him mad and messes up my weekend.
  You-message: You're ruining my weekends because you're too weak to talk to Dad yourself.

- **I-message:** *I feel* lonely *when you* are gone all the time *because I* miss us doing things together.
  You-message: You're always leaving me here alone. You're so selfish.

I-Messages Checklist

A. Did you:

Say in one brief sentence what you were mad about, by

___ describing the specific behavior that was upsetting;

___ telling the person how you felt about the behavior;

___ stating how the behavior affected you?

B. Were you careful not to:

___ blame, put down, or criticize;

___ bring up the past, threaten, or accuse;

___ get caught up in winning rather than solving the conflict?

Group Counseling for School Counselors: A Practical Guide

Session 10
Topic: Suggestions for parents, closure

Resources

- Art supplies
- Suggestions for Parents from Middle School Students handout
- Group Evaluation form (page 10)

Beginning

In a go-round ask students to complete the statement, "One way I have grown since this divorce is . . .".

REVIEW

Have students review the topics discussed in the divorce group and how these issues have affected their lives.

Middle

1. Ask students to draw a picture using symbols, colors, or real images that represent some ways they have grown in their ability to cope with the divorce or get along with their parents or take good care of themselves, or the most important thing they have learned from participating in the group. They may want to draw the picture as a before-and-after or as a then, now, and in the future.

2. Ask students to share their pictures with the group. Encourage the group to give positive feedback to students as they share about their ability to cope with difficulty, their resiliency, or some positive quality they have.

3. Have group generate a list of suggestions to parents from middle school kids of divorce.

4. Have group compare their lists with the Suggestions for Parents handout, which gives suggestions from other middle school students. Provide a copy of this list for each student who wants one.

End

Allow time for students to fill out evaluations. Then invite students to share anything from the evaluation questions or anything else they would like to say to the group.

CLOSURE

Leader wrap-up includes discussion of seeking outside help, having someone to talk to, and problems that parents may be having. Encourage students to come to you individually. You may wish to continue with a once-a-month support group during the year.

Suggestions for Parents from Middle School Students

- Don't have arguments with your ex and then take it out on your kid.

- Do more things with me.

- Spend time with me.

- When you get remarried don't forget I'm still here.

- Don't put bad ideas into my head about my dad/mom.

- Don't put me in the middle.

- Don't tell me things that you don't want my mom/dad to know.

- Don't leave me alone.

- Don't play favorites.

- Don't influence my decision about whom to live with.

- Don't put me on a guilt trip: "If you leave you can't come back!"

2.5
Handling Conflicts

| Grade Level: Middle School | Time Required: 8 Sessions | Author: Greg Brigman |

Purpose

This group is designed to teach self-management skills including conflict management, stress management and related social skills, and self awareness. Role-play with coaching feedback is a key strategy in this group.

Logistics

GROUP COMPOSITION

Students grades 6–8 mixed with regard to activity level and behavior control. Avoid loading group with only overactive behavior problem students. Students need multiple models of appropriate behavior. Groups with only behavior problem students usually do not show significant gains in prosocial behavior. Mixed groups are generally very effective.

GROUP SIZE

6–8 students

GROUP TIME PER SESSION

45 minutes

NUMBER OF SESSIONS

Eight, with optional booster sessions spaced approximately one month apart after regular group ends.

Recommended Resources

Full bibliographic details for these publications are included in the Bibliography at the end of this book.

Carruthers et al., 1996: "Conflict resolution as curriculum."

Cross and Rosenthal, 1999: "Three models of conflict effects on intergroup expectations and attitudes."

Elliot and Mihalic, 1997: "Blueprints for Violence Prevention and Reduction."

Goldstein and McGinnis, 1997: *Skillstreaming the Adolescent.*

Johnson et al., 1997: "The impact of conflict resolution training on middle school students."

McWhirter et al., 1998: *At Risk Youth.*

Masten and Coatsworth, 1998: "The development of competence in favorable and unfavorable environments."

Moote, Smythe, and Wodarsky, 1999: *Social Skills Training with Youth in School Settings.*

Newcomb, Bukowski, and Patee, 1993: "Children's peer relations."

Prout and Brown, 1999: *Counseling and psychotherapy with children and adolescents.*

Prout and Prout, 1998: "A meta-analysis of school-based studies of counseling and psychotherapy."

Slavin, Karweit, and Madden, 1989: "What works for students at risk."

Weisz et al., 1987: "Effectiveness of psychotherapy with children and adolescents."

Weisz et al., 1995: "Effects of psychotherapy with children and adolescents revisited."

Session 1
Topic: Thirty personal characteristics

Resources

- How I See Myself: 30 Characteristics handout
- Processing the 30 Characteristics handout
- Student journals

Beginning

INTRODUCTION

Introduce yourself and welcome the group. Give an overview of the topics covered in the group and how the skills and awareness gained can be used. This is a review of the information covered during pre-group screening with individual group members.

HOUSEKEEPING AND RULES

1. Explain the time and length of meetings and the notebook for journal writing.
2. Ask, "What kind of rules do you think we need for this group to make sure everyone feels safe to share ideas and feels respected? Limit rules to a few key ones, making sure that the following rules are included in some form:
   - Share the talk time.
   - Respect the opinions of others even if you disagree—don't put anyone down.
   - You have the right to pass.
   - What you say in the room is confidential. You can share what *you* say with whomever you choose, but you should not share what *others* say.

INTRODUCTIONS

Have the group divide into pairs and allow students five minutes to get acquainted with their partners. Partners will introduce each other to the group, telling about their interests and hobbies and information that was shared.

Middle

1. Distribute the How I See Myself: 30 Characteristics handout. Read each item and clarify terms when necessary. Students circle their responses. Then have the students write a short paragraph that explains how they see themselves.
2. Next, divide students into pairs. Have partners share with each other how it felt to do this activity and how they see themselves.
3. Discuss these questions with the whole group: "How did you feel when you did this activity?" Students will usually say it felt awkward or embarrassing to grade or judge themselves. Give them permission to grade themselves honestly, to give themselves high scores when they feel that way. "Why does it feel different to give ourselves credit?" Usually we have been taught not to brag, and doing this activity makes you feel as if you are bragging. "Which ones were hardest to do?"
4. Finally, have students complete the processing of the How I See Myself sheets using the Processing the 30 Characteristics handout. Use this sheet to discuss the activity. You may want to have students share answers in pairs, then ask for volunteers to share with the whole group.

End

JOURNAL WRITING

Allow students 2–3 minutes to record their impressions of today's session, responding to these questions:
"What was it like to participate in group today?"
"What were some feelings you had?"
"What are some thoughts you have about the group?"
"What do you hope to gain from the group?"

SUMMARY

Ask volunteers to share with the group their responses to the statement, "One thing I learned today was . . .", and anything they would like from their journal.

Name_____ Date _____

How I See Myself: 30 Characteristics

Directions: Rate yourself on a scale from 1 to 5 on the following 30 characteristics. A rating of 5 means you have a lot of that characteristic. A rating of 1 means you have none, and 3 means about average.

Go with your first impression and be honest. There are no right or wrong answers or good or bad characteristics.

No one will see this list but you unless you want to show it to someone.

Characteristic	Not at All		Average		Very Much
1. Happy	1	2	3	4	5
2. Athletic	1	2	3	4	5
3. Follower	1	2	3	4	5
4. Responsible	1	2	3	4	5
5. Enthusiastic	1	2	3	4	5
6. Creative (artistically or in problem solving)	1	2	3	4	5
7. Intelligent	1	2	3	4	5
8. Good listener	1	2	3	4	5
9. Aggressive	1	2	3	4	5
10. Friendly	1	2	3	4	5
11. Optimistic	1	2	3	4	5
12. Leader	1	2	3	4	5
13. Shy	1	2	3	4	5
14. Helpful	1	2	3	4	5
15. Loner	1	2	3	4	5
16. Competitive	1	2	3	4	5
17. Clumsy	1	2	3	4	5

(continued)

Name_____ Date_____

How I See Myself: 30 Characteristics *(continued)*

Characteristic	Not at All		Average		Very Much
18. Sincere	1	2	3	4	5
19. Good sense of humor	1	2	3	4	5
20. Outgoing	1	2	3	4	5
21. Carefree	1	2	3	4	5
22. Open (willing to share)	1	2	3	4	5
23. Attractive	1	2	3	4	5
24. Worried	1	2	3	4	5
25. Like to be part of a group	1	2	3	4	5
26. Popular	1	2	3	4	5
27. Angry	1	2	3	4	5
28. Dependable	1	2	3	4	5
29. Bored	1	2	3	4	5
30. Confident	1	2	3	4	5

Now write a short paragraph explaining how you see yourself.

_____

_____

_____

_____

_____

_____

_____

Name_____ Date_____

Processing the 30 Characteristics

1. I learned I was more _____ and

   _____ than I thought. I was also less

   _____, _____,

   and _____ than I thought.

2. Write a summary sentence about yourself using what you learned from reviewing your ratings. You may want to begin with:

   I'm the kind of person who is _____

   _____

   _____

   _____

3. Three strengths I have are: _____,

   _____, and _____.

4. The qualities I would like to have more of are _____,

   _____, and _____.

5. With a partner, share some strengths and qualities you'd like more of.

   _____

   _____

   _____

   _____

6. Each person share this with the group:

   I was surprised that _____

   _____

   _____

   _____

   _____

Group Counseling for School Counselors: A Practical Guide

Session 2
Topic: Stress

Resources
- Getting a Handle on Stress handout
- Student journals

Beginning

Have each student in turn tell the group, "My name is . . . and something I do to relax after a stressful day is . . .".

REVIEW

Have each student share what he or she learned in last week's session.

Middle

1. Introduce the topic of stress with the following questions:

   "How many of you feel some stress today?"

   "How do you know when you are under stress?"

   "What are the symptoms?"

   "Name some physical symptoms."

   "Think about the things that cause you stress. Imagine tossing all those words into the center of our circle in a pile. Tell us what causes you stress and throw them on the pile." Some answers that are typically given:

grades	boys/girls
friends	relationships
teachers	school
parents	decisions
time	tests
goals	

2. As students call out different answers, have them explain how that topic causes stress. Say, "Sometimes we feel stress when we think we have to be perfect, expecting perfection of ourselves or others. We may feel disappointed or angry when we feel we have to perform and we don't have the resources for it. Let's look at some ways to handle stress."

3. Hand out the reproducible activity "Getting a Handle on Stress." Say, "As we read the 11 suggestions for dealing with stress,"
   - "Choose your favorites."
   - "Check the ones you already use."
   - "Circle the ones you would like to use more."

4. Have volunteers read each suggestion, using each one as a stimulus to generate student discussion.

5. Have students share their ratings and ask for examples. Discuss which strategies are hardest, easiest, most helpful.

End

JOURNAL WRITING

1. Allow students 1–2 minutes to record their impressions of today's session.

2. Ask students to complete, in their journals, the statements "Today I learned . . ." and "One way I can use what I learned is . . .".

SUMMARY

1. Ask students to share their answers with a partner, then ask for a few volunteers to share with the whole group.

2. Preview the next session.

Name_____ Date _____

Getting a Handle on Stress

Here are some suggestions for how to handle stress.

1. **Work off stress.** If you are angry or upset, try to blow off steam physically through activities such as running or sports. Even taking a walk can help.

2. **Talk out your worries.** It helps to share worries with someone you trust and respect. This may be a friend, family member, teacher, or counselor. Sometimes another person can help you see a new side to your problem and, thus, a new solution.

3. **Learn to accept what you cannot change.** If the problem is beyond your control at this time, try your best to accept it until you can change it. It beats spinning your wheels and getting nowhere.

4. **Get enough sleep and rest.** Lack of sleep can lessen your ability to deal with stress by making you more irritable.

5. **Balance work and recreation.** "All work and no play can make Jack a nervous wreck!" Schedule time for recreation to relax your mind.

6. **Do something for others.** Sometimes when you are distressed, you concentrate too much on yourself and your situation. When this happens, it is often wise to do something for someone else and get your mind off yourself. There is an extra bonus in this technique: It helps to make friends.

(continued)

       Group Counseling for School Counselors: A Practical Guide

Name_____ Date _____

Getting a Handle on Stress *(continued)*

7. **Take one thing at a time.** Many times we set ourselves up for failure by trying to do too many things at the same time. It is defeating to tackle all your tasks at once. Instead, set some aside and work on the most urgent tasks first.

8. **Give in once in a while.** If you find the source of your stress is other people, try giving in instead of fighting and insisting you are always right. You may find that others will begin to give in, too.

9. **Know your abilities and your limitations.** Many times stress is caused by asking yourself to do something you are not able to do. Before agreeing to do something you do not have to do, ask yourself if the task is within your ability to accomplish.

10. **Organize yourself and your time.** Learn ways to help yourself keep up with what you have to do. Plan how you will accomplish the necessary work. Organization can help you avoid wasting time and energy.

11. **Avoid being a perfectionist.** No one person can be perfect at everything. Do your best, but don't be afraid of making a mistake. Everyone makes mistakes, and many times we learn by our mistakes.

Adapted from "Plain Talk About Stress," DHHS Publication No. (ADM) 81-502, and Linda Worley's "The Stress Group." Cobb County Schools, Georgia.

Session 3
Topic: Things I like to do

Resources
- Things I Like to Do handout
- Student journals

Beginning
1. Have each student in turn tell the group, "My name is . . . and how I feel on a scale of 1 to 10 is . . ." (where 1 is the pits and 10 means wonderful.)
2. Also, have each student name something he or she has done for fun in the past week.

REVIEW
Ask students to tell you some things they remember from your last meeting.

Middle
Give a rationale for spending time on things we like to do. "One of the best ways to relieve stress and improve our mood is to routinely do things that we enjoy. Having a clear idea of many things we can do helps us not be bored and to live more healthily."

1. Tell students you'd like them to think about all the things they enjoy doing. Hand out the reproducible activity sheet Things I Like to Do. Let students spend about 2–3 minutes listing as many activities as they can. Lists should include at least 10 activities.
2. After students have listed the things they enjoy doing, ask them to do the following:
   - In the first column on the right, check your five favorite activities.
   - In the second column, put a **P** beside those activities you like to do with people and an **A** beside those that you like to do alone.
   - In the third column, put a **$** sign if the activity costs $5 or more each time you do that activity.
   - In the next column, indicate by a **W** or **M** whether you have done this activity in the past week or month. If you haven't done this activity in a month, leave it blank.
   - Now fill in the lines at the bottom of the activity sheet.
3. When students have finished marking their activity sheets, complete the activity as follows:
   - Go around the circle and have students share the top three things they like to do.
   - Ask how many students found that they enjoy doing more activities with people than alone, and vice versa.
   - How many students had at least five or more activities that don't cost $5 each time they do them? What were these activities?
   - How many of the activities have students done within the last week?
   - Ask students to share with the group what they wrote at the bottom of the activity sheet about being surprised and learning about themselves.

End
1. Allow students 1–2 minutes to record their impressions of today's session.
2. Ask students to complete, in their journals, the statements
   "Today I learned . . ." and "One way I can use what I learned is . . .".
3. Ask volunteers to share their statements with the group.
4. Preview next session.

Name_____ Date _____

Things I Like to Do

Directions: List as many things as you can that you really enjoy doing, that are fun, that make you happy. These can be very simple or complicated; they can be done with people or alone. List at least 10 things.

1.				
2.				
3.				
4.				
5.				
6.				
7.				
8.				
9.				
10.				
11.				
12.				
13.				
14.				
15.				

What did you find out about yourself?

I learned that _____

_____

_____

I was surprised (or pleased) that _____

_____

_____

         Group Counseling for School Counselors: A Practical Guide

Session 4
Topic: Managing ourselves

Resources

- Index cards prepared with role-play questions

Beginning

THE NAME GAME

Go around the circle with students saying their first name and an animal they like. After the first person, the second person says, "That's Tom, he likes gorillas; I'm Venetta and I like horses." Each person begins with the first person and says the name and animal of all persons before him or her. The last person—the group leader— names all the group members and the animals they like.

REVIEW

Ask students to tell you some things they remember from your last meeting.

Middle

1. Ask the group to brainstorm the top 10 reasons students their age get into conflicts with each other. Next ask for some real-life examples they have experienced recently.

2. Ask group members to help decide on one event for the group to role-play. Look for events with the most common ground among group members.

3. Ask the person with the chosen situation to become the director and choose 1–3 group members to help act out the story. The director plays himself/herself and shows/tells the other actors what to do/say. General guidelines for setting the scene and directing the story include answering the following questions. Give these questions on a card for the person who is the director.

QUESTIONS FOR ROLE-PLAY

- What is the setting (where and when)?
- Who are the main characters and how are they feeling at the beginning of the story?
- What is the problem?

- What happens first?
- What are the feelings and reactions of the other characters?
- What do the characters do to try and solve the problem?
- How does the story end and how are the characters feeling?

Limit role-play prep to 2–3 minutes and role-play to 2–3 minutes.

4. After the role-play, have group discuss the pros and cons of how the director handled the situation and explore alternative ways to handle the situation. Both supportive and corrective feedback/coaching are needed to help people improve. Model the sandwich approach: give supportive feedback (bread), then corrective feedback (meat), then finish with supportive feedback (bread).

5. Ask students to use a go-round to share positives about the role-play: "I liked the way you . . .". Then have another go-round for coaching feedback: "You may want to consider . . .".

6. Have group members act out alternative ways of handling the situation and get group feedback as to strengths and things that may need changing.

End

1. Allow students 1–2 minutes to record their impressions of today's session.

2. Ask students to complete, in their journals, the statements

   "Today I learned . . ." and "One way I can use what I learned is . . .".

3. Ask students to rate their energy, mood, what they've eaten, and how much sleep/rest they've gotten, each on a 1–10 scale (10 is the best).

4. Remind students that this is the halfway point of the group sessions, with just four to go.

5. Preview next session.

Session 5
Topic: Handling conflict

Resources

- Handling Conflicts handout

Beginning

1. Ask students to create a weather report that reflects how they are feeling today. They can use wind, all forms of precipitation, temperature, sun, and clouds. *Example:* "Today I am feeling sunny and clear with a slight chance of afternoon thunder-showers," or "partly cloudy with a chance of rain, clearing about 3 P.M., and then warm and sunny."

2. Review last session. Ask, "What do you remember about our last meeting?"

Middle

1. Tell students, "I want to share with you some ideas about how students your age can handle conflicts when they occur. I want us to discuss these ideas and I would like your opinion of each of them. After we finish going over them I would like for us to have a chance to role-play a few situations and use some of the ideas that you find most helpful."

2. Distribute the Handling Conflicts handout. As you go over the items on the handout, ask the following questions:

   - Why is #1 important?
   - What errors in #2 do you most frequently use and which do you most often see used by others?
   - Why is it so difficult to tell someone what you are angry about?
   - Who knows what reflective listening is? Why do you think reflecting/rephrasing someone's ideas would be helpful in settling a conflict? What would an example sound like?

3. After going over the handout, ask for an example of a recent conflict. Choose one that is typical so all group members can benefit from the role-play. Select a student to direct the role-play. First have the student provide the background using the following cues:

   The setting—Where and when and who the main characters were.

   The problem—and what each character was feeling.

   The attempted solution and how each character felt afterward.

4. Now ask the director to try solving the conflict by going through the steps on the Handling Conflicts sheet.

5. Ask the other students to provide feedback—first, on what the director did that was helpful/useful/positive, then any other ideas they have for handling the conflict. Have students role-play the best alternatives, and provide them with feedback.

End

1. Ask students to record their reaction to participating today in their journals. Ask them to respond to the questions, "What did I learn or relearn today?" and "How can I use what I learned?"

2. Also ask them to rate on a 1–10 scale their mood, energy, amount of sleep, exercise, and fun for the week.

3. Ask students to share their answers with a partner.

4. Ask for volunteers to share their reflections with the whole group.

5. Preview the next session.

Name_____ Date_____

Handling Conflicts

Listed below are seven keys to handling conflicts that end in a win-win situation. Adolescents who use these keys regularly tend to have fewer conflicts and better relationships than those who handle their conflicts either more passively or more aggressively. Look over the list and decide which ideas would be most helpful to you.

1. Notice when you start to become angry and rate your anger quickly on a 1–10 scale, where 10 is volcano and 1 is relaxed and peaceful. If you are at 9 or 10, cool off to at least a 7 or 8 before you try to handle the problem with the person with whom you are in conflict.

2. Avoid these common errors in handling the conflict:

   - Interrupting
   - Bringing up the past—"You always . . ."
   - Bringing in allies—"Everybody thinks you . . ."
   - Trying to win rather than trying to solve the problem—work for a win-win solution
   - Blaming—"It's all your fault."
   - Name-calling and other put-downs—"You're so dumb," "That's a stupid idea."
   - Threatening—"If you don't shut up, I'm going to punch you."

3. Tell the person with whom you are in conflict specifically what he or she is doing that is causing you a problem. Keep this very short and to the point. Name the action that bothers you, and the way it affects you: "When you _____,

   then I _____."

(continued)

Name_____ Date_____

Handling Conflicts *(continued)*

4. Expect the other person to defend himself/herself and to want to tell his/her side of the story. Listen respectfully and reflect the other person's point of view—even if you totally disagree with it. You are trying to let her know you heard what she has to say, because you want her to hear what you have to say. The best reflective responses include a paraphrase of what the person said and your best guess as to how he is feeling.

5. Brainstorm possible solutions. Now that the other person knows what your position is and you know what his or her position is, the next step is to see if you can find a solution that will satisfy both. It may not be the perfect solution. You are looking for the best available alternative. "Best available" means both people can live with it. "OK so you want this and I want that—how can we work this out so we both get what we need?"

6. Weigh the pros and cons of each alternative. You are looking for the alternative with the most pros and the fewest cons.

7. Decide on the best alternative and commit to putting it to work. Set a time to check with each other to see how the new plan is working. You may need to alter the new plan when you actually put it into action. Be careful not to throw it out too soon just because it is not perfect. Most new plans take some fine-tuning.

Session 6
Topic: Managing ourselves

Resources

- Chart paper

Beginning

Have students complete the following open-ended sentences in their journals and share them with the group.

"I like being with people who . . ."

"I trust people who . . ."

"I'm a good friend because . . ."

REVIEW

Ask students to tell you some things they remember from your last meeting. If you didn't get a chance to finish the do's and don'ts of handling conflicts, now is the time.

Middle

HANDLING CONFLICTS

1. Ask students to write down typical problems either that they have had with other students at school or that they notice lots of other students have at school. Ask them not to put their names on the lists. Tell them you will collect everyone's ideas in a moment and the group will discuss: (a) if they agree that each problem is typical and (b) some possible solutions.

2. Collect the lists of problems. Read each one and ask if it is a typical problem for this age group. List on a flip chart all the agreed upon typical problems. Ask group members to rank the top three problems in terms of interest to them for discussing possible solutions.

3. Lead a discussion on possible solutions for the selected top three problems. Use a brainstorming technique. List all offered solutions first. Then go back and have the group code each one as "H," helpful, or "HA," harmful to self or others. *Note:* Some will be rated as both. Have group decide if the helpful side outweighs the harmful side.

4. Ask group to divide into pairs and plan a role-play for one of the three problems. The role-play should include one of the helpful solutions. Ask students to use some of the ideas from last week's Handling Conflicts sheet. Allow approximately five minutes for planning.

5. Ask pairs to present their role-plays. Ask the rest of the group to discuss how realistically each problem and solution were portrayed, and to demonstrate additional suggestions for handling the problem. You can also demonstrate various positive alternative ways to handle the situation or coach students in different ways to act. *Note:* It is the role-play and coaching that make this a powerful learning activity.

End

1. Allow students five minutes to record their impressions of today's session.

2. Ask them to rate their energy, mood, what they've eaten, and how much sleep/rest they've gotten, each on a 1–10 scale (where 10 is the best).

3. Ask students to complete, in their journals, the statements "One thing I learned or relearned today was . . ." and "One way I can use what I learned is . . .", then share them with the group.

4. Preview the next session.

Session 7
Topic: More practice in handling conflicts

Resources
- Optional: video camera, TV, VCR

Beginning
1. Ask students to respond to the sentence: "One way I am getting better at handling conflicts is . . ."
2. Review last meeting:

   "What do you remember about what we did last week?"

   "Who tried some of the strategies we practiced? How did it go?"

Middle
1. Say, "Today is our next-to-last meeting and I wanted you to have a chance to put everything you have learned together. I have planned to videotape some of our role-plays and we will get a chance to watch the tape when we finish." (*Note:* You should cover the videotaping during pre-group screening and get parent permission). Taping is not essential but recommended. Students' learning increases when they can see and hear how they act when trying to handle a conflict. The use of videotape speeds up learning and is a great teaching tool.
2. Ask students to think of some typical conflicts that would be good for role-play. With a go-round, hear possible situations for the role-play. Have the group select one that has a lot of common ground.
3. The student whose situation is chosen is the director. Use cues to get the background:

Setting—when, where, and who the main characters are

Problem—in one brief sentence, and how each character is feeling about problem

4. Next have director and other characters role-play their best shot at handling the conflict skillfully and respectfully. When they finish, ask other students if they have any changes they would like to model.
5. Stop the tape, rewind, and show it to group, stopping at spots for group feedback. If you are not taping, then use the normal feedback system. Either way be sure to point out both positive behavior and share ideas for improving.
6. If time permits, repeat the process.

End
1. Allow students five minutes to record their impressions of today's session.
2. Ask them to rate their energy, mood, what they've eaten, and how much sleep/rest they've gotten, each on a 1–10 scale (where 10 is the best).
3. Ask students to complete, in their journals, the statements "One thing I learned or relearned today was . . ." and "One way I can use what I learned is . . ." and then share them with the group.
4. Remind the group that the next meeting is the last weekly meeting for the group.

Session 8
Topic: Wrap-up and evaluation

Resources

- Index cards or sheets of paper
- Group Evaluation form (page 10)

Beginning

REVIEW

1. Students review last meeting. Briefly go over each topic you've covered since the group began, asking for what they remember.

2. Go around the circle, asking students to finish this sentence: "The most important thing I have learned in this group is . . ."

Middle

ACCEPTING AND GIVING COMPLIMENTS

1. Hand out index cards or sheets of paper. Each person is to write down at least one thing they like or appreciate about each other group member. Specific qualities and behaviors are the goal here, not general terms like "you're nice," but what makes that person nice, e.g., "you are friendly, kind, thoughtful, funny."

2. Spotlight: Each group member will say directly to the "spotlighted" person, with eye contact: "[person's name], one thing I like or appreciate about you is . . .".

   After each comment the spotlighted person simply says "thank you," nothing else. (Be sure you get in on this. It feels good.)

3. Process the spotlighting activity. How did it feel receiving compliments? Giving compliments?

End

1. Students complete anonymous evaluation.

2. Concluding remarks: Invite students to make individual appointments if they want.

3. A follow-up meeting in a month is very helpful in maintaining gains. Many counselors set monthly follow-up meetings when their regular weekly meetings end.

Part 3:
Elementary School Group Plans

3.1
Academic and Social Support: Student Success Skills

Grade Level: 3–5	Time Required: 10 Sessions	Author: Greg Brigman

Purpose

To develop academic and social skills with school success. Goal setting, progress monitoring, taking responsibility, social problem solving, and friendship skills and stress management are the focus of the group.

Logistics

GROUP COMPOSITION

Students in grades 3–5, mixed with regard to activity level and behavior control. Avoid loading group with only overactive behavior problem students. Students need multiple models of appropriate behavior. Groups with only behavior problem students usually do not show significant gains in prosocial behavior. Mixed groups are generally very effective.

GROUP SIZE

4–6 students

GROUP TIME PER SESSION

30 minutes

NUMBER OF SESSIONS

Ten, with booster sessions spaced approximately one month apart after regular group ends.

Recommended Resources

Full bibliographic details for these publications are included in the Bibliography at the end of this book.

Brigman, Lane, and Lane, 1994: *Ready to Learn.*

Goldstein and McGinnis, 1997: *Skillstreaming the Adolescent.*

Hattie, Biggs, and Purdie, 1996: "Effects of learning skills interventions on student learning."

Masten and Coatsworth, 1998: "The development of competence in favorable and unfavorable environments."

Prout and Prout, 1998: "A meta-analysis of school-based studies of counseling and psychotherapy."

Prout and Brown, 1999: *Counseling and Psychotherapy with Children and Adolescents.*

Slavin, Karweit, and Madden, 1989: "What works for students at risk."

Wang, Haertel, and Walberg, 1994: "What helps students learn?"

Weisz et al., 1987: "Effectiveness of psychotherapy with children and adolescents."

Weisz et al., 1995: "Effects of psychotherapy with children and adolescents revisited."

Zimmerman and Arunkumar, 1994: "Resiliency research."

Session 1
Topic: Get acquainted, self-evaluation

Resources

- This Is Me handout
- Student Success Skills Self-Evaluation handout

Beginning

INTRODUCTION

Review the purpose of the group (this has been covered individually during the screening): to have fun exploring interests, abilities, strengths, and areas you want to improve. Emphasize that each person is special and unique, and the group will give each person an opportunity to learn more about himself or herself. It will also give each person a chance to understand how to use his/her strengths to be successful in school. We'll play, draw, and talk about topics like friends, stress, and doing well in school.

Go over number of meetings, time, and place.

GROUP RULES

Ask: "What rules do we need to work together, feel safe, and enjoy ourselves?" Be sure to include:

- Confidentiality (You own what you say and can share that with anyone, but what others say stays in the group.)
- Respect others' opinions (no put-downs).
- The right to pass

Secure group consensus on each group rule.

Middle

SKILL-BUILDING OR AWARENESS ACTIVITY 1

1. Distribute the "This Is Me" handout. Students break into pairs. Partners interview one another using the handout, and then each student introduces his or her partner to the group.
2. Discuss similarities and differences. This activity usually works better if you take two items at a time to discuss in pairs, then share with a large group, then discuss next two items in pairs, etc.
3. Get the students involved in looking for what group members have in common.

SKILL-BUILDING OR AWARENESS ACTIVITY 2

1. Introduce the Student Success Skills Self-Evaluation handout. Let the group know that each week they will go over these items and learn how to use problem solving to improve in any area they are not doing as well as they would like.
2. As you go over the form use each item as a discussion starter. These are the behaviors that successful students are able to do well and that struggling students have not yet mastered. Repeated exposure to concrete examples of how to perform these essential skills is the core of this group. If deficits in reading and/or math are present it is advisable to also involve the student with tutoring.

End

1. Ask students the purpose of the group, how many meetings, and so forth.
2. Ask them to share one thing they are looking forward to about the group.
3. Preview the second meeting.

Name _____ Date _____

This Is Me

Name _____

Birthday _____

Favorite TV show _____

Favorite movie _____

Favorite thing to eat _____

Things I like to do (hobbies, sports, etc.) _____

_____

- -

Name _____ Date _____

This Is Me

Name _____

Birthday _____

Favorite TV show _____

Favorite movie _____

Favorite thing to eat _____

Things I like to do (hobbies, sports, etc.) _____

_____

Name_____ Date _____

Student Success Skills Self-Evaluation

Directions: The following skills are all important for doing well in school. Rate yourself on each item. Use a 1–5 scale, in which 5 is the highest/best and 1 is the lowest/worst.

1. I go to class with the materials I need.	1	2	3	4	5
2. I read and understand all assignments.	1	2	3	4	5
3. I have a folder or notebook for each class to help me stay organized.	1	2	3	4	5
4. I turn in all work on time— no zeros.	1	2	3	4	5
5. I keep track of my grades. I know how my teacher decides the final grade.	1	2	3	4	5
6. I listen and focus during class. I usually understand what is being taught.	1	2	3	4	5
7. I ask questions when I do not understand what is being taught. I know when and how to ask questions.	1	2	3	4	5
8. I know what to study for tests and what is expected for reports. I plan ahead for both to avoid last-minute cramming.	1	2	3	4	5
9. I have at least one study buddy in each class.	1	2	3	4	5
10. I work well in pairs or small groups with others in class.	1	2	3	4	5

(continued)

Name_____ Date _____

Student Success Skills Self-Evaluation *(continued)*

My top three strengths from the list on the other page are:

1. _____

_____

2. _____

_____

3. _____

_____

The areas I most want to improve are:

1. _____

_____

2. _____

_____

Session 2
Topic: Process self-evaluation handout

Resources

- Student Success Skills Self-Evaluation handout (page 197)

Beginning

MOVEMENT AND GROUP NORMS

1. Build movement into each group session: a few stretches, follow the leader, Simon Says, and a few slow deep breaths. Suggestions for stretches and breathing: stand and stretch (picking grapes or "head, shoulders, knees and toes" song), shoulder rolls, neck rolls, hand clasped behind back. For breathing—inhale slowly to count of three. Hold to count of three. Exhale slowly to count of three. Hold to count of three. Repeat three times.

2. After modeling these, ask students to take turns leading the others in each one. These can be used at the beginning of each session or during the session when a change of pace is needed.

REINFORCING POSITIVE GROUP NORMS

In a go-round ask students for a five-second response to each of the following stems. Summarize the results at the end.

"When people talk to me, I like for them to . . ."

"A person who talks all the time makes me feel . . ."

"A 'put-down' makes me feel . . ."

"I am willing to listen if . . ."

"When I am not listened to, I feel . . ."

Middle

STUDENT SUCCESS SKILLS SELF-EVALUATION

1. Go through each item, reading it aloud and asking students to rate how they did during the last week. Ask, "Who rated that item 'Good,' who rated it 'OK,' who rated it 'Needs to improve?'"

2. Use the items to stimulate discussion and to clarify problem areas that need to be addressed.

3. Introduce problem solving by asking students to brainstorm solutions to problems raised as you move down the list. Role-playing solutions to problems is a valuable way to help students learn alternative strategies for handling difficult situations. The problem solving can also include how to handle the social problems that come up as the group meets.

End

1. Ask students to write an ending to the following two statements. Ask them to share their answers with a partner. Then ask for volunteers to share what they wrote.

"One thing I learned today was . . ."

"One way I can use what I learned today is . . ."

2. Preview next session.

Session 3
Topic: Drawing and storytelling

Resources

- Paper and markers
- Student Success Skills Self-Evaluation handout (page 197)

Beginning

MOVEMENT, CHECKING GROUP TEMPERATURE, GOAL REPORTING

Stretches, movement, and breathing (student-led), used to balance active and passive activities.

THE NAME GAME

1. Go around the circle asking students to say their first name and an animal they like. After the first person, the second person says, "That's Tom, he likes gorillas, and I'm Mary and I like horses," and so on. Each person begins with the first person and gives the names and animals of all persons coming before. (Pay attention. The leader says all of the names and animals at the end.) It is important to have everyone know and use all the names.

2. In a go-round ask students to rate how they are feeling on the "great, pretty good, not so wonderful, really bad" scale. Be sure to check with any "not so good" or "really bad" to determine if follow-up is needed.

3. Ask, "Who used something we talked about last week during the week? How did it go?"

Middle

DRAWING AND STORYTELLING ABOUT A FRIEND

1. Hand out a blank sheet of paper with markers. Say, "Draw a picture of you and a friend (now or in the past—or the friend you'd like to have) doing something fun." Model by drawing a primitive picture and stressing that the quality of the drawing is not the focus.

2. Ask the students to put the fun event into a story. Put the four Ws and an H questions—who, what, when, where, how—on a chart and go over these questions with the students. Ask them to include the answers in their story.

3. Ask the students to pair up and take turns telling their stories. As the first person finishes the listener summarizes the story by going through the four

Ws and an H questions. Then the listener becomes the storyteller and the process is repeated.

Note: Model storytelling first by listening to a story. Demonstrate eye contact, leaning forward, looking interested, and avoiding distractions. Then summarize by using the four Ws and an H questions—the who, what, when, where, how of the story:

- **who** story was about
- **what** story was about
- **when** story happened, e.g., day, night, spring, summer
- **where** story happened, e.g., inside, outside
- **how** story made storyteller feel, and **how** the story ended

4. Next have pairs tell story (approximately one minute), then lead the group in answering each of the four Ws and an H questions. The storytelling and listening provide practice for key learning skills.

STUDENT SUCCESS SKILLS SELF-EVALUATION

1. Go through each of the items, reading them aloud and asking students to rate how they did that week. Ask "Who rated that item 'Good,' who rated it 'OK,' who rated it 'Needs to improve?'"

2. Use the items to stimulate discussion and to clarify problem areas that need to be addressed.

3. Use group problem solving by asking students to brainstorm solutions to problems students bring up as you move down the list. Role-playing solutions to problems is a valuable way to help students learn alternative strategies for handling difficult situations. The problem solving can also include how to handle the social problems that come up during the group meetings.

End

1. Ask students to write an ending to the following two sentences. Ask them share their answers with a partner. Then ask for volunteers to share what they wrote.

   "One thing I learned today was . . ."

   "One way I can use what I learned today is . . ."

2. Preview next session.

Session 4
Topic: Problem solving

Resources
- Student Success Skills Self-Evaluation handout (page 197)

Beginning
1. Stretches, movement, and breathing (student-led), used to balance active and passive activities.
2. In a go-round ask students to rate how they are feeling on the "great, pretty good, not so good, really bad" scale. Be sure to check with any "not so good" or "really bad" to determine if follow-up is needed.
3. Ask students to tell you some things they remember from last meeting.
4. Ask, "Who used something we talked about last week during the week? How did it go?"

Middle

SOCIAL PROBLEM SOLVING
1. Ask students about problems either that they have had with other students/teachers at school or that they notice lots of other students have with each other at school. Make a list.
2. Ask the group members to rank the top three problems in terms of interest to them for having the group discuss possible solutions.
3. Lead a discussion on possible solutions for the selected top three problems. Use a brainstorming technique. List all offered solutions first. Then go back and have group code each one as "H," helpful, or "HA," harmful to self or others. *Note:* Some will be rated as both. Have group decide if the helpful side outweighs the harmful side.
4. Ask group to divide into pairs and plan a role-play for one of the three problems. The role-play should

include one of the helpful solutions. Allow approximately five minutes for planning.
5. Ask pairs to present their role-plays. Ask the rest of the group to discuss how realistically the problem and solution were portrayed, and to demonstrate additional suggestions for handling the problem. The leader can also demonstrate various positive alternative ways to handle the situation or coach students in different ways to act. *Note:* It is the role-play and coaching that make this a powerful learning activity.

STUDENT SUCCESS SKILLS SELF-EVALUATION
1. Go through each item, reading it aloud and asking students to rate how they did that week. Ask, "Who rated that item 'Good,' who rated it 'OK,' who rated it 'Needs to improve?'"
2. Use the items to stimulate discussion and to clarify problem areas that need to be addressed.
3. Use group problem solving by asking students to brainstorm solutions to problems raised as you move down the list. Role-playing solutions to problems is a valuable way to help students learn alternative strategies for handling difficult situations. The problem solving can also include how to handle the social problems that come up during the group meetings.

End
1. Ask students to write responses to the following two sentences. Ask them share their answers with a partner. Then ask for volunteers to share what they wrote.
   "One thing I learned today was . . ."
   "One way I can use what I learned today is . . ."
2. Preview next session.

Session 5
Topic: Problem-solving role-play

Resources

- Friendship Problems handout
- Student Success Skills Self-Evaluation handout (page 197)

Beginning

1. Stretches, movement, and breathing (student-led), used to balance active and passive activities.

2. In a go-round ask students to rate how they are feeling on the "great, pretty good, not so good, really bad" scale. Be sure to check with any "not so good" or "really bad" to determine if follow-up is needed.

3. Ask students to tell you some things they remember from last meeting.

4. Ask, "Who used something we talked about last week during the week? How did it go?"

5. Have students complete the following statements and share their responses with the group.

   "I like being with people who . . ."

   "I trust people who . . ."

   "I'm a good friend because . . ."

Middle

SOCIAL PROBLEM SOLVING

1. Use the three typical friendship problems on the Friendship Problems handout to stimulate discussion, problem solving, and role-playing of solutions. Divide the group into pairs and ask them to develop a specific solution to the typical problems presented on the handout. The problems are presented as if students had written to a newspaper counselor similar to Dear Abby for advice.

2. After coming up with a solution for each problem, each pair plans a role-play of one of the three problems and the solution. Both role-plays last a maximum of one minute.

3. Each pair presents their role-plays of the problem and their solution. After each problem and solution is role-played the group discusses their reaction to the problem and to the solution as well as to other possible alternatives. Three helpful tips for using role-play:

   - It is important to point out positive reactions and feelings to prosocial solutions and negative reactions and feelings to antisocial solutions.

   - If the original student-generated alternatives are not prosocial, look for students who can model appropriate alternatives. The group leader and other students are important models for appropriate prosocial solutions to typical problems. Students learn best from multiple positive models.

   - The group leader can use the sandwich approach of feedback to respond to each role-play, pointing out all positive aspects and adding alternatives to any inappropriate ideas, followed by a positive summary of the pair's efforts.

4. After all role-plays, the group can generate a list of other typical problems for future problem solving and role-play.

5. To wrap up, the group leader can ask students to discuss what it was like to work together to find solutions:

   - Did any of the pairs have trouble coming to an agreement on any of the solutions or how they would role-play them?

   - How did they work it out?

   - How did they feel about how the disagreement was settled?

   - What suggestions do they have for next time they work in groups to solve problems and present role-plays?

STUDENT SUCCESS SKILLS SELF-EVALUATION

1. Go through each item, reading it aloud and asking students to rate how they did that week. Ask, "Who rated that item 'Good,' who rated it 'OK,' who rated it 'Needs to improve?'"

2. Use the items to stimulate discussion and to clarify problem areas that need to be addressed.

3. Use group problem solving by asking students to brainstorm solutions to problems raised as you move down the list. Role-playing solutions to problems is a valuable way to help students learn alternative strategies for handling difficult situations. The problem solving can also include how to handle the social problems that come up during the group meetings.

End

1. Ask students to write an ending to the following two sentences. Ask them to share their answers with a partner. Then ask for volunteers to share what they wrote.

   "One thing I learned today was . . ."

   "One way I can use what I learned today is . . ."

2. Preview next session.

Friendship Problems

Typical Problem 1

Dear Mary Jo,

My problem is the big J—jealousy:

My friend tries to control whom I spend time with. She threatens to not be my friend if I hang out with certain people. It feels like she wants to keep me all to herself. I really like her but I also want to be friends with other people. What should I do?

Signed,

Confused

Typical Problem 2

Dear Mary Jo,

There are these two kids in my class who are very pushy. Every time we play it has to be by their rules. They always have to go first. When we work in teams they have to be the leader. It's really frustrating. Don't they know how rude they are? I am sick and tired of it. They are smart and could be good friends but they really need to learn to share the lead. What can I do to make them see how bossy they are?

Signed,

Frustrated

Typical Problem 3

Dear Mary Jo,

A couple of my friends have to be the center of attention all the time. It gets boring to be around them because they always have to be the focus. I don't think they know how irritating it is when they won't let me or anyone else have any of the attention. How can I get them to look past themselves and notice how other people feel?

Signed,

Irritated

Session 6
Topic: Dos and don'ts of being a friend

Resources

- Dos and Don'ts of Being a Friend handout
- Chart paper
- My Friendly Environment handout
- Student Success Skills Self-Evaluation handout (page 197)

Beginning

1. Stretches, movement, and breathing (student-led), used to balance active and passive activities.

2. In a go-round, ask students to rate how they are feeling on the "great, pretty good, not so good, really bad" scale. Be sure to check with any "not so good" or "really bad" to determine if follow-up is needed.

3. Ask students to tell you some things they remember from last meeting.

4. Ask, "Who used something we talked about last week during the week? How did it go?"

Middle

DOS AND DON'TS OF BEING A FRIEND

1. Explain to the students that you need their help as consultants. Your friend, Mary Jo, writes a column for a school newspaper about typical problems for elementary school students. You would like their advice on a problem recently sent in to Mary Jo. Give each student a copy of the Dos and Don'ts of Being a Friend handout.

2. In pairs, students brainstorm things to do and things not to do to for keeping friends.

3. Pairs share their lists and a composite list is made on a flip chart. Items are then coded by consensus agreement as "DH," definitely helpful, or "PNH,"

probably not helpful. Discuss the fact that our behaviors toward others create an environment around us. If we want to attract and keep friends we have to maintain an environment that is inviting and friendly so that others will enjoy being around us.

4. Ask students to complete the My Friendly Environment handout.

5. Ask them to share what they wish to from their goal sheets with the group.

STUDENT SUCCESS SKILLS SELF-EVALUATION

1. Go through each item, reading it aloud and asking students to rate how they did that week. Ask "Who rated that item 'Good,' who rated it 'OK,' who rated it 'Needs to improve?'"

2. Use the items to stimulate discussion and to clarify problem areas that need to be addressed.

3. Use group problem solving by asking students to brainstorm solutions to problems raised as you move down the list. Role-playing solutions to problems is a valuable way to help students learn alternative strategies for handling difficult situations. The problem solving can also include how to handle the social problems that come up during the group meetings.

End

1. Ask students to write an ending to the following two sentences. Ask them to share their answers with a partner. Then ask for volunteers to share what they wrote.

   "One thing I learned today was . . ."

   "One way I can use what I learned today is . . ."

2. Preview next session.

Name_____ Date _____

Dos and Don'ts of Being a Friend

Dear Mary Jo,

I am a third grader and things are not going well for me at my school. I am having trouble keeping friends and it is really bothering me a lot. Do you have a list of things that I could do to be accepted more with my friends? Also a list of what not to do would help.

Thanks,
Worried About Friends

Dear Worried About Friends,

I checked with my experts on third-grade friendship and this is what they suggested to help you create the kind of friendly environment that attracts and keeps good friends:

Be sure to do these things:	Be sure not to do these things:
_____	_____
_____	_____
_____	_____
_____	_____
_____	_____
_____	_____
_____	_____
_____	_____
_____	_____

       Group Counseling for School Counselors: A Practical Guide

Name_____ Date_____

My Friendly Environment

Directions: Complete the three areas below and share with a partner. Give this goal sheet to your teacher. You will have a chance next week to share specific examples of things you did to reach your goal.

Three things I already do that create a friendly environment and help me to be a good friend:

1. _____

2. _____

3. _____

Two things I will do more of in the next week to create a friendly environment:

1. _____

2. _____

One thing I will do less of this week to create a friendly environment:

1. _____

A picture of me and my friends in my friendly environment:

Session 7
Topic: Handling stress

Resources

- Chart paper
- Student Success Skills Self-Evaluation handout (page 197)

Beginning

1. Stretches, movement, and breathing (student-led), used to balance active and passive activities.

2. In a go-round ask students to rate how they are feeling on the "great, pretty good, not so good, really bad" scale. Be sure to check with any "not so good" or "really bad" to determine if follow-up is needed.

3. Ask students to tell you some things they remember from last meeting.

4. Ask, "Who used something we talked about last week during the week? How did it go?"

Middle

STRESS

1. Introduce the topic of stress with the following: "What does 'stress' mean? How do you know when you are under stress? What does it feel like? Name some physical symptoms. How many of you feel some stress today?"

2. Storytelling in pairs—a time I felt stressed out. "Think about the things that cause you stress. Tell your partner a story with a beginning, middle, and end about a time when you felt stressed out."

3. Discuss the stressors contained in the stories: "We need a list of things that cause students your age the most stress. Share with the group things from your stories that cause stress. Imagine tossing all those words into the center of our circle in a pile. Tell us what causes you stress and throw them on the pile. We need at least twelve."

Some answers that are typically given:

grades	boys/girls
friends	relationships
teachers	school
parents	decisions
time	tests
goals	performing

As students call out different answers, have them explain how that topic causes stress.

4. Ask, "What are some ways you handle stress?" List group's answers on a flip chart. After listing all their strategies go back through and have them rate each one as "H" for healthy or "HA" for harmful to self or others. Preview next meeting, when they can compare their list with seven other strategies for handling stress that other students their age find helpful.

STUDENT SUCCESS SKILLS SELF-EVALUATION

1. Go through each item, reading it aloud and asking students to rate how they did that week. Ask "Who rated that item 'Good,' who rated it 'OK,' who rated it 'Needs to improve?'"

2. Use the items to stimulate discussion and to clarify problem areas that need to be addressed.

3. Use group problem solving by asking students to brainstorm solutions to problems raised as you move down the list. Role-playing solutions to problems is a valuable way to help students learn alternative strategies for handling difficult situations. The problem solving can also include how to handle the social problems that come up during the group meetings.

End

1. Ask students to write an ending to the following two sentences. Ask them to share their answers with a partner. Then ask for volunteers to share what they wrote.

   "One thing I learned today was . . ."

   "One way I can use what I learned today is . . ."

2. Preview next session.

Session 8
Topic: Ways of handling stress

Resources

- Seven Ways to Handle Stress handout
- Student Success Skills Self-Evaluation handout (page 197)

Beginning

1. Stretches, movement, and breathing (student-led), used to balance active and passive activities.

2. In a go-round ask students to rate how they are feeling on the "great, pretty good, not so good, really bad" scale. Be sure to check with any "not so good" or "really bad" to determine if follow-up is needed.

3. Ask students to tell you some things they remember from last meeting.

4. Ask, "Who used something we talked about last week during the week? How did it go?"

Middle

GETTING A HANDLE ON STRESS

1. Say, "Last meeting we talked about what stress was, some causes of stress, and some strategies you use for handling stress. Let's look at some other ways students your age find helpful to handle stress. How many matches do you see between your list from last meeting and the first six ideas on this list?"

2. Distribute the handout Seven Ways to Handle Stress.

3. Say, "As I read the suggestions for dealing with stress, do the following:

   - Choose your three favorites—put an asterisk (*) by these.

   - Mark the ones you already use with a check (√).

   - Circle (O) the ones you would like to use more."

4. Read each suggestion, using each one as a stimulus to generate student discussion.

5. Have students share their ratings and ask for examples.

STUDENT SUCCESS SKILLS SELF-EVALUATION

1. Go through each item, reading it aloud and asking students to rate how they did that week. Ask "Who rated that item 'Good,' who rated it 'OK,' who rated it 'Needs to improve?'"

2. Use the items to stimulate discussion and to clarify problem areas that need to be addressed.

3. Use group problem solving by asking students to brainstorm solutions to problems raised as you move down the list. Role-playing solutions to problems is a valuable way to help students learn alternative strategies for handling difficult situations. The problem solving can also include how to handle the social problems that come up during the group meetings.

End

1. Ask students to write an ending to the following two sentences. Ask them to share their answers with a partner. Then ask for volunteers to share what they wrote.

   "One thing I learned today was . . ."

   "One way I can use what I learned today is . . ."

2. Preview next session.

Name_____ Date _____

Seven Ways to Handle Stress

Here are seven ideas children your age have used to handle stress. As you look at each idea, decide if it may be useful for you. Then do the following:

A. Choose your top three ideas from the list. Put a * by each of these.

B. Mark the ones you already use with a **check mark (√)**.

C. **Circle** the ones you would like to use more.

_____ 1. **Work it off** by being active—running, playing hard, doing soccer, dance, gymnastics.

_____ 2. **Talk it out** with someone you trust—a parent, teacher, friend, school counselor.

_____ 3. **Get plenty of rest.** You should be getting 9–10 hours of sleep each night.

_____ 4. **Make time for fun,** like playing games with friends or family.

_____ 5. **Expect yourself to make mistakes.** Nobody always does everything perfectly or never makes a mistake. Don't expect that you can always be perfect, either.

_____ 6. **Do something nice for someone**—such as helping around the house, or sending a nice note to a friend.

_____ 7. **Give in once in a while.** Let your friend go first or decide where to go.

Session 9
Topic: Self-evaluation, problem solving

Resources

- Student Success Skills Self-Evaluation handout (page 197)

Beginning

1. Stretches, movement, and breathing (student-led), used to balance active and passive activities.

2. In a go-round ask students to rate how they are feeling on the "great, pretty good, not so good, really bad" scale. Be sure to check with any "not so good" or "really bad" to determine if follow-up is needed.

3. Ask, "Who has been using something we talked about in the group? How did it go?"

Middle

STUDENT SELF-EVALUATION FORM

1. Go through each item, reading it aloud and asking students to rate how they did that week. Ask, "Who rated that item 'Good,' who rated it 'OK,' who rated it 'Needs to improve?'"

2. Use the items to stimulate discussion and to clarify problem areas that need to be addressed.

3. Use group problem solving by asking students to brainstorm solutions to problems raised as you move down the list. Role-playing solutions to problems is a valuable way to help students learn alternative strategies for handling difficult situations. The problem solving can also include how to handle the social problems that come up during the group meetings.

SOCIAL PROBLEM SOLVING

1. Ask students about problems either that they have had with other students/teachers at school or that they notice lots of other children have with each other at school. Make a list.

2. Ask group members to rank the top three problems in terms of interest to them for group to discuss possible solutions.

3. Lead a discussion on possible solutions for the selected top three problems. Use a brainstorming technique. List all offered solutions first. Then go back and have group code each one as "H," helpful, or "HA," harmful to self or others. *Note:* Some will be rated as both. Have group decide if the helpful side outweighs the harmful side.

4. Ask group to divide into pairs and plan a role-play for one of the three problems. The role-play should include one of the helpful solutions. Allow approximately five minutes for planning.

5. Ask each pair to present their role-play. Ask the rest of the group to discuss how realistically the problem and solution were portrayed, and any additional suggestions for handling the problem. The leader can also demonstrate various positive alternative ways to handle the situation or coach students in different ways to act. *Note:* It is the role-play and coaching that make this a powerful learning activity.

End

1. Ask students to write an ending to the following two sentences. Ask them to share their answers with a partner. Then ask for volunteers to share what they wrote.
   "One thing I learned today was . . ."
   "One way I can use what I learned today is . . ."

2. Preview next session.

Session 10
Topic: Review, spotlight, evaluation

Resources

- Index cards or sheets of paper
- Group Evaluation form (page 10)

Beginning

1. Stretches, movement, and breathing (student-led), used to balance active and passive activities.

2. In a go-round ask students to rate how they are feeling on the "great, pretty good, not so good, really bad" scale. Be sure to check with any "not so good" or "really bad" to determine if follow-up is needed.

3. Ask students to tell you some things they remember from last meeting.

4. Ask, "Who used something we talked about last week during the week? How did it go?"

Middle

REVIEW THE LIFE OF THE GROUP

1. Briefly go over each topic you've covered during the last nine weeks, asking for what they remember.

2. Then ask the following questions:

    - What are some the most important things you have learned about yourself?

- What has been the most helpful part of this group for you?
- What is a goal you have set for yourself?

ACCEPTING AND GIVING COMPLIMENTS

1. Hand out index cards or sheets of paper. Each person is to write down at least one thing he or she likes or appreciates about each of the other group members.

2. Spotlight: Ask each group member to say directly to the "spotlighted" person, with eye contact: "[person's name], one thing I like or appreciate about you is . . .". Explain and give examples of the types of qualities you are asking the students to think of and how to say and receive them. Ask students not to use things such as "I like your shirt, shoes, hair," etc., but rather qualities or actions.

3. After each comment, the spotlighted person says "thank you," nothing else. (Be sure you get in on this—it feels good.)

End

1. Process the spotlighting activity. How did it feel receiving compliments? Giving compliments?

2. Students complete anonymous evaluation.

3. Concluding remarks. Invite students to make individual appointments if they want. Remind them of the monthly follow-up sessions.

3.2
Building Math Confidence

Grade Level: 3–5	Time Required: 9 Sessions	Author: Chari Campbell

Purpose

Math proficiency is increasingly important to students in our highly technological society. However, many American students are not performing as well as they might. Although there are many reasons for low performance, math anxiety has been found to play a critical role in mathematics learning. In fact, some researchers in math education have established that a student's attitudes and feelings toward math may, in some cases, play a more important role in math success than any innate aptitude for math.

In addition, school counselors recognize that many of the career-related choices that students make are influenced by their feelings and attitudes toward math. Therefore it is important for school counselors to help students learn strategies that will help them cope with math anxiety.

The following nine-session small group counseling plan is designed to help students manage anxious feelings related to math. In a small group setting, students learn that they are not alone with their math anxiety. They are given a chance to vent their frustration and anger at people and situations that caused them embarrassment and shame related to their math performance. They are taught coping skills and techniques such as deep breathing, deep muscle relaxation, positive self-talk, positive imaging, and journaling to cope with math anxiety. In the beginning stages of the group, negative feelings toward math are recognized and acknowledged. Gradually the focus of the group activities shifts to the positive, with an emphasis on encouraging success.

It is suggested that the counselor hold monthly booster sessions, after the completion of the nine sessions, to reinforce the use of the coping skills. Also, parents and teachers can help children maintain their newly acquired coping skills so that they become well-established habits, which will lead to long-term increased learning and success with math.

Logistics

GROUP COMPOSITION

Students in grades 3–5 who seem to be struggling with math.

GROUP SIZE

4–6 students

GROUP TIME PER SESSION

30 minutes

NUMBER OF SESSIONS

Nine, with booster sessions spaced approximately one month apart after regular group ends.

Recommended Resources

Full bibliographic details for these publications are included in the Bibliography at the end of this book.

Arem, 1993: *Conquering Math Anxiety.*

Campbell, 1991: "Group guidance for academically under-motivated children."

Davidson and Levitov, 2000: *Overcoming Math Anxiety.*

Hebert and Furner, 1997: "Helping high-ability students overcome math anxiety through bibliotherapy."

Tobias, 1995: *Overcoming Math Anxiety.*

Session 1
Topic: Drawing, goal setting

Resources
- Drawing supplies
- Chart paper

Beginning

INTRODUCTION

1. Say, "Today we are going to learn more about each other and the purpose of our group. Let's start with a go-round. Tell us your name, your favorite food, and your least favorite food." Allow a volunteer(s) to repeat everyone's name and their chosen food.

2. "This time when we go around, tell us your favorite subject in school and your least favorite subject." Ask, "Who can remember someone's favorite subject?" until everyone has been remembered. Then ask: "Who can remember someone's least favorite subject?" Point out commonalities. (Since the children in the group were self-referred or referred by teachers because they feared or disliked math, many children will have identified math as their least favorite subject. Help them see that they are not alone.)

3. Explain that in this group we are going to learn ways to enjoy math.

CONFIDENTIALITY, GROUP NAME

Discuss confidentiality.

Say to group, "Let's think of a good name for our group." Let the children brainstorm and vote on a name. (*Examples:* Math Warriors, Math Busters, Rawlings Raiders)

Middle

FEELINGS MURAL

1. Put a sheet of chart paper on the floor or on a table and label it "Feelings Mural." Explain that each child will have her/his own space on the paper to draw.

2. Say, "Draw a picture or just use shapes and colors to describe how you feel when it's time to do math in school or for homework."

3. When the drawings are completed, each child shares his or her feelings while you write the feeling words on a second piece of chart paper.

4. Ask the group to examine the list for commonalities. Point out the ratio of negative to positive feelings listed. Identify the opposite feelings for each of the negative offered (e.g., calm vs. nervous, anticipation vs. dread). Explain that in this group we will learn how to get rid of the unpleasant feelings we have associated with math and replace them with pleasant feelings.

5. Since young children do not have an expansive feelings vocabulary, this activity allows you the opportunity to teach children words they can use to express their feelings. Introduce new words or synonyms for feeling words or phrases that children understand, such as "to anticipate" means "to look forward to."

GOALS

1. Talk about goals, asking "What is a goal?"

2. Discuss general goals for the group: to develop positive feelings about the ability to do math, to get a good grade in math, to like to do math, etc.

3. Ask for student commitment. "Who wants to learn how to relax and love math?"

4. In pairs, have students share their goals for the group. Then ask for volunteers to share.

5. List the group's goals on chart paper to hang on the wall.

WRAP-UP

"What did you learn from today's group?" Lead a discussion group and summarize the session.

HOMEWORK

"Notice how you feel when you are doing your math assignments this week. We will share your feelings at our next meeting."

Session 2
Topic: Math feelings

Resources

- Chart paper or poster board
- Scratch paper cut into small (6" × 8") rectangles
- Markers
- Colored pencils or crayons
- Tape
- Paper or notebook for Math Feelings Journal

Beginning

REVIEW

1. Ask, "Who can remember someone's name and their favorite food?" "Who can remember everyone's name?"

2. "Does anyone want to share your thoughts about our last session?" "At our last session, I asked you to pay attention to your feelings while you were doing math this week. What did you notice?" Lead the discussion and summarize.

Middle

THROW OUT NEGATIVE FEELINGS

1. Put a stack of scratch paper in the center of the group. Ask each member to write as many feeling words as they have to describe the feelings associated with math of which they became aware last week. Write one word per sheet of paper.

2. Ask students to put the positive words in a stack to save.

3. Explain that we are going to get rid of the unpleasant feelings. Students have the option of wadding up, tearing, shredding, or stomping on each of the unpleasant feeling words before throwing them into a trashcan.

4. Ask, "How did that feel?"

MATH POSTER

1. Have students tape any positive feeling words to a large poster paper. Label the poster "Math can be fun" and hang it on the wall, explaining that students can add positive feelings to it each week. "Our group goal will be to cover it with pleasant feelings over time."

2. Children tape pleasant feeling words from the Throwing Out Negative Feelings activity onto the poster chart.

MATH FEELINGS JOURNAL

1. Introduce the Math Feelings Journal.* Fold a piece of paper horizontally, or use the chalkboard to draw a rectangle representing a piece of paper. Draw a line down the middle of it. Label the left side "My Feelings" and the right side "My Work."

2. Tell the children to use words, phrases, or symbols to represent feelings and/or physical symptoms they experience while working on math.

3. Use the chalkboard to brainstorm symbols that might be appropriate, such as happy, sad, or worried faces.

4. Ask students to record their feelings as they move through their work.

5. Ask how the students would feel about sharing their feelings with their teachers. Explain that their teachers are very interested in knowing how students feel because it will make it easier to help them learn.

6. Ask students to keep the Math Feelings Journal daily and to bring it to group next session.

(*Note: The Math Feelings Journal is adapted from Bonnie Donnady's original work at the Wesleyan Math Clinic.)

End

DEAR ABBY

1. Tell the students to pretend that they are going to write an anonymous letter to Dear Abby about their problems with math. Explain that after you collect the letters, you are going to read them all to the group but that we are not going to try to guess who wrote which letter.

2. As you read each letter, ask the students to share how they would feel if the problem were theirs and what they might try to do. This is a chance for each child to receive a large dose of empathy and perhaps some helpful advice.

WRAP-UP

In pairs, ask students to share what they learned from today's session. Then ask for volunteers to share with the group the most important thing they learned today.

HOMEWORK

Remind students to notice their feelings as they work on math and to record them in their Math Feelings Journal (MFJ). *Note:* You should work with the elementary teacher on the best way to use the MFJ. If the teacher requires a special notebook for all math work, then it may be possible to have students use this format for journaling feelings on whatever type of paper or notebook the teacher requires. At the elementary level, the teacher may need to remind students, as they make daily assignments, to use the MFJ. Younger children may need to use a happy, worried, sad face format. Older children should be encouraged to use words to describe their feelings and physical symptoms in their journals.

Session 3
Topic: Learning to relax

Resources
- Optional: tape recorder and blank cassette tape

Beginning
1. Check in with the group. Ask, "How was your week? (Show me on your fingers. Five fingers means it was a great week, one finger means it's been a bummer.)" Ask for volunteers who want to share more about their week.
2. Say, "Share with the person seated next to you some of the feelings you are writing about in your Math Feelings Journal."
3. Next, ask for volunteers to share. Then lead a discussion to help students learn how the journal can help them become more aware of their feelings and how their feelings are related to their thoughts and behavior.

Middle
1. Ask students to identify any physical symptoms of stress they might experience while taking a test or being called on to answer a problem in class. Help students make a common list (such as weak knees, sick stomach, dizziness, blanking out).
2. Introduce the concept of two-word poetry. Ask students to write poems that describe their math anxiety.

   Example:

Rubber Knees	Blanked Out
Shaky hands	Sick Stomach
Cloudy Mind	Achy Head

3. Say, "Today we are going to learn to use our lungs and all of our muscles to train our bodies to relax." Invite the children to close their eyes if they wish, then lead the students through deep breathing exercises. Next lead them through deep muscle relaxation exercises, using the Relaxation Script below.

Relaxation Script
You may wish to make a tape of the relaxation script to play during each succeeding session rather than reading or speaking it each time. Also, copies of the tape may be made for children to take home to practice relaxation. A tape may also be used in the classroom at a learning center where children can practice in their free time.

Say, "Get into the most comfortable position you can in your chair. Uncross your legs and rest your feet flat on the floor. Let your arms rest comfortably in your lap. Now close your eyes and relax. Take several deep, relaxing breaths. I will count while you breathe. Inhale, one, two; hold, three, four; exhale, five, six. (Repeat this three times.)

Now say, "While you're breathing deeply, listen to all the sounds you hear, the noises outside, the noises in the room, the sounds from the person next to you and the noises from yourself. (Pause for 20 seconds) Now just listen to the sounds in the room. (Pause for 20 seconds) Now just listen to your own sounds as you become more and more relaxed until you are completely at peace."

"Focus on your right foot. Notice your toes. Scrunch them as tight as you can, and release. Now arch your foot, tighten, and release. Now, notice your calf. Tighten your calf muscle. Tighter. Now release. Now, be aware of your thigh. Make it as hard and tight as you can. Now release."

Ask the children what that felt like. Let them talk about the experience. Then suggest that they close their eyes again and move to the left foot. Repeat the above paragraph for the left foot. Continue by tightening and relaxing all the muscles in the leg.

Then move up the body to the abdomen (children may refer to it as their stomach) and on to the arms, beginning with the fingers, and on to the shoulders and head. Include the forehead, eyebrows, cheeks, nose, lips, and jaw.

During the deep muscle relaxation, remind children to periodically pay attention to their breathing, telling them to take deep relaxing breaths.

Process the activity. Ask students how they felt while doing the relaxation exercise. Tell students they can use this relaxation technique whenever they feel tense or ill at ease—for example, before starting on their math homework.

Ask students to practice this technique during the week.

End
1. In pairs, have students share what they learned from today's session. Lead the discussion and summarize.
2. For homework remind students to continue with the Math Feelings Journal and to practice relaxing all their muscles for ten minutes in the afternoon before doing their homework.

Session 4
Topic: Using clay to vent anger

Resources

- Clay
- Relaxation script or tape from Session 3
- Poster board or chart paper

Beginning

1. Check in with the group. Ask students to share what they have learned from keeping a Math Feelings Journal thus far.
2. Ask who remembered to practice the relaxation exercises. Ask how it felt.
3. Practice the relaxation exercises with the group.

Middle

VENTING ANGER WITH CLAY

1. Give each student a piece of natural clay (about the size of a baseball). Let them make shapes and squeeze and roll the clay for a few minutes, but ask them not to make an object.
2. After they have enjoyed the clay, show them how they can use the clay to vent anger. Ask the students to stand and throw the clay (onto a safe surface—the table, a wall, wash table, etc.). Ask them to think of something that makes them mad and say: "I feel so angry when . . ." and wham, have them throw the clay as hard as they can.
3. Now ask students, "Can you think of a time you felt 'put down' by someone when you were trying to do math? Don't use their name, but tell us what happened."
4. Then say: "You made me mad when you . . ." And have them slam their clay. Have them say: "I'm really mad at you for doing . . .". Students can all yell their angry phrases and slam the clay for a few minutes. The resulting laughter will feel good and takes some sting from the memory.

5. Next, show students how they can pound (flatten) their clay by beating it with the palms of their hands, their fists, etc. Also they can poke holes in the clay, jab it with pencils or rulers, and pinch it into pieces while expressing anger at someone who they believe made them feel dumb, embarrassed them, or made them angry regarding their attempts at math.

IDEAL MATH TEACHER

1. In pairs, have the students describe an ideal math teacher. What would he or she be like? What kinds of things would the ideal math teacher say and do to make you like math, help you learn math, help you feel confident about your ability to do math?
2. Have the pairs share with the group and collect the descriptions on a poster titled "Wanted—Ideal Math Teacher."

IDEAL MATH CLASSROOM

1. In groups of three, have students describe the ideal math classroom. What would it look like? What activities, games, books, work, etc. would there be for students? Would it be quiet or noisy? Would there be music? Would students work on their own or in groups or pairs?
2. Have the groups report back to the group. Lead a discussion and summarize.

End

Ask: "What did you learn in today's session that you can use to help you feel better about math?" Have the students share with a partner and report back to the group. Summarize student reports.

HOMEWORK

Say, "Practice the relaxation exercises for at least ten minutes every night and we'll talk about it next session."

Session 5
Topic: Self-talk

Resources

- Self-Talk handout
- Chalkboard or chart paper
- 4" × 12" pieces of colored poster board
- Relaxation script or tape from Session 3

Beginning

1. Check in with the group. "How was your week? (Show me on your fingers. Five fingers means it was a great week, one finger means it's been a bummer.)" Ask for volunteers who want to share more about their week.

2. Share the Math Feelings Journals. Say, "Share with the person seated next to you what feelings you are writing about in your Math Feelings Journal." Ask for volunteers to share; then lead a discussion to help students learn how the journal can help them become more aware of their feelings and how their feelings are related to their thoughts and behavior.

3. Practice deep breathing exercise. Ask, "Who practiced?" Then say, "Let's do it together." Play the tape or read the script and go through the exercises with the children.

Middle

SELF-TALK

1. Say, "Today we are going to learn how to recognize some of the negative things we are saying to ourselves about math or our ability to do math that are keeping us from doing our best and feeling good about math. Then we are going to replace those negative thoughts with positive ones and begin to practice thinking positively about ourselves and math."

2. Pass out the Self-Talk handout and ask students to remember some of their math goals. These can be shared aloud to help students select the goals on which they want to work. Sample goals are included on the handout.

3. Next, lead a discussion about negative self-talk. Examples of negative self-talk are provided on the handout.

4. In pairs, have students share some of the negative thoughts that are preventing them from meeting their math goals.

5. When all pairs have finished sharing, have them share all their negative thoughts with the group; record this on the chalkboard or chart paper.

6. Have the group brainstorm positive self-statements to replace each of the negative statements generated by the group. As they generate positive statements, record them on chart paper. (*Note:* Hang this list on the wall and save it for future use.) Students then complete their self-talk handout.

BUMPER STICKER ART

1. Ask each student to select his or her three favorite positive thoughts. Give students pieces of colored poster board on which to design their bumper stickers. They can take these home to hang on the wall above their desk or over their bed.

2. In a go-round, have each student select one of his or her positive thoughts and say it out loud ten times. Encourage students to say the thought in a strong voice and to sound very sure of themselves.

3. If time allows, students can make extra bumper stickers for the classroom, and small ones to use as bookmarks.

End

1. Ask, "What did you learn from today's session that you might be able be able to use tonight when you do your homework, or tomorrow when you take your test?" Summarize the discussion.

2. Ask students to practice saying each positive thought ten times throughout the day.

Name_____ Date_____

Self-Talk

1. My math goals are:

    1. _____

    2. _____

    3. _____

    4. _____

    Examples: to get a good grade in math, to do well on my math test, to learn my multiplication tables.

2. But, my negative thoughts are:

    1. _____

    2. _____

    3. _____

    4. _____

    Examples: "I'm going to fail the test," "I'll never figure out this problem," "I must be a dummy," "I might as well give up."

(continued)

Name_____ Date_____

Self-Talk

3. Change each negative thought to a positive thought.

"I'm going to fail the test."	becomes	"I'm going to pass the test!"
"I never get it right."	becomes	"I'll keep working until I get it right."
"I'm a dummy."	becomes	"I'm smart. I can learn this!"
"I might as well give up."	becomes	"I'll never give up. I'll call a friend for help."

My new, positive thoughts will be:

1. _____

_____

2. _____

_____

3. _____

_____

4. _____

_____

Session 6
Topic: Success imaging

Resources

- Relaxation script or tape from Session 3

Beginning

1. Check in with the group. "How was your week? (Show me on your fingers. Five fingers means it was a great week, one finger means it's been a bummer.)" Ask for volunteers who want to share more about their week.

2. Ask students to share where they put their math "bumper stickers."

3. Ask who remembered to recite each of their positive statements at least ten times. Ask how it felt to do that.

4. Have each student turn to the student seated next to him and share two or three of his favorite positive statements.

5. Next, in a go-round, have each student select one of his or her positive statements and say it aloud to the group three times. Instruct: "Use a strong voice . . . show excitement . . . show your confidence!"

6. Ask: "Who practiced the relaxation exercises?" Then say, "Let's practice together." Play the tape or read the script and go through the exercises with the children, but this time, at the close of the relaxation exercises, ask the children to select one of their positive self-statements and repeat it ten times. Say, "Think your positive self-talk silently to yourself. Say the self-talk slowly. Really believe what you are saying and think about it as you are saying it."

Middle

SUCCESS IMAGES

1. Say, "Today we are going to learn another technique to prepare our minds for success. We are going to use our imaginations to picture ourselves being successful with math. What you are doing is training your mind to have the successful experiences that you want."

2. Say, "Let's practice creating mental pictures. First, get into a comfortable position. Closing your eyes may help you use your imagination while you listen to my voice. I'm going to describe a place and I want you to picture being there."

"It is a glorious morning. The weekend is here and you are going to go biking with your friend. Where is your bike? You've found it. Now you are riding down the road, away from your home. You feel the wind in your face and in your hair. It smells sweet, like freshly mowed grass. You hear birds chirping. They sound as happy and free as you feel. You notice the warmth of the sun on the top of your head and shoulders. You feel like you could ride forever. Take a ride with your friend for a few more minutes. Where will you go? What will you see?" (Give them one or two minutes to mentally ride their bikes. Then say: "In a few more seconds I'm going to ask you to return to this room and then we'll talk about your bike trip.")

3. Ask for volunteers to describe their experiences. What did they see, hear, smell, feel? Did they picture themselves on the bike as though they were looking at a TV screen, or did they seem to be looking out at the scenery through their own eyes? Was it pleasant? Was anything unpleasant? Explain to students that they are completely in control of their own mental pictures, so it can always be a pleasant experience.

4. "Now, let's try using success images to help us obtain our math goals. For example, one of our goals was to remain calm during math exams. Close your eyes while I talk you through the steps. You are smiling and feeling confident. You are practicing your relaxation exercises. You are repeating your favorite positive self-statements. Now the teacher passes out the exam. You continue to use deep relaxing breaths as you work through the problems. When you feel stuck, you repeat your positive self-talk, and guess what? It works! You figure out how to solve the problem and move on to the next one. You complete the test and turn it in. You feel great. You know that you did your best work. You flash your teacher a big smile and leave feeling proud of yourself."

5. Now you are ready to create your own success images. In a go-round, ask each student to share one of her math-related goals for which she wants to create a success image. Ask students to work in pairs to write down the details of their success image. Then each student shares with the group.

6. Say, "Now we are ready to combine relaxation, self-talk, and visualization. We will take a shortcut to relaxation this time. Just get into a comfortable position and stretch and relax your muscles. Now take three relaxation breaths." (The counselor counts: "Inhale 1, 2; — hold 3, 4; — exhale 5, 6, —.") "Good. You are feeling very relaxed. Now practice your positive self-talk." (Allow one minute.) "Now use your imagination and see your success image. Include your positive self-talk where it fits. When you have finished, open your eyes and wait quietly until we are all ready to speak." Ask students to describe what the experience was like.

End

Ask, "What did you learn from today's session that you might be able be able to use tonight when you do your homework, or tomorrow in class?" Summarize the discussion.

HOMEWORK

Say, "Practice, practice, practice! Combine all three techniques and use them each night and in class. Continue to use your Math Feelings Journal."

Session 7
Topic: Creating a math rap song

Resources
- Blank tapes
- Tape recorder
- Relaxation script or tape from Session 3
- Optional: tapes of rap songs, musical instruments

Beginning
1. Check in with the group. "How was your week? (Show me on your fingers. Five fingers means it was a great week, one finger means it's been a bummer.)" Ask for volunteers who want to share more about their week.

2. Ask, "How did your practice go?" Facilitate a discussion, encouraging children to make the practice a routine in their daily lives. Help them find the best time of day to practice. Suggest doing the exercises right before or after taking a shower or brushing their teeth so that they are less likely to forget.

3. Say, "Think of one thing you like about math, or a time you enjoyed doing math. Share that with the person sitting next to you." After the pairs have shared, ask the students to share in a go-round.

4. Practice the entire relaxation exercise; include the positive self-talk and success images. Then process the experience with the children.

5. Inquire about the Math Feelings Journals. What kinds of feelings are they experiencing in class while doing math or taking tests? Suggest that when they notice that they are anxious or feel "stuck," that would be the best time to use the relaxation or success exercises. Ask them to record in their journals what happened when they used the exercises to relax or to get "un-stuck." Tell them to remember so that we can talk about them next time.

Middle

RAP SONGS
1. Ask, "How many of you like rap music? Can anyone teach us how to do it?" Allow volunteers to demonstrate how to set words to the beat.

2. Ask the group to write a math rap song using their positive self-talk in the lyrics. You might ask each student for one line and write them all on the board, or you might start them off with a line and ask for more lines that rhyme. Encourage students to use scenes from their success images in the rap song. Also, they can include positive memories of doing and enjoying math. Encourage them to include positive feeling words and phrases such as proud, trying harder and harder, and motivated.

3. Then add movement to the rap (kicks, jumps, hand-jive, etc.). Say: "You may set it to music if you want." (You may have tapes of rap music that could be used, or borrow basic musical instruments from the music teacher to add to the fun.)

4. Have the group practice the rap song, then record it. Play back the rap song and say/sing along with it. Ask students to picture themselves doing and feeling what the lyrics in the song say.

5. Process the experience. Ask, "How did creating and singing/saying the rap song make you feel? How did creating and singing/saying the song affect your feelings toward math? What new positive affirmations did you hear today? How could you use this song to motivate you to keep trying when you are feeling discouraged?"

End
Remind students that we have two sessions left. Remind them to use the Math Feelings Journal and to practice, practice, practice!

Session 8
Topic: Math is fun mural

Resources

- Tapes/CDs with relaxing music
- Relaxation script or tape from Session 3
- The rap song made by the group
- The chart of positive self-talk made in Session 5
- Paint
- Large sheet of paper

Beginning

1. Check in with the group. "How was your week? (Show me on your fingers. Five fingers means it was a great week, one finger means it's been a bummer.)" Ask for volunteers who want to share more about their week.

2. Ask, "How did your practice go?" Facilitate a discussion.

3. Practice the entire relaxation exercise; include the positive self-talk and success images. Then process the experience with the children.

Middle

A MATH IS FUN MURAL

1. Give students a large sheet of art paper and paint. Tell the students, "Today we are going to make another math mural, but this one will focus on our positive experiences, thoughts, and feelings about math. (Refer to the list of positive self-statements made in Session 3.) Ask students to think of a time that they enjoyed doing math, a time they felt proud, capable, in control. Ask if anyone has experienced feeling successful using the self-talk while doing class work, doing homework, or taking a test. Label the mural "Math is Fun" and allow students to creatively express positive emotions related to math.

2. Before the students begin to paint, play the rap music for inspiration, then play the relaxing music while they are painting.

3. When students have cleaned up, give each child a chance to share what he or she painted.

4. Hang the mural on the wall.

5. Lead a short discussion about recent successes with math, successes they have had at calming themselves when they felt uptight, and experiences of getting "unstuck" when they relaxed while doing their math.

6. Encourage each child by reflecting feelings of growing confidence, even if it is unspoken. Repeat to each child words to the effect of, "You did that on your own! You gained control of your anxious feelings. You must be so proud!"

End

1. Remind students that the next session is the last session of the math confidence-building group and that they may bring party snacks to share.

2. Ask them to continue their relaxation and success exercises and to continue using the Math Feelings Journal. Explain that now that they know how to use these tools to help them conquer math anxiety, they will be able to continue to build their math confidence on their own.

3. Tell students that after the next session we will no longer be able to meet once a week, but that we will meet once a month for a "booster session." Tell them you will want to see their Math Feelings Journals and hear about any new self-talk or success images they are using. Maybe someone will make up a new rap song to share.

Session 9
Topic: Confidence cards, closure

Resources

- Snacks, drinks, and party food for kids
- Colored poster board (4" × 8" or 4" × 12" pieces)
- Markers
- Relaxation script or tape from Session 3

Beginning

1. Check in with the group. "How was your week? (Show me on your fingers. Five fingers means it was a great week, one finger means it's been a bummer.)" Ask for volunteers who want to share more about their week.
2. Ask: "How did your practice go?" Facilitate a discussion.
3. Practice the entire relaxation exercise; include the positive self-talk and success images. Then process the experience with the children. Point out to them that they seem to be able to relax more completely. Explain that if they continue to practice on their own they will be able to achieve complete relaxation in shorter periods of time, so that they can just take three long, relaxing breaths and feel refreshed. Ask students which of the self-statements seem to be the most helpful in getting them "unstuck," to encourage them to work harder, to give them confidence in math.

Middle

1. Ask the children to count with you the number of party foods. Say, "Let's have fun doing math together." Ask, "How many cookies are there? How many snacks are there? So how do we figure out how many of each we get to eat?" Discuss how math played a role in the making of candy, chips, etc. For example, as you are passing out the snacks, ask them to name the jobs of the people who made them (e.g., farmers, cooks, delivery persons, salespeople, accountants). Ask them to describe how those individuals use math on their jobs.
2. While students are enjoying the snacks, lead a group discussion about what it was like to participate in a math confidence group and what students learned as a result of being in the group. Some questions you may ask include: "What have you learned from these sessions that will help you learn math and enjoy the learning process?" "What changes have you noticed in your attitude toward math and taking math tests?" "How did you feel about math at the start of the sessions?" "How do

you feel now?" "How has participating in a math confidence group affected your feelings about math? About yourself? About others?"

End

CONFIDENCE CARDS

1. Have each student write his or her name as decoratively as possible, using colored markers, in the middle of one of the poster board rectangles. Explain that they can decorate each letter, but that they need to leave room for people to write around the edges of the name.
2. Then have the students silently pass the cards to the right and direct them to write a word or phrase that describes a personal strength they have observed about the person whose name is written on the card. If the students have not participated in this type of activity before, take a few minutes to talk about the kinds of personal strengths people have, and give concrete examples, such as: He is kind; she has a good sense of humor; he thinks of others' feelings; she is a good listener; he is creative; she is brave; he is friendly; you can count on her to do what she says. Ask them to be as specific as possible in their feedback to each other.
3. After everyone has his or her card back, ask each student to tell the group (a) the strength of which they are most proud, (b) the strength they were most surprised to see, and (c) a strength of theirs that the group did not mention, if they would like to share it.

CLOSURE

1. Set a date a month from now for a booster session.
2. Tell the students that you would like to stop by their desks periodically to see their Math Feelings Journals. Explain again how the Math Feelings Journal will encourage them to keep working and manage anxious feelings when they crop up.
3. Remind them that everyone sometimes feels uptight about math, even mathematicians. It is how you cope with your anxious feelings that counts.
4. Suggest that if everyone in the group continues to use the Math Feelings Journal to record his successes using relaxation and success exercises, the group can celebrate with a popcorn party at the booster session.
5. Say goodbye.

3.3
Social Problem Solving, K–2

Grade Level: K–2	Time Required: 8 Sessions	Author: Donna Steinberg

Purpose

To develop social problem solving skills and thinking skills. Students use a problem-solving model to apply to typical social problems. Role-play provides practice in applying the new skills.

Logistics

GROUP COMPOSITION

Students grades K–2 mixed with regard to activity level and behavior control. Avoid loading group with only overactive behavior problem students. Students need multiple models of appropriate behavior. Groups with only behavior problem students usually do not show significant gains in prosocial behavior. Mixed groups are generally very effective.

GROUP SIZE

4–6 students

GROUP TIME PER SESSION

30 minutes

NUMBER OF SESSIONS

Eight, with booster sessions spaced approximately one month apart after regular group ends.

Recommended Resources

Full bibliographic details for these publications are included in the Bibliography at the end of this book.

Dinkmeyer and Dinkmeyer, 1982: *Developing Understanding of Self and Others.*

McGinnis and Goldstein, 1997: *Skillstreaming the Elementary School Child.*

Shure, 1992: *I Can Problem-Solve: An Interpersonal Cognitive Problem-Solving Program.*

St. Germain, 1990: *The Terrible Fight.*

Vernon, 1989: *Thinking, Feeling, Behaving: An Emotional Education Curriculum for Children.*

Vernon, 1998: *The Passport Program.*

Session 1
Topic: Getting to know each other

Resources

- Chart paper
- Enough sets of Matching Game Cards for each student to have two cards

Beginning

Before the group begins, have teachers complete a pre-group evaluation.

1. Welcome children to the group. Have them tell the person next to them their name, what they like to be called (could be a nickname), and one thing they like to do for fun. Then children introduce each other.

2. Talk about the purpose of the group. Ask children,

   - "Have you ever had a problem with another person?"
   - "How did you feel when . . . (for example, someone was mean to you)?"

   Say, "In this group, you can learn about solving these kinds of problems. When you make a problem better you are 'solving' the problem."

   - "How do you think this will help you?"

3. Provide a summary of what to expect—sharing, games, stories, role-play, drawing, and puppets.

4. Tell students that today you will talk about rules "that will make our group a happy and safe place to learn. Then we can play a game that will help us think of feeling words and will help us tell the difference between same and different. This can help us with things we will be doing in our group. Does this sound like a good idea?"

Middle

GROUP RULES

1. Discuss rules for the group. Encourage rules that are established by the children.

2. Write the rules on chart paper, making sure to include no put-downs, one person talks at a time, and not talking about what other members say. Children like to sign the rule chart. Talk about confidentiality and limits in concrete terms.

MATCHING FACES GAME

1. Practice with identifying feeling words and understanding same/different are prerequisite skills for upcoming activities. Pass out doubles of picture cards so each member has two pictures. Children hold pictures face down.

2. One child turns a picture for all to see, then chooses a child to show one of his/her pictures. Ask children to name the feeling of the first child's card. Then ask if the second child's picture shows the same or a different feeling. If it is the same, collect the pair of cards. If it is different, turn both cards face down.

3. The last child to show a picture chooses another child. The game continues until all matches are made.

End

Process with members, "What was it like for you to be in group today?" "Who else feels that way?" "What did you learn?" "How do you think our group will help you?"

Name_____ Date _____

Matching Game Cards

         Group Counseling for School Counselors: A Practical Guide

Session 2
Topic: Feelings

Resources

- The Swing illustration

Beginning

1. Review names by greeting each child, for example, "Hi Jamie, I'm glad you are here."

2. Ask children to partner with another and tell how they feel about being in group today. Have them choose a different partner from the last session. Emphasize commonalities in feelings.

3. Ask members what they remember about the last session. Review the rationale for the group, the meaning of "solving a problem," and rules.

4. Provide a rationale for today's activity: "Sometimes pictures are a good way to think about problems people have and their feelings. I have a picture we can look at and talk about. Then we can pretend to be actors and act out a real problem one of you may have had. How do you think this might help us?"

Middle

1. Show the illustration or pass it around for all to see. Ask,
   - "What is the problem in this picture?"
   - "What do you think is happening?"
   - "How do you think this person feels?"
   - "How do you think that person feels?"

2. Ask members, "What kinds of problems have you had where you felt like that?" Using a problem from a member, explain how to role-play. "We can act out Megan's problem. Someone can pretend to be the other person and Megan can play herself. Megan, you tell Lisa what to do."

3. Help children to role-play the incident. Model role-playing the other person if needed. Ask:
   - "What is the problem?"
   - "How does Megan feel?"
   - "How does Lisa feel?"

4. Have players reverse roles. Ask questions like, "How was Lisa thinking about Megan's feelings?"

5. Process the role-play by asking, "What was it like to role-play a problem? What was it like to role-play the other person? How can it help to think about your feelings? How can it help to think about the other person's feelings? What do you think about people having different feelings about the same thing?"

End

Ask children what it was like for them to be in group today. Ask, "What did you learn? How is it going to help you think about how others feel? How can you use what you learned today?"

The Swing

Session 3
Topic: What's the problem

Resources

- Story with problem; recommended: *The Terrible Fight*, by Sharon St. Germain
- Drawing paper

Beginning

1. Ask children how they used what they learned in the last session.

2. Have children tell about a time when they thought about how someone else was feeling. For example, "Who would like to share how they were able to think about the feelings of someone else?"

3. Tell children, "Today I have a story I will read to you. We can learn about solving problems with stories. Some kids have found out that when they know what the problem is, they can understand better. I think this story will help us practice. Does that sound good?"

Middle

1. Use a story with a problem, for example, *The Terrible Fight*, St. Germain (1990).

2. Read the story aloud, stopping at appropriate times to ask:

- "What is the problem?"
- "How do you think ___ feels?"
- "How can you tell?"
- "How did they solve the problem?"
- "What else could they do?"
- "How did it work out?"

3. Focus on who feels the same and who feels different about the same thing. Also elicit responses for ways to find out how someone else feels. Encourage children for listening.

End

1. Ask children, "What have you learned today? What have you learned about getting along with others? How do you feel about our group today? How are you going to use what you learned?"

2. Talk to members about how it can help if they draw a picture of a problem they have for the next time. Talk about examples: "It could be with your teacher, parents, brothers, sisters, or friends." Ask if they think this is a good idea. Distribute drawing paper for students to take with them.

Session 4
Topic: There's more than one way

Beginning

1. Ask children to share their drawings from the last meeting and tell what the problem was.

2. Discuss, "How have you been thinking about how other people feel? Who would like to tell us?"

3. Tell children, "Today we can role-play different ways to solve a problem. Who remembers what role-play is? How will doing this help you when you have a problem with another person?"

Middle

1. Have a member recount the problem picture he or she brought to group; these are best for learning. Or use the following scenario: Samantha is in (grade that applies). She always wants to have her own way. Sometimes she fights with other children or takes things from them. In this problem she cuts in line while she is waiting for lunch. The person she cuts is Andrew. Andrew says, "Hey, that's not fair, you cut." Discuss:

- What is the problem?
- How is Andrew feeling?
- How can you tell?
- How is Samantha feeling?
- How can you tell?

2. Ask for volunteers to role-play. Ask children, "What can Andrew do? Think of as many different things to do as you can and then we can role-play."

3. Have each member role-play his or her solution. Emphasize, "So, it looks like you were able to think about lots of things to do about this problem. How do you think it would help you if you were able to think of different things to do when you are having the problem?"

End

Ask students, "What did you learn today? How can you use what you learned? How do you feel about being in our group? What was it like for you to share in group today?"

Session 5
Topic: What will happen?

Resources

- Two hand puppets
- Small ball

Beginning

1. Ask members to complete the sentence, "I am getting better at getting along with others because . . .".

2. Ask children how they have used what they have learned. "Who would like to tell us about a time when you tried thinking of different things you can do when you have a problem? How did it help you? How do you feel about that?"

3. Tell children, "Today I have some puppets that can show us in a fun way how sometimes people do things that are by accident and what can happen. This can help us to learn and practice solving problems. How do you think getting all the information about your problem will help you?"

Middle

1. You will need two (any kind) of hand puppets. Ask for a volunteer to play a puppet throwing a ball with your puppet. Begin throwing the ball back and forth. Allow the ball to hit your puppet. Then your puppet says angrily, "You hit me in the eye!" Ask group members, "What is the problem?"

2. Give puppets to two children to role-play what might happen next. Talk about feelings and how to find out more information about a problem (asking questions, listening). Refer to examples children presented in their own problems where relevant.

3. Using a child's example problem, have two children role-play the scene with the puppets. "Lisa, would you like to act out the problem you told us about?" Ask questions:

   - What is the problem?
   - How do you know?
   - Do you have all the information?
   - How can you find out?
   - How do you feel?
   - How do you think the other person feels?
   - What can you do about it?
   - What will happen if you do that?
   - What else can you do?
   - Then what will happen?

End

1. Ask, "What did you learn today? How will you use what you learned? What was it like to be in our group today?"

2. Tell children that the group will meet three more times.

Session 6
Topic: The waiting problem

Resources

- Paper
- Drawing materials
- The Swing illustration from Session 2

Beginning

1. Ask members to complete the sentence, "Sometimes when I have to wait I feel . . ."
2. Ask members how they have used what they are learning.
   - Who has had a problem with another person?
   - What can you share with us about the problem?
   - Did you have all the information?
   - What did you do?
3. Ask children, "Have you ever had a problem with another person because she didn't want to wait her turn to talk or to play? Or maybe you can remember a problem when you had a hard time waiting and it got you in trouble. We can draw pictures of those kinds of problems and it can help us figure out what we can do. Does this sound like something that will help?"

Middle

1. Distribute drawing paper. Tell children they will have a few minutes to draw the problem about waiting.
2. Give a two-minute notice when drawing time is over. Have children share their pictures. Problems children have personally experienced are most valuable, but if necessary use the swing illustration as an example of waiting your turn.
3. After hearing a description of the problem, ask children:
   - What is the problem?
   - Do you have all the information?
   - How do you feel?
   - How does the other person feel?
   - What did you do?
   - What happened when you did that?
   - How did you feel when that happened?
   - What else could you do?
   - What will happen then?
4. Discuss as many drawings as time allows. Choose problems that involve taking turns, sharing, and interrupting. Elicit responses where children determine solutions for themselves and acknowledge that their actions can cause responses. Elicit responses that indicate a need to calm down first. Role-play solutions when opportunity is apparent.

End

1. Process, "What did you learn today? How will you use what you learned? What will you do? How do you feel about today's group? For next time, think about problems you may have with other students that happen in your classroom. We can use them in our next group. Does that sound like a good idea?"
2. Remind children that the group will meet two more times.

Session 7
Topic: In the classroom

Resources
- Puppets

Beginning

1. Children complete the sentence, "I am getting better and better at . . ."
2. Ask members how they have used what they are learning about problem solving.
3. Ask children to share problems they have had or have seen in the classroom. Tell members, "So, it sounds like these kinds of problems can get people in trouble and they feel bad about that. We can practice what to do when this happens. What do you think about using the puppets to role-play this kind of problem?"

Middle

1. Have any kind of puppets available. Using a member's experience if possible, role-play a distraction in class with the puppets. Or use the following situation: You are working on your seat-work and the student sitting next to you shows you a toy he has in his backpack. He starts to tell you all about it.
2. Ask for volunteers to role-play this scene with the puppets. Help them with the role-play, "You be the other student, his name is ____. And you be ____. First, pretend you are working on seatwork, then . . ."

3. Ask members:
   - What is the problem?
   - How do you feel?
   - How does the other person feel?
   - What can you do about it?
   - What will happen if you do that?
   - How will you feel about that?
   - What else can you do?
   - Then what will happen?
   - And then how would you feel?
4. Tell children, "I have something for you to think about that has worked for other students. When someone is keeping you from getting your work done or listening to your teacher you can talk to yourself. You can say to yourself: I won't answer, I'm going to do my work. Then when she stops bothering you, you can smile, and say to yourself, I can do it. Who would like to practice this with the puppets?" Allow all group members to role-play this solution with puppets.

End

1. Process, "What did you learn today? How are you going to use what you learned? How do you feel about today's group?"
2. Talk about the group's last meeting and how members would like to say good-bye.

Session 8
Topic: Saying goodbye

Resources

- Refreshments
- Teachers' post-group evaluation form
- Group Evaluation handout (page 239)

Beginning

1. Children share, "When I have a problem with someone, something I do now that I didn't do before this group is . . ."
2. Celebrate success. Ask students to share a time when they used their problem solving. Model complimenting each child and invite members to join in the congratulating.
3. Tell children how you feel about having them in a group. Tell them, "It would help me to know about how you feel and how you think the group has helped you. It will help me with other groups of children who also want to learn about problem solving. And it will help me to know what you learned. I have a few questions that you can answer that will tell me that."

Middle

1. Share snacks. Share, "How do you feel about the group ending?"
2. Ask and record answers to evaluation questions for kindergarten and first grade. Second graders can usually complete the simple form included.

End

1. Children share, "The best part of being in our group was . . .".
2. Tell children that although the group has ended you are there to help with a problem.
3. Have teachers complete post-group evaluation.

Teacher Pre/Post Evaluation

Student _____ Date _____

Teacher _____

Please rate student on a scale of 1–5. Your time is appreciated.

1—Almost Never   5—Almost Always

_____ Behaves positively with classmates

_____ Takes turns/shares

_____ Works well in classroom

_____ Shows understanding of feelings of another person

_____ Is distracted in class

_____ Overreacts frequently

_____ Is involved in fights

_____ Bothers other children

Name_____ Date _____

Social Problem-Solving
Group Evaluation

 Always   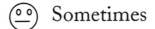 Sometimes    Never

1. I get along with other students.

2. I think about how other people feel.

3. When I have a problem, I think of different things to do.

4. I think about what will happen before I do something about a problem.

5. I think the group has helped me.

Booster Session

Resources

- Chart paper

Beginning

1. Tell students that after a group ends, it is a good idea to check with members to see how they are doing.
2. Remind students that although the group has ended, there are the same rules for this meeting. Ask, "Who would like to remind us of the rules?"

Middle

1. Ask, "How are you using what you learned in the group? What questions do you have? What can we talk about that would help you?"
2. Review briefly, "When you have a problem with another person, what do you do?" Use chart paper to list responses from students. Elicit responses that include: Find out what the problem is. How do you feel? How does the other person feel? What can you do? What will happen if you do that? How will you feel? What else can you do? Then how will you feel? What do you choose to do? How did it work?
3. Ask students to tell about a time when they worked hard to solve a problem. Model a compliment to the speaker and then ask other members, "Who would like to say something to _____ about how he/she did?"

End

1. How did this meeting help you? What did you learn? What was it like to get together again?
2. Remind children they can see you if they need help.

3.4
Social Problem Solving, 3–5

Grade Level: 3–5	Time Required: 8 Sessions	Author: Donna Steinberg

Purpose

To develop social problem-solving skills and thinking skills. Students use a problem-solving model to apply to typical social problems. Role-play provides practice in applying the new skills.

Logistics

GROUP COMPOSITION

Students grades 3–5 mixed with regard to activity level and behavior control. Avoid loading group with only overactive behavior problem students. Students need multiple models of appropriate behavior. Groups with only behavior problem students usually do not show significant gains in prosocial behavior. Mixed groups are generally very effective.

GROUP SIZE

4–6 students

GROUP TIME PER SESSION

30 minutes

NUMBER OF SESSIONS

Eight, with booster sessions spaced approximately one month apart after regular group ends.

Session 1
Topic: Getting started

Resources

- "Think First" Self-Evaluation form (student)
- "Think First" Teacher Pre/Post Evaluation form
- Chart paper

Beginning

1. Students and teachers complete the pre-group evaluations before the group begins. A good time may be after the student has accepted the invitation to the group at the screening interview.

2. Welcome children and let them know you are happy they have chosen to participate. Have them tell a partner their name and something they like to do. Then, members introduce each other.

3. Talk about the purpose of the group. Ask children:
   - "How do you feel when you are having a problem with another person?"
   - "What kinds of problems have you had?"
   - "How do you think a problem-solving group will help you?"

4. Provide a summary of what to expect. "In this group we can learn how to find solutions to problems, how things we do can affect others, how to choose a solution, how to use self-control, and steps for making a decision. Does this sound like something that will help you?"

5. Ask students to "think about what kinds of rules will make our group a happy and safe place to learn."

Middle

1. Discuss rules for the group. Encourage rules that are established by the children. Write the rules on chart paper, making sure to include no put-downs, one person talks at a time, and not talking about what other members say. Talk about confidentiality and limits in concrete terms. Signing the rule chart indicates agreement and adds to cohesion.

2. Tell members, "When we talk about problem-solving, it will help to have real problems you have had or seen. For the next time we meet it would be helpful for each of you to bring an example with you. You can draw a picture of the problem or you can write about it. It can be a problem with a friend, someone at school, or at home."

End

Process with members,
"What was it like for you to be in group today?"
"Who else feels that way?"
"What did you learn?"
"How do you think our group will help you?"

"Think First" Self-Evaluation

Student _____ Date _____

Teacher _____

Rate yourself on the scale indicated. Help yourself by being honest.

1—Almost Never   2—Sometimes   3—Almost Always

_____ I get along well with classmates.

_____ I think about how others are feeling.

_____ I say no in a friendly way when I don't want to do
something that will get me in trouble.

_____ When I have a problem I think first before I do anything
about it.

_____ I think of other ways to solve a problem instead of
fighting.

_____ When I do something I shouldn't have, I admit I did
it and I accept what happens.

_____ I can calm down when I am angry.

_____ I do not pay attention to others when I am doing
my classwork.

_____ When I have a problem I think about how I feel.

_____ When I have a problem I think of different things to
do about it.

_____ When I have a problem I think of what will happen
if I do something about it.

               Group Counseling for School Counselors: A Practical Guide

"Think First" Teacher Pre/Post Evaluation

Student _____ Date _____

Teacher _____

Please rate student on the scale indicated. Your time is appreciated.

1—Almost Never   2—Sometimes   3—Almost Always

_____ Behaves positively with classmates

_____ Shows understanding of how other people feel

_____ Avoids trouble

_____ Acts without thinking

_____ Gets involved in fights

_____ Blames others

_____ Has angry outbursts

_____ Is distracted in class

                   Group Counseling for School Counselors: A Practical Guide

Session 2
Topic: Solutions

Beginning

1. Members complete the sentence, "I can tell when someone is happy when . . ."
2. Explain to members, "Today we will use the problems we have brought with us to learn about identifying a problem, gathering information about a problem, and thinking about solutions for a problem. How do you think this will help us?" Elicit responses that indicate these steps can help to solve the problem.

Middle

1. Have children present their problem: "Who would like to start by telling us about the problem you brought? Tell us what happened without telling us what you did about it." Model telling about a problem without telling the solution. Immediately after the problem is presented, ask, "What is the problem?"
2. Very quickly, ask, "What should _____ do about it?"
3. Tell children, "I asked you to identify the problem and think of a solution very quickly. Now I will give you some time to think about it and answer again." Have children work in pairs. Ask:
   - "What was different about answering without thinking, then having a chance to think about it?"
   - "How is thinking about it better?"
4. Have another child present a problem without telling the solution. Tell members, "This time you can ask (the child presenting the problem) questions

to learn more about the problem." Model asking questions: "How do you feel? How does the other person feel? How can you tell?" After members have asked questions, ask, "What is the problem? What should _____ do about it?"
5. Discuss:
   - How does it help to get all the information about a problem?
   - How does it help to think about how you feel?
   - How does it help to think about how the other person feels?
   - How can you tell how another person feels? (watch, listen, ask)
   - What are some other ways you can know the whole story of a problem? (ask questions)
6. Process remaining problems using questions:
   - How can you get the facts about this problem?
   - What is the problem?
   - How do the people feel?
   - How do you know?
   - What can be done about it?
7. Discuss: What did you notice about the solutions you thought of? Was there more than one solution for a problem? What do you think about that?

End

Ask, "What was it like for you to be in group today?" "What did you learn?" "How will you use what you learned?"

Session 3
Topic: Consequences

Resources
- Andrew's Problem narrative

Beginning
1. Members complete the sentence, "The best thing about last session was . . .".
2. Members share how they have used what they have learned about problem solving.
3. Ask children, "How does it help to think of more than one solution? So it sounds like you are thinking about which one will work best; how do you choose? Today I brought a problem we can use to think about consequences, what will happen if we choose a solution, and to think about how we take responsibility for a problem we have caused. Role-play can be very helpful because it gives us a chance to practice what we are learning. Does this sound like a good idea?"

Middle
1. Read "Andrew's Problem." Discuss:
   - Do you have all the information?
   - What is the problem?
   - How do the people feel?
   - What can Andrew do?
   - What will happen if he does that?
   - What else can he do?

- What will happen then?
2. Continue to consider solutions and consequences.
3. Choose a solution.
4. Model role-playing if necessary. Ask for volunteers to pretend to be Andrew and his brother to role-play the chosen solution.
5. Ask children, "What if I told you Andrew told Sam it wasn't his fault? What do you think about that?" Elicit responses that indicate owning the problem, taking responsibility, and accepting consequences.
6. Continue discussion about responsibility. Ask, "Who chooses how you behave?"
7. Ask children, "Do you think all problems have good solutions? What can you do when this happens?" Elicit responses that indicate doing your best to choose a solution.
8. Ask children, "What if Andrew's brother called him a name? What would you do?" Ask for volunteers to role-play this problem using what they have learned.

End
Ask, "How do you feel about being in group today?"
"Who else feels that way?"
"What did you learn?"
"How are you going to use what you learned?"

Andrew's Problem

Andrew really admired his brother's trading cards. He told his friends at school about the wonderful collection his brother Sam had worked hard to assemble. But his friends said, "You are always bragging about your brother. Nobody has all those cards." This made Andrew feel upset and frustrated because he was telling the truth.

That afternoon after school Andrew asked Sam if he could take his cards to school to show his friends. Sam said, "No way do I let you take my cards anywhere. If your friends want to see my cards, they can come here and I will show them." Andrew felt angry. He felt that Sam was mean to him and didn't trust him with his cards.

The next morning Andrew took Sam's cards from his room and put them in his backpack. He couldn't wait until lunch so he could show everyone the wonderful collection and they would know he was telling the truth. Lunchtime finally came and as everyone at the lunch table was looking at the cards a crowd formed. One person fell into another person. Before Andrew knew what was happening, a pile of gooey beefaroni was all over Sam's cards.

Session 4
Topic: Making a choice

Resources
- Drawing materials

Beginning
1. "Something I am getting better at is . . ."
2. Children share how they are using problem solving.
3. Ask, "Who has ever gotten into a fight with someone? How did you feel? How do you think it will help you to think of different things to do to solve a problem like this without fighting? We can do something different today. I will tell you a problem and you can draw a picture of what you think you could do about it. Then you can tell about your solution. That way we can get ideas. How does that sound?"

Middle
1. Read to children: You are working on your math in class when rubberbands begin to fly by your head from the back of the room. You are trying hard to ignore the distraction and concentrate on the math. Then you feel a strike on the back of your head. You turn around and tell the kid to stop fooling around. You try to get back to your math and feel a sting on your ear.
2. Discuss, "How do you feel?" Distribute drawing paper. Have members draw, "What you will do to solve this problem." For each solution, question the consequences. Emphasize consequences for "hurting back."
3. Members share their solutions. Elicit responses or offer "suggestions to think about" that include:
   - Asking permission to leave the classroom for a short time to calm down and think about what to do
   - Telling the person how you feel without an attitude
   - Talk to yourself—for example, "I am going to keep working. I'm not going to let this kid get to me."
   - Asking the person why they are shooting rubberbands at you—maybe you are not the target
   - Asking for help—deciding who can help best
4. Discuss: "How does it help you to think first in a problem like this?"

End
Ask, "What have you learned?"

"How do you feel about your experience in group today?"

"How is the group helping you?"

"How are you going to use your problem-solving skills?"

Session 5
Topic: Saying no

Beginning

1. Members complete the sentence, "When a friend asks me to do something I don't want to do, I . . .".
2. Members share how they have used problem solving.
3. Ask children, "Who has ever had a problem with someone who wanted you to do something and you didn't want to do it? How is it going to help you to learn about some things you can do? We can role-play your problems and that will help you to practice what you can do the next time it happens."

Middle

1. Suggest that you role-play a problem first to get started and maybe give some ideas to think about. The problem is your friend wants to copy the answers from your homework. Model the problem-solving steps. "OK, first I am thinking about what this problem is. I don't like saying no to my friend. I am pretty sure I have all the information. I am feeling guilty to say no to her. I think she is feeling worried that her homework is not done. Thinking about a solution for this kind of problem, I am going to:
   - Make a decision if I want to do it.
   - Think about why I will or will not do it.
   - Think about consequences.
   - Then I will tell the person no in a way that is friendly.
   - Maybe I will tell the person why I won't do it so they will understand.

2. Ask for a volunteer to play the friend asking to copy homework. Model saying no in an amiable tone: "No, I don't want to do that because the teacher will know you copied when we both hand it in late and we have the same answers. She may even think I copied. And besides, it's kind of like cheating."

3. Role-play the students' problems, allowing everyone the opportunity to practice saying no in a way that is not threatening.

4. Discuss, "Can anyone make you do something? Who chooses how you behave?"

End

1. Process with children, "What was it like to role-play today? How do you feel about group today? What did you learn? How will you use the skills you are learning?"

2. This can be a good time to remind the students they will meet three more times.

Session 6
Topic: Chill out

Resources
- Problem-Solving Steps handout

Beginning
1. Members complete the sentence, "When I get angry I can calm down by . . ."
2. Discuss how members are using problem-solving skills.
3. Ask children, "Who has had a problem with another person that made you so angry that you did something that got you in trouble? Knowing how to calm down can be helpful for these kinds of problems. Today we can practice ways to calm down and chill out. How does that sound?"

Middle
1. Refer to the students' ideas in completing the icebreaker sentence as ways that are successful for them. Suggest other ideas for calming down before dealing with a problem:
   - Count to ten.
   - Recognize how your body feels.
   - Think of things you can do:
     - Leave the area.
     - Use a relaxation activity.
     - Write how you feel in a journal.
     - Talk to someone.
     - Talk to yourself.
     - Choose what you will do to calm down.
2. Discuss ideas with students, and then invite them to try a relaxation exercise. Progressively move from the head to the toes, telling children to tighten muscles and release as they take a breath and let it out. For example: "Scrunch up the muscles in your forehead really tight, take a deep breath. Now let out your breath and relax your forehead. Think about how your head feels now. Now squeeze the muscles all around your eyes and take a deep breath. Let out your breath and relax your eyes. Think about how your eyes feel." Continue with shoulders, arms, etc.
3. Suggest to students that there are ways to relax just by tightening and releasing your fists in your pockets or your arms on your chair if you cannot leave the situation right away. Allow students to practice.
4. Cut the Problem-Solving Steps handout into strips, separating each step. Cut off the numbers. Encourage children to name the ways they have used their skills. Ask, "What have you noticed about the skills you have learned? What do you do when you have a problem?" As members name each step, present the strip indicating the step. Have them put the steps in order.
5. Tell students it would be helpful to the group if they take a problem-solving form with them and complete it with a problem they have or they see happening. Ask students to bring it to the next meeting.

End
1. Ask, "What was it like for you today?"
   "How do you feel about the group?"
   "What did you learn?"
   "How will you use what you learned?"
2. Remind students that two sessions remain.

Name_____ Date_____

Problem-Solving Steps

1. **Calm down.**

   I calmed down by _____

   I feel _____

   I think the other person feels _____

2. **Identify the problem.**

   The problem is _____

   _____

3. **Think about different ways to solve the problem.**

   Solution _____

4. **Consequence**—If I do this, then what might happen?

   _____

5. **What are other things I can do?**

   Solution _____

   Consequence _____

   Solution _____

   Consequence _____

6. **Choose a solution.**

   I think this is the best thing to do because _____

   _____

7. Is the problem solved? How did this work? _____

   _____

8. What would you do differently next time? _____

   _____

     Group Counseling for School Counselors: A Practical Guide

Session 7
Topic: Problem solving

Resources

- Problem-Solving Steps handout from Session 6
- "Think First" Self-Evaluation form (page 243)

Beginning

1. Students complete the sentence, "The best part about what I have learned in our group is . . .".

2. Discuss how children have used their skills by sharing the problem-solving forms. Encourage members to give each other feedback.

3. Ask students, "Who has ever had to make a hard decision? How did you feel when you had to decide? Maybe it was a decision about being invited to two places at the same time. Maybe it was a decision about what to buy with your birthday money. How do you think knowing how to solve a problem can help you make a decision? Today we can practice using what you already know in a different way. Does this sound like a good idea? There is something else I would like to do today that will tell me what you have learned in our group and how I can help others like you. It is a form that will take a few minutes. You may recognize it as the form ("Think First" Self-Evaluation) you completed when I talked to you about joining the group."

Middle

1. Use decisions from members or use those previously stated. Divide the group in half. Have each group use the problem-solving steps to make a decision. Then, discuss:
   - How was making a decision similar to solving a problem?
   - How was it different?
   - How does it help you to look at the steps on paper?

2. Distribute problem-solving handouts. Ask, "Where can you keep this in case you want to look at the steps?"

3. Distribute the "Think First" Self-Evaluation form. Ask students to complete; give directions if necessary.

End

1. How do you feel about the group today? What have you learned? How are you going to use what you learned?

2. Discuss the last session and ask members how they would like to end their group.

Session 8
Topic: Saying goodbye

Resources

- Refreshments
- Group Evaluation form (page 10)
- "Think First" Teacher Pre/Post Evaluation (page 244)

Beginning

1. Members share, "How do you feel about the group ending?" Include yourself in the go-round and validate feelings.

2. Tell members, "We will celebrate as you planned. Then I have a paper (the Group Evaluation) that will take a few minutes for you to complete. It is different from the form you completed last session. Your ideas will help me to know about how you feel and how you think the group has helped you."

Middle

1. Serve snacks. Suggest telling "success stories" using problem-solving skills. Model and encourage children to tell each other what they are doing well, what they liked, what was a good idea, etc.

2. Ask members to complete a Group Evaluation form. "Please be honest about your feelings. You do not have to put your name on it if you don't want to."

End

1. Tell children that although the group is over they can see you if they have a problem.

2. Have teachers complete post-group evaluations.

Booster Session for Problem-Solving Groups

Resources

- Chart paper

Beginning

1. Tell students that after a group ends, it is a good idea to check with members to see how they are doing.
2. Remind students that although the group has ended, there are the same rules for this meeting. Ask, "Who would like to remind us of the rules?"

Middle

1. Ask, "How are you using what you learned in the group? What questions do you have? What can we talk about that would help you?"
2. Review briefly, "When you have a problem with another person, what do you do?" Use chart paper to list responses from students. Elicit responses by inquiring:
   - What is the problem?
   - How do you feel?
   - How does the other person feel?
   - What can you do?
   - What will happen if you do that? How will you feel?
   - What else can you do? Then how will you feel?
   - What do you choose to do?
   - How did it work?
3. Ask students to tell about a time when they worked hard to solve a problem. Encourage feedback. Model a compliment to the speaker and then ask other members, "Who would like to say something to _____ about how he/she did?"

End

1. How did this meeting help you? What did you learn? What was it like to get together again?
2. Remind children that they can see you if they need help.

3.5
Social and Academic Skills Through Storytelling

Grade Level: K–2	Time Required: 8 Sessions	Author: Lori Bednarek

Purpose

To develop the learning skills and social skills that are critical to long-term school success. The skills include attending, listening, asking questions for clarification, and the social skills of encouragement, sharing, empathy, and team work.

Logistics

GROUP COMPOSITION

K–2 students mixed with regard to activity level and behavior control. Avoid loading group with only overactive behavior problem students. Students need multiple models of appropriate behavior. Groups with only behavior problem students usually do not show significant gains in prosocial behavior. Mixed groups are generally very effective.

GROUP SIZE

4–6 students

GROUP TIME PER SESSION

30 minutes

NUMBER OF SESSIONS

Eight, with booster sessions spaced approximately one month apart after regular group ends.

Recommended Resources

Full bibliographic details for these publications are included in the Bibliography at the end of this book.

Brigman, Lane, and Lane, 1994: *Ready to Learn.*
Hutchins, 1993: *My Best Friend.*
Silverstein, 1964: *The Giving Tree.*
Waber, 1988: *Ira Says Goodbye.*

BOOKS ON STORYTELLING

Duke, 1992: *Aunt Isabel Tells a Good One.*
Haley, 1988: *A Story, a Story: An African Tale.*
Long, 1978: *Albert's Story.*
Ziegler, 1993: *Mr. Knocky.*

BOOKS ON FRIENDSHIP

Auch, 1993: *Bird Dogs Can't Fly.*
Carlson, 1992: *Arnie and the New Kid.*
Delton, 1986: *Two Good Friends.*
DePaolo, 1992: *Rosie and the Yellow Ribbon.*
Engel, 1993: *Fishing.*
Henkes, 1990: *Jessica.*
Komaiko, 1988: *Earl's Too Cool for Me.*
Pfister, 1992: *The Rainbow Fish.*
Russo, 1992: *Alex Is My Friend.*
Waber, 1972: *Ira Sleeps Over.*
Wolkstein, 1994: *Step by Step.*

BOOKS ON LISTENING AND PAYING ATTENTION

Gray, 1994: *Small Green Snake.*
Mosel, 1989: *Tikki Tikki Tembo.*
Showers, 1991: *The Listening Walk.*
Vollmer, 1988: *Joshua Disobeys.*

BAD DAY BOOKS

Bourgeois, 1997: *Franklin's Bad Day.*
Hall, 1995: *A Bad, Bad Day.*
Hood, 1999: *Bad Hair Day.*
Mayer, 1995: *Just a Bad Day.*
Michaels, 2000: *Bulbasaur's Bad Day.*
Pellowski, 1986: *Benny's Bad Day.*
Simon, 1998: *The Good Bad Day.*
Viorst, 1972: *Alexander and the Terrible, Horrible, No Good, Very Bad Day.*

WORDLESS PICTURE BOOKS

Asch, 1986: *Goodbye House.*

Goffin, 1991: *Oh!*

McCully, 1988: *The Christmas Gift.*

McCully, 1984: *Picnic.*

Mariotti, 1989: *Hanimations.*

Rohmann, 1994: *Time Flies.*

Turkle, 1976: *Deep in the Forest.*

Ueno, 1973: *Elephant Buttons.*

Ward, 1973: *The Silver Pony: A Story in Pictures.*

Wiesner, 1991: *Tuesday.*

Session 1
Topic: Getting to know you

Resources

- Chart paper
- We Listen with Our Ears handout
- Book with positive theme (recommended: *The Giving Tree*, by Shel Silverstein)

Beginning

1. Introduce yourself and have all the group members say their names.
2. Tell about the purpose of the group. "We are going to be meeting together for eight weeks. In this group we are going to learn about a lot of different things. We are going to learn about making friends, listening to one another, saying positive things to each other, and asking questions. We are also going to learn all about stories. We are even going to be making up our own stories and acting them out!"

Middle

1. "Before we get started we need to talk about some group rules. Who knows what a rule is?" List group members' ideas on chart paper.
2. "Let's come up with some rules together that we can use in our group." With the group brainstorm some general rules. Try to make the list no longer than five rules. Some sample rules are:
   - We listen to each other.
   - No put-downs.
   - Be on time.
   - Respect others.
   - Work cooperatively.
3. Focus on a rule that has to do with listening and introduce the handout "We Listen with Our Ears."

As a group read the poem and talk about what it means to listen with your whole body. Give examples of people who might be listening with their ears, but not with their bodies. Students can practice being active listeners.

4. Next go over the confidentiality rule and its limits. You might say, "We are going to be working together for the next eight weeks. When you leave this group you may talk to your friends or family about anything that **you** say or do in this group. However, you may not talk about anything that **another person** said or did in the group. I will not tell anyone about anything that any of you say in this group except if you are being hurt, or if you could hurt someone else. Whatever we say in our group is confidential. That means private."
5. Share a book with the group that has a positive theme, such as *The Giving Tree* by Shel Silverstein. This story has many positive themes to expand on with the group. During the reading of the story encourage the group members to "listen with their whole bodies."
6. After reading the story check for understanding of the main idea.

End

1. Each student should share what he or she learned about the group rules and confidentiality.
2. Have each group member state what time and day your next meeting will be.
3. Each group member should share one way that he or she is going to use active listening throughout the week.

Name_____ Date_____

We Listen with Our Ears

We listen with our ears of course!

But did you know it's true,

That eyes, and lips, and hands, and feet

Can help us listen too!

Session 2
Topic: Practicing listening and paying attention

Resource

- Book on listening (recommended: *Miss Nelson Is Missing* by H. Allard)
- Four Ws and an H handout
- Feeling Faces sheet (page 9) *or* a poster with similar faces

Beginning

1. Check in with students. Begin by showing the Feeling Faces sheet. Go around the table and ask each student to point to a feeling that he or she is having today. Each student should explain why he or she is feeling that way.

2. Review group rules from the first session.

3. Review listening with the whole body. Have students recite the poem "We listen with our ears."

4. Introduce today's topic. "Today we are going to read a story about a class that is having trouble listening to their teacher. This story will remind us how important listening and paying attention are."

Middle

1. Before reading the story, have students predict what will happen by looking at the pictures.

2. Read the story *Miss Nelson Is Missing* (alternative books on listening/paying attention are listed on page 254).

3. Discuss the story. Explore questions about the book that deal with the social skill of paying attention and listening.

4. Introduce retelling the story. "Pretend that you are telling a friend about this story. This friend has never heard this story before. Let's practice retelling the story so that he or she would know everything that happened in the story."

5. Make three boxes on the chalkboard for the beginning, middle, and end of the story.

Beginning	Middle	End

6. Have students tell what happened in the beginning, middle, and end of the story.

7. Introduce the 4 Ws and an H Questions handout. As a group make sure that the retelling of the beginning, middle, and end contains answers to all the questions on the 4 Ws and an H chart.

End

1. Have students share what they learned about listening and paying attention.

2. Have students share what they learned about the way stories are organized (beginning, middle, and end).

3. Students state one way that they can be good listeners during the next week.

Name_____ Date _____

The 4 Ws and an H Questions

WHO	**Who** was the story about?

WHAT	**What** happened in the story? **What** was the story about?

WHEN	**When** did the story happen? Daytime, nighttime, morning, afternoon, spring, summer, winter, fall?

WHERE	**Where** did the story happen? Inside, outside, city, farm?

HOW	**How** was the person feeling at the beginning of the story? At the end? **How** did the story begin? **How** did the story end?

© Educational Media Corp. This material is used with permission from the authors, Greg Brigman, David Lane, and Donna Lane.

Session 3
Topic: Showing encouragement to friends

Resources

- Feeling Faces sheet (page 9) or poster
- *My Best Friend,* by Pat Hutchins
- Four Ws and an H handout

Beginning

1. Check in with students. Begin by showing the Feeling Faces. Go around the table and ask each student to point to a feeling that he or she is having today. Each student should explain why he or she is feeling that way.
2. Review group rules from the first session.
3. Review listening with the whole body. Have students recite the poem "We listen with our ears."
4. Introduce today's topic. "Today we are going to read a story about two girls who are friends." We are going to talk about how to make friends and why friends are important.

Middle

1. Look at the cover of the book *My Best Friend,* by Pat Hutchins. (Alternative books on friendship are listed on the overview page, p. 254.)

2. Have students predict what will happen in the story by looking at the pictures.
3. Read the story to the group.
4. Discuss the story. Explore questions about the book that deal with the social skill of making and keeping friends.
5. Work through the 4 Ws and an H handout with the group, pointing out the questions (who, what, when, where, how).
6. Explain to the students that all stories contain information about **who** (characters), **what** (plot), **when** (setting), **where** (setting), and **how** (plot). Some students will be familiar with the terms **character** and **setting**.

End

1. Students share what they learned about making friends and why friends are important.
2. Students share what they learned about the way stories are organized.
3. Students state one way that they can be good friends throughout the week.

Session 4
Topic: Making up and telling stories

Resources

- "Feelings" poster or Feeling Faces handout (page 9)
- 4 Ws and an H handout
- Paper and crayons
- We Listen with Our Ears handout (from Session 1)
- Story Beginners handout
- Chart paper

Beginning

1. Check in with students. Begin by showing the Feeling Faces. Go around the table and ask each student to point to a feeling that he or she is having today. Each student should explain why he or she is feeling that way.

2. Goal reporting: Students share one way in which they tried to be good listeners throughout the week.

3. Say, "Today we are going to practice telling stories. Last week we learned that all stories have a beginning, a middle, and an end. We also learned that most stories answer 4 Ws and an H questions. We are going to try to tell stories that answer those questions today."

4. Review the 4 Ws and an H handout with the group.

Middle

1. Model telling a 1–2 minute story. Use one of the story starters below.

> **STORY STARTERS**
>
> One of my favorite things to do at home (outside)
>
> One of my favorite things to do at home (inside)
>
> One of my favorite things to do at school (outside)
>
> One of my favorite things to do at school (inside)
>
> A time I helped someone feel better
>
> A time I made a new friend
>
> A time I invited someone I didn't know well to play or asked to join someone in play
>
> A time I helped someone with schoolwork or working through a problem
>
> A time I started a healthy habit
>
> A time I learned to do something that I thought was too hard or scary

2. The story that you tell should model the 4 Ws and an H story structure. In addition, make sure that your story has a clear beginning, middle, and end.

3. After telling the story, ask the group to answer the who, what, when, where, and how questions, and to identify the beginning, middle, and end of the story.

4. Review the skill of using encouragement. Ask group members how they could show you encouragement as you told your story. Make a list on chart paper of the encouraging things to say and do while listening to a partner's story. Label the list "Encouraging Things to Say and Do."

5. Tell the students that they are now going to get a chance to make up a story on their own. Give the students the following story starter.

> **STORY STARTER:** *A time I made a new friend*

6. Have students use crayons and paper to write/draw their story. Allow 4–5 minutes for this activity. Remind students that their story should contain answers to the 4 Ws and an H questions.

7. Tell students that sometimes starting to tell their stories can be difficult and sometimes it helps to use story-beginning words. Show students the handout Story Beginners. Encourage them to choose one to begin their story.

8. Pair the students up. Have students take turns telling their stories to their partners. Make sure that the listeners pay attention to the storyteller using their active listening skills. (You may want to review the poem "We Listen with Our Ears." Remind the storyteller to include answers to the 4 Ws and an H questions in their story. Allow 1–2 minutes for each student to retell his or her story.

9. To check active listening, have partners report the answers to the 4 Ws and an H questions as they take turns.

10. If time permits, have one or two group members share their stories with the whole group. During this time model encouragement by making two positive compliments about the group member's story.

End

1. Students share what they learned about listening, paying attention, and encouragement.

2. Students share what they learned about the way stories are organized (beginning, middle, and end).

3. Students state one way that they can use encouragement during the week.

Name_____ Date _____

Story Beginners

📖 Once upon a time . . .

📖 One day . . .

📖 One night . . .

📖 Long, long ago . . .

📖 Once there was . . .

📖 Far, far away . . .

Session 5
Topic: Stories with positive and negative social outcomes

Resources

- Feeling Faces handout (page 9) or poster
- Stories with Two Endings handout
- Paper and crayons
- Chart paper

Beginning

1. Check in with students. Begin by showing the Feeling Faces. Go around the table and ask each student to point to a feeling that he or she is having today. Each student should explain why he or she is feeling that way.

2. Goal reporting: Students share one way in which they tried to use encouragement.

3. Tell students, "Today we are going to practice telling stories. Last week we learned how to tell a story. We practiced using encouragement and active listening to help our partners tell their stories. Today we are going to make up some more stories and practice asking questions about those stories."

Middle

1. Introduce the skill of asking questions. Ask group members, "Why is it important to ask questions?" Record their answers on chart paper. Explore this skill by asking them if they ask questions in class and how asking questions can help them learn.

2. Model telling a 1–2 minute story about being mad at your friend *excluding* the ending. Stop your story before you get to resolving the problem. Use the story starter below.

> STORY STARTER: *A time that I was mad at my friend*

3. Use the Stories with Two Endings handout to chart the beginning and middle of the story that you have told. Ask the students to come up with two different endings to your story. One should be a positive outcome and one should be a negative outcome.

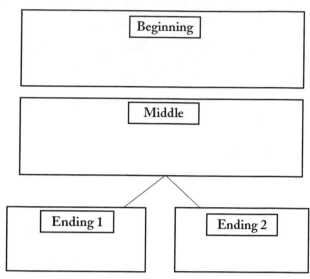

4. Discuss the negative and positive outcomes of your story.

5. Ask the students to choose one of the following story starters.

> STORY STARTERS:
>
> *A time that I got mad at school*
> *A time that I had a problem with a friend*

6. Each student should use paper and crayons to draw out his or her story. Allow 1–2 minutes for this activity.

7. Put students in pairs. Review how to use active listening and encouragement while listening to a partner's story. (Review the poster of encouraging things to say and do that the group made last week). Give each student a chance to tell his or her story to a partner. Encourage them to tell their stories in two different ways. One way should include a positive ending, one should include an ending that was not positive.

8. Check the partners' active listening skills by having them retell the story using the 4 Ws and an H questions.

9. When both partners have had a chance to share, choose one group member to share his or her story out loud. Use the Beginning, Middle, and Two Endings handout to summarize the story.

10. Model good question asking by asking the group member about his or her story. Some good questions to ask might be:

   - Why did you choose the story starter that you did?

   - Is this a real story or make believe?

   - Which ending do you think is the one you would like most to happen?

   - How did the character in this story use encouragement and active listening?

11. Go around the group and have each student ask a question about the story.

End

1. Students share what they learned about listening, paying attention, encouragement, and asking questions.

2. Students share what they learned about making up stories with multiple endings.

3. Students state one way that they can learn more by asking questions during the next week.

Name_____ Date_____

Stories with Two Endings

Beginning

Middle

Ending 1

Ending 2

Session 6
Topic: Dealing with a bad day

Resources
- Feeling Faces handout (page 9) or poster
- Paper and crayons
- Optional: props, puppets

Beginning

1. Check in with students. Begin by showing the Feeling Faces. Go around the table and ask each student to point to a feeling that he or she is having today. Each student should explain why he or she is feeling that way.

2. Goal reporting: Students share one way in which they tried to use asking questions.

3. Say to students, "Today we are going to practice telling stories and then acting those stories out. Last week we practiced telling a story with two different endings. We practiced using encouragement and active listening to help our partners tell their stories. We also learned how to ask questions about those stories. Today we are going to make up some more stories and act those stories out."

Middle

1. Model telling a 1–2 minute story. Use the story starter below.

> **STORY STARTER:**
> *One of my favorite things to do at school*

2. The story should model the 4 Ws and an H story structure. In addition, make sure that your story has a clear beginning, middle, and end.

3. After telling the story, ask the group to answer the who, what, when, where, and how questions, and to identify the beginning, middle, and end of the story.

4. Review the skill of using encouragement. Ask the group members how they could show you encouragement as you told your story.

5. Tell students that they are now going to get a chance to make up a story on their own. Give the students the following story starter.

> **STORY STARTER:** *A very bad day*

6. Tell the students that they are going to make up this story with a partner. Put the students in pairs.

7. Give the students 1–2 minutes to plan their stories using paper and crayons. Remind the students that their stories should have a beginning, middle, and end. In addition they should answer all of the 4 Ws and an H questions. The stories that they make up can have just one ending; we will be adding another ending later.

8. Partners are now going to share their stories with the entire group. Have each pair of students decide who is going to be the storyteller.

9. Remind the group that they need to practice active listening and encouragement during the storytelling process. If necessary, review the poem "We Listen with Our Ears" and the poster of encouraging things to say and do made in Session 4.

10. Go around the group and let each pair tell its story. After each group has told its story, brainstorm with the group alternate endings to each story. Try to guide the group to identify actions of the characters that lead to both positive and negative endings. During this process model using encouragement. In addition, ask questions of each pair and encourage the group members to do the same.

11. After each pair has told its story, tell students that they will now act their stories out. Model this process by using the same story that you told at the beginning of the group. Stand up and enlist volunteers to be characters in your story. Dramatize your story for the group.

12. Give each group time to plan how they will act out their story for the group. You may want to provide props and/or puppets for the group.

13. Let each pair present its dramatization to the group. Again, model using active listening and encouragement during the retelling process.

End

1. Students share what they learned about listening, paying attention, encouragement, and asking questions.

2. Students share what they learned about dramatizing their stories.

3. Students state one way that they can practice using encouragement, active listening, and asking questions throughout the week.

Session 7
Topic: Stories with social themes

Resources

- Feeling Faces handout (page 9) or poster
- Paper and crayons
- Stories with Two Endings handout from Session 5

Beginning

1. Check in with students. Begin by showing the Feeling Faces. Go around the table and ask each student to point to a feeling that he or she is having today. Each student should explain why he or she is feeling that way.

2. Goal reporting: Students share one way in which they tried to use asking questions, encouragement, or active listening during the week.

3. Say to students, "Today we are going to practice making up more stories and acting them out. Last week we had fun making up different endings to stories that your group members made up."

Middle

1. Begin this session by making sure that every group member got a chance to share his or her story during the last session.

2. Tell students that today one partner will be making up the beginning and middle of a story and the other partner will help to make up two different endings to the story.

3. Give students the following prompt.

> **STORY STARTER:**
> *The day my friend made me mad*

4. Give students a chance to plan their stories using paper and crayons. At this point remind them that their story needs to include a beginning and a middle. They should have some ideas for the ending; however, their partners will help them with that later on. Remind the group members of the 4 Ws and an H questions that they need to consider when making up their story.

5. Put the group members in pairs. Remind the pairs of the importance of using active listening and encouragement when their partner is telling a story. After the first partner has told his or her story, the pair of students should chart the story on the Stories with Two Endings handout. The pairs can work together to come up with two different endings to each story.

6. After each pair has shared, have the students work together to act out one of their stories. Allow ten minutes for the students to plan for their presentation. The students should choose one ending to present to the group.

7. Give each pair a chance to act out their story for the group. Model encouragement by giving positive comments for each group. Ask the group to give encouragement to the pair that is sharing.

8. Allow time for group members to ask questions about the performance. Some good questions to include might be:

   - Why did you choose that ending?
   - Did the ending to the story resolve the character's problem? If not, how could a different ending resolve the problem?

End

1. Students share what they learned about listening, paying attention, encouragement, and asking questions.

2. Students share what they learned about getting along with friends.

3. Students state one way that they can practice using encouragement, active listening, and asking questions throughout the week.

4. Students state one way that they can be a good friend.

5. Remind the students that next week is the last session.

Session 8
Topic: Saying good-bye

Resources

- Feeling Faces handout (page 9) or poster
- Story with theme of saying good-bye (recommended: *Ira Says Goodbye* by Bernard Waber)
- Paper and crayons
- End of the Group Assessment handout

Beginning

1. Check in with students. Begin by showing the Feeling Faces. Go around the table and ask each student to point to a feeling that he or she is having today. Each student should explain why he or she is feeling that way.

2. Goal reporting: Students share one way in which they tried to use active listening, encouragement, or asking questions throughout the week.

3. Say to students, "Today is our last session. We are going to read a story about saying good-bye. Then we are going to talk about our favorite parts of this group."

Middle

1. Read the story *Ira Says Goodbye* by Bernard Waber (or another story on good-byes).

2. Discuss the theme of saying good-bye with the group. Have students talk about good-byes that they have said to different people.

3. Tell the group that as a group we are going to make up a story about saying good-bye. Here is our prompt:

> **STORY STARTER:**
> *A time that I had to say good-bye*

4. As a group brainstorm the beginning, middle, and end of the story. Remind the group members to include all the 4 Ws and an H questions.

5. As a group practice telling the good-bye story. If time permits group members can act it out.

6. After the telling of the story, hand out paper and crayons to each group member. Instruct them that they are to draw or write about their favorite part of the group. Allow ten minutes for this activity.

7. After all students are done, have each student share what his or her favorite part of the group was.

End

1. Hand out the End of the Group Assessment. Read each part to the students and have them circle the appropriate face.

2. Ask the students to share one way that they will use what they have learned in the group.

Name_____ Date _____

End of the Group Assessment

 Always    Sometimes    Never

I know how to make friends.

I can listen with my whole body.

I can tell a story with different endings.

I can use encouragement and positive words to help a friend feel better.

I know how to ask good questions.

Saying good-bye is important.

       Group Counseling for School Counselors: A Practical Guide

3.6
Loss/Bereavement

Grade Level: K–5	Time Required: 8 Sessions	Author: Michelle Feldman

Purpose

To help students cope with the death of a loved one. Students are taught about the different types of loss, the stages of grief, feelings associated with loss, ways to say good-bye, and coping skills. Bibliotherapy is used to stimulate sharing thoughts, feelings, and ideas for healing the hurt that the death of a loved one brings.

Children usually do not know how to express their feelings and cope with the stress associated with the death of a loved one. Consequently, school work and participation in school activities are often affected. Therefore, the primary goals of the support group are identifying and validating these feelings and encouraging expression in constructive ways.

Before beginning a support group, the facilitator should be comfortable with his or her own death issues. Any self-disclosure should be limited to promoting group rapport and group cohesion. Be aware that a variety of feelings may arise for the facilitator throughout the sessions; the facilitator's knowledge of his or her own limits, and his or her perception that sharing must be for the betterment of the group, are critical. Creating a safe and loving atmosphere is paramount. Consultation with other professional counselors, along with continued education, is always encouraged.

Encouraging grieving children to externalize their grief is vital. It is crucial that professionals working with these groups are cognizant of the very specific and complex needs of grieving children. Therefore, it is recommended that the facilitator of these groups have grief training, counseling experience, and group skills training.

Logistics

GROUP COMPOSITION

Students in grades K–5 who have recently experienced the death of a loved one

GROUP SIZE

4–6 students

GROUP TIME PER SESSION

30 minutes

NUMBER OF SESSIONS

Eight

Recommended Resources

Full bibliographic details for these publications are included in the Bibliography at the end of this book.

Bernstein and Gullo, 1977: *When People Die.*

Brigman and Earley, 1991: *Group Counseling for School Counselors.*

Brown, 1988: *When Dinosaurs Die.*

Buscaglia, 1982: *The Fall of Freddie the Leaf.*

Cohen, 1987: *I Had a Friend Named Peter.*

Dolbrin, 1971: *Scat!*

Geisel (Dr. Seuss), 1998: *My Many-Colored Days.*

Johnson and Johnson, 1998: *Children Who Grieve Too.*

Loretta and Keating, 1995: *After the Funeral.*

Mellonie and Ingpen, 1987: *Lifetimes, the Beautiful Way to Explain Death to Children.*

Morganette, 1994: *Skills for Living.*

Mudy, 1998: *Sad Isn't Bad.*

O'Rourke and Worzybt, 1996: *Support Groups for Children.*

Palmer and Bourke, 1994: *I Wish I Could Hold Your Hand.*

Silverman, 1999: *Help Me Say Goodbye.*

Skivington and Care, 1998: *Balloons for Trevor.*

Steinberg, 1999: *Grief Group.*

Varley, 1992: *Badger's Parting Gifts.*

Viorst, 1988: *The Tenth Good Thing About Barney.*

Session 1
Topic: Introduction and overview

Resources

- Chart paper
- A poster showing feelings (or use Feeling Faces on page 9)

Beginning

1. Introduce yourself and then say, "This is a group for kids who have had someone special in their life die. We will be coming to my office once a week on _____ (day of the week) at _____ (time of day) for eight weeks to talk a little, play a little, maybe read or color a little bit about how you are feeling."

2. "First, I would like to go around the circle and ask everybody what their name is, the name of the special person that died, and either a thumbs-up (if you're feeling really happy), thumbs to the middle (if you are feeling so-so, not too happy, not too sad), or a thumbs-down (if you are feeling really sad or mad)."

3. "Who has ever been in a group before?" (Some examples you may want to give are Scouts, Brownies, dance class, etc.) "Did you have any rules in that group? Why do you think you have to have rules in groups? In the classroom?" Try to incorporate the idea that rules foster a safe environment and allow everyone a fair share to talk and participate in the group. Say, "Today we are going to have to make up a name for our group and a few rules for our group just to make sure that this is a safe place to talk and play together."

Middle

1. Say, "First, let's come up with some rules." (Have a chalkboard, whiteboard, chart paper, etc., to write answers as they are offered.) "Who can raise their hand and tell me one important rule they think we should have in this group?" Continue to generate answers. Make sure to include the right to pass

(only answer voluntarily), and the idea of confidentiality. ("What you say in here belongs to you and you can tell anyone you want what you say. What other students say in here belongs to them. You should not tell anyone what another student says.")

2. "OK, great, now the fun part. I want everyone to close their eyes and think really hard about a name for our group." (Offer suggestions such as the superstars, whiz kids, second grade sundaes.) "Then I am going to give you three minutes. If you would like to share your answer, you can either come and stand right next to me and tell it to the group, whisper it in my ear, or you can just stay at your seat and share, whichever one you'd like to do." Chart answers and then have students put their heads down on the desk and vote anonymously (by raised hand) to pick their favorite name.

End

1. Display handout or poster of feeling faces and say to the kids, "Well, our time is almost up. For our last activity, I would like to go around the group again and ask you one thing you learned today and how you felt being here today and talking with everyone in group. When I call your name, I would like you to come up and say one thing you learned today" (could be the name of the group, a rule, or even another kid's name) "and then look at the poster and point out which feeling you had today in group." When they point out their feeling, make sure to label that feeling for them if they are not able to: "Oh, John felt mad today in group." If there is time, process that and ask, "What made you so mad today?"

2. Remind kids about when you will see them next. (Day and time) ("Bye everyone, remember, see you next Tuesday, my office at 1:00 sharp!")

Session 2

Topic: *The Fall of Freddie the Leaf*

Resource

- *The Fall of Freddie the Leaf* by Leo Buscaglia

Beginning

1. Welcome everyone back to the group. Remind kids that this is our second meeting and we still have six meetings left. Remind the children of last week's meeting and the name of the group and rules. Have the students do a go-round and say a color that describes how they are doing today (blue = sad, red = mad, yellow = cheerful, etc.).

2. Say, "Many times when someone or something dies, no one really tells us what that means. We know it means they got sick, or hurt, or too old to live, but what does that really mean? Today we are going to read a story and talk a little so we can get a better understanding of death."

Middle

1. Read the story *The Fall of Freddie the Leaf.* Discuss afterwards.

2. As a group, brainstorm what happens when an animal or plant is alive. (It moves around, breathes, barks, grows, etc.) Chart answers.

3. As a group, brainstorm what happens when an animal or plant dies. (Its leaves turn brown, it stops breathing, doesn't move any longer, trees and flowers may rot, etc.) Chart answers.

4. Have the same discussion regarding people.

5. If you have access, take a mini hike and observe leaves, flowers, and trees (both dead and alive). As a group interact with the flowers, leaves, and trees to determine (using the characteristics discussed earlier) whether they are dead or alive.

End

1. Ask students, "How was it to be part of today's group?" "What is one thing you learned today?"

2. Remind kids to be on time and that you will see them next _____ at _____.

Session 3
Topic: Sharing feelings

Resources

- *My Many-Colored Days* by Dr. Seuss (Theodore Geisel)
- Chart paper
- Crayons
- Paper

Beginning

1. Welcome everyone back to the group. Remind kids that this is our third meeting and we still have five meetings left. Have the students do a go-round and say their names and if they are having sunny (happy) feelings today or if they are having cloudy (sad, mad) feelings today. If kids do not understand this idea, explain it to them.

2. Say, "I just want to remind everyone why we are here in this group together. That is because we all have had someone special in our life die. A few things that we would like to learn by being in our group are about feelings, and how to talk about our feelings, learn that we are not the only ones who are going through this tough time, and many other things."

3. "Who here has ever been very sad before? Who here has ever gotten really angry before? Who here has ever been very happy before? Today, we are going to learn all about feelings and how our feelings can really never be wrong."

Middle

1. Read the book *My Many-Colored Days*.

2. Ask for volunteers to raise their hands and share one feeling that they felt when their special person died. (Link and connect answers between students: "Oh, you felt mad just like Marisa did.") Chart answers. Discuss the responses afterward. Point out that everyone will have different feelings and they are all OK to have—even if someone said happy. (Try to process the answers if they seem out of the ordinary, like excited or happy, just to make sure they understand the meaning of those words.)

3. Pass out crayons and paper and instruct the children to draw a picture of how they feel today. Afterwards allow the children to voluntarily share their art and discuss with the group how many of the kids' feelings have changed between the time the person died and today. (This will be encouraging to kids who don't think they will ever feel better.)

End

1. End with a go-round and ask the kids to share one thing that they learned today and their favorite part of group today.

2. Remind kids to be on time and that you will see them next _____ at _____.

Session 4
Topic: Stages of grieving

Resources

- *When People Die* by J.E. Bernstein and S.V. Gullo
- Chart paper
- Crayons or markers
- Paper

Beginning

1. Welcome everyone back to the group. Remind kids that this is our fourth meeting and we are halfway through with group. Review last week's session. Ask the kids to do the thumbs-up check-in (up, middle, down) and then share something really fun that they have done since the last time we were together.

2. Say, "Who here ever felt so sad or mad that they thought they might just feel that way forever?" Since many kids feel that way, it is important to learn that it is normal to feel that way in the beginning but that they will begin to feel better over time.

Middle

1. Brainstorm as a group some of the other losses the children may have experienced—death of a pet, having an item stolen from them, losing a favorite toy. Have the kids discuss their specific situation and what they were feeling during that time. Go further to discuss how they felt when it first happened, then after a little while (days, weeks, months), then after a year or more.

2. Read the book *When People Die* by J. E. Bernstein and S. V. Gullo.

3. According to Dr. Elisabeth Kübler-Ross, in her book *On Death and Dying*, the stages of grief are: **denial, anger, bargaining, depression, acceptance.** On chart paper, list these in a child-friendly manner and explain them:

   (a) **Denial**—You don't believe it has happened— "Nope, she/he is just on vacation," or "It isn't true!"

   (b) **Anger/mad**—"I hate that person for leaving me—she/he said he/she would always take care of me."

   (c) **Bargaining**—Make a trade—"I promise I will never be bad again if she/he comes back" or "I will keep my room clean every day and get all good grades if I can have him/her back."

   (d) **Sadness**—"I don't want to play, I want to be by myself."

   (e) **Acceptance**—Thinking "It's OK, I can smile and remember the person. I am sad about it but I can deal with it."

4. Distribute crayons or markers and paper. Have the students use the paint and paper to show what stage they think they may be in right now.

5. Discuss the completed pictures. Ask the kids what they think a person who has reached the last stage might be thinking or feeling.

End

1. Have students complete the statements, "I learned . . .", "I was surprised that . . .".

2. Remind kids to be on time and that you will see them next _____ at _____.

Session 5
Topic: Ways to say "good-bye"

Resources

- *Scat* by A. Dolbrin
- Chart paper
- Balloons, bubbles, or paper and markers

Beginning

1. Welcome everyone back to the group. Remind kids that this is our fifth meeting and we still have three meetings left. Review last week's session. Ask if there are any questions regarding the stages discussed. Ask the kids to do the thumbs-up check-in (up, middle, down).

2. Say, "Sometimes, when somebody dies suddenly, we don't get the chance to say good-bye, or to tell them certain things that we wanted them to know. Although we can't bring them back, we can still think about all of the things that we would have wanted to tell them and say them out loud, in our minds, or write them down. This activity helps us to say our final thoughts and good-byes."

Middle

1. Read the book *Scat*. Discuss how Scat said good-bye and how it helped him. Also, discuss other ways of saying good-bye. Chart on paper. Do a go-round and process: "What would you say if you had that chance? What else?"

2. Provide balloons, paper and markers, or bubbles as a choice for the children to use to say good-bye to their loved one. They can say their words either aloud or in silence and blow the bubbles, release the balloons, or create a picture or letter to then be "mailed" in a box that you provide.

3. Convene as a group to process the activity: "How did it feel when you blew those bubbles, or released that balloon?"

End

1. Ask students, "How does saying good-bye help someone feel better?"

2. Have them complete the statement, "I can see that I need to . . .".

3. Remind kids to be on time and that you will see them next _____ at _____.

Session 6
Topic: Sharing favorite memories

Resources

- *The Tenth Good Thing About Barney* by J. Viorst
- Paper, prefolded into four sections
- Drawing materials

Beginning

1. Welcome children to group. Remind them that this is the sixth session and we have two sessions left. Briefly review last week's session. Ask if there are any unanswered questions regarding saying good-bye.

2. Have children stand by their seats (or stay seated if they prefer) and state the "weather" of their feelings today (sunny, cloudy, rainy, etc.). Process if need be.

3. Ask the children to raise their hands if they can remember a favorite time that they spent with the person who died. Explain that it is important to think about those good times and to know that it is OK to remember happy/fun things about their special person. So many times when a person dies, there is so much sadness in everyone's heart that it helps to think of fun times that have been shared.

Middle

1. Read the story *The Tenth Good Thing About Barney*. Discuss any thoughts or comments the children may have after reading.

2. Distribute a piece of paper that has been folded into four sections. Have the children draw a picture of a happy memory with their loved one in each section. When the kids complete their picture, allow each child to share memories and to identify one person in their life (preferably home life) with whom they can share these memories. Encourage the importance of thinking and talking about happy memories with self and other people.

End

1. Ask students, "How did it feel today to talk about your happy memories?"

   "What can you do so that you don't forget your memories?"

2. Remind kids to be on time and that you will see them next _____ at _____.

Session 7
Topic: Collage of memories

Resources

- Collage materials—magazines, scissors, glue sticks, construction paper

Beginning

1. Welcome kids to group. Remind them that this is the seventh session and that next week will be the last meeting. Review last week's session and attempt to answer any unanswered questions.

2. Do a go-round and have the kids give a thumbs-up check-up. Have the students also say one fun time that they have had since the last group meeting.

3. Say, "Remember in our last meeting we had a chance to discuss happy memories? We also got a chance to come up with ways to remember our happy memories. One fun thing that I have heard works great for kids who have had someone close to them die is to make a collage of memories. Today, we will make our very own personal collage (collection)."

Middle

1. Provide ample amounts of magazines; be sensitive to race, socioeconomic levels, gender, etc. Explain to the kids that they are to find any pictures in the magazines that remind them of their loved ones— it could be food the person liked, colors they liked, clothes they wore, flowers they enjoyed, makeup or perfume they wore, etc. If they need help cutting, provide assistance.

2. Provide construction paper and glue so that they can paste on their pictures.

3. Have the children share the collages.

End

1. Ask students, "What did you learn about other people's memories? Were they similar to yours? Different?"

2. Have students complete the statement, "I was surprised that . . .".

3. Remind kids to be on time and that you will see them next _____ at _____.

4. Lastly, remind them once again that next week is the last session and that you will celebrate with some snacks and surprises.

Session 8
Topic: Saying good-bye

Resources

- Chart paper
- Refreshments

Beginning

1. Welcome kids back to the last group session. Briefly discuss last week's activity and see if there are any unanswered questions.

2. Go-round—do a color check on students' feelings today (red, blue, yellow?). Have them state one feeling they have about today being the last group.

3. Say, "We have been meeting now for eight weeks and we have covered a lot of information. Today we are going to take a little time to review all of the stuff we have learned and also have the chance to ask any questions we may have about death."

Middle

1. Ask students, "What kinds of things did you learn in group? How did it feel to be in a group? (Beginning, middle, end?)" List on chart paper. "Let me see how you rate this group—thumbs up for really good, closed fist for OK, or thumbs down for not too good." (Use this as an informal evaluation of sorts.)

2. Have the collages posted around the room for all to view (with permission). In the circle, have all of the kids close their eyes and ask them these questions: "When you are in ____ grade (next year's grade), how do you think you will feel then about your special person's death? If you are still sad, what can you do to feel better?" (Talk to someone, look at memory collage, remember those happy memories we talked about in Session 6.) "Whom can you talk to?" (The person identified in Session 6)

3. Enjoy snack with the group and casually discuss how the group ending is similar to losing someone special in your life because we won't be meeting anymore. Also discuss how it is different because we will all see each other around school and will be able to touch base every now and again.

End

Have students complete the statements, "Something I learned from being in this group is . . ." and "My favorite session of all was . . .".

3.7
Divorce/Changing Families

Grade Level: K–5	Time Required: 8 Sessions	Author: Michelle Feldman

Purpose

To help students cope with the stress of parent divorce. Students are taught coping skills and learn how to constructively deal with typical issues associated with divorce. Bibliotherapy is used to stimulate sharing of thoughts, feelings, and positive coping strategies.

Parent divorce is a significant and growing issue affecting children's social and academic development. Parent divorce is one of the most stressful events that can happen to a child. Support groups have been found to be effective in helping students to deal constructively with parent divorce and to return their attention to academic performance and positive peer relations.

The group leader should be comfortable with his or her own issues about divorce. Self-disclosure should be limited to promoting group rapport and cohesion.

Logistics

GROUP COMPOSITION

Students in grades K–5 who have recently experienced the divorce of their parents. Students who are within 1–2 grade levels may be grouped.

GROUP SIZE

4–6 students

GROUP TIME PER SESSION

30 minutes

NUMBER OF SESSIONS

Eight

Recommended Resources

Full bibliographic details for these publications are included in the Bibliography at the end of this book.

Apodaca and Nightingale, 1997: *My Parents Still Love Me Even Though They're Getting Divorced.*

Bienfeld, 1987: *Helping Your Child Succeed after Divorce.*

Blitzer and Shore, 1994: *My Life Turned Upside Down but I Turned It Right Side Up.*

Boulden and Boulden, 1991: *Let's Talk!*

Boulden and Boulden, 1992: *All Together.*

Brigman and Earley, 1991: *Group Counseling for School Counselors.*

Brown, 1988: *Dinosaurs Divorce.*

Friedman and Girard, 1991: *At Daddy's on Saturday.*

Hoctor, 1999: *Changes: My Family and Me.*

Ives, Fassler, and Lash, 1985: *The Divorce Workbook.*

Margolin, 1996: *Complete Group Counseling Program for Children of Divorce.*

Marks, 1995: *Good-bye, Daddy!*

Monroe and Ackelmire, 1998: *Why Don't We Live Together Any More?*

Monroe and Barnet, 1998: *I Have a New Family Now.*

Morganette, 1994: *Skills for Living.*

O'Rourke and Worzybt, 1996: *Support Groups for Children.*

Parkinson and Spelman, 1998: *Mama and Daddy Bears Divorce.*

Poleski, 1983: *The Hurt.*

Robins and Mayle, 1988: *Why Are We Getting a Divorce?*

Rogers and Judkis, 1998: *Let's Talk About It: Divorce.*

Stinson, 1988: *Mom and Dad Don't Live Together Anymore.*

Watson, Switzer, and Hirschberg, 1988: *Sometimes a Family Has to Split Up.*

Session 1
Topic: Introduction and overview

Resources
- Feelings poster (or use Feeling Faces handout on page 9)
- Chalkboard, white board, or chart paper

Beginning
1. Introduce yourself, then say, "This is a group for kids who have had some family changes (give examples of divorce situations, separation situations, as well as stepparent or sibling changes, etc.). We will be coming to my office once a week on _____ (day of the week) at _____ (time of day) for eight weeks to talk a little, play a little, maybe read or color a little bit about how you are feeling."

2. "First I would like to go around the circle and ask everybody what their name is, what kind of changes are happening in their family, and either a thumbs-up (if you're feeling really happy), thumbs to the middle (if you are feeling so-so, not too happy, not too sad) or a thumbs-down (if you are feeling really sad or mad).

3. Ask students, "Who has ever been in a group before?" (Some examples you may want to give are Scouts, Brownies, dance class, etc.) "Did you have any rules in that group? Why do you think you have to have rules in groups? In the classroom?" Try to incorporate the idea that rules foster a safe environment and allow everyone a fair share to talk and participate in the group. Say, "Today we are going to have to make up a name for our group and a few rules for our group just to make sure that this is a safe place to talk and play together."

Middle
1. "First let's come up with some rules." (Have a chalkboard, whiteboard, chart paper, etc., on which to write answers as they are offered.) "Who can raise their hand and tell me one important rule they think we should have in this group?" Continue to generate answers, recording suggestions as they are made. Make sure to include the idea of confidentiality, the right to pass (only answer voluntarily), as well as attendance and tardiness.

2. "OK, great, now the fun part. I want everyone to close their eyes and think really hard about a name for our group." (Offer suggestions such as the superstars, whiz kids, second grade sundaes.) "Then I am going to give you three minutes. If you would like to share your answer, you can come and stand right next to me and tell it to the group, whisper it in my ear, or you can just stay at your seat and share, whichever one you'd like to do." Chart answers and then have students put their heads down on the desk and vote anonymously (by raised hand) to pick their favorite name.

End
1. Display poster of feeling faces and say to the kids, "Well, our time is almost up. For our last activity, I would like to go around the group again and ask you one thing you learned today and how you felt being here today and talking with everyone in group. When I call your name, I would like you to come up and say one thing you learned today" (could be the name of the group, a rule, or even another kid's name) "and then look at the poster and point out which feeling you had today in group." When they point out their feelings, make sure to label that feeling for them if they are not able to: "Oh, Paula felt mad today in group." If there is time, process that and ask, "What made you so mad today?"

2. Remind kids about when you will see them next. (Day and time) ("Bye everyone, remember, see you next Tuesday, my office at 1:00 sharp!")

Session 2
Topic: Family pictures

Resource

- Art materials

Beginning

1. Welcome everyone back to the group. Remind kids, "This is our second meeting and we still have six meetings left." Remind the children of last week's meeting and the name of the group and rules. Have students rate on a scale of 1–10 how they are feeling today (1 being low, 10 being high).

2. Say, "Sometimes it's hard when you have more than one place you call home. Today we are going to talk about different family members that may live in different homes. It's important to understand that even thought they may live in a different home, they are still our family."

Middle

1. Begin a discussion on what each member thinks the word "family" means. Most likely you will get many different spectra of family such as immediate family, extended family, and friends who are so close they are considered family. Place emphasis on family that may not live in the same home as you. Even though many members may live in other homes, cities, countries, etc., they are still your family.

2. Provide children with art materials and allow them to make pictures that show their families and the many different homes they may have.

3. When the pictures are finished, give each child an opportunity to talk about his/her picture and tell more about his/her family.

End

1. Ask students, "How was it to be part of today's group?"
   "What is one thing you learned today?"

2. Point out similarities of group member's situations.

3. Remind kids to be on time and that you will see them next _____ at _____.

Session 3
Topic: Picture album

Resources
- 5 pieces of paper for each student
- Drawing materials

Beginning
1. Welcome everyone back to the group. Remind kids, "This is our third meeting and we still have five meetings left." Have the students do a go-round and say their names and if they are having sunny (happy) feelings today or if they are having cloudy (sad, mad) feelings today. If kids are not familiar with this idea, explain it to them.

2. Say, "I just want to remind everyone why we are here in this group together. That is because we all have had some family changes. One important thing that we would like to learn by being in our group is why people divorce. We can also learn more about our feelings about the situation."

3. "How many people here really understand why there has been a divorce/separation in your family? Many times kids think they are the reason, or really don't know the reason at all why their family has changed. Today we will look at some of the reasons why people divorce."

Middle
1. "Today, we are going to create our very own mini picture album to understand what brought our parents together, and some of the reasons they have had to separate." Pass out five blank pieces of drawing paper so that kids may illustrate. Either prelabel (depending on the children's writing levels) or have the children label each piece of paper with the following headings:

- Why my parents got married
- Why my parents got divorced
- What does the future hold?
- Best time with my family
- Worst time with my family

2. Have children work on each sheet as a group. Read out the first title page and then give them time to illustrate.

3. When all students have completed the first sheet, allow share time to go over what they drew and why. Then continue to the second one.

4. Continue until finished with all five.

5. Make sure to point out and discuss why parents divorce or families have to change. Have the group brainstorm reasons. Some answers you may get are:
- Fighting
- Job situations
- Don't love each other any more
- Want to be married to someone else

Don't forget to explain and make it clear that children are not the cause of divorce.

6. Discuss the following questions: "Have you ever hoped or wished that your parents would get back together? Have you tried anything to do this? How much control do you really have over this situation? What would it be better to do than worry?"

End
1. End with a go-round and ask the kids to share one thing that they learned about their family situation today.

2. Remind kids to be on time and that you will see them next _____ at _____.

Session 4
Topic: Dealing with feelings

Resources

- Chart paper
- *The Hurt* by T. Poleski

Beginning

1. Welcome everyone back to the group. Remind kids, "This is our fourth meeting and we are half-way through with group." Review last week's session. Ask the kids to do the thumbs-up check-in (up, middle, down) and then share something really fun that they have done since the last time we were together.

2. Say, "Kids often have many different feelings when their families go through changes such as separation or divorce. It is important to understand and discuss these feelings, especially with others who are experiencing the same thing."

Middle

1. Ask the children to think about some of the feelings they remember having when they found out their family was about to go through some changes (divorce, separation). Chart the responses. Note similarities (common feelings may include relief, shame, sadness, anger, guilt).

2. Talk about how the children deal or don't deal with their feelings. Read the book *The Hurt*. This book tells the story of a boy who held in a bad feeling and how that affected him. Then it continues to explain how he felt after he talked to someone about his feelings.

3. Discuss things that kids can do to release the bad feelings they may experience (i.e., call a friend, read a favorite story, play a game, write a letter and then throw it out). Then have kids create a Loyal Listener List. This is a list of trustworthy people they can talk to if they need to get something off their chest.

End

1. Do a go-round and have the kids identify one thing they will try in the coming week to release a bad feeling they may get relating to the separation.

2. Remind kids to be on time and that you will see them next _____ at _____.

Session 5
Topic: Stages of dealing with divorce

Resources

- Chart showing stages of divorce

Beginning

1. Welcome everyone back to the group. Remind kids, "This is our fifth meeting and we still have three meetings left." Review last week's session. Ask the kids to rate how they are feeling on a scale of 1–10.

2. Say, "In the last session we discussed feelings about divorce and how important it is to express them instead of keeping them inside. Today, we are going to further discuss feelings and get a better understanding of the stages that most people go through when experiencing a divorce or changing family."

Middle

1. Display a chart that shows the stages of dealing with divorce, based on Bienfeld (1987).

STAGES OF DEALING WITH DIVORCE
1. Disbelief
2. Anxiety
3. Anger
4. Sadness
5. Acceptance

2. Explain what the idea of going through stages means. You may want to give an example such as the stages of learning to ride a bike (tricycle, training wheels, two-wheeler, ten-speed). Or how you feel when you get into a fight with someone (steaming mad, less angry, then sad and missing the friendship, then sometimes even forgetting what the fight was about). Two different stage theories will be explained today; it's best to display both on one poster to allow for comparison and contrast.

3. Go through the chart and explain the meanings of words in terms the children can understand. Have them identify different times when they may have experienced these different stages. Have them identify what stage they may currently be in. Explain that people do not always go through these stages in a set order, or in a certain time frame. Some people stay in stages for much longer than others, some may go back and forth between them.

End

1. Do a go-round and ask each child to share what stage he may be in six months from now and why he feels that way.

2. Ask the kids to say one thing that they think may help them move on to the next stage.

3. Remind kids to be on time and that you will see them next _____ at _____.

Session 6

Topic: Strategies in dealing with divorce

Resources

- *My Life Turned Upside Down, but I Turned It Right Side Up* by Mary Blitzer and Hennie Shore
- Paper and pencils

Beginning

1. Welcome everyone back to the group. Remind kids, "This is our sixth meeting and we still have two meetings left." Review last week's session. Ask if there are any questions regarding the stages discussed. Ask the kids to rate how they are feeling on a scale of 1–10.

2. Say, "Sometimes it's a lot easier to get advice from other people who are going through situations similar to yours. Today we are going to read a story and write letters so we can hear from kids just like us what they would do if they were in our situations."

Middle

1. Read the story *My Life Turned Upside Down, but I Turned It Right Side Up*. Discuss some of the strategies the girl in the story uses to deal with the divorce of her parents. Ask, "Which ones have you tried? Were they successful? Why or why not?"

2. Have the children write anonymous letters to the group. In these letters they will discuss a current problem they are experiencing related to the divorce and ask for advice. Keep the letters to discuss the following week.

End

1. Have students complete the statements,
   "Today I learned . . ."
   "It feels_____knowing I am not the only one going through a divorce/separation."

2. Remind kids to be on time and that you will see them next _____ at _____.

Session 7
Topic: Stepfamilies

Resources

- Story of Cinderella
- Chart paper

Beginning

1. Welcome children to group. Remind them, "This is our seventh session and we have one session left." Briefly review last week's session and ask if there are any unanswered questions.

2. Have each child stand by his or her seat (or stay seated if they prefer) and state the "weather" of their feelings today (sunny, cloudy, rainy, etc.). Process if need be.

3. Say, "First we must finish our activity from last week, but then we need to talk about stepfamilies. Sometimes, when parents divorce or separate, new people come into our lives. We may get a stepparent or stepsibling. Having new additions to your family can be very tough. Today we are going to talk more about stepfamilies."

Middle

1. Process the letters from last week. Have children offer advice to each other in pairs, then with the group.

2. Make sure kids understand the terminology regarding stepfamilies. Explain that this means someone who has married into your family or has married into the family and brought children along (e.g., stepmom, stepdad, stepbrother, stepsister).

3. Read the story of Cinderella. Emphasize the relationship that Cinderella had with her stepmother and stepsisters. Process the story. Ask, "Does this sound as if it could be a true story? Do you know any stepmoms or stepsisters this bad?"

4. Chart some of the tough situations stepfamilies may run into (space, sharing, jealousy regarding attention, respecting new authority, etc.). What are some ways to deal with these stressors?

End

1. Have the kids name one new thing they learned today about stepfamilies.

2. Ask, "Do you feel differently about stepfamilies than you felt before we talked today?"

3. Remind kids to be on time and that you will see them next _____ at _____.

4. Remind that next week is the last session.

Session 8
Topic: Warm-fuzzy collages

Resources

- Collage materials—magazines, scissors, paper, glue sticks

Beginning

1. Welcome kids to group. Remind them that this is our last meeting. Review last week's session and attempt to answer any unanswered questions.

2. Do a go-round and have the kids give a thumbs-up check-up. Have the students also say one fun time that they have had since the last group meeting.

3. Explain to the children that since this is the last group, it is important that we get the chance to say good-bye to each other. Since good-bye is often difficult, and, for children of divorce especially, sometimes a negative experience, we want to have a saying good-bye experience that is positive.

Middle

1. Review the content of the previous sessions.

2. Explain to group members that they are going to create warm fuzzy collages. Explain that warm fuzzys are positive, nice things that people can say to one another or show one another through pictures. Explain that because they shared so much during this eight-week group, they will now have an opportunity to create a warm fuzzy collage for someone in the group (have them draw random names) to wish them a warm good-bye.

3. Provide ample amounts of magazines; be sensitive to race, socioeconomic levels, gender, etc. Explain to the kids that they are to find any pictures in the magazine or create any kind of colorful designs that would make the person they picked feel good. It could be a picture of friends, a warm sunshine, a picture of flowers, or a game that they mentioned they liked.

4. Provide construction paper and glue so that they can paste on their pictures.

5. Have the children present and share the collages individually when they are complete.

End

1. Ask, "How did it feel to be presented with this warm fuzzy collage?"

2. Tell the children that you thank them for participating and that there might be rough times ahead. Point out that now they have a support team and, if appropriate, let them know that you will be available after the group to help them individually.

Part 4:
Group Plans for All Levels

4.1
New Student Programs

Grade Level: 3–12	Time Required: 2 small group sessions, with follow-up options	Authors: Greg Brigman and Barbara Earley Goodman

There are many ways counselors can help facilitate a new student's adjustment to moving and getting started in a new school. We have developed a four-part program that combines (a) a two-session small group model led by trained peer helpers, with follow-up using (b) a peer buddy system for monitoring academic and social progress, (c) a classroom buddy program, and (d) a mentoring system pairing seniors and freshmen, which can be modified for middle and elementary levels; see Transition—The Buddy System, in this book, for a full description of this component.

The two-session small group plan follows the explanation of the peer helper system and classroom buddy plan.

PEER HELPER SYSTEM

Trained peer helpers lead small group meetings to welcome new students. Approximately 4–6 weeks after this meeting (usually just after report cards), the peer helpers who led the group sessions meet individually with each group member. Each peer helper completes the following structured outline as he/she discusses how things are going for the new student. This system provides a means to monitor the progress of new students and to refer them appropriate support services if needed.

Introduction and Rationale

Use this approach for a follow-up individual meeting by peer helper and new student after first grade reporting period.

Hi _____, good to see you again. As we said during the new student group, I am meeting with you to check on how things are going. If it is OK with you I want to ask you to rate how things are going with grades, teachers, and peers, and getting involved in the school/community.

New Student_____ Date _____

1. How are your grades? You have received a report card by now.

Math_____ Science_____ Social Studies_____
Lang Arts_____ Elective_____ Elective _____

Rate how satisfied you are with your grades on a 1–10 scale, 1 meaning not at all satisfied and 10 meaning very satisfied_____.

If student rates satisfaction with grades at below 7, ask if he/she would like to have a peer tutor. Explain peer tutoring. Yes_____ No _____
What subject? _____

2. How are things going with you and your teachers? 1–10 _____

If not satisfactory to student, peer helper helps student explore what could be done to improve relations with the teacher. Peer asks, "Would you like to talk with a counselor about getting along with your teachers?"

Yes_____ No_____ Explain who the counselors are and how to see them.

3. How satisfied are you with making friends here? 1–10 _____

If student is not satisfied, peer helper listens, explores the student's problem, discusses what activities the student is involved in or might like to try.

4. How satisfied are you with getting involved in school and community activities? 1–10_____

If rating is high, ask about the types of activities they have found to participate in. If the rating is not high, ask about their interests and talk about other activities in and out of school that are available.

5. Peer helper summarizes meeting and tells new student about next meeting in six weeks and any follow-up before then. *Example:* "One of the counselors will get in touch with you regarding peer tutoring, or to discuss how things are going with teachers and friends."

Throughout this meeting the peer helper is using the listening and other communication skills taught in peer helper training. The goal is to have a warm, personal meeting and to give some positive life to the above structured outline.

Recommended Resources

Full bibliographic details for these publications are included in the Bibliography at the end of this book.

Combs, 1993: "A middle school transition program."

Jett, Pulling, and Ross, 1994: "Preparing high schools for eighth grade students."

Rollenhagen, 1989: "FOTP: A school transition program that works."

Roth, 1991: *Middle Level Transition: Policies, Programs, and Practices.*

Classroom Buddy Plan

The classroom buddy system is a plan to help new students feel more comfortable and become better acquainted with their new school. Each classroom teacher selects two students (one male, one female) who agree to be classroom buddies.

The following is a lesson plan for a training session for classroom buddies.

Classroom Buddy System: Introductory Meeting

1. Introduce counselors, administrator, and person in charge of registration.

2. "Congratulations on being chosen as a buddy or thank you for volunteering. Being a buddy to new students shows your care and concern about others and that you want them to feel a part of this school."

3. Questions to provide background and rationale for classroom buddy system. Divide into pairs. Ask partners to discuss the following questions.

   - How many of you remember being a new student?

   - What did you think on the first day?

   - How were you treated?

   - How long before you felt comfortable here?

   - What do we do in our classes when a new student walks in?

   - What were some things you worried about before coming to school the first day? *Examples:*

     What would students wear?

     Would I make friends?

     Would I like my teachers?

     Would I get lost?

     Would I be afraid?

     Would I be able to open my locker?

4. Discuss these items and have the partners share their answers.

5. Talk with the new classroom buddies about how new students sometimes act aloof. Why do you think they might appear that way? (Because they are frightened and are trying to look as though they're comfortable.)

Role of the Buddy

"Since this is the beginning of the school year, we have about 100 new students who have registered during the summer and the first week of school. We'll give you a list of those students so you can meet them and talk with them. As new students come in during the year, you can meet with them on the first day and help them find everything.

"You have a list of suggested activities (see next page for list) that might be helpful to a new student. Please get a partner and come up with some ideas for items 4, 7, and 8 of the suggested activities page. At the end, brainstorm other things you could do to help new students feel comfortable and welcome. I'll give you ten minutes, and at the end of that time we'll share our ideas with the whole group."

Other Services for New Students

- Peer helpers' new-student group
- Peer helpers talking individually with new students
- Referral to counselors if new students are not adjusting to school
- Counselors talk to parents and teachers of new students
- Friendship groups by the counselors
- Coupon book that students can redeem for items such as bookmarks from librarians or cookies from the cafeteria

"The responsibility for helping new students is not yours alone. Enlist the help of your friends, help students get involved in clubs and activities, and let them know what is offered in the community.

"You have an important job and are providing a much-needed service for new students. We'll be in touch with you throughout the year to see how things are going. If you see that a new student is having a difficult time at school or at home, we would like you to let one of the counselors know."

Name_____ Date _____

Classroom Buddy System Suggested Activities

1. Sit next to new students in class (for the first week).

2. Help with locker combinations (demonstrate).

3. Take students to class or match them with a student who is going to their class.

4. Find out their interests and introduce them to others who share the interest(s).

5. Include them with your friends at lunch.

6. Give the new students a phone call to check on how things are going (after first and second week). Ask how you can be helpful.

7. Inform the students of activities after school and in the community in which they may have an interest.

8. Tell students about who is available to help new students (e.g., peer tutors, counselors, teachers).

Classroom Buddy System

To: Homeroom Teachers

From: Counselors

Re: Classroom Buddy System

To help our new students feel more comfortable and become better acquainted with our school, we would like to begin a Classroom Buddy System.

Most of you already have a procedure for helping new students. We want to extend that program with some specific activities, phone calls, notes, and being in touch. We'll also have peer helpers working with new students in a group and then individually.

Please select a boy and a girl to be buddies for your homeroom. Please choose students who are open, caring, and who want to be a buddy.

We will meet with them and go over this list of duties. You might want to read them this list.

CLASSROOM BUDDY ROLE: (SOME SUGGESTED ACTIVITIES)

1. Sit next to new students in class (for first week).

2. Help with locker combinations.

3. Take new students to class or match them with a student who is going to their class.

4. Include them with your friends at lunch.

5. Phone once a week for the first 2–3 weeks.

6. Share some activities after school (how to join).

7. Tell students where they can get extra help (i.e., peer tutoring, counselors, teachers).

Please turn in two names to one of the counselors by _____.

We will meet with these students on _____ during period _____.

Homeroom Teacher _____

Classroom Buddy System

Name _____

Name _____

         Group Counseling for School Counselors: A Practical Guide

Session 1
Topic: Get acquainted, get involved

Note: These are lesson plans conducted by trained peer helpers working in pairs as described on page 290. Each new student group is lead by a pair of peer helpers. Each group has approximately six students.

Beginning

INTRODUCTION

1. Introduce self, go over purpose of group; use a go-round for group members to say names and where there are moving from.

   After go-round ask: Who came from the farthest away? Closest?

2. Students interview each other in pairs, then introduce partner to group. The following information is used for introductions:

   - brothers, sisters, and ages
   - hobbies, interests, what they do for fun
   - pets

3. After each introduction, group leader asks person introduced if anything was left out. Thank person doing introduction.

4. Discuss with group:

   - What were some things you noticed people had in common?
   - What were some things you noticed that were different?

Middle

Discuss with group:

- How many have moved more than once? Determine who has moved the most.
- What are some fun things about moving?
- What are some things about moving that you don't like?

When leader gets answers to the above, ask:

- How many of you have felt that way, or agree with that?
- When did you feel that way?
- How have you found the people here?
- How many have found at least one friend already?
- What are some ways you go about making new friends? (Spend some time on this question.)

- What are some things about this school that are like your old school? Different?
- How long do you think it usually takes to get used to a new school, to feel comfortable? What is one thing you can do to make that time shorter?
- What are some things people can do to help you feel comfortable here?
- What's one thing you like about this school? (Give them a moment to think, then go around the circle for responses.)

GETTING INVOLVED

Students who have been new in the past tell us that getting involved in activities with other students helps them feel connected and is helpful in fitting in.

- What are some activities that are available for you to join?

After group brainstorms activities and how to join, each leader shares list, pointing out any not mentioned.

KNOWLEDGE ABOUT SCHOOL

- Do you all know who the principal is?
- Do you all know the school's colors and mascot?
- How many know where the clinic is?
- If you lose something, do you know where lost-and-found is?
- Have you met any of the counselors here? Their names are _____. They can be helpful if you need to talk individually. They offer groups and come to classrooms. Peer tutoring is also available.

End

"Think about one thing you've learned about this school today, and one thing you can do to speed up the process of getting settled here. We'll go around the circle in a moment and ask each of you to share your ideas on these two areas."

"I enjoyed meeting you today and look forward to seeing you again. Each of you will have a peer helper buddy who will check with you in a couple of weeks to see how things are going."

Session 2
Topic: Making friends

Resources
- Making Friends handout

Beginning

INTRODUCTION

1. Go around the circle. Have students say their names and one positive thing that has happened to them since the last meeting.
2. Say, "Today we'll be talking about friendship. Most people moving into a new place are anxious to make new friends. How many of you feel that way?"

VOTING ACTIVITY

"Let's take a look at how you think and feel about friends. We'll start with a voting activity—raise your hand if you agree."

How many of you:

- have a best friend?
- have a good friend of the opposite sex?
- have had an argument with a good friend lately?
- have a friend that you can talk to about your problems?
- have ever had a day when you felt as if you didn't have any friends?

- think a friend is someone who will do whatever you say?
- think a friend should always agree with you?
- have a brother or sister who is also your friend?

Middle

1. Ask students to brainstorm at least ten positive ways to make new friends. After each suggestion ask group, "How many think this is a positive way to make friends? How many have used this technique before?"
2. Distribute the Making Friends handout.

   "Let's compare our list to the list on this page. As we read each technique for making friends put a check by it if it is one you use and circle it if it is sometimes hard for you." Read each item and ask, "How many have used this one, and how many find this one hard to do?"

End

1. Ask, "From the all the different ways we have discussed for making friends, which 1–2 ways work best for you?"
2. Ask each group member to complete the statements "Today I learned or relearned . . ." and "One way I can use what I learned is . . .".
3. Remind group of scheduled follow-up and how they can contact counselors if needed.

Name_____ Date _____

Making Friends

1. Think about a friend you have now or used to have. Recall when, where, and how

    you met. _____

    _____

    _____

    Share your story with the group. Be sure to include what you did to help develop the
    friendship.

2. Check the boxes that are next to the techniques you like for meeting people, making
    friends, and keeping friends. Circle the boxes that are next to the techniques that are
    hardest for you.

    ❑ Smile. Smiling can do more to communicate that you are friendly and
    approachable than almost any other thing you can do.

    ❑ Listen. Being a good listener is very important. Listening says "I care" and
    makes the person feel important. Listening takes concentration and energy,
    but it's worth it.

    ❑ Introduce yourself. Usually others are just as cautious as you about starting
    a conversation. Most of the time they will be glad you got things started.

    ❑ Remember names and use them often.

    ❑ Spend time at places where people with some of your interests go. Spending
    time with people doing things you both enjoy builds friendship.

    ❑ Invite people to do things with you. Try to match what you like with people who
    like the same kinds of activities. Try short time periods first to find out if you
    enjoy spending time together.

    ❑ Be a complimenter. Give honest compliments. A phony compliment can lead to
    trouble. Letting people know you admire and appreciate something about them
    builds goodwill and shows you care.

    ❑ Share the talk time. Shoot for a 50/50 talk-listen ratio. Nobody likes the non-
    stop talker. Not talking isn't helpful either—people wonder if you're interested
    or care.

    ❑ Give parties. Invite people you think might be interesting. Ask the people you
    know to invite one of their friends.

    ❑ Get involved in after-school clubs or activities.

         Group Counseling for School Counselors: A Practical Guide

4.2
Personal Growth for Teachers

Time Required: 8 Sessions	Authors: Barbara Earley Goodman and Greg Brigman

How This Group Developed

Because teachers frequently experience stress and burnout, we decided to offer an after-school personal-growth group. Offering the group shows teachers your concern for their well-being, which is appreciated. Working with adults is rewarding for the counselor and gives teachers opportunities to share ideas. Serving refreshments and modeling a relaxed atmosphere is in itself therapeutic. It is certainly an excellent way to get to know each other.

Several Methods for Quick and Easy Teacher Groups

If you feel hesitant or uncertain about offering groups for teachers, your first experience could be to have speakers for each session. You might begin by offering an activity once a month or having four sessions offered weekly. There could be four speakers on one topic such as stress, or a different topic each time. Consult your local mental health agency, hospital speakers' bureau, a private therapist, or ask another school counselor. Your responsibilities would include: conducting an icebreaker with the group; discussing objectives; introducing the speaker; leading a discussion after the speaker; and concluding with a summary and written evaluation.

Another idea is to offer a series of video- or audiotapes based on a particular topic of interest to the participants.

As you begin to feel more comfortable leading groups, you could offer a staff-development course such as *Cooperative Discipline* by Linda Albert, published by American Guidance Services. If time does not allow for a 50-hour course, you could do small segments on topics such as encouragement or the democratic classroom.

An easy and ready-for-use group lesson plan is *The Encouragement Book* by Don Dinkmeyer. The activities in this book are great for motivating participants to be more loving, motivating, respectful, and encouraging to themselves and others. Cover a chapter per week. If you obtain copies for each participant, you can begin with a discussion of the reading. Next, lead the group through the chapter's activities. If participants do not have copies, summarize the key points before and/or after the activities.

A good standard format for group sessions is:

- Icebreaker
- Review of last session
- Discussion and activity
- Summary

Group Objectives

- To get to know other faculty members better
- To learn about yourself
- To develop personal growth goals and plans

TIME

Eight one-hour meetings after school

GROUP COMPOSITION

Faculty members

GROUP RULES

Rules for adult groups are similar to rules for student groups. The rules need to come from the participants and should include confidentiality, right to pass or not participate, and respect of others' opinions (no put-downs).

Recommended Resources

Griswold: *Taking Control of Your Life* (audiocassette).

Session 1
Topic: Introduction, get acquainted

Resources

- Index cards
- What Are You Doing for the Rest of Your Life handout

Beginning

INTRODUCTION AND OVERVIEW

1. Introduce the group by outlining its purpose. *Example:* "We'll be meeting for the next eight weeks from 3–4 P.M. During this time I hope you'll become more aware of your strengths and look for some areas that you may want to enhance. Our meeting together in a personal-growth group indicates that we are healthy individuals who have high expectations about the quality of life. We all have times of stress and disappointments. We also have goals that we may not pursue because of our busy lives. The group time will provide an opportunity for you to look more closely at yourself and those goals. Meeting together each week will help us get to know each other in a personal and nonthreatening manner. You will decide how open you want to be with the group. A feeling of trust will help us be more open with each other. The trust will develop as we come to feel that group members will keep what we say here confidential."

2. Establish—as a group—some group rules. Members will come up with the same rules that students do: confidentiality, respect for each other, and no put-downs. (Members should all agree on the rules.)

3. Housekeeping: Group members may take turns bringing refreshments. Encourage them to be on time.

4. Explain the purpose and advantages of keeping a journal. *Example:* "It is helpful to keep a journal while you are in the group. You will have opportunities to write down your thoughts while we are doing an activity and to write an 'I learned' statement at the end of each session. During the week, as you work on an assignment or have thought about the group, writing in the journal will help bring focus to your ideas."

NAME TAG ACTIVITY

Sample Name Tag		
Place where you spent five days of bliss: _____ _____		Something you have planned that you are looking forward to: _____ _____
	Name: _____	
Most serene, peaceful place in home: _____ _____		List places you have lived: _____ _____

Give members a 5" × 8" index card on which to write information. (See above for a sample name tag.) The leader gives directions for each corner of the card. When the group has finished, each person joins with a partner and shares what he/she has written. Have the group spend some time with the details. For example, in the corner that asks "list places you have lived," have participants choose the one that meant most to them. Perhaps it was the place where the most growth occurred, a happy place, or a place where there was a crisis.

Back in the big group, have group members share an "I learned . . ." statement.

Middle

"WHAT ARE YOU DOING FOR THE REST OF YOUR LIFE?"

1. Group members list 20 things they would like to do in their lives that they haven't done yet. Allow 10–15 minutes for them to list the activities. In the spaces after listing the activities, have them make marks indicating:
   - one you can begin right away
   - one you would like to begin in five years
   - how many require money
   - which ones you would have chosen five years ago

   The additional spaces can be used if you have time, and might include topics such as:
   - which ones you prefer doing alone
   - which ones you prefer doing with people
   - which ones a spouse or significant other would choose
   - which ones require additional training and education

2. Ask participants to share some of the categories with a partner or with the larger group.

3. Ask the group to share aloud. Who had one that was about:
   - travel
   - profession/career
   - relationships
   - physical activity
   - spiritual life
   - intellectual pursuit

End

1. Ask participants to complete these sentences in their journals:

   "I learned . . ."

   "I was surprised that . . ."

   "One activity I want to start right away . . ."

   Ask for volunteers to share journal entries with the group.

2. Put on music (soft, instrumental) for 60 seconds. Ask participants to picture themselves doing that one thing that they want to begin right away.

ASSIGNMENT

Share your 20 things with a spouse or significant other, or spend time thinking about how to begin on this new task.

Name_____ Date_____

What Are You Doing for the Rest of Your Life?

List in the first column below 20 things that you would like to do, experience, achieve, try, or enjoy before you die.

What did you find out about yourself? I learned that _____

_____

_____

I was surprised (or pleased) that _____

_____

_____

         Group Counseling for School Counselors: A Practical Guide

Session 2
Topic: Connectedness network

Resources
- My Connectedness Network handout

Beginning
1. "My name is . . . and the high point of my week was . . ."
2. Volunteers share how their assignment of sharing their 20 things went.
3. Introduce main activity:

   "Alfred Adler believed that our primary goal in life was to feel a sense of belonging. Adler stated that there were three tasks in life: work, friends, and intimate relationships. Most of us have an imbalance among these three areas. Nobody is perfect. One way of checking our satisfaction with our lives is to look at these three areas. Then we need to decide which area needs the most attention right now."

Middle
A feeling of connectedness is essential for self-esteem. To be happy, we have to feel that we belong. Our connectedness network includes our family, friends, and coworkers.

1. The leader asks the following four questions, one at a time. After each question, ask participants to write a brief impression in their journals. After approximately one minute for writing, ask for volunteers to share. This sharing should not be a go-round. There should be no pressure to share.
   - How do you feel connected to your family of origin? Close your eyes and picture yourself approaching the family at a reunion. Are you welcomed with open arms and positive comments, or do you anticipate cutting remarks and disapproval?
   - How does it feel walking up to your front door at the end of the day?
   - What do your friends mean to you? Do you have friends for confidantes, for fun, and as models?
   - How do you relate to your coworkers? If you were out of work for three days, would you be missed?

2. **Connectedness handout.** Explain one category at a time and have the group list people for each area. For example:
   - *Confidantes* are those people you can really trust with your intimate feelings, and thoughts, those with whom you can share joys and sorrows.
   - *Intellectual Stretchers* are people with whom you philosophize, those who expand your knowledge and your creative thinking.
   - *Health* people are those who hand you your running shoes, who inspire and encourage your taking care of yourself.
   - *Fun and Adventure* people enjoy life, try new things, and encourage you to take part.
   - *Spiritual* has to do with those people in your life who cause you to examine and expand your beliefs and thoughts.
   - *Chicken soup* people are those who would visit you if you were sick and bring you chicken soup. These are the people who are always there to help you out.
   - *Mentors/Guides* are people whom you want to learn from. They have talents and skills that they want to share with you.

End
Ask participants to share in pairs their responses to the following three questions related to today's group meeting:
   "I learned . . ."
   "I relearned . . ."
   "I can see that I need to . . ."
After pair share, ask for a few volunteers to share with group.

Name_____ Date_____

My Connectedness Network

Family	Friends	Coworkers and Others
Confidantes		
Intellectual Stretchers		
Health		
Fun and Adventure		
Spiritual		
Chicken Soup		
Mentors/Guides		

       Group Counseling for School Counselors: A Practical Guide

Session 3
Topic: Connectedness continued

Resources

- Identifying Connections handout

Beginning

1. "Today I'm a . . . on a 1–10 scale, and one thing I'm looking forward to in the next week is . . . ."
2. Review last session.

Middle

1. Connectedness handout, continued. Usually this activity requires time this session for completion (see last session).

2. Identifying Connections handout: Ask group members to take a few minutes to complete this sheet. After completing, have participants get into groups of three to share the responses to each section. Remind the group that everyone has the right to pass on any part of the handout.

End

Ask group to return to larger circle and share how it felt to complete the Connectedness sheet and the Identifying Connections sheet.

Name_____ Date _____

Identifying Connections

Four people who love you

_____   _____

_____   _____

Three people you have learned a lot from

_____

_____

_____

Three people who have learned something from you

_____

_____

_____

Four people who usually smile at you

_____   _____

_____   _____

Two people who have helped you in an important way

_____   _____

Three people who are usually kind to you

_____

_____

_____

           Group Counseling for School Counselors: A Practical Guide

Session 4
Topic: Relaxation training

Resources

- *Taking Control of Your Life* audiocassette by Robert Griswold
- Cassette player

Beginning

1. Ask participants to complete the following sentence stem in a go-round:

   "One quality about myself that I'm proud of is . . .".

2. Review last week's meeting.

Middle

RELAXATION TRAINING

1. Introduce the importance of learning to relax deeply. Mention regular practice, how images are helpful, and how relaxation creates your inner sanctuary.

   Many relaxation techniques are readily available. Two of the most popular are the Relaxation Response (Herbert Benson) and Progressive Relaxation (Edmund Jacobson).

There are also many useful cassette tapes that incorporate relaxation training and positive imagery—some with helpful ideas on avoiding self-defeating behavior and improving self-esteem. You may want to guide the relaxation with or without imagery.

2. Ask the participants to listen for 2–3 important ideas and to be ready to discuss their choices after the tape. After going through the tape, ask who was able to relax deeply, to clearly see the images described.

   Ask each person to identify his or her favorite image. Then, one by one, share 1–3 important ideas from the tape.

End

Ask group members to complete one of the following:

"One thing I learned or relearned today was . . .".
"Something that surprised me was . . .".

Session 5
Topic: Irrational beliefs

Resources

- Irrational Beliefs handout

Beginning

1. Ask participants to complete the following sentence stem in a go-round:

   "One (non school-related) thing I could teach someone else is . . .".

2. Review last meeting.

Middle

IRRATIONAL BELIEFS

1. Ask the participants to read the irrational beliefs by Albert Ellis and choose the 2–3 that cause them the most trouble, or that they can't see anything wrong with, or that influence their life the most.

2. In groups of 3–4, ask members to share the above. For irrational beliefs that seem appropriate to some, the other group members provide reasons that the belief is irrational or can cause problems. Designate a spokesperson to give a summary of small group to large group. Ask the small groups to give a summary of their discussion.

3. If time permits, give a brief overview of Ellis's ABC model. See any of the numerous books by Ellis on R.E.T. (Rational Emotive Therapy).

End

Ask participants to record a summary of key points and their feelings about the meeting in their journal. Ask for volunteers to share their entries with the group.

Irrational Beliefs

It is essential that one be loved or approved of by virtually everyone in the community.

One must be perfectly competent, adequate, and achieving to consider oneself worthwhile.

Some people are bad, wicked, or villainous, and therefore should be blamed and punished. It is a terrible catastrophe when things are not as one wants them to be.

Unhappiness is caused by outside circumstances, and the individual has no control over it.

Dangerous or fearsome things are causes for great concern, and their possibility must be continually dwelt upon.

It is easier to avoid certain difficulties and self-responsibilities than to face them.

One should be dependent on others and one must have someone stronger on whom to rely.

Past experiences and events are the determiners of present behavior; the influence of the past cannot be eradicated.

One should be quite upset over other people's problems and disturbances.

There is always a right or perfect solution to every problem and it must be found or the results will be catastrophic.

". . . people do not get upset but instead upset themselves by insisting that (a) they should be outstandingly loved and accomplished, (b) other people should be incredibly fair and giving, and (c) the world should be exceptionally easy and munificent."—Albert Ellis, 1973.

Session 6
Topic: Writing a five-year plan

Resources

- Enjoying Your Life script
- Picturing Your Ideal Self script

Beginning

1. Ask participants to respond to the following question in a go-round: What three things do you want for your children? for students in your class? for young people today?

2. Review Session 5 and ask:

   - Who has done something about an item on his or her list of 20 things (What Are You Doing for the Rest of Your Life handout)?

   - Who has set up some times to get together with some of their important connection people?

- Who has tried any relaxation techniques?
- Who has caught himself or herself holding any irrational beliefs?

Middle

1. Guided Imagery: Enjoying Your Life script (to be read to the group).

2. Read the Picturing Your Ideal Self script to the group. Tell members to write a plan for reaching their ideal selves in five years.

End

Ask each participant to complete the following and to share with the group: "One thing I learned today was . . .".

Script: Enjoying Your Life

Developing your skills in relaxation and imagery is extremely beneficial in your quest to get more joy and satisfaction from your life. Now we will go through a series of five imagery exercises, each lasting from 15 seconds to 2 minutes.

Following this series, we will use our imagination to look at our "ideal self" and develop a five-year plan for approaching our image. You will have an opportunity to share part of your plan in groups of three. Let's begin.

Take several slow, deep breaths, get into a comfortable position, and close your eyes as we practice using our imagination.

1. Picture yourself in your favorite chair. See the color, feel the texture and comfortable feelings you have when you sit there. (pause 15–20 seconds)

2. Picture an ideal place—a place where you feel tranquil, serene, and balanced. This can be a place you've been or a place you create in your imagination. (pause 30–60 seconds)

3. Picture a fun experience you've had recently. (pause 30 seconds)

4. Picture a beautiful sunrise—see the pinks and blues, the clouds—feel the wind, hear the birds. (pause 30 seconds)

5. Picture yourself on the beach alone. Watch the waves, listen to the rhythm, feel the warmth of the sand. As you inhale, imagine the incoming waves bringing you energy, peace, happiness; as you exhale, imagine the receding waves taking away your worries, concerns, stress. (pause 2–3 minutes)

Script: Picturing Your Ideal Self

Picture yourself in your ideal place, the one you created just a few moments ago. Now picture yourself as already having all the positive qualities or traits you believe are important. This is your ideal self. Don't hold back—see yourself just as you want to be. What are you doing? Who is around, if anyone?

Feel the gracefulness of your movement—the poise and balance. Feel the confidence, the courage you have to be yourself, to say and do what you feel and think even if others disapprove.

What are some of your ideal self's self-talk messages? How are these self-talk messages similar to your current self? How are they different?

Feel yourself relaxed and at ease, alert and aware, with tremendous energy. See yourself taking action on the things that are important in your life.

How is your ideal self similar to your current self? How is it different? How are the most important things in your ideal self picture similar to your current most important things list?

Feel the contentment of knowing you do whatever it takes to take good care of yourself, because you know that without good self-care, there won't be anything to share with others. Deeply relax and allow these positive feelings to soak in.

In a moment I will ask you to write out a plan for reaching this state within the next five years. Picture what steps are needed. Break your plan into easy-to-achieve chunks. Set a time to begin one small part. Don't overload—trying too much at once is a key to discouragement. (pause 2–3 minutes)

In just a moment I will ask you to open your eyes. (pause 10–15 seconds)

Now slowly open your eyes and slowly move around and stretch in your chair. Take a moment to write yourself some notes on your plan. In groups of three, share your plans (allow enough time for everyone to share.) Now complete your plan write-up. Be specific, clear, and realistic.

Session 7
Topic: Birth order

Resources
- Chart paper and pens

Beginning
1. Ask participants to rate how they are feeling on a scale of 1–10, and to share one thing they have done to nurture themselves lately.
2. Review last meeting.

Middle
1. Participants get into groups according to birth order—oldest children, middle children, youngest children, and only children. Each group lists the characteristics of that position and how it felt to grow up in that position.
2. Each group has a recorder, who reports the characteristics to the whole group. One way to accomplish this reporting is to have each group list their characteristics on a poster or blackboard. After all groups have reported, post the lists side by side for easy comparison. The discussion can evolve into how these positions carry over into adult life and how these characteristics are seen in participants' own children.
3. Sometimes participants may not feel that they fit neatly into a profile of only, youngest, oldest, or middle child. Refer to your readings of Adlerian psychology, which explains that it may be your perception of your position in the family, rather than the actual birth order, that influences behavior. *Example:* Ask a sibling or parent how they saw you, and you may get a different perception from yours. The psychological birth order may be more significant than the physical birth order. For instance, the second child may exhibit characteristics of the oldest child.

End
Ask participants to complete one of the following:
"One thing I learned was . . ."
"One thing I relearned was . . ."
"One thing that surprised me was . . ."
The idea that birth order affects our personality development is an Adlerian concept. For additional information, you may want to read:

Parenting Young Children: Systematic Training for Effective Parenting (STEP) of Children Under Six by Don Dinkmeyer

Parenting Teenagers: Systematic Training for Effective Parenting (STEP) of Teens by Don Dinkmeyer

Adlerian Family Counseling by Oscar Christenson

Session 8
Topic: Strength bombardment

Resources

- My Strengths handout
- Group Evaluation form (page 10)

Beginning

1. Ask participants to complete the following sentence stem in a go-round: "One thing I'm looking forward to is . . .".

2. Review the last seven sessions. Ask teachers to recall some of the activities that were meaningful to them and share. After sharing the activities that were most meaningful, ask: "What changes can you start right away?" Ask participants to write these changes down and then share them with the group. Ask them to identify longer-range changes and what they need to do. After listing these changes, have them share in the group.

Middle

1. Pass out strength circles (My Strengths handout). Ask each teacher to sign his/her name on a strength circle and pass it to the next teacher. Each teacher writes positive qualities about every other teacher as the strength circles are passed around.

These positive comments are written in the outer circle, leaving the inner circle blank. After everyone finishes the strength circles, give them back to their owners.

2. We call this next part "Spotlighting" or "Strength Bombardment." One by one the group focuses on a teacher. Each participant tells the focus teacher one or more things that they appreciate about him or her. After everyone has spoken, the next person is spotlighted.

   Instructions for giving and receiving compliments: Direct eye contact, say "[person's name], one thing I really like about you is . . ." or "One thing I appreciate about you is . . .". The receiver simply smiles and says "thank-you."

3. To conclude this activity, ask teachers to write in the center of the circle the three most important strengths or positive qualities they see in themselves.

End

1. Have participants fill out a group evaluation.

2. Ask for volunteers to share closing comments with the group.

My Strengths

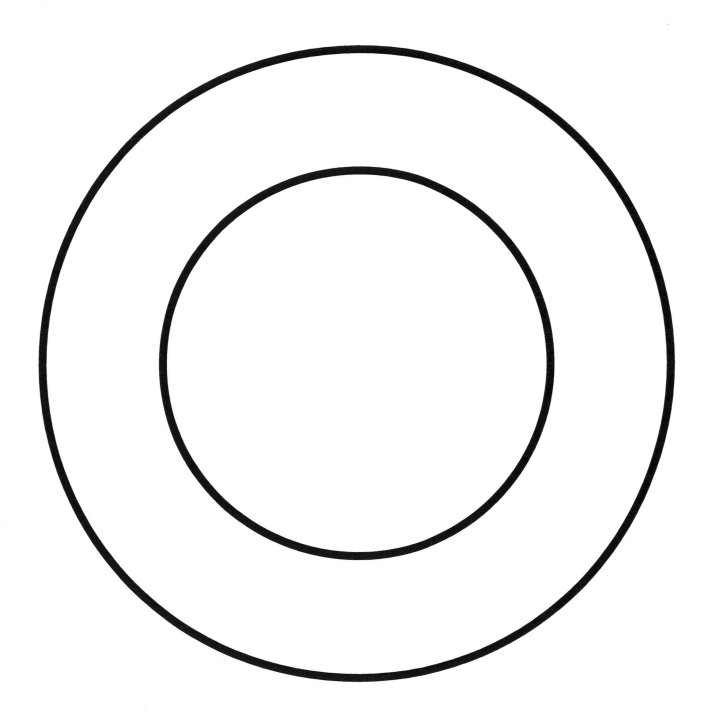

Bibliography

Admunson-Beckman, K., and A. R. Lucas. 1989. Gaining a foothold in the aftermath of divorce. *Social Work in Education, 12,* 5–15.

Albert, L. 1989. *A Teacher's Guide to Cooperative Discipline: How to Manage Your Classroom and Promote Self-Esteem.* Circle Pines, MN: American Guidance Service.

Albert, L. 1996. *Cooperative Discipline.* Circle Pines, MN: American Guidance Service.

Allard, H., and J. Marshall. 1977. *Miss Nelson Is Missing.* Boston, MA: Houghton Mifflin.

Alpert-Gillis, L. J., J. L. Pedro-Carroll, and E. L. Cowen. 1989. The Children of Divorce Intervention Program: Development, implementation, and evaluation of a program for young urban children. *Journal of Counseling and Clinical Psychology, 57,* 583–589.

Apodaca, B., and L. V. Nightingale. 1997. *My Parents Still Love Me Even Though They're Getting Divorced.* Yorba Linda, CA: Nightingale Rose Publishing.

Arem, C. 1993. *Conquering Math Anxiety.* Pacific Grove, CA: Brooks/Cole.

Asch, F. 1986. *Goodbye House.* Englewood Cliffs, NJ: Prentice-Hall.

Auch, M. J. 1993. *Bird Dogs Can't Fly.* New York: Holiday House.

Begun, R. 1996. *Ready to Use Social Skills Lessons and Activities.* West Nyack, NY: The Center for Applied Research in Education.

Begun, R. W., and F. J. Huml, eds. 1999. *Violence Prevention Skills: Lessons and Activities.* West Nyack, NY: The Center for Applied Research in Education.

Bernstein, J. E., and S. V. Gullo. 1977: *When People Die.* New York: Dutton.

Bete, C. L. 1997. *When Anger Heats Up.* South Deerfield, MA: Channing L. Bete Co., Inc.

Bienfeld, Florence. 1987. *Helping Your Child Succeed After Divorce.* Clairmont, CA: Hunter House.

Blitzer, M., and H. Shore. 1994. *My Life Turned Upside Down but I Turned It Right Side Up.* King of Prussia, PA: The Center for Applied Psychology.

Bloom, G. 1984. *Community Mental Health.* Belmont, CA: Brooks/Cole.

Borders, L., and S. Drury. 1992. Comprehensive school counseling programs: A review for policy makers and practitioners. *Journal of Counseling and Development, 70,* 487–489.

Boulden, J., and J. Boulden. 1991. *Let's Talk!* Santa Rosa, CA: Boulden Publishing.

Boulden, J., and J. Boulden. 1992. *All Together.* Santa Rosa, CA: Boulden Publishing.

Bourgeois, P. 1997. *Franklin's Bad Day.* New York: Scholastic, Inc.

Bowman, R., et al. 1998. *Aggressive and Violent Students.* Columbia, SC: Youthlight Inc.

Brigman, G., and B. Earley. 1990. *Peer Helping: A Training Guide.* Portland, ME: J. Weston Walch, Publisher.

Brigman, G., and B. Earley. 1991. *Group Counseling for School Counselors: A Practical Guide.* Portland, ME: J. Weston Walch, Publisher.

Brigman, G., D. Lane, and D. E. Lane. 1994. *Ready to Learn.* Minneapolis, MN: Educational Media.

Brown, D. 1999a. Improving academic achievement: What school counselors can do. Greensboro, NC: ERIC Clearinghouse on Counseling and Student Services.

Brown, D. 1999b. *Proven Strategies for Improving Learning and Academic Achievement.* Greensboro, NC: CAPS Publications.

Brown, L, and M. Brown. 1986. *The Dinosaurs Divorce.* Washington, MO: Paperbacks for educators.

Brown, M. T. 1988. *Dinosaurs Divorce.* Boston: Atlantic Monthly Press.

Brown, M. 1988. *When Dinosaurs Die.* Boston: Atlantic Monthly Press.

Buscaglia, Leo. 1982. *The Fall of Freddie the Leaf.* Washington, MO: Charles Slack and Paperbacks for Educators.

Campbell, C. A. 1991. Group guidance for academically under-motivated children. *Elementary School Guidance and Counseling,* 25, 302–307.

Campbell, C., and C. Dahir. 1997. *Sharing the Vision: The National Standards for School Counseling Programs.* Alexandria, VA. American School Counseling Association.

Carlson, N. L. 1992. *Arnie and the New Kid.* New York: Puffin Books.

Carruthers W., et al. 1996. Conflict resolution as curriculum: A definition, description, and process for integration in core curriculum. *The School Counselor,* 43, 326–344.

Casey, R., and J. Berman. 1985. The outcome of psychotherapy with children. *Psychological Bulletin,* 98, 388–400.

Christenson, Oscar, ed. 1993. *Adlerian Family Counseling: A Manual for Counselor, Educator, and Psychotherapist.* Minneapolis: Educational Media Corp.

Clark, B. 1998. *When Your Parents Divorce.* Minneapolis, MN: Educational Media.

Cohen, J. 1987. *I Had a Friend Named Peter.* New York: Morrow Junior Books.

Combs, H. 1993. A middle school transition program: Addressing the social side of schooling. *ERS Spectrum,* Winter, 12–21.

Cordell, A. S., and B. Bergman-Meador. 1991. The use of drawings in group intervention for children of divorce. *Journal of Divorce and Remarriage,* 17, 139–155.

Crosbie-Burnett, M., and L. L. Newcomer. 1990. Group counseling children of divorce: The effects of a multimodal intervention. *Journal of Divorce,* 13, 69–78.

Cross, S., and R. Rosenthal. 1999. Three models of conflict effects on intergroup expectations and attitudes. *Journal of Social Issues,* 55 (3), 561–580.

Curran, D., 1983. *Traits of a Healthy Family.* New York: Ballantine Books.

Dahir, C., C. Sheldon, and M. Valiga. 1998. *Vision into Action: Implementing the National Standards for School Counseling Programs.* Alexandria, VA: American School Counseling Association.

Davidson, R., and E. Levitov, 2000. *Overcoming Math Anxiety.* New York: Addison Wesley Longman.

Delton, J. 1986. *Two Good Friends.* New York: Crown.

DePaolo, P. 1992. *Rosie and the Yellow Ribbon.* Boston: Little, Brown.

DiClemente, R. J., Ed. 1992. *Adolescents and AIDS: A Generation in Jeopardy.* Thousand Oaks, CA: Sage Publications.

Dinkmeyer, D., and D. Dinkmeyer Jr. 1982. *Developing Understanding of Self and Others* (rev. ed.). Circle Pines, MN: American Guidance Service.

Dinkmeyer, D.C., and L.E. Losoncy. 1980. *The Encouragement Book: Becoming a Positive Person.* Englewood Cliffs, NJ: Prentice Hall.

Dinkmeyer, D.C., and G.D. McKay. 1998. *Parenting Teenagers: Systematic Training for Effective Parenting (STEP) of Teens.* Circle Pines, MN: American Guidance Service.

Dinkmeyer, D.C., G.D. McKay, and J.S. Dinkmeyer. 1997. *Parenting Young Children: Systematic Training for Effective Parenting (STEP) of Children Under Six.* Circle Pines, MN: American Guidance Service.

Dolbrin, A. 1971. *Scat!* New York: Four Winds Press.

Duke, K. 1992. *Aunt Isabel Tells a Good One.* New York: Dutton Children's Books.

Eggert, L. L. 1994. *Anger Management for Youth: Stemming Aggression and Violence.* Bloomington, IN: National Educational Service.

Elkind, D., 1988. *The Hurried Child: Growing Up Too Fast Too Soon.* Reading, MA: Addison-Wesley.

Elliot, D., and S. Mihalic. 1997. *Blueprints for Violence Prevention and Reduction: The Identification and Documentation of Successful Programs.* Boulder, CO: Center for the Study and Prevention of Violence.

Engel, D. 1993. *Fishing.* New York: Macmillan.

Friedman, J., and L. W. Girard. 1991. *At Daddy's on Saturday.* Morton Grove, IL: Albert Whitman and Company.

Gardner, R. 1971. *The Boys and Girls Book About Divorce.* Washington, DC: Paperbacks for Educators.

Garvin, V., D. Leber, and N. Kalter. 1991. Children of divorce: Predictors of change following preventative intervention. *American Journal of Ortopsychiatry,* 61, 438–447.

Geisel, T. (Dr. Seuss). 1998. *My Many-Colored Days.* New York, NY: Knopf Publishing.

Gladding, S. 1999. *Group Work: A Counseling Specialty.* Upper Saddle River, NJ: Prentice Hall.

Goffin, J. 1991. *Oh!* New York: H.N. Abrams.

Goldstein, A. P., and J. C. Conoley, eds. 1997. *School Violence Intervention: A Practical Handbook.* New York: The Guilford Press.

Goldstein, A., and E. McGinnis. 1997. *Skillstreaming the Adolescent: New Strategies and Perspectives for Teaching Prosocial Skills.* Champaign, IL: Research Press.

Gootman, M. 1994. *When a Friend Dies: A Book for Teens About Grieving and Healing.* Minneapolis, MN: Free Spirit.

Gray, L. M. 1994. *Small Green Snake.* New York: Orchard Books.

Griswold, R. *Taking Control of Your Life* (audiocassette). Bonita Springs, FL: Effective Learning Systems, Inc.

Grollman, E. 1993. *Straight Talk About Death for Teenagers: How to Cope with Losing Someone You Love.* Boston, MA: Beacon Press.

Grollman, E. 1995. *Bereaved Children and Teens: A Support Guide for Parents and Professionals.* Boston, MA: Beacon Press.

Grych, J. H., and F. D. Fincham. 1992. Interventions for children of divorce: Toward greater integration of research and action. *Psychological Bulletin,* 111, 434–454.

Guidance Club for Teens. 1993. *Anger, Temper Tantrums and Violent Emotions* (videocassette). Santa Monica, CA: Ready Reference Press.

Gumaer, J. 1986. Group workers' perceptions of ethical and unethical behavior of group leaders. *Journal for Specialists in Group Work,* 11(3), 139–50.

Haley, G. E. 1988. *A Story, a Story: An African Tale.* New York: Aladdin Books.

Hall, K. 1995. *A Bad, Bad Day.* New York: Scholastic.

Hattie, J., J. Biggs, and N. Purdie. 1996. Effects of learning skills interventions on student learning: A meta analysis. *Review of Educational Research,* 66, 99–136.

Hawkins, W. E. 1986. *Circle of Friends Project.* Des Moines, IA: Iowa Department of Public Instruction.

Hebert, T. P., and J. M. Furner. 1997. Helping high-ability students overcome math anxiety through bibliotherapy. *The Journal of Secondary Gifted Education,* 4, 164–178.

Hechinger, F. M. 1992. *Fateful Choices.* New York: Carnegie Corporation of New York.

Heegaard, M. 1990. *When Mom and Dad Separate.* Minneapolis, MN: Woodland Press.

Heegaard, M. 1993. *When a Parent Marries Again.* Minneapolis, MN: Woodland Press.

Henkes, K. 1990. *Jessica.* New York: Puffin Books.

Hipp, E. 1995. *Help for the Hard Times: Getting Through Loss.* Center City, MN: Hazelden.

Hoctor, S. K. 1999. *Changes: My Family and Me.* Washington, DC: Child Welfare League.

Hood, S. 1999. *Bad Hair Day.* New York: Grosset & Dunlap.

Hutchins, P. 1993. *My Best Friend.* New York: Greenwillow Books.

Ives, S. B., D. Fassler, and M. Lash. 1985. *The Divorce Workbook.* Burlington, VT: Waterfront Books.

Ivey, A., P. Pedersen, and M. Ivey. 2001. *Intentional Group Counseling: A Microskills Approach.* Belmont, CA: Brooks/Cole.

Jackson, A. 1998. *When Your Parents Split Up.* Washington, MO: Stern Sloan and Paperbacks for Educators.

Jackson, T. 1993. *Activities That Teach.* Washington, MO: Red Rock Publishing, Paperbacks for Educators.

Jackson, T. 1995. *More Activities That Teach.* Washington, MO: Red Rock Publishing, Paperbacks for Educators.

Jacobs, E., 1992. *Creative Counseling Techniques: An Illustrated Guide.* Odessa, FL: Psychological Assessment Resources, Inc.

Jacobs, E., R. Masson, and R. Harvill. 1998. *Group Counseling Strategies and Skills.* Pacific Grove, CA: Brooks/Cole.

Jett, D., D. Pulling, and J. Ross. 1994. Preparing high schools for eighth grade students. *National Association of Secondary School Principals Bulletin,* December, 85–91.

Johnson, D., et al. 1997. The impact of conflict resolution training on middle school students. *The Journal of Social Psychology,* 137 (1), 11–21.

Johnson, J., and M. Johnson. 1998. *Children Who Grieve Too: A Book for Families Who Have Experienced a Death.* Omaha, NE: Centering Corp.

Kivel, P., et al. 1997. *Making the Peace.* Washington, MO: Paperbacks for Educators.

Komaiko, L. 1988. *Earl's Too Cool for Me.* New York: Harper & Row.

Korb-Khalsa, K., S. Azok, and E. Leutenberg. 1991. *Life Management Skills II.* Beachwood, OH: Wellness Reproductions Inc.

Kramer, P. 1994. *The Dynamics of Relationships.* Baltimore, MD: Equal Partners.

Kroen, W. 1996. *Helping Children Cope with the Loss of a Loved One.* Minneapolis, MN: Free Spirit.

Kübler-Ross, E. 1974. *On Death and Dying.* New York: MacMillan Publishing Co.

Lee, V. E., L. F. Winfield, and T. C. Wilson. 1991: Academic behaviors among high-achieving African-American students. *Education and Urban Society* 24, no. 1, 65–86.

Le Shan, E.J. 1976. *Learning to Say Good-Bye: When a Parent Dies.* New York: Simon and Schuster.

Long, C. 1978. *Albert's Story.* New York: Delacorte Press.

Loretta, J., and P. Keating. 1995. *After the Funeral.* New York, NY: Paulist Press.

McCully, E. A. 1984. *Picnic.* New York: Harper & Row.

McCully, E. A. 1988. *The Christmas Gift.* New York: Harper & Row.

McGinnis, E., and A. P. Goldstein. 1997. *Skillstreaming the Elementary School Child: New Strategies and Perspectives for Teaching Prosocial Skills.* (rev. ed.) Champaign, IL: Research Press.

McWhirter, J. J., et al. 1998. *At Risk Youth: A Comprehensive Response.* (2nd ed.) Pacific Grove, CA: Brooks/Cole.

Margolin, S. 1996. *Complete Group Counseling Program for Children of Divorce.* West Nyack, NY: Center for Applied Research in Education.

Mariotti, M. 1989. *Hanimations.* Brooklyn, NY: Kane/Miller Book Publishers.

Marks, A. 1995. *Good-bye, Daddy!* New York: North South Books.

Marta, S. Y., and M. Laz. 1997: *Rainbows: Facilitator Component Module.* Schaumburg, IL: Rainbows.

Masten, A., and J. Coatsworth. 1998. The development of competence in favorable and unfavorable environments: Lessons from research on successful children. *American Psychologist,* 53, (2), 205–220.

Mayer, G., and M. Mayer. 1995. *Just a Bad Day.* Westport, CT: Reader's Digest Kids.

Mellonie, B., and R. Ingpen. 1987. *Lifetimes, the Beautiful Way to Explain Death to Children.* Toronto, NY: Bantam Doubleday Dell.

Merrill, K. 1992. *School Social Behavior Scales.* Austin, TX: PRO-ED, Inc.

Michaels, B. 2000. *Bulbasaur's Bad Day.* Mahwah, NJ: Troll Associates.

Miller, B. C., et al. 1992. *Preventing Adolescent Pregnancy: Model Programs and Evaluations.* Newbury Park, CA: Sage Publications.

Monroe, R. P., and C. Ackelmire. 1998. *Why Don't We Live Together Any More?: Understanding Divorce.* St. Louis, MO: Concordia Publishing House.

Monroe, R. P., and N. Barnet. 1998. *I Have a New Family Now.* St. Louis, MO: Concordia Publishing House.

Moote, G. T., N. J. Smythe, and J. S. Wodarsky. 1999. *Social Skills Training with Youth in School Settings: A Review.* Thousand Oaks, CA: Sage Publications, Inc.

Morganette, R. 1990. *Skills for Living: Young Adolescents: Group Counseling Activities.* Champaign, IL: Research Press.

Morganette, R. S. 1994. *Skills for Living: Group Counseling Activities for Elementary Students.* Champaign, IL: Research Press.

Mosel, A. 1989. *Tikki Tikki Tembo.* New York: H. Holt and Co.

Mudy, M. 1998. *Sad Isn't Bad.* St. Meinrad, IN: Abbey Press.

Musick, J. S. 1993. *Young, Poor, and Pregnant.* New Haven, CT: Yale University Press.

Myrick, R. 1998. *Developmental Guidance and Counseling: A Practical Approach.* Minneapolis, MN: Educational Media.

National Peer Helpers Association, P.O. Box 32272, Kansas City, MO 64171, peerhelping.org.

Newcomb, A., W. Bukowski, and L. Patee. 1993. Children's peer relations: A meta-analytic review of popular, rejected, neglected, controversial, and average sociometric status. *Psychological Bulletin*, 113, 99–128.

Oates, M. 1993. *Death in the School Community: A Handbook for Counselors, Teachers, and Administrators.* Alexandria, VA: American Counseling Association.

O'Rourke, K., and J. C. Worzybt. 1996. *Support Groups for Children.* Philadelphia, PA: Accelerated Development.

Palmer, P., and D. Burke. 1994. *I Wish I Could Hold Your Hand.* Atascadero, CA: Impact Publishers Inc.

Parkinson, K., and C. Spelman. 1998. *Mama and Daddy Bears Divorce.* Morton Grove, IL: Albert Whitman and Company.

Pellowski, M. 1986. *Benny's Bad Day.* Mahwah, NJ: Troll Associates.

Peterson, J. S. 1995. *Talk With Teens About Feelings, Family, Relationships, and the Future.* Denver, CO: Free Spirit Publishing, Inc.

Pfister, M. 1992. *The Rainbow Fish.* Translated by J. Alison James. New York: North-South Books.

Poleski, T. 1983. *The Hurt.* Mahwah, NJ: Paulist Press.

Prout, S., and R. A. DeMartino. 1986. A meta-analysis of school-based studies of counseling and psychotherapy: An update. *Journal of School Psychology*, 24, 285–292.

Prout, S., and T. Prout. 1998. A meta-analysis of school-based studies of counseling and psychotherapy: An update. *Journal of School Psychology*, 36, 121–136.

Prout, T., and D. Brown. 1999. *Counseling and Psychotherapy with Children and Adolescents.* New York: John Wiley and Sons.

Rizzon-Toner, P. 1993. *Stress Management and Self-Esteem Activities* (Unit 5). New York: The Center for Applied Research in Education.

Robins, A., and P. Mayle. 1988. *Why Are We Getting a Divorce?* New York: Harmony Books.

Rogers, F., and J. Judkis. 1998. *Let's Talk About It: Divorce.* New York: Paper Star.

Rohmann, E. 1994. *Time Flies.* New York: Crown.

Rollenhagen, L. 1989. FOTP: A school transition program that works. *National Association of*

Secondary School Principals Bulletin, November, 130–132.

Romain, T. 1999. *What on Earth Do You Do When Someone Dies?* Minneapolis, MN: Free Spirit.

Rose, S. 1998. *Group Counseling with Children and Adolescents.* Thousand Oaks, CA: Sage Publications.

Rose, S. R. 1998. *Group Work with Children and Adolescents: Prevention and Intervention in School and Community Systems.* Thousand Oaks, CA: Sage Publications, Inc.

Roth, L. 1991. *Middle Level Transition: Policies, Programs, and Practices.* Reston, VA: National Association of Secondary School Principals.

Russo, M. 1992. *Alex Is My Friend.* New York: Greenwillow Books.

Schilling, D., and G. Dunne. 1992. *Understanding Me.* San Francisco, CA: Innerchoice Publishing.

Schneider, M., and J. Zuckerberg. 1996. *Difficult Questions Kids Ask and Are Too Afraid to Ask About Divorce.* Washington, MO: Fireside and Paperbacks for Educators.

Showers, P. 1991. *The Listening Walk.* New York: HarperCollins.

Shure, M. B. 1992. *I Can Problem-Solve: An Interpersonal Cognitive Problem-Solving Program.* Champaign, IL: Research Press.

Silverman, J. 1999. *Help Me Say Goodbye: Activities for Helping Kids Cope When a Special Person Dies.* Minneapolis, MN: Fairview Press.

Silverstein, S., 1964. *The Giving Tree.* New York: Harper & Row.

Simon, C. 1998. *The Good Bad Day.* Brookfield, CT: Millbrook Press.

Skivington, J., and A. Care. 1998. *Balloons for Trevor.* St. Louis, MO: Concordia Publishing House.

Slavin, R. E., N. L. Karweit, and N. A. Madden. 1989. What works for students at risk: A research synthesis. *Educational Leadership, 46* (5), 4–13.

Smead, R. 1994. *Skills for Living: Group Counseling Activities for Elementary Students.* Champaign, IL: Research Press.

Smead, R. 1995. *Skills and Techniques for Group Work with Children and Adolescents.* Champaign, IL: Research Press.

Smead, R., 2000. *Skills for Living, Volume Two: Group Counseling Activities for Young Adolescents.* Champaign, IL: Research Press.

Stern, Z., and E. Stern. 1997. *Divorce Is Not the End of the World.* Berkeley, CA: Tricycle Press.

St. Germain, S. 1990. *The Terrible Fight.* Boston, MA: Houghton Mifflin.

Steinberg, D. 1999. *Grief Group.* Ft. Lauderdale, FL: Unpublished manuscript.

Stinson, K. 1988. *Mom and Dad Don't Live Together Anymore.* Toronto, Canada: Firefly Books.

Sunburst Communications. 1991. *If Your Parents Break Up.* (videocassette): Pleasantville, NY: Sunburst Communications.

Sunburst Communications. 1993. *When You're Mad! Mad! Mad!* (videocassette) Pleasantville, NY: Sunburst Communications.

Sunburst Communications. 1995. *Anger: You Can Handle It.* (videocassette, teacher's guide) Pleasantville, NY: Sunburst Communications.

Sunburst Communications. 1995. *When Anger Turns to Rage.* (videocassette): Pleasantville, NY: Sunburst Communications.

Sunburst Communications. 1997. *Handling Your Anger.* (videocassette, teacher's guide, handouts) Pleasantville, NY: Sunburst Communications.

Sunburst Communications. 1998. *Anger Management Skills.* (videocassette) Pleasantville, NY: Sunburst Communications.

Taylor, J. F. 1994. *Anger Control Training for Children and Teens.* Warminster, PA: Mar-Co Products, Inc.

Tindall, J. 1995. *Peer Counseling.* Muncie, IN: Accelerated Development.

Tobias, S. 1995. *Overcoming Math Anxiety.* New York: Norton.

Traisman, E. S. 1992. *Fire in My Heart Ice in My Veins: A Journal for Teenagers Experiencing a Loss.* Omaha, NE: Centering Corporation.

Turkle, B. 1976. *Deep in the Forest.* New York: Dutton.

Ueno, N. 1973. *Elephant Buttons.* New York: Harper & Row.

Varley, S. 1992. *Badger's Parting Gifts.* New York: Mulberry Books.

Vernon, A. 1998. *The Passport Program: A Journey Through Emotional, Social, Cognitive, and Self-Development.* Champaign, IL: Research Press.

Vernon, A. 1989. *Thinking, Feeling, Behaving: An Emotional Education Curriculum for Children.* Champaign, IL: Research Press.

Viorst, J. 1972. *Alexander and the Terrible, Horrible, No Good, Very Bad Day.* New York: Atheneum.

Viorst, J. 1988. *The Tenth Good Thing About Barney.* New York: Aladdin.

Vollmer, D. 1988. *Joshua Disobeys.* Kansas City, MO: Landmark Editions.

Waber, B. 1972. *Ira Sleeps Over.* Boston: Houghton Mifflin.

Waber, B. 1988. *Ira Says Goodbye.* Boston: Houghton Mifflin.

Wang, M. C., G. D. Haertel, and H. J. Walberg. 1994. *Educational Resilience in Inner City America: Challenges and Prospects.* Hillsdale, NJ: Lawrence Erlbaum Associates.

Wang, M. C., G. D. Haertel, and H. J. Walberg, 1994. What helps students learn? *Educational Leadership,* 51 (4), 74–79.

Ward, L. 1973. *The Silver Pony: A Story in Pictures.* Boston: Houghton Mifflin.

Watson, J. W., R. E. Switzer, and J. C. Hirschberg. 1988. *Sometimes a Family Has to Split Up.* New York: Crown Publishers.

Weisz, J. R., et al. 1987. Effectiveness of psychotherapy with children and adolescents: A meta-analysis for clinicians. *Journal of Consulting and Clinical Psychology* 55, 542–549. EMBASE

Weisz, J. R., B. Weiss, and G. R. Donenberg. 1992. The lab versus the clinic: Effects of child and adolescent psychotherapy. *American Psychologist* 47, 1578–1585.

Weisz, J. R., et al. 1995. Effects of psychotherapy with children and adolescents revisited: A meta-analysis of treatment outcome studies. *Psychological Bulletin* 177, 450–468.

Whitehouse, E., et al. 1996. *A Volcano in My Tummy: Helping Children to Handle Anger.* Gabriola Island, BC, Canada: New Society Publishers.

Wiesner, D. 1991. *Tuesday.* New York: Clarion Books.

Wilde, J. 1994. *Hot Stuff to Help Kids Chill Out.* Washington, MO: Paperbacks for Educators.

Wilde, J. 1995. *Anger Management in Schools.* Lancaster, PA: Technomic Publishing Co.

Wilson, J. 1982. School counselor interventions with low-achieving and underachieving elementary, middle, and high school students: A review of the research literature. *The School Counselor,* 30(2), 113–120.

Wittmer, J. 1993. *Managing Your School Counseling Program.* Minneapolis, MN: Educational Media, Inc.

Wolkstein, D. 1994. *Step by Step.* New York: Morrow Junior Books.

Zimmerman, M., and R. Arunkumar. 1994. Resiliency research: Implications for schools and policy. *Social Policy Report: Society for Research in Child Development,* 8 (4), 1–17.

Ziegler, J. 1993. *Mr. Knocky.* New York: Macmillan.

Share Your Bright Ideas with Us!

We want to hear from you! Your valuable comments and suggestions will help us meet your current and future classroom needs.

Your name_____Date_____

School name_____Phone_____

School address_____

Grade level taught_____Subject area(s) taught_____Average class size_____

Where did you purchase this publication?_____

Was your salesperson knowledgeable about this product?   Yes_____   No_____

What monies were used to purchase this product?

___School supplemental budget   ___Federal/state funding   ___Personal

Please "grade" this Walch publication according to the following criteria:

Quality of service you received when purchasing	A	B	C	D	F
Ease of use	A	B	C	D	F
Quality of content	A	B	C	D	F
Page layout	A	B	C	D	F
Organization of material	A	B	C	D	F
Suitability for grade level	A	B	C	D	F
Instructional value	A	B	C	D	F

COMMENTS:_____

_____

What specific supplemental materials would help you meet your current—or future—instructional needs?

_____

Have you used other Walch publications? If so, which ones?_____

May we use your comments in upcoming communications?   ___Yes   ___No

Please **FAX** this completed form to **207-772-3105**, or mail it to:

Product Development, J. Weston Walch, Publisher, P.O. Box 658, Portland, ME 04104-0658

We will send you a **FREE GIFT** as our way of thanking you for your feedback. **THANK YOU!**

Contents

Contents

Contents

Before You Begin

Congratulations! You have in your hands a powerful tool to ensure your best chances of getting a great score on the Public Safety Dispatcher/911 Operator exam. By working through this book, taking time to practice the sample exercises, and studying the various strategies and techniques for tackling various question types, you will put yourself at a significant advantage for achieving a top-notch score.

HOW TO USE THIS BOOK

This book is designed as a teach-yourself training course, complete with test-taking tips and strategies, exercises, and two full-length Practice Tests.

Part I is a review of jobs with the municipal (city), state, and federal governments and private industry. You'll find information on the various types of public safety dispatcher careers available, with descriptions of the typical dispatcher work environment, earnings potential, and the hiring process. If you are new to public safety dispatching, the number of job opportunities available in this field may surprise you. Did you know that almost 300,000 jobs in the United States are in the field of dispatching?

Part II explains the civil service exams. It describes how to take a civil service exam and provides tips for maximizing your score. By learning about the civil service exam process, you will be better prepared to do well on your particular test.

Part III is a review of the specific types of questions you're most likely to see on the public safety dispatcher exam. Because qualifying exams for public safety dispatchers vary greatly from state to state and from one municipality to another, we cannot predict exactly what question types you'll encounter on your exam. Each sector has its own requirements and tests, but as you will see, certain types of questions will appear on most civil service exams, regardless of the type of test you're taking. If you thoroughly review the test question types in this section of the book, you will be well prepared when you take the exam. We suggest you review this section carefully to get a good idea of where your strengths and weaknesses lie, so that you'll know where to focus your studies.

Part IV provides two full-length practice tests, including detailed answer explanations for each question. These tests are closely patterned after actual public safety dispatcher exams. Time limits, level of difficulty, question styles, and scoring methods all conform to the examinations for which they are meant to prepare you.

Try to set aside the full amount of time for each exam and take it in one sitting, as you would on your actual test day. Time yourself, and stop working when time is up. Check your answers against the correct answers provided in the book. Carefully study all the answer explanations—even for questions you answered correctly. You'll develop a better understanding about how best to answer actual exam questions and the reasoning behind the correct answer choices.

Regardless of which test you think you'll be taking, try to get through all of the practice exercises and both of the full-length exams in this book. It may seem like a lot of extra work, but you never know where you may end up. You may be interested in a job with a local city government but end up working for a private company instead. Or perhaps the exam you are hoping to take will not be administered for another year, but another type of test is scheduled for next month. It's always best to be prepared.

The Appendixes at the end of the book provide information on finding and getting a job with the federal government or with a state, municipal, or local government. We also provide a glossary of definitions for some of the most important and frequently used terms you can expect to see when studying for your exam, and a list of 400 frequently misspelled words that you may encounter in the spelling section of your exam.

SPECIAL STUDY FEATURES

Master the Public Safety Dispatcher/911 Operator Exam is designed to be as user-friendly as it is complete. To this end, it includes two features to make your preparation more efficient.

Overview

Each chapter begins with a bulleted overview listing the topics covered in the chapter. This will allow you to quickly target the areas in which you are most interested.

Bonus Information

As you work your way through the book, check the margins to find bonus information and advice. You'll find the following kinds of information:

Note

Notes highlight need-to-know information about the public safety dispatcher/911 operator exams, whether it's details about applying and scoring or the structure of a question type.

Tip

Tips provide valuable strategies and insider information to help you score your best on your exam.

Alert!

Alerts do just what they say—alert you to common pitfalls and misconceptions you might face or hear regarding these exams.

Summing It Up

Each chapter ends with a point-by-point summary that reviews the most important items in the chapter. The summaries offer a convenient way to review key points.

YOU'RE WELL ON YOUR WAY TO SUCCESS

You've made the decision to become a public safety dispatcher or 911 operator. *Peterson's® Master the Public Safety Dispatcher/911 Operator Exam* will help prepare you for the steps you'll need to take to achieve your goal—from scoring high on the exam to finding the best dispatcher or operator job for you. Good luck!

GIVE US YOUR FEEDBACK

Peterson's publishes a full line of books—test prep, education exploration, financial aid, and career preparation. Peterson's publications can be found at high school guidance offices, college libraries and career centers, and your local bookstore and library. In addition, you can find Peterson's products online at www.petersonsbooks.com. Peterson's books are also available as ebooks.

We welcome any comments or suggestions you may have about this publication. Please call our customer service department at 800-338-3282 Ext. 54229 or send an e-mail message to custsvc@petersons.com. Your feedback will help us make educational dreams possible for you—and others like you.

PART I
WORKING FOR THE GOVERNMENT

Jobs with Federal, State, and Local Governments

OVERVIEW

- Where the jobs are: Federal civilian employment
- The merit system
- Where the jobs are: State and local governments
- Where to find out about government job openings
- The format of the government job announcement
- Summing it up

Government service is one of the nation's largest sources of employment. About 17 million employed persons in the United States work in some form of civilian government service. Of those government employees, over 80 percent are employed by state or local governments. The remainder work for the federal government.

Government employees represent a significant portion of the nation's workforce. They are present in cities, small towns, and remote and isolated places such as lighthouses and forest ranger stations. A small number of federal employees even work overseas. In this chapter, we will outline the various types of careers available in the federal, state, and local governments of the United States.

WHERE THE JOBS ARE: FEDERAL CIVILIAN EMPLOYMENT

According to the U.S. Census Bureau, the federal government is the nation's largest employer, with nearly 3 million full-time civilian workers in the United States, including postal employees. Although the headquarters of most federal departments and agencies are in the Washington, DC, area, eight out of ten federal jobs are located outside the nation's capital. Federal jobs exist throughout the United States—and throughout the world. In fact, approximately 90,000 federal employees work outside the United States, most of them in embassies or defense installations.

Many federal occupations are similar to jobs in the private sector, such as those in accounting, computer programming, and health care. Other types of employment opportunities are unique to the federal government, such as regulatory inspectors, Foreign Service officers, and Internal Revenue Service agents. More than 100 agencies and bureaus exist within the federal government, and each has specific employment needs. The numerous job opportunities with the federal government include careers in the executive, legislative, and judicial branches.

chapter 1

The executive branch employs the majority of federal workers. This includes the Office of the President, the cabinet departments, and about 100 independent agencies, commissions, and boards. The executive branch is responsible for administering federal laws, handling international relations, conserving natural resources, treating and rehabilitating disabled veterans, delivering U.S. mail, conducting scientific research, maintaining the flow of supplies to the Armed Forces, and administering other programs that promote the health and welfare of the people of the United States.

The Department of Defense, which includes the Joint Chiefs and the Departments of the Army, Navy, Air Force, and Marines, is the largest department in the executive branch of the federal government. It employs about 30 percent of all civilian government workers. Employees of the U.S. Postal Service account for another 20 percent of federal workers. Other federal jobs are distributed among other agencies in the government, including large employers such as the Department of Veterans Affairs, the Department of Homeland Security, and the Department of the Treasury.

Some agencies in the executive branch do not fall under the jurisdiction of these large departments. These independent agencies, such as the Social Security Administration, the National Aeronautics and Space Administration (NASA), and the Environmental Protection Agency (EPA), account for fewer than 200,000 federal jobs, but they should be considered when searching for government employment.

Federal civilian employment is also available in the legislative branch, which includes Congress, the Government Printing Office, the Government Accountability Office, and the Library of Congress. The judicial branch, the smallest employer of the federal government, hires people for work within the courts system.

Professional Occupations

Because of its wide range of responsibilities, the federal government employs professional workers in a broad variety of occupational fields. Professional jobs account for approximately 90 percent of all federal civilian jobs. According to the Bureau of Labor Statistics, one fourth of all federal employees work in management, finance, or business.

Management

Upper-level managers are responsible for directing the activities of government agencies; mid-level managers supervise various government programs and projects. Senators and legislators are considered part of management because they are responsible for overseeing the executive branch of the government.

Finance and Business

Accountants and auditors with the federal government analyze financial reports and investigate government spending and inefficiencies. The Government Accountability Office, the Internal Revenue Service, and the Department of the Treasury employ accounting experts and budget administrators.

Additional business experts work in purchasing, cataloging, storage, and supply distribution, which occur on a large scale in the federal government. These include managerial and administrative positions—such as supply management officers, purchasing officers, and inventory management specialists—and a great number of specialized clerical positions. Most of these jobs are with the Department of Defense.

NOTE

Although the headquarters of most government departments and agencies are in Washington, DC, only a small percentage of federal employees work there. Federal employees are stationed in all parts of the United States and its territories and in many other countries, as well.

Professions Requiring Specialized Training

Another one fourth of federal workers include professionals who have earned a specialized degree, including lawyers, doctors, computer experts, scientists, and engineers. The majority of these employees work in life sciences, physical sciences, or social science.

Life Sciences

Biologists, geologists, and forest technicians determine the effectiveness of new medications, predict hurricanes, and prevent forest fires in national parks and other federally owned land. The federal government, mostly in the Departments of Agriculture and Interior, employs about 60,000 biological and agricultural science workers, many of whom work in forestry and soil conservation. Others administer farm assistance programs.

Physical Sciences

The Departments of Defense, Interior, and Commerce typically employ physical scientists such as chemists, physicists, meteorologists, and cartographers. Opportunities also exist for physical science technicians, meteorological technicians, and cartography technicians.

Approximately 137,000 federal employees are nurses, surgeons, and physicians who work in hospitals or in medical, dental, and public health services. Other occupations in this field include dieticians, technologists, and physical therapists. Technician and aide jobs include medical technicians, medical laboratory aides, and dental assistants. Health-care employees work primarily for the Veterans Administration; others work for the Department of Defense and the Department of Health and Human Services.

Social Sciences

Economists and other social science experts are employed throughout the government. Psychologists and social workers work primarily for the Veterans Administration; foreign affairs and international relations specialists typically find employment with the Department of State. Social insurance administrators are employed largely by the Department of Health and Human Services.

Engineering and Mathematics

Many government departments require the expertise of engineers to construct bridges, develop computer systems, and design spacecraft. The Department of Defense employs experts in electronics, surveying, and drafting. Computer software engineers and computer network administrators are necessary throughout the government to write computer programs, analyze data, and ensure that computer systems run smoothly.

Professional mathematicians, statisticians, mathematics technicians, and statistical clerks work in the federal government, primarily with the Departments of Defense, Agriculture, Commerce, and Health and Human Services.

Law

The federal government employs thousands of people in the legal field: attorneys, paralegals, passport examiners, and tax law specialists among many others. In addition, federal positions are available for claims examiners.

Other Professional Fields

Nearly 30 percent of all federal jobs consist of office and administrative support. Employees in this area assist management with administrative duties. All federal departments and agencies employ general clerical workers, such as information and record clerks and administrative assistants. Office machine operators, stenographers, clerk-typists, mail- and file-clerks, telephone operators, and workers in computer and related occupations are categorized as office support personnel. However, according to the Bureau of Labor Statistics, administrative support jobs are declining because of the increased use of automation and computers.

Some government workers are engaged in administrative work related to private business and industry. They arrange and monitor contracts with and purchase goods and services from companies in the private sector. Administrative occupations in this area include contract and procurement specialists, production control specialists, and Internal Revenue Service officers.

Eight percent of federal employees work in service occupations, including officers at federal prisons, criminal investigators, and health regulatory inspectors, many of whom are employed by the Departments of Justice or Agriculture. Local and state governments are the primary employers of firefighters, police officers, and prison guards.

Employment Requirements

Requirements for professional jobs with the federal government vary widely, from a postsecondary degree to a high school diploma. An undergraduate or advanced degree is usually required for occupations in physics, engineering, ecology, and law. Office clerk positions may not require a specific level of education or experience; other federal jobs may require some combination of education and experience for job consideration.

Prospective employees for administrative and managerial positions are usually not required to have knowledge of a specialized field. Instead, they must indicate a potential for future development by having obtained an undergraduate degree from a four-year college or by having responsible job experience. New employees usually begin as trainees and learn their duties on the job. Typical entry-level positions in management include budget analyst, claims examiner, purchasing specialist, administrative assistant, and personnel specialist.

Job seekers with a high school diploma or the equivalent can find entry-level government work as technicians, clerical workers, or aides/assistants. Many of these positions require no previous experience or training. Entry-level positions are usually trainee spots. Individuals with junior college or technical school training or who have specialized skills may enter these occupations at higher levels. Typical jobs include engineering technicians, supply clerks, clerk-typists, and nursing assistants.

Skilled-Labor Occupations

Skilled-labor occupations in fields such as construction, janitorship, and some service jobs provide full-time employment for nearly 300,000 federal workers. About 75 percent of these government workers are employed with the Department of Defense in naval shipyards, arsenals, Army depots, and in construction, harbor, flood control, irrigation, or reclamation projects. Others work for the Veterans Administration, the Postal Service, the General Services Administration, the Department of the Interior, and the Tennessee Valley Authority.

The largest single skilled-worker group consists of manual laborers. Many others are employed in machine tool and metalwork, motor vehicle operation, warehousing, and food preparation and service. The federal government employs workers in maintenance and repair work—such as electrical and electronic equipment installation and repair—and in vehicle and industrial equipment maintenance and repair. Each of these fields requires a range of skill levels and employs workers in a variety of occupations comparable to those in the private sector.

Although the federal government employs skilled workers in many different fields, about half are concentrated within a small number of occupations. The largest group consists of skilled mechanics, who work as air-conditioning, aircraft, automobile, truck, electronics, sheet metal, and general maintenance mechanics. Another large group is employed as painters, pipefitters, carpenters, electricians, and machinists. Others are warehouse workers, truck drivers, general laborers, janitors, and food service workers.

Employment Requirements

Prospective employees who have previous training in a skilled trade may apply for a position with the federal government at the journey level. Those with no previous training may apply for appointment to one of several apprenticeship programs. These programs generally last four years, during which trainees receive classroom and on-the-job training. After completing an apprenticeship, an employee is eligible for a journey-level position. A number of federal positions require little or no prior training or experience; these include janitors, maintenance workers, and messengers.

THE MERIT SYSTEM

More than 90 percent of jobs in the federal government fall under a merit system. The Civil Service Act, administered by the U.S. Office of Personnel Management (OPM), covers six out of ten federal titles. This act was passed by Congress to ensure that federal employees are hired based on individual merit and fitness. It provides for competitive examinations and the selection of new employees from among the most qualified applicants.

Some federal jobs are exempt from civil service requirements, either by law or by action of the OPM. However, most of these positions are covered by separate merit systems for other agencies, such as the Foreign Service of the U.S. Department of State, the Federal Bureau of Investigation (FBI), the Nuclear Regulatory Commission (NRC), and the Tennessee Valley Authority (TVA).

Earnings, Advancement, and Working Conditions

Several decades ago, most federal civilian employees were paid according to one of three major pay systems: the General Pay Schedule, the Federal Wage System, or the Postal Service Schedule. Today, however, new pay plans have been developed that are unique to their individual agencies. Because we are focusing specifically on public safety dispatcher positions, we will discuss only the General Pay Schedule and the Federal Wage System as they currently operate.

General Pay Schedule

Most federal workers are paid under the General Schedule (GS), a pay scale for workers in professional, administrative, technical, and clerical jobs, as well as for those working as guards and messengers. GS jobs are divided by the OPM into fifteen grades, according to the difficulty of duties and responsibilities and the knowledge, experience, and skills required of the workers in that pay grade. GS pay rates are set by Congress, and they apply to government workers nationwide. Pay rates are reviewed annually to determine whether they are comparable to salaries of equivalent workers in the private sector. They are generally subject to upward adjustment for regions where the cost of living is very high; in areas with a low cost of living, GS pay may exceed that of private-sector workers.

Most employees receive within-grade pay increases at one-, two-, or three-year intervals if their work is acceptable. Within-grade increases may also be given in recognition of high-quality service. Some managers and supervisors receive increases based on job performance rather than on time served in a specific grade level.

High school graduates with no related work experience usually start at the GS-2 level. Some who have specialized skills begin at grade GS-3. Graduates of two-year colleges and technical schools often begin at the GS-4 level; those who have a bachelor's degree and are appointed to professional and administrative jobs such as statisticians, economists, writers and editors, budget analysts, accountants, and physicists typically enter the government workforce at grades GS-5 or GS-7, depending on experience and academic record. A master's degree, Ph.D., or equivalent experience enables people to begin working for the government at the GS-9 or GS-11 level. Advancement to higher grades generally depends upon ability, work performance, and high-level job openings.

GENERAL SCHEDULE
(Range of Salaries)

Effective as of January 1, 2015

GS Rating	Low	High
1	$18,161	$22,712
2	20,419	25,698
3	22,279	28,966
4	25,011	32,517
5	27,982	36, 379
6	31,192	40,552
7	34,662	45,057
8	38,387	49,907
9	42,399	55,116
10	46,691	60,695
11	51,298	66,688
12	61,486	79,936
13	73,115	95,048
14	86,399	112,319
15	101,630	132,122

The Federal Wage System

Most federal skilled laborers are paid according to the Federal Wage System. Under this system, craft, service, and manual workers earn hourly wages based on the local prevailing rates paid by private employers for similar work. As a result, the federal government wage rate for an occupation varies by locality. This commitment to meeting the local wage scale allows federal wage earners to bring home a weekly paycheck comparable to what they would earn in the private sector while receiving the benefits and security of a government job. The federal wage earner has the best of all possible worlds in this regard. Federal government employees work a standard 40-hour week. Employees who are required to work overtime may receive premium rates for the additional time or compensatory time off later. Most employees work 8 hours a day, five days a week, Monday through Friday. In some cases, the nature of the work requires a modified workweek. Annual earnings for most full-time federal workers are not affected by seasonal factors.

Federal employees earn thirteen days of vacation time each year during their first three years of service, twenty days each year until the end of their fifteenth year of service, and twenty-six days each year of service thereafter. In addition, workers who are members of military reserve organizations are granted up to fifteen days of paid military leave annually for training purposes. Although federal layoffs are uncommon, any federal worker who is laid off is entitled to unemployment compensation similar to what is available for employees in the private sector.

Other benefits available to most federal employees include a contributory retirement system, optional participation in low-cost group life and health insurance programs, which are partly supported by the government (as the employer), and training programs to develop maximum job proficiency and help workers achieve their highest potential. These training programs may be conducted in government facilities or at private educational facilities, at the government's expense.

WHERE THE JOBS ARE: STATE AND LOCAL GOVERNMENTS

According to the U.S. Census Bureau, state and local governments provide an enormous and expanding source of job opportunities in a wide variety of occupational fields. State and local government agencies in the United States employ about 14 million people; nearly three fourths of these employees work in units of local government, such as counties, municipalities, towns, and school districts. Job distribution varies greatly from that of federal government service. Defense, international relations and commerce, immigration, and mail delivery are virtually nonexistent in state and local governments. By contrast, state and local governments have a greater need for employees in education, health, social services, transportation, construction, and sanitation.

Educational Services

About one half of all jobs in state and local governments fall under educational services. Employees in education work in public schools, colleges, and various extension services. About 60 percent of all education workers in state and local governments are instructional personnel. School systems, colleges, and universities also employ administrative personnel, librarians, guidance counselors, nurses, dieticians, clerks, and maintenance workers.

Health Services

After educational services, the next-largest field of state and local government employment is health services. This includes physicians, nurses, medical lab technicians, dieticians, kitchen and laundry workers, and hospital attendants.

Social services make up another aspect of health and welfare. The need for workers in welfare and human services departments has increased dramatically over the past few years. As the need grows, so do the opportunities for social workers and their affiliated administrative and support staff.

Government Control/Financial Activities

Almost 1 million workers in state and local governments are employed in general governmental control and financial activities. These include chief executives and their staff workers, legislative representatives, and those in justice administration, tax enforcement and other finances, and general administration. These positions require lawyers, judges, court officers, city managers, property assessors, budget analysts, stenographers, and clerks.

Streets and Highways

Road construction and maintenance are major concerns for local and state governments. Building and maintaining roads improves the safety and efficiency of a community. Highway workers include civil engineers, surveyors, equipment operators, truck drivers, concrete finishers, carpenters, and construction laborers. In some areas of the nation, snow removers perform essential tasks. Toll collectors are usually state or county employees (unless they are employed by private firms working on behalf of a state or county). Municipal mass transit in and between cities and outlying suburbs is also the province of local government. A large and varied workforce is required to maintain and staff the vehicles, as well as to maintain the roadbeds and signaling systems.

Police and Fire Protection Services

More than 1 million people are employed in police and fire departments throughout the United States. Along with uniformed officers, local fire and police departments require the assistance of support staff, such as administrative, clerical, maintenance, and custodial personnel.

Miscellaneous State and Local Occupations

Local utilities, parks and recreation, sanitation, corrections, libraries, sewage disposal, and housing and urban renewal employ hundreds of thousands of workers in state and local governments. These jobs may require economists, electrical engineers, electricians, pipefitters, clerks, foresters, and drivers as employees.

Clerical, Administrative, Maintenance, and Custodial Workers

A great percentage of employment in local and state government agencies consists of clerical, administrative, maintenance, and custodial jobs. These include administrative assistants, data processors, IT specialists, office managers, fiscal and budget administrators, bookkeepers, accountants, carpenters, painters, plumbers, guards, and janitors, among many others.

Residents of a state or locality typically fill most positions in state and local governments because of residency requirements within each locality, although most agencies make exceptions for persons with skills that are in special demand.

Earnings

The job conditions and earnings of state and local government employees vary widely depending upon occupation and locality. Salaries vary from state to state and within each state because of differences in the prevailing wage level and the cost of living of each locality.

As with the federal government, a majority of state and local government positions are filled through some type of formal civil service test; that is, employees are hired and promoted based on merit. State and local government workers have the same protections as federal government workers: they cannot be refused employment because of race;

they cannot be denied promotion because another individual made a greater political contribution; and they cannot be let go because the boss's son or daughter needs a job. The classification level of a particular position provides the salary base. Periodic performance reviews are standard. Nearly every group of employees has access to a union or other labor organization, but the functions and powers of these units vary greatly.

Benefits packages offered to state and local government employees differ widely. These workers often participate in retirement plans or the federal social security program, and health coverage is a common benefit. Local and state employees typically work a standard 40-hour week and may earn overtime pay or compensatory time off for additional hours of work.

WHERE TO FIND OUT ABOUT GOVERNMENT JOB OPENINGS

Most federal, state, and municipal units have recruitment procedures for filling civil service positions. Agencies have developed a number of methods to publicize job opportunities. Here are some suggestions on where you can look for a government job:

1. Online federal job boards. Numerous online resources exist to assist job seekers in locating open federal positions, including the federal government's official job site at USAJOBS.gov and the U.S. Office of Personnel Management at opm.gov.

2. State Employment Offices. There are almost 2,000 state employment offices in the United States, each administered by the state in which it is located, with financial assistance from the federal government. These offices provide support for job seekers and employers. Each state employment office is named and organized differently, but their essential services are the same. You can find the address of the one closest to you in your telephone book or online.

3. Your state Civil Service Commission. Address your inquiry to the capital city of your state.

4. Your city Civil Service Commission. In cities, this commission is sometimes called by another name, such as the Department of Personnel—but you will be able to identify it in your telephone directory or online under the listing of city departments.

5. Your municipal building and your local library.

6. Complete listings are carried by newspapers such as *The Chief-Leader* (published in New York City) and by other city and statewide publications devoted to civil service employees. Many local newspapers also run a section on regional civil service news.

7. State and local agencies seeking competent employees will contact schools, professional societies, veterans' organizations, unions, and trade associations.

8. Go directly to school boards and boards of education, which employ the greatest number of all state and local personnel, for job openings in education.

You will find more in-depth information about this at the end of this book.

THE FORMAT OF THE GOVERNMENT JOB ANNOUNCEMENT

When a government position is open and a civil service examination will be administered for the position, notice of examination or a job announcement is posted (for federal jobs, announcements are posted on http://www.usajobs.gov). This announcement explains everything an applicant needs to know about the position. The announcement begins with the job title and salary. A typical announcement then describes the work, the location of the position, the education and experience requirements, the kind of examination applicants must take, and the system of rating. It may also refer to veteran preferences and age specifications. The announcement indicates which application form you should fill out, where to get the form, and where and when to file it.

Study each job announcement carefully. It will answer most of your questions about the position and will help you decide whether you are interested in and/or qualified for the job. Sample job announcements are included later in this chapter.

Don't bother applying for a position and taking the required exam if you do not want to work in the community where the job is located. If the location of a job is unappealing to you, simply continue searching. Focus on positions that will give you an opportunity to work in a place of your choice. Keep in mind that a civil service job that is close to home gives you the additional advantage of receiving preference as a local resident.

The front page of a job announcement may include the words **Optional Fields**—or sometimes just the word **Options.** This means that you have a choice of whether to apply for a particular position in which you are especially interested. It usually means that the duties of various positions are quite different even though they bear the same broad title. A public relations clerk, for example, performs different tasks than a payroll clerk, although they are in the same general area of work.

Not every announcement has options; however, in each announcement, the precise duties are described in detail, usually under the heading **Description of Work.** Make sure that these duties fall within the range of your experience and ability.

Most job requirements indicate a **deadline for filing** an application. No application mailed past a deadline date will be considered. Others may include the phrase **No Closing Date** at the top of the first page. This means that instead of adhering to a set deadline, the hiring agency will accept applications for the position until its needs are met. In some cases, a public notice is issued when a certain number of applications have been received.

Every job announcement has a detailed section on **education and experience requirements** for the particular job and for the optional fields. Make sure that in both education and experience, you meet the minimum qualifications for the position being advertised. If you do not meet the given standards for one job, other job openings may be more suitable. If you are a military veteran and the job announcement does not mention **veteran preference,** it's a good idea to inquire whether such a provision exists in your state or municipality so that you can be sure you'll receive any preference offered. In some cases, preference is given only to disabled veterans; in some jurisdictions, spouses of disabled (or deceased) veterans are given preference as well. All such information can be obtained through the agency that issues the job announcement.

Applicants may be denied examinations and eligible candidates may be denied appointments for any of the following reasons:

- making intentional false statements
- being deceptive or fraudulent in examination or appointment

TIP

The official employment website of the U.S. federal government is USAJOBS: www.usajobs.gov.

- using intoxicating beverages to the extent that ability to perform the duties of the position is impaired
- conducting oneself in a criminal, villainous, dishonest, immoral, or notoriously disgraceful manner

The announcement describes the **kind of test** given for the particular position. Pay special attention to this section, because it describes what will be included in the written test and lists the specific subjects that will be tested. Sometimes sample questions are provided—and these can be extremely helpful in preparing for your test.

Usually, a job announcement states whether the examination is to be **assembled** or **unassembled.** In an assembled examination, applicants gather in the same place at the same time to take a written or performance test. In an unassembled examination, an applicant does not take a test; instead, he or she receives a rating based on education, experience, and records of previous achievements.

In an assembled competitive examination, all applicants for a position compete with one another—meaning that the higher your score, the better your chance of being appointed. (Competitive examinations are also administered to determine an existing employee's eligibility for promotion.)

Civil service written tests are graded on a scale of 1–100, with 70 usually considered a passing score.

Filling Out the Application Form

You've studied a job announcement carefully and you've decided that you want the position and are qualified for it. Your next step is to get an application form or to apply online. The job announcement indicates how to acquire the application.

Overall, civil service application forms differ little between states and localities. The questions tend to be simple and direct, and they are designed to elicit as much information as possible about the applicant. Many prospective civil service employees have failed to get the job they wanted because of slipshod, erroneous, incomplete, misleading, or untruthful answers. Give each application serious attention—it is the first and most important step to getting the job you want.

Here, along with some helpful comments, are the questions you will see on the average application form (although not necessarily in this order):

- **Name of examination or kind of position for which applying.** This information appears in large type on the first page of the job announcement.
- **Optional job** (if mentioned in the announcement). If you wish to apply for an option, simply copy the title from the announcement. If you are not interested in an option, write None.
- **Primary place of employment for which applying.** The location of the position is usually mentioned in the announcement. The announcement may list more than one location in which the same job is available. If you would accept employment in any of the places, list them all; otherwise, list the specific place or places where you would be willing to work.
- **Name and address.** Provide your full name, including your middle name and/or maiden name if applicable.
- **Home and office phones.** If none, write None.

NOTE

On your application, you may be asked whether someone may contact your present employer. If you say no, it will not affect your employment opportunities—but try to provide some form of evaluation or letter of recommendation to compensate.

- **Legal or voting residence.** The state in which you vote is the one you list here.
- **Height without shoes, weight, sex.** Answer accurately.
- **Date of birth.** Give the exact day, month, and year of your birth.
- **Lowest grade or pay you will accept.** Although the salary is clearly stated in the job announcement, there may be another opening in the same occupation with less responsibility and a lower entrance salary. You will not be considered for a job paying less than the amount you provide as an answer to this question.
- **Will you accept temporary employment if offered you for (a) one month or less, (b) one to four months, (c) four to twelve months?** Temporary positions arise frequently. Decide whether you want to be available should one open up.
- **Will you accept less than full-time employment?** Part-time work comes up occasionally. Consider whether you want to accept such a position while waiting for a full-time position.
- **Were you in active military service in the Armed Forces of the United States?** Veteran's preference, if given, is usually limited to active duty service during a war or during particular service periods. If you are a veteran, you may qualify for 5-point preference or 10-point preference, depending on whether you meet specific criteria.
- **Do you claim disabled veterans credit?** If you do, you have to show proof of a war-incurred disability compensable by at least 10 percent. This is done via certification by the Veterans Administration.
- **Special qualifications and skills.** Even though these are not directly related to the position for which you are applying, the agency requests information about licenses and certificates obtained for teacher, pilot, registered nurse, and other positions. List your experience in machinery and equipment and whatever other skills you may have acquired. Also list any published writings, public speaking experience, membership in professional societies, and honors and fellowships you may have received.
- **Education.** List your entire educational history, including all diplomas, degrees, and special courses taken in any accredited or Armed Forces school. Also provide information regarding any additional college or graduate-level course credits you have earned.
- **References.** List the names of people who can provide information about you, including their occupation, business address, and contact information.
- **Medical history.** You are expected to have the physical and psychological capacity to perform the job for which you are applying. Standards vary, of course, depending on the requirements of the position. A physical handicap usually will not bar an applicant from a job unless the safety of the public is involved.
- **Work history.** Considerable space is allotted on the form for applicants to describe previous employment experiences. Examiners check these answers closely, so don't embellish or falsify your history. If you were ever fired, say so. It is better for you to state this openly than for the examiners to find out the truth from a former employer.

Many civil service applications for jobs at all levels of government are now processed online. To give you an idea of the questions asked, the following pages contain hard copy samples of an Ohio Civil Service Application for State and County Agencies and a state application from Louisiana.

TIP

Include a college transcript only if the job announcement requests one.

TIP

Experience you acquired more than fifteen years ago may be summarized in one block if it is not applicable to the type of position for which you are applying.

Ohio Civil Service Application
for State and County Agencies
GEN-4268 (REVISED 01/12)

The State of Ohio is an Equal Opportunity Employer and provider of ADA services.

POSITION:	AGENCY:	POSITION NUMBER:

Please submit one application per position or examination to the address indicated on the job posting or examination announcement. Copies are acceptable. Applications lacking sufficient information will not be processed. Please ensure your application is received or postmarked by the closing date, as required by the hiring agency. Please be sure to complete the entire application. Also note that, once submitted to a governmental agency, this completed form will be subject to all applicable public records laws.

PLEASE TYPE OR PRINT IN INK

NAME: (Last, First, Middle)	DATE OF BIRTH - Year Not Required Month Day

ADDRESS: (Street, City, State, ZIP Code)

HOME PHONE:	ALTERNATE PHONE:	E-MAIL ADDRESS:

DRIVER'S LICENSE: ☐ Yes ☐ No STATE: CLASS:	LEGAL RIGHT TO WORK IN THE U. S.: ☐ Yes ☐ No

PREFERENCES

PREFERRED SALARY:

ARE YOU WILLING TO RELOCATE?
☐ Yes ☐ No ☐ Maybe

WHAT TYPE OF JOB ARE YOU LOOKING FOR?
☐ Regular ☐ Temporary

TYPES OF WORK YOU WILL ACCEPT:
☐ Full-Time ☐ Part-Time

SHIFTS YOU WILL ACCEPT:
☐ Day ☐ Evening ☐ Night ☐ Rotating ☐ Weekends ☐ On Call (as needed)

EDUCATION

HIGH SCHOOL NAME:	LOCATION: (City, State)	DID YOU GRADUATE? ☐ Yes ☐ No
CHECK YEAR COMPLETED: ☐ 9 ☐ 10 ☐ 11 ☐ 12		OBTAINED GED? ☐ Yes ☐ No

SCHOOL NAME (College/University):		LOCATION: (City, State)
CHECK YEAR COMPLETED: ☐ 1 ☐ 2 ☐ 3 ☐ 4 ☐ 5 ☐ 6	DID YOU GRADUATE? ☐ Yes ☐ No	MAJOR:
DEGREE RECEIVED:		NUMBER OF QUARTER/SEMESTER HOURS COMPLETED:

SCHOOL NAME (College/University):		LOCATION: (City, State)
CHECK YEAR COMPLETED: ☐ 1 ☐ 2 ☐ 3 ☐ 4 ☐ 5 ☐ 6	DID YOU GRADUATE? ☐ Yes ☐ No	MAJOR:
DEGREE RECEIVED:		NUMBER OF QUARTER/SEMESTER HOURS COMPLETED:

SCHOOL NAME (College/University):		LOCATION: (City, State)
CHECK YEAR COMPLETED: ☐ 1 ☐ 2 ☐ 3 ☐ 4 ☐ 5 ☐ 6	DID YOU GRADUATE? ☐ Yes ☐ No	MAJOR:
DEGREE RECEIVED:		NUMBER OF QUARTER/SEMESTER HOURS COMPLETED:

EMPLOYMENT HISTORY

Please list your work experience beginning with your most recent employment. Military experience and volunteer work may also be included as employment. **NOTE:** To be considered for employment, you must fill in the information below, accurately and completely. You may submit a résumé *in addition* to completing this section. If applying for a civil service examination, only the information provided below will be considered. A résumé may not be used. **If you need additional space, attach extra sheets to this application.**

DATES: From: To:	EMPLOYER:	POSITION TITLE:
ADDRESS: (Street, City, State, ZIP Code)		
COMPANY URL:	PHONE NUMBER:	SUPERVISOR:
HOURS PER WEEK:	SALARY:	MAY WE CONTACT THIS EMPLOYER: ☐ Yes ☐ No
DUTIES:		
REASON FOR LEAVING:		

DATES: From: To:	EMPLOYER:	POSITION TITLE:
ADDRESS: (Street, City, State, ZIP Code)		
COMPANY URL:	PHONE NUMBER:	SUPERVISOR:
HOURS PER WEEK:	SALARY:	MAY WE CONTACT THIS EMPLOYER: ☐ Yes ☐ No
DUTIES:		
REASON FOR LEAVING:		

DATES: From: To:	EMPLOYER:	POSITION TITLE:
ADDRESS: (Street, City, State, ZIP Code)		
COMPANY URL:	PHONE NUMBER:	SUPERVISOR:
HOURS PER WEEK:	SALARY:	MAY WE CONTACT THIS EMPLOYER: ☐ Yes ☐ No
DUTIES:		
REASON FOR LEAVING:		

EMPLOYMENT HISTORY (Continued)

DATES: From: To:	EMPLOYER:	POSITION TITLE:
ADDRESS: (Street, City, State, ZIP Code)		
COMPANY URL:	PHONE NUMBER:	SUPERVISOR:
HOURS PER WEEK:	SALARY:	MAY WE CONTACT THIS EMPLOYER: ☐ Yes ☐ No
DUTIES:		
REASON FOR LEAVING:		

DATES: From: To:	EMPLOYER:	POSITION TITLE:
ADDRESS: (Street, City, State, ZIP Code)		
COMPANY URL:	PHONE NUMBER:	SUPERVISOR:
HOURS PER WEEK:	SALARY:	MAY WE CONTACT THIS EMPLOYER: ☐ Yes ☐ No
DUTIES:		
REASON FOR LEAVING:		

CERTIFICATES AND LICENSES

TYPE:	
LICENSE NUMBER:	ISSUING AGENCY:
TYPE:	
LICENSE NUMBER:	ISSUING AGENCY:

SKILLS

OFFICE SKILLS: Typing Speed: Data Entry Speed:
COMPUTER SKILLS:
OTHER SKILLS:
LANGUAGE(S):

The purpose of questions 1-11 is to obtain information relevant to employment with the State of Ohio. **Responses to these questions are required.**

1. Please indicate your county of residence. _____

2. **Summary of Qualifications** - In the area below, briefly describe the experience, education, training and other factors that qualify you for the position or examination for which you are applying. Refer to the **Minimum Qualifications** and any **position-specific qualifications** posted for this position or examination. If you need additional space, attach an extra sheet to this application.

3. Please list below the specific course work areas at the high school level or beyond relevant to the position or examination for which you are applying. Also indicate the number of courses you have successfully completed in each area. **Note:** A transcript may not be substituted for this section, although you may be required to submit a transcript.

4. Are you a current State of Ohio employee?
   ____Yes, I'm a permanent employee
   ____Yes, I'm an interim or intermittent employee
   ____Yes, I'm a temporary, seasonal or project employee
   ____Yes, I'm a fixed term or established term employee
   ____No, I'm not a State of Ohio employee

5. If you are a current State of Ohio employee, please provide your eight (8) digit, OAKS ID number. If you are not a current State of Ohio employee, **please type N/A.** _____

6. If you are not a current State of Ohio employee, have you ever been employed by the State of Ohio? (If you are a current State of Ohio employee, please select N/A.)
   ____ Yes ____ No ____N/A

7. If you were previously employed by the State of Ohio, please choose one of the following:
   ____ Employment ended prior to 12-01-2004.
   ____ Employment ended on or after 12-01-2004.
   ____ N/A - Not previously employed by the State of Ohio or current state employee.

8. If you were previously employed by the State of Ohio, have you ever plead guilty or been convicted of a misdemeanor, for violation of Ohio Revised Code 1347.15 (H)(1) and/or (H)(2) - Access rules for confidential personal information?
   ____ Yes ____ No

9. Have you ever been convicted of a felony? (A felony conviction may not automatically exclude you from consideration.)
   ____ Yes ____No

10. If you answered Yes to the previous question, please give date(s) of conviction(s) and explain. **If you answered No, please type N/A.**

11. How did you learn about this employment or examination opportunity?
   ____ careers.ohio.gov   ____ Monster.com   ____ Trade journal   ____ Walk-in
   ____ Ohiomeansjobs.com   ____ Other Internet Web site ____ State of Ohio Employee Referral   ____ Other
   ____ GovernmentJobs.com   ____ Newspaper   ____ Civil Service test announcement

CERTIFICATION

I certify that the answers I have made to all of the questions in this application are true and complete to the best of my knowledge. I understand that if this application is not completed in its entirety, it will not be processed and I will be automatically disqualified. I understand that I am responsible for the correctness of this application. I also understand that a background check may be required prior to employment and that, in accordance with the Drug-Free Workplace Program, drug testing may be required. I waive all provisions of law forbidding colleges or universities which I attended, or past employers, from disclosing any information which they acquired relevant to my employment. I consent that they may disclose such information to the Human Resources Division, Ohio Department of Administrative Services, and/or the agency that holds the vacancy for which I am applying and to appropriate officials for recruitment purposes. I understand that any offer of employment is conditional upon proof of legal authorization to work in the United States as required by the Immigration Reform and Control Act.

Signature of Applicant _____ Date _____

STATE OF OHIO
EQUAL EMPLOYMENT OPPORTUNITY

Responses to questions 12-17 are **OPTIONAL**. These questions are included to assist our equal employment opportunity efforts. Providing this information is **VOLUNTARY** and will in no way affect the processing of your application or your being considered for employment. Human Resources will process your responses to these confidential questions separately. Responses will be used for statistical purposes only.

Position Applied For _____   Date _____

Agency _____   Position Number_____

12. **OPTIONAL**: Sex

___Male   ___Female

13. **OPTIONAL**: Please select your age group.

☐ Under 18
☐ 18-25
☐ 26-39
☐ 40-54
☐ 55-69
☐ 70+

14. **OPTIONAL**: Race/Ethnicity

☐ **WHITE**: All persons having origins in any of the original peoples of Europe, North Africa or the Middle East.

☐ **BLACK or AFRICAN AMERICAN**: All persons having origins in any of the Black racial groups of Africa.

☐ **HISPANIC or LATINO**: All persons of Mexican, Puerto Rican, Cuban, Central or South America or other Spanish culture or origin, regardless of race.

☐ **ASIAN**: All persons having origins in any of the original peoples of the Far East, Southeast Asia, the Indian Subcontinent (for example, China, India, Japan and Korea).

☐ **NATIVE HAWAIIAN or PACIFIC ISLANDER**: All persons having origins in any of the original peoples of the Hawaiian Islands and Pacific Islands (for example, Hawaii, Philippine Islands and Samoa).

☐ **AMERICAN INDIAN or ALASKAN NATIVE**: All persons having origins in any of the original peoples of North America and who maintain cultural identification through tribal affiliation or community recognition.

☐ **OTHER**: Please self define. _____

15. **OPTIONAL**: Are you an individual with a physical or mental impairment which substantially limits one or more of your major life activities?

___Yes   ___No

16. **OPTIONAL**: Are you a veteran?

___Yes   ___No

17. **OPTIONAL**: If you answered Yes to the previous question, please indicate if one or more of the following apply.

☐ **MILITARY STATUS**: The performance of duty in a uniformed service, to include active duty, active duty for training, initial active duty for training, inactive duty for training, full-time National Guard duty.

☐ **DISABLED VETERAN**: A person whose discharge or release from active duty was for a disability incurred or aggravated in the line of duty.

☐ **DESERT STORM/SHIELD VETERAN**: A person whose active duty was performed after August 2, 1990, in the Persian Gulf Conflict.

☐ **VIETNAM ERA VETERAN**: A person served on active duty for a period of more than 180 days, any part of which occurred between August 5, 1964, and May 7, 1975.

State of Louisiana
Employment Application

civilservice.la.gov

Position applying for: (Please print and attach supplemental questions included in the posting for which you are applying)

*Job Title: _____

*Agency: _____ *Location: _____

Contact Information

*Name _____

                First   Middle Initial   Last

*Mailing Address _____

             Street   City   State   Zp Code

*Email Address _____

*Home Phone _____ Alternative Phone _____

*Social Security Number (Full # Required) _____

*By which method would you prefer to be notified about application status, testing dates and examination results? (Note: if you select 'E-mail,' you may still continue to receive paper notices from certain employers, depending on their preference.)

Please check one of the following options: _____ E-mail   _____ Mail

Other Personal Information

*Do you possess a valid Driver's License? (Please check one)

_____ Yes, I possess a valid Driver's License.   _____ No, I do not possess a valid Driver's License.

If Yes, Please provide the State and number _____

*Class: _____1   _____2   _____3   _____4   _____A   _____A CDL

        _____B   _____B CDL   _____C   _____C CDL   _____CM   _____D

        _____E   _____E (Learner)   _____F   _____M1   _____M2

        _____Motorcycle   _____R   _____None

I consent to the release of information concerning my capacity and/or all aspects of prior job performance by employers, educational institutions, law enforcement agencies, and other individuals and agencies to duly accredited investigators, human resources staff, and other authorized employees of the state government for the purpose of determining my eligibility and suitability for employment.

I certify that all statements made on this application and any attached papers are true and complete to the best of my knowledge. I understand that the information on this application may be subject to investigation and verification and that any misrepresentation or material omission may cause my application to be rejected, my name to be removed from the eligible register and/or subject me to dismissal from state service.
I have read the statements above carefully before signing this application:

Signature of Applicant _____ **Date** _____

* Required field

Additional Information

*Can you, after employment, submit proof of your legal right to work in the United States? (Please check one)
_____Yes   _____No

*Please check the types of employment you will accept:_____Permanent   _____Temporary

Certificates and Licenses

Type	License Number	Issued By	Date Issued	Date Expires

Additional Skills _____

_____

*Are you currently at least 18 years old?_____Yes   _____No

The State of Louisiana requests the information below so we may comply with federal Equal Employment Opportunity law requirements. The information is strictly voluntary and in no way influences employment prospects.

Gender:_____Male   _____Female   _____Decline to state

Ethnicity:_____Hispanic or Latino   _____Non-Hispanic or Non-Latino   _____Decline to state

Race:_____White/Caucasian   _____Asian   _____American Indian/Alaskan Native

_____Black or African American   _____Native Hawaiian or other Pacific Islander

_____2 or more races   _____Decline to state

Date of Birth (Month/Day/Year):_____/_____/_____

How did you find out about this job?   _____Civil Service website   _____Paper announcement at agency
_____Newspaper ad   _____Flier_____Career Fair   _____Word of mouth _____Other
Please select all that apply to you:
_____I am a certified Vocational Rehabilitation Client. (Rule 22.8(a))
_____I have a 3.5 GPA or higher for my baccalaureate degree. (Rule 22.8(c))
_____I am an active duty member of the armed forces, or a veteran of the armed forces who has served at least
      90 days of active service for purposes other than training and who has been honorably discharged from active
      duty within the previous 12 months. (Rule 22.8(d))
_____I am eligible for Non-competitive Re-employment. (Rule 23.13)
_____I am a current permanent classified state employee in a job which requires the same Civil Service test as this
      vacancy, and I have been in this job for at least the last six months.
_____None of the above.
*Are you an *Army Pays* participant?   _____Yes   _____No
*Are you claiming Veteran's Preference points on this application?   _____Yes   _____No
If claiming Veteran's Preference points, were you honorably discharged or discharged under honorable conditions
from the Armed Forces of the United States?   _____Yes   _____No   _____Does not apply
Are you an honorably discharged veteran who served either in peace or in war and who has one or more
disabilities recognized as service-connected by the Veteran's Administration?   _____Yes   _____No

Required field

During which period did you serve? (check all that apply)

_____In the wartime period April 6, 1917 through November 11, 1918

_____In the wartime period September 16, 1940 through July 25, 1947

_____In the wartime period June 27, 1950 through January 31, 1955

_____In the wartime period July 1, 1958 through May 7, 1975

_____In a peacetime campaign or expedition for which campaign badges are authorized

_____Post 09/11/01 for 90 days or more and for purposes other than training

_____Does not apply/None of the above

Please select all that apply:

_____I am the spouse of a veteran whose physical condition precludes his or her appointment to a civil service job in his or her usual line of work.

_____I am the unmarried widow of a deceased veteran who served in a war period as defined in the question above, or in a peacetime campaign or expedition.

_____I am the un-remarried widowed parent of any person who died in active wartime or peacetime service or who suffered total and permanent disability in active wartime or peacetime service.

_____I am the divorced or separated parent of any person who died in wartime or peacetime service or who became totally and permanently disabled in wartime or peacetime service.

_____None of the above

*Are you currently holding or running for an elective public office?   _____Yes   _____No

*Have you ever been on probation or sentenced to jail/prison as a result of a felony conviction or guilty plea to a felony charge?   _____Yes   _____No

If "Yes", please give the law enforcement authority (city, police, sheriff, FBI, etc.), the offense, place, and disposition of case below.

_____

*Have you ever been fired from a job or resigned to avoid dismissal?_____Yes   _____No
If "Yes", please explain below. A "Yes" answer will not necessarily bar you from state employment.

_____

*If you are a male from the ages 18 through 25, please answer the following question "Yes" or "No". If you are not a male in this group, select "Does not apply". Are you registered with the Selective Service System?

_____Yes   _____No   _____Does not apply

In which parishes are you available for employment?

			_____Acadia	_____Allen	_____Ascension
_____Assumption	_____Avoyelles	_____Beauregard	_____Bienville	_____Bossier	_____Caddo
_____Calcasieu	_____Caldwell	_____Cameron	_____Catahoula	_____Claiborne	_____Concordia
_____DeSoto	_____E. Baton Rouge	_____E. Carroll	_____E. Feliciana	_____Evangeline	_____Franklin
_____Grant	_____Iberia	_____Iberville	_____Jackson	_____Jefferson	_____Jeff Davis
_____Lafayette	_____Lafourche	_____LaSalle	_____Lincoln	_____Livingston	_____Madison
_____Morehouse	_____Natchitoches	_____Orleans	_____Ouachita	_____Plaquemines	_____Pointe Coupee
_____Rapides	_____Red River	_____Richland	_____Sabine	_____St. Bernard	_____St. Charles
_____St. Helena	_____St. James	_____St. John	_____St. Landry	_____St. Martin	_____St. Mary
_____St. Tammany	_____Tangipahoa	_____Tensas	_____Terrebonne	_____Union	_____Vermillion
_____Vernon	_____Washington	_____Webster	_____W. Baton Rouge	_____W. Carroll	_____W. Feliciana
_____Winn					

Required field

Education

*High School Name_____ Location_____

Have you received a high school diploma or equivalency certificate?_____Yes _____No

Give the name and address of the school, major course of study, and degree achieved:

Undergraduate University _____   Graduate School_____

College Major _____   Area of Study _____

Degree Attained_____   Degree Attained _____

Year_____   Year_____

Undergraduate Semester Hours Completed	Undergraduate Quarter Hours Completed	Graduate Semester Hours Completed	Graduate Quarter Hours Completed

Work History

Describe your work experience, beginning with your current or most recent job. Include military service, volunteer work, self-employment, and part-time employment.

1. Name of Present or Last
Employer_____

Job Title_____

Address_____   _____

Phone_____Supervisor _____

From (Month/Year)_____/_____To_____/_____Hours Per Week _____

Salary _____   Number of Employees Supervised _____

May we contact this employer?_____Yes_____No

Job Duties (give details)

_____

_____

_____

Reason For Leaving_____

2. Your Next Most Recent
Employer_____

Job Title_____

Address_____

Phone_____Supervisor _____

From (Month/Year)_____/_____To_____/_____Hours Per Week _____

Salary _____   Number of Employees Supervised _____

May we contact this employer?_____Yes_____No

Required field

Job Duties (give details)

_____

_____

Reason For Leaving_____

3. Your Next Most Recent

Employer_____

Job Title_____

Address_____

Phone_____Supervisor _____

From (Month/Year)_____/_____To_____/_____Hours Per Week _____

Salary _____   Number of Employees Supervised _____

May we contact this employer?_____Yes_____No

Job Duties (give details)

_____

_____

Reason For Leaving_____

4. Your Next Most Recent

Employer_____

Job Title_____

Address_____

Phone_____Supervisor _____

From (Month/Year)_____/_____To_____/_____Hours Per Week _____

Salary _____   Number of Employees Supervised _____

May we contact this employer?_____Yes_____No

Job Duties (give details)

_____

_____

Reason For Leaving_____

5. Your Next Most Recent

Employer_____

Job Title_____

Address_____

Phone_____Supervisor _____

From (Month/Year)_____/_____To_____/_____Hours Per Week _____

Salary _____   Number of Employees Supervised _____

May we contact this employer?_____Yes_____No

Job Duties (give details)

_____

_____

Reason For Leaving_____

Required field

SUMMING IT UP

- The government is one of the nation's largest sources of employment, with about 17 million employed people working in some type of civilian government service. Government employees work in cities, small towns, and remote and isolated places; some work overseas.

- Many federal occupations are similar to jobs in the private sector, such as those in accounting, computer programming, and health care. Others are unique to the federal government, such as regulatory inspectors, Foreign Service officers, and Internal Revenue Service agents.

- The executive branch of the federal government employs the majority of federal workers. The Department of Defense, the largest department in the executive branch, employs about 30 percent of all civilian government workers; the U.S. Postal Service accounts for another 20 percent.

- Federal civilian employment is also available in the legislative branch, which includes Congress, the Government Printing Office, the Government Accountability Office, and the Library of Congress. The judicial branch, the smallest employer of the federal government, hires people for work within the courts system.

- Professional positions account for approximately 90 percent of all federal civilian jobs and include work in management, finance, business, law, medicine, computer technology, the sciences, and engineering. All federal departments and agencies employ general clerical workers, some of whom arrange and monitor contracts with and purchase goods and services from private industries.

- Requirements for professional federal jobs vary from a postsecondary degree to a high school diploma. An undergraduate or advanced degree is usually required for specialized occupations in areas such as physics, engineering, ecology, and law. Office clerk positions may not require a specific level of education or experience; other federal jobs may require some combination of education and experience.

- More than 90 percent of jobs in the federal government fall under the merit system, established by an act of Congress to ensure that federal employees are hired based on individual merit.

- Most federal workers are paid under the General Schedule (GS). GS jobs are divided into fifteen grades, according to the difficulty of duties and responsibilities and the knowledge, experience, and skills required of the workers in that pay grade. GS pay rates are set by Congress, and they apply to government workers nationwide.

- State and local government agencies in the United States employ about 14 million people, three fourths of whom work in counties, municipalities, towns, and school districts. State and local governments have a greater need than does the federal government for employees in education, health, social services, transportation, construction, and sanitation.

- Most federal, state, and municipal government units have recruitment procedures for filling civil service positions. The best places to seek a government job include federal online job resources, state employment offices, your state's or city's Civil Service Commission, your local municipal building or public library, job newspapers such as New York City's *The Chief-Leader*, schools, professional societies, veterans' organizations, unions, trade associations, and local boards of education.

- Follow the steps outlined in this chapter to learn how to read government job announcements and apply for desired positions. The announcement will tell you whether you need to take a test to qualify for consideration and what kind of test it will be. In an assembled competitive examination, all applicants for a position compete with one another; the higher your score, the better your chance of being appointed.

What Public Safety Dispatchers and 911 Operators Do

OVERVIEW

- The nature of the work
- Employment and job outlook
- The public safety dispatcher hiring process
- Summing it up

THE NATURE OF THE WORK

Public Safety Dispatcher, 911 Operator, Police Communications Technician, E911 Call-taker/Dispatcher (in New York City), and other similar job titles refer to people who collect information about emergency situations and relay that information to the divisions that can provide emergency help. Clearly, those who manage emergency assistance control centers serve a vital public purpose. They earn good wages, and they gain the psychological reward of knowing that they are truly helping people.

Dispatchers act as a link between the public requesting assistance and the appropriate service provider. They see that each request for service is carried out quickly and accurately. Their specific duties depend on the type of service being rendered.

Police, fire, and ambulance dispatchers—called public safety dispatchers—are usually the first people contacted in an emergency. They receive reports from the public concerning crimes, fires, and medical emergencies; broadcast orders to units near the scene of the event to respond or investigate; and relay information or orders to proper officials. Public safety dispatchers manage emergency calls in a variety of settings, including police stations, fire stations, hospitals or other health care centers, and centralized city communications centers.

In many cities, the police department serves as the communications center. In such situations, all 911 calls go to the police department, where a dispatcher handles the emergency police-related calls and screens all other calls before transferring them to the appropriate service or department. Dispatchers carefully question each caller to determine the type, seriousness, and location of the emergency. The dispatcher then quickly determines the type and number of response units needed, locates the closest and most suitable ones, and sends them to the scene of the emergency.

chapter 2

Dispatchers remain in contact with response units until the emergency has been handled, in case further instructions are needed. When appropriate, they stay in close contact with other service providers as well. For example, a police dispatcher would monitor the response of the fire department during a major fire. In a medical emergency, dispatchers stay in contact not only with the responding ambulance team but also with the caller who reported the emergency. They often provide extensive first-aid instructions while the caller is waiting for the ambulance. Dispatchers give continual updates on the patient's condition to ambulance personnel and provide a link between the medical staff at the hospital where a patient will be taken and the emergency medical technicians in the ambulance.

For more helpful information about the nature of public safety dispatcher work, you may want to explore the following options:

- Do a "sit along" or "ride along" with one or more emergency agencies.

- Attend a citizen's academy and find out about any 911 courses you can complete online.

- Take one or more criminal justice courses.

The following is a typical job description for a police communications technician. Read through it for additional insight into the duties and responsibilities associated with public safety dispatchers.

Typical Job Description

Police Communications Technician Occupational Group

Police Communications Technician

GENERAL STATEMENT OF DUTIES AND RESPONSIBILITIES

In a police department, under direct supervision, serves as an emergency operator and radio dispatcher; performs all clerical, administrative, and other duties related to the provision of emergency service; performs related work.

Incumbents may be required to work varied tours—including nights, weekends, and holidays—depending upon the needs of the department.

EXAMPLES OF TASKS

- Receives calls from the public for emergency assistance.

- Evaluates each call for assistance; checks accuracy of information with caller, and checks computer for prior entries on incorrect or incomplete information that may have been entered.

- Inputs information into computer terminal.

- Operates computer terminal and other equipment in support of the request for emergency assistance.

continued

- Maintains liaison with other emergency services for the provision of appropriate assistance.

- Refers callers to other agencies for provision of nonemergency assistance.

- Operates computer, radio, telephone, FATN, and other equipment as required.

- Consults computer to ascertain pending assignments and changing situations.

- Dispatches police resources to emergencies.

- Interacts with operating personnel to provide and receive information and assistance in support of the provision of emergency response.

- Reviews priority listing of assignments for accuracy and possible reevaluation of priority codes.

- Communicates with other agencies concerning involvement in emergency situations.

- Performs responsible clerical duties and maintains statistics in support of the 911 emergency function.

- Operates office apparatus, including telephone, alarm board, and related equipment.

- Maintains logbooks, receipt books, and other records and ledgers.

- Reviews and verifies written information and writes reports and other communication documents.

- Instructs and assists other personnel in the performance of their duties.

- Attends training sessions.

QUALIFICATION REQUIREMENTS

1. High school graduation or evidence of having passed an examination for a High School Equivalency Diploma or United States Armed Forces GED certificate with a score of at least 35 on each of the five tests and an overall score of at least 225 in the examination for the certificate, plus the following:

   - one year of full-time experience performing clerical duties, **or**

   - one year of full-time paid responsible experience in public contact work requiring the obtaining of information from persons, **or**

   - the successful completion of 30 college credits in an accredited college, **or**

   - two years of active military duty.

2. Education and/or experience equivalent to "1" above. However, high school graduation or its equivalent as described above is required of all candidates. In addition, all candidates will be required to pass a qualifying fitness assessment.

Physical Requirements

A public safety dispatcher must have keen hearing. He or she must be able to filter out a message even with a great deal of background noise or interference on the phone line. In this position, a worker seldom has the luxury of asking the caller to repeat his or her message. Because good hearing is so important, many jurisdictions administer a hearing test to applicants. Poor hearing may disqualify a candidate.

A speech impairment may also lead to a candidate's disqualification. During emergencies, dispatchers must speak on the telephone to citizens who need assistance and to police officers, firefighters, and other emergency personnel. It is imperative that a dispatcher be easily understood by those he or she is assisting.

Work Environment

The work of dispatchers can be very hectic, especially when many calls come in at the same time. The job of public safety dispatchers is particularly stressful because a slow or improper response to a call may result in serious injury or further harm to another person or people. Callers who are anxious, panicky, or afraid may become too excited or upset to provide needed information; in such difficult circumstances, some may even become abusive. Despite such challenges, dispatchers must remain calm, objective, and in control of the situation.

Dispatchers sit for long periods, using telephones, computers, and two-way radios. Much of their time is spent at video display terminals, viewing monitors, and observing traffic patterns. Because they work for long stretches with computers and other electronic equipment, dispatchers may experience significant eyestrain and back discomfort.

Most dispatchers work a 40-hour week; however, rotating shifts and compressed work schedules are common in this line of work. Alternative work schedules are necessary to accommodate evening, weekend, and holiday work and 24-hours-a-day, seven-days-a-week operations.

Most public safety dispatchers are entry-level workers who are trained on the job and need no more than a high school diploma. However, many states require specialized training or certification.

Education and Training

Public safety dispatchers usually develop the necessary skills on the job. This informal training lasts from several days to a few months, depending on the complexity of the position. While working with an experienced dispatcher, new employees monitor calls and learn how to operate a variety of communications equipment, including telephones, two-way radios, and various wireless devices. As trainees gain confidence, they are permitted to handle calls themselves. Many public safety dispatchers also participate in structured training programs sponsored by an employer. Increasingly, public safety dispatchers are also trained in stress and crisis management as well as in family counseling. The skills they learn from this training help them provide more effective services to others—and these skills also help them manage the stress that comes with the work they do.

Licensure

Several states require their public safety dispatchers to undergo specific types of training or secure certification from a professional association. Certification often requires several months in a classroom for instruction in computer-assisted dispatching and other emerging technologies, in addition to courses on radio dispatching and stress management.

Other Qualifications

State or local government civil service regulations usually govern police, fire, and emergency medical dispatching job requirements. Candidates for these positions may have to pass written, oral, and performance tests. They may also be asked to attend training classes to qualify for advancement. Residency in the city or county of employment is often required for public safety dispatchers.

Communication skills and the ability to work under pressure are important personal qualities for dispatchers. Those who work in the transportation industry must also be able to deal with sudden influxes of shipments and disruptions of shipping schedules caused by bad weather, road construction, or accidents.

Certification and Advancement

Although no mandatory licensing requirements exist for public safety dispatchers, some states require them to be certified to work on a state network, such as the Police Information Network. Many dispatchers participate in these programs as a means of improving their prospects for advancement.

Dispatchers who work for private firms (usually small businesses) generally have few opportunities for advancement. By contrast, a public safety dispatcher may be promoted to shift or divisional supervisor or may be eligible to become chief of communications. Public safety dispatchers may also move to higher-paying administrative jobs. Some ultimately become police officers or firefighters.

EMPLOYMENT AND JOB OUTLOOK

Dispatchers held about 284,000 jobs in 2013. About one third of these worked as police, fire, and ambulance dispatchers in local and state governments. Dispatcher positions are also available outside the scope of law enforcement agencies. School districts, universities, and city parks require the skills of dispatchers to manage minor and major emergencies. Public safety dispatcher positions are available in national parks across the United States, where campers may become lost or sustain injuries or where traffic accidents may occur, especially during peak travel seasons. Similar positions are available at local and long-distance trucking companies and with bus lines, telephone, electric, and gas utility companies, and wholesale and retail establishments. Although dispatchers work throughout the United States, most positions are in metropolitan areas. Large communications centers and private businesses that require dispatching services are often based in urban areas.

Employment of dispatchers is expected to increase 7 percent between 2012 and 2022, according to the Bureau of Labor Statistics. Population growth and economic factors are expected to stimulate employment growth for all types of dispatchers. In addition, an aging general population will require greater need for emergency services and is expected to spur job growth for police, fire, and ambulance dispatchers. Job openings will also increase as more workers transfer to other occupations or retire. Successful public safety dispatchers are promoted into supervisory positions or other roles with greater responsibility—and as they move up, their former positions become available.

Once you have served successfully as a public safety operator or dispatcher, you, too, can look forward to promotion or perhaps a move into private industry.

Current competition for public safety dispatcher jobs is intense. The job security of public safety dispatchers is unlikely to be affected by a sluggish economy. By contrast, employment opportunities for dispatchers who work in transportation industries may decrease with an economic downturn. To be considered for a public safety dispatcher position, you must earn a high score on a competitive exam and rank near the top of the list of eligible candidates. You must also demonstrate good typing and computer skills. And perhaps most important, you must impress interviewers with your communication skills, good judgment, patience, and tact.

Information about job opportunities for police, fire, and public safety dispatchers is available from state and local civil service commissions and police departments. This information is generally distributed in the form of Official Job Announcements. On the next few pages, you'll see a sample Notice of Examination and a job announcement from two cities in different parts of the United States. As you read the announcements, note the similarities—and significant differences—among job descriptions and the qualifying exams. Keep these in mind as you search actual job postings in and around your locality.

Earnings

The profession of public safety dispatching is exciting and challenging—but it can be tedious and stressful as well. Being a public safety dispatcher is a difficult job that takes time and patience to learn. However, successful dispatchers can earn a comfortable living and serve their communities at the same time. When reviewing the requirements and salaries for public safety dispatching jobs, remember that both aspects of the profession vary greatly by agency and location.

According to the Bureau of Labor Statistics, median annual wage-and-salary earnings of dispatchers (except police, fire, and ambulance dispatchers) as of May 2013 were $36,390. The middle 50 percent earned between $27,800 and $47,080 annually. The lowest-paid dispatchers earned $21,700; the highest-paid 10 percent earned $60,090 annually.

Median annual wage-and-salary earnings of police, fire, and ambulance dispatchers as of 2013 were $37,040. The middle 50 percent earned between $29,140 and $46,890. The lowest-paid public safety dispatchers earned less than $23,830; the highest-paid 10 percent earned more than $58,020 annually.

THE PUBLIC SAFETY DISPATCHER HIRING PROCESS

As with any government job, state and federal laws regulate the hiring process. A candidate should know which questions a potential employer is legally allowed to ask and which topics are forbidden. Applicants should understand their rights during each step of the process. The Fair Inquiry Guidelines established by the Equal Employment Opportunity Commission (EEOC) help clarify what an employer can ask during an interview. Browsing the EEOC website (www.eeoc.gov) may provide useful information regarding interview questions.

The process of applying, testing, and screening for a public safety dispatcher position involves a number of steps. Most of them are designed to determine whether a candidate can perform the specific tasks required of a public safety dispatcher. A candidate who meets the initial requirements is typically given a "conditional job offer." This candidate may then take an additional series of tests to determine whether he or she meets the necessary qualifications to be an employee of the city, county, or state.

The typical employment process for a government job involves the following steps. Not every government agency follows all these steps to fill job openings; for example, many agencies do not require candidates to undergo a polygraph exam.

1 application

2 written test

3 practical test

4 interview

5 conditional job offer

6 full job offer

7 medical exam

8 psychological test

9 polygraph test

10 background check

Since the events of September 11, 2001, and the establishment of the Department of Homeland Security (DHS), numerous new rules and regulations have gone into effect. Stringent hiring policies and procedures may affect the hiring process for a federal, state, regional, or local job in which you're interested. These rules and regulations generally fall under the jurisdiction of the DHS, and they should be set forth in writing at every level of the application process.

NOTE: Federal labor law requires that a medical, psychological, or polygraph exam be administered only *after* a conditional job offer—not before. The Employee Polygraph Protection Act of 1988 prohibits private firms from subjecting job candidates or employees to lie detector tests in most circumstances. However, the law does not cover federal, state, and local governments. Therefore, an applicant for a public safety dispatcher position may be required to take a polygraph test as part of the screening process.

Sample Dispatcher Qualifications

Many government agencies set minimum standards for skills, abilities, related experience, or education before an applicant is accepted for a position as a public safety dispatcher. The following samples come from actual job announcements for public safety dispatcher positions. Each describes the typical qualifications a public safety dispatcher must meet to be considered for employment.

Sample 1

Knowledge of standard radio and telephone communications receiving and transmitting equipment, standard broadcasting procedures and rules, operation of common radio dispatch equipment, public safety classification codes, basic provisions of the vehicle and penal code.

Sample 2

Ability to interpret and give both verbal and written instructions. Excellent verbal and written communication skills. Bilingual skills strongly desired. Ability to speak clearly and concisely over the radio and telephone. Have prioritization skills and ability to multitask. Ability to make sound decisions using all available information. Knowledge of FCC laws, regulations, procedures, and practices applicable to basic radio-telephone operation. Skill to accomplish tasks in a controlled, effective manner while working under stress. Ability to read maps. Ability to develop and maintain cooperative working relationships with coworkers and customers. Keyboard skills.

Sample 3

Knowledge of operational procedures and methods used in operation of a public safety communications center, general functions of public safety agencies, use and proper care of computer and radio-telephone equipment, geography of the county/city. Working knowledge of FCC regulations applicable to the operation of public safety radio-telephone communications equipment, all computer assisted dispatch (CAD) files, commonly used law violations. Some knowledge of supervision and training practices. Skill to accurately type a minimum of 25 wpm, operate a CAD computer, keep accurate records of information received via computer, operate a variety of communications equipment. Ability to remain calm, think clearly, quickly assess and evaluate situations, organize thoughts, and respond quickly in emergency and stressful situations; effectively coordinate emergency dispatch of public safety equipment and personnel; prepare work schedules for all shifts for routine assignments and emergency situations. Prepare written reports and trainee evaluations; recommend training methods; interpret and apply rules and regulations; establish and maintain cooperative working relationships; communicate clearly and effectively with the general public, safety officials, and other governmental and private staff persons. Take and transmit clear and complete directions and information. Perform a variety of tasks simultaneously.

Sample 4

Knowledge of modern office practices and procedures; CAD equipment operation; proper English usage, diction, grammar, spelling, and punctuation; demonstrated proficiency in alphabetic, chronological, and numeric filing systems; techniques, procedures, and methods used in the operation of a highly technical communications center; community resources; emergency response procedures; department procedures and activities; effective communication techniques; specialized police network computer operations; the law enforcement culture and its nuances; the rank structure within a police agency; automated systems dedicated to law enforcement; maintenance of standard operating procedure (SOP) integrity while working under emotional conditions; various penal, vehicle, health and safety codes as well as alpha mnemonics; map reading; listening and interrogation techniques to control direction and length of telephone calls; personal computer operating systems and software applications.

Ability and skills that accompany speaking and hearing clearly; demonstrate excellent interpersonal skills, including communicating effectively with those contacted in the course of work; analyze situations quickly and make sound decisions in emergency and routine situations; perform two or more tasks concurrently; input and retrieve computer data quickly; learn the techniques, procedures, and methods used in the operation of a highly technical communications center; quickly read and retain information; quickly interpret maps and floor layouts; relate effectively to coworkers; recognize and discern various emotional states when dealing with citizens in person and while on 911, emergency, and business lines; recognize the voices of field units; use patience and tact in dealing with the public; quickly operate electronic data processing equipment and radio consoles; read and disseminate court orders and warrant information; use personal computers and computer software to perform word processing and spreadsheet functions. The ability to understand and speak Spanish is preferred.

Sample 5

Knowledge of public safety dispatching methods using various communications equipment, including CAD or similar equipment. Ability to operate CAD equipment under stress; type at a corrected speed of 30 words per minute. Skill in establishing and maintaining effective working relationships with a variety of individuals, including police and fire personnel, other city employees, and the public. Skill in reading, writing, and communicating in English at an appropriate level.

Certain features of public safety dispatcher work are common throughout all agencies. Here are sample descriptions of some of these features.

Stationary work: Dispatchers are required to sit at telephone/radio consoles for extended periods.

Most work is verbal: Dispatchers must receive, evaluate, and produce verbal information.

Work is random and reactive: Dispatchers do not choose calls/situations to be handled; they do not know ahead of time what the situation will be.

Must be able to multitask: Dispatchers are required to perform multiple activities simultaneously and work with frequent interruptions.

Dispatchers are required to **interact with many different people** on a daily basis, often at the same time.

Work structure is rigid: Dispatchers must work within a framework of many rules, procedures, and regulations.

Dispatchers have a **high visibility** for their actions and decisions—performance is taped.

Dispatchers have a high level of responsibility, and there will be **serious consequences if an error** is made.

Dispatchers must deal with **unpleasant situations.**

Work is often repetitive and alternates between periods of high activity and low activity.

Dispatchers have access to **sensitive information.**

A dispatcher must, with little time to spare, **provide information, make decisions, and perform duties** that may be critical to the safety of the public and field officers.

Dispatchers are often the only contact citizens have with the police department. They are in a **public relations role.** The dispatcher's demeanor and competence in handling calls from the public combine to form what is often the first impression that people have about law enforcement agencies.

SAMPLE NOTICE OF EXAM AND JOB ANNOUNCEMENTS (SEE NEXT PAGE)

THE CITY OF NEW YORK
DEPARTMENT OF CITYWIDE
ADMINISTRATIVE SERVICES
APPLICATION UNIT
1 CENTRE STREET, 14ᵀᴴ FLOOR
NEW YORK, NY 10007

BILL DE BLASIO
Mayor

STACEY CUMBERBATCH
Commissioner

N O T I C E
O F
E X A M I N A T I O N

POLICE COMMUNICATIONS TECHNICIAN

Exam Nos. 5330 and 5331

YOU ARE RESPONSIBLE FOR READING THIS NOTICE IN ITS ENTIRETY BEFORE YOU SUBMIT YOUR APPLICATION.

WHEN TO APPLY: On the date of the test

APPLICATION FEE: $47.00
Payable only at a Computer-based Testing & Applications Center on the day of the test by credit card, bank card, debit card, gift card, or money order payable to DCAS (EXAMS). If you choose to pay the application fee with a credit/bank/debit/gift card, you will be charged a fee of 2.49% of the payment amount. This fee is nonrefundable.

THE TEST SCHEDULE: Testing for the title of Police Communications Technician will be held periodically throughout the year depending on the hiring needs of the agency. Below is the schedule of testing for Police Communications Technician:

Exam No.	Filing and Testing Period
5330	November 1, 2014 - December 31, 2014
5331	April 1, 2015 - May 31, 2015

Monthly Schedule: A monthly schedule of the days and times of filing will be available beginning on the 1ˢᵗ day of each month when testing is being held at www.nyc.gov/dcas and at the DCAS Computer-based Testing & Applications Centers.

DCAS COMPUTER-BASED TESTING & APPLICATIONS CENTERS: This exam will be administered at the DCAS Computer-based Testing & Applications Centers:

Manhattan
2 Lafayette Street
17ᵗʰ Floor
New York, NY 10007

Brooklyn
210 Joralemon Street
4ᵗʰ Floor
Brooklyn, NY 11201

Seating is limited. Once the Computer-based Testing & Applications Centers are filled to capacity, no more candidates will be admitted. You are encouraged to take the test earlier in the month since there is generally more seating available at that time.

You may take the Police Communications Technician test at either location, but you may only take each exam number once. If you take a test with the same exam number more than once, only your first test will be rated and your additional filing fee will not be refunded.

Warning: You are not permitted to enter the test site with cellular phones, beepers, pagers, cameras, portable media players, or other electronic devices. Calculators are **not** permitted. Electronic devices with an alphabetic keyboard or with word processing or data recording capabilities such as planners, organizers, etc. are prohibited. If you use any of these devices in the building at any time before, during or after the test, you may not receive your test results, your test score may be nullified, and your application fee will not be refunded.

You may not have any other person, including children, present with you while you are being processed for or taking the test, and no one may wait for you inside of a Computer-based Testing & Applications Center while you are taking the test.

Required Identification: **You are required to bring one (1) form of valid (non-expired) signature and photo bearing identification to the test site.** The name that was used to apply for the exam must match the first and last name on the photo ID. A list of acceptable identification documents is provided below. **If you do not have an acceptable ID, you may be denied testing.** Acceptable forms of identification (bring one) are as follows: State issued driver's license, State issued identification card, US Government issued Passport, US Government issued Military Identification Card, US Government issued Alien Registration Card, Employer ID with photo, or Student ID with photo.

Leaving: You must leave the test site once you finish the test. If you leave the test site after being fingerprinted but before finishing the test, you will not be permitted to re-enter. If you disregard this instruction and re-enter the test site, you may not receive your test results, your test score may be nullified, and your application fee will not be refunded.

Test dates and times are subject to change.

READ CAREFULLY AND SAVE FOR FUTURE REFERENCE

WHAT THE JOB INVOLVES: Police Communications Technicians, working under direct supervision in the Police Department Communications Section, serve as 911 emergency call-takers; obtain necessary information from callers in order to initiate emergency assistance; serve as radio dispatchers of police resources; perform clerical, administrative and other duties related to the provision of emergency service; and perform related work.

Some of the physical activities performed by Police Communications Technicians and environmental conditions experienced are: sitting for extended periods of time with headset on while monitoring a computer screen; typing information into the computer using a computer keyboard; coordinating eye/hand movements while handling emergency calls for the efficient use of console and computer; speaking calmly and clearly in order to elicit information and giving instructions to a continuous flow of callers under stress; listening carefully to clearly understand emergency information; making responsible judgments where timing is critical; and sitting within hearing distance of other call-takers working under similar conditions.

Special Working Conditions: You will be required to work various tours around the clock, including Saturdays, Sundays and holidays, and you will be required on occasion to work overtime tours depending on the needs of the Department.

(This is a brief description of what you might do in this position and does not include all the duties of this position.)

THE SALARY: The current minimum salary is $34,678 per annum. This rate is subject to change.

HOW TO APPLY: You will receive an exam application and filing instructions when you arrive at a DCAS Computer-based Testing & Applications Center.

The administration of the test is subject to change in the event of an unforeseen occurrence. If you wish to verify the test date and time, you may call the DCAS Interactive Voice Response (IVR) system at (212) 669-1357 two hours before the test session you wish to attend to hear if the test is not being administered at that time. The recorded message will be heard after the "Thank you for calling" greeting. If there is no message regarding testing at the Centers, it means that testing will be administered as scheduled for that day.

Special Circumstances Guide: This guide gives important information about requesting an alternate test date because of religious observance or a special test accommodation for disability, claiming Veterans' or Legacy credit, and notifying DCAS of a change in your mailing address. Follow all instructions on the Special Circumstances Guide that pertain to you when you complete your Application for Examination.

HOW TO QUALIFY: You will be given the test before we verify your qualifications. You are responsible for determining whether or not you meet the qualification requirements for this examination prior to submitting your application. If you are marked "Not Qualified," your application fee will not be refunded.

Education and Experience Requirements: By the **last day of the Filing and Testing Period for the exam number you are taking,** you must have a four-year high school diploma or its educational equivalent, plus

1. one year of satisfactory full-time experience performing clerical, typing, or secretarial work; or
2. one year of satisfactory full-time experience dealing with the public, including the obtaining of information from persons; or
3. the successful completion of 30 college semester credits from an accredited college or university; or
4. two years of active U.S. military duty with honorable discharge; or
5. a satisfactory combination of education and/or experience that is equivalent to 1, 2, 3, or 4 above.

However, all candidates must have a four-year high school diploma or its educational equivalent.

High School education must be approved by a State's Department of Education or a recognized accrediting organization. College education must be from an accredited college or university, accredited by regional, national, professional or specialized agencies recognized as accrediting bodies by the U.S. Secretary of Education, and by the Council for Higher Education Accreditation (CHEA).

If you were educated outside the United States, you must have your foreign education evaluated at your own expense to determine its equivalence to education obtained in the United States. You will receive instructions from the Police Department during the pre-employment screening process regarding the approved evaluation services that you may use for foreign education.

Education and experience will be investigated by the Police Department during the pre-employment screening process.

Medical and Psychological Requirements: Medical and psychological guidelines have been established for the position of Police Communications Technician. You will be examined to determine whether you can perform the essential functions of the position of Police Communications Technician. Where appropriate, a reasonable accommodation will be provided for a person with a disability to enable him or her to take the examination and/or to perform the essential functions of the job.

Drug Screening Requirement: You must pass a drug screening in order to be appointed.

Residency Requirement Advisory: Under New York City Administrative Code Section 12-120, you might need to be a resident of the City of New York within 90 days of the date you are appointed to this position. Since residency requirements vary by title, appointing agency and length of service, consult the **appointing agency's personnel office** at the time of the appointment interview to find out if City residency is required.

English Requirement: You must be able to understand and be understood in English.

Proof of Identity: Under the Immigration Reform and Control Act of 1986, you must be able to prove your identity and your right to obtain employment in the United States prior to employment with the City of New York.

THE TEST: You will be given a multiple-choice test at a computer terminal. Your score on this test will be used to determine your place on an eligible list. You must achieve a score of at least 70% to pass the test. The multiple-choice test will include questions which may require the use of any of the following abilities:

Written Comprehension: understanding written sentences and paragraphs.

Written Expression: using English words or sentences in writing so that others will understand.

Memorization: remembering information, such as words, numbers, pictures and procedures. Pieces of information can be remembered by themselves or with other pieces of information.

Problem Sensitivity: being able to tell when something is wrong or is likely to go wrong. It includes being able to identify the whole problem as well as elements of the problem.

Deductive Reasoning: applying general rules to specific problems and coming up with logical answers. It involves deciding if an answer makes sense.

Inductive Reasoning: combining separate pieces of information, or specific answers to problems, to form general rules or conclusions. It involves the ability to think of possible reasons for why things go together.

Information Ordering: following correctly a rule or set of rules or actions in a certain order. The rule or set of rules used must be given. The things or actions to be put in order can include numbers, letters, words, pictures, procedures, sentences, and mathematical or logical operations.

THE TEST RESULTS: If you pass the multiple-choice test, your name will be placed in final score order on an eligible list and you will be given a list number. You will be notified by mail of your test results. If you meet all requirements and conditions, you will be considered for appointment when your name is reached on the eligible list.

CHANGE OF MAILING AND/OR EMAIL ADDRESS: It is critical that you promptly notify DCAS of any change to your mailing address and/or email address. You may miss important information about your exam(s) or consideration for appointment, including important information that may require a response by a specified deadline, if we do not have your correct mailing and/or email address. Change of mailing and/or email address requests submitted to any place other than DCAS, such as your Agency or to the United States Postal Service will NOT update your records with DCAS. To update your mailing and/or email address with DCAS, you must submit a change request by mail or in person. Your request must include your full name, social security number, exam title(s), exam number(s), old mailing and/or email address, and your new mailing and/or email address. Your request can be mailed to DCAS Records Room, 1 Centre Street, 14th Floor, New York, NY 10007 or brought in person to the same address Monday through Friday from 9AM to 5PM.

ADDITIONAL INFORMATION:

Selective Certification for Spanish: If you can speak Spanish, you may be considered for appointment to positions requiring this ability through a process called Selective Certification. If you pass a qualifying test, you may be given preferred consideration for positions requiring this ability. Follow the instructions given to you on the day of the test to indicate your interest in such Selective Certification. This requirement may be met at any time during the duration of the list. If you meet the Selective Certification requirement at some future date, please submit documentation by mail to DCAS Bureau of Examinations - USEG, 1 Centre Street, 14th Floor, New York, NY 10007. Please include the examination title and number, and your social security number on your correspondence.

Investigation: This position is subject to investigation before appointment. At the time of investigation, you will be required to pay a $91.50 fee for fingerprint screening.

Probationary Period: The probationary period for Police Communications Technician is 18 months. You will be required to pass a 911 emergency call-taker training course and a radio dispatcher training course. If you fail to successfully complete the training courses, you will be terminated.

SPECIAL TEST ACCOMMODATIONS: If you plan to request special testing accommodations due to disability, you must notify the Exam Support Group by e-mail at testingaccommodations@dcas.nyc.gov or by fax at (212) 313-3241. Please refer to the **Special Circumstances Guide** http://www.nyc.gov/html/dcas/downloads/pdf/misc/exam_special_circumstances.pdf for information on what to include in your request. Your request must be received at least fifteen business days before the date of your test.

PENALTY FOR MISREPRESENTATION: Any intentional misrepresentation on the application or examination may result in disqualification, even after appointment, and may result in criminal prosecution.

POLICE SERVICE REPRESENTATIVE

Job Description: Police Service Representatives are civilian employees of the Police Department assigned to the Communications Division or to a geographic area police station. They receive and analyze telephone and in-person requests for service from citizens, field officers, and other agencies; take crime and other reports; handle referral calls and dispatch patrol units using radio, digital terminal, and other methods; and perform related station duties.

Notes:

1. Police Service Representatives' initial assignments will be to the Communications Division in positions that have been designated as temporary training positions by the Civil Service Commission. Employment in such positions will be limited to six months, during which time employees must successfully complete a comprehensive training program for Police Service Representatives. Upon completion of the training program, employees will receive regular appointments to the class of Police Service Representative and begin a six-month probationary period in the Communications Division.

2. Police Service Representatives must be available to work weekend, holiday, day, night, and early-morning shifts on a rotating basis. You will not necessarily be assigned to the permanent shift of your choice.

Distinguishing Features: A Police Service Representative is a civilian employee of the police department who may wear a uniform but carries no weapon. An employee of this class, when assigned to a public counter of a geographic police station, is usually the first person to assist visitors and receive most telephone calls. A Police Service Representative also prepares crime and traffic reports based on information provided by citizens and other agencies and must be able to deal effectively with emergency situations that arise.

When assigned to the Communications Division, a Police Service Representative receives citizens' requests, responds to the citizens' concerns, and, if necessary, dispatches patrol units using radio, digital terminal, and other methods. An employee of this class must make independent decisions that affect the safety of police officers, citizens, and property—such as those involved in determining the urgency of requests received—and the appropriate action to take. A Police Service Representative receives extensive training in police communications procedures, arrest and report follow-up, search procedures, and interview techniques.

Examples of Duties:

- Takes both telephone and in-person reports of crimes from citizens and other agencies.

- Dispatches urgent calls to the proper unit or section.

- Assists persons who enter the station in need of police assistance or general information.

- Screens individuals who enter the station.

- Receives, reviews, and routes messages.

continued

- Updates the station supervisor's message board.

- Directs station record clerks to send messages; answers questions from field officers.

- Maintains police department logs.

- Reviews daily field activity reports for accuracy and completeness.

- Ensures that reports are submitted in a timely and accurate manner.

- Monitors police department radio transmissions to keep informed of field situations requiring station personnel action.

- May verify and resolve discrepancies on bail monies received; deposits bail money; completes and authorizes bank checks; forwards checks, security bonds, and other necessary documents to appropriate court; maintains the divisional bail file, schedule, and instructional booklet; may, at an area station, interview persons (in person or by telephone) who have previously reported crime incidents or who were alleged witnesses to reported incidents, and prepare and forward appropriate reports to concerned department entities; and, if required in connection with such interviews, search and retrieve information from the department's Automated Information System.

- Forwards subpoenas to the proper supervisors or units for service; accepts the returned, served, or unserved subpoenas and forwards them to the concerned court; maintains liaison with concerned courts to ensure station personnel appear as scheduled; may maintain a subpoena control log; and may pick up and deliver evidential or other documents to police stations using an automobile.

- May act as a communications dispatch center operator responsible for receiving calls from the public requesting services and taking crime and other reports; analyzes the caller's request for service to determine if any emergency exists and if the call should result in a dispatch of a police unit, or if the call should be transferred to another department or person; uses radio, digital terminal, and other methods to dispatch field units to the scene, if necessary; handles referral calls and uses appropriate computer systems.

- May assist with other departmental duties as necessary.

Requirements: Experience that includes assisting and referring telephone or two-way radio callers and entering and retrieving computer data using video display terminals is desired but not required.

Notes:

1. Prior to appointment, eligible candidates will be given two opportunities to pass a typing test with a speed requirement of 32 net words per minute.

2. Some of the positions to be filled by this examination may require the ability to speak or write a language other than English. Only persons who have

continued

the necessary language skills may be posted on the eligible list to fill such positions. If you have the ability to speak or write a language other than English, indicate this language in the appropriate box on the application. Proficiency in Spanish is especially desired.

Application Information: Application may be made by mail or in person. Filing may close without prior notice any time after a sufficient number of applications have been received. Immediate vacancies will be filled from among those who apply first. Candidates will be scheduled for the next available written test. The written test will be given approximately every two months.

The Examination: The multiple-choice written test will cover the following: speed and accuracy in matching numerical and alphabetical sequences; spelling and vocabulary; reading comprehension; the ability to learn, apply, and make decisions based on rules; and the ability to follow verbal and written directions. Also included will be a test of approximately 30 minutes in length, which measures personal characteristics required for the position of Police Service Representative.

The interview will consist of an evaluation of your oral communication skills and the extent to which your work experience and training demonstrate the abilities to deal tactfully and effectively with the public, officials, and city employees; make decisions under various situations; perform multiple tasks with frequent interruptions; retrieve and provide information; and perform other necessary tasks.

Examination Weights:

Written Test	50%
Interview	50%

You may take the written test and interview only once in a calendar year. Your name may be removed from the open competitive eligible list after 180 calendar days.

SUMMING IT UP

- Public safety dispatchers go by many titles, including 911 Operator, Police Communications Technician, and E911 Call-taker/Dispatcher. All of these titles refer to people who collect information in emergency situations and relay that information to those who can provide immediate assistance. Dispatchers are the link between citizens requesting help and the appropriate service provider.

- Police, fire, and ambulance dispatchers are usually the first people contacted in an emergency. They receive reports from the public concerning crimes, fires, and medical emergencies; broadcast orders to units near the scene of the event to respond or investigate; and relay information or orders to proper officials.

- Dispatchers remain in contact with response units until the emergency has been handled, in case further instructions are needed. When appropriate, they stay in close contact with other service providers as well.

- Dispatcher work can be extremely busy, but it can also be monotonous and repetitive. It's particularly stressful because a slow or improper response to a call may result in serious injury or further harm to another person or people, and callers may be fearful, anxious, upset, or even abusive. Dispatchers must remain calm, objective, and in control in all situations.

- Dispatchers sit for long periods and use telephones, computers, and two-way radios almost constantly. The job often requires evening, weekend, and holiday shifts.

- Public safety dispatchers are often trained on the job. Many also attend structured training programs sponsored by an employer, and they are increasingly being trained in stress and crisis management and in family counseling.

- Some states require public safety dispatchers to undergo specific types of training or secure certification from a professional association. Candidates for police, fire, and emergency medical dispatching positions may have to pass written, oral, and performance tests. They may also be asked to attend training classes to qualify for advancement.

- Although dispatchers who work for private firms often have few opportunities for advancement, public safety dispatchers may be promoted to shift or divisional supervisors or may be eligible to become chief of communications. Public safety dispatchers may also move to higher-paying administrative jobs, and some become police officers or firefighters.

- Employment of dispatchers is expected to increase 7 percent between 2012–2022, according to the Bureau of Labor Statistics. Population growth and economic factors are expected to stimulate employment growth for all types of dispatchers.

- Current competition for public safety dispatcher jobs is intense. To be considered for a position, you must earn a high score on a competitive exam and rank near the top of the list of eligible candidates.

- State and federal laws regulate the public safety dispatcher hiring process. The steps involved in the hiring process include the application, a written test, a practical test, an interview, a conditional job offer, a full job offer, a medical exam, a psychological test, a polygraph test, and a background check. Not every government agency follows all these steps to fill job openings; for example, many agencies do not require candidates to undergo a polygraph exam.

PART II
ALL ABOUT CIVIL SERVICE EXAMS

Civil Service Exams Explained

OVERVIEW

- Taking a civil service exam
- Manage your test time
- Should you guess?
- How your exam is scored
- Twelve tips to raise your score
- Summing it up

TAKING A CIVIL SERVICE EXAM

Many factors contribute to a civil service test score—but the most important factor, of course, is the ability to answer the questions correctly, which in turn indicates the ability to learn and perform the duties of the job for which you are being evaluated. Assuming that you have this ability, knowing what to expect on the exam and becoming familiar with the techniques of effective test taking should give you the confidence you need to do your best on your public safety dispatcher exam.

There is no quick substitute for long-term study and development of your skills and abilities to prepare you for doing well on such tests. However, you can take some steps to help you gain an edge over others who will be taking the exam. These steps fall into four major categories:

1. Being prepared
2. Avoiding careless errors
3. Managing your test time wisely
4. Taking educated guesses

Be Prepared

Do not make your exam more difficult than it has to be by not preparing yourself. You are taking a very important step in preparing for a public safety dispatcher career by reading this book and taking the sample tests we've included. This will help you to become familiar with the tests and the kinds of questions you will have to answer—and therefore more comfortable taking the actual test on exam day.

chapter 3

As you use this book, carefully and thoroughly read the sample questions and directions for taking the test. Read every word, even if you think you know what the question is asking. When you're ready to take the full-length Practice Tests, find a quiet place where you're not likely to be interrupted and time yourself, to simulate as closely as possible the atmosphere you'll experience on exam day.

As you work through the sample questions in this book, avoid checking the answer keys and explanations before you've attempted to answer them correctly on your own. Doing otherwise might fool you into believing that you fully understand a question. Once you've completed the question or the exam, compare your answers with the ones provided. This will help you determine where you might need additional practice and which question types are most difficult for you. Remember, in a sample test, you are your own grader; you gain nothing by pretending to understand something that you don't.

What to Expect on Exam Day

ALERT!

Make sure you complete all required forms before you arrive at the test site. If necessary, have all forms ready to turn in.

On exam day (a test date will be assigned to you), allow the exam itself to be the main attraction of the day. Avoid fitting it in between other activities. The night before the exam, lay out all the materials you'll need to bring with you—your admission card, identification, sharpened pencils, directions to the test center—and place them where you're unlikely to forget them in the rush to get out the door. Get a good night's sleep and leave your house in plenty of time to get to the test center before the exam begins (in fact, it's a good idea to leave a bit early, to account for traffic tie-ups or other unforeseen situations). Arriving rested, relaxed, and on time for your exam will go a long way toward making you feel confident and in control.

At the testing center, the administrator will hand out forms for you to complete. Next, he or she will give you the exam instructions and explain how to fill in the answer sheet or how to provide computerized responses. He or she will explain time limits and timing signals. Don't hesitate to ask questions if you don't understand something the administrator is telling you. Remember, complete understanding is one key to scoring high, so it makes no sense not to be sure you're completely clear on what you have to do.

You must follow instructions *exactly*. If you are completing paper forms, fill in the grids on the forms carefully and accurately. Mis-gridding may lead to a loss of veteran's credits to which you may be entitled or a misaddressing of your test results. Don't begin the exam until you are told to do so, and stop as soon as the administrator tells you to. Don't turn pages unless you're told to do so, and don't return to parts of the exam that you've already completed unless you are instructed that you may do so. Any infraction of the rules is considered cheating—and that disqualifies you from eligibility for the job you're seeking.

Avoid Careless Errors

Don't reduce your score by making careless mistakes. Be very careful when marking your answer sheet that you're filling in the correct space for the question you're answering. Always read the directions for each test section carefully—even when you think you already know what the directions are. It is why we stress throughout this book that it is important to understand the directions for the different question types before you go into the actual exam. Following these two pieces of advice will not only help you reduce errors, but it will also save you time—time you will need for answering exam questions.

Marking Your Answer Sheet

If you are taking a paper-and-pencil test, keep in mind that the answer sheets for most multiple-choice exams are scored by machine. Be sure to fill out your answer sheet clearly and correctly. After all, you can't "explain" your answers to a scoring machine.

1 Blacken your answer space firmly and completely. ● is the only correct way to mark the answer sheet. ◑, ⊗, ◍, and ⦸ are unacceptable. The machine might not read them at all, or might read them incorrectly.

2 Mark only one answer for each question; otherwise your answer is read as incorrect.

3 If you change your mind about an answer, erase your mark completely; don't cross it out. An incomplete erasure might be read as a second answer, and you will end up being marked incorrect for that question.

4 All of your answers should be in the form of blackened spaces. The machine cannot "read" English, so avoid making notes in the margins of the answer sheet.

5 Answer each question in the right place. This is one of the most frequent reasons why test takers' questions are scored as incorrect. Question 1 must be answered in space 1; question 2 in space 2, and so on. If you should skip an answer space and mark a series of answers in the wrong places, you'll need to erase all your answers and mark your answer sheet all over again, with answers in the proper spaces. Remember, however, that you're being timed—you cannot afford to use your limited test time doing this. Instead, keep rechecking as you go along that you're filling in the correct answer space for the question you're answering. Look at the question number, check that you are marking your answer in the proper space, and then move on.

6 If your exam includes a typing test, type steadily and carefully. Avoid rushing through the test—that's when you're most likely to make errors. Keep in mind that each error subtracts 1 word per minute (wpm) from your final typing score.

Reading and Following Directions

What if you don't understand the directions on the exam? You risk answering incorrectly for an entire test section. For example, vocabulary questions sometimes ask about synonyms (words that are similar in meaning) but sometimes ask about antonyms (words with opposite meanings). You can easily see how misunderstanding directions in this case could make a whole set of answers incorrect.

If you have time, reread any complicated instructions after you complete the first few questions to check that you really do understand them. If you're still stumped, do not hesitate to ask the examiner to clarify anything you find confusing.

Other mistakes may affect only the response to particular questions—but you still want to avoid them. For instance, some test takers are prone to making what are called "response errors." A response error usually stems from a momentary lapse of concentration.

TIP

Check often to be sure that the question number matches the answer space and that you have not skipped a space by mistake.

Example

The question states, "The capital of Massachusetts is ...." The correct answer is **(D)** Boston, but you mark **(B)** because "B" is the first letter of the word "Boston."

Example

The question states, "$8 - 5 = ...$" The correct answer is **(A)** 3, but you mark **(C)** thinking "third letter of the alphabet."

A common error in reading comprehension questions is inadvertently bringing your own knowledge into the question. This usually happens when you encounter a passage that discusses a subject you know something about. In exam questions like this, you are instructed to rely *solely* on information within the passage to answer correctly. Although knowing a bit about the subject of the passage can make it easier for you to read and understand, it can also tempt you to rely on your own knowledge rather than on the information provided in the passage. In fact, sometimes an "incorrect" answer to a question is actually based on true information about the subject—but that information is not given in the passage. Keep in mind that test makers are assessing your reading ability, not your general knowledge of a subject, and be sure to answer based on information in the passage—whether or not it is accurate in real life.

MANAGE YOUR TEST TIME

TIP

During the exam, keep track of the time, but try not to constantly think about how much time you have left.

Before you begin the exam, take a moment to plan your progress. In most timed exams, you are not expected to get to all of the questions on a test, but you should at least form an idea of how much time you can spend on each question in order to answer them all. For example, if your exam contains 60 questions and you have 30 minutes to complete the exam, you have about one-half minute to spend on each question. Making a quick calculation like this will help you stay on track and avoid getting bogged down on any one question.

Keep track of the time using your watch or a clock in the exam room—but try not to fixate on how much time you have left. Your task is to answer questions. Avoid spending too much time on any one question: if you feel stuck on a particular question, avoid taking it as a personal challenge. Make an educated guess (we'll discuss this in a moment) or skip the question and move on. Then, if you have time at the end of the exam or section, you can return to the question and give it another try. If you do skip the question, remember to skip the appropriate answer space on your answer sheet as well.

Answering Multiple-Choice Questions

Almost all of the questions on most civil service exams are multiple-choice format. You'll usually have four or five answer choices per question—but remember that there is only one correct answer for each multiple-choice question. Because the exam you're taking has been administered repeatedly, the test developers have a good sense of which types of questions work well and which do not—so it's rare to see ambiguous answer choices. The questions may be complex or somewhat confusing at first, but you will always have only one correct answer choice. Let's review a basic technique for answering this question type that may help you feel less stressed when taking your exam.

First, look at the question and read it thoroughly without reviewing the answer choices. Try to come up with the correct answer *without* reading any of the answer choices.

Now, with a tentative answer in mind, review all the answer choices provided. If your answer is among the choices provided, chances are pretty good that the one it's most similar to is the correct answer choice for that question.

This may work especially well with questions involving math or other calculations. Try to solve the problem without reading the answer choices. If your answer is among the choices, that answer choice is probably the correct one. Pay careful attention to function signs (addition, subtraction, multiplication, division) and to whether numbers are negative or positive to avoid being tripped up when choosing from among the answer choices provided. Some will *appear* to be the correct answer because they result from a common error in calculation.

SHOULD YOU GUESS?

What if you don't know the correct answer? You could use what is called the process of elimination. First, take a moment to eliminate answers that you know are incorrect. Then quickly consider and guess from the remaining choices. Having fewer viable choices is likely to increase your odds of choosing the correct answer. Once you've decided to make a guess—whether it's an educated guess or a wild stab, do it right away and move on. Don't dwell on a particular question; you will be wasting valuable time. A good idea is to use your scratch paper to keep track of questions for which you've guessed the answer. If you have time at the end of the exam or the section, you can quickly return to them and try again.

You may be wondering whether it is wise to guess when you're not sure of an answer (even if you have reduced the odds to 50 percent) or whether it is better to skip a question you're unsure of. Whether you should guess depends for the most part on the method used to score your exam. Civil service exams generally are scored in one of three ways:

1. rights only
2. rights minus wrongs
3. rights minus a fraction of wrongs

If the score is *rights only*, that means it's based only on correct answers. In other words, you are given one point for each correct answer and do not lose points or fractions of points for incorrect ones. In such a case, it's smart to make a guess, even if it isn't an educated one. Of course, you should still read the question and all of the answer choices carefully and try to eliminate choices you believe are wrong before you guess—but if you are not penalized for incorrect answers, even a "lucky" guess might help you gain a point.

In fact, on exams for which you receive no penalty for incorrect answers, you should try to fill in all the answer spaces. If it appears that you will run out of time before completing such an exam, fill in all the remaining answer spaces with the same letter. According to the law of averages, you should get some portion of those questions right and gain points toward your final score.

On the other hand, if the scoring method for your exam is *rights minus wrongs*, meaning that you receive a point for each question answered correctly but have a point subtracted for each incorrect answer, your best bet is to *avoid* guessing. In this type of exam, a wrong answer counts heavily against you. Never fill answer spaces randomly at the end of such an exam. Instead, work as quickly as possible and concentrate on accuracy. Keep working carefully until time is up; then stop and leave the remaining answer spaces blank.

On some exams, you are given a point for questions you answer correctly and have a fraction of a point subtracted from your score for each question you answer incorrectly. In this type of exam, taking educated guesses is acceptable, but you may want to avoid making wild guesses.

Consider: A correct answer gives you one point. A skipped answer gives you nothing, but it also costs you nothing except the chance of getting a correct answer. An incorrect answer costs you 1/4 point. If you're uncomfortable with guessing on this type of exam, you should skip the question—but of course, remember to skip the corresponding answer space as well. However, the risk of losing your place if you skip many questions is so great that you may want to try and guess, even if you are not sure of the answer. If you find that you are spending too much time on any one question for fear of answering incorrectly, you may decide to take a guess, simply to avoid becoming bogged down. If you run short of time, *avoid* filling in answer spaces for uncompleted questions. Work steadily and accurately until time is up.

Finding out which of these scoring methods will be used to grade your exam will go a long way toward helping you establish a test-taking strategy that will help you raise your score.

HOW YOUR EXAM IS SCORED

We mentioned that most civil service exams are machine scored and consist of multiple-choice questions. If your exam is a short-answer written exam, however, such as those often used by companies in the private sector, your answers may be scored by a personnel officer trained in grading test questions. If you blackened spaces on the separate answer sheet accompanying a multiple-choice exam, your answer sheet will be machine scanned or hand scored using a punched card stencil. Then a raw score will be calculated using the scoring formula that applies to that test or test portion— rights only, rights minus wrongs, or rights minus a fraction of wrongs. The raw scores of test sections are then added together for a total raw score.

A raw score is neither a final score nor the score that finds its way onto an eligibility list. The civil service testing authority, U.S. Postal Service, or other testing body converts raw scores to a scaled score, according to an unpublicized formula. The scaling formula allows for slight differences in difficulty of questions from one form of the exam to another and allows for equating the scores of all candidates. The entire process of conversion from raw to scaled score is confidential. The score you receive for your exam does not tell you the number of correct responses you had or a percentage of those responses, even though it is a 1–100 grade.

If you are entitled to veterans' service points, these points are added to your *passing* scaled score to boost your rank on the eligibility list. Veterans' points are added only to passing scores. A failing score cannot be brought to passing level by adding veterans' points. The score earned, plus any veterans' service points, is the score that will be on the eligibility list rankings. Highest scores go to the top of the list.

TWELVE TIPS TO RAISE YOUR SCORE

1 Get to the test center early. Give yourself plenty of time to get there, park your car, and even grab a cup of coffee before the test.

2 Listen to the test administrator and follow his or her instructions carefully.

3 Read *every word* of the instructions. Read *every word of every question.*

4 On a paper-and-pencil test, mark your answers by completely darkening the answer space of your choice. Do not use the test paper to work out your answers or make notes.

5 Mark *only one* answer for each question, even if you think that more than one answer is correct. You *must* choose only one. If you mark more than one answer, you will be marked incorrect for that question.

6 If you change your mind about an answer, erase your previous answer mark completely. Leave no doubt as to which answer you choose.

7 If your test administrator permits you to use scratch paper or the margins of the test booklet for figuring, don't forget to mark your final answer on the answer sheet as well. Only the answer sheet is scored.

8 As you work, check often to be sure that the question number matches the answer space and that you haven't skipped a space accidentally.

9 Guess according to the suggestions described in this chapter (see "Should You Guess?"). Find out before or on exam day what method of scoring is used to grade your exam.

10 Stay alert. Be careful not to mark a wrong answer because you had a momentary lapse of concentration.

11 If you run out of time to finish any part of the exam before time is called, don't panic. If your responses are accurate, you can do well even without finishing a section. It is even possible to earn a scaled score of 100 without entirely finishing an exam section if you are very accurate. At any rate, do not let your performance on any one section of an exam affect your performance on any other section.

12 Check and recheck your answers as time permits. If you finish any section of your exam before time is called, use the remaining time to be sure you've answered each question in the right space and that you've chosen only one answer for each question. If time still remains, return to the most difficult questions and take another shot at them.

SUMMING IT UP

- Knowing what to expect on a civil service exam and becoming familiar with the techniques of effective test taking will help you do your best on your public safety dispatcher exam. Follow the steps outlined in this chapter to help you gain an edge over others who will be taking the exam: be prepared, avoid careless errors, manage your test time wisely, and know when and how to make educated guesses.

- Don't make your exam more difficult by not preparing for it. Read this book and take the sample tests to become familiar with the kinds of questions you are likely to encounter on your public safety dispatcher exam. When taking the Practice Tests—and especially on your exam day—carefully and thoroughly read every word of directions, even if you think you know what the question is asking. Find a quiet place where you're not likely to be interrupted and time yourself to simulate as closely as possible the test conditions on exam day.

- While practicing for your exam, avoid checking the answer keys and explanations before you've attempted to answer questions correctly on your own. Once you've completed the exam, compare your answers with those provided to determine where you might need additional practice and which question types are most difficult for you.

- Careless mistakes from momentary inattention can lower your test score. Be very careful when marking your answer sheet that you're filling in the correct space for the question you're answering, and read all directions carefully. Following these two pieces of advice will help you reduce errors and save you valuable time on exam day.

- Before you begin the exam, take a moment to plan your progress. Form an idea of how much time you can spend on each question in order to answer them all. This will help you stay on track and avoid getting bogged down on any one question. During the exam, keep track of the time, but try not to fixate on how much time you have left. If you feel stuck on a particular question, make an educated guess or skip the question and move on. If you have extra time, you can give it another try.

- Whether you should guess at answers depends on the method by which your exam is scored. Civil service exams generally are scored as rights only, rights minus wrongs, or rights minus a fraction of wrongs. Follow the tips in this chapter to make the best of whatever scoring method is used for your exam.

PART III

PREPARING FOR THE PUBLIC SAFETY DISPATCHER EXAM

Reading
Comprehension

In Chapter 3, we explained what you can expect when taking a civil service exam and reviewed a few basic strategies for answering multiple-choice questions. In this chapter, we'll take a closer look at the types of questions you'll see on the public safety dispatcher exam.

READING COMPREHENSION ON THE PUBLIC SAFETY DISPATCHER EXAM

A recent survey of dispatcher exams administered nationwide indicates that the subject matter of these exams varies widely. The single common question type, however, is reading comprehension. Some exams include classic reading comprehension questions, in which you are presented with a passage and then asked to answer questions about what you've read. Other exams require candidates to determine a dispatcher's or other public safety officer's appropriate response based on a reading of printed procedures and regulations. A third type of reading comprehension question requires the test taker to predict the next step in a process or procedure based on the information presented in a passage. Of course, questions of judgment in emergency and non-emergency situations rely heavily on reading as well.

Before you begin studying strategies for answering reading-based questions, think about your present reading habits and skills. Of course, you already know how to read. But how *well* do you read? Do you concentrate on reading? Do you get the point on your first reading? Do you notice details?

If you answered negatively to any of those last three questions, you'll probably need to improve your reading concentration and comprehension before exam day. It's not as difficult as you might think. Your daily newspaper provides an excellent source to help improve your reading. Begin by making a point of reading all the way through any article that you begin. Don't be satisfied with skimming the first paragraph or two. Read with a pen in hand and underline details and ideas that seem crucial to the meaning of the article. Notice points of view, arguments, and supporting information. When you finish the article, summarize it for yourself. Do you know the purpose of the article? The main idea presented? The attitude of the writer? Any points of controversy? Did you find certain information lacking? As you answer these questions, review your underlined text. Did you focus on important words and ideas? Did you read with comprehension?

Try to repeat this process each day. Before long, you'll find that you'll become more efficient in and glean more information from your reading.

Changing Your Reading Habits

You can't simply sit down the night before a test containing reading comprehension questions and cram for it. The only way to strengthen your reading skill is to practice systematically. The gains you make will show, not only in an increased score on the test but also when you read for study or pleasure.

Trying to change reading habits you've probably had your whole life can be difficult and discouraging. Don't attempt to employ every reading comprehension suggestion presented here all at once. Take it a little at a time, as the program here suggests.

❶ Set aside 15 minutes a day to practice new reading techniques.

❷ Start with a short, easy-to-read article from a magazine or newspaper. Note the amount of time you take to read and understand the article. At the end of this practice session, time yourself on another short article, and record both times.

❸ Read an editorial or a review of a book, movie, or performance in a literary magazine or newspaper. This type of article always expresses the author's (or the paper's) point of view, so it's good practice for seeking the main idea of a reading passage. After you've finished, see whether you can come up with a good title for the article, and jot down in one sentence the author's main idea.

❹ Find one new word and write the sentence in which it appears. Try to determine its meaning from the context in which it's used. Then look up the definition in a dictionary. Form your own sentence using the word; then try to use the word in conversation at least twice the next day.

If you follow this program daily, you'll find that your test score will show the improvements you have made in reading comprehension.

Reading Includes Vocabulary

Building your vocabulary is one of the most effective ways to strengthen your reading comprehension. The most effective readers have a rich, extensive vocabulary. As you read, make a list of words you come across that are unfamiliar. Include in the list any words that you understand within the context of the article, but that you cannot readily define. Also include words that you do not understand at all. When you put aside your article, refer to a dictionary and look up every new and unfamiliar word you encountered. In a special notebook, write down each word and its definition: Writing helps seal the information in your memory far better than simply reading, and the notebook will be a handy reference. Being sensitive to the meaning of words and trying to understand each word you encounter will make reading easier and more enjoyable—even if none of the words you learn in this process crops up on your exam. In fact, the practice of vocabulary building is a good lifetime habit to develop.

Five Steps to Answering Reading Comprehension Questions

Success with reading-based questions on the public safety dispatcher exam depends on more than simply understanding what you read; you must also know how to draw the correct answers to the questions from the reading selection and how to distinguish the best answer from a number of answers that seem correct—or from several answers that all seem incorrect. Follow these five steps to help you score your highest on the reading comprehension section of your exam:

1 **Read the questions first.** Strange as it may seem, it's a good idea to approach reading comprehension questions by reading the questions—not the answer choices, just the questions—before you read the passage. Doing so alerts you to specific details, ideas, and points of view that you'll need to know to answer correctly. Use a pencil to underline key words in the questions; it will help you focus your attention as you read.

2 **Scan the reading passage quickly.** This gives you an idea of the passage's subject matter and organization before you read it more thoroughly. If key words or ideas pop out at you, underline them, but try not to search for details in this preliminary skim.

3 **Read for detail.** Next, read the passage carefully, with comprehension as your main goal. Underline the most significant words, just as you have been doing in your newspaper readings.

4 **Return to the questions.** Read each question carefully. Be sure you understand what it asks: Misreading questions is a major cause of errors on reading comprehension questions. Then, read *all* the answer choices and eliminate the obviously incorrect answers. You may be left with only one possible answer. If you have more than one possible answer left, reread the question, focusing on catching words that might destroy the validity of a seemingly acceptable answer. These include expressions like *under all circumstances, at all times, never, always, under no condition, absolutely, entirely,* and *except when.*

5 **Scan the passage again.** Finally, skim the passage once more, focusing on the underlined segments. By now, you should be able to conclude which answer is best.

Quick Tips

After you follow the five steps listed above, keep in mind these tips for answering reading comprehension questions.

- If the author quotes material from another source, make sure that you understand the purpose of the quote. Does the author agree or disagree with the substance of the quote?

- Avoid inserting your own judgments into your answers. Even if you disagree with the author or spot a factual error in the selection, remember that you are being asked to answer based only on what is stated or implied in the selection.

- Don't spend too much time on any one question. If reviewing the passage doesn't help you determine the correct answer, try to make an educated guess from among the answers remaining after you eliminate the obviously incorrect choices. Then mark your answer in the test booklet or answer sheet and move on. If you have time at the end of the section or the exam, you can return to the passage and take another shot at the question. Often, a fresh look provides new insights.

ALERT!

Misreading questions is one of the major reasons test-takers answer questions incorrectly.

Types of Reading-Based Questions

Reading-based questions are presented in a number of forms. Here's a look at the most commonly used types:

❶ **Question of fact or detail.** You may have to mentally rephrase or rearrange the words of a passage to answer this type of question, but the answer can always be found in the body of the passage.

❷ **Best title or main idea.** The answer may be obvious, but the incorrect answer choices for the "main idea" question are often half-truths that you might easily confuse with the main idea. They may misstate the idea, omit part of the idea, or even offer a supporting idea quoted directly from the text. The correct answer is the one that deals with the largest portion of the selection.

❸ **Interpretation.** You will be asked what the selection means rather than what it states outright.

❹ **Inference.** This is the most difficult type of reading-based question. It asks you to go beyond what the selection says and predict what might happen next. You may have to choose the best course of action to take based on given procedures and a factual situation, or you may have to judge the actions of others. In any case, your answer must be based on the information in the selection and on your own common sense—but not on any other information outside of the passage that you may have or know. A variation of the inference question might begin with the phrase, "The author would expect that. . . ." To answer this question type, you must first determine the author's viewpoint and then make an inference from that viewpoint based on the information in the selection.

❺ **Vocabulary.** Some reading questions directly or indirectly ask for the meanings of certain words that appear in the selection.

PRACTICE READING COMPREHENSION QUESTIONS

Let's take a look at some typical reading comprehension passages and questions.

QUESTIONS 1–4 ARE BASED ON THE FOLLOWING PASSAGE.

The recipient gains an impression of a typewritten letter before beginning to read the message. Factors that give a good first impression include margins and spacing that are visually pleasing, formal parts of the letter that are correctly placed according to the style of the letter, copy that is free of obvious erasures and overstrikes, and transcript that is even and clear. The problem for the typist is how to produce that first positive impression of his or her work.

There are several general rules that a typist can follow when he or she wishes to prepare a properly spaced letter on a sheet of letterhead. The width of a letter ordinarily should not be less than four inches nor more than six inches. The side margins should also have a proportionate relation to the bottom margin, as should the space between the letterhead and the body of the letter. Usually the most appealing arrangement is when the side margins are even and the bottom margin is slightly wider than the side margins. In some offices, however, a standard line length is used for all business letters, and the typist then varies the spacing between the date line and the inside address according to the length of the letter.

1. The best title for the preceding passage is
   (A) Writing Office Letters.
   (B) Making Good First Impressions.
   (C) Judging Well-Typed Letters.
   (D) Good Placing and Spacing for Office Letters.

2. According to the passage, which of the following might be considered the way that people quickly judge the quality of work that has been typed?
   (A) By measuring the margins to see whether they are correct
   (B) By looking at the spacing and cleanliness of the typescript
   (C) By scanning the body of the letter for meaning
   (D) By reading the date line and address for errors

3. According to the passage, what would be definitely undesirable as the average line length of a typed letter?
   (A) 4 inches
   (B) 5 inches
   (C) 6 inches
   (D) 7 inches

4. According to the preceding paragraphs, when the line length is kept standard, the typist
   (A) does not have to vary the spacing at all because this also is standard.
   (B) adjusts the spacing between the date line and inside address for different lengths of letters.
   (C) uses the longest line as a guideline for spacing between the date line and inside address.
   (D) varies the number of spaces between the lines.

Helpful Hints

Begin by skimming the questions and underlining key words. Your underlined questions should look more or less like this:

1. The <u>best title</u> for the preceding passage is. . . .

2. According to the passage, which of the following might be considered the way that people <u>quickly judge the quality</u> of work that has been typed?

3. According to the passage, what would be definitely <u>undesirable</u> as the <u>average line length</u> of a typed letter?

4. According to the preceding paragraphs, <u>when the line length is kept standard</u>, the typist. . . .

Now skim the selection. A quick reading should give you an idea of the structure of the selection and of its overall meaning.

Next, read the selection carefully and underline words that seem important or that you think hold keys to the answers. Your underlined selection should look something like this:

> The recipient gains an impression of a typewritten letter before beginning to read the message. <u>Factors that give a good first impression</u> include <u>margins and spacing that are visually pleasing</u>, formal parts of the letter that are <u>correctly placed</u> according to the style of the letter, copy that is <u>free of obvious erasures and overstrikes</u>, and transcript that is <u>even and clear</u>. The problem for the typist is how to produce that first, positive impression of his or her work.

> There are several general rules that a typist can follow when he or she wishes to prepare a properly spaced letter on a sheet of letterhead. The width of a letter ordinarily <u>should not be less than four inches nor more than six inches</u>. The side margins should also have a proportionate relation to the bottom margin, as well as the space between the letterhead and the body of the letter. Usually the most appealing arrangement is when the <u>side margins are even</u> and the <u>bottom margin is slightly wider</u> than the side margins. In some offices, however, a <u>standard line length is used for all business letters</u>, and the clerk then <u>varies the spacing between the date line and the inside address</u> according to the length of the letter.

Now go back and read the questions and answer choices again, and try to choose the correct answer for each question. The answers and explanations can be found on page 70.

QUESTIONS 5–9 ARE BASED ON THE FOLLOWING PASSAGE.

Cotton fabrics treated with the XYZ Process have features that make them far superior to any previously known flame-retardant-treated cotton fabrics. XYZ Process-treated fabrics endure repeated laundering and dry cleaning; are glow resistant as well as flame resistant; form tough, pliable, and protective chars when exposed to flames or intense heat; are inert physiologically to persons handling or exposed to the fabric; are only slightly heavier than untreated fabrics; and are susceptible to further wet and dry finishing treatments. In addition, the treated fabrics exhibit little or no adverse change in feel, texture, and appearance and are shrink-, rot-, and mildew-resistant. The treatment reduces strength only slightly. Finished fabrics have "easy care" properties in that they are wrinkle resistant and dry rapidly.

5. It is most accurate to state that the author of the preceding selection presents

   (A) facts but reaches no conclusion concerning the value of the process.

   (B) a conclusion concerning the value of the process and facts to support that conclusion.

   (C) a conclusion, unsupported by facts, concerning the value of the process.

   (D) neither facts nor conclusions, but merely describes the process.

6. Of the following articles, for which is the XYZ Process most suitable?

   (A) nylon stockings

   (B) woolen shirts

   (C) silk ties

   (D) cotton bedsheets

7. Of the following aspects of the XYZ Process, which is NOT discussed in the preceding selection?

   (A) costs

   (B) washability

   (C) wearability

   (D) the human body

8. The main reason for treating a fabric with the XYZ Process is to

   (A) prepare the fabric for other wet and dry finishing treatments.

   (B) render it shrink-, rot-, and mildew-resistant.

   (C) increase its weight and strength.

   (D) reduce the chance that it will catch fire.

9. Which of the following would be considered a minor drawback of the XYZ Process?

   (A) It forms chars when exposed to flame.

   (B) It makes fabrics mildew-resistant.

   (C) It adds to the weight of fabrics.

   (D) It is compatible with other finishing treatments.

Helpful Hints

Skim the questions and underline the words or phrases that you consider important. The questions should look something like this:

5. It is most accurate to state that the author of the preceding selection <u>presents</u>. . . .

6. Of the following articles, for which is the <u>XYZ Process most suitable</u>?

7. Of the following aspects of the XYZ Process, which is <u>NOT discussed</u> in the preceding selection?

8. The <u>main reason for treating</u> a fabric with the XYZ Process is to. . . .

9. Which of the following would be considered a <u>minor drawback</u> of the XYZ Process?

Skim the reading selection. Get an idea of the subject matter of the selection and of how it is organized. Now read the selection carefully and underline the words that you think are especially important. The passage might be underlined like this:

<u>Cotton fabrics treated</u> with the <u>XYZ Process</u> have <u>features</u> that make them far superior to any previously known <u>flame-retardant-treated cotton fabrics</u>. XYZ Process treated fabrics <u>endure repeated laundering</u> and <u>dry cleaning</u>; are <u>glow resistant</u> as well as <u>flame resistant</u>; <u>form tough, pliable</u>, and <u>protective chars</u> when exposed to flames or intense heat; are <u>inert physiologically to persons handling</u> or exposed to the fabric; are only <u>slightly heavier than untreated fabrics</u>; and are <u>susceptible to further wet</u> and <u>dry finishing treatments</u>. In addition, the treated fabrics exhibit <u>little</u> or <u>no adverse change in feel, texture</u>, and <u>appearance</u> and are <u>shrink-, rot-, and mildew-resistant</u>. The treatment <u>reduces strength only slightly</u>. Finished fabrics have "easy care" <u>properties</u> in that they are <u>wrinkle resistant</u> and <u>dry rapidly</u>.

Now go back and read these questions and answer choices again, and try to choose the correct answer for each question. The answers and explanations are on pages 70–71.

You should be getting better at reading and answering questions. Try the next questions on your own. The answers and explanations for questions 10–18 can be found on pages 71–72.

QUESTIONS 10–12 ARE BASED ON THE FOLLOWING PASSAGE.

Language performs an essentially social function: It helps us get along together, communicate, and achieve a great measure of concerted action. Words are signs that have significance by convention, and those people who do not adopt the conventions simply fail to communicate. They do not "get along," and a social force arises that encourages them to achieve the correct associations. By "correct," we mean as used by other members of the social group. Some of the vital points about language are brought home to an English visitor to America, and vice-versa, because our vocabularies are nearly the same—but not quite.

10. As defined in the preceding selection, usage of a word is "correct" when it is

(A) defined in standard dictionaries.

(B) used by the majority of persons throughout the world who speak the same language.

(C) used by the majority of educated persons who speak the same language.

(D) used by other persons with whom we are associating.

11. In the preceding selection, the author is concerned primarily with the

(A) meaning of words.

(B) pronunciation of words.

(C) structure of sentences.

(D) origin and development of language.

12. According to the preceding selection, the main language problem of an English visitor to America stems from the fact that an English person

(A) uses some words that have different meanings for Americans.

(B) has different social values than the Americans.

(C) has had more exposure to non-English speaking persons than Americans.

(D) pronounces words differently than Americans.

QUESTIONS 13–18 ARE BASED ON THE FOLLOWING PASSAGE.

Because almost every office once had some contact with data-processed records, a senior stenographer had to have some understanding of the basic operations of data processing. Data processing systems once handled about one-third of all office paperwork. On punched cards, magnetic tape, or other media, data were recorded before being fed into the computer for processing. A machine such as the keypunch was used to convert the data written on the source document into the coded symbols on punched cards or tapes. After data were converted, they had to be verified to guarantee absolute accuracy of conversion. In this manner, data became a permanent record that could be read by computers that compared, stored, computed, and otherwise processed data at high speeds. One key person in a computer installation was a programmer, the man or woman who put business and scientific problems into special symbolic languages that could be read by the computer. Jobs done by the computer ranged from payroll operations to chemical process control, but most computer applications were directed toward management data. About half of the programmers employed by business came to their positions with college degrees; the remaining half were promoted to their positions, without regard to education, from within the organization on the basis of demonstrated ability.

13. Of the following, the best title for the preceding selection is

(A) The Stenographer as Data Processor.

(B) The Relation of Key Punching to Stenography.

(C) Understanding Data Processing.

(D) Permanent Office Records.

14. According to the passage, a senior stenographer had to understand the basic operations of data processing because

(A) almost every office had contact with data-processed records.

(B) any office worker might have been asked to verify the accuracy of data.

(C) most offices were involved in the production of permanent records.

(D) data may have been converted into computer language by typing on a keypunch.

15. According to the passage, the data that the computer understands were most often expressed as
    (A) a scientific programming language.
    (B) records or symbols punched on tape, cards, or other media.
    (C) records on cards.
    (D) records on tape.

16. According to the passage, computers were used most often to handle
    (A) management data.
    (B) problems of higher education.
    (C) the control of chemical processes.
    (D) payroll operations.

17. Computer programming was taught in many colleges and business schools. The passage implies that programmers in industry
    (A) had to have professional training.
    (B) needed professional training to advance.
    (C) had to have at least a college education to do adequate programming tasks.
    (D) did not need college education to do programming work.

18. According to the passage, data to be processed by computer should have been
    (A) recent.
    (B) complete.
    (C) basic.
    (D) verified.

POLICE-RELATED PRACTICE READING COMPREHENSION QUESTIONS

On exams that are written specifically for dispatchers in the police department, many reading passages will relate to legal definitions, laws, and police procedures. When reading these passages, you must pay special attention to details relating to exceptions, special preconditions, combinations of activities, choices of actions, and prescribed time sequences. Sometimes the printed procedure specifies that certain actions are to be taken only when there is a combination of factors, such as that a person actually breaks a window *and* has a gun. At other times, the procedures give choices of action under specific circumstances. You must read carefully to determine whether the passage requires a combination of factors or gives a choice, then make the appropriate judgment. When a time sequence is specified, be certain to follow that sequence in the prescribed order.

The following passages are based on police-specific questions. Beyond requiring reading comprehension skills, they require the special police exam emphasis we have just discussed.

QUESTIONS 19–23 ARE BASED ON THE FOLLOWING PASSAGE.

If we are to study crime in its widest social setting, we will find a variety of conduct that, although criminal in the legal sense, is not offensive to the moral conscience of a considerable number of persons. Traffic violations, for example, do not brand the offender as guilty of a moral offense. In fact, the recipient of a traffic ticket is usually simply the subject of some good-natured joking by friends. Although there may be indignation among certain groups of citizens against gambling and liquor law violations, these activities are often tolerated, if not openly supported, by the more numerous residents of the community. Indeed, certain social and service clubs regularly conduct gambling games and lotteries for the purpose of raising funds. Some communities regard violations involving the sale of liquor with little concern because they may stand to profit from increased license fees and taxes paid by dealers. The thousand and one forms of political graft and corruption that infest our urban centers only occasionally arouse public condemnation and official action.

19. According to the passage, all types of illegal conduct are

   (A) condemned by all elements of the community.

   (B) considered a moral offense, although some are tolerated by a few citizens.

   (C) violations of the law, but some are acceptable to certain elements of the community.

   (D) found in a social setting and therefore not punishable by law.

20. According to the passage, traffic violations are generally considered by society to be

   (A) crimes requiring the maximum penalty set by the law.

   (B) more serious than violations of the liquor laws.

   (C) offenses against the morals of the community.

   (D) relatively minor offenses requiring minimal punishment.

21. According to the passage, a lottery conducted for the purpose of raising funds for a church

   (A) is considered a serious violation of the law.

   (B) may be tolerated by a community that has laws against gambling.

   (C) may be conducted under special laws demanded by the more numerous residents of a community.

   (D) arouses indignation in most communities.

22. On the basis of the passage, the most likely reaction in the community to a police raid on a gambling casino would be

   (A) more an attitude of indifference than interest in the raid.

   (B) general approval of the raid.

   (C) condemnation of the raid by most people.

   (D) demand for further action, since this raid is not sufficient to end gambling activities.

23. Of the following, which best describes the central thought behind this passage and would be most suitable as a title?

   (A) Crime and the Police

   (B) Public Condemnation of Graft and Corruption

   (C) Gambling Is Not Always a Vicious Business

   (D) Public Attitudes Toward Law Violations

QUESTIONS 24–26 ARE BASED ON THE FOLLOWING PASSAGE.

The law enforcement agency is one of the most important agencies in the field of juvenile delinquency prevention. This is so, however, not because of the social work connected with this problem—for this is not a police matter—but because the officers are usually the first to come in contact with the delinquent. The manner of arrest and detention makes a deep impression on the delinquent and affects his or her lifelong attitude toward society and toward the law. The juvenile court is perhaps the most important agency in this work. Contrary to general opinion, however, it is not primarily concerned with putting children into correctional schools. The main purpose of the juvenile court is to save the child and to develop his or her emotional makeup so that he or she can grow up to be a decent and well-balanced citizen. The system of probation is the means by which the court seeks to accomplish these goals.

24. According to the passage, police work is an important part of a program to prevent juvenile delinquency because

(A) social work is no longer considered important in juvenile delinquency prevention.

(B) police officers are the first to have contact with the delinquent.

(C) police officers jail the offender so that they can change his or her attitude toward society and the law.

(D) it is the first step in placing the delinquent in jail.

25. According to the passage, the chief purpose of the juvenile court is to

(A) punish the child for the offense.

(B) select a suitable correctional school for the delinquent.

(C) use available means to help the delinquent become a better person.

(D) provide psychiatric care for the delinquent.

26. According to the passage, the juvenile court directs the development of delinquents under its care chiefly by

(A) placing the child on probation.

(B) sending the child to a correctional school.

(C) keeping the delinquent in prison.

(D) returning the child to his or her home.

QUESTION 27 IS BASED ON THE FOLLOWING PASSAGE.

When a person commits a traffic infraction, a police officer should

1. inform the violator of the offense committed.

2. request the violator to show his or her driver's license, vehicle registration, and insurance identification card. Failure to produce this required material may result in additional tickets. (Taxis, buses, and other rented vehicles do not require insurance identification cards.)

3. enter only one infraction on each ticket.

4. use a separate ticket for each additional infraction.

27. Police Officer Herrmann has been assigned to curb traffic violations at the intersection of Main Street and Central Avenue. Officer Herrmann observes a taxicab going through a red light at this intersection and signals the driver to pull over. The officer informs the cab driver of his violation and asks for the required material. The driver surrenders his license and registration to the officer. Police Officer Herrmann should

(A) issue the cab driver a ticket for the red light violation and issue him a separate ticket for not surrendering his insurance card.

(B) issue the cab driver one ticket including both the red light violation and the absence of the insurance card.

(C) issue the cab driver a ticket only for the red light violation.

(D) issue the cab driver a ticket only for not having an insurance card.

ANSWER KEY AND EXPLANATIONS

1. D	7. A	13. C	18. D	23. D
2. B	8. D	14. A	19. C	24. B
3. D	9. C	15. B	20. D	25. C
4. B	10. D	16. A	21. B	26. A
5. B	11. A	17. D	22. A	27. C
6. D	12. A			

1. **The correct answer is (D).** The best title for any reading passage is one that takes in all of the ideas presented without being too broad or too narrow. Choice (D) provides the most inclusive title for this passage. A look at the other choices shows you why. Choice (A) can be eliminated because the passage discusses typing a letter, not writing one. Although the first paragraph states that a letter should make a good first impression, the passage is clearly devoted to the letter, not the first impression, so choice (B) also can be eliminated. Choice (C) puts the emphasis on the wrong aspect of the typewritten letter. The passage concerns how to type a properly spaced letter, not how to judge one.

2. **The correct answer is (B).** Both spacing and cleanliness are mentioned in the first paragraph as ways to judge the quality of a typed letter. The first paragraph states that the margins should be "visually pleasing" in relation to the body of the letter, but that does not imply margins of a particular measure, so choice (A) is incorrect. Meaning is not discussed in the passage, only the look of the finished letter, so choice (C) is incorrect. The passage makes no mention of uncorrected errors, only the avoidance of erasures and overstrikes, so choice (D) is incorrect.

3. **The correct answer is (D).** The second sentence in the second paragraph states that the width of a letter "should not be less than four inches nor more than six inches." According to this rule, seven inches is an undesirable length.

4. **The correct answer is (B).** The answer to this question is stated in the last sentence of the reading passage. When a standard line length is used, the clerk "varies the spacing between the date line and the inside address according to the length of the letter." The passage offers no support for any other choice.

5. **The correct answer is (B).** This is a combination main idea and interpretation question. If you cannot answer this question readily, reread the selection. The author clearly thinks that the XYZ Process is terrific and says so in the first sentence. The rest of the selection presents a wealth of facts to support the initial claim.

6. **The correct answer is (D).** At first glance, you might think that this is an inference question requiring you to make a judgment based upon the few drawbacks of the process. Closer reading, however, shows that there is no contest for a correct answer here. This is a simple question of fact. The XYZ Process is a treatment for cotton fabrics.

7. **The correct answer is (A).** The text you chose to underline should help you with this question of fact. Cost is not mentioned; all other aspects of the XYZ Process are. If you are having trouble finding mention of the effect of the XYZ Process on the human body,

add to your vocabulary list "inert" and "physiologically."

8. **The correct answer is (D).** This is a main-idea question. You must distinguish between the main idea and the supporting and incidental facts.

9. **The correct answer is (C).** A drawback is a negative feature. The selection mentions only two negative features. The treatment reduces strength slightly, and it makes fabrics slightly heavier than untreated fabrics: Only one of these negative features is offered among the answer choices.

10. **The correct answer is (D).** The answer to this question is stated in the next-to-last sentence of the selection.

11. **The correct answer is (A).** This is a main-idea question. From reading the passage you should have gleaned that the reading was primarily about the meaning of words.

12. **The correct answer is (A).** This is a question of fact. The phrasing of the question is different from the phrasing of the last sentence, but the meaning is the same.

13. **The correct answer is (C).** Choosing the best title for this selection is not easy. Although the senior stenographer is mentioned in the first sentence, the selection is really not concerned with stenographers or with their relationship to key punching. Thus, choices (A) and (B) can be eliminated. Permanent office records are mentioned in the selection, but only along with other equally important uses for data processing. This fact eliminates choice (D). When in doubt, the most general title is usually correct.

14. **The correct answer is (A).** This is a question of fact. Any one of the answer choices could be correct, but the answer is given almost verbatim in the first sentence. Take advantage of answers that are handed to you in this way.

15. **The correct answer is (B).** This is a question of fact, but it is a tricky one. The program language is a symbolic language, not a scientific one. Reread carefully and eliminate choice (A). Choice (B) includes more of the information in the selection than either choice (C) or (D), and so is the best answer.

16. **The correct answer is (A).** This is a question of fact. The answer is stated in the next-to-last sentence.

17. **The correct answer is (D).** Remember that you are answering the questions on the basis of the information given in the selection. In spite of any information you may have to the contrary, the last sentence of the selection states that half the programmers employed in business achieved their positions by moving up from the ranks without regard to education.

18. **The correct answer is (D).** The answer appears in the second-to-last sentence in the first paragraph: "After data were converted, they had to be verified to guarantee absolute accuracy of conversion."

19. **The correct answer is (C).** The words "although" and "occasionally," which pop up in this passage, are the clues to the answer. Although illegal conduct is, by definition, a violation of law, much illegal conduct is not repulsive to many elements of the community. Choice (A) is a direct contradiction of the meaning of the passage, as is choice (B). Choice (D) is unsupported by the passage.

20. **The correct answer is (D).** The third sentence supports this answer. The fourth sentence directly contradicts choice (B) in its statement that gambling and liquor law violations may raise some indignation.

21. **The correct answer is (B).** The clear implication is that law-abiding citizens readily engage in gambling and lotteries for fund-raising purposes. Nothing

is said about special laws enabling this activity, so (C) is not a correct choice.

22. **The correct answer is (A).** Since gambling is not considered a serious criminal activity by the bulk of the populace, a raid on a gambling establishment would meet with indifference rather than approval or disapproval.

23. **The correct answer is (D).** Choice (A) is too broad; the passage deals specifically with certain kinds of crime. Choice (B) is opposite in thought to the content of the passage. Choice (C) is too narrow since other crimes are discussed in addition to gambling.

24. **The correct answer is (B).** The correct answer is stated in the second sentence: "… officers are usually the first to come in contact with the delinquent." The point with reference to social work is not that social work is unimportant, but that it is not a police matter. Choices (C) and (D) are in direct contradiction to the passage.

25. **The correct answer is (C).** The purpose of the juvenile court is to choose the best possible method to "save the

child." The passage implies that punishment and reform school are not the methods of choice—that probation is preferred. While psychiatric care may be the correct method in some cases, it is not mentioned in the passage and is not the best answer choice.

26. **The correct answer is (A).** The last sentence in the passage clearly states that probation is the method that the juvenile courts use to direct the development of delinquents.

27. **The correct answer is (C).** The taxi driver violated the law by going through a red light. Officer Herrmann correctly informed the driver of this infraction and must issue a ticket. If the violator had been driving a private automobile, Officer Herrmann would have had to issue a separate ticket for his not producing an insurance card. (See rules 3 and 4.) However, in this case, an exception applies. The exception is that taxis, along with buses and rented vehicles, do not need to have insurance identification cards.

MORE PRACTICE QUESTIONS

Just as all exams for similar positions are not alike, and all reading-based questions are not alike, so all traditional-style reading questions are not alike. Some traditional reading comprehension questions introduce novel situations and totally unfamiliar information. Others construct reading passages that use vocabulary and situations immediately relevant to the position for which the exam is testing. Some base each question upon a single reading passage, others use a series of questions based upon one passage. In the two exercises that follow, you will have an opportunity to review a variety of reading comprehension styles. In each exercise, circle the letter of the correct answer to each question. You will find correct answers and answer explanations at the end of each exercise.

Exercise 1

Directions: Read the passages below, then answer the questions that follow.

In a pole-vaulting competition, the judge decides on the minimum height to be jumped. The vaulter may attempt to jump any height above the minimum. Using flexible fiberglass poles, vaulters have jumped as high as 18 feet, 8¼ inches.

1. The passage best supports the statement that pole vaulters

   (A) may attempt to jump any height in competition.

   (B) must jump higher than 18 feet, 8¼ inches to win.

   (C) must jump higher than the height set by the judge.

   (D) must use fiberglass poles.

Only about one tenth of an iceberg is visible above the water. Eight to nine times as much ice is hidden below the water line. In the Antarctic Ocean, near the South Pole, some icebergs rise as high as 300 feet above the water line.

2. The passage best supports the statement that icebergs in the Antarctic Ocean

   (A) are usually 300 feet high.

   (B) can be as much as 3,000 feet high.

   (C) are difficult to spot.

   (D) are hazards to navigation.

You can tell a frog from a toad by its skin. In general, a frog's skin is moist, smooth, and shiny, while a toad's skin is dry, dull, and rough or covered with warts. Frogs are also better at jumping than toads are.

3. The passage best supports the statement that you can recognize a toad by its

   (A) great jumping ability.

   (B) smooth, shiny skin.

   (C) lack of warts.

   (D) dry, rough skin.

Thomas Edison was responsible for more than 1,000 inventions in his 84-year lifespan. Among the most famous of his inventions are the phonograph, the electric light bulb, motion picture film, the electric generator, and the battery.

4. The passage best supports the statement that Thomas Edison

    (A) was the most famous inventor.

    (B) was responsible for 84 inventions.

    (C) invented many things in his short life.

    (D) was responsible for the phonograph and motion picture film.

Amateur sportsmen or sportswomen are those who take part in sports purely for enjoyment, not for financial reward. Professionals are people who are paid to participate in sports. Most athletes who compete in the Olympic Games are amateurs.

5. The passage best supports the statement that one example of an amateur in sports might be

    (A) an Olympic champion.

    (B) a member of the Philadelphia Eagles.

    (C) the holder of the heavyweight boxing crown.

    (D) a participant in the World Series.

A year—the time it takes the Earth to go exactly once around the sun—is not 365 days. It is actually 365 days, 6 hours, 9 minutes, 9½ seconds—or 365¼ days. Leap years make up for this discrepancy by adding an extra day once every four years.

6. The passage best supports the statement that the purpose of leap years is to

    (A) adjust for the fact it takes 365¼ days for the Earth to circle the sun.

    (B) make up for time lost in the work year.

    (C) occur every four years.

    (D) allow for differences in the length of a year in each time zone.

Scientists are taking a closer look at the recent boom in the use of wood for heating. Wood burning, it seems, releases high-level pollutants. It is believed that burning wood produces a thousand times more CO—carbon monoxide—than natural gas does when it burns.

7. The passage best supports the statement that CO is

    (A) natural gas.

    (B) wood.

    (C) carbon monoxide.

    (D) heat.

The average American family makes a major move every ten years. This means that family history becomes scattered. In some cases, a person searching for his or her family's past must hire a professional researcher to track down his or her ancestors.

8. The passage best supports the statement that every few years
   (A) somebody tries to trace his or her family's history.
   (B) the average American family moves.
   (C) family history becomes scattered.
   (D) professional researchers are hired to track down ancestors.

When gas is leaking, any spark or sudden flame can ignite it. This can create a "flashback," which burns off the gas in a quick puff of smoke and flame. But the real danger is in a large leak, which can cause an explosion.

9. The passage best supports the statement that the real danger from leaking gas is a(n)
   (A) flashback.
   (B) puff of smoke and flame.
   (C) explosion.
   (D) spark.

With the exception of Earth, all of the planets in our solar system are named for gods and goddesses in Greek or Roman legends. This is because the other planets were thought to be in heaven, like the gods, and our planet lay beneath, like the earth.

10. The passage best supports the statement that all the planets except Earth
    (A) were part of Greek and Roman legends.
    (B) were thought to be in heaven.
    (C) are part of the same solar system.
    (D) were worshiped as gods.

The Supreme Court was established by Article 3 of the Constitution. Since 1869 it has been made up of 9 members—the Chief Justice and 8 associate justices—who are appointed for life. Supreme Court justices are named by the President and must be confirmed by the Senate.

11. The passage best supports the statement that the Supreme Court
    (A) was established in 1869.
    (B) consists of 9 justices.
    (C) consists of justices appointed by the Senate.
    (D) changes with each presidential election.

The sport of automobile racing originated in France in 1894. There are five basic types of competition: (1) the Grand Prix, a series of races that leads to a world championship; (2) stock car racing, which uses specially equipped standard cars; (3) midget car racing; (4) sports car racing; and (5) drag racing. The best-known U.S. race is the Indianapolis 500, first held in 1911.

12. The passage best supports the statement that the sport of auto racing

(A) started with the Indianapolis 500 in 1911.

(B) uses only standard cars, which are specially equipped.

(C) holds its championship race in France.

(D) includes five different types of competition.

The brain controls both voluntary behavior, such as walking and talking, and most involuntary behavior, such as the beating of the heart and breathing. In higher animals, the brain is also the site of emotions, memory, self-awareness, and thought.

13. The passage best supports the statement that in higher animals, the brain controls

(A) emotions, memory, and thought.

(B) voluntary behavior.

(C) most involuntary behavior.

(D) all of the above.

The speed of a boat is measured in knots. One knot is equal to a speed of one nautical mile per hour. A nautical mile is equal to 6,080 feet, while an ordinary mile is 5,280 feet.

14. The passage best supports the statement that

(A) a nautical mile is longer than an ordinary mile.

(B) a speed of 2 knots is the same as 2 miles per hour.

(C) a knot is the same as a mile.

(D) the distance a boat travels is measured in knots.

There are only two grooves on an LP—one on each side. The groove is cut in a spiral on the surface of the record. For stereo sound, a different sound is recorded in each wall of the groove. The pick-up produces two signals, one of which goes to the left speaker and one to the right speaker.

15. The passage best supports the statement that stereo sound is produced by

(A) cutting extra grooves in an LP.

(B) recording different sounds in each wall of the groove.

(C) sending the sound to two speakers.

(D) having left and right speakers.

The overuse of antibiotics today represents a growing danger, according to many medical authorities. Patients everywhere, stimulated by reports of new wonder drugs, continue to ask their doctors for antibiotics to relieve a cold, flu, or any other viral infections that occur during the course of a bad winter. But, for the common cold and many other viral infections, antibiotics have no effect.

16. The passage best supports the statement that

(A) the use of antibiotics is becoming a health hazard.

(B) antibiotics are of no value in the treatment of many viral infections.

(C) patients should ask their doctors for a shot of one of the new wonder drugs to relieve the symptoms of the flu.

(D) the treatment of colds and other viral infections by antibiotics will lessen their severity.

A prompt report of every unusual occurrence on a train will be made by telephone to the Station Supervisor's office, whether or not a written report is used. The telephone report should include the time and place and a concise statement of the circumstances and actions taken, including the names and addresses of passengers and the names and badge numbers of all employees and police officers involved. Details will be confirmed in a written report when requested. No unusual occurrence is too trivial to report.

17. The passage best supports the statement that when reporting an unusual occurrence, a railroad clerk need not say

(A) where it happened.

(B) what was done about it.

(C) when it occurred.

(D) why it happened.

Alertness and attentiveness are essential qualities for success as a telephone operator. The work the operator performs often requires careful attention under conditions of stress.

18. The passage best supports the statement that a telephone operator

(A) always works under great strain.

(B) cannot be successful unless he or she memorizes many telephone numbers.

(C) must be trained before he or she can render good service.

(D) must be able to work under difficulties.

To prevent accidents, safety devices must be used to guard exposed machinery, the light in the plant must be adequate, and mechanics should be instructed in safety rules that they must follow for their own protection.

19. The passage best supports the statement that industrial accidents

(A) are always avoidable.

(B) may be due to ignorance.

(C) usually result from inadequate machinery.

(D) cannot be entirely overcome.

The leader of an industrial enterprise has two principal functions. He or she must manufacture and distribute a product at a profit, and he or she must keep individuals and groups of individuals working effectively together.

20. The passage best supports the statement that an industrial leader should be able to

(A) increase the distribution of his or her plant's products.

(B) introduce large-scale production methods.

(C) coordinate the activities of employees.

(D) profit by the experience of other leaders.

ANSWER KEY AND EXPLANATIONS

1. C	5. A		9. C	13. D		17. D	
2. B	6. A		10. B	14. A		18. D	
3. D	7. C		11. B	15. B		19. B	
4. D	8. B		12. D	16. B		20. C	

1. **The correct answer is (C).** The judge decides on the minimum height to be jumped, so pole vaulters must jump higher than the height set by the judge.

2. **The correct answer is (B).** Since some icebergs in the Antarctic Ocean rise as high as 300 feet above the water, and since only one tenth of an iceberg is visible above the water, there are icebergs in the Antarctic Ocean that are as much as 3,000 feet high altogether.

3. **The correct answer is (D).** A toad's skin is dry, dull, and rough or covered with warts.

4. **The correct answer is (D).** The phonograph and motion picture film are listed among Thomas Edison's inventions. Since Edison lived 84 years, his was not a short life. While Edison may well be in the running for designation as the most famous inventor, such a statement is not supported by the paragraph.

5. **The correct answer is (A).** Since the other three options involve monetary gain for the athlete, the correct answer is (A).

6. **The correct answer is (A).** This is a restatement of the paragraph. The other choices have no relevance whatsoever to the paragraph.

7. **The correct answer is (C).** The answer is stated in the last sentence.

8. **The correct answer is (B).** While all four statements are somewhat supported by the paragraph, the *best* support is from the statement that the average American family moves every few years.

9. **The correct answer is (C).** See the last sentence.

10. **The correct answer is (B).** Choice (B) is a restatement of the last sentence.

11. **The correct answer is (B).** The other three choices are incorrect statements. The date 1869 refers to the establishment of the current 9-member court. Justices are appointed by the President, are confirmed by the Senate, and serve for life.

12. **The correct answer is (D).** Most of the paragraph is devoted to describing the five different types of competition.

13. **The correct answer is (D).** The word *also* in the last sentence is the key to the fact that in higher animals the brain controls voluntary behavior, involuntary behavior, emotions, memory, and thought.

14. **The correct answer is (A).** Because 6,080 feet is longer than 5,280 feet, the correct answer is choice (A).

15. **The correct answer is (B).** Stereophonic sound is *transmitted* by sending the sound to two speakers and is received by having left- and right-hand speakers, but it is *produced* by recording different sounds in each wall of the groove.

16. **The correct answer is (B).** The paragraph may open by mentioning that there is a growing danger in the overuse of antibiotics; however, the paragraph does not expand on this theme. The quote mainly focuses on the ineffectiveness of antibiotics against viral infections. Because more than twice as much of the paragraph is devoted to the second theme, choice (B) is the best answer.

17. **The correct answer is (D).** The report must include place (A), action taken (B), and time (C). The cause of the unusual occurrence need not be part of the report.

18. **The correct answer is (D).** The paragraph states that the work of the operator often requires careful attention under conditions of stress. This means that the operator must be able to work under difficulties. The paragraph does not state that the work must always be performed under stress.

19. **The correct answer is (B).** The answer to this question is implied in the statement that "mechanics be instructed in safety rules that they must follow for their own protection." If the mechanics must be instructed, then accidents may occur if they have not been instructed (that is, if they are ignorant).

20. **The correct answer is (C).** Keeping individuals and groups of individuals working together effectively is coordinating the activities of employees. This answer is stated. The other choices require more interpretation and more stretching than necessary to choose the correct answer. Introduction of large-scale production methods and increasing distribution of products may very well increase profits, but not necessarily.

Exercise 2

Directions: Read the passages below, then answer the questions that follow.

The force reconciling and coordinating all human conflicts and directing people in the harmonious accomplishment of their work is the supervisor. To deal with people successfully, the first person a supervisor must learn to work with is himself or herself.

1. According to the passage, the most accurate of the following conclusions is

    (A) human conflicts are the result of harmonious accomplishment.

    (B) a supervisor should attempt to reconcile all the different views subordinates may have.

    (C) a supervisor who understands himself or herself is in a good position to deal with others successfully.

    (D) the reconciling force in human conflicts is the ability to deal with people successfully.

Law must be stable and yet it cannot stand still.

2. This sentence means most nearly that

    (A) law is a fixed body of subject matter.

    (B) law must adapt itself to changing conditions.

    (C) law is a poor substitute for justice.

    (D) the true administration of justice is the firmest pillar of good government.

The treatment to be given to the offender cannot alter the fact of the offense, but we can take measures to reduce the chance of similar acts occurring in the future. We should banish the criminal, not to exact revenge nor directly to encourage reform, but to deter that person and others from further illegal attacks on society.

3. According to the passage, prisoners should be punished to

    (A) alter the nature of their offenses.

    (B) banish them from society.

    (C) deter them and others from similar illegal attacks on society.

    (D) directly encourage reform.

On the other hand, the treatment of prisoners on a basis of direct reform is doomed to failure. Neither honest persons nor criminals will tolerate a bald proposition from anyone to alter their characters or habits, least of all if we attempt to gain such a change by a system of coercion.

4. According to this passage, criminals

    (A) are incorrigible.

    (B) are incapable of being coerced.

    (C) are not likely to turn into law-abiding citizens.

    (D) possess very firm characters.

While much thought has been devoted to the question of how to build walls high enough to keep persons temporarily in prison, we have devoted very little attention to the treatment necessary to enable them to come out permanently cured—inclined to be friends rather than enemies of their law-abiding fellow citizens.

5. According to this passage, much thought has been devoted to the problem of prisons as

(A) vengeful agencies.

(B) efficient custodial agencies.

(C) efficient sanatoriums.

(D) places from which society's friends might issue.

Community organization most often includes persons whose behavior is unconventional in relation to generally accepted social definition, if such persons wield substantial influence with the residents.

6. The inference one can most validly draw from this statement is that

(A) influential persons are often likely to be unconventional.

(B) the success of a community organization depends largely on the democratic processes employed by it.

(C) a gang leader may sometimes be an acceptable recruit for a community organization.

(D) the unconventional behavior of a local barkeeper may often become acceptable to the community.

The safeguard of democracy is education. The education of youth during a limited period of more or less compulsory attendance at school does not suffice. The educative process is a lifelong one.

7. The statement most consistent with this passage is:

(A) The school is not the only institution that can contribute to the education of the population.

(B) All democratic people are educated.

(C) The entire population should be required to go to school throughout life.

(D) If compulsory education were not required, the educative process would be more effective.

The police officer's art consists in applying and enforcing a multitude of laws and ordinances in such degree or proportion and in such manner that the greatest degree of social protection will be secured. The degree of enforcement and the method of application will vary with each neighborhood and community.

8. According to this statement,

(A) each neighborhood or community must judge for itself to what extent the law is to be enforced.

(B) a police officer should only enforce those laws that are designed to give the greatest degree of social protection.

(C) the manner and intensity of law enforcement is not necessarily the same in all communities.

(D) all laws and ordinances must be enforced in a community with the same degree of intensity.

As a rule, police officers, through service and experience, are familiar with the duties and the methods and means required to perform them. Yet, left to themselves, their aggregate effort would disintegrate and the vital work of preserving the peace would never be accomplished.

9. According to this statement, the most accurate of the following conclusions is:

   (A) Police officers are sufficiently familiar with their duties as to need no supervision.

   (B) Working together for a common purpose is not efficient without supervision.

   (C) Police officers are familiar with the methods of performing their duties because of rules.

   (D) Preserving the peace is so vital that it can never be said to be completed.

ANSWER QUESTIONS 10–12 ON THE BASIS OF THE INFORMATION GIVEN IN THE FOLLOWING PASSAGE.

Criminal science is largely the science of identification. Progress in this field has been marked and sometimes spectacular because new techniques, instruments, and facts flow continuously from the scientific community. But the crime laboratories are understaffed, trade secrets still prevail, and inaccurate conclusions are often the result. However, modern gadgets cannot substitute for the skilled, intelligent investigator; he or she must be their master.

10. According to this passage, criminal science

    (A) excludes the field of investigation.

    (B) is primarily interested in establishing identity.

    (C) is based on the equipment used in crime laboratories.

    (D) uses techniques different from those used in other sciences.

11. According to the passage, advances in criminal science have been

    (A) extremely limited.

    (B) slow but steady.

    (C) unusually reliable.

    (D) outstanding.

12. According to the passage, a problem that has not been overcome completely in crime work is

    (A) unskilled investigators.

    (B) the expense of new equipment and techniques.

    (C) an insufficient number of personnel in crime laboratories.

    (D) inaccurate equipment used in laboratories.

ANSWER QUESTION 13 USING THE INFORMATION PRESENTED IN THE FOLLOWING PASSAGE.

While the safe burglar can ply his or her trade the year round, the loft burglar has more seasonal activities, since only at certain periods of the year is a substantial amount of valuable merchandise stored in lofts.

13. The generalization that this statement best illustrates is

    (A) nothing is ever completely safe from a thief.

    (B) there are safe burglars and loft burglars.

    (C) some types of burglary are seasonal.

    (D) the safe burglar considers safe-cracking a trade.

ANSWER QUESTIONS 14–17 ON THE BASIS OF THE INFORMATION GIVEN IN THE FOLLOWING PASSAGE.

When a vehicle has been disabled in a tunnel, the officer on patrol in this zone shall press the emergency truck light button. In the fast lane, red lights will go on throughout the tunnel; in the slow lane, amber lights will go on throughout the tunnel. The yellow zone light will go on at each signal control station throughout the tunnel and will flash the number of the zone in which the stoppage has occurred. A red flashing pilot light will appear only at the signal control station at which the emergency truck button was pressed. The emergency garage will receive an audible and visual signal indicating the signal control station at which the emergency truck button was pressed. The garage officer shall acknowledge

receipt of the signal by pressing the acknowledgment button. This will cause the pilot light at the operated signal control station in the tunnel to cease flashing and to remain steady. It is an answer to the officer at the operated signal control station that the emergency truck is responding to the call.

14. According to this passage, when the emergency truck light button is pressed,

    (A) amber lights will go on in every lane throughout the tunnel.

    (B) emergency signal lights will go on only in the lane in which the disabled vehicle is located.

    (C) red lights will go on in the fast lane throughout the tunnel.

    (D) pilot lights at all signal control stations will turn amber.

15. According to this passage, the number of the zone in which the stoppage has occurred is flashed

    (A) immediately after all the lights in the tunnel turn red.

    (B) by the yellow zone light at each signal control station.

    (C) by the emergency truck at the point of stoppage.

    (D) by the emergency garage.

16. According to the passage, an officer near the disabled vehicle will know that the emergency tow truck is coming when

    (A) the pilot light at the operated signal control station appears and flashes red.

    (B) an audible signal is heard in the tunnel.

    (C) the zone light at the operated signal control station turns red.

    (D) the pilot light at the operated signal control station becomes steady.

17. Under the system described in the passage, it would be correct to conclude that

   (A) officers at all signal control stations are expected to acknowledge that they have received the stoppage signal.

   (B) officers at all signal control stations will know where the stoppage has occurred.

   (C) all traffic in both lanes of that side of the tunnel in which the stoppage has occurred must stop until the emergency truck has arrived.

   (D) there are two emergency garages, each able to respond to stoppages in traffic going in one particular direction.

ANSWER QUESTIONS 18–20 USING THE INFORMATION PRESENTED IN THE FOLLOWING PASSAGE.

The use of a roadblock is simply an adaptation of the military practice of encirclement by the police. Successful operation of a roadblock plan depends almost entirely on the amount of advance study and planning given to such operations. A thorough and detailed examination of the roads and terrain under the jurisdiction of a given police agency should be made in advance, and the locations of potential roadblocks pinpointed. The first principle to be borne in mind in the location of each roadblock is the time element. The roadblock's location must be at a point beyond which the fugitive could not have possibly traveled in the time elapsed from the commission of the crime to the arrival of the officers at the roadblock.

18. According to the passage,

   (A) military operations have made extensive use of roadblocks.

   (B) the military practice of encirclement is an adaptation of police use of roadblocks.

   (C) the technique of encirclement has been widely used by military forces.

   (D) a roadblock is generally more effective than encirclement.

19. According to the passage,

   (A) advance study and planning are of minor importance in the success of roadblock operations.

   (B) a thorough and detailed examination of all roads within a radius of fifty miles should precede the determination of a roadblock location.

   (C) consideration of terrain features is important in planning the location of roadblocks.

   (D) a roadblock operation can seldom be successfully undertaken by a single police agency.

20. According to the passage,

   (A) the factor of time is the sole consideration in the location of a roadblock.

   (B) the maximum speed possible in the method of escape is of major importance in roadblock location.

   (C) the time the officers arrive at the site of a proposed roadblock is of little importance.

   (D) a roadblock should be situated as close to the scene of the crime as the terrain will permit.

ANSWER QUESTIONS 21 AND 22 USING THE INFORMATION PRESENTED IN THE FOLLOWING PASSAGE.

A number of crimes, such as robbery, assault, rape, certain forms of theft, and burglary are high visibility crimes in that it is apparent to all concerned that they are criminal acts prior to or at the time they are committed. In contrast to these, check forgeries, especially those committed by first offenders, have low visibility. There is little in the criminal act or in the interaction between the check passer and the person cashing the check to identify it as a crime. Closely related to this special quality of the forgery crime is the fact that, while it is formally defined and treated as a felonious or "infamous" crime, it is informally held by the legally untrained public to be a relatively harmless form of crime.

21. According to the passage, crimes of "high visibility"

    (A) are immediately recognized as crimes by the victims.

    (B) take place in public view.

    (C) always involve violence or the threat of violence.

    (D) are usually committed after dark.

22. According to the passage,

    (A) the public regards check forgery as a minor crime.

    (B) the law regards check forgery as a minor crime.

    (C) the law distinguishes between check forgery and other forgery.

    (D) it is easier to spot inexperienced check forgers than other criminals.

ANSWER QUESTIONS 23 AND 24 USING THE INFORMATION PRESENTED IN THE FOLLOWING PASSAGE.

The racketeer is primarily concerned with business affairs—legitimate or otherwise—and preferably those that are close to the margin of legitimacy. The racketeer gets the best opportunities from business organizations that meet the need of large sections of the public for goods or services that are defined as illegitimate by the same public, such as prostitution, gambling, illicit drugs, or liquor. In contrast to the thief, the racketeer and the establishments controlled deliver goods and services for money received.

23. It can be deduced from the passage that suppression of racketeers is difficult because

    (A) victims of racketeers are not guilty of violating the law.

    (B) racketeers are generally engaged in fully legitimate enterprises.

    (C) many people want services that are not obtainable through legitimate sources.

    (D) laws prohibiting gambling and prostitution are unenforceable.

24. According to the passage, racketeering, unlike theft, involves

    (A) objects of value.

    (B) payment for goods received.

    (C) organized gangs.

    (D) unlawful activities.

ANSWER QUESTION 25 USING THE INFORMATION PRESENTED IN THE FOLLOWING PASSAGE.

In examining the scene of a homicide, one should not only look for the usual, standard traces—fingerprints, footprints, and so on—but also have eyes open for details that at first glance may not seem to have any connection with the crime.

25. The most logical inference to be drawn from this statement is that

(A) in general, standard traces are not important.

(B) sometimes one should not look for footprints.

(C) usually only the standard traces are important.

(D) one cannot tell in advance what will be important.

ANSWER QUESTIONS 26 AND 27 USING THE INFORMATION PRESENTED IN THE FOLLOWING PASSAGE.

If a motor vehicle fails to pass inspection, the owner will be given a rejection notice by the inspection station. Repairs must be made within ten days after this notice is issued. It is not necessary to have the required adjustment or repairs made at the station where the inspection occurred. The vehicle may be taken to any garage. Reinspection after repairs may be made at any official inspection station, not necessarily the same station that made the initial inspection. The

registration of any motor vehicle for which an inspection sticker has not been obtained as required, or that is not repaired and inspected within ten days after inspection indicates defects, is subject to suspension. A vehicle cannot be used on public highways while its registration is under suspension.

26. According to the passage, the owner of a car that does not pass inspection must

(A) have repairs made at the same station that rejected the car.

(B) take the car to another station and have it reinspected.

(C) have repairs made anywhere and then have the car reinspected.

(D) not use the car on a public highway until the necessary repairs have been made.

27. According to the passage, which of the following situations may be cause for suspension of the registration of a vehicle?

(A) An inspection sticker was issued before the rejection notice had been in force for ten days.

(B) The vehicle was not reinspected by the station that rejected it originally.

(C) The vehicle was not reinspected either by the station that rejected it originally or by the garage that made the repairs.

(D) The vehicle has not had defective parts repaired within ten days after inspection.

ANSWER QUESTION 28 USING THE INFORMATION PRESENTED IN THE FOLLOWING PASSAGE.

A statute states: "A person who steals an article worth less than $100 where no aggravating circumstances accompany the act is guilty of petty larceny. If the article is worth $100 or more, it may be larceny second degree."

28. If all you know is that Edward Smith stole an article worth $100, it may reasonably be said that
   (A) Smith is guilty of petty larceny.
   (B) Smith is guilty of larceny second degree.
   (C) Smith is guilty of neither petty larceny nor larceny second degree.
   (D) precisely what charge will be placed against Smith is uncertain.

ANSWER QUESTIONS 29 AND 30 USING THE INFORMATION PRESENTED IN THE FOLLOWING PASSAGE.

The city police department will accept for investigation no report of a person missing from his or her residence if such residence is located outside of the city. The person reporting same will be advised to report such fact to the police department of the locality where the missing person lives, which will, if necessary, communicate officially with the city police department. However, a report will be accepted of a person who is missing from a temporary residence in the city, but the person making the report will be instructed to make a report also to the police department of the locality where the missing person lives.

29. According to the passage, a report to the city police department of a missing person whose permanent residence is outside of the city will
   (A) always be investigated, provided that a report is also made to local police authorities.
   (B) never be investigated, unless requested officially by local police authorities.
   (C) be investigated in cases of temporary residence in the city, but a report should always be made to local police authorities.
   (D) always be investigated, and a report will be made to the local police authorities by the city police department.

30. Mr. Smith of Oldtown and Mr. Jones of Newtown have an appointment in the city, but Mr. Jones doesn't appear. Mr. Smith, after trying repeatedly to phone Mr. Jones the next day, believes that something has happened to him. According to the passage, Mr. Smith should apply to the police of
   (A) Oldtown.
   (B) Newtown.
   (C) Newtown and the city.
   (D) Oldtown and the city.

A police department rule reads as follows: "A Deputy Commissioner acting as Police Commissioner shall carry out the orders of the Police Commissioner, previously given, and such orders shall not, except in cases of extreme emergency, be countermanded."

31. This rule means most nearly that, except in cases of extreme emergency,

(A) the orders given by a Deputy Commissioner acting as Police Commissioner may not be revoked.

(B) a Deputy Commissioner acting as Police Commissioner should not revoke orders previously given by the Police Commissioner.

(C) a Deputy Commissioner acting as Police Commissioner is vested with the same authority to issue orders as the Police Commissioner.

(D) only a Deputy Commissioner acting as Police Commissioner may issue orders in the absence of the Police Commissioner.

A crime is an act committed or omitted in violation of a public law either forbidding or commanding it.

32. This statement implies most nearly that

(A) crimes can be omitted.

(B) a forbidding act, if omitted, is a crime.

(C) an act of omission may be criminal.

(D) to commit an act not commanded is criminal.

"He who by command, counsel, or assistance procures another to commit a crime is, in morals and in law, as culpable as the visible actor himself; for the reason that the criminal act, whichever it may be, is imputable to the person who conceived it and set the forces in motion for its actual accomplishment."

33. Of the following, the most accurate inference from this statement is that

(A) a criminal act does not have to be committed for a crime to be committed.

(B) acting as counselor for a criminal is a crime.

(C) the mere counseling of a criminal act can never be a crime if no criminal act is committed.

(D) a person acting only as an adviser may be guilty of committing a criminal act.

A felony is a crime punishable by death or imprisonment in a state prison, and a misdemeanor is a crime punishable by fine or imprisonment in a municipal or county jail.

34. According to this passage, the decisive distinction between "felony" and "misdemeanor" is the

(A) degree of criminality.

(B) type of crime.

(C) manner of punishment.

(D) judicial jurisdiction.

ANSWER QUESTION 35 USING THE INFORMATION PRESENTED IN THE FOLLOWING PASSAGE.

If the second or third felony is such that, upon a first conviction, the offender would be imprisoned for any term less than his or her natural life, then such person must be sentenced to imprisonment for an indeterminate term. The minimum of this term shall not be less than one half of the longest term prescribed upon a first conviction, and the maximum shall not be longer than twice such longest term. However, the minimum sentence imposed upon the second or third felony offender shall in no case be less than five years; except that where the maximum punishment for a second or third felony offender hereunder is five years or less, the minimum sentence must be not less than two years.

35. According to this passage, a person who has a second felony conviction shall receive as a sentence for that second felony an indeterminate term

(A) not less than twice the minimum term prescribed upon a first conviction as a maximum.

(B) not less than one half the minimum term of the first conviction as a maximum.

(C) not more than twice the minimum term prescribed upon a first conviction as a minimum.

(D) with a maximum of not more than twice the longest term prescribed for a first conviction for this crime.

ANSWER KEY AND EXPLANATIONS

1. C	8. C	15. B	22. A	29. C
2. B	9. B	16. D	23. C	30. B
3. C	10. B	17. B	24. B	31. B
4. C	11. D	18. C	25. D	32. C
5. B	12. C	19. C	26. C	33. D
6. C	13. C	20. B	27. D	34. C
7. A	14. C	21. A	28. D	35. D

1. **The correct answer is (C).** Before understanding and working with others, one must first understand one's own motivation and working habits. The supervisor with good self-understanding is an effective supervisor.

2. **The correct answer is (B).** To adapt means to change in response to changing conditions without a total change of substance.

3. **The correct answer is (C).** This passage expresses the philosophy that the purpose of punishment is neither to make the offender "pay for his/her crime" nor to reform the offender, but rather to protect society from the specific criminal and to serve, by example, as a deterrent to others.

4. **The correct answer is (C).** The philosophy expressed here is "Once a criminal, always a criminal." Attempts at reform and rehabilitation are futile. (Remember: Answer questions based on the information in the passages. You may disagree; you may even know that the information is incorrect. However, your answer must be based on the passage, not upon your opinions or your knowledge.)

5. **The correct answer is (B).** This question deals with a philosophy contrary to those expressed in the previous two questions. It states that we have devoted attention to the means of making prisons secure places in which to keep offenders, but have not given much thought to rehabilitation.

6. **The correct answer is (C).** You may find this principle difficult to accept, but it represents accepted practice in many quarters. The concept is that if the person with leadership qualities—even if combined with antisocial behaviors—is drawn into the mainstream, that person can learn to accept certain norms of the majority and transmit these more acceptable attitudes and behaviors to the group that respects him or her. The term used to describe the drawing into the inner circle of the unconventional leader is "co-opting."

7. **The correct answer is (A).** Since education continues throughout life, yet schooling is of limited duration, obviously education occurs in places other than schools.

8. **The correct answer is (C).** The needs and desires of communities vary; therefore, degree and manner of enforcement of different laws in different communities will also vary.

9. **The correct answer is (B).** The meaning of this passage is that good intentions and thorough knowledge of duties are not sufficient. Organization

and supervision are vital to efficient operation of the police function.

10. **The correct answer is (B).** The science of identification is primarily interested in establishing identity.

11. **The correct answer is (D).** Marked and spectacular progress is outstanding.

12. **The correct answer is (C).** Understaffed laboratories have insufficient personnel.

13. **The correct answer is (C).** The concept may be novel to you, but the question itself is an easy one. The answer is stated directly in the paragraph.

14. **The correct answer is (C).** See the second sentence. When a reading passage is crammed with details, most of the questions will be strictly factual.

15. **The correct answer is (B).** See the third sentence.

16. **The correct answer is (D).** See the last two sentences.

17. **The correct answer is (B).** The yellow zone light goes on at each signal control station and flashes the number of the zone in which the stoppage has occurred, so all officers receive this information.

18. **The correct answer is (C).** If the military practice of encirclement was adapted for use by the police, we may assume that it was widely and successfully used. Choice (B) reverses the order of the adaptation.

19. **The correct answer is (C).** This is the clear implication of the third sentence.

20. **The correct answer is (B).** The roadblock must be placed beyond the point that the fugitive could have possibly reached, so maximum speed of escape is vitally important in the establishment of a roadblock.

21. **The correct answer is (A).** See the first sentence.

22. **The correct answer is (A).** See the last sentence.

23. **The correct answer is (C).** The racketeer provides goods and services that are officially illegal, but that are desired by otherwise respectable members of the general public. Since the public wants these services, active effort to suppress the providers is unlikely.

24. **The correct answer is (B).** See the last sentence.

25. **The correct answer is (D).** The police officer must always be observant and alert to both abnormalities and routine details in the environment. This useful quality in a police officer is the reason many police officer exams include a section testing powers of observation and memory.

26. **The correct answer is (C).** The state is not concerned with who makes repairs or with who does the inspection, only that these be accomplished.

27. **The correct answer is (D).** See the next-to-last sentence.

28. **The correct answer is (D).** Beware of qualifying words and definite statements. If the article is worth $100 or more, it *may* be larceny second degree, but not necessarily.

29. **The correct answer is (C).** See the last sentence.

30. **The correct answer is (B).** Mr. Jones is a resident of Newtown, so the missing person report must be filed with the Newtown police. The meeting of Smith and Jones was to have taken place in the city, but Jones was not a temporary resident of the city, so the city police are not involved in this case.

31. **The correct answer is (B).** The word "countermand" means "revoke." The Deputy Commissioner carries out the orders of the Police Commissioner and revokes them only in cases of extreme emergency.

32. The correct answer is (C). An act of omission, if it is in violation of a public law commanding said act, is a crime. The act of omission is not a crime if it is not in violation of a public law.

33. The correct answer is (D). The person who conceives and sets in motion the forces for the accomplishment of a crime—in other words, the adviser who convinced another to commit a criminal act—may well be deemed guilty of committing the criminal act.

34. The correct answer is (C). Crimes are defined by the level and manner of punishment the offender receives.

35. The correct answer is (D). You may have to do some very careful reading and rereading to find the answer to this question. You will find it in the the end of the second sentence: ". . . and the maximum shall not be longer than twice such longest term."

SUMMING IT UP

- The single most common question type in dispatcher exams is reading comprehension. Before you begin studying strategies for answering reading-based questions, think about whether you need to sharpen your present reading habits and skills. If so, try to work on that task before exam day. Read articles in your daily newspaper all the way through rather than skimming the first paragraph or two. Underline details and ideas that seem crucial to the meaning of the article. Notice points of view, arguments, and supporting information. If you do this every day, you're bound to become more efficient in your reading comprehension.

- Don't try to tackle every reading comprehension suggestion in this chapter all at once. Take on a little at a time and work systematically for best results. You may need just 15 minutes a day—even this small amount of time will be helpful.

- Remember that reading includes building your vocabulary—one of the most effective ways to strengthen your comprehension. Make a point of listing words with which you're unfamiliar as you read. Then look up those words and write them in a separate notebook with their definitions. This will help you "lock" the information into your memory and will provide a handy reference.

- Follow the five steps to answering reading comprehension questions outlined in this chapter: read the questions first; scan the reading passage quickly; read the passage for detail; return to the questions; and scan the passage again.

- Carefully review the five most common types of reading comprehension questions (question of fact or detail, best title or main idea, interpretation, inference, and vocabulary) and practice answering each type using the sample questions in this chapter and in the Practice Tests in this book. This will help you be at your best on exam day.

- Exams written specifically for dispatchers in the police department will contain reading passages related to legal definitions, laws, and police procedures. If you encounter these on your exam, pay special attention to details relating to exceptions, special preconditions, combinations of activities, choices of actions, and prescribed time sequences. You'll need to determine whether the passage requires a combination of factors or gives a choice, then make the appropriate judgment. When a time sequence is specified, be certain to follow that sequence in the prescribed order.

Vocabulary and Spelling

VOCABULARY ON THE PUBLIC SAFETY DISPATCHER EXAM

A public safety dispatcher must be readily understood by everyone with whom he or she speaks. Aside from having clear pronunciation and diction, dispatchers must have a strong command of the language. Perhaps even more important, public safety dispatchers must clearly understand others and must be able to draw the meaning from an excited, garbled message.

The words that appear on employment tests may not be those that an employee will need on the job. Generally, the vocabulary used in exams is more complex than what is required for a civil service position. The theory behind testing with words that are more difficult than what one uses in everyday life is that if you know the meaning of more obscure words, you will most certainly be fluent and proficient with simpler words. Test makers also use more difficult words in exams to tap into the test taker's logical thinking and reasoning powers.

Synonym questions are the most commonly used measure of vocabulary on the exam.

Synonyms

Synonyms are two words with similar meanings. A synonym can replace another word or phrase in a sentence without significantly changing the meaning of the sentence. Most exams make use of two types of synonym questions:

❶ **A key word followed by a number of answer choices.** In this type of question, you must select the word or phrase that is exactly the same as, or closest in meaning to, the key word. If you are not sure about the meaning of the word, try to eliminate one or more choices. Perhaps you recognize a part of the word from your study of word stems, for example, or you might try to use the word in a sentence.

2 **A sentence containing one word in UPPERCASE.** In this type of question, you are to choose the answer choice that is the best synonym for the uppercased word. Sentence questions offer more clues than key word questions. The overall meaning of the sentence may provide clues to the word's definition, and the way in which the word is used in the sentence will tell you whether it is a noun, a verb, or a modifier.

Nine Steps to Answering Synonym Questions

1 Read each question carefully.

2 Eliminate answer choices that you know are wrong.

3 Use all of the clues provided in the question stem. If the question is a sentence, consider the part of speech and the context of the word. For both sentence and non-sentence items, see whether any word parts are familiar to you. Recall where you have seen or heard the word used. Create your own sentence using the word.

4 From the answer choices that seem possible, select the one that most nearly means the same as the given word, even if this choice is not part of your normal vocabulary. The correct answer may not be a perfect synonym, but it is closest in meaning to the given word.

5 Test your answer by putting it in place of the given word in the question sentence or the sentence you have created. Is the meaning of the new sentence the same or similar to that of the original? If so, you probably have the correct answer.

6 If the word is not part of a sentence or the sentence does not help you to define the word, you must rely on other clues. Perhaps you have seen or heard the word but were never sure of its meaning. Now look at the word carefully. Is there any part of the word whose meaning you know?

7 If the word is not used in a sentence, try creating your own sentence using the given word. Then try substituting the answer choices in your sentence.

8 If you're stumped by a question, move on to the next question and answer the least difficult ones first. Then go back to work on the questions with answers you did not immediately recognize.

9 When all else fails, take an educated guess.

PRACTICE VOCABULARY QUESTIONS

Directions: Choose the answer that means most nearly the same as the word that appears in UPPERCASE letters.

1. REMEDIAL measures need to be taken to clean up air pollution in the area.
   - (A) reading
   - (B) slow
   - (C) corrective
   - (D) graceful

2. The increased use of computers has greatly REDUCED the need for typewriters.
   - (A) enlarged
   - (B) canceled
   - (C) lessened
   - (D) expanded

3. Although a complex response was required to the difficult question, she answered with EQUANIMITY.
   - (A) composure
   - (B) anger
   - (C) pauses
   - (D) doubts

4. The UNIFORMITY of the students' answers suggested they had not considered the many possible responses.
   - (A) military appearance
   - (B) slowness
   - (C) great variety
   - (D) sameness

5. The surface of the TRANQUIL lake was as smooth as glass.
   - (A) cold
   - (B) muddy
   - (C) deep
   - (D) calm

6. The manager ordered a GROSS of pencils from the office supplies store.
   - (A) disgusting
   - (B) all-inclusive
   - (C) twelve dozen
   - (D) monster

7. To send a note of apology is the only DECENT thing to do in these circumstances.
   - (A) proper
   - (B) going down
   - (C) children
   - (D) inclination

8. The speaker had an ABRASIVE voice.
   - (A) tuneful
   - (B) high-pitched
   - (C) loud
   - (D) harsh

9. Her DOMICILE was very well maintained.
   - (A) clothing
   - (B) residence
   - (C) appearance
   - (D) office

10. DISINTERESTED
    - (A) sympathetic
    - (B) young
    - (C) objective
    - (D) poor

11. TEMPORIZE
    - (A) increase
    - (B) consider
    - (C) flatter
    - (D) stall

12. ABOMINATE
    (A) adore
    (B) help
    (C) abide
    (D) hate

13. SALIENT
    (A) prominent
    (B) true
    (C) meaningful
    (D) respectable

14. The President nominates candidates for JUDICIAL positions in the federal courts.
    (A) engineering
    (B) philosophical
    (C) technician
    (D) judge

15. When hula hoops were a fad, these toys were UBIQUITOUS in school playgrounds.
    (A) rare
    (B) enjoyed
    (C) abundant
    (D) broken

16. An efficient manager knows how to DELEGATE responsibilities.
    (A) representative
    (B) give to a subordinate
    (C) hire
    (D) elect to office

17. TRANSCRIPT
    (A) journey
    (B) videotape
    (C) correction
    (D) written copy

18. The city purchased a SITE for the new public library building.
    (A) reference
    (B) location
    (C) job
    (D) book

19. INSUFFICIENT
    (A) excessive
    (B) having enough
    (C) lacking
    (D) nonexistent

20. DETRIMENTAL
    (A) favorable
    (B) lasting
    (C) harmful
    (D) temporary

ANSWER KEY AND EXPLANATIONS

1. C	5. D	9. B	13. A	17. D
2. C	6. C	10. C	14. D	18. B
3. A	7. A	11. D	15. C	19. C
4. D	8. D	12. D	16. B	20. C

1. **The correct answer is (C).** First eliminate *reading*. Its use in this sentence does not make sense, although you may associate *remedial* with remedial reading. Because pollution is a serious problem, *slow* would not be a good choice. Why would one delay solving such a problem? *Graceful* describes a physical trait, so it is not appropriate in this sentence. After you eliminate these choices, even if you are not sure of exactly what *remedial* means, you should be able to choose (C) as the best synonym in this context.

2. **The correct answer is (C).** The meaning of the sentence should cause you to immediately rule out choice (A), *enlarged,* and (D), *expanded.* Choice (B), *canceled,* implies that there is no need at all for typewriters. If this were the case, then the modifier *greatly* would be unnecessary. Therefore, choice (C), *lessened,* is the best synonym for *reduced.*

3. **The correct answer is (A).** Even if you are not sure what *equanimity* means, you can eliminate choices (C) and (D) because the word *although* in the first part of the sentence tells you that the response was not affected by the difficulty of the question. Choice (B) is not a good choice because the emotion of the person answering is not related to difficulty of the question.

4. **The correct answer is (D).** Although *uniform* may make you think of the armed forces, clothing has nothing to do with the meaning of this sentence,

so (A) is not a possible choice. Choice (C) is an incorrect choice because the sentence says that *not* many were considered. Choice (B) makes sense in the sentence, but *slowness* changes the meaning of the sentence. Thus, the best choice based on the meaning of the sentence is choice (D), *sameness.*

5. **The correct answer is (D).** Any of these choices might substitute for the word *tranquil,* and the sentence would still make sense. However, if the surface of the lake was as smooth as glass, the water would have to be very *calm.* Thus, while a *cold, muddy,* or *deep* lake could have a smooth surface, it is most reasonable to assume, on the basis of the sentence, that *tranquil* means *calm* and that (D) is the correct answer.

6. **The correct answer is (C).** In this example, the sentence is absolutely necessary to the definition of the word. Without the sentence, you could not know if the word *gross* is the noun, which means "twelve dozen," or the adjective, which can mean "crude and disgusting" or "total" depending on the context. The sentence tells you *gross* is a noun. Choices (A) and (B) are adjectives, so they cannot be correct. Choice (D) is tricky. *Monster* is sometimes used as slang for many or a large amount, but this is an incorrect use of the word. *Monster* does not appear in dictionaries as an adjective. As a noun, a *monster* could also be a beast, but that would not fit in a sentence about pencils. Therefore, choice (C), *twelve dozen,* is the only possible correct answer.

7. **The correct answer is (A).** As in the previous example, the sentence helps you to decide on the best synonym because *decent* is an adjective describing what someone will do. Thus, you will know not to confuse *decent* with a noun that sounds nearly the same, although spelled differently, *descent*, which means a downward path, or another similar-sounding noun, *descendants*—one's children. Choice (A) is the only adjective and therefore the correct answer.

8. **The correct answer is (D).** Sometimes a sentence may be of little or no use in helping you to choose the best synonym. The sentences may help you to determine the part of speech of the indicated word, but not its meaning, This sentences shows that *abrasive* is used to describe a voice, but it gives you no clue that *abrasive* means *harsh*. In this instance, you simply need to understand the meaning of *abrasive*.

9. **The correct answer is (B).** In this example, it is clear that a *domicile* is something that belongs to someone, but there is no information in the sentence to help you decide what that is. Although any of the choices could be substituted for *domicile*, the correct answer is (B), *residence*.

10. **The correct answer is (C).** When you see the word *disinterested*, you will recognize the word part "interested," which means concerned. Since the prefix *dis-* often means "not," you can eliminate choice (A). A *sympathetic* person is interested in a person or situation. You cannot immediately eliminate choice (D), *poor*, but before selecting an answer, consider all the possibilities. Since *dis-* is a negative prefix, look for a negative word as the meaning of *disinterested*. There is no choice meaning "not interested," so you should look for a negative kind of interest. To be objective is to have no interest in the outcome of a situation. An objective person is one who makes decisions without considering personal consequences; thus to be *objective* means to be *disinterested*, and choice (C) is therefore the correct answer.

11. **The correct answer is (D).** When you see *temporize*, you will recognize the word part *tempo*, which means time. You may think of a word like "temporary," which means for a short period of time. Thus, you should look for an answer that involves the concept of time. To *stall* is to hesitate or delay before responding, so it involves time. Therefore, (D) is the correct choice.

12. **The correct answer is (D).** *Abominate* means to loathe or hate. If you think of other variations of the word, such as abominable, you might think of the abominable snowman, which you know to be a despicable monster. The word "hate" would be the only word to which you could then relate the word "abominate."

13. **The correct answer is (A).** *Salient* means prominent.

14. **The correct answer is (D).** Because the sentence tells you that these positions are in courts, you need to find a synonym for someone who works in a court. While *engineers* or *technicians* might be important witnesses to a case, they're not court employees. Some people who work in courts may have a *philosophical* character or change of mind, but that is not a description of a job. Thus you can decide that choice (D), *judge*, is the best answer.

15. **The correct answer is (C).** The word in the sentence that most helps in choosing the correct answer is *fad*. A *fad* is something that is enjoyed by many people. Thus choice (C), *abundant,* is the best choice. While choice (B), *enjoyed*, makes sense in the sentence, there are many toys that children may enjoy that do not become *ubiquitous*. Choice (A), *rare*, contradicts the idea of a fad. And while toys

may get broken while they are being played with, so that the second part of the sentence would make sense, choice (D), *broken*, changes the meaning of the sentence.

16. **The correct answer is (B).** Looking at the sentence, it is clear that *delegate* is a verb. Therefore, although you may have heard of a delegate as a person who attends a convention, choice (A), *representative*, is incorrect. While choice (C), *hiring*, may be one of a manager's duties, responsibilities are duties, not something that can be hired. Similarly, responsibilities can not be *elected to office*, so choice (D) is also incorrect. To *delegate* means to authorize someone to act in one's place or take over one's responsibilities. Therefore, choice (B), *give to a subordinate*, is the best answer.

17. **The correct answer is (D).** When you see the word *transcript*, you will probably recognize the word part *script*, which means writing. You may think of a script for a movie. Since the word includes writing, choice (B), *videotape*, which is not a writing, could be eliminated. Although *tran-* may make you think of trains or transportation, there is no choice that means anything like moving writing, so choice (A), *journey*, can be eliminated. This leaves you with choices (C) and (D). Think about where you have heard or seen the word. Newspapers often print *transcripts* of speeches, which give a complete text of what a speaker said. Thus, a *transcript* is a written copy, and choice (D) is the correct answer.

18. **The correct answer is (B).** When you read the sentence, you may confuse the word *site* and *cite*. Although they may sound the same, their meanings are different. *Cite* is a verb that means to summon or quote. Because *reference* does not fit the meaning of the sentence, you can eliminate choice (A). Choice (C), *job*, is a synonym for a *situation*, which sounds like site, but a building cannot hold a job. Although you would find a book in a library, it does not make sense to buy a book to create a new building. Since these choices can be eliminated, choice (B), *location*, should be the answer you select.

19. **The correct answer is (C).** The word *sufficient* means enough, and the prefix *in-* often means not. So *insufficient* means not enough. Choices (A) and (B) are opposites of not enough. Choice (D) means *having none at all*, which does not mean the same thing as *not enough*. A choice meaning *not enough* is the best answer, and (C), *lacking*, means not enough, so (C) is the correct choice.

20. **The correct answer is (C).** Detrimental means harmful.

MORE PRACTICE QUESTIONS

Now try some synonym questions for yourself.

Directions: Choose the answer that means most nearly the same as the word that appears in UPPERCASE letters.

1. CARDIGAN means most nearly
   (A) storm coat.
   (B) sleeveless sweater.
   (C) turtleneck.
   (D) buttoned sweater.

2. GRAPHIC means most nearly
   (A) vivid.
   (B) unclear.
   (C) repetitious.
   (D) sickening.

3. REFRAIN means most nearly
   (A) join in.
   (B) sing along.
   (C) abstain.
   (D) retire.

4. PUNCTUAL means most nearly
   (A) polite.
   (B) prompt.
   (C) thoughtful.
   (D) neat.

5. INFRACTION means most nearly
   (A) violation.
   (B) whole.
   (C) interpretation.
   (D) part.

6. IMPASSE means most nearly
   (A) agreement.
   (B) compromise.
   (C) signed contract.
   (D) deadlock.

7. TEMERITY means most nearly
   (A) shyness.
   (B) enthusiasm.
   (C) rashness.
   (D) self-control.

8. ALLEGIANCE means most nearly
   (A) freedom.
   (B) loyalty.
   (C) defense.
   (D) protection.

9. RESCINDED means most nearly
   (A) revised.
   (B) implemented.
   (C) canceled.
   (D) confirmed.

10. VINDICTIVE means most nearly
    (A) prejudiced.
    (B) petty.
    (C) revengeful.
    (D) crude.

11. INNOCUOUS means most nearly
    (A) forceful.
    (B) harmless.
    (C) offensive.
    (D) important.

12. STRINGENT means most nearly
    (A) lengthy.
    (B) rigid.
    (C) vague.
    (D) ridiculous.

13. ORTHODOX means most nearly
    (A) pious.
    (B) godly.
    (C) traditional.
    (D) heretical.

14. ELICITED means most nearly
    (A) eliminated.
    (B) drawn out.
    (C) illegal.
    (D) confirmed.

15. REPRISAL means most nearly
    (A) retaliation.
    (B) warning.
    (C) denial.
    (D) losing.

16. IMPAIR means most nearly
    (A) improve.
    (B) conceal.
    (C) inflate.
    (D) weaken.

17. ABHOR means most nearly
    (A) tolerate.
    (B) try to change.
    (C) avoid.
    (D) hate.

18. INANE means most nearly
    (A) incessant.
    (B) argumentative.
    (C) polished.
    (D) foolish.

19. DECAY means most nearly
    (A) burning.
    (B) disposal.
    (C) rotting.
    (D) piling.

20. PROXIMITY means most nearly
    (A) nearness.
    (B) worldliness.
    (C) charisma.
    (D) fame.

ANSWER KEY AND EXPLANATIONS

1. D	5. A	9. C	13. C	17. D
2. A	6. D	10. C	14. B	18. D
3. C	7. C	11. B	15. A	19. C
4. B	8. B	12. B	16. D	20. A

1. **The correct answer is (D).** A cardigan is a collarless sweater that opens the full length of the center front and ordinarily is closed with buttons. A cardigan could be sleeveless, but the sleeves do not enter into the definition of a cardigan.

2. **The correct answer is (A).** Graphic means *vivid* or *picturesque*. A graphic description may well be false or sickening, but what makes it graphic is its vividness.

3. **The correct answer is (C).** To refrain from an act is to *keep oneself from doing it* or to *abstain*.

4. **The correct answer is (B).** Punctual means *on time* or *prompt*.

5. **The correct answer is (A).** An infraction is a *breaking of the rules* or a *violation*. You have probably heard of punishments for infractions of traffic regulations, so you know what this word means. If you did not know the word, you might well pull it apart into "not a fraction" and choose whole. Sometimes trying to figure out a meaning does not work.

6. **The correct answer is (D).** An impasse is a predicament offering no obvious escape, hence a *deadlock*. The etymology here is quite simple. The negative prefix *im-* appears before pass. If you can't pass, you are stuck.

7. **The correct answer is (C).** If you do not know the word *temerity*, you are likely to get this wrong. Temerity is in no way related to *timidity* or *shyness* except as an opposite. *Enthusiasm* might be a reasonable synonym, but

rashness, boldness, recklessness, and *nerve* are better.

8. **The correct answer is (B).** Allegiance means *devotion* or *loyalty.*

9. **The correct answer is (C).** The prefix should help you narrow your choices. The prefix *re-*, meaning *back*, narrows the choices to (A) or (C). To rescind is to *take back* or to *cancel*.

10. **The correct answer is (C).** Vindictive means *spiteful* or *seeking revenge*.

11. **The correct answer is (B).** The prefix *in-*, meaning *not*, is your chief clue. Innocuous means *inoffensive* or *harmless*.

12. **The correct answer is (B).** Stringent means *tight* or *rigid*. Perhaps you can see the basis of "strict" in the word. If you did not know this word and guessed on the basis of its looks, you would probably choose (A) or (B). This would be a sensible way to guess, and it would give you a 50 percent chance of being right.

13. **The correct answer is (C).** One who is orthodox is *conventional, conservative,* and *traditional*. Although an Orthodox Jew may indeed be pious, choice (A), pious is not the meaning of the word *orthodox*.

14. **The correct answer is (B).** To elicit is to *draw out*, to *evoke*, or to *extract*.

15. **The correct answer is (A).** Reprisal literally means *taking back*. Stretch that meaning and you arrive at *getting back at* or *retaliation*.

16. **The correct answer is (D).** To impair is to *make worse*, to *injure*, or to *weaken*.

17. **The correct answer is (D).** To abhor is to *loathe*, to *reject*, or to *hate*.

18. **The correct answer is (D).** Inane means *empty*, *insubstantial*, *silly*, or *foolish*.

19. **The correct answer is (C).** Decay is *deterioration*, *decomposition*, or just plain *rotting*.

20. **The correct answer is (A).** You should be able to look at the word, see "approximate," and choose *nearness* as the meaning of proximity.

SPELLING ON THE PUBLIC SAFETY DISPATCHER EXAM

Spelling is not a major component of the public safety dispatcher position. When speed is of the essence, perfect spelling, punctuation, and even grammar are clearly secondary. On the other hand, spelling cannot be so bizarre that words will be misread. Grammar must be sufficiently accurate so that there is no doubt about who is the victim and who the suspect, and there must be no doubt about the sequence of events.

Most public safety dispatchers keep records. Some dispatchers prepare full-fledged daily reports. Reports must be correct in content and in form. In positions in which keeping logs or preparing reports is a regular part of the job description, spelling questions may appear on the exam. As in vocabulary testing, spelling words on the exam may be more challenging than the words you need to use in everyday work situations. Again, the theory is that if you can spell difficult words, you can spell easier ones.

Some fortunate individuals seem to be "natural" spellers. They are able to picture a word and instinctively spell it correctly. Most of us must memorize rules and rely on a dictionary. It is *not* a sign of weakness to consult a dictionary when you are in doubt about the spelling of a word. On the other hand, constant use of the dictionary does slow your work. Under the pressure of emergency communications, referring to a dictionary may be impossible.

Here are a few rules you can learn to help you improve your spelling:

1 The letter *i* comes before *e* except after *c*, or when sounding like *ay*, as in *neighbor* or *weigh*.

> *Exceptions:* Neither, leisure, seize, weird, height.
>
> **NOTE:** This rule does not apply when the *ie* combination is pronounced *eh* (as in *foreigner*), even if *ie* immediately follows the letter *c*.
>
> *Examples:* ancient, conscience, deficient, efficient, foreigner, proficient.

2 If a word ends in a *y* that is preceded by a vowel, keep the *y* when adding a suffix.

> *Examples:* day, days; attorney, attorneys; spray, sprayer.

3 If a word ends in a *y* that is preceded by a consonant, change the *y* to *i* before adding a suffix.

> *Examples:* try, tries, tried; lady, ladies; dainty, daintiest; steady, steadily; heavy, heavier; study, studious; ally, alliance; defy, defiant; beauty, beautiful; justify, justifiable.
>
> *Exceptions:* dry, dryly, dryness; shy, shyly; sly, slyly, slyness; spry, spryly.
>
> **NOTE:** This rule does not apply before the suffixes *-ing* and *-ish*. To avoid double *i*, retain the *y* before *-ing* and *-ish*.
>
> *Examples:* fly, flying; baby, babyish; relay, relaying.

4 A silent *e* at the end of a word is usually dropped before a suffix that begins with a vowel.

    Examples:

    dine + ing = dining

    locate + ion = location

    use + able = usable

    relieve + ed = relieved

    admire + ation = admiration

    Exceptions:

    Words ending in *ce* and *ge* retain the *e*.

    Words ending in *-able* and *-ous* to retain the soft sounds of *c* and *g*.

    Examples:

    peace + able = peaceable

    courage + ous = courageous

5 The silent *e* is usually kept when followed by a suffix that begins with a consonant.

    Examples:

    care + less = careless

    late + ly = lately

    one + ness = oneness

    game + ster = gamester

    manage + ment = management

    NOTE: This is a case where exceptions must simply be memorized. Some exceptions to rules 4 and 5 are *truly, duly, awful, argument, wholly, ninth, mileage, dyeing, acreage, canoeing,* and *judgment.*

6 In a one-syllable word that ends in a single consonant that is preceded by a single vowel, you must double the final consonant before a suffix beginning with a vowel or with *y*.

    Examples: hit, hitting; drop, dropped; big, biggest; mud, muddy; quit, quitter.

    Exceptions: *help* becomes *helping*, because *help* ends in *two* consonants; and *need* becomes *needing*, because the final consonant is preceded by *two* vowels.

7 In a multi-syllable word that ends in a single consonant preceded by a single vowel and in which the last syllable is accented, you must double the final consonant when adding a suffix beginning with a vowel.

    Examples: begin, beginner; admit, admitted; control, controlling; excel, excellence; recur, recurrent; admit, admittance; transmit, transmittal

    Exceptions: *enter* becomes *entered* because the accent is *not* on the last syllable; *divert* becomes *diverted* because the word ends in *two* consonants; *refrain* becomes *refraining* because *two* vowels precede the final consonant; and *equip* becomes *equipment* because the suffix begins with a consonant.

8 In a word ending in *-er* or *-ur,* you must double the *r* in the past tense if the accent falls on the last syllable.

   Examples: occur, occurred; prefer, preferred; transfer, transferred

9 In a word ending in *-er,* do not double the *r* in the past tense if the accent falls on any syllable other than the last.

   Examples: answer, answered; offer, offered; differ, differed

10 When *-full* is added to the end of a noun to form an adjective, the final *l* is dropped.

   Examples: cheerful, cupful, hopeful

11 All words beginning with *over* should be spelled as one unhyphenated word.

   Examples: overcast, overcharge, overhear

12 All words beginning with the prefix *self-* should be hyphenated.

   Examples: self-control, self-defense, self-evident

13 The letter *q* is always followed by *u.*

   Examples: quiz, bouquet, acquire

14 *Percent* is never hyphenated. It may be spelled as one word (*percent*) or as two words (*per cent*).

15 *Welcome* is one word with one *l.*

16 *All right* is always two words. Some critics have insisted that *alright* is all wrong; however, many writers do use *alright* now.

17 *Already* means "prior to a specified or implied time." *All ready* means "completely ready." The words are not interchangeable.

   Examples: By the time I was *all ready* to go to the play, he had *already* left.

18 *Altogether* means "entirely." *All together* means "in sum" or "collectively." The words are not interchangeable.

   Examples: There are *altogether* too many people to seat in this room when we are *all together.*

19 *Their* is the possessive of *they.* *They're* is the contraction for *they are.* *There* is *that place.* They are not interchangeable.

   Examples: *They're* going to put *their* books over *there.*

20 *Your* is the possessive of *you.* *You're* is the contraction for *you are.* They are not interchangeable.

   Examples: *You're* planning to leave *your* muddy boots outside, aren't you?

21 *Whose* is the possessive of *who.* *Who's* is the contraction for *who is.* They are not interchangeable.

   Examples: Do you know *who's* ringing the doorbell or *whose* car is in the street?

22 *Its* is the possessive of *it.* *It's* is the contraction for *it is.* They are not interchangeable.

   Examples: *It's* not I who doesn't like *its* style.

Of course, these aren't the only spelling rules for the English language, but this is a good start. Studying these rules and practicing them while learning spelling will see you through thousands of perplexing situations. One final hint: If you find that you must look up certain words every time you use them, write them down, correctly spelled, on the inside front cover of your dictionary to save valuable time. Consult this list of your personal spelling "devils" the day before your exam. Chances are, the words that trouble you also perplex others—and that means they may appear on your exam.

If you are following the advice in this book, you've begun compiling a list of words that tend to stump you consistently: your spelling devils. Many of these words may appear on the list, "400 Frequently Misspelled Words," in the Appendix section of this book. These are words that have proven troublesome for most test takers and that frequently appear on civil service exam spelling sections. Reviewing this list before exam day will help you tackle many of the most vexing words.

PRACTICE SPELLING QUESTIONS

Now that you've reviewed some of the most basic spelling rules and exceptions, try your hand at these practice questions.

Exercise 1

Directions: Circle the letter of the correct spelling. If no suggested spelling is correct, circle choice (D). The answers are at the end of the exercise.

1.
   (A) occassional
   (B) ocassional
   (C) occasional
   (D) none of these

2.
   (A) Wensday
   (B) Wednesday
   (C) Wendesday
   (D) none of these

3.
   (A) rythym
   (B) ryhthm
   (C) rhthym
   (D) none of these

4.
   (A) matinee
   (B) mattinee
   (C) matinnee
   (D) none of these

5.
   (A) availble
   (B) available
   (C) availible
   (D) none of these

6.
   (A) conscience
   (B) consceince
   (C) concience
   (D) none of these

7.
   (A) wholly
   (B) wholey
   (C) wholley
   (D) none of these

8.
   (A) basiclly
   (B) basicaly
   (C) basically
   (D) none of these

9.

(A) bookeeper
(B) bookeepper
(C) bookkeeper
(D) none of these

10.

(A) picknicing
(B) picnicking
(C) picnicing
(D) none of these

11.

(A) sacreligious
(B) sacrelegious
(C) sacrilegious
(D) none of these

12.

(A) February
(B) Ferbuary
(C) Febuary
(D) none of these

13.

(A) obsolescensce
(B) obsolecense
(C) obsolescence
(D) none of these

14.

(A) interferance
(B) interferrence
(C) interference
(D) none of these

15.

(A) outrageous
(B) outragous
(C) outrageouse
(D) none of these

16.

(A) vacuum
(B) vacume
(C) vaccuume
(D) none of these

17.

(A) vegtable
(B) vegertable
(C) vegitable
(D) none of these

18.

(A) caffiene
(B) caffeinn
(C) caffeine
(D) none of these

19.

(A) gauge
(B) guage
(C) gaugue
(D) none of these

20.

(A) exzema
(B) exzcema
(C) ezxema
(D) none of these

ANSWER KEY AND EXPLANATIONS

1. C	5. B	9. C	13. C	17. D
2. B	6. A	10. B	14. C	18. C
3. D	7. A	11. C	15. A	19. A
4. A	8. C	12. A	16. A	20. D

1. **The correct answer is (C).** The correct spelling is *occasional*.
2. **The correct answer is (B).** The correct spelling is *Wednesday*.
3. **The correct answer is (D).** The correct spelling is *rhythm*.
4. **The correct answer is (A).** The correct spelling is *matinee*.
5. **The correct answer is (B).** The correct spelling is *available*.
6. **The correct answer is (A).** The correct spelling is *conscience*.
7. **The correct answer is (A).** The correct spelling is *wholly*.
8. **The correct answer is (C).** The correct spelling is *basically*.
9. **The correct answer is (C).** The correct spelling is *bookkeeper*.
10. **The correct answer is (B).** The correct spelling is *picnicking*.
11. **The correct answer is (C).** The correct spelling is *sacrilegious*.
12. **The correct answer is (A).** The correct spelling is *February*.
13. **The correct answer is (C).** The correct spelling is *obsolescence*.
14. **The correct answer is (C).** The correct spelling is *interference*.
15. **The correct answer is (A).** The correct spelling is *outrageous*.
16. **The correct answer is (A).** The correct spelling is *vacuum*.
17. **The correct answer is (D).** The correct spelling is *vegetable*.
18. **The correct answer is (C).** The correct spelling is *caffeine*.
19. **The correct answer is (A).** The correct spelling is *gauge*.
20. **The correct answer is (D).** The correct spelling is *eczema*.

Exercise 2

Directions: In each of the following groups, there is one misspelled word. Write the letter of that word on the line provided.

1. _____
   - (A) refferee
   - (B) eligible
   - (C) excitement
   - (D) reign

2. _____
   - (A) eighth
   - (B) acheivement
   - (C) aching
   - (D) readiness

3. _____
   - (A) imune
   - (B) orator
   - (C) ascertain
   - (D) pierce

4. _____
   - (A) wield
   - (B) gradually
   - (C) tumbleing
   - (D) philosophical

5. _____
   - (A) superior
   - (B) traffic
   - (C) interminable
   - (D) admittence

6. _____
   - (A) standardize
   - (B) peaceable
   - (C) fatigue
   - (D) involvment

7. _____
   - (A) arbitrary
   - (B) blemish
   - (C) testamony
   - (D) deprivation

8. _____
   - (A) apparently
   - (B) demolition
   - (C) resturant
   - (D) visibility

9. _____
   - (A) vacancy
   - (B) incredible
   - (C) minature
   - (D) interpreter

10. _____
   - (A) allottment
   - (B) baggage
   - (C) equitable
   - (D) colossal

Directions: In the following section, some words are spelled correctly and some are misspelled. If a word is spelled correctly, write the word "correct" on the line to the right. If a word is misspelled, write the correct spelling.

11. enrolement _____
12. grease _____
13. goalkeeper _____
14. qualitey _____
15. disatisfied _____
16. whisle _____
17. abundant _____
18. intellectuel _____
19. antena _____
20. cieling _____
21. controlled _____
22. disgise _____
23. physicain _____
24. noticable _____
25. nineteenth _____
26. consience _____
27. renounce _____
28. enamies _____
29. allergick _____
30. spagetti _____

31. apalogy _____
32. concerning _____
33. pianoes _____
34. celabration _____
35. license _____
36. privilege _____
37. sophmore _____
38. acheiving _____
39. lonliness _____
40. surroundings _____
41. prarie _____
42. legitamate _____
43. secretarial _____
44. dissagreeable _____
45. coincidence _____
46. concientious _____
47. comparision _____
48. salaries _____
49. creditted _____
50. forthcoming _____

ANSWERS AND EXPLANATIONS

1. **The correct answer is (A).** Refferee should be *referee*.

2. **The correct answer is (B).** Acheivement should be *achievement*.

3. **The correct answer is (A).** Imune should be *immune*.

4. **The correct answer is (C).** Tumbleing should be *tumbling*.

5. **The correct answer is (D).** Admittence should be *admittance*.

6. **The correct answer is (D).** Involvment should be *involvement*.

7. **The correct answer is (C).** Testamony should be *testimony*.

8. **The correct answer is (C).** Resturant should be *restaurant*.

9. **The correct answer is (C).** Minature should be *miniature*.

10. **The correct answer is (A).** Allottment should be *allotment*.

11. **The correct spelling is** *enrollment*.

12. **Correct as written.**

13. **Correct as written.**

14. **The correct spelling is** *quality*.

15. **The correct spelling is** *dissatisfied*.

16. **The correct spelling is** *whistle*.

17. **Correct as written.**

18. **The correct spelling is** *intellectual*.

19. **The correct spelling is** *antenna*.

20. **The correct spelling is** *ceiling*.

21. **Correct as written.**

22. **The correct spelling is** *disguise*.

23. **The correct spelling is** *physician*.

24. **The correct spelling is** *noticeable*.

25. **Correct as written.**

26. **The correct spelling is** *conscience*.

27. **Correct as written.**

28. **The correct spelling is** *enemies*.

29. **The correct spelling is** *allergic*.

30. **The correct spelling is** *spaghetti*.

31. **The correct spelling is** *apology*.

32. **Correct as written.**

33. **The correct spelling is** *pianos*.

34. **The correct spelling is** *celebration*.

35. **Correct as written.**

36. **Correct as written.**

37. **The correct spelling is** *sophomore*.

38. **The correct spelling is** *achieving*.

39. **The correct spelling is** *loneliness*.

40. **Correct as written.**

41. **The correct spelling is** *prairie*.

42. **The correct spelling is** *legitimate*.

43. **Correct as written.**

44. **The correct spelling is** *disagreeable*.

45. **Correct as written.**

46. **The correct spelling is** *conscientious*.

47. **The correct spelling is** *comparison*.

48. **Correct as written.**

49. **The correct spelling is** *credited*.

50. **Correct as written.**

SUMMING IT UP

- A public safety dispatcher must be clearly and easily understood and must have a strong command of the language. He or she must also readily understand others and be able to draw meaning from excited or garbled messages or speech. This is why vocabulary and spelling are assessed on the public safety dispatcher exam.

- The vocabulary you'll encounter on the exam is more complex than what most people use in everyday speech—but if you know the meaning of more obscure words, you will most certainly be fluent and proficient with simpler words.

- Synonym questions are the most commonly used measure of vocabulary on the public safety dispatcher exam. Test takers use two types of synonym questions. One consists of a key word followed by several answer choices; you must select the word or phrase that is exactly the same as or closest in meaning to the key word. Another question type consists of a sentence containing one uppercased word; you must choose the answer choice that is the best synonym for that word.

- Spelling is not a major component of the public safety dispatcher position, but it's important that your spelling is accurate enough that it's unlikely to be misread or misinterpreted. Dispatchers who prepare written reports must ensure that the reports are correct in content and form; if you are testing for this type of position, you'll probably see spelling questions on your exam.

- Learn and review the spelling rules in this chapter and the 400-word spelling list in the Appendix section of this book. The list consists of words that many test takers find troublesome and that frequently appear on civil service exams.

Clerical Skills

OVERVIEW

- Typing on the Public Safety Dispatcher Exam
- Typing exercises
- Address checking on the Public Safety Dispatcher Exam
- Address-checking practice sets
- Address-checking exercises
- Name and number comparison questions on the Public Safety Dispatcher Exam
- Name and number comparison exercises
- Summing it up

TYPING ON THE PUBLIC SAFETY DISPATCHER EXAM

Facility in typing is so important to the job of the public safety dispatcher that some municipalities rely solely on a typing test to select candidates for the position. Very few cities waive proof of a candidate's typing skills.

The typing test, like the written test, can take many different forms. It is usually administered on a computer keyboard. Since computers and typing test programs vary, you will receive specific instructions and ample time to practice on the testing equipment before the scored portion of your typing test begins.

An effective public safety dispatcher must be an accurate and swift typist. Some municipalities require a speed as minimal as 25 words per minute (wpm), but these municipalities generally demand 100 percent accuracy: A single error at 25 wpm is enough to disqualify a candidate. If you hope to do well on the typing test, it's imperative that you practice as much as time permits. The more you practice, the more proficient you will become.

To prepare for the typing test, practice both copying and typing from dictation, and be sure to include words and numbers. Limber up by typing whatever pops into your head, or copy the text of the day's junk mail. Aim for total accuracy. The usual rule in scoring typing tests is that a corrected error is still an error; ideally, you should make no mistakes at all. Corrections you make while typing on a computer keyboard are generally not recorded. Watch the screen closely for errors, however. If you make an error, correct it as quickly as possible and keep moving. Any time you lose in making a correction will do you less harm than letting the error pass.

One variety of this test is called a "plain copy" typing test. You're given a few paragraphs to type exactly as you see them on the copy. You must reproduce spacing, paragraph breaks, spelling, punctuation, capitalization, and line breaks precisely as they appear on the original copy. Most plain copy typing tests take 5 minutes. Try practicing this type of test with the exercises that follow. Make sure you correct any errors you spot, and be sure to time yourself (or have someone do it for you).

TYPING EXERCISES

TIP

The best preparation for any typing test is simply to practice typing. Choose any material and practice copying it exactly as it is presented, with the same punctuation, line breaks, spaces, capitalization, and spelling. Try timing yourself and aim for speed balanced with accuracy.

> **Directions:** Space, paragraph, spell, punctuate, capitalize, and begin and end each line precisely as shown in the exercise. Allow exactly 5 minutes to type as many copies of the text as you can. Each time you complete the paragraph, hit the return key twice and begin again. Continue typing until five minutes have elapsed.

Exercise 1

Your position at the computer is of prime importance. You

should sit easily and naturally, with your hips back in the

chair, your body erect, and both feet flat on the floor. One

foot may be somewhat in front of the other. Your shoulders

should be relaxed, your upper arms close to your body, and

your forearms parallel to the slope of the keyboard. Your

hands should never rest on the keyboard.

Exercise 2

This is an example of the type of material that will be

presented to you at the actual typing examination.

Each competitor will be required to type the practice

material exactly as it appears on the copy. You will be

asked to space, capitalize, punctuate, spell, and begin and

end each line exactly as it is presented in the copy. Each

time you reach the end of the paragraph, you should begin

again and continue to practice typing the paragraph until

the test administrator tells you to stop. You are advised

that it is more important to type accurately than to type

rapidly.

Exercise 3

Because they have often learned to know types of architecture
by decoration, casual observers sometimes fail to
realize that the significant part of a structure is not the
ornamentation but the body itself. Architecture, because of
its close contact with human lives, is peculiarly and intimately
governed by climate. For instance, a home built for
comfort in the cold and snow of the northern areas of this
country would be unbearably warm in a country with weather
such as that of Cuba. A Cuban house, with its open court,
would prove impossible to heat in a northern winter.
Because the purpose of architecture is the construction of
shelters in which human beings may carry on their numerous
activities, the designer must consider not only climatic
conditions, but also the function of a building. Thus,
although the climate of a certain locality requires that an
auditorium and a hospital have several features in common,
the purposes for which they will be used demand some difference
in structure. For centuries, builders have first
complied with these two requirements and later added whatever
ornamentation they wished. Logically, we should see as
mere additions, not as basic parts, the details by which we
identify architecture.

Listening and Typing

Because the work of a public safety dispatcher relies heavily upon information received
via telephone, your typing test is just as likely to be based on typing from dictation
as it is to be a copying test. To practice typing from dictation, ask a friend or family
member to read short passages at varying speeds (but fairly rapidly at times). Find
passages that include names, addresses, and telephone numbers. They might also
include short sections of reported information, such as "burglary in progress," "my
child can't breathe," or "there's a fire in the house across the street." Your friend could
read names, addresses, and telephone numbers directly from a phone book and from
the clerical speed and accuracy exercises in the next section. The reader should also
dictate some longer passages, such as those you practiced keying in the plain copy
exercises. Ask your friend to read these passages more slowly and with expression and
appropriate pauses so that you can punctuate correctly. If a friend or family member
isn't available to dictate, read some material into a recorder and then play it back to
yourself.

Typing Numbers

Listening to numbers and relaying them in the same order is very important in the work of a public safety dispatcher, so your exam may contain a section emphasizing number entry. The number line is the keyboard section with which most people are least familiar and least skilled in using. In routine typing, number keys are not used as frequently as letter keys; however, to perform the duties of a public safety dispatcher, it's vital to be comfortable with the number keys.

Type Exercise 4 again and again, making sure you include the spacing and punctuation exactly as they appear here. At first, aim for perfect accuracy; then focus on increasing your typing speed. In the beginning, you may have to look at the number keys on your typewriter. If your computer has an extended keyboard with a numerical keypad, consider using that instead of the row of numbered keys above the lettered section of the keyboard. The numerical keypad is set up like a calculator, and you may find it easier to use than the row of numbers on the basic keyboard. Regardless of which set of keys you choose, be sure that you know how to use both for typing numbers.

Your goal for Exercise 4 should be to type the entire passage correctly, looking only at the paper from which you're copying and the computer screen—not the keyboard or keypad. Proofread it carefully, either on screen or printed out. Repeat this exercise until you are satisfied with your speed and accuracy. Then try typing the same numbers from dictation.

Exercise 4

8321	9547	6503	8402	0886
9723	7531	7158	4602	0284
1570	2580	8400	4790	4273
682,412	598,211	890,142	797,501	204,673
212 - 1237	914 - 17862	516 - 1418	203 - 9834	4 - 8308
336 - 1451	773 - 4801	926 - 1862	302 - 0964	8 - 2593
$510.66	$923.45	$256.99	$812.59	$908.45@
#67,532	#909,482	#856,304	#168,451	#93,715
21.33%	100%	99.44%	155%	83.8%
@230	@490	@82	@92140	@810

The Alphanumeric Typing Test

On your public safety dispatcher exam, you may also encounter an alphanumeric, computer-administered section. The format explained here is one of several for this test type.

As the test begins, you'll see on the screen an explanation of which keys you will be using and how they function. You need to use the letter, number, shift, return (or enter), delete (or backspace), and caps lock keys. A test administrator will remain in the room to answer questions.

The computer program will then display an explanation of the typing task itself. A letter-and-number code will appear on the upper right of the screen. You must type the code exactly as you see it, then hit return to bring up the next code. When you see the next code, type that exactly as you see it and hit return, and so on.

The codes generally consist of four letters and three numbers; for example TYHR346 or BZIP801. The more quickly you enter them and hit return, the more quickly the next code will come up and the more codes you'll be able to enter before the test ends. In the explanation phase of the exam, you will have 15 seconds in which to copy five codes. The computer program will tell you how many you copied correctly.

After the explanation phase, you'll be offered a practice session. You're allowed 5 minutes to correctly copy as many codes as you can (again, one at a time). The 5-minute practice session does not count toward your exam score, so this is your chance to experiment.

Follow these four simple steps when taking an alphanumeric typing test:

1. Look at the code and quickly memorize it; four letters and three numbers should pose no problem for such a short-term memory task.

2. Type in the code, keeping your eyes at the center of the screen where the letters and numbers appear.

3. Delete and retype if you spot an error.

4. Hit the return button and repeat the process.

When your 5 minutes have elapsed, your score will flash on the screen. If you scored 14 or higher, you can feel confident about taking the actual exam; you've done well. If your score is lower than 14, don't panic. Remember that this session does not count toward your exam score, and that you used this time to practice. Look at it this way: You now have 5 minutes to use the system with which you have already become comfortable. Your second score—the score that *does* count—will be higher. The actual test session is exactly like the practice session, but with new sets of codes.

Exercise 5 is a sample of the kind of content you'll encounter on a computer-based alphanumeric typing test. Use it as a model to prepare more exercises for additional practice.

Exercise 5

RJKF566	BVEI155	GKZP876
YTMN068	FUQS478	EDBJ582
FULLD727	JMGE610	OLDE751
TTHU950	SQWP010	LEAP274
NORT707	BDEY851	PHYX593
FLIR015	CZDT874	BLDV592
OYJXO55	FTTD123	KHTP805
GYKN094	RHVZ417	IFWK173
WEST301	TGIF629	YCWI142
DRHK967	PDQD157	OLZT809
AVNB893	EAST383	VMHW649
RKBY775	GSAP013	HTCQ858
LGBU919	UQFP180	JFTA862

ADDRESS CHECKING ON THE PUBLIC SAFETY DISPATCHER EXAM

It is impossible to overemphasize the need for speed and accuracy in the work of a dispatcher. Public safety dispatchers must be able to hear, type, and read accurately. Without these skills, the public safety dispatcher could, for example, transpose numbers and potentially send an assisting emergency vehicle to the wrong address. Or misspelling a name might lead the police to detain an innocent person as a suspect in a crime.

When a public safety dispatcher listens to information on the telephone, he or she must be able to immediately enter the information into a computer and promptly relay it to another party. An applicant's ability to perform these tasks accurately and quickly is tested in several ways. Some municipalities give only paper-and-pencil tests of speed and accuracy in checking names, numbers, or both. These types of tests often involve complex instructions.

Other municipalities test for clerical speed and accuracy with a typing test. We've already reviewed what a typing test might entail for a public safety dispatcher position. In this section, we'll look at how you can conquer clerical speed and accuracy exam questions.

Five Steps for Answering Address-Checking Questions

Address-checking questions are not difficult, but they require great speed and often carry heavy penalties for inaccuracy. Some may also have rather complicated directions. To answer address-checking questions swiftly and accurately, you need to learn to spot differences very quickly and make firm, fast decisions. Let's review five steps you can use to improve your speed and accuracy with address-checking questions. Once you have learned this "system," practice will help you build up speed.

❶ Read exactly what you see. The best way to read addresses is to read exactly what you see and sound out words by syllable. For example:

- If you see "St.," read "es-tee, period," not "street."

- If you see "NH," read "en aich," not "New Hampshire."

- If you see "1035," read "one zero three five," not "one thousand thirty-five."

Why do this? Let's say you read the abbreviation "Pky" as "Parkway," the word it stands for. Very likely, this means you'll also read "Pkwy" as "Parkway"—and you won't notice the difference between the two abbreviations. Your mind will complete the word without allowing you to focus on the letters. If, however, you read each abbreviation *as* an abbreviation, you will begin to notice that the two abbreviations are not the same. Similarly, if you read "Kansas City, MO" as "Kansas City, Missouri," you are unlikely to catch the difference between it and "Kansas City, MD." But if you read "Kansas City em oh," you will readily pick up the difference between that phrase and "Kansas city em dee."

Read aloud at first so that you'll develop an ear for what you're reading. As you practice, you'll learn to "hear" the correctly sounded addresses in your mind.

❷ Use your hands. Because speed is so important in answering address-checking questions, and since it is so easy to lose your place, use both hands during your work on questions with this format. In the hand with which you write, hold your pencil poised at the number on your answer sheet. Run the index finger of your other hand under the addresses being compared. This helps you to focus on one line at a time and will help you avoid jumping from one line to another. By holding your place on both the question and answer sheet, you're less likely to skip a question or fill in the wrong answer space.

One effective way to tackle address-checking questions quickly and accurately is to look for differences in just one area at a time. Every address consists of numbers and words. If you narrow your focus to compare only the numbers or only the words, you are more likely to notice differences and less apt to see what you expect to see rather than what is actually printed on the page.

❸ Look for differences in numbers. Look first at the numbers. Read the number in the left column, then skip immediately to the number in the right column. Do the two numbers contain the same number of digits? Are they in the same order? Is any digit out of place?

❹ Look for differences in abbreviations. When you are satisfied that the numbers are alike, and if no other difference has "struck you between the eyes," turn your attention to the abbreviations. Keep alert for subtle differences. For example:

Rd   Dr

Wy   Way

NH   NM

❺ Look for differences in street or city names. If you've compared the numbers and the abbreviations but have not spotted any differences, look next at the main words of the address. Are the words in the two addresses really the same words?

TIP

When you are reading and comparing names, numbers, and addresses, read them phonetically, syllable by syllable. If you see "Rd.," don't read it as "road" but as "are-dee period." You're more likely to notice differences this way.

Sound out the words by syllables or spell them out. Is the spelling exactly the same? Are the same letters doubled? Are two letters reversed?

Here are four sets of questions so you can practice looking for differences in numbers, abbreviations, and street or city names (Steps 3, 4, and 5 on the previous page).

ADDRESS-CHECKING PRACTICE SETS

Practice Set 1

Directions: In the questions that follow, choose **(A)** if the two numbers are exactly alike or **(D)** if the numbers differ in any way.

1.	2003	2003
2.	75864	75864
3.	7300	730
4.	50106	5016
5.	2184	2184
6.	7516	7561
7.	80302	80302
8.	19832	18932
9.	6186	6186
10.	54601	54601
11.	16830	16830
12.	94936	94636
13.	3287	3285
14.	54216	54216
15.	32341	33341

ANSWER KEY AND EXPLANATIONS

1. A	4. D	7. A	10. A	13. D
2. A	5. A	8. D	11. A	14. A
3. D	6. D	9. A	12. D	15. D

1. **The correct answer is (A).** Both are the same.

2. **The correct answer is (A).** Both are the same.

3. **The correct answer is (D).** The first, 7300, is four digits; the second, 730, is three digits.

4. **The correct answer is (D).** The first, 50106, is five digits; the second, 5016, is four digits and does not have a second 0.

5. **The correct answer is (A).** Both are the same.

6. **The correct answer is (D).** The first, 7516, ends in 16; the second ends in 61.

7. **The correct answer is (A).** Both are the same.

8. **The correct answer is (D).** The first, 19832, begins with 198; the second begins with 189.

9. **The correct answer is (A).** Both are the same.

10. **The correct answer is (A).** Both are the same.

11. **The correct answer is (A).** Both are the same.

12. **The correct answer is (D).** The first, 94936, has 9 as its middle (third) digit; the second, 94636, has 6 as its middle digit.

13. **The correct answer is (D).** The first, 3287, ends in 7; the second, 3285, ends in 5.

14. **The correct answer is (A).** Both are the same.

15. **The correct answer is (D).** The first, 32341, has 2 as its second digit; the second, 33341, has 3 as its second digit.

Practice Set 2

Directions: In the following set of practice questions, all differences are in the numbers. Work quickly, focusing only on the numbers. You may find any of the three varieties of differences just described. Place an **(A)** next to the question if the items are alike, and a **(D)** if they are different.

1. 3685 Brite Ave — 3865 Brite Ave
2. Ware MA 08215 — Ware MA 08215
3. 4001 Webster Rd — 401 Webster Rd
4. 9789 Bell Rd — 9786 Bell Rd
5. Scarsdale NY 10583 — Scarsdale NY 10583
6. 1482 Grand Blvd — 1482 Grand Blvd
7. Milwaukee WI 53202 — Milwaukee WI 52302
8. 3542 W 48th St — 3542 W 84th St
9. 9461 Hansen St — 9461 Hansen St
10. 32322 Florence Pkwy — 3232 Florence Pkwy
11. Portland OR 97208 — Portland OR 99208
12. 3999 Thompson Dr — 3999 Thompson Dr
13. 1672 Sutton Pl — 1972 Sutton Pl
14. Omaha NE 68127 — Omaha NE 68127
15. 1473 S 96th St — 1743 S 96th St
16. 3425 Geary St — 3425 Geary St
17. Dallas TX 75234 — Dallas TX 75234
18. 4094 Horchow Rd — 4904 Horchow Rd
19. San Francisco CA 94108 — San Francisco CA 94108
20. 1410 Broadway — 141 Broadway
21. 424 Fifth Ave — 4240 Fifth Ave
22. Westport CT 06880 — Westport CT 06880
23. 1932 Wilton Rd — 1923 Wilton Rd
24. 2052 Victoria Sta — 2502 Victoria Sta
25. 1982 Carlton Pl — 1982 Carlton Pl

ANSWER KEY AND EXPLANATIONS

1. D	6. A	11. D	16. A	21. D
2. A	7. D	12. A	17. A	22. A
3. D	8. D	13. D	18. D	23. D
4. D	9. A	14. A	19. A	24. D
5. A	10. D	15. D	20. D	25. A

1. **The correct answer is (D).** The first address includes the number 3685; in the second address, the middle two digits of this number are transposed (3865).

2. **The correct answer is (A).** Both are the same.

3. **The correct answer is (D).** The first address includes a four-digit number, 4001; the second includes a three-digit number, 401.

4. **The correct answer is (D).** The number in the first address, 9789, ends in 9; the number in the second address ends in 6.

5. **The correct answer is (A).** Both are the same.

6. **The correct answer is (A).** Both are the same.

7. **The correct answer is (D).** In the ZIP Code in the first address, the second digit is 3 and third is 2; in the ZIP Code in the second address, the second digit is 2 and the third is 3.

8. **The correct answer is (D).** The number in the first address is 48; the number in the second is 84.

9. **The correct answer is (A).** Both are the same.

10. **The correct answer is (D).** The first address includes a five-digit number, 32322; the second address includes a four-digit number, 3232.

11. **The correct answer is (D).** In the ZIP Code in the first address, the second digit is 7; in the ZIP Code in the second address, the second digit is 9.

12. **The correct answer is (A).** Both are the same.

13. **The correct answer is (D).** In the number of the first address, the second digit is 6; in the number in the second address, the second digit is 9.

14. **The correct answer is (A).** Both are the same.

15. **The correct answer is (D).** The second and third digits of the two address numbers have been transposed: 47 and 74.

16. **The correct answer is (A).** Both are the same.

17. **The correct answer is (A).** Both are the same.

18. **The correct answer is (D).** The second and third digits of the two address numbers have been transposed: 09 and 90.

19. **The correct answer is (A).** Both are the same.

20. **The correct answer is (D).** The first address has a four-digit number, 1410; the second has a three-digit number, 141.

21. **The correct answer is (D).** The first address has a three-digit number, 424; the second has a four-digit number, 4240.

22. The correct answer is (A). Both are the same.

23. The correct answer is (D). The third and fourth digits of the two address numbers have been transposed: 32 and 23.

24. The correct answer is (D). The second and third digits of the two address numbers have been transposed: 05 and 50.

25. The correct answer is (A). Both are the same.

Practice Set 3

Directions: For each question, look for any discrepancies between abbreviations. Remember to sound out the abbreviations exactly as you see them.

1.	3238 NW 3rd St	3238 NE 3rd St
2.	7865 Harkness Blvd	7865 Harkness Blvd
3.	Seattle WA 98102	Seattle WY 98102
4.	342 Madison Ave	342 Madison St
5.	723 Broadway E	723 Broadway E
6.	4731 W 88th Dr	4731 W 88th Rd
7.	Boiceville NY 12412	Boiceville NY 12412
8.	9021 Rodeo Dr	9021 Rodeo Dr
9.	2093 Post St	2093 Post Rd
10.	New Orleans LA 70153	New Orleans LA 70153
11.	5332 SW Bombay St	5332 SW Bombay St
12.	416 Wellington Pkwy	416 Wellington Hwy
13.	2096 Garden Ln	2096 Garden Wy
14.	3220 W Grant Ave	3220 W Grant Ave
15.	Charlotte VT 05445	Charlotte VA 05445
16.	4415 Oriental Blvd	4415 Oriental Blvd
17.	6876 Raffles Rd	6876 Raffles Rd
18.	891 S Hotel Hwy	891 E Hotel Hwy
19.	9500 London Br	9500 London Br
20.	24A Motcomb St	24A Motcomb St
21.	801 S Erleigh Ln	801 S Erleigh La
22.	839 Casco St	839 Casco St
23.	Freeport ME 04033	Freeport NE 04033
24.	3535 Island Ave	3535 Island Av
25.	2186 Missourie Ave NE	2186 Missourie Ave NW

ANSWER KEY AND EXPLANATIONS

1. D	6. D	11. A	16. A	21. D
2. A	7. A	12. D	17. A	22. A
3. D	8. A	13. D	18. D	23. D
4. D	9. D	14. A	19. A	24. D
5. A	10. A	15. D	20. A	25. D

1. **The correct answer is (D).** The first address includes NW (for Northwest); the second includes NE (for Northeast).

2. **The correct answer is (A).** Both are the same.

3. **The correct answer is (D).** The first address is in WA (Washington); the second address is in WY (Wyoming).

4. **The correct answer is (D).** The first address includes Ave (for Avenue); the second includes St (for Street).

5. **The correct answer is (A).** Both are the same.

6. **The correct answer is (D).** The first address includes Dr (for Drive); the second includes Rd (for Road).

7. **The correct answer is (A).** Both are the same.

8. **The correct answer is (A).** Both are the same.

9. **The correct answer is (D).** The first address includes St (for Street); the second includes Rd (for Road).

10. **The correct answer is (A).** Both are the same.

11. **The correct answer is (A).** Both are the same.

12. **The correct answer is (D).** The first address includes Pkwy (for Parkway); the second includes Hwy (for Highway).

13. **The correct answer is (D).** The first address includes Ln (Lane); the second includes Wy (Way).

14. **The correct answer is (A).** Both are the same.

15. **The correct answer is (D).** The first address is located in VT (Vermont); the second is located in VA (Virginia).

16. **The correct answer is (A).** Both are the same.

17. **The correct answer is (A).** Both are the same.

18. **The correct answer is (D).** The first address is on S (South) Hotel; the second is on E (East) Hotel.

19. **The correct answer is (A).** Both are the same.

20. **The correct answer is (A).** Both are the same.

21. **The correct answer is (D).** The two addresses contain different abbreviations for Lane (Ln vs. La).

22. **The correct answer is (A).** Both are the same.

23. **The correct answer is (D).** The first address is located in ME (Maine); the second is located in NE (Nebraska).

24. **The correct answer is (D).** The addresses contain different abbreviations for Avenue (Ave vs. Av).

25. **The correct answer is (D).** The first address is on Missourie Ave NE (Northeast); the second is on Missourie Ave NW (Northwest).

Practice Set 4

Directions: Look for discrepancies in the following list. Place an **(A)** next to the question if the items are alike, and a **(D)** if they are different.

1. Brookfield   Brookville
2. Wayland   Wayland
3. Ferncliff   Farmcliff
4. Spring   Springs
5. New City   New City
6. Beech   Beach
7. Torrington   Torington
8. Brayton   Brayton
9. Collegaite   Collegiate
10. Weston   Wetson

ANSWER KEY AND EXPLANATIONS

1. D	3. D	5. A	7. D	9. D
2. A	4. D	6. D	8. A	10. D

1. **The correct answer is (D).** The first is Brook*field*; the second is Brook*ville*.

2. **The correct answer is (A).** Both are the same.

3. **The correct answer is (D).** The first is *Fern*cliff; the second is *Farm*cliff.

4. **The correct answer is (D).** The first is Spring; the second ends in an *s*.

5. **The correct answer is (A).** Both are the same.

6. **The correct answer is (D).** The first, Beech, is spelled with *ee*; the second is spelled with *ea*.

7. **The correct answer is (D).** The first contains a double *r*; the second does not.

8. **The correct answer is (A).** Both are the same.

9. **The correct answer is (D).** In the first word, Collegaite, *a* comes before *i* (fourth- and third-to-last letters); in the second word, Collegiate, the order of these two letters is reversed.

10. **The correct answer is (D).** In the first word, Weston, the *s* comes before the *t*; in the second, the *t* comes before the *s*.

ADDRESS-CHECKING EXERCISES

In these questions, you may find differences in the two addresses in numbers, abbreviations, or main words, or you may find no difference at all. Work quickly, but do not time yourself on these practice questions.

Exercise 1

Directions: Look for discrepancies in the following list. Place an **(A)** next to the question if the items are alike, and a **(D)** if they are different.

1.	8690 W 134th St	8960 W 134th St
2.	1912 Berkshire Wy	1912 Berkshire Wy
3.	5331 W Professor St	5331 W Proffesor St
4.	Philadelphia PA 19124	Philadelphia PN 19124
5.	7450 Saguenay St	7450 Saguenay St
6.	8650 Christy St	8650 Christey St
7.	Lumberville PA 18933	Lumberville PA 19833
8.	114 Alabama Ave NW	114 Alabama Av NW
9.	1756 Waterford St	1756 Waterville St
10.	2214 Wister Wy	2214 Wister Wy
11.	2974 Repplier Rd	2974 Repplier Dr
12.	Essex CT 06426	Essex CT 06426
13.	7676 N Bourbon St	7616 N Bourbon St
14.	2762 Rosengarten Wy	2762 Rosengarden Wy
15.	239 Windell Ave	239 Windell Ave
16.	4667 Edgeworth Rd	4677 Edgeworth Rd
17.	2661 Kennel St SE	2661 Kennel St SW
18.	Alamo TX 78516	Alamo TX 78516
19.	3709 Columbine St	3709 Columbine St
20.	9699 W 14th St	9699 W 14th Rd
21.	2207 Markland Ave	2207 Markham Ave
22.	Los Angeles CA 90013	Los Angeles CA 90018
23.	4608 N Warnock St	4806 N Warnock St
24.	7118 S Summer St	7118 S Summer St
25.	New York, NY 10016	New York, NY 10016
26.	4514 Ft Hamilton Pk	4514 Ft Hamilton Pk
27.	5701 Koszciusko St	5701 Koscusko St

28.	5422 Evergreen St	4522 Evergreen St
29.	Gainesville FL 32611	Gainesville FL 32611
30.	5018 Church St	5018 Church Ave
31.	1079 N Blake St	1097 N Blake St
32.	8072 W 20th Rd	8072 W 20th Dr
33.	Onoro ME 04473	Orono ME 04473
34.	2175 Kimbell Rd	2175 Kimball Rd
35.	1243 Mermaid Rd	1243 Mermaid St
36.	4904 SW 134th St	4904 SW 134th St
37.	1094 Hancock St	1049 Hancock St
38.	Des Moines IA 50311	Des Moines IA 50311
39.	4832 S Rinaldi Rd	4832 S Rinaldo Rd
40.	2015 Dorchester Rd	2015 Dorchester Rd
41.	5216 Woodbine St	5216 Woodburn St
42.	Boulder CO 80302	Boulder CA 80302
43.	4739 N Marion St	479 N Marion St
44.	3720 Nautilus Wy	3720 Nautilus Way
45.	3636 Gramercy Pk	3636 Gramercy Pk
46.	757 Johnson Ave	757 Johnston Ave
47.	3045 Brighton 12th St	3054 Brighton 12th St
48.	237 Ovington Ave	237 Ovington Ave
49.	Kalamazoo MI 49007	Kalamazoo MI 49007
50.	Missoula MT 59812	Missoula MS 59812
51.	Stillwater OK 74704	Stillwater OK 47404
52.	4746 Empire Blvd	4746 Empire Bldg
53.	6321 St Johns Pl	6321 St Johns Pl
54.	2242 Vanderbilt Ave	2242 Vanderbilt Ave
55.	542 Ditmas Blvd	542 Ditmars Blvd
56.	4603 W Argyle Rd	4603 W Argyle Rd
57.	653 Knickerbocker Ave NE	653 Knickerbocker Ave NE
58.	3651 Midwood Terr	3651 Midwood Terr
59.	Chapel Hill NC 27514	Chaple Hill NC 27514
60.	3217 Vernon Pl NW	3217 Vernon Dr NW
61.	1094 Rednor Pkwy	1049 Rednor Pkwy
62.	986 S Doughty Blvd	986 S Douty Blvd

63.	Lincoln NE 68508	Lincoln NE 65808
64.	1517 LaSalle Ave	1517 LaSalle Ave
65.	3857 S Morris St	3857 S Morriss St
66.	6104 Saunders Expy	614 Saunders Expy
67.	2541 Appleton St	2541 Appleton Rd
68.	Washington DC 20052	Washington DC 20052
69.	6439 Kessler Blvd S	6439 Kessler Blvd S
70.	4786 Catalina Dr	4786 Catalana Dr
71.	132 E Hampton Pkwy	1322 E Hampton Pkwy
72.	1066 Goethe Sq S	1066 Geothe Sq S
73.	1118 Jerriman Wy	1218 Jerriman Wy
74.	5798 Gd Central Pkwy	5798 Gd Central Pkwy
75.	Delaware OH 43015	Delaware OK 43015
76.	Corvallis OR 97331	Corvallis OR 97331
77.	4231 Keating Ave N	4231 Keating Av N
78.	5689 Central Pk Pl	5869 Central Pk Pl
79.	1108 Lyndhurst Dr	1108 Lyndhurst Dr
80.	842 Chambers Ct	842 Chamber Ct
81.	Athens OH 45701	Athens GA 45701
82.	Tulsa OK 74171	Tulsa OK 71471
83.	6892 Beech Grove Ave	6892 Beech Grove Ave
84.	2939 E Division St	2939 W Division St
85.	1554 Pitkin Ave	1554 Pitkin Ave
86.	905 St Edwards Plz	950 St Edwards Plz
87.	1906 W 152nd St	1906 W 152nd St
88.	3466 Glenmore Ave	3466 Glenville Ave
89.	Middlebury VT 05753	Middlebery VT 05753
90.	Evanston IL 60201	Evanston IN 60201
91.	9401 W McDonald Ave	9401 W MacDonald Ave
92.	5527 Albermarle Rd	5527 Albermarle Rd
93.	9055 Carter Dr	9055 Carter Rd
94.	Greenvale NY 11548	Greenvale NY 11458
95.	1149 Cherry Gr S	1149 Cherry Gr S

ANSWER KEY AND EXPLANATIONS

1. D	20. D	39. D	58. A	77. D
2. A	21. D	40. A	59. D	78. D
3. D	22. D	41. D	60. D	79. A
4. D	23. D	42. D	61. D	80. D
5. A	24. A	43. D	62. D	81. D
6. D	25. A	44. D	63. D	82. D
7. D	26. A	45. A	64. A	83. A
8. D	27. D	46. D	65. D	84. D
9. D	28. D	47. D	66. D	85. A
10. A	29. A	48. A	67. D	86. D
11. D	30. D	49. A	68. A	87. A
12. A	31. D	50. D	69. A	88. D
13. D	32. D	51. D	70. D	89. D
14. D	33. D	52. D	71. D	90. D
15. A	34. D	53. A	72. D	91. D
16. D	35. D	54. A	73. D	92. A
17. D	36. A	55. D	74. A	93. D
18. A	37. D	56. A	75. D	94. D
19. A	38. A	57. A	76. A	95. A

1. **The correct answer is (D).** The first address number is 8690; in the second address, the number is 8960.

2. **The correct answer is (A).** Both are the same.

3. **The correct answer is (D).** The first address contains Professor with a double *s;* the second contains Proffesor with a double *f.*

4. **The correct answer is (D).** The first address contains PA; the second contains PN.

5. **The correct answer is (A).** Both are the same.

6. **The correct answer is (D).** The first address contains Christy with no *e;* the second spells Christey with an *e.*

7. **The correct answer is (D).** The ZIP Code in the first address is 18933; in the second, the ZIP Code is 19833 (second and third digits transposed).

8. **The correct answer is (D).** The first has Ave as an abbreviation for Avenue; the second uses Av.

9. **The correct answer is (D).** The first address is on Waterford; the second is on Waterville.

10. **The correct answer is (A).** Both are the same.

11. **The correct answer is (D).** The first address is a Road (Rd); the second is a Drive (Dr).

12. **The correct answer is (A).** Both are the same.

13. **The correct answer is (D).** The number of the first address is 7676; the number of the second is 7616.

14. **The correct answer is (D).** The first address includes Rosengarten spelled with a *t*; the second includes Rosengarden spelled with a *d*.

15. **The correct answer is (A).** Both are the same.

16. **The correct answer is (D).** The number of the first address is 4667; the number of the second is 4677.

17. **The correct answer is (D).** The first address is Kennel St *SE*; the second is Kennel St *SW*.

18. **The correct answer is (A).** Both are the same.

19. **The correct answer is (A).** Both are the same.

20. **The correct answer is (D).** The first address is a Street (St); the second is a Road (Rd).

21. **The correct answer is (D).** The street name in the first address is Markland; in the second, it is Markham.

22. **The correct answer is (D).** The ZIP Code in the first address is 90013; in the second, it is 90018.

23. **The correct answer is (D).** The street number in the first address is 4608; in the second, it is 4806.

24. **The correct answer is (A).** Both are the same.

25. **The correct answer is (A).** Both are the same.

26. **The correct answer is (A).** Both are the same.

27. **The correct answer is (D).** The street name in the first address is Koszciusko; in the second, it is Koscusko.

28. **The correct answer is (D).** The number in the first address is 5422; in the second, it is 4522.

29. **The correct answer is (A).** Both are the same.

30. **The correct answer is (D).** The first address is a Street (St); the second is an Avenue (Ave).

31. **The correct answer is (D).** The number in the first address is 1079; in the second, it is 1097.

32. **The correct answer is (D).** The first address is a Road (Rd); the second is a Drive (Dr).

33. **The correct answer is (D).** The town name in the first address is Onoro; in the second, it is Orono.

34. **The correct answer is (D).** The first address is on Kimbell; the second is on Kimball.

35. **The correct answer is (D).** The first address is a Road (Rd); the second is a Street (St).

36. **The correct answer is (A).** Both are the same.

37. **The correct answer is (D).** The number of the first address is 1094; the number of the second is 1049.

38. **The correct answer is (A).** Both are the same.

39. **The correct answer is (D).** The first address is Rinaldi; the second is Rinaldo.

40. **The correct answer is (A).** Both are the same.

41. **The correct answer is (D).** The first address contains Woodbine; the second contains Woodburn.

42. **The correct answer is (D).** The first address is in Colorado (CO); the second is in California (CA).

43. **The correct answer is (D).** The number in the first address is four digits long (4739); in the second, it is three digits (479).

44. **The correct answer is (D).** In the first address, Way is abbreviated (Wy); in the second, it is spelled out.

45. **The correct answer is (A).** Both are the same.

46. **The correct answer is (D).** The first address is on Johnson; the second is on Johnston (with a *t*).

47. **The correct answer is (D).** The number in the first address is 3045; in the second, it is 3054.

48. **The correct answer is (A).** Both are the same.

49. **The correct answer is (A).** Both are the same.

50. **The correct answer is (D).** The first address is in Montana (MT); the second is in Mississippi (MS).

51. **The correct answer is (D).** The ZIP Code of the first address is 74704; the ZIP Code of the second is 47404.

52. **The correct answer is (D).** The first address refers to a Boulevard (Blvd); the second refers to a Building (Bldg).

53. **The correct answer is (A).** Both are the same.

54. **The correct answer is (A).** Both are the same.

55. **The correct answer is (D).** The first address is on Ditmas; the second is on Ditmars.

56. **The correct answer is (A).** Both are the same.

57. **The correct answer is (A).** Both are the same.

58. **The correct answer is (A).** Both are the same.

59. **The correct answer is (D).** The first address is in Chapel Hill; the second is in Chaple Hill.

60. **The correct answer is (D).** The first address is a Place (Pl); the second is a Drive (Dr).

61. **The correct answer is (D).** The number of the first address is 1094; the number of the second is 1049.

62. **The correct answer is (D).** The first address is on Doughty; the second is on Douty.

63. **The correct answer is (D).** The ZIP Code of the first address is 68508; the ZIP Code of the second is 65808.

64. **The correct answer is (A).** Both are the same.

65. **The correct answer is (D).** The first address is on Morris; the second is on Morriss.

66. **The correct answer is (D).** The number of the first address is 6104 (four digits); the number of the second is 614 (three digits).

67. **The correct answer is (D).** The first address is a Street (St); the second is a Road (Rd).

68. **The correct answer is (A).** Both are the same.

69. **The correct answer is (A).** Both are the same.

70. **The correct answer is (D).** The first address is on Catalina; the second is on Catalana.

71. **The correct answer is (D).** The number of the first address is 132 (three digits); the number of the second is 1322 (four digits).

72. **The correct answer is (D).** The first address is on Goethe; the second is on Geothe.

73. **The correct answer is (D).** The number of the first address is 1118; the number of the second is 1218.

74. **The correct answer is (A).** Both are the same.

75. **The correct answer is (D).** The first address is in Ohio (OH); the second is in Oklahoma (OK).

76. **The correct answer is (A).** Both are the same.

77. **The correct answer is (D).** In the first address, Avenue is abbreviated Ave; in the second, it is abbreviated Av.

78. **The correct answer is (D).** The number of the first address is 5689; the number of the second is 5869.

79. **The correct answer is (A).** Both are the same.

80. **The correct answer is (D).** The first address is on Chambers; the second is on Chamber (no *s*).

81. **The correct answer is (D).** The first address is in Ohio (OH); the second is in Georgia (GA).

82. **The correct answer is (D).** The ZIP Code of the first address is 74171; the ZIP Code of the second is 71471.

83. **The correct answer is (A).** Both are the same.

84. **The correct answer is (D).** The first address is on *E* Division; the second is on *W* Division.

85. **The correct answer is (A).** Both are the same.

86. **The correct answer is (D).** The number of the first address is 905; the number of the second is 950.

87. **The correct answer is (A).** Both are the same.

88. **The correct answer is (D).** The first address is on Glenmore; the second is on Glenville.

89. **The correct answer is (D).** The first address is in Middlebury; the second is in Middlebery.

90. **The correct answer is (D).** The first address is in Illinois (IL); the second is in Indiana (IN).

91. **The correct answer is (D).** The first address is on McDonald; the second is on MacDonald.

92. **The correct answer is (A).** Both are the same.

93. **The correct answer is (D).** The first address is a Drive (Dr); the second is a Road (Rd).

94. **The correct answer is (D).** The ZIP Code of the first address is 11548; the ZIP Code of the second is 11458.

95. **The correct answer is (A).** Both are the same.

Exercise 2

Directions: Each question consists of a set of names and addresses. In each question, the name and address in Column II should be exactly like the name and address in Column I. However, some addresses in Column II contain mistakes.

- Write **(A)** next to the question number if there is a mistake *only* in the NAME.

- Write **(B)** next to the question number if there is a mistake *only* in the ADDRESS.

- Write **(C)** next to the question number if there are mistakes in *both* NAME *and* ADDRESS.

- Write **(D)** next to the question number if there are NO MISTAKES.

Column I	Column II
1. Mrs. Myrna McCardle 332 East 128th St. Chicago, IL 60637	Mrs. Myra McCardle 332 East 128th St. Chicago, IL 60637
2. Jorge T. Garcia, M.D. 843 Alameda Street Austin, TX 78712	Jorge T. Garcia, M.D. 843 Alameda Street Austin, TX 78712
3. Ms. Lillian Loomis 862 S.E. Byram Blvd Durham, NC 27706	Ms. Lillian Loomia 862 S.E. Bryan Blvd. Durham, NC 27706
4. Prof. Jeanette Jesperson 761 Palo Alto Drive Stanford, CA 94305	Prof. Jeanette Jesperson 716 Palo Alto Drive Stamford, CA 94305
5. Mr. Brett H. Meyers 72 Nannyhagen Road Haverford, PA 19042	Mr. Brett H. Meyers 72 Nannyhagen Road Haverford, PA 19402
6. George and Sylvia Shields 362 West 96th Street New York, NY 10028	George and Sylvia Sheilds 362 West 96th Street New York, NY 10028
7. Dr. and Mrs. P.J. Clarke 2146 Old Lyme Highway New London, CT 06320	Dr. and Mrs. P.J. Clarke 2146 Old Lyme Highway New London, CA 06320

8. Mr. Milton F. Gladstone
   72 Conshohocken Rd.
   Athens, OH 45701

   Mr. Milton P. Gladstone
   72 Conshohocken Rd.
   Athena, OH 45701

9. Francis X. O'Rourke
   1918 Meridian Way
   Norman, OK 73069

   Francis X. O'Rourke
   1918 Meridian Way
   Norman, OK 73069

10. Mrs. Anne C. Warren
    38-42 Marvela Drive
    Santa Cruz, CA 95064

    Mrs. Anna C. Warren
    38-42 Marvella Drive
    Santa Cruz, CA 95064

11. Miss Maude Silverstone
    48601 Maryland Ave. NW
    Washington, DC 20052

    Miss Maude Silverstone
    48610 Maryland Ave. NW
    Washington, DC 20052

12. Hoh Sun-Wah, Ph.D.
    4862 Southern Artery
    Omaha, NE 68178

    Moh Sun-Wah, Ph.D.
    4862 Southern Arterial
    Omaha, NE 68178

13. Sr. Mary Donohue
    378 Brigham Drive
    Provo, UT 84601

    Sr. Mary Donoghue
    378 Brigham Drive
    Provo, UT 86401

14. Mr. Thomas Trimmingham
    603 East Taunton Street
    Atlanta, GA 30322

    Mr. Thomas Trimingham
    603 East Taunton Street
    Atlanta, GA 30322

15. Miss Sussana Oliviero
    215 Sorority Way
    Tallahassee, FL 32306

    Miss Sussana Oliviero
    215 Sorority Way
    Tallahassee, FL 32306

ANSWER KEY AND EXPLANATIONS

1. A	4. B	7. B	10. C	13. C
2. D	5. B	8. C	11. B	14. A
3. C	6. A	9. D	12. C	15. D

1. **The correct answer is (A).** The first name of the addressee in Column I is Myrna; in the second, it is Myra.

2. **The correct answer is (D).** No errors.

3. **The correct answer is (C).** The last name of the addressee in Column I is Loomis; in the second, it is Loomia. Also, the first address is on Byram; the second is on Bryan.

4. **The correct answer is (B).** The number of the first address is 761; the number of the second is 716. Also, the first address is in Stanford; the second is in Stamford.

5. **The correct answer is (B).** The ZIP Code of the first address is 19042; the ZIP Code of the second is 19402.

6. **The correct answer is (A).** The last name of the addressees in Column I is Shields; in the second, it is Sheilds.

7. **The correct answer is (B).** The first address is in CT; the second is in CA.

8. **The correct answer is (C).** The middle initial of the addressee in Column I is F; the middle initial of the addressee in Column II is P. Also, the first address is in Athens, OH; the second is in Athena, OH.

9. **The correct answer is (D).** No errors.

10. **The correct answer is (C).** The first name of the addressee in Column I is Anne; the first name of the addressee in Column II is Anna. Also, the address in Column I is on Marvela; in Column II, it is on Marvella.

11. **The correct answer is (B).** The house number in Column I is 48601; in Column II, it is 48610.

12. **The correct answer is (C).** The addressee's first name in Column I is Hoh; in Column II, it is Moh. Also, the address in Column I is on Artery; in Column II, it is on Arterial.

13. **The correct answer is (C).** The last name of the addressee in Column I is Donohue; the last name in Column II is Donoghue. Also, the ZIP Code of the address in Column I is 84601; in Column II, it is 86401.

14. **The correct answer is (A).** The addressee's last name in Column I is Trimmingham; in Column II, it is Trimingham.

15. **The correct answer is (D).** No errors.

NAME AND NUMBER COMPARISON QUESTIONS ON THE PUBLIC SAFETY DISPATCHER EXAM

You may see name-and-number and number-and-letter comparison questions in one of many different formats and question styles. In general, though, the basic comparison task is always the same. The biggest difference lies in the directions. It is unlikely that you will find more than one form of comparison question on your exam, but there is no way of predicting which kind of question you will encounter. Therefore, if you find any comparison questions on your exam, it's extremely important that you *read the directions* very carefully.

Try the five comparison exercises that follow. Each has a different style of question. Each has different directions that you must master before you attempt to answer the questions. For the most part, the strategies that you learned for address checking will work well here, too. Of course, if you are not comparing columns, you must adjust to the requirements of the exercise. The final exercise is considerably more complicated than the others in terms of directions.

NAME AND NUMBER COMPARISON EXERCISES

Exercise 1

Directions: Each question consists of letters or numbers in Columns I and II. For each question, compare each line of Column I with its corresponding line in Column II. Decide how many lines in Column II are exactly the same as their counterparts in Column I.

- Choose **(A)** if only ONE line in Column II is exactly the same as its corresponding line in Column I.

- Choose **(B)** if TWO lines in Column II are exactly the same as their corresponding lines in Column I.

- Choose **(C)** if THREE lines in Column II are exactly the same as their corresponding lines in Column I.

- Choose **(D)** if ALL FOUR lines in Column II are exactly the same as their corresponding lines in Column I.

Column I	Column II
1. 3816	3816
5283	5832
4686	4868
1252	1252
2. acdt	acdt
xuer	xuer
Itbf	Ibtf
oypn	oypn

3. 9063   9063

    itop   itop

    nzne   nzne

    7549   7549

4. TYBF   TYIF

    5631   5361

    BcOp   BcOP

    ag7B   ag7B

5. Ibct   lbct

    1803   1803

    Xtux   Xtux

    45NM   45NM

6. AbuR   AbuR

    52VC   52VC

    rehg   rehg

    3416   3416

7. awg3   awg3

    tyE3   ty3E

    abhn   abnh

    24po   24op

8. 6tru   6tru

    sw4k   sw4K

    lgh8   lgh8

    u2up   u2up

9. agxp   agXp

    ruy5   ruy5

    aglb   agLb

    8a9c   8z9c

10. agbt   agbt

    SsiI   sSiI

    ty4f   ty4f

    arwd   erwd

11. 4tT4	4tt4
mp8s	mp8s
bh43	bh43
9ewz	9ewz
12. r2D2	R2D2
zboc	zboc
LQ6t	Lq6T
0851	0851
13. tzng	yzng
5F09	5F09
bAIr	bAlr
6406	6406
14. 151Y	151Y
Pti7	Pti7
4uy3	4uyE
htmn	hynm
15. rvC8	rvC8
pg53	pg53
1080	1080
ednp	edhp
16. rTux	rTux
lgad	lgab
84fp	84fb
uEms	uEms
17. rpIt	rlpt
8eoz	8oez
agew	agew
T59v	T59v

18. 38mo   38m0

    Sebc   Sbce

    UPRF   URPF

    a5y3   a5y3

19. 25dq   25bq

    uz4R   uz4R

    ylng   yLng

    stRe   sire

20. 4fKD   4fKd

    swhC   swhC

    nbQt   bNQt

    L073   L073

ANSWER KEY AND EXPLANATIONS

1. B	5. C	9. A	13. B	17. B
2. C	6. D	10. B	14. B	18. A
3. D	7. A	11. C	15. C	19. A
4. A	8. C	12. B	16. B	20. B

1. **The correct answer is (B).** Alike: 3816, 3816; 1252, 1252. Different: 5283, 5832; 4686, 4868.

2. **The correct answer is (C).** Alike: acdt, acdt, xuer, xuer; oypn, oypn. Different: Itbf, Ibtf.

3. **The correct answer is (D).** All alike.

4. **The correct answer is (A).** Alike: ag7B, ag7B. Different: TYBF, TYIF; 5631, 5361; BcOp, BcOP.

5. **The correct answer is (C).** Alike: 1803, 1803; Xtux, Xtux; 45NM, 45NM. Different: Ibct, lbct.

6. **The correct answer is (D).** All alike.

7. **The correct answer is (A).** Alike: awg3, awg3. Different: tyE3, ty3E; abhn, abnh; 24po, 24op.

8. **The correct answer is (C).** Alike: 6tru, 6tru; lgh8, lgh8; u2up, u2up. Different: sw4k, sw4K.

9. **The correct answer is (A).** Alike: ruy5, ruy5. Different: agxp, agXp; aglb, agLb; 8a9c, 8z9c.

10. **The correct answer is (B).** Alike: agbt, agbt; ty4f, ty4f. Different: SsiI, sSiI; arwd, erwd.

11. **The correct answer is (C).** Alike: mp8s, mp8s; bh43, bh43; 9ewz, 9ewz. Different: 4tT4, 4tt4.

12. **The correct answer is (B).** Alike: zboc, zboc; 0851, 0851. Different: r2D2, R2D2; LQ6t, Lq6T.

13. **The correct answer is (B).** Alike: 5F09, 5F09; 6406, 6406. Different: tzng, yzng; bAIr, bAlr.

14. **The correct answer is (B).** Alike: 151Y, 151Y; Pti7, Pti7. Different: 4uy3, 4uyE; htmn, hynm.

15. **The correct answer is (C).** Alike: rvC8, rvC8, pg53, pg53; 1080, 1080. Different: ednp, edhp.

16. **The correct answer is (B).** Alike: rTux, rTux; uEms, uEms. Different: lgad, lgab; 84fp, 84fb.

17. **The correct answer is (B).** Alike: agew, agew; T59v, T59v. Different: rpIt, rlpt; 8eoz, 8oez.

18. **The correct answer is (A).** Alike: a5y3, a5y3. Different: 38mo, 38m0; Sebc, Sbce; UPRF, URPF.

19. **The correct answer is (A).** Alike: uz4R, uz4R. Different: 25dq, 25bq; ylng, yLng; stRe, sire.

20. **The correct answer is (B).** Alike: swhC, swhC; L073, L073. Different: 4fKD, 4fKd; nbQt, bNQt.

Exercise 2

Directions: Each of the following questions consists of three sets of names and name codes. For each question, the two names and name codes on the same line should be exactly the same. Look carefully at each set of names and codes and mark your answer next to the question number.

- Write **(A)** if ALL THREE sets contain mistakes.
- Write **(B)** if TWO of the sets contain mistakes.
- Write **(C)** if only ONE set contains mistakes.
- Write **(D)** if NO MISTAKES are in any of the sets.

	Column I		Column II	
1.	Macabe, John N.	V 53162	Macade, John N.	V 53162
	Howard, Joan S.	J 24791	Howard, Joan S.	124791
	Ware, Susan B.	A 45068	Ware, Susan B.	A 45968
2.	Powell, Michael C.	78537 F	Powell, Michael C.	78537 F
	Martinez, Pablo J.	24435 P	Martinez, Pablo J.	24435 P
	MacBane, Eliot M.	98674 E	MacBane, Eliot M.	98674 E
3.	Fitz-Kramer Machines	259090	Fitz-Kramer Machines	259090
	Marvel Cleaning Service	482657	Marvel Cleaning Service	482657
	Donato, Carl G.	637418	Danato, Carl G.	687418
4.	Davison Trading Corp.	43108 T	Davidson Trading Corp.	43108 T
	Cotwald Lighting Fixtures	76065 L	Cotwald Lighting Fixtures	70056 L
	R. Crawford Plumbers	23157 C	R. Crawford Plumbers	23157 G
5.	Fraiman Eng. Corp.	M4773	Friaman Eng. Corp.	M4773
	Neuman, Walter B.	N7745	Neumen, Walter B.	N7745
	Pierce, Eric M.	W6304	Pierce, Eric M.	W6304
6.	Constable, Eugene	B 64837	Comstable, Eugene	B 64837
	Derrick, Paul	H 27119	Derrik, Paul	H 27119
	Heller, Karen	S 49606	Heller, Karen	S 46906
7.	Hernando Delivery Co.	D 7456	Hernando Delivery Co.	D 7456
	Barettz Electrical Supplies	N 5392	Barettz Electrical Supplies	N 5392
	Tanner, Abraham	M 4798	Tanner, Abraham	M 4798

8.	Kalin Associates	R 38641	Kaline Associates	R 38641
	Sealey, Robert E.	P 63533	Sealey, Robert E.	P 63553
	Scalsi Office Furniture	R 36742	Scalsi Office Furniture	R 36742
9.	Janowsky, Philip M.	742213	Janowsky, Philip M.	742213
	Hansen, Thomas H.	934816	Hanson, Thomas H.	934816
	L. Lester and Son Inc.	294568	L. Lester and Son Inc.	294568
10.	Majthenyi, Alexander	P 4802	Majthenyi, Alexander	B 4802
	Prisco Pools, Inc.	W 3641	Frisco Pools, Inc.	W 3641
	DePaso, Nancy G.	X 4464	DePasoa, Nancy G.	X 4464
11.	Hardy, Thomas G.	374093	Hardy, Thomas G.	374093
	Carlin, Oren F.	581158	Carling, Oren F.	581158
	van Rijn, Marike	248652	von Rijn, Marike	248652
12.	Kozy Kitchens, Inc.	Z 48621	Kozy Kitchens, Inc.	Z 46821
	Mullins, Iris	L 51790	Mollins, Iris	L 51790
	The Cheese Shop	M 48164	The Cheese Shop	M 48614
13.	Bryant College	431798	Bryant College	431798
	Harbison, James T.	468319	Harbinson, James T.	468319
	Riverfront Stadium	791645	Riverside Stadium	791645
14.	Brunswick Lanes	T 44198	Runswick Lanes	T 44198
	T. Greisis & Son	Q 53817	T. Greisis & Son	Q 53817
	DiPasquale, Gino	B 43921	DiPasquale, Gino	B 43921
15.	Hisogi, Mitsuki	563141	Hisogi, Mitsuki	536141
	Janover, Richard L.	453120	Janover, Richard L.	453210
	Britten, Barbara B.	673498	Brittan, Barbara B.	673498

ANSWER KEY AND EXPLANATIONS

1. A	4. A	7. D	10. A	13. B
2. D	5. B	8. B	11. B	14. C
3. C	6. A	9. C	12. A	15. A

1. **The correct answer is (A).** Maca<u>b</u>e, Maca<u>d</u>e; <u>J</u>24791, <u>1</u>24791; A 45<u>0</u>68, A 45<u>9</u>68.

2. **The correct answer is (D).** No errors.

3. **The correct answer is (C).** D<u>o</u>nato, D<u>a</u>nato; 6<u>3</u>7418; 6<u>8</u>7418.

4. **The correct answer is (A).** Davison, Davi<u>d</u>son; 7<u>60</u>65 L, 7<u>00</u>56 L; 23157 <u>C</u>, 23157 <u>G</u>.

5. **The correct answer is (B).** Fr<u>ai</u>man, Fr<u>ia</u>man; Neum<u>a</u>n, Neum<u>e</u>n.

6. **The correct answer is (A).** Con<u>s</u>table, Com<u>s</u>table; Derri<u>c</u>k, Derrik; S 49<u>6</u>06, S 46<u>9</u>06.

7. **The correct answer is (D).** No errors.

8. **The correct answer is (B).** Kalin, Kalin<u>e</u>; P 635<u>3</u>3, P 635<u>5</u>3.

9. **The correct answer is (C).** Han<u>s</u>en, Han<u>s</u>on.

10. **The correct answer is (A).** <u>P</u> 4802, <u>B</u> 4802; <u>P</u>risco, <u>F</u>risco; DePaso, DePaso<u>a</u>.

11. **The correct answer is (B).** Carlin, Carlin<u>g</u>; v<u>a</u>n Rijn, v<u>o</u>n Rijn.

12. **The correct answer is (A).** Z 4<u>8</u>621, Z 4<u>6</u>821; Mullins, Mollins; M 48<u>1</u>64, M 48<u>6</u>14.

13. **The correct answer is (B).** Harbison, Harbi<u>n</u>son; Riverfr<u>ont</u>, Rivers<u>ide</u>.

14. **The correct answer is (C).** <u>B</u>runswick, <u>R</u>unswick.

15. **The correct answer is (A).** 5<u>63</u>141, 5<u>36</u>141; 453<u>120</u>, 453<u>210</u>; Britt<u>e</u>n, Britt<u>a</u>n.

Exercise 3

Directions: Each question lists four names or numbers. The names or numbers may or may not be exactly the same. Compare the four names or numbers in each question, and next to the question number:

- Write **(A)** if ALL FOUR names or numbers are DIFFERENT.
- Write **(B)** if TWO of the names or numbers are exactly the same.
- Write **(C)** if THREE of the names or numbers are exactly the same.
- Write **(D)** if all FOUR names or numbers are exactly the same.

1. W.E. Johnston
   W.E. Johnson
   W.E. Johnson
   W.B. Johnson

2. Vergil L. Muller
   Vergil L. Muller
   Vergil L. Muller
   Vergil L. Muller

3. 5261383
   5263183
   5623183
   5263183

4. Atherton R. Warde
   Asheton R. Warde
   Atherton P. Warde
   Athertin P. Warde

5. 8125690
   8126690
   8125609
   8125609

6. E. Owens McVey
   E. Owen McVey
   E. Owen McVay
   E. Owen McVey

7. Emily Neal Rouse
   Emily Neal Rowse
   Emily Neal Roose
   Emily Neal Rowse

8. Francis Ramsdell
   Francis Ransdell
   Francis Ramsdell
   Francis Ramsdell

9. 2395890
   2395890
   2395890
   2395890

10. 1926341
    1962341
    1963241
    1926341

11. H. Merritt Audubon
    H. Merriott Audobon
    H. Merritt Audobon
    H. Merritt Audubon

12. 6219354
    6219354
    6219345
    6219354

13. Cornelius Detwiler
    Cornelius Detwiler
    Cornelius Detwiler
    Cornelius Detwiler

14. 2312793
    2312973
    2312973
    2312973

15. Drusilla S. Ridgeley
    Drusilla S. Ridgeley
    Drucilla S. Ridgeley
    Drucilla S. Ridgely

16. Andrei I. Tourantzev
    Andrei I. Toumantzev
    Andrei I. Toumantzov
    Andrei I. Tourantzov

17. 0065407
    1065407
    0065407
    0064507

18. 6452054
    6452054
    6452654
    6452054

19. 8501268
    8501286
    8501268
    8501268

20. Ella Burk Newham
    Ella Burk Newnam
    Ella Burk Newham
    Ella Burk Newham

ANSWER KEY AND EXPLANATIONS

1. B	5. B	9. D	13. D	17. B
2. D	6. B	10. B	14. C	18. C
3. B	7. B	11. B	15. B	19. C
4. A	8. C	12. C	16. A	20. C

1. **The correct answer is (B).** Same: W.E. Johnson, W.E. Johnson. Different: W.E. Johnston; W.B. Johnson.

2. **The correct answer is (D).** All alike.

3. **The correct answer is (B).** Same: 5263183, 5263183. Different: 5261383, 5623183.

4. **The correct answer is (A).** Different: Atherton R., Asheton R., Atherton P., Athertin P.

5. **The correct answer is (B).** Same: 5609, 5609. Different: 5690, 6690.

6. **The correct answer is (B).** Same: E. Owen McVey, E. Owen McVey. Different: E. Owens McVey, E. Owen McVay.

7. **The correct answer is (B).** Same: Rowse, Rowse. Different: Rouse, Roose.

8. **The correct answer is (C).** Same: Ramsdell, Ramsdell, Ramsdell. Different: Ransdell.

9. **The correct answer is (D).** All alike.

10. **The correct answer is (B).** Same: 263, 263. Different: 623, 632.

11. **The correct answer is (B).** Same: H. Merritt Audubon, H. Merritt Audubon. Different: H. Merriott Audobon, H. Merritt Audobon.

12. **The correct answer is (C).** Same: 54, 54, 54. Different: 45.

13. **The correct answer is (D).** All alike.

14. **The correct answer is (C).** Same: 973, 973, 973. Different: 793.

15. **The correct answer is (B).** Same: Drusilla Ridgeley, Drusilla Ridgeley. Different: Drucilla Ridgeley, Drucilla Ridgely.

16. **The correct answer is (A).** Different: Tourantzev, Toumantzev, Toumantzov, Tourantzov

17. **The correct answer is (B).** Same: 00654, 00654. Different: 10654, 00645.

18. **The correct answer is (C).** Same: 054, 054, 054. Different: 654.

19. **The correct answer is (C).** Same: 68, 68, 68. Different: 86.

20. **The correct answer is (C).** Same: Newham, Newham, Newham. Different: Newnam.

Exercise 4

Directions: Each question gives the name and identification number of an employee. Choose the ONE answer that has exactly the same identification number and name as those given in the question, and circle the letter of your answer.

1. 176823 Katherine Blau
   (A) 176823 Catherine Blau
   (B) 176283 Katherine Blau
   (C) 176823 Katherine Blau
   (D) 176823 Katherine Blaw

2. 673403 Boris T. Frame
   (A) 673403 Boris P. Frame
   (B) 673403 Boris T. Frame
   (C) 673403 Boris T. Fraim
   (D) 673430 Boris T. Frame

3. 498832 Hyman Ziebart
   (A) 498832 Hyman Zeibart
   (B) 498832 Hiram Ziebart
   (C) 498832 Hyman Ziebardt
   (D) 498832 Hyman Ziebart

4. 506745 Barbara O'Dey
   (A) 507645 Barbara O'Day
   (B) 506745 Barbara O'Day
   (C) 506475 Barbara O'Day
   (D) 506745 Barbara O'Dey

5. 344223 Morton Sklar
   (A) 344223 Morton Sklar
   (B) 344332 Norton Sklar
   (C) 344332 Morton Sklaar
   (D) 343322 Morton Sklar

6. 816040 Betsy B. Voight
   (A) 816404 Betsy B. Voight
   (B) 814060 Betsy B. Voight
   (C) 816040 Betsy B. Voight
   (D) 816040 Betsey B. Voight

7. 913576 Harold Howritz
   (A) 913576 Harold Horwitz
   (B) 913576 Harold Howritz
   (C) 913756 Harold Horwitz
   (D) 913576 Harald Howritz

8. 621190 Jayne T. Downs
   (A) 621990 Janie T. Downs
   (B) 621190 Janie T. Downs
   (C) 622190 Janie T. Downs
   (D) 621190 Jayne T. Downs

9. 004620 George McBoyd
   (A) 006420 George McBoyd
   (B) 006420 George MacBoyd
   (C) 006420 George McBoid
   (D) 004620 George McBoyd

10. 723495 Alice Appleton
    (A) 723495 Alice Appleton
    (B) 723594 Alica Appleton
    (C) 723459 Alice Appleton
    (D) 732495 Alice Appleton

11. 856772 Aaron B. Haynes
    (A) 856722 Aaron B. Haynes
    (B) 856722 Arron B. Haynes
    (C) 856722 Aaron B. Haynes
    (D) 856772 Aaron B. Haynes

12. 121434 Veronica Pope
    (A) 121343 Veronica Pope
    (B) 121434 Veronica Pope
    (C) 121434 Veronica Popa
    (D) 121343 Veronica Popa

13. 376900 Barry R. Jantzen
    - (A) 376900 Barry R. Jantsen
    - (B) 379600 Barry R. Jantzen
    - (C) 376900 Barry R. Jantzen
    - (D) 376900 Barry R. Jantzon

14. 804866 Margery Melton
    - (A) 804866 Marjery Melton
    - (B) 808466 Margery Melton
    - (C) 804866 Margery Mellon
    - (D) 804866 Margery Melton

15. 762409 Philip L. Phillipi
    - (A) 762409 Philip L. Philippi
    - (B) 762409 Phillip L. Philipi
    - (C) 762490 Philip L. Philippi
    - (D) 762409 Philip L. Phillipi

ANSWER KEY AND EXPLANATIONS

1. C	4. D	7. B	10. A	13. C
2. B	5. A	8. D	11. D	14. D
3. D	6. C	9. D	12. B	15. D

1. **The correct answer is (C).** 176823 Katherine Blau. The different items in the other answer choices are as follows: (A) Catherine; (B) 176283; (D) Blaw.

2. **The correct answer is (B).** 673403 Boris T. Frame. The different items in the other answer choices are as follows: (A) P.; (C) Fraim; (D) 673430.

3. **The correct answer is (D).** 498832 Hyman Ziebart. The different items in the other answer choices are as follows: (A) Zeibart; (B) Hiram; (C) Ziebardt.

4. **The correct answer is (D).** 506745 Barbara O'Dey. The different items in the other answer choices are as follows: (A) 507645 O'Day; (B) O'Day; (C) 506475 O'Day.

5. **The correct answer is (A).** 344223 Morton Sklar. The different items in the other answer choices are as follows: (B) 344332 Norton; (C) 344332 Sklaar; (D) 343322.

6. **The correct answer is (C).** 816040 Betsy B. Voight. The different items in the other answer choices are as follows: (A) 816404; (B) 814060; (D) Betsey.

7. **The correct answer is (B).** 913576 Harold Howritz. The different items in the other answer choices are as follows: (A) Horwitz; (C) 913756 Horwitz; (D) Harald.

8. **The correct answer is (D).** 621190 Jayne T. Downs. The different items in the other answer choices are as follows: (A) 621990 Janie; (B) Janie; (C) 622190 Janie.

9. **The correct answer is (D).** 004620 George McBoyd. The different items in the other answer choices are as follows: (A) 006420; (B) 006420 MacBoyd; (C) 006420 McBoid.

10. **The correct answer is (A).** 723495 Alice Appleton. The different items in the other answer choices are as follows: (B) 723594 Alica; (C) 723459; (D) 732495.

11. **The correct answer is (D).** 856772 Aaron B. Haynes. The different items in the other answer choices are as follows: (A) 856722; (B) 856722 Arron; (C) 856722.

12. **The correct answer is (B).** 121434 Veronica Pope. The different items in the other answer choices are as follows: (A) 121343; (C) Popa; (D) 121343 Popa.

13. **The correct answer is (C).** 376900 Barry R. Jantzen. The different items in the other answer choices are as follows: (A) Jantsen; (B) 379600; (D) Jantzon.

14. **The correct answer is (D).** 804866 Margery Melton. The different items in the other answer choices are as follows: (A) Marjery; (B) 808466; (C) Mellon.

15. **The correct answer is (D).** 762409 Philip L. Phillipi. The different items in the other answer choices are as follows: (A) Philippi; (B) Phillip Philipi; (C) 762490 Philippi.

Exercise 5

This final exercise is considerably more complicated than the previous comparison questions because of the complexity of the directions. The procedure you must follow is somewhat related to the one you followed in the address-checking questions at the beginning of this chapter. Note also that this exercise offers you five answer choices rather than the four in the previous exercises.

Directions: In the following questions, compare the three names or numbers and mark your answer next to the question number.

Write **(A)** if ALL THREE names or numbers are exactly ALIKE.

Write **(B)** if only the FIRST and SECOND names or numbers are exactly ALIKE.

Write **(C)** if only the FIRST and THIRD names or numbers are exactly ALIKE.

Write **(D)** if only the SECOND and THIRD names or numbers are exactly ALIKE.

Write **(E)** if ALL THREE names or numbers are DIFFERENT.

Tips To Get You Started

- When comparing names, look first for the shortest, easiest comparisons. If the name has first or middle initials, check them first. Then look for Jr., Sr., II, M.D., and the like.

- The next area for easy comparison is names that include Mc, Mac, Van, von, de, De, and so on. If you find a difference between first and second names in any of these regards, mark a minus sign (–) in the space between the names to keep track. Then do the same for any differences between the second and third names.

- If after the "easy" comparisons, you already have minus signs between first and second and between second and third, you can concentrate on comparing first and third; first along "easy" lines, then the main names.

- If the first and third differ as well, you can choose (E) with confidence and move on to the next question.

- If after making the "easy" comparisons you have no minus signs or only one, then look at the names themselves. Start with the first names or last names, but do so consistently. Be on the lookout for added or dropped "e" or "s" in particular. Check for spelling, double letters, and letters dropped into the middle of names. Again, mark a minus sign between first and second and between second and third names if you find any differences. The minus signs help you eliminate comparisons and narrow your field.

- Two minus signs in a question signal you to compare the first and third names, and choose (C) or (E) as indicated. The absence of minus signs tells you immediately that you must choose (A). If the first and second names are exactly alike and the second and third names are exactly alike, then the first and third must be exactly alike.

Take a look at the following examples.

A. Henry H. Liede   Henry M. Liede   Henry H. Leide

Begin with the "easy" comparisons. You see a middle initial, which is a good starting place. The middle initial of the first name is H, whereas that of the second name is M, so put a minus sign between the first and second names. The middle initial of the second name is M, but that of the third name is H, so put a minus also between the second and third names. Your only possible comparison is between the first and third names. You already know that they have the same middle initial. A very quick look tells you that the first name, Henry, is alike in both. Look carefully, though, at the spellings of the last names. In the first name it is spelled Liede; in the third name it is spelled Leide. All three names are different, so the answer is (E). NOTE: Do not bother to look at the spelling of the last name in the second name. It is already out of the comparison because of the middle initial.

B. Gerald M. Rosmarin   Gerald M. Rosmarin   Gerald M. Rosemarin

Start with the middle initials. All three are M. Next, look at first names: Differences tend to be more obvious among first names. All three are alike. Now look carefully at the last names. The first and second are identical; however, the third name has an *e* that does not appear in name two. Mark a minus sign between two and three, and mark (B) as the correct answer. Do not waste time comparing names three and one, because you've already determined that the first name is the same as the second.

C. Frima V. Spiner, M.D.   Frima V. Spiner, M.D.   Frima V. Spiner, M.D.

With a single glance, you can make two "easy" comparisons in this set. All three names have the middle initial V, and all three end with M.D. The first name is short although uncommon. You can easily see that all three are alike. So far, you have marked no minus signs. Next, check the third name. There are no differences between the third and the other two. The first is the same as the second, and the second is the same as the third. Therefore, the first and third must also be alike. The answer is (A).

D. Emilio Scaramuzza   Emilio Scaramuzzo   Emilio Scaramuzza

None of the names in this set has a middle initial, so begin by comparing first names. All three are alike. Compare last names, paying special attention to doubled letters. You might expect that in one name, the letter "z" might not be doubled or that the letter "r" might be doubled in addition to or instead of the *z*. In this example, though, this is not the case. Look carefully and you'll see that the first name ends with the letter *a* and the second ends with the letter *o*. Put a minus sign between one and two. Now, the second name ends with the letter *o,* and the third ends with an *a*. Mark a minus sign between the second and third names. You cannot answer (E) just because you have placed minus signs in two places, however. You must still compare the last names of the first and third names. One and three are exactly alike, so the answer is (C).

E. Craig R. Curcio   Graig R. Curcio   Graig R. Curcio

The middle initials are alike, so check first names. The first name starts with Craig (beginning with a C); in the second name you have Graig (beginning with a G). Place a minus sign between name one and two. The third name begins with G, just like the second. Now compare the second and third last names. Both are alike and you've completed your comparison of the second and third names, so the answer is (D). Do not bother to compare any part of the third name with the first. If the third name is exactly like the second, and the second name differs from the first, the first and third cannot be alike.

Comparing numbers is essentially the same as comparing names, except that the task is not as neatly divided into steps. There is no easy comparison with which to begin; at the outset, you must be alert for number reversals and actual number differences. You may find it worthwhile to divide each number into segments when comparing; this helps you develop a rhythm for reading them and may make differences easier to spot.

F.   5282864   5282864   5282684

Compare one and two. They are identical. Compare two and three. Three reverses the numbers 8 and 6. Place a minus sign between two and three, and do not bother to compare one and three. The correct answer is (B).

G.   6983429   6985429   6983429

Compare the first and second numbers. The middle digit of the first number is 3; the middle digit of the second is 5. Mark a minus sign between the first and second numbers, and compare the second to the third. The middle digit of the second is 5; the middle digit of the third is 3. Mark another minus sign. Now compare one and three. They are exactly alike, so the answer is (C).

Now try some practice questions on your own.

1.	Cyriac Aleyamma	Cyriac Aleyamma	Cyriac Aleyamma
2.	Eric O. Hartman	Eric O. Hartman	Eric O. Harpman
3.	Stephen Mescall	Steven Mescall	Stephan Mescall
4.	Frank E. Roemer	Frank F. Roemer	Frank F. Reomer
5.	Rose T. Waldhofer	Rose T. Waldhofer	Rose T. Walderhofer
6.	4726840	4728640	4726840
7.	9616592	9616952	9616592
8.	8349135	8319435	8349135
9.	4243275	4243275	4243275
10.	3245270	3245270	3245270
11.	Susan B. Vizoski	Susan B. Vizoski	Suzan B. Vizoski
12.	M.R. vonWeisenseel	M.R. vonWeisenseel	M.R. vonWeisensteel
13.	Barbara T. Scarry	Barbara T. Scarey	Barbara T. Scarrey
14.	Roy L. Gildesgame	Roy L. Gildegame	Roy L. Gildesgame
15.	Jaime Chiquimia	Jaime Chiquimia	Jaime Chiquimia
16.	7621489	7624189	7621849
17.	9625874	9625974	9625874
18.	5767140	5761740	5761740
19.	2454308	2454308	2454380
20.	7622378	7622378	7622378

ANSWER KEY AND EXPLANATIONS

1. A	5. B	9. A	13. E	17. C
2. B	6. C	10. A	14. C	18. D
3. E	7. C	11. B	15. A	19. B
4. E	8. C	12. B	16. E	20. A

1. **The correct answer is (A).** All alike.

2. **The correct answer is (B).** Alike: Eric O. Hartman, Eric O. Hartman. Different: Eric O. Harpman.

3. **The correct answer is (E).** Different: Stephen, Steven, Stephan.

4. **The correct answer is (E).** Different: E. Roemer, F. Roemer, F. Reomer.

5. **The correct answer is (B).** Alike: Waldhofer, Waldhofer. Different: Walderhofer

6. **The correct answer is (C).** Alike: 4726840, 4726840. Different: 4728640

7. **The correct answer is (C).** Alike: 9616592, 9616592. Different: 9616952.

8. **The correct answer is (C).** Alike: 8349135, 8349135. Different: 8319435.

9. **The correct answer is (A).** All alike.

10. **The correct answer is (A).** All alike.

11. **The correct answer is (B).** Alike: Susan B. Vizoski, Susan B. Vizoski. Different: Suzan.

12. **The correct answer is (B).** Alike: M.R. vonWeisenseel, M.R. vonWeisenseel. Different: vonWeisensteel.

13. **The correct answer is (E).** Different: Scarry, Scarey, Scarrey.

14. **The correct answer is (C).** Alike: Gildesgame, Gildesgame. Different: Gildegame.

15. **The correct answer is (A).** All alike.

16. **The correct answer is (E).** Different: 1489, 4189, 1849.

17. **The correct answer is (C).** Alike: 9625874, 9625874. Different: 9625974.

18. **The correct answer is (D).** Alike: 5761740, 5761740. Different: 5767140.

19. **The correct answer is (B).** Alike: 2454308, 2454308. Different: 2454380.

20. **The correct answer is (A).** All alike.

SUMMING IT UP

- An effective public safety dispatcher must be an accurate and swift typist. If you hope to do well on the typing section of the public safety dispatcher exam, be sure to practice as much as you can, and practice both copying and typing from dictation. Include words and numbers in your drills and aim for total accuracy. The typing section of the public safety dispatcher exam may take one of several forms: plain copy typing, typing from dictation, numbers typing, or alphanumeric typing.

- The usual rule in scoring typing tests is that a corrected error is still an error; ideally, you should make no mistakes. Corrections you make on a computer keyboard are generally not recorded. Watch the screen closely for errors, however. If you make an error, correct it as quickly as possible and keep moving.

- Address-checking questions require great speed and may carry heavy penalties for inaccuracy. You may need to follow complicated directions. Follow these five steps to increase your accuracy: (1) read exactly what you see; (2) use your hands; (3) look for differences in numbers; (4) look for differences in abbreviations; (5) look for differences in street or city names. Practice with the exercises in this chapter so that you're able to spot differences quickly and make firm, fast decisions.

- Your exam may include name-and-number and number-and-letter comparison questions; these can appear in one of a number of different formats, but the basic comparison task is always the same. The biggest difference lies in the directions. With name-and-number and number-and-letter comparison questions, it is extremely important that you read the directions thoroughly and carefully. For the most part, the strategies you learn for address checking will work well here, too. Follow "Tips to Get You Started" in this chapter for help in answering this type of question quickly and accurately.

Following Oral Directions

OVERVIEW

- Oral directions exercises on the Public Safety Dispatcher Exam
- Tips for answering oral directions exercises
- Summing it up

ORAL DIRECTIONS EXERCISES ON THE PUBLIC SAFETY DISPATCHER EXAM

Every written exam tests your ability to follow written directions. Some directions are quite simple; others are complex. In any event, it's important that you read each set of directions carefully and be absolutely certain that you know what is expected of you before you begin answering the questions. If the directions are complex, you may need to refer to them as you answer questions. Rereading directions takes time, but it is time well spent if it prevents you from answering incorrectly because you misunderstood what was expected of you.

Similarly, because the responsibilities of the public safety dispatcher are so heavily telephone-based, many public safety dispatcher qualification exams include a section that measures a test taker's ability to follow oral directions. The example we provide in this book is one of the many forms in which you might encounter this type of exam section. The questions and type of directions on your actual exam may differ from the exercise that follows, but it will nonetheless give you a fair idea of what you can expect.

The key to success with questions testing your ability to follow oral directions is to maintain total concentration on the task at hand. Many of the instructions consist of asking you to take one step on the worksheet followed by another step on the answer sheet. For example, you may hear oral directions similar to this:

> Find the smallest number on line 3 and draw one line under that number. Now, on your answer sheet, find the number under which you just drew one line and blacken space (C).

This is a relatively simple set of instructions. The moment you hear the words "line 3," you should direct your attention there and begin searching for the lowest number. But you must not stop paying attention to the rest of the instructions, or you will not know what to do with that number on line 3.

chapter 7

"Draw one line" is uncomplicated. The two-second pause that a reader takes after announcing this instruction should be adequate time for you to find the smallest number and draw a single line under it. The second part of the instruction is also uncomplicated—but remember, you cannot let your attention be drawn away from listening to what you must do next. You need to concentrate on what the reader is saying to find out which lettered space you must blacken. You then have 5 seconds to find the number and blacken the space.

If you hear more complicated directions, you are generally given slightly more time to follow them. For example, if the reader instructs you to circle each even number between 12 and 25, you will be given at least 10 seconds to find the numbers and actually circle them. In the example above, after the instructions that tell you what letters to darken, you are allowed 5 seconds for each combination.

The most difficult directions to follow are those with several steps, such as this:

> If January comes before June, and Monday comes after Wednesday, write the letter E in the box on the left; if not, write the letter A in the circle on the right.

Take questions like these one step at a time. Yes, January comes before June, so the first part of the opening phrase is true. Monday does *not* come after Wednesday, so the second part of this phrase is false. The instructions, however, use *and* to connect these two parts, so what immediately follows should only be performed if both parts of the statement are true. In this statement, one part is false, so you must perform the second action: Write the letter A in the circle on the right.

TIPS FOR ANSWERING ORAL DIRECTIONS EXERCISES

Try your best to stay calm during this section of your public safety dispatcher exam. If you miss part of an instruction, try to follow through as best you can, or just let that instruction pass and be ready for the next one. Your reader is not permitted to repeat an instruction, so you will hear it only once. Still, a missed question here or there in this section is not likely to rule out your candidacy. Take it in stride and resolve to focus carefully on the next set of instructions.

To practice taking this part of the public safety dispatcher exam, you'll need someone to read aloud the oral instructions in this chapter and in the Practice Tests at the end of the book. On the actual exam, you will not see or hear the oral instructions before exam day—so to get the most out of your practice, you should treat the "oral instructions" questions in this book as if they were actual exam questions. Do not look at them before answering the practice questions, and do not record yourself reading the instructions to play back for practice.

Answer Sheet for Following Oral Directions Exercise

Following Oral Directions Worksheet

1. Ⓐ Ⓑ Ⓒ Ⓓ Ⓔ   24. Ⓐ Ⓑ Ⓒ Ⓓ Ⓔ   47. Ⓐ Ⓑ Ⓒ Ⓓ Ⓔ   70. Ⓐ Ⓑ Ⓒ Ⓓ Ⓔ
2. Ⓐ Ⓑ Ⓒ Ⓓ Ⓔ   25. Ⓐ Ⓑ Ⓒ Ⓓ Ⓔ   48. Ⓐ Ⓑ Ⓒ Ⓓ Ⓔ   71. Ⓐ Ⓑ Ⓒ Ⓓ Ⓔ
3. Ⓐ Ⓑ Ⓒ Ⓓ Ⓔ   26. Ⓐ Ⓑ Ⓒ Ⓓ Ⓔ   49. Ⓐ Ⓑ Ⓒ Ⓓ Ⓔ   72. Ⓐ Ⓑ Ⓒ Ⓓ Ⓔ
4. Ⓐ Ⓑ Ⓒ Ⓓ Ⓔ   27. Ⓐ Ⓑ Ⓒ Ⓓ Ⓔ   50. Ⓐ Ⓑ Ⓒ Ⓓ Ⓔ   73. Ⓐ Ⓑ Ⓒ Ⓓ Ⓔ
5. Ⓐ Ⓑ Ⓒ Ⓓ Ⓔ   28. Ⓐ Ⓑ Ⓒ Ⓓ Ⓔ   51. Ⓐ Ⓑ Ⓒ Ⓓ Ⓔ   74. Ⓐ Ⓑ Ⓒ Ⓓ Ⓔ
6. Ⓐ Ⓑ Ⓒ Ⓓ Ⓔ   29. Ⓐ Ⓑ Ⓒ Ⓓ Ⓔ   52. Ⓐ Ⓑ Ⓒ Ⓓ Ⓔ   75. Ⓐ Ⓑ Ⓒ Ⓓ Ⓔ
7. Ⓐ Ⓑ Ⓒ Ⓓ Ⓔ   30. Ⓐ Ⓑ Ⓒ Ⓓ Ⓔ   53. Ⓐ Ⓑ Ⓒ Ⓓ Ⓔ   76. Ⓐ Ⓑ Ⓒ Ⓓ Ⓔ
8. Ⓐ Ⓑ Ⓒ Ⓓ Ⓔ   31. Ⓐ Ⓑ Ⓒ Ⓓ Ⓔ   54. Ⓐ Ⓑ Ⓒ Ⓓ Ⓔ   77. Ⓐ Ⓑ Ⓒ Ⓓ Ⓔ
9. Ⓐ Ⓑ Ⓒ Ⓓ Ⓔ   32. Ⓐ Ⓑ Ⓒ Ⓓ Ⓔ   55. Ⓐ Ⓑ Ⓒ Ⓓ Ⓔ   78. Ⓐ Ⓑ Ⓒ Ⓓ Ⓔ
10. Ⓐ Ⓑ Ⓒ Ⓓ Ⓔ   33. Ⓐ Ⓑ Ⓒ Ⓓ Ⓔ   56. Ⓐ Ⓑ Ⓒ Ⓓ Ⓔ   79. Ⓐ Ⓑ Ⓒ Ⓓ Ⓔ
11. Ⓐ Ⓑ Ⓒ Ⓓ Ⓔ   34. Ⓐ Ⓑ Ⓒ Ⓓ Ⓔ   57. Ⓐ Ⓑ Ⓒ Ⓓ Ⓔ   80. Ⓐ Ⓑ Ⓒ Ⓓ Ⓔ
12. Ⓐ Ⓑ Ⓒ Ⓓ Ⓔ   35. Ⓐ Ⓑ Ⓒ Ⓓ Ⓔ   58. Ⓐ Ⓑ Ⓒ Ⓓ Ⓔ   81. Ⓐ Ⓑ Ⓒ Ⓓ Ⓔ
13. Ⓐ Ⓑ Ⓒ Ⓓ Ⓔ   36. Ⓐ Ⓑ Ⓒ Ⓓ Ⓔ   59. Ⓐ Ⓑ Ⓒ Ⓓ Ⓔ   82. Ⓐ Ⓑ Ⓒ Ⓓ Ⓔ
14. Ⓐ Ⓑ Ⓒ Ⓓ Ⓔ   37. Ⓐ Ⓑ Ⓒ Ⓓ Ⓔ   60. Ⓐ Ⓑ Ⓒ Ⓓ Ⓔ   83. Ⓐ Ⓑ Ⓒ Ⓓ Ⓔ
15. Ⓐ Ⓑ Ⓒ Ⓓ Ⓔ   38. Ⓐ Ⓑ Ⓒ Ⓓ Ⓔ   61. Ⓐ Ⓑ Ⓒ Ⓓ Ⓔ   84. Ⓐ Ⓑ Ⓒ Ⓓ Ⓔ
16. Ⓐ Ⓑ Ⓒ Ⓓ Ⓔ   39. Ⓐ Ⓑ Ⓒ Ⓓ Ⓔ   62. Ⓐ Ⓑ Ⓒ Ⓓ Ⓔ   85. Ⓐ Ⓑ Ⓒ Ⓓ Ⓔ
17. Ⓐ Ⓑ Ⓒ Ⓓ Ⓔ   40. Ⓐ Ⓑ Ⓒ Ⓓ Ⓔ   63. Ⓐ Ⓑ Ⓒ Ⓓ Ⓔ   86. Ⓐ Ⓑ Ⓒ Ⓓ Ⓔ
18. Ⓐ Ⓑ Ⓒ Ⓓ Ⓔ   41. Ⓐ Ⓑ Ⓒ Ⓓ Ⓔ   64. Ⓐ Ⓑ Ⓒ Ⓓ Ⓔ   87. Ⓐ Ⓑ Ⓒ Ⓓ Ⓔ
19. Ⓐ Ⓑ Ⓒ Ⓓ Ⓔ   42. Ⓐ Ⓑ Ⓒ Ⓓ Ⓔ   65. Ⓐ Ⓑ Ⓒ Ⓓ Ⓔ   88. Ⓐ Ⓑ Ⓒ Ⓓ Ⓔ
20. Ⓐ Ⓑ Ⓒ Ⓓ Ⓔ   43. Ⓐ Ⓑ Ⓒ Ⓓ Ⓔ   66. Ⓐ Ⓑ Ⓒ Ⓓ Ⓔ   89. Ⓐ Ⓑ Ⓒ Ⓓ Ⓔ
21. Ⓐ Ⓑ Ⓒ Ⓓ Ⓔ   44. Ⓐ Ⓑ Ⓒ Ⓓ Ⓔ   67. Ⓐ Ⓑ Ⓒ Ⓓ Ⓔ   90. Ⓐ Ⓑ Ⓒ Ⓓ Ⓔ
22. Ⓐ Ⓑ Ⓒ Ⓓ Ⓔ   45. Ⓐ Ⓑ Ⓒ Ⓓ Ⓔ   68. Ⓐ Ⓑ Ⓒ Ⓓ Ⓔ
23. Ⓐ Ⓑ Ⓒ Ⓓ Ⓔ   46. Ⓐ Ⓑ Ⓒ Ⓓ Ⓔ   69. Ⓐ Ⓑ Ⓒ Ⓓ Ⓔ

answer sheet

Directions: Listening carefully to each set of instructions, mark each item on this worksheet as directed. Then complete each question by marking the answer sheet as directed. For each answer, you will darken the answer for a number-letter combination. Should you fall behind and miss an instruction, don't panic. Let it go and listen for the next one. If, when you start to darken a space, you find that you have already darkened another space for that number, either erase the first mark and darken the space for the new combination or let the first mark stay and do not darken a space for the new combination. Write with a pencil that has a clean eraser. When you finish, you should have no more than one space darkened for each number.

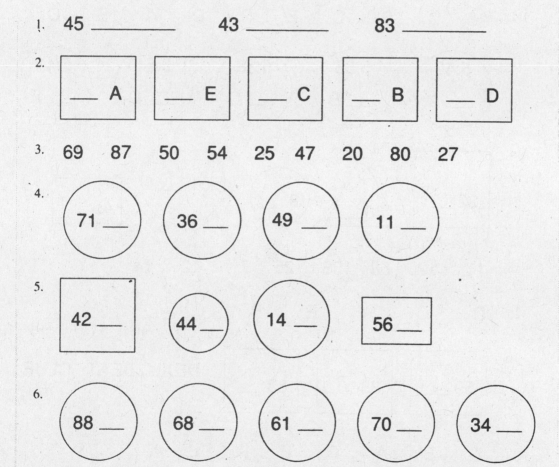

1. 45 _____   43 _____   83 _____

2. [__ A] [__ E] [__ C] [__ B] [__ D]

3. 69   87   50   54   25   47   20   80   27

4. (71 __)   (36 __)   (49 __)   (11 __)

5. [42 __]   (44 __)   (14 __)   [56 __]

6. (88 __)   (68 __)   (61 __)   (70 __)   (34 __)

7. 28   67   29   77   26

answer sheet

8.

| A CHESTNUT STREET _____ | B HYDE PARK _____ | C PRUDENTIAL PLAZA _____ |

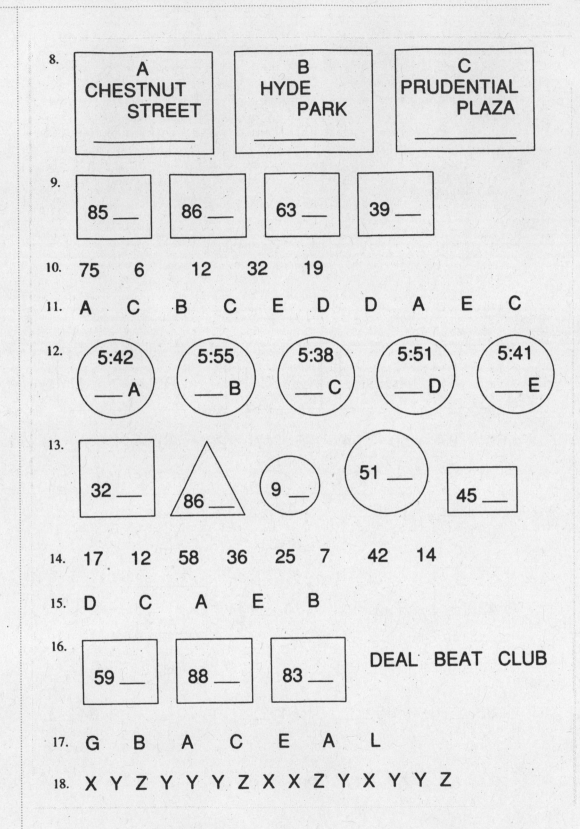

9.   85 ___   86 ___   63 ___   39 ___

10.   75   6   12   32   19

11.   A   C   B   C   E   D   D   A   E   C

12.   5:42 ___A   5:55 ___B   5:38 ___C   5:51 ___D   5:41 ___E

13.   32 ___   86 ___   9 ___   51 ___   45 ___

14.   17   12   58   36   25   7   42   14

15.   D   C   A   E   B

16.   59 ___   88 ___   83 ___   DEAL BEAT CLUB

17.   G   B   A   C   E   A   L

18.   X   Y   Z   Y   Y   Y   Z   X   X   Z   Y   X   Y   Y   Z

Following Oral Directions Exercise

Total Time: *25 minutes*

Directions: Give the following instructions to a friend and have him or her read them aloud to you at 80 words per minute. Do NOT read them to yourself. Your friend will need a timepiece that measures seconds. Listen carefully and do exactly what your friend tells you to do with the worksheet *and* with the answer sheet. Your friend will tell you what to do with each item on the worksheet. After each set of instructions, your friend will give you time to mark your answer by darkening a circle on the answer sheet. **Before proceeding further, tear out the worksheet on pages 165–166 of this test. Then hand this book to your friend.**

To the Reader: The directions are to be read at a rate of 80 words per minute. Do not read aloud the material that is in parentheses. Once you have begun the test itself, do not repeat any directions. The next three paragraphs consist of approximately 120 words. Read these three paragraphs aloud to the candidate in about one and one-half minutes.

On the job, you will have to listen to directions and then do what you have been told to do. In this test, I will read instructions to you. Try to understand them as I read them; I cannot repeat them. Once we begin, you may not ask any questions until the end of the test.

On the job, you won't have to deal with pictures, numbers, and letters like those in the test, but you will have to listen to instructions and follow them. We are using this test to see how well you can follow instructions.

You are to mark your test booklet according to the instructions that I'll read to you. After each set of instructions, I'll give you time to record your answers on the separate answer sheet.

The actual test begins now.

Look at line 1 on your worksheet. (*Pause slightly.*) Next to the left-hand number write the letter "E." (*Pause 2 seconds.*) Now, on your answer sheet, find the space for the number beside which you wrote, and darken space "E." (*Pause 5 seconds.*)

Now look at line 2 on your worksheet. (*Pause slightly.*) There are five boxes. Each box has a letter. (*Pause slightly.*) In the fifth box, write the answer to this question: Which of the following numbers is largest: 18, 9, 15, 19, or 13? (*Pause 5 seconds.*) Now, on your answer sheet, darken the space for the number-letter combination that is in the box in which you just wrote. (*Pause 5 seconds.*) In the fourth box on the same line, do nothing. In the third box, write "5." (*Pause 2 seconds.*) Now, on your answer sheet, darken the space for the number-letter combination that is in the box in which you just wrote. (*Pause 5 seconds.*) In the second box, write the answer to this question: How many hours are there in a day? (*Pause 2 seconds.*) Now, on your answer sheet, darken the space for the number-letter combination that is in the box in which you just wrote. (*Pause 5 seconds.*)

Look at line 3 on your worksheet. (*Pause slightly.*) Draw a line under every number that is greater than 50 but less than 85. (*Pause 12 seconds.*) Now, on your answer sheet, for each number under which you drew a line, darken space "D" as in dog. (*Pause 25 seconds.*)

Look at line 4 on your worksheet. (*Pause slightly.*) Write a "B" as in baker in the third circle. (*Pause 2 seconds.*) Now, on your answer sheet, find the number in that circle, and darken space "B" as in baker for that number. (*Pause 5 seconds.*)

Look at line 4 again. (*Pause slightly.*) Write "C" in the first circle. (*Pause 2 seconds.*) Now, on your answer sheet, find the number in that circle and darken space "C" for that number. (*Pause 5 seconds.*)

Look at line 5 on your worksheet. (*Pause slightly.*) There are two circles and two boxes of different sizes with numbers in them. (*Pause slightly.*) If 4 is more than 6 and if 9 is less than 7, write "D" as in dog in the smaller box. (*Pause slightly.*) Otherwise write "A" in the larger circle. (*Pause 2 seconds.*) Now, on your answer sheet, darken the space for the number-letter combination for the box or circle in which you just wrote. (*Pause 5 seconds.*)

Now look at line 6 on your worksheet. (*Pause slightly.*) Write an "E" in the second circle. (*Pause 2 seconds.*) Now, on your answer sheet, find the number in that circle and darken space "E" for that number. (*Pause 5 seconds.*)

Now look at line 6 again. (*Pause slightly.*) Write a "B" as in baker in the middle circle. (*Pause 2 seconds.*) Now, on your answer sheet, find the number in that circle and darken space "B" as in baker for that number. (*Pause 5 seconds.*)

Look at line 7 on your worksheet. (*Pause slightly.*) Draw a line under the largest number in the line. (*Pause 2 seconds.*) Now, on your answer sheet, find the number and darken space "C" for that number. (*Pause 5 seconds.*)

Now look at line 7 again. (*Pause slightly.*) Draw a circle around the smaller number in the line. (*Pause 2 seconds.*) Now, on your answer sheet, find the number around which you just drew a circle and darken space "A" for that number. (*Pause 5 seconds.*)

Now look at line 8 on your worksheet. (*Pause slightly.*) There are three boxes with words and letters in them. (*Pause slightly.*) Each box represents a station in a large city. Station A delivers mail in the Chestnut Street area, Station B delivers mail in Hyde Park, and Station C delivers mail in the Prudential Plaza. Mr. Adams lives in Hyde Park. Write the number 30 on the line inside the box that represents the station that delivers Mr. Adams' mail. (*Pause 2 seconds.*) Now, on your answer sheet, find number 30 and darken the space for the letter that is in the box in which you just wrote. (*Pause 5 seconds.*)

Now look at line 9 on your worksheet. (*Pause slightly.*) Write a "D" as in dog in the third box. (*Pause 2 seconds.*) Now, on your answer sheet, find the number that is in the box you just wrote in, and darken space "D" as in dog for that number. (*Pause 5 seconds.*)

Look at line 10 on your worksheet. (*Pause slightly.*) Draw a line under all the even numbers in line 10. (*Pause 5 seconds.*) Find the second number with a line drawn under it. (*Pause 2 seconds.*) On your answer sheet, blacken space "C" for that number. (*Pause 5 seconds.*)

Look at line 11 on your worksheet. (*Pause slightly.*) Count the number of "Cs" in line 11 and write the number at the end of the line. (*Pause 3 seconds.*) On your answer sheet, blacken the letter "E" for that number. (*Pause 5 seconds.*)

Now look at line 12 on your worksheet. (*Pause slightly.*) The time written in each circle represents the last pickup of the day from a particular street box. Write the last two numbers of the earliest pickup time on the line next to the letter in that circle.

(*Pause 2 seconds.*) Now on your answer sheet blacken the space for the number-letter combination in the circle in which you just wrote. (*Pause 5 seconds.*)

Look at line 12 on your worksheet again. (*Pause slightly.*) Find the second earliest pickup time and write the last two numbers of the second earliest pickup time on the line next to the letter in that circle. (*Pause 2 seconds.*) Now, on your answer sheet, blacken the space for the number-letter combination in the circle in which you just wrote. (*Pause 5 seconds.*)

Look at line 13 on your worksheet. (*Pause slightly.*) If there are 365 days in a leap year, write the letter "B" as in baker in the small circle. (*Pause 2 seconds.*) If not, write the letter "A" in the triangle. (*Pause 2 seconds.*) Now, on your answer sheet, blacken the space for the letter-number combination in the figure in which you just wrote. (*Pause 5 seconds.*)

Look at line 13 again. (*Pause slightly.*) Write the letter "D" as in dog in the box with the lower number. (*Pause 2 seconds.*) Now, on your answer sheet, blacken the space for the letter-number combination in the figure in which you just wrote. (*Pause 5 seconds.*)

Look at line 14 on your worksheet. (*Pause slightly.*) Draw two lines under all the numbers that are greater than 12, but less than 41. (*Pause 8 seconds.*) Count the number of numbers under which you drew two lines and blacken the letter "B" as in baker for that number on your answer sheet. (*Pause 10 seconds.*)

Still on line 14 of the worksheet, (*pause slightly*) circle all the even numbers. (*Pause 2 seconds.*) Count all the numbers that you marked in any way, and blacken the letter "E" for that number on your answer sheet. (*Pause 10 seconds.*)

Look at line 15 on your worksheet. (*Pause slightly.*) Circle the fourth letter in the line. (*Pause 2 seconds.*) Add together the number of hours in a day, the number of months in a year, and the number of days in a week. (*Pause 10 seconds.*) Now on your answer sheet, blacken the circled letter for that number. (*Pause 5 seconds.*)

Look at line 16 on your worksheet. (*Pause slightly.*) Write the first letter of the third word in the second box. (*Pause 5 seconds.*) On your answer sheet, mark the number-letter combination in the box in which you just wrote. (*Pause 5 seconds.*)

Look again at line 16. (*Pause slightly.*) Write the third letter of the second word in the first box. (*Pause 5 seconds.*) On your answer sheet, mark the number-letter combination in the box in which you just wrote. (*Pause 5 seconds.*)

Look once more at line 16. (*Pause slightly.*) Write the second letter of the second word in the third box. (*Pause 5 seconds.*) Now, on your answer sheet, mark the number-letter combination in the box in which you just wrote. (*Pause 5 seconds.*)

Look at line 17 on your worksheet. (*Pause slightly.*) Draw a wavy line under the middle letter in the line. (*Pause 2 seconds.*) On your answer sheet, blacken that letter for answer space 36. (*Pause 5 seconds.*)

Look at line 18 on your worksheet. (*Pause slightly.*) Count the number of "Ys" in the line and write the number at the end of the line. (*Pause 2 seconds.*) Add 27 to that number (*pause 2 seconds*) and blacken "B" as in baker for the space that represents the total of 27 plus the number of "Ys." (*Pause 5 seconds.*)

END OF EXAMINATION

Correctly Filled Worksheet

1. 45 __*E*__   43 _____   83 _____

2.
| __ A | *24* E | *5* C | __ B | *19* D |

3. <u>69</u> 87 50 <u>54</u> 25 47 20 <u>80</u> 27

4.
(71 __*C*__)   (36 __)   (49 __*B*__)   (11 __)

5.
[42 __]   (44 __)   (14 __*A*__)   [56 __]

6.
(88 __)   (68 __*E*__)   (61 __*B*__)   (70 __)   (34 __)

7. 28 67 29 <u>77</u> (26)

8.
| **A** CHESTNUT STREET _____ | **B** HYDE PARK *30* _____ | **C** PRUDENTIAL PLAZA _____ |

9.
| 85 __ | 86 __ | 63 __*D*__ | 39 __ |

10. 75 <u>6</u> <u>12</u> <u>32</u> 19

11. A C B C E D D A E C *3*

12.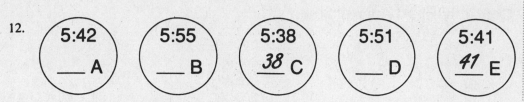

13.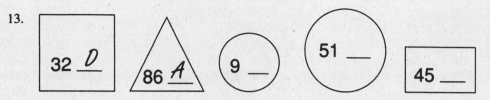

14. <u>17</u> (12) (58) (36) <u>25</u> 7 (42) (14)

15. D   C   A   (E)   B

16.

| 59 _A_ | 88 _C_ | 83 _E_ | DEAL BEAT CLUB |

17. G   B   A   <u>C</u>   E   A   L

18. X Y Z Y Y Z X X Z Y X Y Y Z   _7_

Correctly Filled Answer Sheet

1. Ⓐ Ⓑ Ⓒ Ⓓ ●	31. Ⓐ Ⓑ Ⓒ Ⓓ ●	61. Ⓐ ● Ⓒ Ⓓ Ⓔ
2. Ⓐ Ⓑ Ⓒ Ⓓ ●	32. Ⓐ Ⓑ Ⓒ ● Ⓔ	62. Ⓐ Ⓑ Ⓒ Ⓓ ●
3. Ⓐ Ⓑ Ⓒ Ⓓ ●	33. Ⓐ Ⓑ Ⓒ Ⓓ ●	63. Ⓐ Ⓑ Ⓒ ● Ⓔ
4. Ⓐ ● Ⓒ Ⓓ Ⓔ	34. Ⓐ ● Ⓒ Ⓓ Ⓔ	64. Ⓐ Ⓑ Ⓒ Ⓓ ●
5. Ⓐ Ⓑ ● Ⓓ Ⓔ	35. Ⓐ Ⓑ Ⓒ Ⓓ ●	65. Ⓐ Ⓑ Ⓒ Ⓓ ●
6. Ⓐ Ⓑ Ⓒ Ⓓ ●	36. Ⓐ Ⓑ ● Ⓓ Ⓔ	66. Ⓐ Ⓑ Ⓒ Ⓓ ●
7. Ⓐ Ⓑ Ⓒ Ⓓ ●	37. Ⓐ Ⓑ Ⓒ Ⓓ ●	67. Ⓐ Ⓑ Ⓒ Ⓓ ●
8. Ⓐ Ⓑ Ⓒ Ⓓ ●	38. Ⓐ Ⓑ ● Ⓓ Ⓔ	68. Ⓐ Ⓑ Ⓒ Ⓓ ●
9. Ⓐ Ⓑ Ⓒ Ⓓ ●	39. Ⓐ Ⓑ Ⓒ Ⓓ ●	69. Ⓐ Ⓑ Ⓒ ● Ⓔ
10. Ⓐ Ⓑ Ⓒ Ⓓ ●	40. Ⓐ Ⓑ Ⓒ Ⓓ ●	70. Ⓐ Ⓑ Ⓒ Ⓓ ●
11. Ⓐ Ⓑ Ⓒ Ⓓ ●	41. Ⓐ Ⓑ Ⓒ Ⓓ ●	71. Ⓐ ● Ⓒ Ⓓ Ⓔ
12. Ⓐ Ⓑ ● Ⓓ Ⓔ	42. Ⓐ Ⓑ Ⓒ Ⓓ ●	72. Ⓐ Ⓑ Ⓒ Ⓓ ●
13. Ⓐ Ⓑ Ⓒ Ⓓ ●	43. Ⓐ Ⓑ Ⓒ Ⓓ ●	73. Ⓐ Ⓑ Ⓒ Ⓓ ●
14. ● Ⓑ Ⓒ Ⓓ Ⓔ	44. Ⓐ Ⓑ Ⓒ Ⓓ ●	74. Ⓐ Ⓑ Ⓒ Ⓓ ●
15. Ⓐ Ⓑ Ⓒ Ⓓ ●	45. Ⓐ Ⓑ Ⓒ Ⓓ ●	75. Ⓐ Ⓑ Ⓒ Ⓓ ●
16. Ⓐ Ⓑ Ⓒ Ⓓ ●	46. Ⓐ Ⓑ Ⓒ Ⓓ ●	76. Ⓐ Ⓑ Ⓒ Ⓓ ●
17. Ⓐ Ⓑ Ⓒ Ⓓ ●	47. Ⓐ Ⓑ Ⓒ Ⓓ ●	77. Ⓐ Ⓑ ● Ⓓ Ⓔ
18. Ⓐ Ⓑ Ⓒ Ⓓ ●	48. Ⓐ Ⓑ Ⓒ Ⓓ ●	78. Ⓐ Ⓑ Ⓒ Ⓓ ●
19. Ⓐ Ⓑ Ⓒ ● Ⓔ	49. Ⓐ ● Ⓒ Ⓓ Ⓔ	79. Ⓐ Ⓑ Ⓒ Ⓓ ●
20. Ⓐ Ⓑ Ⓒ Ⓓ ●	50. Ⓐ Ⓑ Ⓒ Ⓓ ●	80. Ⓐ Ⓑ Ⓒ ● Ⓔ
21. Ⓐ Ⓑ Ⓒ Ⓓ ●	51. Ⓐ Ⓑ Ⓒ Ⓓ ●	81. Ⓐ Ⓑ Ⓒ Ⓓ ●
22. Ⓐ Ⓑ Ⓒ Ⓓ ●	52. Ⓐ Ⓑ Ⓒ Ⓓ ●	82. Ⓐ Ⓑ Ⓒ Ⓓ ●
23. Ⓐ Ⓑ Ⓒ Ⓓ ●	53. Ⓐ Ⓑ Ⓒ Ⓓ ●	83. Ⓐ Ⓑ Ⓒ Ⓓ ●
24. Ⓐ Ⓑ Ⓒ Ⓓ ●	54. Ⓐ Ⓑ Ⓒ ● Ⓔ	84. Ⓐ Ⓑ Ⓒ Ⓓ ●
25. Ⓐ Ⓑ Ⓒ Ⓓ ●	55. Ⓐ Ⓑ Ⓒ Ⓓ ●	85. Ⓐ Ⓑ Ⓒ Ⓓ ●
26. ● Ⓑ Ⓒ Ⓓ Ⓔ	56. Ⓐ Ⓑ Ⓒ Ⓓ ●	86. ● Ⓑ Ⓒ Ⓓ Ⓔ
27. Ⓐ Ⓑ Ⓒ Ⓓ ●	57. Ⓐ Ⓑ Ⓒ Ⓓ ●	87. Ⓐ Ⓑ Ⓒ Ⓓ ●
28. Ⓐ Ⓑ Ⓒ Ⓓ ●	58. Ⓐ Ⓑ Ⓒ Ⓓ ●	88. Ⓐ Ⓑ ● Ⓓ Ⓔ
29. Ⓐ Ⓑ Ⓒ Ⓓ ●	59. ● Ⓑ Ⓒ Ⓓ Ⓔ	89. Ⓐ Ⓑ Ⓒ Ⓓ ●
30. Ⓐ ● Ⓒ Ⓓ Ⓔ	60. Ⓐ Ⓑ Ⓒ Ⓓ ●	90. Ⓐ Ⓑ Ⓒ Ⓓ ●

SUMMING IT UP

- Because a large part of a public safety dispatcher's job consists of recording and relaying information by telephone, it's likely that you will see a section on your public safety dispatcher exam that measures your ability to follow oral directions.

- The questions and type of directions you encounter on your actual exam may differ from those in the exercise in this chapter, but this exercise will nonetheless help train you to listen carefully and follow directions as they are spoken.

- On your actual exam, don't panic if you miss part of an instruction. Try to follow through as best you can, or just let that instruction pass and prepare for the next one.

- Keep in mind that your reader is not permitted to repeat an instruction, so you will hear it only once.

- To practice taking this part of the public safety dispatcher exam, enlist the help of a friend or colleague to read aloud the oral instructions. Treat the "oral instructions" questions in this book as if they were actual exam questions: Do not look at them before answering the practice questions, and do not record yourself reading the instructions to play back for practice.

Personality Assessments

OVERVIEW

- Personality assessments on the Public Safety Dispatcher Exam
- Personality assessment variations
- How personality assessments differ from interviews
- Sample personality assessment
- Reviewing your responses
- Summing it up

PERSONALITY ASSESSMENTS ON THE PUBLIC SAFETY DISPATCHER EXAM

Some public safety dispatcher jobs require that applicants for the position undergo a personality assessment. Many municipalities rely on an oral interview to assess whether a candidate has the emotional and psychological stability and the personality type to deal with the rigors and stresses of a public safety dispatcher job. However, some agencies administer assessments—in paper-and-pencil, audiocassette or CD recording, or computer-based format—in conjunction with or as a replacement for oral interviews. These assessments aim to evaluate the behaviors and personalities of candidates to help determine whether they will be successful as public safety dispatchers.

PERSONALITY ASSESSMENT VARIATIONS

Personality assessments for the type of person generally sought for a public safety dispatcher position save government agencies time and money. Entry-level dispatchers receive extensive training, so it is to an agency's benefit to determine before this training period which candidates are best for the job—those who will not only learn quickly but will also adapt easily to the many mental and emotional challenges involved in dispatching. Because the occupation is often stressful and fast-paced, agencies want to ensure that they are hiring individuals who have the personality traits needed to remain calm under pressure. Let's look at some of the types of questions you might encounter on a personality assessment.

chapter 8

True-or-False Questions

You probably already know that you should not try to second-guess questions on a personality assessment. There are no "correct" responses, even if certain answers *seem* to be correct. Moreover, inconsistency in answering questions that purport to probe specific attitudes and behaviors may indicate that you're being untruthful. It's best simply to strive to be as honest as possible when answering the questions.

The MMPI

The most commonly used standardized personality assessment is the Minnesota Multiphasic Personality Inventory (MMPI). The most recent version of the MMPI, the MMPI-2-RF, consists of 338 questions (older versions, such as the MMPI-2, may include up to 567 questions) to which test takers must answer "True" or "False." The statements are free-ranging. No single answer is of special significance; what's important is the totality of the pattern that emerges from all answers.

Here are some sample MMPI-type questions for which you would answer True (T) or False (F).

_____ I like school.

_____ I like to cook.

_____ Someone is trying to poison me.

_____ I like to tease animals.

_____ I would rather win than lose in a game.

_____ I do not like everyone I know.

_____ I am not afraid of mice.

_____ I like repairing a door latch.

_____ I dread the thought of an earthquake.

_____ My parents often objected to the kind of people I went around with.

A variation of the MMPI might be a locally constructed assessment, on which you would answer "Yes" or "No" rather than "True" or "False" for each statement:

_____ I often have difficulty making decisions.

_____ I often think that someone is out to get me.

_____ I enjoy going to plays more than to parties.

_____ I sometimes feel self-conscious.

_____ Most people are dishonest.

_____ We had a lot of family trouble when I was young.

_____ I often have headaches.

The HPI

The Hogan Personality Inventory (HPI) is another widely used personality assessment. The HPI consists of 206 true-or-false items that aim to predict occupational success. It assesses the following seven personality characteristics:

1. adjustment
2. ambition
3. sociability
4. interpersonal sensitivity
5. prudence
6. inquisitiveness
7. learning approach

It also assesses six personality factors that may help predict a candidate's potential for job success:

1. service orientation
2. stress tolerance
3. reliability
4. clerical potential
5. sales potential
6. managerial potential

HPI assessment questions are similar to the true-and-false statements you would see on the MMPI:

_____ I enjoy making friends.

_____ I consider myself a lively person.

_____ I do not have a great deal of self-confidence.

_____ I think crowded public events (rock concerts, sports events) are very exciting.

_____ I try to get details correct in my work.

Self-Evaluation

Some personality assessments require candidates to evaluate a variety of behaviors and character traits in themselves. This requires not only self-assessment but also an understanding of how your elders and peers might rate you regarding certain traits. The traits evaluated in such assessments often relate to a candidate's energy, adventuresomeness, fearfulness, friendliness, gentleness, and compassion.

HOW PERSONALITY ASSESSMENTS DIFFER FROM INTERVIEWS

Standardized personality assessments require only true-false or multiple-choice responses. You do not need to calculate or use logic to determine your answers. As a result, scores can be derived quickly—almost immediately if the test is computer-based. These tests usually don't rely on the answers to individual questions for interpretation but rather on the sum of responses to a group of questions, such as those related to personal integrity—although key questions may be scattered throughout the personality assessment (we'll discuss this later in the chapter).

Length of Assessment

Standardized tests don't probe as deeply as subjective tests that require you to write your answers or explain them verbally to an interviewer. You are responding to very narrowly phrased questions. The examiner cannot explore the meaning of your true-or-false (or yes-or-no) responses, and you don't have the opportunity to explain them. To help counteract the fact that such responses can be misunderstood, personality assessments generally include a great number of questions (usually hundreds).

On the other hand, a standardized personality assessment can cover a much larger field than a more subjective assessment. It doesn't take long to answer several hundred true-or-false questions. (The HPI, for example, is administered over 15 to 20 minutes.) From an employer's point of view, the more information one can gather about an applicant, the better.

Time Limits

For the sample questions in this chapter, you are given no time limit. However, an actual personality assessment is timed. The idea is to answer quickly without dwelling too much on any one question; a time limit is intended to keep you moving through the questions without thinking too much. A timed personality assessment doesn't allow you the luxury of analyzing each question in depth or agonizing over your answer, but you usually have enough time to read each question and briefly consider which is the most truthful response.

That said, don't answer questions without considering what your response means. For example, let's say you receive a warning from the test administrator that your time is nearly up. Avoid feeling pressured into speeding through the rest of the questions and answering without reading thoroughly. With a personality assessment, you're far better off having not answered some questions than having accidentally labeled yourself a dishonest or unscrupulous person.

SAMPLE PERSONALITY ASSESSMENT

The following are sample questions drawn from a variety of standardized personality assessments. Find a quiet place where you're unlikely to be disturbed, and answer these questions without pausing, as if you were taking an official personality assessment. Although there is no time limit, work through them as efficiently as possible, and try not to spend too much time on any one question.

Directions: Please answer all questions in the space provided or on a separate sheet of paper. If you are using a separate sheet, number it from 1–30 before you start. Answer these questions by circling "Y" for "Yes" or "N" for "No."

1. Y N   Would you jump (or go under) a subway turnstile if you were sure you wouldn't be caught?

2. Y N   Have you ever found a crook so clever or entertaining that you rooted for him or her to get away with a crime?

3. Y N   Is taking damaged goods from your employer all right?

4. Y N   Do you always tell the truth?

5. Y N   Have you ever been tempted to take company property but didn't?

6. Y N   Do you think that police officers are usually honest?

7. Y N   While shopping, have you ever been tempted to take something without paying?

8. Y N   Is it okay to cheat on your taxes?

9. Y N   Did anyone ever show you how you could cheat your company out of money?

10. Y N   Have you ever thought about committing a burglary?

Directions: For the following items, please circle "Y" for "Yes" or "N" for "No" concerning any of the following activities you may have been involved in within the last six years. IN THE LAST SIX YEARS, DID YOU:

11. Y N   Sell illegal drugs?

12. Y N   Steal?

13. Y N   Get drunk?

14. Y N   File a false insurance claim deliberately?

15. Y N   Smoke pot?

16. Y N   Knowingly buy stolen or "hot" merchandise?

17. Y N   Give a friend company merchandise without charging for it?

18. Y N   Snort cocaine?

19. Y N   Do something only to cause trouble in your workplace?

20. Y N   Threaten somebody or use force to take something of value?

Directions: For the following items, please indicate your choice by circling the letter in front of the option you have selected. Be sure to answer all questions honestly.

21. What color is marijuana?
    (A) black
    (B) white
    (C) green
    (D) red

22. What color is cocaine?
    (A) black
    (B) white
    (C) green
    (D) red

23. Cocaine makes the user
    (A) hyperactive.
    (B) lazy.
    (C) hungry.
    (D) none of the above.

24. What was the worth of the most valuable thing you have stolen?
    (A) $2000 or more
    (B) $1000 to $2000
    (C) $100 to $1000
    (D) $25 to $100
    (E) $0 to $25

25. Have you ever taken a towel from a hotel or motel?
    (A) Yes
    (B) No

26. "If given a chance, everybody would cheat on their taxes." This statement is
    (A) definitely true.
    (B) mostly true.
    (C) uncertain.
    (D) mostly false.
    (E) definitely false.

27. "Everybody would steal if given the chance to do it without being caught." This statement is
    (A) definitely true.
    (B) mostly true.
    (C) uncertain.
    (D) mostly false.
    (E) definitely false.

28. "The reason people steal lies with the environment and the society in which we live." This statement is
    (A) definitely true.
    (B) mostly true.
    (C) uncertain.
    (D) mostly false.
    (E) definitely false.

29. "A person who will lie will steal." This statement is
    (A) definitely true.
    (B) mostly true.
    (C) uncertain.
    (D) mostly false.
    (E) definitely false.

30. A fellow employee is caught taking something from your employer that is worth about three dollars. This is the first time it has happened. What should be done?
    (A) The person's employment should be terminated.
    (B) The person should be severely reprimanded.
    (C) The person should be warned that more serious action will be taken if he or she does it again.
    (D) The person should give back what he or she has taken with no further consequences.

REVIEWING YOUR RESPONSES

Take a look at your answers to the sample questions. As we've discussed, there are no correct answers to any of these questions—but some answers may be better than others. Below, we'll discuss why this is true.

Key Questions

Earlier in this chapter, we mentioned the concept of key questions. You'll very likely encounter several of them in any personality assessment you take. In the sample inventory you just took, Question 4 was a key question: *Do you always tell the truth?* Look at your response. If you answered "Yes," read the question again until you completely understand what your answer means.

The key word here is *always*. Of course, the average person *usually* tells the truth—but this question asks whether you *always* tell the truth. On personality assessments, you'll find that statements containing the words *always* or *never* are almost never true for you. Words like *sometimes, usually, often, infrequently,* or *rarely* provide a "hedge" and are thus a lot "safer" to answer with a definite "True" or "False" (or "Yes" or "No").

The main point to remember about key questions is that, although they are expressed in absolute terms *(always* or *never)*, they describe behavior that may be *often* but *not always* correct or incorrect. To the question "Have you ever killed someone?" you can easily give a clear "No" response—but to the key question "Have you ever told a lie?" it's likely that you cannot truthfully and absolutely respond with "No." Key questions are used to test the value of the rest of your responses. Claiming that you always and without question tell the truth may cast serious doubt on the truthfulness of the rest of your responses.

Questions of Integrity and Honesty

The first twenty questions in the sample assessment above relate to honesty, integrity, and possible criminal behavior. Questions 1–10 are intended to assess a person's attitudes toward different types of behavior; they aren't meant to question whether you've done anything wrong. By contrast, the second group (Questions 11–20) ask directly whether you have committed certain acts, some of which are crimes.

You may have noticed that some questions may appear to be variations on the same theme and are simply worded differently. Questions 3, 5, 7, and 10 of the sample assessment all seek to determine your attitude—to varying degrees—toward stealing. For instance, Question 3 asks about taking from an employer something that doesn't belong to you; Question 10 asks about burglary, which is a serious crime. In a personality assessment containing about 100 questions of this type, you can expect to see several questions at the level of Question 3. You might be asked whether it is okay to use your employer's postage stamps, or whether it is okay to take your employer's pencils for your own use.

You need not worry about being consistent in your responses to these questions. Perhaps you believe that taking your employer's pencils is okay but that using your employer's postage stamps is not. Most people have mixed views on what constitutes stealing, and those who write and administer personality assessments recognize this fact. Scoring is not based on consistency of response, but on a continuum from "angel" to "thief." The angel is unbelievable—but nobody wants to hire a thief.

Question 5 illuminates a curious aspect of integrity and honesty questions. Suppose you were tempted to take something and gave in to the temptation. In that case, the appropriate answer is "No." However, if you were never tempted in the first place, the appropriate answer is also "No." In fact, technically, if we were to substitute the word *merchandise* for *property,* you would also answer "No" if you had never worked in a wholesale or retail firm—and therefore never even had the opportunity to be tempted to take your employer's merchandise. The point here is that you must always respond to the question or statement exactly as it is written. Don't read anything into the question that isn't there.

The Importance of Following Directions

As we discussed above, Questions 3, 5, 7, and 10 explore your attitudes about theft. By contrast, Questions 12 and 17 ask directly whether you have stolen anything. This is a good example of the importance of carefully reading the directions that precede groups of questions. The instructions before Questions 11–20 read as follows:

> For the following items, please circle "Y" for "Yes" or "N" for "No" concerning any of the following activities you may have been involved in within the last six years. IN THE LAST SIX YEARS, DID YOU:

These instructions are particularly clear; the same point is made twice. The first sentence refers to *activities you may have been involved in within the last six years.* The second sentence asks outright, "DID YOU?" It's clear here that the questions that follow will ask whether you personally have done any of the things listed. If you don't read the directions carefully, you can easily misinterpret what these questions are asking.

Two examples are Question 14, which includes the word *deliberately,* and Question 16, which includes the word *knowingly.* Both of them exclude actions you may have committed accidentally. Be sure to answer them accordingly. For example, if you filed twice for the same insurance claim because you forgot about the first filing or because the company took a long time to pay, it's true that you may have filed a false claim—but you didn't do it *deliberately,* so your honest answer is "No."

Another example is Question 17, which concerns a situation that's likely to occur only if you have experience in a retail position (the phrase "company merchandise" suggests this). Answer the question *exactly* as it is written. In this question, you weren't asked to admit whether you might have given away company merchandise if you had the opportunity; you were asked whether you actually *did* do it. A personality assessment may contain many such questions. Be sure that you avoid putting yourself into the situation outlined in the question if you've never been in that situation.

Pay Attention to Shades of Meaning

Questions 21–30 of the sample assessment demonstrate the reasoning behind the careful phrasing of personality assessment questions.

In Questions 21–23, you are asked about your knowledge of illegal drugs. The theory is that an applicant whose responses suggest that he or she knows a great deal about this subject is probably using drugs, and one who claims to know absolutely nothing may be trying to hide his or her knowledge of it. Although that is the theory, most administrators seek confirming evidence before tagging an applicant as a drug user based on questions of this sort. That's because none of these questions asks directly whether you have ever used an illegal drug. Knowing about a drug doesn't necessarily mean that you have used it. It's quite possible that you picked up what you know from books, movies, or a school course on drug use.

Questions of this type can have very fine shades of meaning. Changing a word or two can produce a totally different question. For instance, Question 23 might have read:

Cocaine makes <u>you</u>

(A) hyperactive.

(B) lazy.

(C) hungry.

(D) none of the above.

Note the underlined word here. The original question stem reads: "Cocaine makes *the user,*" not "you"; it is asking about your knowledge of the subject, not about your personal experience with cocaine. The lesson here is to read each question very carefully before choosing your response.

Questions 24 and 25 ask directly whether you have ever stolen anything and whether you believe that taking an item of low value is okay. But note how Question 24 is phrased: *What was the worth of the most valuable thing <u>you have stolen</u>?* The question already assumes that you will have stolen something. The only way to answer in the negative—that is, that you have never stolen anything—is to choose response (E). The *$0* in "$0 to $25" is an indirect way to say that, but it's the only response that allows you to do so.

Questions 26–30 offer the opportunity to "shade" your responses. In general, test administrators assume that an applicant who believes that everybody (or almost everybody) is dishonest is by definition including himself or herself in that category. On the other hand, everyone knows that some people *are* dishonest. Unlike the first twenty questions, these multiple-choice questions allow you to choose a non-absolute response. Note, too, that Question 30 differs in format from Questions 26–29, which present generalized statements and ask you to assess your belief in them. Question 30 presents a real-life (albeit hypothetical) situation, and asks you to judge what should be done.

You may find some questions on personality assessments intrusive—or worse. For instance, Questions 11–20 in this chapter may strike you as being of questionable legality, because some of the response choices appear to require that test takers incriminate themselves. Thus far, no one who has taken such personality assessments has legally challenged this sort of question, however, and these particular questions haven't been proven illegal. In any case, the administrators of a personality assessment are not looking to entrap test takers; they are seeking the best candidate for the job. You may choose not to answer certain questions, but bear in mind that this will likely result in your not getting the job for which you're applying.

SUMMING IT UP

- Many municipalities and agencies administer standardized personality assessments instead of, or in conjunction with, interviews. Entry-level dispatchers receive extensive training, so it benefits an agency to determine before the training period which candidates are best for the job.

- The most commonly used standardized personality assessment is the Minnesota Multiphasic Personality Inventory. Another widely used standardized personality assessment, the Hogan Personality Inventory, aims to predict occupational success. On these assessments, the question format requires a true or false (or yes or no) response. Another type of personality assessment requires candidates to evaluate their own behaviors and character traits, both from their own perspective and from the perspectives of their elders and peers.

- The scores for standardized personality assessments are based less on answers to individual questions than on the sum of responses to a group of questions, such as those related to personal integrity. You are responding to narrowly phrased questions and given a time limit on such assessments because you are meant to answer quickly without dwelling too much on any one question.

- Although you should not spend too much time on any one question in a personality assessment, avoid answering any question unless you have the time to read the directions completely and thoroughly. It's better to have run out of time to complete all the questions than to have accidentally labeled yourself unfit or unsuitable for a public safety dispatcher position.

- Key questions, though expressed in absolute terms (using words such as *always* or *never*) nonetheless describe behavior that may be *often* but *not always* correct or incorrect. For this reason, be absolutely sure that you answer them as honestly as you can. For example, claiming that you *always* tell the truth may cast serious doubt on whether the rest of your responses are truthful.

- Questions meant to evaluate honesty and integrity may be phrased to determine your attitudes toward different types of behavior, or they may directly ask whether you have committed certain acts. Don't worry about being consistent in your responses. However, it's vital that you respond to the question or statement exactly as it is written and that you carefully and thoroughly read every set of directions. Misreading directions can easily cause you to misinterpret what the questions are asking.

Scenario Questions

OVERVIEW

- Scenario questions on the Public Safety Dispatcher Exam
- Practice scenario questions
- Summing it up

SCENARIO QUESTIONS ON THE PUBLIC SAFETY DISPATCHER EXAM

Scenario questions may or may not appear on your exam. The inclusion of these questions depends on the jurisdiction in which you are taking the exam and the position for which you are testing. These questions draw from real-life experiences and test several aspects of being a successful dispatcher.

One of the abilities measured in Scenario questions is reading comprehension. You will be asked to read a set of rules, incidents, or situations in order to come up with the best answer for the scenario. It is important to carefully read the rules for each scenario, as they will vary from question to question. Try not to skim over the reading material because some questions will be detail-oriented.

Another critical skill measured in this section of the exam is your use of logic—your ability to make inferences and draw conclusions based on the facts and evidence given. Logic questions assess your aptitude for evaluating situations and thinking critically to arrive at a solution. Scenario questions also involve classification and series reasoning. These skills include the ability to recognize sequences and put items in order or to categorize items based on information given. For example, you may be asked to put a series of incidents in order of priority determined by their severity.

Lastly, when answering scenario questions, you will be required to utilize your information-retrieval skills. Some scenarios will be presented to you and you will be given a certain amount of time to absorb the information. After that time, you will answer the questions without the scenario information in front of you. These types of questions measure your ability to recall information from memory. They are generally less focused on complex facts than questions that can be answered with the information in front of you.

Scenario questions give you examples of what you may experience as a 911 dispatcher. They reflect some of the day-to-day job decisions you may have to make. While it is not required that you possess preexisting job knowledge for this exam, the scenarios presented assess your aptitude for this kind of work.

chapter 9

As a 911 dispatcher, you may often find yourself in a pressurized situation where time is of the essence. The scenarios provided help assess your ability to react quickly to these types of situations. For instance, some of the questions ask you to assign field units to a certain call type. In a real-life scenario, you might find yourself in a position where you must assign police units to an appropriate call quickly. You may receive a call and a number of significant facts in a short amount of time. Being careful and thorough with your work will be necessary skills for good performance in your job. Scenario questions regarding similar situations can help determine how well you pay attention to detail and how likely you are to succeed in the field.

Some scenario questions test your mastery of the English language. Excellent communication is a must when dealing with emergency situations. When transcribing a call, you will need to write clearly and effectively to gather all of the information necessary. You will also be asked to translate policies into actions, including where and when to assign emergency assistance. This is when your keen logic skills will come into play.

Five Steps to Answering Scenario Questions

1. **Read the directions.** The directions will be different for each question. It is extremely important to read through the directions before proceeding to the scenario and question(s). Some instructions will apply to more than one question, but you should still read and refer back to them before answering.

2. **Read the scenario.** Carefully read over the scenario and absorb the information given. Some questions will present you with a bulletin that you will be asked to draw information from for answers. Others will give facts used to determine a conclusion. You should read through the scenario thoroughly without taking too much time. Leave yourself enough time to answer the question while making sure you understand the scenario information.

3. **Make notes about the scenario.** Writing notes about the scenario will allow you to conceptualize the ideas in your mind. Some people prefer to use diagrams as a means of remembering and processing information. Others prefer to simply underline the relevant information for a reference. Whatever your learning style may be, find what works best for you and be sure to put it into practice on the exam.

4. **Read the questions.** Read each question carefully and make sure you understand what the question is asking. After you understand the question, read through all of the answers. If possible, try to eliminate answers that you are sure are incorrect. You may not be able to eliminate any answers on certain scenario questions. For example, one question type asks you to prioritize emergency situations, and each situation must be prioritized. You are not able to eliminate any answers for this question type.

5. **If you have time, check your work.** If you finish with enough time, you should go back and review your answers. Depending on how the test is administered, you may be able to check your work after each section. If you are not able to do this, check your work after you complete a series of questions.

Types of Scenario Questions

These are five common types of scenario questions that may be on the exam. Most of the questions ask you to read a set of preexisting rules or facts to determine the answers. Listed below are descriptions of some of the scenario questions that you may see on your test:

1 **Sentence Clarity.** You will compare two versions of similarly written sentences. One sentence is written without certain information or with unclear information while the other is more straightforward. You are asked to determine which sentence is more precisely written. It is important to pay attention to details in answering this question type.

2 **Public Safety Bulletin.** For these questions, you are given 3 minutes to read a brief description of events. Next, you will answer factual questions based on the details of the incidents given. You will need to draw upon your memory for this question type.

3 **Assigning Field Units.** In these questions, you will review a list of rules and assign a unit or units if the criteria are met in an incident. The rules may vary from selecting a choice based on geographic location to specifying what kinds of calls can be assigned. It is important to read through all of the rules before making your decision. This question type requires logic and critical-thinking skills.

4 **Evaluating Facts.** You will read a list of facts and then deduce whether certain conclusions are true, false, or undetermined on the basis of the facts. The facts might apply to more than one question. Be sure to read the directions to determine how many questions are based on a single set of facts.

5 **Setting Priorities.** This question type asks you to determine the urgency of three incidents according to a set of rules. You will not be able to eliminate any answers for this question type. You must read the incidents carefully and deduce the order in which the incidents should be prioritized.

PRACTICE SCENARIO QUESTIONS

Directions: Compare two versions of the same sentence. Which of the following is more clearly written?

1. **(A)** Peter's bag was stolen on his way home by an unidentified man. He was on a motorcycle last night.

   (B) Peter was on his way home last night when an unidentified man on a motorcycle stole his bag.

2. **(A)** The bank was robbed this morning by two men wearing masks. The men were last seen driving a blue car.

   (B) They drove away in a car after robbing the bank.

3. **(A)** Jack Monroe notified police immediately after he crashed into Gabriel Gonzalez's grey Honda Accord on the corner of 13th and Market.

   (B) Jack Monroe crashed into Gabriel Gonzalez's grey Honda Accord on the corner of 13th and Market. He called immediately to report it.

4. **(A)** Paolo returned home to find an intruder inside. He ran quickly to his neighbor's house.

   (B) When Paolo returned home this afternoon, he found an intruder inside and ran quickly to his neighbor's house.

5. **(A)** Amir said he was attacked by a man. He had a brown coat on.

   (B) Amir said he was attacked by a man wearing a brown coat.

ANSWER QUESTIONS 6–11 BASED ON THE INFORMATION PROVIDED BELOW.

Directions: You will have 3 minutes to review this information. After reading the bulletin, answer the questions from memory.

February 5–7 Notable Incidents

Burglary:
An unknown person entered Tommy's Pizza on 410 Steele Street at 2:06 a.m. on February 7th with a gun. The suspect took three wallets from restaurant patrons. The total amount stolen is unknown. Police were called at 2:10 a.m. when the suspect left the restaurant.

Criminal Damage to Property:
Two teenage males broke the windows of a red Toyota Corolla, license plate unknown, Friday morning February 6th between 4:10 and 4:20 a.m. The car was parked on the 6200 block of Hiatus Road.

Disorderly Conduct:
An unknown man shouted obscenities and threats at two females on the corner of 16th and Cabrillo at 10:30 p.m. on February 5th. The women described the man as middle-aged and wearing a black coat.

6. In the burglary incident, how much money was stolen from the pizza restaurant?

   (A) $35
   (B) $700
   (C) $100
   (D) amount unknown

7. In the burglary incident, what was the name of the pizza restaurant?

   (A) Tina's Pizza
   (B) Tommy's Pizza
   (C) Jay's Pizza
   (D) Jimmy's Pizza

8. In the criminal damage to property incident, what street was the car parked on?

   (A) Nob Hill Rd.
   (B) University Dr.
   (C) Adams St.
   (D) Hiatus Rd.

9. In the criminal damage to property incident, what color was the damaged car?

   (A) Blue
   (B) Black
   (C) Red
   (D) White

10. In the disorderly conduct incident, how many women were victimized?

    (A) Three
    (B) Two
    (C) One
    (D) Information not given

11. What time of day did the disorderly conduct incident take place?

    (A) Morning
    (B) Afternoon
    (C) Evening
    (D) Information not given

ANSWER QUESTIONS 12–17 BASED ON THE INFORMATION PROVIDED BELOW.

Directions: You will have 3 minutes to review this information. After reading the bulletin, answer the questions from memory.

February 10–11 Notable Incidents

Burglary:
Early Wednesday morning, February 11th, two teenage female suspects were seen leaving Home Depot with multiple bags of building supplies. The store manager estimated $500 worth of stolen property.

Deceptive Practices:
First Bank on 19th street reported a male, mid-30s, attempting to deposit $8,000 worth of counterfeit bills. The suspect was using fraudulent identification when opening his account. Bank teller Jennifer Ribiero was the employee who discovered the bills were counterfeit.

Disorderly Conduct:
A group of teenagers were found using graffiti on an office building on the 4200 block of Market Street. Witnesses told police the incident occurred at 10 p.m. on February 10th. The group was seen driving away in a white SUV.

12. In the burglary incident, what store did the suspects rob?

(A) Macy's
(B) Video Plus
(C) Home Depot
(D) Office Max

13. How old were the suspects in the burglary incident?

(A) 20s
(B) 30s
(C) Teenagers
(D) Middle-aged

14. In the deceptive practices incident, how much money was the suspect attempting to deposit?

(A) $200
(B) $2,000
(C) $800
(D) $8,000

15. What was the name of the bank in the deceptive practices incident?

(A) Compass Bank
(B) Bank of America
(C) Pine Tree Bank
(D) First Bank

16. What time of day did the suspects graffiti the building in the disorderly conduct incident?

(A) Morning
(B) Afternoon
(C) Evening
(D) Information not given

17. What type of car were the suspects in the disorderly conduct seen in?

(A) Sedan
(B) SUV
(C) Sports car
(D) Information not given

ANSWER QUESTIONS 18–22 BASED ON THE FOLLOWING INFORMATION.

There are three field units: A, B, and C. Each unit is selected to cover one or more areas as follows:

> **Unit A**—North and West
> **Unit B**—East
> **Unit C**—South

Rules for assigning units are listed below.

- Units are assigned only to the area(s) in which they are designated, except in the case of emergency calls.

- Units are to be assigned to a call only if they are currently available.

- Every available unit is to be assigned to an emergency call.

Directions: Assign the appropriate field unit or units to each example incident listed. When assigning the unit(s), consider the rules above. On your answer sheet, mark the letters that refer to the corresponding units. If an incident requires more than one unit to be assigned, mark more than one letter on your answer sheet for that item. When no units are to be assigned, mark "D" for no units to be assigned.

18. Area: West
    Type of Call: Emergency
    Current Assignments:
    Unit A: Available
    Unit B: Non-Emergency
    Unit C: Unavailable

19. Area: South
    Type of Call: Emergency
    Unit A: Available
    Unit B: Unavailable
    Unit C: Available

20. Area: East
    Type of Call: Non-Emergency
    Unit A: Unavailable
    Unit B: Available
    Unit C: Available

21. Area: North
    Type of Call: Emergency
    Unit A: Available
    Unit B: Available
    Unit C: Unavailable

22. Area: South
    Type of Call: Non-Emergency
    Unit A: Unavailable
    Unit B: Available
    Unit C: Unavailable

ANSWER QUESTIONS 23–26 BASED ON THE INFORMATION PROVIDED BELOW.

Directions: Read the list of facts and then evaluate the conclusions that follow. Indicate whether the conclusions are true, false, or cannot be determined.

Facts:
All robberies are considered crimes.
Some robberies are nonviolent.
Violent crimes require a police report.
Nonviolent crimes require an incident write-up.

23. Conclusion: If a nonviolent robbery occurred last night, no police report is required.

    (A) It is true based on facts given.

    (B) It is false based on facts given.

    (C) On the basis of the facts, it cannot be determined whether the statement is true or false.

24. Conclusion: If Officer Randall is solving a violent crime, he should write an incident write-up to give his supervisor.

    (A) It is true based on the facts given.

    (B) It is false based on the facts given.

    (C) On the basis of the facts, it cannot be determined whether the statement is true or false.

25. Conclusion: If Julia Morris reports a robbery at her storefront to the police, then Officer Book should write a police report.

    (A) It is true based on the facts given.

    (B) It is false based on the facts given.

    (C) On the basis of the facts, it cannot be determined whether the statement is true or false.

26. Conclusion: If a violent robbery occurred at Caleb's Diner, then the officer reporting should write an incident write-up.

    (A) It is true based on the facts given.

    (B) It is false based on the facts given.

    (C) On the basis of the facts, it cannot be determined whether the statement is true or false.

ANSWER QUESTIONS 27–32 BASED ON THE INFORMATION PROVIDED BELOW.

Directions: Read priority codes A, B, and C. Assign priorities to the events listed below.

Events are to be prioritized as follows:

Code A—Highest priority: Events that involve injury or are life-threatening.

Code B—Second priority: Events that involve property loss or damage.

Code C—Lowest priority: Other events that do not involve injury, threat to life, or property loss or damage.

27. A family of possums is found in caller's backyard.

28. A man is breaking into a closed storefront.

29. A serious car crash occurs on highway.

30. A man discovers his car was hit in the middle of the night.

31. A bicyclist was struck by a vehicle and is unconscious.

32. A caller reports a fallen tree that did not harm anyone or cause any damage.

ANSWER KEY AND EXPLANATIONS

1. B	8. D	15. D	22. D	28. B
2. A	9. C	16. C	23. A	29. A
3. A	10. B	17. B	24. B	30. B
4. B	11. C	18. A	25. C	31. A
5. B	12. C	19. A and C	26. B	32. C
6. D	13. C	20. B	27. C	
7. B	14. D	21. A and B		

1. **The correct answer is (B).** The second sentence clarifies who stole Peter's bag and when it was stolen. In choice (A), it is not clear who the "he" refers to: Peter or the thief.

2. **The correct answer is (A).** The first sentence clarifies when the bank was robbed and describes the suspects.

3. **The correct answer is (A).** The first sentence clarifies who reported the accident to the police, Jack Monroe.

4. **The correct answer is (B).** Choice (B) describes when Paolo returned home and explains that it was Paolo who ran to the neighbor's.

5. **The correct answer is (B).** The second sentence clarifies that the man who attacked Amir was wearing a brown coat.

6. **The correct answer is (D).** According to the description of the burglary, the number of wallets was listed but not the specific amount of money.

7. **The correct answer is (B).** The restaurant name is cited as "Tommy's Pizza" in the description.

8. **The correct answer is (D).** The car was parked on Hiatus Road in the property damage incident.

9. **The correct answer is (C).** The property damage incident describes a red Toyota Corolla.

10. **The correct answer is (B).** In the disorderly conduct description, two women were listed as victims.

11. **The correct answer is (C).** The incident documented occurred at 10:30 p.m. on Friday.

12. **The correct answer is (C).** Home Depot is the store described in this incident.

13. **The correct answer is (C).** The suspects in the burglary incident are reported as teenagers.

14. **The correct answer is (D).** The suspect tried to deposit $8,000 to the bank in the description.

15. **The correct answer is (D).** First Bank is the name of the bank described in the deceptive practices incident.

16. **The correct answer is (C).** According to the description, the graffiti incident occurred at 10 p.m.

17. **The correct answer is (B).** The suspects were seen leaving in a white SUV in the disorderly conduct incident.

18. **The correct answer is (A).** The incident is an emergency call and located in the West area, which is covered by Unit A. Unit B only takes non-emergency calls, and Unit C is unavailable.

19. **The correct answers are (A) and (C).** The call is an emergency, and every available unit is to be assigned to an emergency call even if the call is not

in the unit's designated area. Units A and C are both available, while Unit B is unavailable.

20. **The correct answer is (B).** The incident is located in the East area, which is covered by Unit B. Unit A is unavailable, and Unit C does not need to be assigned because this is a non-emergency call.

21. **The correct answers are (A) and (B).** Both Units A and B are available and can be assigned an emergency call. All units available are to be assigned to emergency calls.

22. **The correct answer is (D).** No units can be assigned because the call is a non-emergency and Unit C, which covers the South area, is unavailable.

23. **The correct answer is (A).** The conclusion is true because the facts state that only violent crimes require a police report.

24. **The correct answer is (B).** The conclusion is false because violent crimes require police reports, not incident write-ups.

25. **The correct answer is (C).** The conclusion cannot be determined as true or false because it does not state whether the crime was violent or non-violent. It is therefore not clear which type of document should be written, a police report or an incident write-up.

26. **The correct answer is (B).** The conclusion is false because violent crimes require a police report.

27. **The correct answer is (C).** The event described does not involve any life-threatening injury or property loss.

28. **The correct answer is (B).** The event described involves potential property loss.

29. **The correct answer is (A).** The event described involves potential life-threatening injury.

30. **The correct answer is (B).** The incident portrays property damage.

31. **The correct answer is (A).** An unconscious bicyclist is a potentially life-threatening situation.

32. **The correct answer is (C).** The caller reported a situation that is not life-threatening and does not involve property loss or damage.

SUMMING IT UP

- A public safety dispatcher must possess certain skills and a keen eye for detail in order to be successful. The scenario questions on the exam will test your aptitude for these skills through various types of questions. Some of the questions will focus on reading comprehension, logic, information retrieval, and attention to detail. The questions present possible real-life situations that you may encounter as a public safety dispatcher.

- There are five scenario question types discussed in this chapter. The first is Sentence Clarity; for these questions, you will be asked to choose a more clearly written sentence. For the Public Safety Bulletin questions, you will read a brief description of events and then answer questions based on your ability to retrieve information. The Assigning Field Units questions ask you to read a set of rules and assign units based on the criteria given. For Evaluating Facts questions, you will read the facts listed and determine if the conclusions given are true or false. Lastly, when answering the Setting Priorities questions, you will determine the priority level of an incident.

- You are not expected to use job-related knowledge for these question types. While the scenarios presented may involve emergency-related content, you are not being tested on your prior knowledge. You are, however, being tested on your ability to follow rules and procedures.

- Read the directions carefully. Some directions may apply to several questions, while others may apply only to one. Be sure to read through the directions and then the related information for the question or questions.

- Read the scenarios in their entirety and pay attention to details. Some questions might inquire about specific details related to an incident. It might be helpful to take notes or underline important information so that you can answer the questions correctly.

- Familiarize yourself with the different question types. While not all of these types may appear on the exam, the questions listed in this chapter are a good indicator of situations you may encounter on the job.

PART IV
TWO PRACTICE TESTS

ANSWER SHEET PRACTICE TEST 1

1. Ⓐ Ⓑ Ⓒ Ⓓ	21. Ⓐ Ⓑ Ⓒ Ⓓ	41. Ⓐ Ⓑ Ⓒ Ⓓ	61. Ⓐ Ⓑ Ⓒ Ⓓ
2. Ⓐ Ⓑ Ⓒ Ⓓ	22. Ⓐ Ⓑ Ⓒ Ⓓ	42. Ⓐ Ⓑ Ⓒ Ⓓ	62. Ⓐ Ⓑ Ⓒ Ⓓ
3. Ⓐ Ⓑ Ⓒ Ⓓ	23. Ⓐ Ⓑ Ⓒ Ⓓ	43. Ⓐ Ⓑ Ⓒ Ⓓ	63. Ⓐ Ⓑ Ⓒ Ⓓ
4. Ⓐ Ⓑ Ⓒ Ⓓ	24. Ⓐ Ⓑ Ⓒ Ⓓ	44. Ⓐ Ⓑ Ⓒ Ⓓ	64. Ⓐ Ⓑ Ⓒ Ⓓ
5. Ⓐ Ⓑ Ⓒ Ⓓ	25. Ⓐ Ⓑ Ⓒ Ⓓ	45. Ⓐ Ⓑ Ⓒ Ⓓ	65. Ⓐ Ⓑ Ⓒ Ⓓ
6. Ⓐ Ⓑ Ⓒ Ⓓ	26. Ⓐ Ⓑ Ⓒ Ⓓ	46. Ⓐ Ⓑ Ⓒ Ⓓ	66. Ⓐ Ⓑ Ⓒ Ⓓ
7. Ⓐ Ⓑ Ⓒ Ⓓ	27. Ⓐ Ⓑ Ⓒ Ⓓ	47. Ⓐ Ⓑ Ⓒ Ⓓ	67. Ⓐ Ⓑ Ⓒ Ⓓ
8. Ⓐ Ⓑ Ⓒ Ⓓ	28. Ⓐ Ⓑ Ⓒ Ⓓ	48. Ⓐ Ⓑ Ⓒ Ⓓ	68. Ⓐ Ⓑ Ⓒ Ⓓ
9. Ⓐ Ⓑ Ⓒ Ⓓ	29. Ⓐ Ⓑ Ⓒ Ⓓ	49. Ⓐ Ⓑ Ⓒ Ⓓ	69. Ⓐ Ⓑ Ⓒ Ⓓ
10. Ⓐ Ⓑ Ⓒ Ⓓ	30. Ⓐ Ⓑ Ⓒ Ⓓ	50. Ⓐ Ⓑ Ⓒ Ⓓ	70. Ⓐ Ⓑ Ⓒ Ⓓ
11. Ⓐ Ⓑ Ⓒ Ⓓ	31. Ⓐ Ⓑ Ⓒ Ⓓ	51. Ⓐ Ⓑ Ⓒ Ⓓ	71. Ⓐ Ⓑ Ⓒ Ⓓ
12. Ⓐ Ⓑ Ⓒ Ⓓ	32. Ⓐ Ⓑ Ⓒ Ⓓ	52. Ⓐ Ⓑ Ⓒ Ⓓ	72. Ⓐ Ⓑ Ⓒ Ⓓ
13. Ⓐ Ⓑ Ⓒ Ⓓ	33. Ⓐ Ⓑ Ⓒ Ⓓ	53. Ⓐ Ⓑ Ⓒ Ⓓ	73. Ⓐ Ⓑ Ⓒ Ⓓ
14. Ⓐ Ⓑ Ⓒ Ⓓ	34. Ⓐ Ⓑ Ⓒ Ⓓ	54. Ⓐ Ⓑ Ⓒ Ⓓ	74. Ⓐ Ⓑ Ⓒ Ⓓ
15. Ⓐ Ⓑ Ⓒ Ⓓ	35. Ⓐ Ⓑ Ⓒ Ⓓ	55. Ⓐ Ⓑ Ⓒ Ⓓ	75. Ⓐ Ⓑ Ⓒ Ⓓ
16. Ⓐ Ⓑ Ⓒ Ⓓ	36. Ⓐ Ⓑ Ⓒ Ⓓ	56. Ⓐ Ⓑ Ⓒ Ⓓ	76. Ⓐ Ⓑ Ⓒ Ⓓ
17. Ⓐ Ⓑ Ⓒ Ⓓ	37. Ⓐ Ⓑ Ⓒ Ⓓ	57. Ⓐ Ⓑ Ⓒ Ⓓ	77. Ⓐ Ⓑ Ⓒ Ⓓ
18. Ⓐ Ⓑ Ⓒ Ⓓ	38. Ⓐ Ⓑ Ⓒ Ⓓ	58. Ⓐ Ⓑ Ⓒ Ⓓ	78. Ⓐ Ⓑ Ⓒ Ⓓ
19. Ⓐ Ⓑ Ⓒ Ⓓ	39. Ⓐ Ⓑ Ⓒ Ⓓ	59. Ⓐ Ⓑ Ⓒ Ⓓ	79. Ⓐ Ⓑ Ⓒ Ⓓ
20. Ⓐ Ⓑ Ⓒ Ⓓ	40. Ⓐ Ⓑ Ⓒ Ⓓ	60. Ⓐ Ⓑ Ⓒ Ⓓ	80. Ⓐ Ⓑ Ⓒ Ⓓ

answer sheet

Practice Test 1

80 Questions • 180 Minutes

Directions: Choose the best answer to each question based upon the accompanying information and your own judgment. Regulations, codes, and procedures are not necessarily accurate for the municipality in which you are taking this exam. You must accept the rules as stated; do *not* base answers upon any actual knowledge that you may have.

1. Under certain circumstances, a dispatcher should make specific recommendations for special action to be taken. A dispatcher should recommend that an extra contingent of rescue workers be sent to the scene of a flaming one-story building that houses
   - (A) 80 high school students.
   - (B) 80 kindergarten children.
   - (C) 80 residents of a nursing home.
   - (D) 80 office workers.

2. A hysterical woman advises you that her son's dog is sick. You should refer her to
   - (A) the animal hospital.
   - (B) the local children's hospital.
   - (C) the ambulance service.
   - (D) none of the above.

3. 911 operator Maria Ruiz receives the following information on her computer screen:

   Place of Occurrence: 1520 Clarendon Road, Brooklyn
   Time of Occurrence: 6:32 a.m.
   Type of Building: Two-family frame dwelling
   Event: Fire, suspected arson

   Suspect: Male, white, approx. 6-feet tall, wearing blue jeans
   Witness: Mary Smith of 1523 Clarendon Road, Brooklyn

   Operator Ruiz is about to notify the fire department and to radio an alert for the suspect. Which of the following expresses the information *most clearly* and *accurately*?
   - (A) At 6:32 a.m. Mary Smith of 1523 Clarendon Road, Brooklyn, saw a white male wearing approximately 6-foot blue jeans running from the building across the street.
   - (B) A white male wearing blue jeans ran from the house at 1520 Clarendon Road at 6:32 a.m. Mary Smith saw him.
   - (C) At 6:32 a.m. a 6-foot white male wearing blue jeans ran from a burning two-family frame structure at 1520 Clarendon Road, Brooklyn. He was observed by a neighbor, Mary Smith.
   - (D) A two-family frame house is on fire at 1520 Clarendon Road in Brooklyn. A white male in blue jeans probably did it. Mary Smith saw him run.

4. Operator Warren Wu receives an emergency call from a token clerk. From the information the clerk gives, Wu types the following into his computer:

Time of Occurrence: 1:22 a.m.

Place of Occurrence: Uptown-bound platform, 59th Street Station, 7th Avenue line

Victim: Juana Martinez

Crime: Purse-snatching

Description of Suspect: Unknown, male, fled down steps to lower platform

Operator Wu will now radio the transit police. Which of the following expresses the information *most clearly* and *accurately*?

(A) Juana Martinez had her purse snatched on the subway platform at 59th Street Station. She didn't see him.

(B) A purse was just snatched by a man who ran down the steps from the 7th Avenue token booth at 59th Street Station. Her name is Juana Martinez.

(C) It is 1:22 a.m. The person who snatched Juana Martinez's purse is downstairs at 59th Street Station.

(D) Call from the 59th Street Station, uptown-bound 7th Avenue token booth. A Juana Martinez reports that her purse was just snatched by a man who fled down the steps to a lower platform.

ANSWER QUESTIONS 5–10 ON THE BASIS OF THE FOLLOWING PASSAGE.

Police officers Brown and Redi are on patrol in a radio car on a Saturday afternoon in the fall. They receive a radio message that a burglary is in progress on the fifth floor of a seven-floor building on the corner of 7th Street and Main. They immediately proceed to that location to investigate and take appropriate action.

The officers start for the fifth floor, using the main elevator. As they reach that floor and open the door, they hear noises, followed by the sound of the freight elevator door in the rear of the building closing and the **elevator** descending. They quickly run through the open door of the Fine Jewelry Company and observe that the office safe is open and empty. The officers then proceed to the rear of the building and use the rear staircase to reach the ground floor. They open the rear door and go out onto the street where they observe four individuals running up the street, crossing at the corner. At that point, the police officers get a clear view of the suspects. There are three males and one female. One of the males appears to be white, one is Hispanic, and the other male is black. The female is white.

The white male is bearded. He is dressed in blue jeans, white sneakers, and a red and blue jacket. He is carrying a white duffel bag on his shoulder. The Hispanic male limps slightly and has a large dark moustache. He is wearing brown pants, a green shirt, and brown shoes. He is carrying a blue duffel bag on his shoulder. The black male is clean-shaven, wearing black pants, a white shirt, a green cap, and black shoes. He is carrying what appears to be a toolbox. The white female is carrying a sawed-off shotgun, has long brown hair, and is wearing white jeans, a blue blouse, and blue sneakers. She has a red kerchief around her neck.

The officers chase the suspects for two blocks without being able to catch them. They then quickly return to their radio car to report what has happened. Dispatcher Marian Koslowksi takes their report and sends out a bulletin to all cars in the area. Her bulletin alerts officers to watch for a/an:

5. armed suspect. This suspect is a
   (A) white female.
   (B) black male.
   (C) Hispanic male.
   (D) white male.

6. female suspect whose hair is
   (A) short and light in color.
   (B) long and light in color.
   (C) short and dark in color.
   (D) long and dark in color.

7. suspect who limps while running. This suspect is a
   (A) white female.
   (B) black male.
   (C) Hispanic male.
   (D) white male.

8. bearded white male carrying a
   (A) blue duffel bag.
   (B) yellow duffel bag.
   (C) red duffel bag.
   (D) white duffel bag.

9. female wearing
   (A) a green cap.
   (B) a red jacket.
   (C) blue sneakers.
   (D) a white shirt.

10. black male carrying a
    (A) crowbar.
    (B) sawed-off shotgun.
    (C) red kerchief.
    (D) toolbox.

11. Waynesboro Hospital calls 911 to say that they have a person in the emergency room with a gunshot wound to the head. This is a case of
    (A) robbery.
    (B) harassment.
    (C) larceny.
    (D) assault.

12. The superintendent of Smith View Apartments was seen changing the locks on a woman's apartment because she refused to pay her rent. This is considered
    (A) aggravated harassment.
    (B) illegal eviction.
    (C) theft of service.
    (D) larceny.

13. A group of teenagers were pickpocketing people who were waiting on line at the roller rink. This is a case of
    (A) criminal mischief.
    (B) robbery.
    (C) larceny.
    (D) burglary.

14. Mr. Gleason and his family went to dinner at the Shore Rock Restaurant. When dinner was finished, they left without paying. They stated that they did not like the service. This is considered
    (A) larceny.
    (B) robbery.
    (C) theft of service.
    (D) assault.

15. Sometimes the calls that are made to the emergency number are not really emergencies at all. The emergency operator should refer these callers to the proper agencies. Which one of the following callers should be referred to another agency?

   (A) A caller reporting a leak in the bedroom ceiling.

   (B) A caller reporting that an occupied elevator is stuck between floors.

   (C) A caller reporting a man snapping a large whip on the sidewalk.

   (D) A caller reporting a strong odor of gas.

16. Operator Juana Diaz receives a telephoned complaint about poor emergency service. The facts as she records them are as follows:

   Date of Event: June 26

   Time of Event: 8:30 a.m.

   Complainant: Martha Brown

   Address: 1030 Whitcomb Street, Apt. 7A

   Complaint: Requested ambulance took 35 minutes to arrive

   Operator Diaz must prepare a report on this call for her supervisor to investigate or to turn over to the dispatcher of Emergency Services. Which one of the following expresses the above information *most clearly* and *accurately*?

   (A) Martha Brown said on June 26 an ambulance took 35 minutes to come at 8:30 a.m.

   (B) On June 26, an ambulance came at 8:30 a.m. after 35 minutes to 1030 Whitcomb Street, said Martha Brown.

   (C) To 1030 Whitcomb Street came an ambulance at 8:30 a.m. after 35 minutes on June 26. Martha Brown said it.

   (D) According to Martha Brown of 1030 Whitcomb Street, an ambulance requested on June 26 took 35 minutes, arriving at 8:30 a.m.

ANSWER QUESTIONS 17–21 ON THE BASIS OF THE FOLLOWING PASSAGE.

PROCEDURES CONCERNING TARDINESS, VACATION, PERSONAL DAYS, AND ATTENDANCE

As a new employee, you are allowed 13 sick days, 5 personal days, and 25 vacation days. After 1 year of service, you are allowed 27 days vacation. When you are reporting sick for work, you must notify your command within 10 hours prior to the start of your tour. If you fail to report to your command, you will be reported as AWOL (absent without leave). When returning to work, you must notify your command within 5 hours before reporting back. If you fail to follow this procedure, you will receive a report of violation.

Lateness is not tolerated. When reporting late for work, you must notify your command 2 hours before the start of your tour. If you are in a training class, you must also make a courtesy call to the training center to advise them of your lateness. If you fail to follow this procedure, you will be docked 1 hour of pay for every hour that you are late.

17. Operator John King was to report to work at 11:30 p.m. At 10:30 p.m. he reported to the command that he would be late. Operator King was

    (A) right by notifying the command at 10:30 p.m.

    (B) right because he notified the training class of his lateness.

    (C) wrong because he failed to give 2 hours' notice.

    (D) None of the above.

18. Operator John King will now be

    (A) docked for every hour he is late.

    (B) marked AWOL.

    (C) fired from the job.

    (D) None of the above.

19. Operator Randolph Hill is a new employee in training. He is to report to work at 12:00 a.m. He notified the command at 2:00 p.m. that he was reporting sick. Did he correctly follow the sick procedure?

    (A) No, because he failed to notify the command according to procedure.

    (B) No, because he failed to also notify the training center.

    (C) Yes, because he notified the command within the required time.

    (D) None of the above.

20. Operator Joyce Collins is a new employee. According to procedure, how many times can she call in late?

    (A) 13 times per year.

    (B) 1 time per year.

    (C) 5 times per year.

    (D) None.

21. Operator Gwen McClain has been on the job for two years. How many vacation days can she take?

    (A) 25 days.

    (B) 30 days.

    (C) 15 days.

    (D) None of the above.

ANSWER QUESTION 22 ON THE BASIS OF THE FOLLOWING INFORMATION.

The procedure to be followed upon receipt of the information that a suicide is being attempted is the following:

1. Ask the precise location where the attempt is occurring.

2. Ask for the sex and race of the attempter, plus approximate age and name if known.

3. Ask for the name of the person reporting the attempt.

4. Request the address from which the report is coming.

5. Ask if the caller knows the victim. If so, (a) ask about motive; and (b) request names of others who might be of influence in dissuading the victim.

6. Notify the nearest appropriate rescue squad.

22. 911 operator Henry Hansen receives the message: "Someone is about to jump off the bridge." Hansen first asks, "Which bridge?" He then asks, "Is the jumper a man or a woman? Of what race? About how old is the person? What is his name?" Operator Hansen then asks the caller for his name and from what address he/she is calling. Hansen's next question is, "Do you know this person?" The caller responds, "No, I just happened to be looking out the window." Henry Hansen should now

(A) notify the newspapers about the attempted suicide.

(B) ask the caller why the jumper is attempting suicide.

(C) alert the rescue squad.

(D) ask for the race and age of the caller.

23. It is December 14 and a 911 operator has transmitted the following set of facts to Fire Dispatcher Mary Carey:

Location of fire: 122 Barley Road

Time of report: 4:18 a.m.

Type of structure: Chemicals factory

Origin of fire: Unknown

Extent of involvement: Active and total; heavy, foul-smelling smoke

Fire Dispatcher Carey has committed three full detachments to the scene. She is now preparing a written report of the night's activity. Which of the following conveys all the information *most clearly* and *accurately*?

(A) A chemical factory caught fire all by itself at 4:18 a.m. on Barley Road. Three fire engines put it out.

(B) At 4:18 a.m. on December 14, a fire of unknown origin was reported at a chemicals factory at 122 Barley Road. I dispatched three detachments to the scene and cautioned about the possibility of toxic fumes.

(C) There was a big fire in the chemicals factory at 122 Barley Road early this morning. It was not dangerous because no one is at work at that time, but I sent three detachments to put it out.

(D) Three detachments went to put out the fire at the chemicals factory on Barley Road this morning. The 911 operator told me that the cause was unknown.

24. Emergency communications technician Rita Mulligan receives four very excited calls in rapid succession. Each caller reports that a man has been running back and forth on the block of West 47th Street between 7th and 8th Avenues, shouting obscenities and waving a small handgun. The four descriptions vary in some details. Which of the following four descriptions should Ms. Mulligan choose to transmit to the police radio dispatcher?

(A) White, 40 years old, wearing a black hat and red sneakers.

(B) Black, 25 years old, wearing a black hat and red sneakers.

(C) White, 25 years old, wearing a black hat and red sneakers.

(D) White, 30 years old, wearing a red hat and black sneakers.

ANSWER QUESTION 25 ON THE BASIS OF THE FOLLOWING INFORMATION.

When an emergency radio dispatcher receives word from the 911 operator that a suspicious package has been noticed at a specific location, the dispatcher must do the following:

1. Notify the police bomb-disarming unit.

2. Check the police jurisdiction grid to identify the precinct in which the suspicious package is located.

3. Pinpoint the nearest squad car and direct it to the location.

4. Check the fire jurisdiction grid to identify the fire company that protects the location.

5. Notify the firehouse for standby alert.

25. In a clear and accurate message, a 911 operator has informed Dispatcher Pedro Melendez of the address, precise location, and description of a suspicious package. Melendez has directed the bomb unit to the scene and has ascertained that the package is in the 35th precinct. Pedro Melendez should now

(A) call the 35th precinct and request that a squad car be sent to the scene to direct evacuation if necessary.

(B) call the 35th precinct and ask for the location of the nearest fire house.

(C) notify the nearest fire company as to the action in progress.

(D) search for the nearest patrol car and send it to the "bomb" site.

ANSWER QUESTION 26 ON THE BASIS OF THE FOLLOWING INFORMATION.

When a police dispatcher receives a call for reinforcements, the dispatcher must do the following:

1. Ask for the calling officer's badge number to be sure that the request is not a diversionary tactic.

2. Ask if an ambulance is needed.

3. Press 222, the emergency signal.

4. Press 456, the signal for all available cars to call in immediately.

5. Tell the location of the action to all responding cars.

6. Notify the hostage negotiation team to be ready.

26. Car 66 has arrived at the scene of a bank robbery in progress, and officers Klein and Carilli realize that there are a number of well-armed robbers inside. Officer Klein radios the police dispatcher and requests that reinforcements be sent at once. Dispatcher Barbara Blake asks Officer Klein for her badge number. Ms. Blake then asks if an ambulance is needed and learns that one is not necessary at this time. The next step dispatcher Blake should take is to

(A) send an ambulance on a nonemergency alert.

(B) press 222, then 456.

(C) broadcast the location of the action to all cars in the area.

(D) tell the location of the action individually to each responding car.

27. At 11 a.m. on Saturday, June 11, Dispatcher Frances Szulk receives a bulletin with the following information:

Location: Bicycle path alongside Shady Parkway, approximately 3,000 yards south of Highland train station

Occurrence: Discovery of body of fully clothed Hispanic female in early 20s

Reporter: Bill Sawyer, age 12

Identity of Victim: Unknown

Dispatcher Szulk must now send a patrol car to the scene. Which of the following conveys all the information *most clearly* and *accurately*?

(A) A woman was found by Bill Sawyer on the Shady Parkway. He doesn't know her.

(B) There is a body on the bicycle path on Shady Parkway near the train station. She is a Hispanic woman and Bill Sawyer, a 12-year-old, found her.

(C) The body of an unknown Hispanic woman was found at 11 a.m. by 12-year-old Bill Sawyer, on the bicycle path of Shady Parkway south of the Highland train station.

(D) On Saturday, June 11, Bill Sawyer found a dead body of a woman on the bicycle path. He called to say he didn't know her or why she died, but she had her clothes on.

28. An emergency operator receives many calls. Many of these calls do require action by the operator, but some are greater emergencies than others. Of the following calls, to which should an operator assign *lowest* priority?

(A) A dog is running loose in a residential neighborhood.

(B) An open fire hydrant is gushing into the roadway.

(C) There is a panhandler at the bus stop.

(D) A wire of unknown purpose is dangling over the sidewalk.

ANSWER QUESTION 29 ON THE BASIS OF THE FOLLOWING INFORMATION.

When a 911 operator receives notice of an accident that has just occurred in the street, the operator must do the following:

1. Ask for the exact location of the accident.

2. Ask about the number of people involved.

3. Inquire about the extent of the injuries.

4. If there are serious injuries, send ambulance(s).

5. Dispatch two patrol cars.

6. Ask if there is fire.

7. If there is fire, sound the alarm at the firehouse.

8. Ask if there are seriously disabled vehicles.

9. If necessary, send tow trucks.

29. 911 operator Tim Weitz receives a call informing him that a taxi has just hit a boy on a bicycle. Weitz learns the precise location of the accident and finds out that the boy seems badly hurt, but that the cabby is standing over him and no one else was involved. Operator Weitz sends an ambulance to the scene and dispatches the nearest two patrol cars. Then he asks if the cab is on fire and is assured that it is not. The next thing Tim Weitz must do is

(A) send a fire engine.

(B) send a tow truck.

(C) ask about the condition of the cab.

(D) ask if the bicycle has been damaged.

ANSWER QUESTION 30 ON THE BASIS OF THE FOLLOWING INFORMATION.

If the caller on the line is threatening to kill someone, the operator must

1. ask the caller for street address and apartment number.

2. write these alongside code 202 and pass the slip of paper to the nearest operator so that he or she can dispatch the police at once.

3. ask for the name of the caller.

4. ask questions about the intended victim and the situation leading to the threat.

5. keep the caller on the telephone until police arrive.

30. The caller screams at operator Jenny Wong that her son has just come home high again and he is rummaging through her pocketbook, and this time she will kill him. Operator Wong asks the woman where she lives. Next, Jenny Wong should

(A) press code 202.

(B) write down the exact address.

(C) tell the operator next to her to send the police.

(D) ask the woman what kind of drugs her son takes.

ANSWER QUESTIONS 31–36 ON THE BASIS OF THE FOLLOWING PASSAGE.

The following memorandum is on the police dispatcher's desk. The dispatcher must become thoroughly familiar with its content in order to alert both police officers assigned to the court house and patrol officers to the situation and to rapidly process any reports of sightings that may come in from the field.

MEMORANDUM

This memorandum concerns the murder trial of George Jackson that is now in progress. Information has been received from reliable sources that the accused may attempt to escape from the courtroom, aided by members of the "Blue Circle" gang with which the accused was connected prior to his arrest.

Known members of this gang include Patsy "Boots" Brescia, a short, swarthy individual who invariably dresses conservatively. Although this member of the gang has no arrest record, he is known to carry firearms at all times and is now wanted by authorities in this state.

Fred Fick, alias Frederick Fidens: This individual is 6 feet, 4 inches tall; weighs 230 pounds; and may be identified by a knife scar on the right cheek. He has been convicted of felonious assault, manslaughter, and burglary.

Patrick Ahern: This individual is 6 feet, 2 inches tall and weighs 145 pounds. He is known to be extremely dangerous when under the influence of drugs. Ahern's convictions include those for robbery, breaking and entering, and Sullivan Law violation. He is wanted for kidnapping by the California authorities.

All officers, including those not assigned to the murder trial, are expected to be on the lookout for anyone acting peculiarly. If you observe anyone who answers any of the descriptions given above, or anyone else whose actions arouse your suspicion, send another officer to call the chief court officer. Avoid any indication that you are suspicious. Above all, avoid any action that may even remotely jeopardize the safety of spectators. While every precaution will be taken to prevent the admission to the courtroom of anyone carrying arms, do not gamble on the success of these precautions. These men are dangerous and, if convinced that their own safety is in peril, will not hesitate to use their weapons.

31. The memorandum indicates that, of the members of the "Blue Circle" gang mentioned,
- **(A)** all have been arrested at least once.
- **(B)** only one has never been arrested.
- **(C)** two have never been arrested.
- **(D)** three have never been arrested.

32. Of the members of the gang mentioned in the memorandum,
- **(A)** at least one, if apprehended, may be extradited (returned to another state).
- **(B)** at least two are said to be wanted by authorities in other states.
- **(C)** at least three have been guilty of felonies.
- **(D)** any one is likely to act peculiarly.

33. The memorandum does not state that Fred Fick has ever been convicted of
(A) burglary.
(B) manslaughter.
(C) robbery.
(D) felonious assault.

34. From information given in the memorandum, Patrick Ahern may best be described as
(A) short and stocky.
(B) tall and heavy.
(C) tall and thin.
(D) short and thin.

35. According to the memorandum, the member of the "Blue Circle" gang who is known to use drugs is
(A) "Boots" Brescia.
(B) Patrick Ahern.
(C) Fred Fick.
(D) George Jackson.

36. "Boots" Brescia may most readily be identified by
(A) his swarthy complexion.
(B) the scar on his right cheek.
(C) his flashy clothes.
(D) his footwear.

ANSWER QUESTIONS 37–39 BASED ON THE FOLLOWING INFORMATION.

When receiving information from a caller in regard to a ringing alarm, the information should be taken in the following order:

1. What is the address or location of the ringing alarm?

2. How long has the alarm been ringing?

3. Is the alarm coming from a building or car?

4. If the alarm is coming from a building, find out if there are any open doors.

5. If the alarm is coming from a car, obtain the color, plate number, and type of auto.

6. Get name and address of the caller.

37. An anonymous caller states that an alarm is coming from the house across the street. He is unable to sleep and would like the police to respond to the location as soon as possible. What will your next course of action be?
(A) Ask the caller for his name.
(B) Ask how long has the alarm been ringing.
(C) Obtain the address of the house.
(D) None of the above.

38. What would be your next course of action?
(A) Find out how long the alarm has been ringing.
(B) Find out if anyone is in the house.
(C) Obtain the color, plate number, and type of auto.
(D) None of the above.

39. Your final course of action should be to
(A) tell the caller the police are responding.
(B) get the name and address of the caller.
(C) get the caller's name.
(D) None of the above.

ANSWER QUESTION 40 ON THE BASIS OF THE FOLLOWING INFORMATION.

When a 911 operator receives a call in a familiar foreign language, the operator should do the following:

1. If not certified in that language, transfer the call to an operator who is certified in that language.

2. If certified:

   a. Ask the caller for telephone number, name, and address.

   b. Ask about the nature of the emergency.

3. Determine which emergency service is appropriate to the problem.

4. Transmit the information to the appropriate dispatcher.

40. Operator Marisol Gonzalez receives a call from a distraught woman who tells her, in Spanish, that drug sales are being carried on in the hallway outside her apartment door. Operator Gonzalez is fluent in Spanish, though not certified, and easily obtains from the woman her telephone number, name, and address. Then Ms. Gonzalez transmits this information to a police dispatcher so that the drug sales can be observed in progress and the suspects arrested. Marisol Gonzalez's actions are

(A) correct; she is perfectly competent to deal with the Spanish-speaking woman, and action must be taken quickly when dealing with drug sales.

(B) incorrect; if she is not certified, her Spanish is not adequate for dealing with the excited woman.

(C) correct; it would be too upsetting to the distraught woman to have her call transferred to another operator.

(D) incorrect; the rules require that only foreign language–certified operators handle foreign language calls.

41. An emergency operator transmits the following information to the police dispatcher, who must radio it to patrol cars and ambulance:

Location: Intersection of Grand Street and Torrance Avenue

Occurrence: Hit and run accident

Victim: Very old Asian man

Witness: Joan Johnson of 332 Grand Street, Apt. 3B

Vehicle: Red sports car with out-of-state license plates

Which of the following expresses the information *most clearly* and *accurately*?

(A) A very old Asian man was hit by Joan Johnson in a red sports car at 332 Grand Street, Apt. 3B.

(B) Joan Johnson was hit by a very old Asian man at the intersection of Grand Street and Torrance Avenue. The red sports car was from out of state.

(C) Joan Johnson of 332 Grand Street, Apt. 3B, reports that a very old Asian man was hit by a red sports car at Grand and Torrance.

(D) A red sports car from out of state hit an old Asian man in front of Joan Johnson of 332 Grand Street, Apt. 3B.

ANSWER QUESTION 42 ON THE BASIS OF THE FOLLOWING INFORMATION.

When an emergency operator receives a call reporting a fire, the operator must ask for the following information in this order:

1. The exact address of the building or the nearest intersection.

2. The kind of building—apartment, private house, factory, store, theater, school, etc.

3. The number of floors—2-story, low-rise, mid-rise, or high-rise.

4. If the building is customarily occupied, vacant, or abandoned.

5. Whether or not the building is actually occupied.

6. Identity of the owner of the building.

7. Identity of the caller.

42. Operator Hans Kohl has received a report of a fire and has asked the caller where the fire is. He has learned that the building is a boarded-up small apartment house. Operator Kohl's next question should be

(A) Is the fire out yet?
(B) Do you know if anyone was living there?
(C) How did the fire start?
(D) Do you know who owns the building?

43. Police officer George Mullins arrives at the scene of a jewelry store robbery. Witnesses surround him, all eager to give descriptions of the getaway car. Officer Mullins must call the dispatcher to broadcast the description of the car throughout the city. Which of the following descriptions should he assume to be correct?

(A) White Ford, 2-door, California plate 482-ACE
(B) Cream Buick, 2-door, New York plate 483-GE
(C) Yellow Mercury, 4-door, New Jersey plate 495-BGF
(D) Cream Ford, 2-door, New Jersey plate 482-BCE

ANSWER QUESTION 44 ON THE BASIS OF THE FOLLOWING INFORMATION.

If an operator receives a call from a woman about to give birth, the operator must do the following in the following order:

1. Ask the caller for her telephone number, address, and name. If an apartment building, ask apartment number.

2. Ask how emergency personnel can gain entrance to building and unit.

3. Ask about any problems that may require immediate special services—prematurity or heavy bleeding, for instance.

4. Transmit information to police and ambulance services.

5. Ask caller if anyone else—doctor, family member—should be alerted.

44. Operator Raoul Castellano receives a call from a woman who tells him that she is in heavy labor and the baby is coming very fast. Operator Castellano asks the woman for her telephone number, name, and address. Then he learns that the apartment house front door is always open and the woman has unlocked her own apartment door. In answer to Castellano's inquiry, the woman says that she is just entering her seventh month of pregnancy. Operator Castellano's next act should be to

(A) call the hospital to alert them of the imminent arrival of a premature newborn.

(B) ask the woman for the name and number of her doctor.

(C) transmit all the information to the police and emergency medical services.

(D) ask who is caring for the other children.

45. The following information appears on the screen in front of Police Dispatcher Mike Thorkelson:

Occurrence: Dog bite, left calf

Victim: Calliope Petropolis, age 9

Address of Victim: 730 Ninth Avenue, Apt. 5G

Location of occurrence: In front of 680 Tenth Avenue

Caller: Artemis Canellos, 688 Tenth Avenue

Description of dog: Terrier-sized brown-and-white mongrel

Location of dog: Unknown

Thorkelson must transmit this information to the police canine control unit. Which of the following expresses this information *most completely* and *accurately*?

(A) A brown-and-white mongrel bit Artemis Canellos at 730 Ninth Avenue. She is 9. It bit her left leg.

(B) Calliope Petropolis, a 9-year-old of 730 Ninth Avenue, Apt. 5G, was bitten on the leg by a brown-and-white mongrel. The occurrence took place near 680 Tenth Avenue and was reported by one Artemis Canellos of #688. The dog is at large.

(C) Nine-year-old Calliope Petropolis was bitten by a brown-and-white mutt at 730 Ninth Avenue. Artemis Canellos reported that it was her left calf. She doesn't know where the dog is.

(D) A dog bit Calliope Petropolis in front of 680 Tenth Avenue. Calliope is 9, reported Artemis Canellos of Apt. 5G. No one knows where the dog is.

46. 911 operator Jim Goldman receives a call from a citizen who complains of a foul odor coming from the trunk of a car parked in his neighborhood. This is not an emergency situation, but operator Goldman takes down information to pass on to the police department. The caller is Frank Connolly of 923 188th Road. The car is a nearly new blue Lincoln Town Car. It has been parked at the same spot, in front of 947 188th Road, for at least two weeks. The car bears New York license plate SBT-383. With which of the following will operator Goldman express the information *most clearly* and *accurately*?

(A) Frank Connolly of 923 188th Road reports an odor coming from a blue Lincoln Town Car, NY SBT-383, parked in front of 947 188th Road for two weeks.

(B) A blue Lincoln at 923 188th Road has a bad smell for two weeks. Its number is SBT-383. Mr. Connolly told about it.

(C) License plate SBT-383 from New York is on a blue Lincoln Town Car. It smells, says Frank Connolly of 923 188th Road.

(D) Frank Connolly complains that a blue Lincoln with New York license plate SBT-383 has been smelling bad for two weeks. He lives at 923; it is at 947.

ANSWER QUESTION 47 ON THE BASIS OF THE FOLLOWING INFORMATION.

When a caller to 911 makes a bizarre or highly improbable report, the operator must follow a special line of questioning to determine if the caller is a danger to the public, requiring massive, immediate response, or to himself or herself, requiring a nonintimidating reaction. The order of questioning is as follows:

1. Telephone number of phone being used and location from which call is being made.

2. Name, address, and home phone number of caller.

3. Detailed description of event being reported.

   a. If alien landing, description, how many, how armed.

   b. Demands being made of caller.

4. What the caller is planning to do about it.

47. 911 operator Akeel Hakim receives a call from an agitated citizen who reports that a space ship has just touched down in the vacant lot across the street and that aliens are pouring out of it. Hakim gets from the caller the phone number and address from which he is calling and determines that these are the home number and address of the caller. Next he should ask:

(A) What are you going to do about it?

(B) Do they speak English?

(C) Tell me what they look like and how many there are.

(D) What do they want?

48. Mrs. Wood calls 911 and states that the unoccupied elevator in her building is not working. You should

    (A) send a patrol car to check the elevator.

    (B) tell her to call back in 1 hour if the elevator is still not working.

    (C) tell her to call building repair or superintendent/landlord of the building

    (D) hang up on her.

49. On July 21 at 10:30 p.m., emergency operator Lorraine Wilson receives a call from a furious citizen who complains about nighttime activity in the church parking lot next door. He says that his name is Peter Lynch and he lives at 168 Cayman Road. He says that the parking lot of St. Mary's church at 170 Cayman Road is "sin center" at night. He demands that the parking lot gate be locked at night to discourage the drag racing, drinking, and sexual activity that have been going on there. Operator Wilson knows that this is not an emergency and that she needn't pass the call to a dispatcher, but as long as she has the information, she prepares a written report. Which of the following expresses the information *most clearly* and *accurately*?

    (A) Peter Lynch of St. Mary's on 170 Cayman Road says the parking lot should be locked at 10:30 p.m. People drink there at night.

    (B) Peter Lynch of 168 Cayman Road complains of nighttime rowdiness in the parking lot of St. Mary's at 170 Cayman. He requests that the lot be padlocked at night.

    (C) There is drinking and sex in the St. Mary's parking lot at night at 170 Cayman Road. Peter Lynch says it should be padlocked on July 21st.

    (D) Padlocking the parking lot of St. Mary's is the solution to nightly disturbances at 170 Cayman Road, according to Peter Lynch of 168 Cayman Road at 10:30 p.m. on July 21st.

50. Mrs. Swanson calls 911 to find out if alternate street parking is suspended today. You should

    (A) ask the operator next to you, because she drives.

    (B) tell her that you think so, because of all the snow outside.

    (C) tell her to watch the news.

    (D) refer her to the alternate street parking hotline.

ANSWER QUESTIONS 51–55 ON THE BASIS OF THE FOLLOWING PASSAGE.

EMPLOYEE LEAVE REGULATIONS

As a full-time permanent City employee under the Career and Salary Plan, operator Peter Smith earns an annual leave allowance. This consists of a certain number of days off per year with pay and may be used for vacation, personal business, or for observing religious holidays. As a newly appointed employee, during his first 8 years of City service he will earn an annual leave allowance of 20 days off per year (an average of 1-2/3 days off per month). After he has finished 8 full years of working for the City, he will begin earning an additional 5 days off per year. His annual leave allowance will then be 25 days per year and will remain at this amount for 7 full years. He will begin earning an additional 2 days off per year after he has completed a total of 15 years of City employment. Therefore, in his sixteenth year of working for the City, Smith will be earning 27 days off a year as his 'annual leave allowance' (an average of 2-1/4 days off per month).

A sick leave allowance of 1 day per month is also given to Operator Smith, but it can be used only in case of actual illness. When Smith returns to work after using sick leave allowance, he must have a doctor's note if the absence is for a total of more than 3 days, but he may also be required to show a doctor's note for absences of 1, 2, or 3 days.

51. According to the preceding passage, Mr. Smith's annual leave allowance consists of a certain number of days off per year that he

    (A) does not get paid for.

    (B) gets paid for at time and a half.

    (C) may use for personal business.

    (D) may not use for observing religious holidays.

52. According to the preceding passage, after Mr. Smith has been working for the City for 9 years, his annual leave allowance will be

    (A) 20 days per year.

    (B) 25 days per year.

    (C) 27 days per year.

    (D) 37 days per year.

53. According to the preceding passage, Mr. Smith will begin earning an average of 2-1/4 days off per month as his annual leave allowance after he has worked for the City for

    (A) 7 full years.

    (B) 8 full years.

    (C) 15 full years.

    (D) 17 full years.

54. According to the preceding passage, Mr. Smith is given a "sick leave allowance" of

    (A) 1 day every 2 months.

    (B) 1 day per month.

    (C) 1-2/3 days per month.

    (D) 2-1/4 days per month.

55. According to the preceding passage, when he uses sick leave allowance, Mr. Smith may be required to show a doctor's note

    (A) even if his absence is for only 1 day.

    (B) only if his absence is for more than 2 days.

    (C) only if his absence is for more than 3 days.

    (D) only if his absence is for 3 days or more.

56. By far the greatest number of calls to 911 are calls intended for the police department. Which of the following emergency calls should be directed to someone other than the police department?

    (A) A call reporting a man going up the fire escape at a neighboring building

    (B) A call reporting a group of young people burning an American flag in the park

    (C) A call reporting youths breaking car windows

    (D) A call reporting a customer who appears to have suffered a heart attack in a department store

57. Off-duty police officer Howard Kenzie notices an apparently unsupervised small boy wandering aimlessly on East 18th Street between Avenue P and Kings Highway. He asks the child his name and is told "Jimmy." The child, who appears to be no more than 3 years old, has curly blond hair and is wearing striped pants and a white T-shirt with Bugs Bunny on the front. The youngster cannot tell his last name or where he lives. Officer Kenzie calls the police dispatcher from the nearest call box and asks the dispatcher to check with the local precinct, and possibly other precincts as well, to see if a child matching this description has been reported missing. Which of the following statements expresses this information to the precincts *most clearly* and *accurately*?

    (A) Jimmy is all alone on East 18th Street between Avenue P and Kings Highway. Has anyone missed him?

    (B) A small, blond boy wearing striped pants and a Bugs Bunny T-shirt and identifying himself as "Jimmy" is wandering on East 18th Street between Avenue P and Kings Highway. Has he been reported missing?

    (C) Police Officer Howard Kenzie, who is not on duty, has little Jimmy on East 18th Street between Avenue P and Kings Highway in striped pants. He is blond.

    (D) An off-duty little boy named Jimmy is with Police Officer Howard Kenzie at a call box near East 18th Street and Kings Highway. He likes Bugs Bunny and wears striped pants.

ANSWER QUESTIONS 58–60 ON THE BASIS OF THE FOLLOWING INFORMATION.

In the event of a bank robbery, the emergency operator must follow this procedure:

1. Determine the precise location of the bank.

2. Ask for the name of the bank.

3. Ask for a description of the bank robber.

4. Ask if any weapons were used and obtain a description of the weapons.

5. If there are serious injuries, send an ambulance.

6. Dispatch three police cars to the location.

7. If the bank robber has left the bank, determine how the suspect left the scene and the direction of travel.

8. Obtain a description of any vehicle(s) involved.

9. Request name, location, and telephone number from which call is being made.

10. Request that the caller remain on that telephone if it is safe to do so.

58. Operator Tina Green received a call from someone who says there is a man standing at a bank teller window with a gun pointed at the cashier. Operator Green's first course of action should be to

   (A) ask the caller the name of the bank.

   (B) ask if an ambulance is needed.

   (C) ask the caller the address of the bank.

   (D) None of the above.

59. Operator Green's next step should be to

   (A) send several police cars to the location, because the bank robber is still in the bank.

   (B) advise his supervisor, because a bank robbery is a newsworthy event.

   (C) get the description of the bank robber.

   (D) get the name of the bank.

60. After Operator Green gets the description of the bank robber, he will

   (A) find out if anyone is injured.

   (B) find out if any weapon was used. If so, get a description of the weapon, etc.

   (C) find out how the bank robber got away.

   (D) None of the above.

61. An emergency operator must be able to size up calls very quickly, refer true emergencies to the proper departmental dispatchers, and rapidly dispose of non-emergency calls with referrals or suggestions. Sometimes, however, the best course is for the emergency operator to consult the supervisor. Which one of the following calls should the operator turn to his or her supervisor?

   (A) A call complaining of rudeness by another operator

   (B) A call complaining that there is no hot water in the building

   (C) A call reporting that a helicopter has just crashed into the river

   (D) A call reporting an explosion in a toy factory

ANSWER QUESTION 62 ON THE BASIS OF THE FOLLOWING INFORMATION.

In the event of a maritime accident, the emergency operator must follow this procedure:

1. Determine the precise location of the accident.

2. Ask for an estimate of the number of victims involved.

3. Ask if there is fire.

4. Notify police boats, fireboats, and helicopters.

5. Request name, location, and telephone number from which call is being made.

6. Request that the caller remain by that telephone in case there are problems in locating victims.

practice test

62. A pleasure craft has just collided with a garbage scow traveling down the river. Sarah Small, who was looking out her office window at the time, dials 911. Emergency operator Brian Isco asks Ms. Small which river, and with what street it is in line. He then learns from Ms. Small that the boat has capsized, tossing about five people into the water and that neither vessel is on fire at this time. Operator Isco instantly alerts police boats, fireboats, and police helicopter services. He then asks Ms. Small for her name, home address, and home telephone number. Operator Isco has acted

(A) correctly; he did everything required in the proper order.

(B) incorrectly; there was no fire; so he should not have sent fire boats.

(C) incorrectly; he should have asked Sarah Small for her office address and telephone number.

(D) incorrectly; he should have told Ms. Small to stay right where she was.

63. Operator James Monroe takes a call from a woman who has just been raped. Here are the details:

> **Location:** 583 Cooper Terrace, elevator
>
> **Time:** 2:15 p.m.
>
> **Occurrence:** Rape and robbery
>
> **Weapon:** Knife
>
> **Perpetrator:** White male, approx. 25 yrs. old, slight build, medium height, wearing blue jeans and red T-shirt
>
> **Items stolen:** Pocketbook, pearl ring, cameo brooch
>
> **Victim:** Bella Luciano, age 67, of 583 Cooper Terrace

Operator Monroe is preparing a bulletin for police officers. Which of the following expresses the information *most clearly* and *accurately*?

(A) A 25-year-old white male raped 67-year-old Bella Luciano in the elevator with a knife. He robbed her, too.

(B) At 2:15 p.m. a man raped Bella Luciano in the elevator of 583 Cooper Terrace and robbed her of her pocketbook, pearl ring, and cameo brooch.

(C) A pocketbook, pearl ring, and cameo brooch were stolen at knifepoint from Bella Luciano when a man raped her in the elevator. He was 67 years old, medium sized, and wearing blue jeans and a red T-shirt.

(D) A white male, approximately 25 years of age, slightly built and of medium height, wearing blue jeans and a red T-shirt, robbed and raped at knifepoint Bella Luciano, age 67, in the elevator of 583 Cooper Terrace at 2:15 p.m. Items stolen were a pocketbook, pearl ring, and cameo brooch.

ANSWER QUESTION 64 ON THE BASIS OF THE FOLLOWING INFORMATION.

The main role of the emergency operator is to receive information and to pass it on to the appropriate services or dispatchers. Occasionally, the operator should take it upon himself or herself to give emergency instructions. If it appears to the operator that a caller might be in danger by remaining at the location from which the call is being made, the operator should do the following:

1. Ask for the name of the caller and the address of the emergency.

2. Tell the caller to leave the premises at once and to call from the nearest available telephone at another location.

3. Dispatch the police at once.

4. Alert all other emergency operators to expect the call back.

   a. Inform other operators as to the nature of the situation and what has been done so far.

   b. Ask to have the call transferred to you if your line is not occupied when the caller calls back.

5. Get additional information to complete the call information report when the caller calls back.

64. Operator Sirhan Amin receives a call from a woman who says that she is certain that she locked the front door when she left to take her husband to the airport for a business trip 3 hours earlier, and she has just returned to a wide-open door. Operator Amin takes down the woman's name and address

and tells her to get out immediately in case there are burglars in the house and to call from her cell phone or the home of her nearest neighbor. Operator Amin then dispatches police to the woman's home and begins to tell other emergency operators about the situation. While Amin is briefing the operators, he receives a call from a man whose kitchen curtains have blown into the flames on his gas range. Just as Amin is taking down location information from the man with the kitchen fire, the first woman calls back. Operator Shirley Hyacinth receives the call. Operator Hyacinth should

(A) interrupt Sirhan Amin to tell him that his caller is back on the line.

(B) ask the woman more questions about the appearance of the house, possible activity, pets inside, etc.

(C) ask the woman to hold, because operator Amin is busy but will be available soon.

(D) tell the woman that the police are on the way.

65. A park should be a restful, safe place, but sometimes emergency situations may arise. On this balmy Sunday afternoon, the emergency call box is constantly busy. To which of the following emergencies should the dispatcher **not** send an ambulance?

(A) A jogger has fallen unconscious on the running path.

(B) A man is systematically stopping cyclists, robbing them with a heavy stick in hand, then releasing them.

(C) A child went sailing off an actively swinging swing and cannot get up.

(D) A teenager was hit in the eye by a baseball and says he cannot see with that eye.

ANSWER QUESTIONS 66–70 ON THE BASIS OF THE INFORMATION IN THE FOLLOWING PASSAGE AND ON THE INFORMATION IN THE QUESTIONS THEMSELVES. EACH QUESTION STANDS BY ITSELF UNLESS OTHERWISE STATED.

The city is divided into six police precincts roughly gridded:

4	5	6
1	2	3

The circumstances of each precinct are different, so each has a unique allotment of personnel and equipment.

The first precinct encompasses the business district. The daytime needs in the first tend to be limited to traffic control; however, burglary and assault on pedestrians are nighttime problems. Twenty-four patrol cars serve this precinct along with 5 motorcycles and, of course, foot patrols.

The second precinct includes municipal, state, and federal buildings. Daytime pedestrian traffic is heavy here, and there are frequent demonstrations and protests of various sorts. The precinct is served by 10 patrol cars, 8 motorcycles, 6 horses for mounted police, a bomb squad, 2 patrol wagons for transporting suspects and for transferring prisoners, and 6 specially trained sharpshooters.

The third precinct is a well-to-do apartment house district in which each building has some sort of security of its own. This precinct is served by 16 patrol cars, along with a full complement of detectives, investigators, and foot patrols.

The fourth precinct is a congested apartment house district. There is heavy unemployment here, with consequent loitering, criminal activity, and drug use and trade. Though the precinct is geographically small, its population and police needs are high. The precinct has 40 patrol cars and many officers assigned to foot patrol. The fourth precinct is also the home base of the narcotics squad.

The fifth precinct contains the city's warehouses and docks. It is also the center of the red-light district. Much of the crime here is at night in the form of hijacking and large-scale burglary. This precinct boasts a canine squad, undercover agents, and 2 patrol wagons, along with 14 patrol cars.

The sixth precinct consists mainly of one- and two-family dwellings and neighborhood stores. The police needs of this precinct are best served by 30 patrol cars and 2 motorcycles. The police maintenance garage is located in the sixth precinct. It can service up to 25 vehicles at one time but is seldom full.

It is the dispatcher's job to send the closest available appropriate vehicles or services to wherever they are needed, without leaving any precinct unprotected.

66. The President of the United States has come to the city. He entered through the first precinct and is en route to the federal buildings. His motorcade is being escorted by 8 motorcycles and 30 patrol cars. Sharpshooters are stationed strategically on area roofs. The mounted police are all in the federal area for crowd control. The patrol cars should have been drawn from the precincts as follows:

(A) 22 from the first; 8 from the second.

(B) 10 from the first; 5 from the second; 3 from the third; 2 from the fourth; 5 from the fifth; 5 from the sixth.

(C) 12 from the first; 5 from the second; 2 from the third; 6 from the fourth; 5 from the fifth.

(D) 5 from each of the six precincts.

67. Under the scenario of question 66, the dispatcher suddenly receives a call reporting a heavily armed bank robbery in progress in the first precinct. The foot patrols in the area request immediate reinforcement and cover from 8 cars. (Some of these could be drawn from the President's escort, if necessary.) The best array of cars for the dispatcher to send in order to supply 8 cars quickly and to not expose other areas unduly is

(A) 4 from the first, 4 from the second.

(B) 8 from the first.

(C) 8 from the fourth.

(D) 8 from the sixth.

68. It is 10 p.m. A 9-year-old girl seated in a car in the fourth precinct has just been caught in a drug-related crossfire and has been shot and killed. The neighbors have chased down the perpetrators and are beating them severely. The violence is rapidly

escalating as angry, frustrated residents of the neighborhood break windows, overturn cars, and start fires. Fourteen cars from the fourth precinct have already converged on the scene, but much more help is needed. The dispatcher should send

(A) more cars from the fourth, motorcycles from the first and second, and cars and paddy wagons from the second.

(B) cars from the third and sharpshooters and motorcycles from the first.

(C) cars from the sixth, a paddy wagon from the fifth, and the mounted police.

(D) the canine unit, the bomb squad, and cars and motorcycles from the first.

69. A police officer in the sixth precinct suspects that drugs are entering a neighborhood grocery on his post and major drug dealing is going on in the store. This is not an emergency situation, but the dispatcher should arrange assistance for the sixth precinct from units in the

(A) second and fourth precincts.

(B) first and second precincts.

(C) second and fifth precincts.

(D) fourth and fifth precincts.

70. A citizen has called to report finding two burglars inside his premises at 8:30 p.m. This call is least likely to originate from the

(A) first precinct.

(B) second precinct.

(C) third precinct.

(D) fourth precinct.

71. At 5:17 p.m. on May 3, Operator Krikor Mardikian takes a call that warns that a bomb has been placed under a third-row seat at the Savoy Theater on Main Street. The theater is showing an R-rated movie of which the caller disapproves. The caller tells Operator Mardikian that the bomb should go off within 1-1/2 hours. Krikor Mardikian must notify the police, bomb squad, and theater management. Which of the following bulletins expresses the information *most clearly* and *accurately*?

(A) It is May 3 at 5:17 p.m. The bomb at the Savoy Theater will go off at 6:47 p.m.

(B) The bomb in the third row of the Savoy Theater on Main Street will go off in an hour and a half.

(C) Report has been received of a bomb under a third-row seat in the Savoy Theater on Main Street. It is 5:17 p.m.

(D) At 5:17 p.m. a bomb with a 1-1/2-hour fuse was reported to have been placed under a third-row seat of the Savoy Theater on Main Street.

ANSWER QUESTION 72 ON THE BASIS OF THE FOLLOWING INFORMATION.

In the event of a major disaster, the emergency operator should take the following steps in this order:

1. Determine the precise location of the disaster.

2. Estimate the numbers of victims involved.

3. Notify and alert the following services citywide:

   a. firefighters

   b. emergency medical services (ambulances)

   c. police

   d. hospitals

4. Request state police assistance in keeping access routes open for emergency vehicles.

72. 911 Operator Kimberly Kane receives a horrifying report that a large passenger train has just derailed in a residential area. Operator Kane learns the basic location of the wreckage and realizes that hundreds will be affected, including passengers and residents of the neighborhood. Kane immediately sends out the alert for all available fire companies to rush to the scene and also sounds the alarm for emergency ambulances. The next step Operator Kane must take is to

(A) notify police in the precinct in which the wreckage is strewn.

(B) notify police citywide.

(C) contact state police.

(D) alert hospitals to prepare for trauma victims.

ANSWER QUESTIONS 73–78 BASED ON THE INFORMATION PROVIDED BELOW.

CRIME DEFINITIONS

Criminal mischief	Intentionally damages another's property
Burglary	Enters or remains unlawfully in a dwelling with intent to commit a crime
Assault	Causes injury to another person or persons
Robbery	Forcible stealing of another's property
Harassment	Strikes, shoves, kicks, or subjects another to physical contact but without causing injury
Larceny	Deprives another of property by wrongfully taking, obtaining, or withholding it from the other party (no physical force involved)
Aggravated harassment	To harass or annoy another by means of a tele-communications device
Theft of service	To avoid payment for services
Illegal eviction	When a person evicts or attempts to evict without a warrant

73. Mary Newman calls 911 and states her husband just slapped her, but that she is not injured. Under the crime definitions, this is considered

   (A) criminal mischief.
   (B) larceny.
   (C) harassment.
   (D) assault.

74. Mr. Jim Jones reports that he just came home from work and found that his apartment was broken into. Under the crime definitions, this is considered

   (A) robbery.
   (B) burglary.
   (C) larceny.
   (D) illegal eviction.

75. The school nurse calls 911 and states that several kids are spray painting the side of the school building. Under the crime definitions, this is considered

   (A) aggravated harassment.
   (B) theft of service.
   (C) larceny.
   (D) criminal mischief.

76. An elderly women states that her pocketbook was taken from her at gunpoint. Under the crime definitions, this is considered

   (A) robbery.
   (B) assault.
   (C) larceny.
   (D) theft of service.

77. The gas station owner advises that he just filled up a car with a tank of gas, and the driver left without paying. Under the crime definitions, this is considered

   (A) larceny.
   (B) theft of service.
   (C) harassment.
   (D) aggravated harassment.

78. Mrs. Francois is receiving numerous phone calls from her estranged husband. He is threatening to kill her. Under the crime definitions, this is considered

   (A) aggravated harassment.
   (B) harassment.
   (C) criminal mischief.
   (D) assault.

79. Operator Irene Tortino receives a call from a woman who complains bitterly of obscene phone calls. Operator Tortino takes down the following information:

> **Complaint:** Unsolicited phone calls with heavy breathing and obscene questions and suggestions
>
> **Complainant:** Dorothy Hultz of 17-12 Highland Way
>
> **Phone number being called:** 555-6686
>
> **Caller:** Unknown male with husky voice, no particular accent
>
> **Target of calls:** Any female answering phone
>
> **Time of day calls take place:** Between 7 and 9 p.m.

Operator Tortino recommends to Ms. Hultz that she instruct all household members to hang up immediately when they receive these calls. Then Ms. Tortino prepares an information report for the police department and telephone company. Which of the following expresses the information *most clearly* and *accurately*?

(A) An unidentified male with a husky voice has been making obscene phone calls to 555-6686, the home of Dorothy Hultz at 17-12 Highland Way between 7 and 9 p.m.

(B) Dorothy Hultz gets obscene calls from a husky-man at 555-6686 at 17-12 Highland Way.

(C) A husky voice breathes hard and is obscene between 7 and 9 p.m., says Dorothy Hultz.

(D) Between 7 and 9 p.m., any female receives a husky voice at 555-6686 from 17-12 Highland Way by Dorothy Hultz.

ANSWER QUESTION 80 ON THE BASIS OF THE FOLLOWING INFORMATION.

911 operators are given the following instructions with regard to telephoned complaints about lack of heat.

1. If the outside temperature is above 30 degrees Fahrenheit (°F), give the caller the telephone number of the Buildings Department.

2. If the outside temperature is below 30°F, ask the following:

   a. name of caller

   b. address of premises without heat

   c. number of units in building

   d. number of people in unit and their ages

   e. if there are any special health problems among occupants

   f. if occupants have enough blankets

3. If any occupant of the unit is over the age of 65 or under the age of 18 months, or if there is severe illness in the household, notify the Health Department.

4. Ask the name of the landlord and the address to which rent is paid.

5. Notify the Buildings Department and the mayor's emergency heat force.

80. The outside temperature is 24°F when Operator Aliza Chatzky receives a call from a woman complaining that there is no heat in the apartment, that there has been no heat for more than a week, and that furthermore some windows are broken. Operator Chatzky learns the woman's name and the address of the building. The building has 24 apartments, none of which has heat. There are 8 people living in this apartment, all between the ages of 4 and 55. The woman's 8-year-old daughter is running a fever of 105 degrees. The family has piled all of its blankets on the little girl because she has chills. Aliza Chatzky next asks the name of the landlord. Operator Chatzky's action is

(A) incorrect, because no one in the apartment is under the age of 18 months or over the age of 65 years.

(B) incorrect, because the 8-year-old girl is sick.

(C) correct, because there are plenty of blankets.

(D) correct, because the mayor's emergency heat force will need to know the name of the landlord in order to compel him or her to provide heat.

ANSWER KEY AND EXPLANATIONS

1. C	17. C	33. C	49. B	65. B
2. A	18. A	34. C	50. D	66. B
3. C	19. B	35. B	51. C	67. C
4. D	20. D	36. A	52. B	68. A
5. A	21. D	37. C	53. C	69. D
6. D	22. C	38. A	54. B	70. C
7. C	23. B	39. B	55. A	71. D
8. D	24. C	40. D	56. D	72. B
9. C	25. D	41. C	57. B	73. C
10. D	26. B	42. B	58. C	74. B
11. D	27. C	43. D	59. D	75. D
12. B	28. C	44. C	60. B	76. A
13. C	29. C	45. B	61. A	77. B
14. C	30. B	46. A	62. C	78. A
15. A	31. B	47. C	63. D	79. A
16. D	32. A	48. C	64. B	80. B

1. **The correct answer is (C).** Small children may disobey, but they are mobile on their own or can be scooped up easily. Kindergartens are generally adequately staffed to deal with quick evacuation. Nursing home residents, on the other hand, often are disabled or even bedridden. The staff is unlikely to be able to remove all residents unaided. Many rescue workers are needed right away.

2. **The correct answer is (A).** The ambulance services and the children's hospital are for people, not pets. You should refer her to the local animal hospital.

3. **The correct answer is (C).** This statement tells what happened, where, and when. It gives a brief description of the suspect and identifies the witness. Choices (A) and (B) neglect to mention the fire; choice (D) omits the height of the suspect, an important fact, and does not identify the relationship of the witness for later questioning, if necessary.

4. **The correct answer is (D).** This statement gives the precise location, what took place, and a direction in which the suspect might be traced. Since the statement says that the event just occurred, the time is irrelevant. The recipient of the message knows to move quickly. Choice (A) does not give enough details to be of use; choice (B) makes a disjointed statement; choice (C) makes a flat statement that is not necessarily true. The purse-snatcher may have exited by another route.

5. **The correct answer is (A).** The white female is armed with a sawed-off shotgun.

6. **The correct answer is (D).** The white female has long brown hair.

7. **The correct answer is (C).** The police officers observed the suspects running. The Hispanic male ran with a slight limp.

8. **The correct answer is (D).** The white male was bearded and carried a white duffel bag. The Hispanic male carried the blue duffel bag.

9. **The correct answer is (C).** The female wore blue sneakers.

10. **The correct answer is (D).** The black male carried the toolbox.

11. **The correct answer is (D).** Because someone caused injury to this person, it is considered an assault.

12. **The correct answer is (B).** The superintendent was attempting to evict the person without a warrant by tampering with the lock.

13. **The correct answer is (C).** The kids were wrongfully taking property and no force was used.

14. **The correct answer is (C).** Regardless of the reason they didn't pay, because they avoided payment for their meal, this would be considered a theft of service.

15. **The correct answer is (A).** The water leak should be reported and repaired, but it does not constitute an emergency. The caller should be referred to the Buildings Department. An occupied elevator that is stuck between floors represents a clear emergency situation. The man cracking the whip could injure people. A gas odor may indicate an imminent explosion. The fire department and/or utility company should be summoned on an emergency basis.

16. **The correct answer is (D).** This statement gives all the relevant information in logical order. Choice (A) omits the location. Choices (B) and (C) are garbled messages.

17. **The correct answer is (C).** He gave only 1 hour notice, and therefore he was wrong.

18. **The correct answer is (A).** He will be docked, because he failed to follow the late procedure.

19. **The correct answer is (B).** He is in training and therefore must also notify the training center.

20. **The correct answer is (D).** Lateness is not tolerated.

21. **The correct answer is (D).** In the first year, you are allowed 25 vacation days. After 1 year of service, you receive 27 days. This answer was not a choice.

22. **The correct answer is (C).** Henry Hansen has followed procedures correctly to step 5. Since the caller does not know the victim, it would be pointless to ask about motive or ask for suggestions as to whom to call for assistance with this particular victim. The next step is to call out the rescue squad.

23. **The correct answer is (B).** This statement includes date, time, place, problem, and action taken. Choices (A) and (C) make assumptions that are not necessarily true. Choice (D) is incomplete.

24. **The correct answer is (C).** Look for the points of agreement. Three callers agree that the man is white, three agree that he is youthful, and all agree that he is wearing a hat and sneakers. It certainly appears that caller (D) simply reversed colors and descriptions. Choice (C) contains all points on which there is agreement.

25. **The correct answer is (D).** The narrative has brought dispatcher Melendez up to step 3. It is his responsibility to locate the nearest squad car and dispatch it to the site.

26. **The correct answer is (B).** This choice combines two steps of the procedure, but since these two steps do indeed follow in rapid succession in this order, the choice is correct.

27. **The correct answer is (C).** While not complete in every detail, this report is quite adequate to direct police to the scene and to tell them what they are looking for. Choice (A) does not even say that the woman is dead and does not give adequate directions. Choice (B) is inadequate only in that it does not identify the train station. Choice (D) gives no location at all.

28. **The correct answer is (C).** A panhandler at the bus stop presents no emergency. First priority should be given to the dangling wire; it might be a live electric wire.

29. **The correct answer is (C).** Tim Weitz has correctly followed all steps through step 6. Since there is no fire, he must skip over step 7 and ask about the cab. If the cab is only dented, there is no need for a tow truck. The bicycle, even if totally destroyed, does not require a tow truck.

30. **The correct answer is (B).** Jenny Wong must write the address as given and pass it to another operator with the code 202. The code gives notice of the urgency of the matter to the other operator. Wong must maintain contact with the caller to distract her from carrying out her threat.

31. **The correct answer is (B).** Patsy "Boots" Brescia has no arrest record. Fick and Ahern have previous convictions, so they obviously have been previously arrested. Jackson is under arrest right now.

32. **The correct answer is (A).** Patrick Ahern is wanted for kidnapping in California and, if apprehended, may be extradited to California. No mention is made of any other gang member's being wanted by another state.

33. **The correct answer is (C).** Fred Fick's list of convictions does not include robbery.

34. **The correct answer is (C).** A person who stands 6 feet, 2 inches, yet weighs only 145 pounds, is tall and thin.

35. **The correct answer is (B).** If Patrick Ahern is known to be extremely dangerous when under the influence of drugs, then he must be a user.

36. **The correct answer is (A).** Brescia is a conservative dresser with a swarthy complexion. Fick is the one with a knife scar. We were not told how Brescia got his nickname.

37. **The correct answer is (C).** According to the information provided, the address or location is the first thing to ask.

38. **The correct answer is (A).** According to the information provided, your next course of action is to find out how long the alarm has been ringing.

39. **The correct answer is (B).** According to the information provided, the last thing you need to know is the name and address of the caller.

40. **The correct answer is (D).** Rules are rules. Even though Marisol Gonzalez may have been perfectly able to handle this caller and perfectly correct in her choice of referral, she was not permitted to carry through with this call.

41. **The correct answer is (C).** Even though this report neglects the fact that the car had out-of-state plates, it is clearly the most complete and accurate. Choice (D) identifies the witness by name and address but does not give the location of the accident.

42. **The correct answer is (B).** A boarded-up building *should* be empty, but squatters often take advantage of such shelter. There is a real possibility that someone may be trapped inside. The question at step 5 is a very important one and must not be overlooked.

43. **The correct answer is (D).** Choose the answer through elimination. Color is not the determinant; people's

descriptions of colors vary. However, Ford and Mercury are built by the same company, and three witnesses agree that it was one of these two makes, so eliminate the Buick in choice (B). Three witnesses agree that it was a 2-door car, so eliminate choice (C). You are left with choices (A) and (D). The plate numbers are similar. Two witnesses identified the plate as being from New Jersey, so Mullins should go with choice (D).

44. **The correct answer is (C).** With important information in hand, the operator must transmit all details to police and emergency medical services. The police or ambulance crew will take over notifying the receiving hospital of unique circumstances.

45. **The correct answer is (B).** It is important that the right name be connected with the right address, the location of the occurrence be reported accurately, and the dog be described as completely as possible.

46. **The correct answer is (A).** To be useful, the information must be organized, complete, and correct.

47. **The correct answer is (C).** An open question such as "What do they look like?" satisfies the requirement of 3a and helps the operator determine if this is a dangerous delusion. If the caller reports that there are 8 little green men, each 2 feet high and waving a flag, there need be less concern than if the caller "sees" 15 creatures that look like gorillas and are carrying machine guns.

48. **The correct answer is (C).** Operators should be aware that not all calls to 911 represent an emergency. Police are not elevator repairmen. If the elevator is not working in an hour, the police still can't help. The superintendent or landlord is responsible for repairs to the building. A professional operator does not hang up on a caller, regardless of the nature of the call.

49. **The correct answer is (B).** Choice (D) is also accurate, but choice (B) is clearer and more easily interpreted. Choices (A) and (C) are garbled.

50. **The correct answer is (D).** You, or the operator next to you, should not be giving out this type of information because this does not involve 911. A parking hotline is set up to give callers this information.

51. **The correct answer is (C).** See the second sentence.

52. **The correct answer is (B).** From 8 to 15 years of service, the annual leave is 25 days.

53. **The correct answer is (C).** The sixteenth year, in which leave is earned at the rate of 2-1/4 days per month, comes after fifteen full years.

54. **The correct answer is (B).** See the first sentence of the second paragraph.

55. **The correct answer is (A).** See the last sentence.

56. **The correct answer is (D).** This is a situation for emergency medical services, paramedics, or ambulances. While police might easily be called to this scene as well, you must consider the question in light of the other answer choices. All others are strictly police concerns.

57. **The correct answer is (B).** This statement gives a full description of the child and the location at which he was found. None of the others is so complete.

58. **The correct answer is (C).** According to procedure, the first question to ask is the location of the bank.

59. **The correct answer is (D).** The bank name is the second thing you should ask for, according to the procedure.

60. **The correct answer is (B).** According to procedure, after obtaining a description of the bank robber, you then should ask for a description of the weapon(s).

answers practice test 1

61. **The correct answer is (A).** The complaint about another operator can only be handled by the supervisor. The hot water call is a non-emergency referral to the buildings department or the health department. Police and emergency squads should be rushed to the scene of the helicopter crash, and the fire department should be dispatched to the toy factory.

62. **The correct answer is (C).** Sarah Small is calling from her office, and step 5 requires the operator to obtain location and telephone number from which the call is being made. There is no stated qualification that fireboats need not be alerted if there is no fire. Fire could break out at any time. However, it is important for the operator to be able to tell the fireboats that there is no fire right now, so that they can determine which boats and how many to send.

63. **The correct answer is (D).** This report is correct and complete. Choice (A) gives neither description nor address; choice (B) misses describing the perpetrator; and choice (C) describes the man incorrectly and omits the location.

64. **The correct answer is (B).** Since Sirhan Amin is handling another emergency call, the conditions of step 4b lead directly to step 5. Operator Hyacinth must now obtain additional information about the caller and the premises involved. It would be entirely reasonable for her to tell the caller that the police are on the way, but that is not the next step on the mandated order of procedure.

65. **The correct answer is (B).** The armed robber is only threatening—not hurting—his victims, so they do not require an ambulance. A police car should be sent to intercept the robber. The unconscious jogger clearly requires an ambulance. The child who was fallen from the swing may have sustained a back injury that should be handled only by a trained ambulance crew, not by a police car. Similarly, the eye injury might be a detached retina, so the teenager should be moved with care.

66. **The correct answer is (B).** This arrangement allows for the best distribution. The activity is taking place in the first and second precincts, so they can spare the greatest number of cars from regular patrol. Those cars could rapidly be redirected if necessary. Choice (A) takes too many cars from regular patrol; choice (C) takes too many from the fourth, which cannot spare them, and none at all from the sixth, which can; Choice (D) makes no sense. The bulk of the protection should be supplied from within the precincts involved.

67. **The correct answer is (C).** This question takes some thinking. Since speed is of the essence and the sixth precinct is far away, eliminate choice (D). Many of the cars from the first and second are guarding the president. Pulling them from the motorcade would take time; sending so many of the remaining cars to one spot would underprotect the remainder of the precincts. The fourth is close by. While the fourth will have difficulty sparing 8 cars, it did start with 40 before the president came to town, so presumably will not be left with no police protection.

68. **The correct answer is (A).** The problem is in the fourth precinct, which is a geographically small area. More cars from the fourth can help to quell the riot. There are no motorcycles in the fourth; however, motorcycles move quickly in narrow areas, so they should be called in. Generally, a riot culminates with a roundup of rioters. Paddy wagons will be needed. Sharpshooters, dogs, and the bomb squad would be inappropriate for a riot. Mounted police are very helpful in crowd control, but they must be planned for well in advance. Mounted police are for parades and rock concerts, not for riots.

69. The correct answer is (D). The sixth precinct could use help from the Narcotics Unit, which is based in the fourth, and from the Canine Unit (for sniffing drugs), which is based in the fifth.

70. The correct answer is (C). The question indicates private ownership. The answer presupposes that the dispatcher will know that since no citizen owns the premises of municipal, state or federal buildings, a citizen would not be calling from the second precinct. Of the precincts that a citizen would be calling from, the third precinct is the least likely because buildings in the third precinct have doormen and other security. Thus, burglars are least likely to have gained access there.

71. The correct answer is (D). There is not much information to report, but it must be totally accurate and complete. Choice (A) makes an unwarranted assumption. We know only how long the timer was set for, not when it was set. Choice (B) makes a similar leap. Choice (C) does not impart the urgency required.

72. The correct answer is (B). This disaster requires massive response. The local police precinct cannot handle it alone. Following the prescribed order of calls, Kimberly Kane must next call out the police citywide, then alert hospitals, then bring in the state police for further assistance.

73. The correct answer is (C). This is harassment, since no injury was sustained.

74. The correct answer is (B). When someone enters a building with the intent to commit a crime, it is a burglary.

75. The correct answer is (D). If there is intent to damage another's property, it would be considered criminal mischief.

76. The correct answer is (A). Because her property was taken from her by force, it would be considered a robbery.

77. The correct answer is (B). The driver avoided payment for services, and thus, it was a theft of service.

78. The correct answer is (A). He is harassing her by means of a telecommunications device and, according to the definitions, this is aggravated harassment.

79. The correct answer is (A). Choice (B) leaves out the critical time of day; choice (C) omits phone number and address; choice (D) is garbled.

80. The correct answer is (B). A fever of 105 degrees constitutes illness. The health department should be notified.

ANSWER SHEET PRACTICE TEST 2

Part One

1. Ⓐ Ⓑ Ⓒ Ⓓ Ⓔ 31. Ⓐ Ⓑ Ⓒ Ⓓ Ⓔ 61. Ⓐ Ⓑ Ⓒ Ⓓ Ⓔ 91. Ⓐ Ⓑ Ⓒ Ⓓ Ⓔ
2. Ⓐ Ⓑ Ⓒ Ⓓ Ⓔ 32. Ⓐ Ⓑ Ⓒ Ⓓ Ⓔ 62. Ⓐ Ⓑ Ⓒ Ⓓ Ⓔ 92. Ⓐ Ⓑ Ⓒ Ⓓ Ⓔ
3. Ⓐ Ⓑ Ⓒ Ⓓ Ⓔ 33. Ⓐ Ⓑ Ⓒ Ⓓ Ⓔ 63. Ⓐ Ⓑ Ⓒ Ⓓ Ⓔ 93. Ⓐ Ⓑ Ⓒ Ⓓ Ⓔ
4. Ⓐ Ⓑ Ⓒ Ⓓ Ⓔ 34. Ⓐ Ⓑ Ⓒ Ⓓ Ⓔ 64. Ⓐ Ⓑ Ⓒ Ⓓ Ⓔ 94. Ⓐ Ⓑ Ⓒ Ⓓ Ⓔ
5. Ⓐ Ⓑ Ⓒ Ⓓ Ⓔ 35. Ⓐ Ⓑ Ⓒ Ⓓ Ⓔ 65. Ⓐ Ⓑ Ⓒ Ⓓ Ⓔ 95. Ⓐ Ⓑ Ⓒ Ⓓ Ⓔ
6. Ⓐ Ⓑ Ⓒ Ⓓ Ⓔ 36. Ⓐ Ⓑ Ⓒ Ⓓ Ⓔ 66. Ⓐ Ⓑ Ⓒ Ⓓ Ⓔ 96. Ⓐ Ⓑ Ⓒ Ⓓ Ⓔ
7. Ⓐ Ⓑ Ⓒ Ⓓ Ⓔ 37. Ⓐ Ⓑ Ⓒ Ⓓ Ⓔ 67. Ⓐ Ⓑ Ⓒ Ⓓ Ⓔ 97. Ⓐ Ⓑ Ⓒ Ⓓ Ⓔ
8. Ⓐ Ⓑ Ⓒ Ⓓ Ⓔ 38. Ⓐ Ⓑ Ⓒ Ⓓ Ⓔ 68. Ⓐ Ⓑ Ⓒ Ⓓ Ⓔ 98. Ⓐ Ⓑ Ⓒ Ⓓ Ⓔ
9. Ⓐ Ⓑ Ⓒ Ⓓ Ⓔ 39. Ⓐ Ⓑ Ⓒ Ⓓ Ⓔ 69. Ⓐ Ⓑ Ⓒ Ⓓ Ⓔ 99. Ⓐ Ⓑ Ⓒ Ⓓ Ⓔ
10. Ⓐ Ⓑ Ⓒ Ⓓ Ⓔ 40. Ⓐ Ⓑ Ⓒ Ⓓ Ⓔ 70. Ⓐ Ⓑ Ⓒ Ⓓ Ⓔ 100. Ⓐ Ⓑ Ⓒ Ⓓ Ⓔ
11. Ⓐ Ⓑ Ⓒ Ⓓ Ⓔ 41. Ⓐ Ⓑ Ⓒ Ⓓ Ⓔ 71. Ⓐ Ⓑ Ⓒ Ⓓ Ⓔ 101. Ⓐ Ⓑ Ⓒ Ⓓ Ⓔ
12. Ⓐ Ⓑ Ⓒ Ⓓ Ⓔ 42. Ⓐ Ⓑ Ⓒ Ⓓ Ⓔ 72. Ⓐ Ⓑ Ⓒ Ⓓ Ⓔ 102. Ⓐ Ⓑ Ⓒ Ⓓ Ⓔ
13. Ⓐ Ⓑ Ⓒ Ⓓ Ⓔ 43. Ⓐ Ⓑ Ⓒ Ⓓ Ⓔ 73. Ⓐ Ⓑ Ⓒ Ⓓ Ⓔ 103. Ⓐ Ⓑ Ⓒ Ⓓ Ⓔ
14. Ⓐ Ⓑ Ⓒ Ⓓ Ⓔ 44. Ⓐ Ⓑ Ⓒ Ⓓ Ⓔ 74. Ⓐ Ⓑ Ⓒ Ⓓ Ⓔ 104. Ⓐ Ⓑ Ⓒ Ⓓ Ⓔ
15. Ⓐ Ⓑ Ⓒ Ⓓ Ⓔ 45. Ⓐ Ⓑ Ⓒ Ⓓ Ⓔ 75. Ⓐ Ⓑ Ⓒ Ⓓ Ⓔ 105. Ⓐ Ⓑ Ⓒ Ⓓ Ⓔ
16. Ⓐ Ⓑ Ⓒ Ⓓ Ⓔ 46. Ⓐ Ⓑ Ⓒ Ⓓ Ⓔ 76. Ⓐ Ⓑ Ⓒ Ⓓ Ⓔ 106. Ⓐ Ⓑ Ⓒ Ⓓ Ⓔ
17. Ⓐ Ⓑ Ⓒ Ⓓ Ⓔ 47. Ⓐ Ⓑ Ⓒ Ⓓ Ⓔ 77. Ⓐ Ⓑ Ⓒ Ⓓ Ⓔ 107. Ⓐ Ⓑ Ⓒ Ⓓ Ⓔ
18. Ⓐ Ⓑ Ⓒ Ⓓ Ⓔ 48. Ⓐ Ⓑ Ⓒ Ⓓ Ⓔ 78. Ⓐ Ⓑ Ⓒ Ⓓ Ⓔ 108. Ⓐ Ⓑ Ⓒ Ⓓ Ⓔ
19. Ⓐ Ⓑ Ⓒ Ⓓ Ⓔ 49. Ⓐ Ⓑ Ⓒ Ⓓ Ⓔ 79. Ⓐ Ⓑ Ⓒ Ⓓ Ⓔ 109. Ⓐ Ⓑ Ⓒ Ⓓ Ⓔ
20. Ⓐ Ⓑ Ⓒ Ⓓ Ⓔ 50. Ⓐ Ⓑ Ⓒ Ⓓ Ⓔ 80. Ⓐ Ⓑ Ⓒ Ⓓ Ⓔ 110. Ⓐ Ⓑ Ⓒ Ⓓ Ⓔ
21. Ⓐ Ⓑ Ⓒ Ⓓ Ⓔ 51. Ⓐ Ⓑ Ⓒ Ⓓ Ⓔ 81. Ⓐ Ⓑ Ⓒ Ⓓ Ⓔ 111. Ⓐ Ⓑ Ⓒ Ⓓ Ⓔ
22. Ⓐ Ⓑ Ⓒ Ⓓ Ⓔ 52. Ⓐ Ⓑ Ⓒ Ⓓ Ⓔ 82. Ⓐ Ⓑ Ⓒ Ⓓ Ⓔ 112. Ⓐ Ⓑ Ⓒ Ⓓ Ⓔ
23. Ⓐ Ⓑ Ⓒ Ⓓ Ⓔ 53. Ⓐ Ⓑ Ⓒ Ⓓ Ⓔ 83. Ⓐ Ⓑ Ⓒ Ⓓ Ⓔ 113. Ⓐ Ⓑ Ⓒ Ⓓ Ⓔ
24. Ⓐ Ⓑ Ⓒ Ⓓ Ⓔ 54. Ⓐ Ⓑ Ⓒ Ⓓ Ⓔ 84. Ⓐ Ⓑ Ⓒ Ⓓ Ⓔ 114. Ⓐ Ⓑ Ⓒ Ⓓ Ⓔ
25. Ⓐ Ⓑ Ⓒ Ⓓ Ⓔ 55. Ⓐ Ⓑ Ⓒ Ⓓ Ⓔ 85. Ⓐ Ⓑ Ⓒ Ⓓ Ⓔ 115. Ⓐ Ⓑ Ⓒ Ⓓ Ⓔ
26. Ⓐ Ⓑ Ⓒ Ⓓ Ⓔ 56. Ⓐ Ⓑ Ⓒ Ⓓ Ⓔ 86. Ⓐ Ⓑ Ⓒ Ⓓ Ⓔ 116. Ⓐ Ⓑ Ⓒ Ⓓ Ⓔ
27. Ⓐ Ⓑ Ⓒ Ⓓ Ⓔ 57. Ⓐ Ⓑ Ⓒ Ⓓ Ⓔ 87. Ⓐ Ⓑ Ⓒ Ⓓ Ⓔ 117. Ⓐ Ⓑ Ⓒ Ⓓ Ⓔ
28. Ⓐ Ⓑ Ⓒ Ⓓ Ⓔ 58. Ⓐ Ⓑ Ⓒ Ⓓ Ⓔ 88. Ⓐ Ⓑ Ⓒ Ⓓ Ⓔ 118. Ⓐ Ⓑ Ⓒ Ⓓ Ⓔ
29. Ⓐ Ⓑ Ⓒ Ⓓ Ⓔ 59. Ⓐ Ⓑ Ⓒ Ⓓ Ⓔ 89. Ⓐ Ⓑ Ⓒ Ⓓ Ⓔ 119. Ⓐ Ⓑ Ⓒ Ⓓ Ⓔ
30. Ⓐ Ⓑ Ⓒ Ⓓ Ⓔ 60. Ⓐ Ⓑ Ⓒ Ⓓ Ⓔ 90. Ⓐ Ⓑ Ⓒ Ⓓ Ⓔ 120. Ⓐ Ⓑ Ⓒ Ⓓ Ⓔ

ANSWER SHEET PRACTICE TEST 2

Part Two

1. Ⓐ Ⓑ Ⓒ Ⓓ Ⓔ
2. Ⓐ Ⓑ Ⓒ Ⓓ Ⓔ
3. Ⓐ Ⓑ Ⓒ Ⓓ Ⓔ
4. Ⓐ Ⓑ Ⓒ Ⓓ Ⓔ
5. Ⓐ Ⓑ Ⓒ Ⓓ Ⓔ
6. Ⓐ Ⓑ Ⓒ Ⓓ Ⓔ
7. Ⓐ Ⓑ Ⓒ Ⓓ Ⓔ
8. Ⓐ Ⓑ Ⓒ Ⓓ Ⓔ
9. Ⓐ Ⓑ Ⓒ Ⓓ Ⓔ
10. Ⓐ Ⓑ Ⓒ Ⓓ Ⓔ
11. Ⓐ Ⓑ Ⓒ Ⓓ Ⓔ
12. Ⓐ Ⓑ Ⓒ Ⓓ Ⓔ
13. Ⓐ Ⓑ Ⓒ Ⓓ Ⓔ
14. Ⓐ Ⓑ Ⓒ Ⓓ Ⓔ
15. Ⓐ Ⓑ Ⓒ Ⓓ Ⓔ
16. Ⓐ Ⓑ Ⓒ Ⓓ Ⓔ
17. Ⓐ Ⓑ Ⓒ Ⓓ Ⓔ
18. Ⓐ Ⓑ Ⓒ Ⓓ Ⓔ
19. Ⓐ Ⓑ Ⓒ Ⓓ Ⓔ
20. Ⓐ Ⓑ Ⓒ Ⓓ Ⓔ
21. Ⓐ Ⓑ Ⓒ Ⓓ Ⓔ
22. Ⓐ Ⓑ Ⓒ Ⓓ Ⓔ
23. Ⓐ Ⓑ Ⓒ Ⓓ Ⓔ

24. Ⓐ Ⓑ Ⓒ Ⓓ Ⓔ
25. Ⓐ Ⓑ Ⓒ Ⓓ Ⓔ
26. Ⓐ Ⓑ Ⓒ Ⓓ Ⓔ
27. Ⓐ Ⓑ Ⓒ Ⓓ Ⓔ
28. Ⓐ Ⓑ Ⓒ Ⓓ Ⓔ
29. Ⓐ Ⓑ Ⓒ Ⓓ Ⓔ
30. Ⓐ Ⓑ Ⓒ Ⓓ Ⓔ
31. Ⓐ Ⓑ Ⓒ Ⓓ Ⓔ
32. Ⓐ Ⓑ Ⓒ Ⓓ Ⓔ
33. Ⓐ Ⓑ Ⓒ Ⓓ Ⓔ
34. Ⓐ Ⓑ Ⓒ Ⓓ Ⓔ
35. Ⓐ Ⓑ Ⓒ Ⓓ Ⓔ
36. Ⓐ Ⓑ Ⓒ Ⓓ Ⓔ
37. Ⓐ Ⓑ Ⓒ Ⓓ Ⓔ
38. Ⓐ Ⓑ Ⓒ Ⓓ Ⓔ
39. Ⓐ Ⓑ Ⓒ Ⓓ Ⓔ
40. Ⓐ Ⓑ Ⓒ Ⓓ Ⓔ
41. Ⓐ Ⓑ Ⓒ Ⓓ Ⓔ
42. Ⓐ Ⓑ Ⓒ Ⓓ Ⓔ
43. Ⓐ Ⓑ Ⓒ Ⓓ Ⓔ
44. Ⓐ Ⓑ Ⓒ Ⓓ Ⓔ
45. Ⓐ Ⓑ Ⓒ Ⓓ Ⓔ
46. Ⓐ Ⓑ Ⓒ Ⓓ Ⓔ

47. Ⓐ Ⓑ Ⓒ Ⓓ Ⓔ
48. Ⓐ Ⓑ Ⓒ Ⓓ Ⓔ
49. Ⓐ Ⓑ Ⓒ Ⓓ Ⓔ
50. Ⓐ Ⓑ Ⓒ Ⓓ Ⓔ
51. Ⓐ Ⓑ Ⓒ Ⓓ Ⓔ
52. Ⓐ Ⓑ Ⓒ Ⓓ Ⓔ
53. Ⓐ Ⓑ Ⓒ Ⓓ Ⓔ
54. Ⓐ Ⓑ Ⓒ Ⓓ Ⓔ
55. Ⓐ Ⓑ Ⓒ Ⓓ Ⓔ
56. Ⓐ Ⓑ Ⓒ Ⓓ Ⓔ
57. Ⓐ Ⓑ Ⓒ Ⓓ Ⓔ
58. Ⓐ Ⓑ Ⓒ Ⓓ Ⓔ
59. Ⓐ Ⓑ Ⓒ Ⓓ Ⓔ
60. Ⓐ Ⓑ Ⓒ Ⓓ Ⓔ
61. Ⓐ Ⓑ Ⓒ Ⓓ Ⓔ
62. Ⓐ Ⓑ Ⓒ Ⓓ Ⓔ
63. Ⓐ Ⓑ Ⓒ Ⓓ Ⓔ
64. Ⓐ Ⓑ Ⓒ Ⓓ Ⓔ
65. Ⓐ Ⓑ Ⓒ Ⓓ Ⓔ
66. Ⓐ Ⓑ Ⓒ Ⓓ Ⓔ
67. Ⓐ Ⓑ Ⓒ Ⓓ Ⓔ
68. Ⓐ Ⓑ Ⓒ Ⓓ Ⓔ
69. Ⓐ Ⓑ Ⓒ Ⓓ Ⓔ

70. Ⓐ Ⓑ Ⓒ Ⓓ Ⓔ
71. Ⓐ Ⓑ Ⓒ Ⓓ Ⓔ
72. Ⓐ Ⓑ Ⓒ Ⓓ Ⓔ
73. Ⓐ Ⓑ Ⓒ Ⓓ Ⓔ
74. Ⓐ Ⓑ Ⓒ Ⓓ Ⓔ
75. Ⓐ Ⓑ Ⓒ Ⓓ Ⓔ
76. Ⓐ Ⓑ Ⓒ Ⓓ Ⓔ
77. Ⓐ Ⓑ Ⓒ Ⓓ Ⓔ
78. Ⓐ Ⓑ Ⓒ Ⓓ Ⓔ
79. Ⓐ Ⓑ Ⓒ Ⓓ Ⓔ
80. Ⓐ Ⓑ Ⓒ Ⓓ Ⓔ
81. Ⓐ Ⓑ Ⓒ Ⓓ Ⓔ
82. Ⓐ Ⓑ Ⓒ Ⓓ Ⓔ
83. Ⓐ Ⓑ Ⓒ Ⓓ Ⓔ
84. Ⓐ Ⓑ Ⓒ Ⓓ Ⓔ
85. Ⓐ Ⓑ Ⓒ Ⓓ Ⓔ
86. Ⓐ Ⓑ Ⓒ Ⓓ Ⓔ
87. Ⓐ Ⓑ Ⓒ Ⓓ Ⓔ
88. Ⓐ Ⓑ Ⓒ Ⓓ Ⓔ
89. Ⓐ Ⓑ Ⓒ Ⓓ Ⓔ
90. Ⓐ Ⓑ Ⓒ Ⓓ Ⓔ

FOLLOWING ORAL DIRECTIONS: WORKSHEET

25 Minutes

Directions: While listening carefully to each set of instructions, mark each item on this worksheet as directed. Then complete each question by marking the answer sheet as directed. For each answer, you will darken the answer for a number-letter combination. Should you fall behind and miss an instruction, don't be alarmed. Let that one go and listen for the next one. When you start to darken a space number, if you find that you have already darkened another space for that number, either erase the first mark and darken the space for the new combination or let the first mark stay and do not darken a space for the new combination. Write with a pencil that has a clean eraser. When you finish, you should have no more than one space darkened for each number.

1. 59   35   62   58   8

2.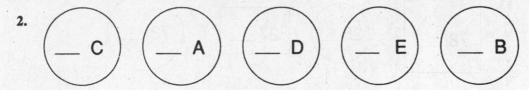

3. 15 _____   20 _____

4. [83 __]   [37 __]   [36 __]   CURE   DAMP   BEAR

5. A   C   B   A   B   D   C   E   D

6. [48 __]   [28 __]   [22 __]   [43 __]

7. 51 _____   69 _____   50 _____

8.

65 ___   13 ___   87 ___   31 ___   17 ___

9.

55 ___   44 ___   74 ___   25 ___

10.   40   85   17   87   52   55   80   45   75

11.

65 ___   37 ___   12 ___   4 ___

12.   X O O O X O O X X O X O X

13.

78 ___   25 ___   27 ___   73 ___

14.   88   2   69   84   34

15.

63 ___   38 ___   76 ___   53 ___   57 ___

16.

435 ___ B   466 ___ C   474 ___ E   467 ___ A   489 ___ D

17.   79 _____   39 _____

18.

___ C   ___ E   ___ A   ___ D   ___ B

Practice Test 2

Part One

120 Questions • 150 minutes

> **Directions:** Choose the best answer to each question and darken its letter on your answer sheet.

1. FLEXIBLE means most nearly
   - (A) breakable.
   - (B) flammable.
   - (C) pliable.
   - (D) weak.

2. OPTION means most nearly
   - (A) use.
   - (B) choice.
   - (C) value.
   - (D) blame.

3. To VERIFY means most nearly to
   - (A) examine.
   - (B) explain.
   - (C) confirm.
   - (D) guarantee.

4. INDOLENT means most nearly
   - (A) moderate.
   - (B) hopeless.
   - (C) selfish.
   - (D) lazy.

5. RESPIRATION means most nearly
   - (A) recovery.
   - (B) breathing.
   - (C) pulsation.
   - (D) sweating.

Directions: Find the correct spelling of the word, and darken the proper answer space. If no suggested spelling is correct, darken space (E).

6. (A) corregated
   (B) corrigated
   (C) corrugated
   (D) corriegated
   (E) none of these

7. (A) accumalation
   (B) accumulation
   (C) accumullation
   (D) accumilation
   (E) none of these

8. (A) consumation
   (B) consumeation
   (C) consummation
   (D) consummacion
   (E) none of these

9. (A) retorical
   (B) rhetorrical
   (C) rehtoricle
   (D) retoricle
   (E) none of these

10. (A) hieght
    (B) height
    (C) heighth
    (D) hieghth
    (E) none of these

Directions: Compare the names or numbers and darken on your answer sheet the letter

(A) if ALL THREE names or numbers are exactly ALIKE.

(B) if only the FIRST and SECOND names or numbers are exactly ALIKE.

(C) if only the FIRST and THIRD names or numbers are exactly ALIKE.

(D) if only the SECOND and THIRD names or numbers are exactly ALIKE.

(E) if ALL THREE names or numbers are DIFFERENT.

11. Robert F. Taft	Robert F. Taft	Robert P. Taft
12. Eduardo Ingles	Eduardo Inglese	Eduardo Inglese
13. Roger T. DeAngelis	Roger T. D'Angelis	Roger T. DeAngeles
14. 7692138	7692138	7692138
15. 2633342	2633432	2363342

Directions: Choose the best answer to each question, and darken its letter on your answer sheet.

16. VIGILANT means most nearly
    (A) sensible.
    (B) watchful.
    (C) suspicious.
    (D) restless.
    (E) unhappy.

17. VEGETATION means most nearly
    (A) food.
    (B) plant life.
    (C) moisture.
    (D) bird life.
    (E) mixture.

18. MARSHY means most nearly
    (A) swampy.
    (B) sandy.
    (C) wooded.
    (D) rocky.
    (E) soft.

19. INCIDENTAL means most nearly
    (A) independent.
    (B) needless.
    (C) infrequent.
    (D) casual.
    (E) happening.

20. PREFACE means most nearly
    (A) title page.
    (B) introduction.
    (C) table of contents.
    (D) appendix.
    (E) justification.

Directions: Find the correct spelling of the word, and darken the proper answer space. If no suggesting spelling is correct, darken space (E).

21. (A) faciliatate
    (B) facilitate
    (C) faceilitate
    (D) fasilitate
    (E) none of these

22. (A) proletarian
    (B) prolatarian
    (C) proleterian
    (D) prolaterian
    (E) none of these

23. (A) occasionally
    (B) occassionally
    (C) ocasionally

    (D) occasionaly
    (E) none of these

24. (A) esential
    (B) essential
    (C) essencial
    (D) essensial
    (E) none of these

25. (A) ommision
    (B) omission
    (C) ommission
    (D) omitsion
    (E) none of these

Directions: Compare the names or numbers and darken:

(A) if ALL THREE names or numbers are exactly ALIKE.

(B) if only the FIRST and SECOND names or numbers are exactly ALIKE.

(C) if only the FIRST and THIRD names or numbers are exactly ALIKE.

(D) if only the SECOND and THIRD names or numbers are exactly ALIKE.

(E) if ALL THREE names or numbers are DIFFERENT.

26. Yoshihito Saito	Yoshito Saito	Yoshihito Saito
27. Helmut V. Lochner	Helmut V. Lockner	Helmut W. Lochner
28. 2454803	2548403	2454803
29. 9670243	9670423	9670423
30. 2789350	2789350	2798350

Directions: Read the paragraph and the five suggested answers to the question. Choose the answer that is best supported by the paragraph, and darken the proper space on the answer sheet.

31. Through advertising, manufacturers exercise a high degree of control over consumers' desires. However, the manufacturer assumes enormous risks in attempting to predict what consumers will want, and in producing goods in quantity and distributing them in advance of final selection by the consumers.

The paragraph best supports the statement that manufacturers

(A) can eliminate the risk of overproduction by advertising.

(B) distribute goods directly to the consumers.

(C) must depend upon the final consumers for the success of their undertakings.

(D) can predict with great accuracy the success of any product they put on the market.

(E) can produce whatever consumers want, whenever they want.

32. Economy once in a while is just not enough. I expect to find it at every level of responsibility, from cabinet member to the newest and youngest recruit. Controlling waste is something like bailing out a boat: you have to keep at it. I have no intention of easing up on my insistence on getting a dollar's worth of value for each dollar we spend.

The paragraph best supports the statement that

(A) we need not be concerned about items that cost less than a dollar.

(B) it is advisable to buy the cheaper of two items.

(C) the responsibility of economy is greater at high levels than at low levels.

(D) economy is a continual responsibility.

(E) bailing out a boat is economical.

33. What constitutes skill in any line of work is not always easy to determine; economy of time must be carefully distinguished from economy of energy, as the quickest method may require the greatest expenditure of muscular effort, and it may not be essential or at all desirable.

The paragraph best supports the statement that

(A) the most efficiently executed task is not always the one done in the shortest time.

(B) energy and time cannot both be conserved in performing a single task.

(C) a task is well done when it is performed in the shortest time.

(D) skill in performing a task should not be acquired at the expense of time.

(E) more effort and time put into a task will guarantee success.

34. It is a common assumption that city directories are prepared and published by the cities concerned. However, the directory business is as much a private business as is the publishing of dictionaries and encyclopedias. The companies financing the publication make their profits through the sales of the directories themselves and through the advertising in them.

The paragraph best supports the statement that

(A) the publication of a city directory is a commercial enterprise.

(B) the size of a city directory limits the space devoted to advertising.

(C) many city directories are published by dictionary and encyclopedia concerns.

(D) city directories are sold at cost to local residents and business people.

(E) city directories are published by nonprofit organizations.

35. It is difficult to distinguish between bookkeeping and accounting. In attempts to do so, bookkeeping is called the art, and accounting the science, of recording business transactions. Bookkeeping gives the history of the business in a systematic manner and accounting classifies, analyzes, and interprets the facts thus recorded.

The paragraph best supports the statement that

(A) accounting is less systematic than bookkeeping.

(B) accounting and bookkeeping are closely related.

(C) bookkeeping and accounting cannot be distinguished from one another.

(D) bookkeeping has been superseded by accounting.

(E) science is more important than art, especially in business.

36. "White collar" is a term used to describe one of the largest groups of workers in American industry and trade. It distinguishes those who work with the pencil and the mind from those who depend on their hands and the machine. It suggests occupations in which physical exertion and handling of materials are not primary features of the job.

The paragraph best supports the statement that "white collar" workers are

(A) not so strong physically as those who work with their hands.

(B) those who supervise workers handling materials.

(C) all whose work is entirely indoors.

(D) not likely to use heavy machines so much as are other groups of workers.

(E) a rapidly expanding minority in American labor.

37. Any business not provided with capable substitutes to fill all-important positions is a weak business. Therefore, a supervisor should train each worker not only to perform his or her own particular duties but also to do those of two or three positions.

The paragraph best supports the statement that

(A) dependence on substitutes is a sign of a weak organization.

(B) training will improve the strongest organization.

(C) the supervisor should be the most expert at any particular job under him or her.

(D) vacancies in vital positions should be provided for in advance.

(E) a weak business should hire more substitutes.

38. Some fire-resistant buildings, although wholly constructed of materials that will not burn, may be completely gutted by the spread of fire through their contents by way of hallways and other openings. They may even suffer serious structural damage by the collapse of metal beams and columns.

The paragraph best supports the statement that some fire-resistant buildings

(A) can be damaged seriously by fire.

(B) have specially constructed halls and doors.

(C) afford less protection to their contents than would ordinary buildings.

(D) will burn readily.

(E) are not structurally sound.

39. According to Congressman Johnson, "Too much of our taxpayers' money is spent on the rehabilitation of drug addicts. This is no way to solve the problem. Most of the people who spend time in rehabilitation centers go right back to taking narcotics after they leave. Instead of wasting money on rehabilitation, we should be using it to get rid of the drug peddlers."

The paragraph best supports the statement that Congressman Johnson implies that the way to solve the problem of drug addiction is to

(A) create more rehabilitation centers.

(B) do away with rehabilitation centers.

(C) put drug addicts in jail.

(D) tax drug peddlers.

(E) eliminate the source of the drugs.

40. When gas is leaking, any spark or sudden flame can ignite it. This can create a "flashback," which burns off the gas in a quick puff of smoke and flame. But the real danger is in a large leak that can cause an explosion.

    The paragraph best supports the statement that the real danger from leaking gas is a(n)

    (A) flashback.

    (B) puff of smoke and flame.

    (C) explosion.

    (D) spark.

    (E) ignition.

41. The indiscriminate or continual use of any drug without medical supervision is dangerous. Even drugs considered harmless may result in chronic poisoning if used for a period of years. Prescriptions should not be refilled without consulting your doctor. A given amount was prescribed in order to limit your use of the drug to a certain time. Never use a drug prescribed for someone else just because your symptoms appear similar. There may be differences, apparent to an expert but hidden from you, that indicate an entirely different ailment requiring different medication.

    The paragraph best supports the statement that

    (A) the use of drugs is very dangerous.

    (B) if a physician prescribes a drug, it is safe to refill the prescription.

    (C) people with similar symptoms are usually suffering from the same ailment.

    (D) a drug considered harmless may be dangerous if taken over a long period of time without supervision.

    (E) doctors always limit the use of prescription drugs to a definite period of time.

42. Civilization started to move ahead more rapidly when people freed themselves of the shackles that restricted their search for the truth.

    The statement best supports the idea that the progress of civilization

    (A) came as a result of people's dislike for obstacles.

    (B) did not begin until restrictions on learning were removed.

    (C) has been aided by people's efforts to find the truth.

    (D) is based on continually increasing efforts.

    (E) was enhanced when slavery was abolished.

43. Federal investigators must direct their whole effort toward success in their work. If they wish to succeed in each investigation, their work will be by no means easy, smooth, or peaceful; on the contrary, they will have to devote themselves completely and continuously to a task that requires all their ability.

    The paragraph best supports the statement that an investigator's success depends most upon

    (A) ambition to advance rapidly in the service.

    (B) persistence in the face of difficulty.

    (C) training and experience.

    (D) willingness to obey orders without delay.

    (E) superior ability.

44. Since the government can spend only what it obtains from the people and this amount is ultimately limited by their capacity and willingness to pay taxes, it is very important that the people be given full information about the work of the government.

The paragraph best supports the statement that

(A) governmental employees should be trained not only in their own work, but also in how to perform the duties of other employees in their agency.

(B) taxation by the government rests upon the consent of the people.

(C) the release of full information on the work of the government will increase the efficiency of governmental operations.

(D) the work of the government, in recent years has been restricted because of reduced tax collections.

(E) the foundation of our government is abhorrence of the principle of taxation without representation.

45. Foreign-born adults hold on to the habits, preferences, and loyalties of their homelands. Their speech, if they learn English at all, reflects the accent and idiom of their land of origin. Children, on the other hand, acquire English without a trace of accent and, through their playmates and school life, learn to prefer American clothing and mannerisms to the customs and dress of their parents.

The paragraph best supports the statement that

(A) American customs are more complicated than the customs of other countries.

(B) immigrant children do not respect their parents.

(C) it is nearly impossible for foreigners to adopt American ways.

(D) foreign-born adults seldom learn English.

(E) foreign-born children become Americanized more quickly than their parents.

Directions: Compare two versions of the same sentence. Which of the following is more clearly written?

46. (A) Annette crashes into Karla's car during rush hour on the highway. She calls the police.

(B) During rush hour, Annette crashes into Karla's car on the highway and immediately calls the police.

47. (A) Officer Lee filed a police report after taking a call from a witness.

(B) Officer Lee spoke to a witness. He filed police report and took a call.

48. (A) Patricia heard the window shatter. Two men were breaking into her apartment building.

(B) She heard the window shatter and from the sound, it was being broken into.

ANSWER QUESTIONS 49–51 BASED ON THE FOLLOWING INFORMATION.

Directions: You will have 3 minutes to review this information. After reading the bulletin, answer the questions from memory.

March 10–14 Notable Incidents

Burglary:
On Saturday morning, March 14th, a middle-aged couple robbed Lester's Jewelry Store of more than $50,000 worth of diamonds. Owner Lester McIntyre reported that necklaces, earrings, and bracelets were among the stolen items.

Deceptive Practices:
Robert Taylor of 32 Maple Street cashed fraudulent checks at Bank of America on March 10th. He received $6,500 before the manager realized the checks were fake.

Disorderly Conduct:
Three male youths were seen egging houses on 16th Avenue between Geary and Clement streets. Neighbors said the boys were egging the houses between 9:00 and 9:30 p.m. on March 11th. Ten houses in total were vandalized.

49. In the burglary incident, what store did the suspects rob?
   (A) Pa's Pet Shop
   (B) Lester's Jewelry Store
   (C) Lina's Book Barn
   (D) Octavio's Paper Supply

50. In the deceptive practices incident, what was Robert Taylor using to get money from the bank?
   (A) Counterfeit bills
   (B) His ATM card
   (C) Fraudulent checks
   (D) Information not given

51. In the disorderly conduct incident, what time of day were the male youths egging houses?
   (A) Morning
   (B) Afternoon
   (C) Evening
   (D) Information not given

ANSWER QUESTIONS 52–54 BASED ON THE FOLLOWING INFORMATION.

There are three field units: A, B, and C. Each unit is selected to cover one or more areas as follows:

Unit A—North and West

Unit B—East

Unit C—South

Rules for assigning units are listed below.

- Units are assigned only to the area(s) in which they are designated, except in the case of emergency calls.

- Units are to be assigned to a call only if they are currently available.

- Every available unit is to be assigned to an emergency call.

Directions: Assign the appropriate field unit or units to each example incident listed. When assigning the unit(s), consider the rules above. On your answer sheet, mark the letters that refer to the corresponding units. If an incident requires more than one unit to be assigned, mark more than one letter on your answer sheet for that item. When no units are to be assigned, mark "D" for no units to be assigned.

52. Area: Southeast
Type of Call: Emergency
Current Assignments:
Unit A: Unavailable
Unit B: Available
Unit C: Available

53. Area: North
Type of Call: Non-Emergency
Current Assignments:
Unit A: Unavailable
Unit B: Unavailable
Unit C: Unavailable

54. Area: West
Type of Call: Emergency
Unit A: Unavailable
Unit B: Unavailable
Unit C: Available

ANSWER QUESTIONS 55–57 BASED ON THE INFORMATION PROVIDED BELOW.

Directions: Read the list of facts and then evaluate the conclusions that follow. Indicate whether the conclusions are true, false, or cannot be determined.

Facts:
All arrests are entered in the criminal database system. Most arrests lead to a criminal or civil charge. Criminal charges receive a red flag in the system.

55. Conclusion: If a suspect is arrested, the suspect will incur a criminal or civil charge.
   (A) It is true based on the facts given.
   (B) It is false based on the facts given.
   (C) On the basis of the facts, it cannot be determined whether the statement is true or false.

56. Conclusion: If an arrest is made on Saturday morning, then the suspect will not be charged and will not be entered in the system.
   (A) It is true based on the facts given.
   (B) It is false based on the facts given.
   (C) On the basis of the facts, it cannot be determined whether the statement is true or false.

57. Conclusion: If a file for a charge against a male suspect is entered, then it should be given a red flag.
   (A) It is true based on the facts given.
   (B) It is false based on the facts given.
   (C) On the basis of the facts, it cannot be determined whether the statement is true or false.

ANSWER QUESTIONS 58–60 BASED ON THE INFORMATION PROVIDED BELOW.

Directions: Read priority codes A, B, and C. Assign priorities to the events listed below.

Events are to be prioritized as follows:

Code A—Highest priority: Events that involve injury or are life threatening.

Code B—Second priority: Events that involve property loss or damage.

Code C—Lowest priority: Other events that do not involve injury, threat to life, or property loss or damage.

58. All four tires of a caller's truck have been slashed.

59. A pedestrian is hit by a car running a red light.

60. A caller reports a dent in a "yield" sign.

Directions: Choose the best answer to each question, and darken its letter on your answer sheet.

61. SHORE means most nearly
(A) gulf.
(B) coast.
(C) inlet.
(D) beach.
(E) edge.

62. AIM means most nearly
(A) bulls-eye.
(B) goal.
(C) duty.
(D) promise.
(E) trajectory.

63. ACUTE means most nearly
(A) dull.
(B) slight.
(C) alarming.
(D) sharp.
(E) charming.

64. COMPEL means most nearly
(A) tempt.
(B) persuade.
(C) force.
(D) disable.
(E) rate.

65. AROMA means most nearly
(A) flavor.
(B) warmth.
(C) fragrance.
(D) steam.
(E) texture.

Directions: Choose the word in each group of four that is spelled correctly and darken its letter on your answer sheet. If no word is spelled correctly, darken (E).

66. (A) unconsiously
(B) pamflet
(C) asess
(D) adjacent
(E) none of these

67. (A) mortgages
(B) infalible
(C) eradecated
(D) sourse
(E) none of these

68. (A) predescessor
(B) obsolete
(C) unimpared
(D) sporadicaly
(E) none of these

69. (A) impenitrable
(B) recognisable
(C) paresite
(D) buisness
(E) none of these

70. (A) accross
(B) manefold
(C) anxieties
(D) expence
(E) none of these

Directions: Compare the names or numbers and darken on your answer sheet the letter

    (A) if ALL THREE names or numbers are exactly ALIKE.

    (B) if only the FIRST and SECOND names or numbers are exactly ALIKE.

    (C) if only the FIRST and THIRD names or numbers are exactly ALIKE.

    (D) if only the SECOND and THIRD names or numbers are exactly ALIKE.

    (E) if ALL THREE names or numbers are DIFFERENT.

71. Desean Louis Green	DeSean Lewis Greene	Desean Louis Green
72. Fernando Silva, Jr.	Fernando Silva, Jr.	Fernand Silva, Jr.
73. PT090901	PT090901	PT1090901
74. 2789327	2879327	2789327
75. 5927681	5927861	5927681

Directions: For questions 76–80, carefully read the rules for use of the community room and the information about the applications that were received on July 1. On the basis of the rules and the facts, determine the disposition of each application. Darken the letter of the answer you choose.

RULES FOR USE OF COMMUNITY ROOM (CR)

Note: Assume that, in order to be granted use of the CR, a tenant group ("TG") must comply fully with all the rules.

Rule 1. The head of the TG must submit a signed application in writing at least 20 days before the date requested.

Rule 2. The application must state the number of persons expected to attend and the general nature, date, and time of the requested use.

Rule 3. Included as part of the application must be a money order in the amount of $25, payable to the housing authority, to help defray the expense of cleanup after the use of the CR.

Rule 4. No TG may have use of the community room for more than 6 consecutive hours. No use will be permitted between 11 p.m. and 8 a.m.

Rule 5. Provided an application is otherwise acceptable, priority will be granted where applications conflict in the following order: senior citizen TGs, youth TGs, civic TGs, social TGs, athletic TGs.

The following applications were received on July 1:

  1. A civic TG's head has sent a signed application, accompanied by a money order for $25, payable to the housing authority, requesting the CR for a political discussion to be attended by 100 people on August 12 from 7 p.m. to 10 p.m.

2. A youth TG's head has sent a signed application, accompanied by his personal check for $25, payable to the housing authority, requesting the CR for a film showing to be attended by 70 people on August 12 from 7:30 p.m. to 11:30 p.m.

3. A senior citizen TG's head has sent a signed application, accompanied by a money order for $25, payable to the housing authority, requesting the CR for a cake sale to be attended by 80 people on July 18 from 2 p.m. to 8:30 p.m.

4. An athletic TG's head has sent a signed application, accompanied by a money order for $25, payable to the housing authority, requesting the CR for a weight-lifting contest to be attended by 50 people on July 31 from 4 p.m. to 7 p.m.

5. A social TG's head has sent a signed application, accompanied by a money order for $25, payable to the housing authority, requesting the CR for a singles' party to be attended by 60 people on July 31 from 2 p.m. to 5 p.m.

76. The first application should be
(A) granted.
(B) denied: it does not comply with Rules 1 and 5.
(C) denied: it does not comply with Rules 2 and 4.
(D) denied: it does not comply with Rule 3.
(E) denied: it does not comply with Rules 1 and 4.

77. The second application should be
(A) granted.
(B) denied: it does not comply with Rules 1 and 2.
(C) denied: it does not comply with Rules 3 and 4.
(D) denied: it does not comply with Rule 5.
(E) denied: it does not comply with Rule 3.

78. The third application should be
(A) granted.
(B) denied: it does not comply with Rules 1 and 4.
(C) denied: it does not comply with Rules 2 and 5.

(D) denied: it does not comply with Rule 3.
(E) denied: it does not comply with Rules 2 and 4.

79. The fourth application should be
(A) granted.
(B) denied: it does not comply with Rules 1 and 3.
(C) denied: it does not comply with Rules 2 and 4.
(D) denied: it does not comply with Rule 5.
(E) denied: it does not comply with Rule 2.

80. The fifth application should be
(A) granted.
(B) denied: it does not comply with Rule 1.
(C) denied: it does not comply with Rules 2 and 5.
(D) denied: it does not comply with Rules 3 and 4.
(E) denied: it does not comply with Rules 1 and 2.

Directions: For questions 81–83, read the rules governing clinic appointments, and make the decisions required by the questions that follow. Darken the letter of each answer you choose.

RULES GOVERNING CLINIC APPOINTMENTS

1. No more than eight appointments should be scheduled for each 3-hour clinic session for each dentist who will be on duty.

2. A new patient's first appointment should allow time for a complete examination by the dentist.

3. Appointments should not be made fewer than four days apart for any patient without the consent of the dentist.

4. Appointments should be made in person or over the telephone whenever possible, so that the patient may give his or her consent while the appointment is being made. If a request for an appointment is made in any other manner, it must contain a statement of the date(s) and term(s) acceptable to the patient in order to be approved. No patient shall be given an appointment to which he or she does not consent.

5. A card stating the place, date, and time of the appointment shall be given to or mailed to the patient on the same day on which the appointment is made.

6. If a patient fails to keep three appointments in a row, his or her case is to be terminated, and no further appointments are to be made for him or her unless a new authorization is received.

81. A patient calls to request an appointment at a clinic session for which 8 patients are scheduled for each dentist who will be on duty. As the appointments receptionist you should

   (A) give the patient the appointment since he or she has already consented to it.

   (B) tell the patient that he or she cannot be given an appointment at that clinic session.

   (C) give the patient an appointment at another session without his or her consent.

   (D) tell the patient to come in without an appointment and hope for a cancellation.

   (E) ask for authorization to make an appointment for the patient.

82. A patient requests that he be given appointments on three successive days. You must deny this request if

   (A) the schedule for each of those days is already partly filled.

   (B) the dentist has treated the patient only once previously.

   (C) the patient has requested the appointments by mail.

   (D) this is a new patient.

   (E) the dentist does not give his or her consent to the appointments.

83. A patient has failed to keep three successive appointments. You should

   (A) send her a card stating the place, date, and time of the next appointment.

   (B) not give her another appointment without a new authorization.

   (C) give her an emergency appointment.

   (D) not give her another appointment unless she appears in person to make the appointment.

   (E) insist upon payment in advance.

Directions: Read the following rules governing pharmacists, and answer questions 84–90 as if you were a pharmacist. Darken the letter of your answer choice.

1. No person shall compound or dispense any drug or a prescription in which any drug is stated in a code name or a name not generally recognized in the pharmaceutical profession; nor shall any ingredient be substituted for another in any prescription.

2. Drugs compounded or dispensed on a written prescription shall bear a label containing the name and place of business of the dispenser, the serial number and date of compounding such prescription, the direction for use, and the name of the practitioner. In the case of barbiturates, the label shall contain in addition the name and address of the patient, and—if such a drug was prescribed for an animal—a statement showing the species of the animal.

3. In addition to any other records required to be kept by this article or by any other law, every prescription when filled shall be kept on file by the pharmacist for at least two (2) years and shall be open to inspection by a representative of the Department of Health or such other agency as is authorized by law. Every prescription for a barbiturate shall be endorsed with the name of the compounder of the prescription and, if refilled, the name of the person compounding the prescription at the time of the refilling, together with the date thereof.

84. In labeling a drug dispensed on a written prescription, you must include

(A) a description of the ingredients.

(B) a statement of the amount of each ingredient.

(C) the name of the practitioner.

(D) the name, address, and telephone number of the pharmacy.

(E) the age of the patient.

85. A regulation that you must keep in mind is that

(A) you must not keep prescriptions on file for a period longer than two years.

(B) if you do not have in stock an ingredient named in a prescription, you may use an equivalent ingredient.

(C) when filling a prescription for a barbiturate, you should sign your name on the label.

(D) you must write the directions for use on the label when filling the prescription for a barbiturate.

(E) code names for drugs must not be disclosed to the public.

86. If you are refilling a prescription for a barbiturate, you should write on the prescription

(A) the name and address of the pharmacy, the date of the refilling, and the species of the animal.

(B) the date of the original filling of the prescription, the name of the person who filled it, and the doctor's name.

(C) the directions for use and the name and address of both doctor and patient.

(D) the date of inspection by the Department of Health.

(E) your name and the date.

87. A patient hands you a prescription for an unfamiliar drug. You should

(A) call the Department of Health.

(B) type onto the label the serial number, date of compounding, directions for use, and doctor's name.

(C) substitute a well-known product.

(D) refuse to fill it.

(E) write down the name and address of the patient.

88. The prescription handed to you orders barbiturates for a dog. The information you type onto the label must include

(A) the directions for use, your name, and the date.

(B) the name, address, and serial number of the dog.

(C) the doctor's name, directions for use, and designation that the patient is a dog.

(D) the names of the doctor, dog, owner, and pharmacist.

(E) the name of the pharmacist, the date of refilling, and the description of dog by breed.

89. If the drug is not a barbiturate, you need not

(A) sign the prescription.

(B) put directions for use on the label.

(C) assign a serial number to the prescription.

(D) fill it precisely as written.

(E) keep the prescription on file.

90. Every prescription label must include

(A) the name of the substance, the date, and the name of the doctor.

(B) the name and address of the pharmacy, the date, and the directions for use.

(C) the name and address of the pharmacist, the serial number of the prescription, and the name of the doctor.

(D) the name and address of the patient, the date, and the directions for use.

(E) the list of ingredients, the name and address of the pharmacy, the date, and the name of the patient.

Directions: Choose the best answer to each question, and darken its letter on your answer sheet.

91. To ACCENTUATE means most nearly to

(A) modify.

(B) hasten.

(C) sustain.

(D) intensify.

92. BANAL means most nearly

(A) commonplace.

(B) tranquil.

(C) original.

(D) indifferent.

93. INCORRIGIBLE means most nearly

(A) intolerable.

(B) retarded.

(C) irreformable.

(D) brazen.

94. NOTORIOUS means most nearly

(A) convicted.

(B) dangerous.

(C) well known.

(D) escaped.

(E) decorated.

95. CREVICE means most nearly

(A) plant.

(B) uneven spot.

(C) crack.

(D) puddle.

(E) shellfish.

Directions: In each group of words, one word may be spelled incorrectly. Choose the word that is spelled incorrectly, and darken its letter on your answer sheet. If no word is spelled incorrectly, darken (E).

96. **(A)** executive
    (B) rainbow
    (C) irigation
    (D) multiply
    (E) none of these

97. **(A)** acquarium
    (B) aerial
    (C) livery
    (D) declaration
    (E) none of these

98. **(A)** final
    (B) foundation
    (C) hardships
    (D) deodorant
    (E) none of these

99. **(A)** salary
    (B) weakly
    (C) swallow
    (D) wilderness
    (E) none of these

100. **(A)** seashore
     (B) picnicking
     (C) chopping
     (D) lipstick
     (E) none of these

Directions: Compare the names or numbers and darken on your answer sheet the letter

  (A) if ALL THREE names or numbers are exactly ALIKE.

  (B) if only the FIRST and SECOND names or numbers are exactly ALIKE.

  (C) if only the FIRST and THIRD names or numbers are exactly ALIKE.

  (D) if only the SECOND and THIRD names or numbers are exactly ALIKE.

  (E) if ALL THREE names or numbers are DIFFERENT.

101. Franklin D. Roosevelt	Franklyn D. Roosevelt	Franklin D. Roosevelt
102. Lambent Forman, M.D.	Lambent Forman, M.D.	Lambent Forman, M.D.
103. Joseph A. Gurreri	Joseph A. Gurreri	Joseph A. Gurreri
104. 4xy932958	4xy939258	4xy932758
105. 9631695	9636195	9631695

Directions: Choose the best answer to each question, and darken its letter on your answer sheet.

106. UNIFORM means most nearly
  (A) increasing.
  (B) unchanging.
  (C) unusual.
  (D) neat.
  (E) ignorant.

107. UNITE means most nearly
  (A) improve.
  (B) serve.
  (C) uphold.
  (D) combine.
  (E) open.

108. GRATITUDE means most nearly
  (A) thankfulness.
  (B) excitement.
  (C) disappointment.
  (D) sympathy.
  (E) politeness.

109. EMBELLISH means most nearly
  (A) exaggerate.
  (B) play down.
  (C) scrutinize.
  (D) facilitate.
  (E) sympathize.

110. ASSEMBLE means most nearly
  (A) examine carefully.
  (B) bring together.
  (C) locate.
  (D) fill.
  (E) make.

Directions: In each group of words, one word may be spelled incorrectly. Choose the word that is spelled incorrectly, and darken its letter on your answer sheet. If no word is spelled incorrectly, darken (E).

111. (A) innate
  (B) cannoneer
  (C) passtime
  (D) auditorium
  (E) none of these

112. (A) hinderance
  (B) offered
  (C) embarrass
  (D) syllabus
  (E) none of these

113. (A) privilege
  (B) pavilion
  (C) underrate
  (D) questionnaire
  (E) none of these

114. (A) dilletante
  (B) liquefy
  (C) physiology
  (D) proscribe
  (E) none of these

115. (A) harass
  (B) vilify
  (C) similar
  (D) superceed
  (E) none of these

Directions: Compare the names or numbers and darken on your answer sheet the letter

    (A) if ALL THREE names or numbers are exactly ALIKE.

    (B) if only the FIRST and SECOND names or numbers are exactly ALIKE.

    (C) if only the FIRST and THIRD names or numbers are exactly ALIKE.

    (D) if only the SECOND and THIRD names or numbers are exactly ALIKE.

    (E) if ALL THREE names or numbers are DIFFERENT.

116.	Sylnette Lynch	Sylnette Lynch	Sylnette Lynch
117.	7370527	7375027	7370537
118.	Zion McKenzie, Jr.	Zion McKenzie, Sr.	Zion MacKenzie, Jr.
119.	2799379	2739779	2799379
120.	J. Randolph Rea	J. Randolph Rea	J. Randolphe Rea

End of Part One

If you finish before time is up, check over your work on this part only.

PART TWO

Total Time: *25 Minutes*

> **Directions:** When you are ready to try this part of the exam, give the following instructions to a friend and have the friend read them aloud to you at 80 words per minute. Do NOT read them to yourself. Your friend will need a watch with a second hand. Listen carefully and do exactly what your friend tells you to do with the worksheet and with the answer sheet. Your friend will tell you some things to do with each item on the worksheet. After each set of instructions, your friend will give you time to mark your answer by darkening a circle on the answer sheet. **Before proceeding further, tear out the worksheet on pages 237–238. Then hand this book to your friend.**

To the Reader: The directions are to be read at the rate of 80 words per minute. Do not read aloud the material that is in parentheses. Once you have begun the test itself, do not repeat any directions. The next three paragraphs consist of approximately 120 words. Read these three paragraphs aloud to the candidate in about one and one-half minutes.

On the job, you will have to listen to directions and then do what you have been told to do. In this test, I will read instructions to you. Try to understand them as I read them; I cannot repeat them. Once we begin, you may not ask any questions until the end of the test.

On the job you won't have to deal with pictures, numbers, and letters like those in the test, but you will have to listen to instructions and follow them. We are using this test to see how well you can follow instructions.

You are to mark your test booklet according to the instructions that I'll read to you. After each set of instructions, I'll give you time to record your answers on the separate answer sheet.

The actual test begins now.

Look at line 1 on your worksheet. (Pause slightly.) Draw a line under the largest number in the line. (Pause 2 seconds.) Now on your answer sheet, find the number under which you just drew a line and darken space "D" as in dog for that number. (Pause 5 seconds.)

Look at line 1 on your worksheet again. (Pause slightly.) Draw two lines under the smallest number in the line. (Pause 2 seconds.) Now on your answer sheet, find the number under which you just drew two lines and darken space "E." (Pause 5 seconds.)

Look at the circles in line 2 on your worksheet. (Pause slightly.) In the second circle, write the answer to this question: How much is 6 plus 4? (Pause 8 seconds.) In the third circle, write the answer to this question: Which of the following numbers is largest: 67, 48, 15, 73, or 61? (Pause 5 seconds.) In the fourth circle, write the answer to this question: How many months are there in a year? (Pause 2 seconds.) Now, on your answer sheet, darken the number-letter combinations that are in the circles in which you wrote. (Pause 10 seconds.)

Look at line 3 on your worksheet. (Pause slightly.) Write the letter "C" on the blank next to the right-hand number. (Pause 2 seconds.) Now on your answer sheet, find the space for the number beside which you wrote and darken space "C." (Pause 5 seconds.)

Now look at line 3 on your worksheet again. (Pause slightly.) Write the letter "B" as in baker on the blank next to the left-hand number. (Pause 2 seconds.) Now on your answer sheet, find the space for the number beside which you just wrote and darken space "B" as in baker. (Pause 5 seconds.)

Look at the boxes and words in line 4 on your worksheet. (Pause slightly.) Write the first letter of the second word in the third box. (Pause 2 seconds.) Write the last letter of the first word in the second box. (Pause 2 seconds.) Write the first letter of the third word in the first box. (Pause 2 seconds.) Now on your answer sheet, darken the space for the number-letter combinations that are in the three boxes in which you just wrote. (Pause 10 seconds.)

Look at the letters on line 5 on your worksheet. (Pause slightly.) Draw a line under the fifth letter on the line. (Pause 2 seconds.) Now on your answer sheet, find the number 56 (pause 2 seconds) and darken the space for the letter under which you drew one line. (Pause 5 seconds.)

Look again at the letters on line 5 on your worksheet. (Pause slightly.) Draw two lines under the fourth letter in the line. (Pause 2 seconds.) Now on your answer sheet, find the number 66 (pause 2 seconds) and darken the space for the letter under which you drew two lines. (Pause 5 seconds.)

Look at the drawings on line 6 on your worksheet. (Pause slightly.) The four boxes indicate the number of buildings in four different office parks. In the box for the office park with the fewest number of buildings, write an "A." (Pause 2 seconds.) Now on your answer sheet, darken the space for the number-letter combination that is in the box in which you just wrote. (Pause 5 seconds.)

Now look at line 7 on your worksheet. (Pause slightly.) If fall comes before summer, write the letter "B" as in baker on the line next to the middle number. (Pause slightly.) Otherwise, write an "E" on the blank next to the left-hand number. (Pause 5 seconds.) Now on your answer sheet, darken the space for the number-letter combination that you have just written. (Pause 5 seconds.)

Now look at line 8 on your worksheet. (Pause slightly.) Write a "D" as in dog in the circle with the lowest number. (Pause 2 seconds.) Now on your answer sheet, darken the space for the number-letter combination that is in the circle in which you just wrote. (Pause 5 seconds.)

Look at the drawings on line 9 on your worksheet. The four boxes are planes for carrying mail. (Pause slightly.) The plane with the highest number is to be loaded first. Write an "E" in the box with the highest number. (Pause 2 seconds.) Now on your answer sheet, darken the space for the number-letter combination that is in the box in which you just wrote. (Pause 5 seconds.)

Look at line 10 on your worksheet. (Pause slightly.) Draw a line under every number that is more than 35 but less than 55. (Pause 12 seconds.) Now on your answer sheet, for each number under which you drew a line, darken space "A." (Pause 25 seconds.)

Now look again at line 10 on your worksheet. (Pause slightly.) Draw two lines under every number that is more than 55 and less than 80. (Pause 12 seconds.) Now on your answer sheet for each number under which you drew two lines, darken space "C." (Pause 25 seconds.)

Look at line 11 on your worksheet. (Pause slightly.) Write an "E" in the last box. (Pause 2 seconds.) Now on your answer sheet, find the number in that box and darken space "E" for that number. (Pause 5 seconds.)

Look at line 12 on your worksheet. (Pause slightly.) Draw a line under every "X" in the line. (Pause 5 seconds.) Count the number of lines that you have drawn, add 3, and write that number at the end of the line. (Pause 5 seconds.) Now on your answer sheet, find that number and darken space "E" for that number. (Pause 5 seconds.)

Look at line 13 on your worksheet. (Pause slightly.) If the number in the right-hand box is larger than the number in the left-hand circle, add 4 to the number in the left-hand circle, and change the number in the circle to this number. (Pause 8 seconds.) Then write "C" next to the new number. (Pause slightly.) Otherwise, write "A" next to the number in the smaller box. (Pause 3 seconds.) Now on your answer sheet, darken the space for the number-letter combination that is in the box or circle in which you just wrote. (Pause 5 seconds.)

Look at line 14 on your worksheet. (Pause slightly.) Draw a line under the middle number on the line. (Pause 2 seconds.) Now on your answer sheet, find the number under which you just drew the line and darken space "D" as in dog for that number. (Pause 5 seconds.)

Look at line 15 on your worksheet. (Pause slightly.) Write a "B" as in baker in the third circle. (Pause 2 seconds.) Now on your answer sheet, find the number in that circle and darken space "B" as in baker for that number. (Pause 5 seconds.)

Now look at line 15 again. (Pause slightly.) Write a "C" in the last circle. (Pause 2 seconds.) Now on your answer sheet, find the number in that circle and darken space "C" for that number. (Pause 5 seconds.)

Look at the drawings on line 16 on your worksheet. The number in each box is the number of employees in an office. (Pause slightly.) In the box for the office with the smallest number of employees, write on the line the last two figures of the number of employees. (Pause 5 seconds.) Now on your answer sheet, darken the space for the number-letter combination that is in the space in which you just wrote. (Pause 5 seconds.)

Now look at line 17 on your worksheet. (Pause slightly.) Write an "A" on the line next to the right-hand number. (Pause 2 seconds.) Now on your answer sheet, find the space for the number next to which you just wrote and darken space "A." (Pause 5 seconds.)

Look at line 18 on your worksheet. (Pause slightly.) In the fourth box, write the answer to this question: How many feet are in a yard? (Pause 2 seconds.) Now on your answer sheet, darken the space for the number-letter combination that is in the space in which you just wrote. (Pause 5 seconds.)

Look at line 18 again. (Pause slightly.) In the second box, write the number 32. (Pause 2 seconds.) Now on your answer sheet, find the number-letter combination that is in the space in which you just wrote. (Pause 5 seconds.)

END OF EXAMINATION

ANSWER KEY AND EXPLANATIONS

Part One

1. C	25. B	49. B	73. B	97. A
2. B	26. C	50. C	74. C	98. D
3. C	27. E	51. C	75. C	99. E
4. D	28. C	52. B and C	76. A	100. E
5. B	29. D	53. D	77. C	101. C
6. C	30. B	54. C	78. B	102. A
7. B	31. C	55. B	79. D	103. A
8. C	32. D	56. B	80. A	104. E
9. E	33. A	57. C	81. B	105. C
10. B	34. A	58. B	82. E	106. B
11. B	35. B	59. A	83. B	107. D
12. D	36. D	60. C	84. C	108. A
13. E	37. D	61. B	85. D	109. A
14. A	38. A	62. B	86. E	110. B
15. E	39. E	63. D	87. D	111. C
16. B	40. C	64. C	88. C	112. A
17. B	41. D	65. C	89. A	113. E
18. A	42. C	66. D	90. B	114. A
19. D	43. B	67. A	91. D	115. D
20. B	44. B	68. B	92. A	116. A
21. B	45. E	69. E	93. C	117. E
22. A	46. B	70. C	94. C	118. E
23. A	47. A	71. C	95. C	119. C
24. B	48. A	72. B	96. C	120. B

Part One

1. **The correct answer is (C).** Flexible means *adjustable* or *pliable*. An office that offers flexible hours may operate from 6 a.m. to 10 p.m.

2. **The correct answer is (B).** An option is a *choice*. When you cast your vote, you are exercising your option.

3. **The correct answer is (C).** To verify is to *check the accuracy of* or to *confirm*. A notary stamp verifies that the signature on the document is the signature of the person named.

4. **The correct answer is (D).** Indolent means *idle* or *lazy*. An indolent person is not likely to become a productive employee.

5. **The correct answer is (B).** Respiration is *breathing*. Respiration is the process by which animals inhale and exhale air.

6. **The correct answer is (C).** The correct spelling is *corrugated*.

7. **The correct answer is (B).** The correct spelling is *accumulation*.

8. **The correct answer is (C).** The correct spelling is *consummation*.

9. **The correct answer is (E).** The correct spelling is *rhetorical*.

10. **The correct answer is (B).** The correct spelling is *height*. This word is one of the few exceptions to the rule: "*I* before *e* except after *c* or when sounded like *ay*." If you do not know the exceptions to the rule, you must memorize them.

11. **The correct answer is (B).** The first two names are exactly alike, but the third name has a different middle initial.

12. **The correct answer is (D).** "Inglese" of the second and third names is different from "Ingles" of the first name.

13. **The correct answer is (E).** Look carefully at the last names: DeAngelis; D'Angelis; DeAngeles.

14. **The correct answer is (A).**

15. **The correct answer is (E).** The first number ends in 342, the second in 432. The first two numbers begin with 263, the third with 236.

16. **The correct answer is (B).** Vigilant means *alert* or *watchful*. A worker must remain vigilant to avoid accidents on the job.

17. **The correct answer is (B).** The term vegetation includes all *plant life*. The jungle is characterized by lush vegetation.

18. **The correct answer is (A).** Marshy means *boggy* or *swampy*. The marshy area around the inlet is a breeding ground for mosquitoes.

19. **The correct answer is (D).** Incidental means *happening in connection with something else* or *casual*. Having the windshield washed is incidental to filling the gas tank and checking the oil.

20. **The correct answer is (B).** A preface is an *introduction*. The preface of the book was very interesting.

21. **The correct answer is (B).** The correct spelling is *facilitate*.

22. **The correct answer is (A).** The correct spelling is *proletarian*.

23. **The correct answer is (A).** The correct spelling is *occasionally*.

24. **The correct answer is (B).** The correct spelling is *essential*.

25. **The correct answer is (B).** The word *omission is* based upon the word *omit*, which contains only one "*m*." The accent

in *omit* falls upon the second syllable, so the final consonant is doubled in adding *-ion.*

26. **The correct answer is (C).** The "Yoshito" of the second name is different from the first and third name. It is missing the middle "ih" of "Yoshihito."

27. **The correct answer is (E).** The "Lockner" of the second name is different from the "Lochner" of the first and third names. The middle initial "W" of the third name is different from the middle initial "V" of the first and second names.

28. **The correct answer is (C).** The "254" of the beginning of the second number is different from the "245" opening of the first and third numbers.

29. **The correct answer is (D).** The "243" ending of the first number is different from the "423" ending of the second and third numbers.

30. **The correct answer is (B).** The "2798" opening of the third number is different from the "2789" opening of the first and second numbers.

31. **The correct answer is (C).** Since manufacturers are assuming risks in attempting to predict what consumers will want, their success depends on the ultimate purchases made by the consumers.

32. **The correct answer is (D).** See the first sentence.

33. **The correct answer is (A).** Time and effort cannot be equated. Efficiency must be measured in terms of results.

34. **The correct answer is (A).** The business of publishing city directories is a private business operated for profit. As such, it is a commercial enterprise.

35. **The correct answer is (B).** The first sentence of the paragraph makes this statement.

36. **The correct answer is (D).** The answer suggested by the paragraph is that "white collar" workers work with their pencils and their minds, rather than with their hands and machines.

37. **The correct answer is (D).** The point of this paragraph is that a business should be prepared to fill unexpected vacancies with pretrained staff members.

38. **The correct answer is (A).** The paragraph presents the problems of fire in fire-resistant buildings. It suggests that the contents of the buildings may burn even though the structural materials themselves do not, and the ensuing fire may even cause the collapse of the buildings. The paragraph does not compare the problem of fire in fire-resistant buildings with that of fire in ordinary buildings.

39. **The correct answer is (E).** When Congressman Johnson suggests that money be spent to "get rid of the drug peddlers," he is suggesting eliminating the source of the drugs.

40. **The correct answer is (C).** The last sentence makes this statement.

41. **The correct answer is (D).** See the second sentence. Choice (E) may appear to say the same thing, but it is a categorical statement that is not supported by the paragraph in an unqualified way.

42. **The correct answer is (C).** The search for truth has speeded the progress of civilization. Choice (B) is incorrect in its statement that "civilization did not begin until ...." Civilization moved ahead slowly even before restrictions on learning were removed.

43. The correct answer is (B). In saying that investigators must devote themselves completely though the work may not be easy, smooth, or peaceful, the paragraph is saying that they must be persistent in the face of difficulty.

44. The correct answer is (B). According to the paragraph, the government can spend only what it obtains from the people. The government obtains money from the people by taxation. If the people are unwilling to pay taxes, the government has no source of funds.

45. The correct answer is (E). Foreign-born adults hold on to their old ways; children adapt to the language, clothing, and mannerisms of their playmates. In other words, the children become Americanized more quickly than their parents.

46. The correct answer is (B). Choice (B) is clear about who calls the police, Annette.

47. The correct answer is (A). The first sentence explains when Officer Lee wrote the police report: after he took a call from a witness. The second sentence is less clear regarding the order in which the events occurred.

48. The correct answer is (A). The first sentence gives more specific and clear information. Patricia is the subject of the first sentence, whereas "she" is the subject of the second, and it is not clear who "she" is. Also, the first sentence describes what the two men broke into—Patricia's apartment building.

49. The correct answer is (B). The incident describes Lester's Jewelry Store as the setting for the burglary. The incident lists the types of jewelry that were reported stolen for further context clues.

50. The correct answer is (C). Robert Taylor cashed fraudulent checks at Bank of America to receive money.

51. The correct answer is (C). According to the incident description, neighbors said the boys were egging houses between 9:00 and 9:30 p.m.

52. The correct answers are (B) and (C). Both South and East units are available for an emergency call, and the incident occurs in their regions. Unit A is unavailable and is not assigned the call.

53. The correct answer is (D). No units need to be assigned because the call is non-emergency and no units are available.

54. The correct answer is (C). Any available unit is to be assigned to an emergency call. Unit C is the only available unit; therefore, it must be assigned the call.

55. The correct answer is (B). The conclusion is false because the facts state that most arrests lead to charges. Some individuals who are arrested might not be charged.

56. The correct answer is (B). The statement is false because the facts state that all arrests, regardless of charge, need to be entered into the system.

57. The correct answer is (C). There is not enough information given about the charge to determine if it needs a red flag. In order to know whether the charge should receive a red flag, we would need to know whether the charge was criminal or civil.

58. The correct answer is (B). The event involves property damage but no injury.

59. The correct answer is (A). The incident describes a potentially life-threatening situation.

answers practice test 2

60. The correct answer is (C). The event describes a situation with neither property damage nor life-threatening injuries.

61. The correct answer is (B). The shore is the *land bordering a body of water,* in other words, the *coast.* The sailors reached the shore in a landing barge.

62. The correct answer is (B). An aim is an *intention* or a *goal.* To aim is to direct toward the goal. The aim of the enlistee was to join the navy.

63. The correct answer is (D). An acute pain is a *sharp* pain. When I lifted the rock, I felt an acute pain in my back.

64. The correct answer is (C). To compel is to *require,* to *coerce,* or to *force.* Compel is a much stronger word than persuade. The law compels all 18-year-old males to register.

65. The correct answer is (C). An aroma is a *pleasing smell* or *fragrance.* I love the aroma of fresh-brewed coffee.

66. The correct answer is (D). Other correct spellings are
(A) unconsciously
(B) pamphlet
(C) assess

67. The correct answer is (A). Other correct spellings are
(B) infallible
(C) eradicated
(D) source

68. The correct answer is (B). Other correct spellings are
(A) predecessor
(C) unimpaired
(D) sporadically

69. The correct answer is (E). Correct spellings are
(A) impenetrable
(B) recognizable
(C) parasite
(D) business

70. The correct answer is (C). Other correct spellings are
(A) across
(B) manifold
(D) expense

71. The correct answer is (C). The second name used a capital "S" in DeSean, Lewis is spelled differently, and an "e" is added to Greene.

72. The correct answer is (B). "Fernand" of the third name is different from "Fernando" of the first and second names.

73. The correct answer is (B). The first and second selections begin with PT190; the third begins with PT109.

74. The correct answer is (C). The "287" beginning of the second number is different from the "278" beginning of the first and third numbers.

75. The correct answer is (C). The "861" ending of the second number is not the same as the "681" ending of the first and third numbers.

76. The correct answer is (A). This application complies with all the rules. It is signed and submitted far more than 20 days before the date requested; includes the proper money order; states purpose, date, time, and expected number of people; and makes a request for permitted hours.

77. The correct answer is (C). The $25 must be submitted by money order; a personal check is not acceptable. The CR must be used only until 11 p.m.; 11:30 is too late.

78. The correct answer is (B). The rules require 20 days' notice; July 18th is not 20 days from July 1. A time stretch from 2 p.m. to 8:30 p.m. is 6-1/2 hours; this is in excess of the permitted 6 consecutive hours.

79. The correct answer is (D). The problem here lies not with the application itself but with a conflict in priorities. You must look not only at the rules but also at the other applications. Application 5 from a social TG asks for the CR during a period of time that overlaps with that of the athletic TG's request. Since social TG's have priority over athletic TG's, the fourth application must be denied.

80. **The correct answer is (A).** This request complies with all the rules.

81. **The correct answer is (B).** Rule 1 allows for no exceptions.

82. **The correct answer is (E).** Rule 3 requires that appointments must be at least four days apart unless the dentist consents otherwise. Appointments on three consecutive days must clearly be denied without the dentist's consent.

83. **The correct answer is (B).** Rule 6 is very clear on this point.

84. **The correct answer is (C).** Rule 2 requires that the name of the practitioner (doctor) appear on every prescription label. The telephone number of the pharmacy is not required, though it generally is preprinted on the labels along with name and address.

85. **The correct answer is (D).** The directions for use must appear on the label for all prescription drugs. The pharmacist's name must be recorded on the prescription for the barbiturate, not on the label. The requirement is that prescriptions must be kept on file for at least two years; there is no limit.

86. **The correct answer is (E).** You must write your own name and the date on the prescription when refilling the prescription for a barbiturate. The date of original filling and the name of that pharmacist should already be on the prescription.

87. **The correct answer is (D).** Rule 1 is clear on this point.

88. **The correct answer is (C).** The doctor's name and directions for use go on all prescription labels. The second part of Rule 2 requires that barbiturates prescribed for a dog must be labeled with that information.

89. **The correct answer is (A).** Only the prescription for barbiturates need be signed by the dispensing pharmacist. The other choices refer to rules that govern all prescriptions.

90. **The correct answer is (B).** Only this choice includes items that must appear on all labels.

91. **The correct answer is (D).** To accentuate is to *stress, emphasize,* or *intensify.* Life is more pleasant when those we deal with accentuate the positive.

92. **The correct answer is (A).** Banal means *insipid* or *commonplace.* His commentary was so banal that I had to stifle many yawns.

93. **The correct answer is (C).** One who is incorrigible *cannot be changed or corrected;* the person is *irreformable.* Incorrigible offenders should be sentenced to prison for life.

94. **The correct answer is (C).** Notorious means *well known,* generally in an unfavorable sense. The face on the poster was that of a notorious bank robber.

95. **The correct answer is (C).** A crevice is a *narrow opening* or *crack.* The climbers caught their axes in several crevices in the rocks.

96. **The correct answer is (C).** The correct spelling is *irrigation.*

97. **The correct answer is (A).** The correct spelling is *aquarium.*

98. **The correct answer is (D).** The correct spelling is *deodorant*.

99. **The correct answer is (E).**

100. **The correct answer is (E).**

101. **The correct answer is (C).** "Franklyn" of the second name is different from "Franklin" of the first and third names.

102. **The correct answer is (A).**

103. **The correct answer is (A).**

104. **The correct answer is (E).** The three numbers end 2958, 9258, and 2758.

105. **The correct answer is (C).** The first and third numbers end 1695; the second ends 6195.

106. **The correct answer is (B).** Uniform means *all the same, consistent,* or *unchanging*. The cyclist pedaled at a uniform rate.

107. **The correct answer is (D).** To unite is to *put together,* to *combine,* or to *join.* At their marriage, two people unite to create a family.

108. **The correct answer is (A).** Gratitude is the *state of being grateful* or *thankfulness.* In gratitude for his good health, he made a donation to his church.

109. **The correct answer is (A).** Embellish means to *exaggerate.* She embellished the truth when she told him how much money she earned.

110. **The correct answer is (B).** To assemble is to *congregate,* to *convene,* or to *bring together.* During a fire drill, we assemble the whole school on the front lawn.

111. **The correct answer is (C).** The correct spelling is *pastime*.

112. **The correct answer is (A).** The correct spelling is *hindrance*.

113. **The correct answer is (E).**

114. **The correct answer is (A).** The correct spelling is *dilettante*.

115. **The correct answer is (D).** The correct spelling is *supersede*.

116. **The correct answer is (A).**

117. **The correct answer is (E).** The three numbers end in 0527, 5027, and 0537.

118. **The correct answer is (E).** The second name is Sr., while the first and third names are Jr. The third surname begins with "Mac," while the first and second names begin with "Mc."

119. **The correct answer is (C).** The first and third numbers are identical; the second number differs in a number of digits.

120. **The correct answer is (B).** "Randolphe" in the third name is different from "Randolph" of the first and second names.

Part Two

1. Ⓐ Ⓑ Ⓒ Ⓓ Ⓔ
2. Ⓐ Ⓑ Ⓒ Ⓓ Ⓔ
3. Ⓐ Ⓑ Ⓒ ● Ⓔ
4. Ⓐ Ⓑ Ⓒ Ⓓ ●
5. Ⓐ Ⓑ Ⓒ Ⓓ Ⓔ
6. Ⓐ Ⓑ Ⓒ Ⓓ Ⓔ
7. Ⓐ Ⓑ Ⓒ Ⓓ Ⓔ
8. Ⓐ Ⓑ Ⓒ Ⓓ ●
9. Ⓐ Ⓑ Ⓒ Ⓓ ●
10. ● Ⓑ Ⓒ Ⓓ Ⓔ
11. Ⓐ Ⓑ Ⓒ Ⓓ Ⓔ
12. Ⓐ Ⓑ Ⓒ Ⓓ ●
13. Ⓐ Ⓑ Ⓒ ● Ⓔ
14. Ⓐ Ⓑ Ⓒ Ⓓ Ⓔ
15. Ⓐ ● Ⓒ Ⓓ Ⓔ
16. Ⓐ Ⓑ Ⓒ Ⓓ Ⓔ
17. Ⓐ Ⓑ Ⓒ Ⓓ Ⓔ
18. Ⓐ Ⓑ Ⓒ Ⓓ Ⓔ
19. Ⓐ Ⓑ Ⓒ Ⓓ Ⓔ
20. Ⓐ Ⓑ ● Ⓓ Ⓔ
21. Ⓐ Ⓑ Ⓒ Ⓓ Ⓔ
22. ● Ⓑ Ⓒ Ⓓ Ⓔ
23. Ⓐ Ⓑ Ⓒ Ⓓ Ⓔ
24. Ⓐ Ⓑ Ⓒ Ⓓ Ⓔ
25. Ⓐ Ⓑ Ⓒ Ⓓ Ⓔ
26. Ⓐ Ⓑ Ⓒ Ⓓ Ⓔ
27. Ⓐ Ⓑ Ⓒ Ⓓ Ⓔ
28. Ⓐ Ⓑ Ⓒ Ⓓ Ⓔ
29. Ⓐ Ⓑ ● Ⓓ Ⓔ
30. Ⓐ Ⓑ Ⓒ Ⓓ Ⓔ

31. Ⓐ Ⓑ Ⓒ Ⓓ Ⓔ
32. Ⓐ Ⓑ Ⓒ Ⓓ ●
33. Ⓐ Ⓑ Ⓒ Ⓓ Ⓔ
34. Ⓐ Ⓑ Ⓒ Ⓓ Ⓔ
35. Ⓐ ● Ⓒ Ⓓ Ⓔ
36. Ⓐ Ⓑ Ⓒ ● Ⓔ
37. Ⓐ Ⓑ Ⓒ Ⓓ ●
38. Ⓐ Ⓑ Ⓒ Ⓓ Ⓔ
39. ● Ⓑ Ⓒ Ⓓ Ⓔ
40. ● Ⓑ Ⓒ Ⓓ Ⓔ
41. Ⓐ Ⓑ Ⓒ Ⓓ Ⓔ
42. Ⓐ Ⓑ Ⓒ Ⓓ Ⓔ
43. Ⓐ Ⓑ Ⓒ Ⓓ Ⓔ
44. Ⓐ Ⓑ Ⓒ Ⓓ Ⓔ
45. ● Ⓑ Ⓒ Ⓓ Ⓔ
46. Ⓐ Ⓑ Ⓒ Ⓓ Ⓔ
47. Ⓐ Ⓑ Ⓒ Ⓓ Ⓔ
48. Ⓐ Ⓑ Ⓒ Ⓓ Ⓔ
49. Ⓐ Ⓑ Ⓒ Ⓓ Ⓔ
50. Ⓐ Ⓑ Ⓒ Ⓓ Ⓔ
51. Ⓐ Ⓑ Ⓒ Ⓓ ●
52. ● Ⓑ Ⓒ Ⓓ Ⓔ
53. Ⓐ Ⓑ Ⓒ Ⓓ Ⓔ
54. Ⓐ Ⓑ Ⓒ Ⓓ Ⓔ
55. Ⓐ Ⓑ Ⓒ Ⓓ Ⓔ
56. Ⓐ ● Ⓒ Ⓓ Ⓔ
57. Ⓐ Ⓑ ● Ⓓ Ⓔ
58. Ⓐ Ⓑ Ⓒ Ⓓ Ⓔ
59. Ⓐ Ⓑ Ⓒ Ⓓ Ⓔ
60. Ⓐ Ⓑ Ⓒ Ⓓ Ⓔ

61. Ⓐ Ⓑ Ⓒ Ⓓ Ⓔ
62. Ⓐ Ⓑ Ⓒ ● Ⓔ
63. Ⓐ Ⓑ Ⓒ Ⓓ Ⓔ
64. Ⓐ Ⓑ Ⓒ Ⓓ Ⓔ
65. Ⓐ Ⓑ Ⓒ Ⓓ Ⓔ
66. ● Ⓑ Ⓒ Ⓓ Ⓔ
67. Ⓐ Ⓑ Ⓒ Ⓓ Ⓔ
68. Ⓐ Ⓑ Ⓒ Ⓓ Ⓔ
69. Ⓐ Ⓑ Ⓒ ● Ⓔ
70. Ⓐ Ⓑ Ⓒ Ⓓ Ⓔ
71. Ⓐ Ⓑ Ⓒ Ⓓ Ⓔ
72. Ⓐ Ⓑ Ⓒ Ⓓ Ⓔ
73. Ⓐ Ⓑ Ⓒ ● Ⓔ
74. Ⓐ Ⓑ Ⓒ Ⓓ ●
75. Ⓐ Ⓑ ● Ⓓ Ⓔ
76. Ⓐ ● Ⓒ Ⓓ Ⓔ
77. Ⓐ Ⓑ Ⓒ Ⓓ Ⓔ
78. Ⓐ Ⓑ Ⓒ Ⓓ Ⓔ
79. Ⓐ Ⓑ Ⓒ Ⓓ Ⓔ
80. Ⓐ Ⓑ Ⓒ Ⓓ Ⓔ
81. Ⓐ Ⓑ Ⓒ Ⓓ Ⓔ
82. Ⓐ Ⓑ Ⓒ Ⓓ Ⓔ
83. Ⓐ ● Ⓒ Ⓓ Ⓔ
84. Ⓐ Ⓑ Ⓒ Ⓓ Ⓔ
85. Ⓐ Ⓑ Ⓒ Ⓓ Ⓔ
86. Ⓐ Ⓑ Ⓒ Ⓓ Ⓔ
87. Ⓐ Ⓑ Ⓒ Ⓓ Ⓔ
88. Ⓐ Ⓑ Ⓒ Ⓓ Ⓔ
89. Ⓐ Ⓑ Ⓒ Ⓓ Ⓔ

Part Two

1. 59   35   <u>62</u>   58   <u style="border-bottom: double">8</u>

2. (__ C) (<u>10</u> A) (<u>73</u> D) (<u>12</u> E) (__ B)

3. 15 _____*B*_____   20 _____*C*_____

4. [83 <u>*B*</u>]   [37 <u>*E*</u>]   [36 <u>*D*</u>]   CURE   DAMP   BEAR

5. A   C   B   <u>A</u>   <u>B</u>   D   C   E   D

6. [48 __]   [28 __]   [22 <u>*A*</u>]   [43 __]

7. 51 _____*E*_____   69 _____   50 _____

8. (65 __) (13 <u>*D*</u>) (87 __) (31 __) (17 __)

9. [55 __]   [44 __]   [74 *E*]   [25 __]

10. <u>40</u>   85   17   87   <u>52</u>   55   80   <u>45</u>   <u style="border-bottom: double">75</u>

11. [65 __]   [37 __]   [12 __]   [4 *E*]

12. <u>X</u> O O O <u>X</u> O O <u>X</u> <u>X</u> O <u>X</u> O <u>X</u>   9

13.

78 ___   25 29 C   27 ___   73 ___

14. 88   2   <u>69</u>   84   34

15.

63 ___   38 ___   76 *B*   53 ___   57 *C*

16.

| 435 <u>35</u> B | 466 ___ C | 474 ___ E | 467 ___ A | 489 ___ D |

17. 79 _____   39 ___ *A* ___

18.

| ___ C | <u>32</u> E | ___ A | <u>3</u> D | ___ B |

PART V

APPENDIXES

Career Information Resources

Finding a job is very often a combination of luck, direction, and skill. Sometimes, it seems as though you simply stumble upon an opening that seems perfect for you; other times, you'll find that you need to conduct a great deal of research to find what you're interested in.

If you want to become a public safety dispatcher, you may not know where to look for the type of openings that will likely yield success. The best places to start your search for dispatcher opportunities are your local police and fire departments. The following tips will help you make the most of your time and effort as you seek information about public safety dispatcher/911 operator positions.

HOW TO GET A GOVERNMENT JOB

The procedure for seeking a government job varies little from one position to another or from one level of government to another. There are variations in details, of course, but certain steps are common to all. Let's review them here.

The Notice of Examination or Announcement

A Notice of Examination, often called an announcement, will be posted for each government position. Once you find what you're looking for, read it very carefully. Make a copy for yourself if you can; if not, take detailed notes and be sure you've made a note of every detail listed. Each Notice of Examination provides a brief job description, including the title of the job and a description of the basic duties and responsibilities of the position. Based on this description, you can decide whether you want to apply.

If the job appeals to you, concentrate on the following aspects of the Notice of Examination:

- **Education and experience requirements.** If you cannot meet these requirements, do not apply. Government service can be very competitive. The government receives thousands of job applications, and it will not waive requirements for you.
- **Age requirements.** Discrimination based on age is illegal. However, certain types of work demand a great deal of sustained physical effort. These positions carry an entry age limit. If you are already beyond that age, do not apply. If you are too young to qualify but are still interested, ask about the average time span between applying and hiring. It's possible that you may reach the minimum age by the time the position will be filled.
- **Citizenship requirements.** Many government jobs are open to anyone eligible to work in the United States, but all law enforcement jobs and most federal jobs are open only to U.S. citizens. If you are well along in the process of becoming a U.S. citizen and you expect to be naturalized soon, you should ask about your exact status with respect to the job.
- **Residency requirements.** If a Notice of Examination mentions a residency requirement, you must live within the prescribed limits or be willing to move

to that area. If you are not willing to live in the area defined on the notice, do not bother to apply for the position.

- **Required forms.** The announcement of the position for which you are applying will specify the form of application you're required to submit. For most federal jobs, you may be required to submit a resume. For other than federal jobs, the Notice of Examination may tell you where you must go or whom you need to contact to get the necessary paperwork. Make sure you get everything you need. The application might be a simple form that asks for nothing more than name, address, citizenship, and Social Security number, or it may be a more complex form, such as an Experience Paper. As the name implies, an Experience Paper requires extensive information about your education, job training and experience, and life experiences. Typically, an Experience Paper does not ask for identification by name, gender, or race; the only identifying mark is your Social Security number. This is done to avoid bias of any sort to enter into the weighting of responses. The Experience Paper generally follows a short form of application that requires your name. When the rating process is completed, the two forms are matched by Social Security number.

- **Filing date, place, and fee.** There is great variation in this area. Some openings allow you to file your application at any time; others state a specific filing period or deadline. For the latter, filing too early or too late disqualifies your application. If you are completing an online application, be sure to check the deadline dates as well. You may also have to pay an application fee for an online submission.

- **How to qualify.** This portion of the notice explains the basis on which a candidate will be chosen. There are two types of qualifying scores. Some scores are the result of the total of weighted education and experience factors. This is called an "unassembled exam" score because candidates for the position do not assemble in one place to take a qualifying test. Instead, the score is based on your responses on the application and supplementary forms. (Obviously, though, to receive full credit for your education, experience, and accomplishments, you must fill out these forms completely.) A Notice of Examination may state that a qualifying exam is necessary in addition to an unassembled, written, or performance test. Alternatively, the notice may inform you of a competitive exam that consists of a written, performance, or combined test. Depending on the notice, the competitive exam may be described in very general terms or in great detail; in some cases, a few sample questions are included. If the date of the assembled exam has been set, that date will appear on the notice. Make sure you write it down.

Once you have the proper application forms, review the questions and write or type out practice answers before submitting the application. This way, you can correct mistakes or make changes before you submit your final form. Do your best to fit what you have to say into the space allowed. Do not exaggerate, but be sure to give yourself credit for responsibilities you have assumed, for cost-saving ideas you may have devised for a previous employer, or for any other accomplishments. Be clear and thorough in communicating what you have learned and what you can do.

When you are satisfied with your draft, copy the application onto the original form(s). Be sure to include any required documentation. However, do not send more "evidence" than is truly needed to support your claims of qualification. Your application must be complete according to the requirements of the announcement, but it should not be overwhelming. You want to command attention by conforming to requirements, not by overdoing it.

Check all forms for neatness and completeness, and sign wherever indicated. Submit the fee, if required.

When the civil service commission or personnel office to which you submitted your application receives it, an official will date, stamp, log, and open your file. The office may acknowledge receipt with more forms, with sample exam questions, or with a simple notice of receipt. It's not uncommon, however, to hear nothing at all for months.

Eventually, you will receive a testing date or an interview appointment. Write or type these dates on your calendar so that you do not let them slip by. If you receive an admission ticket for an exam, put it in a safe place but keep it in sight so that you don't forget to take it with you to the exam. Begin studying and preparing immediately, if you have not already done so.

If you are called for an exam, arrive promptly and dress appropriately. Neatness is always appropriate; however, you need not "dress up" for a performance or written exam. If you will do manual work for your performance exam, wear clean work clothes. For a written exam, neat, casual clothing will do.

PUBLIC SAFETY DISPATCHER JOBS

The nation's public safety communications centers have been facing staffing shortages. These shortages are the direct result of an overall increase in number of positions, competition with the part of private-sector employment that offers similar but higher-paying jobs, and a large turnover rate for existing employees. As a result, nearly every communications center in the United States is seeking qualified candidates who may not have relevant experience but who can be trained to perform the job. Of course, having prior public contact or public safety experience makes you a more attractive candidate, but most agencies hire dispatchers at entry-level positions, for which only a high school diploma and a clean background check are required.

So where do you start your search for public safety dispatcher openings? Here are some tips:

1. **Find your local dispatch center**. Check a phone directory for the phone number of your local police department. (If your city or town is small, it may not have its own police department, so look for the nearest sheriff's department instead.)

2. **Speak with someone on the job.** Call the non-emergency phone number at the local police or sheriff's department and ask to speak with the dispatch or communications supervisor. (In some areas, this person may be a sergeant or lieutenant.) If he or she is unavailable, ask to speak with a senior dispatcher.

3. **Get all the details you need.** Once you have the appropriate person on the phone, explain politely that you're interested in becoming a dispatcher and would like information. Here are some "starter" questions:

   a. Are you presently hiring? If not, when do you expect to be doing so?

   b. What are the requirements in your department for becoming a dispatcher?

   c. Is a typing certificate required? If so, where can I get one? (Some agencies will accept typing certificates only from certain certifying companies.)

   d. Are training courses available for preparing to become a dispatcher? If so, where can I find them?

   e. Does your agency allow people who are interested in being dispatchers to observe workers on the job? If so, how can I arrange to do so?

JOB REQUIREMENTS FOR PUBLIC SAFETY DISPATCHERS

Many states hold dispatchers to the same hiring standards as law officers—and every city, county, and state has different policies. For this reason, try to be as flexible as you can about meeting specific requirements.

Any or all of the following may be required of applicants seeking public safety dispatcher positions:

- an exam (may be written, computerized, or oral)
- an interview (typically with a panel of officials)
- a medical exam
- a psychological exam
- a polygraph test
- a background investigation
- an interview with the communications manager, police chief, or sheriff

Public Safety Dispatcher Job Resources

- Job listings are posted on the websites of the following organizations: National Emergency Number Association (www.nena.org); Association of Public-Safety Communications Officials (www.apcointl.org); *9-1-1 Magazine* (www.9-1-1magazine. com); *DISPATCH Magazine On-line* (www.911dispatch.com); and Jobs in 911 (www. jobsin911.com).

- The *Occupational Outlook Handbook,* published by the Bureau of Labor Statistics (BLS), posts an annual analysis of job availability. This and other useful information can be viewed online at http://stats.bls.gov/ooh (http://stats.bls.gov/oco/ocos138.htm for information specific to public safety dispatchers). For current pay rates, check the Bureau of Labor Statistics' Occupational Employment Statistics page at www. bls.gov/oes. Search on this page for the phrase "public safety dispatchers" to find the latest salary and job outlook information.

- Enter the search term "public safety dispatcher" into your favorite search engine to find hundreds of sites with information on agency job descriptions and job openings in the field.

- The O*NET OnLine website (http://online.onetcenter.org) has occupational information about dispatching, including an interesting list of skills, abilities, and other requirements, at online.onetcenter.org/link/summary/43-5031.00.

- *DISPATCH Magazine On-line* (www.911dispatch.com) provides facts and figures about public safety dispatchers as well as current job listings.

- The *Journal of Emergency Medical Services (JEMS)*, online at www.jems.com, lists current salary surveys that include call taker and radio dispatcher positions, as well as job listings.

- Check the website www.payscale.com for median pay information for public safety dispatchers.

Federal Positions

For federal jobs, start your search with the Office of Personnel Management (OPM). The OPM updates its list of job openings daily. Although it is not responsible for hiring employees, the OPM provides access to each hiring agency in the federal government. From the hiring agencies, you can acquire specific details about each open position. On the OPM website, www.opm.gov, click on "Job Seekers" on the left side of the page.

You can also access thousands of federal job announcements directly by checking out the official job website of the U.S. Federal Government: www.usajobs.gov. The site allows you to search for positions by agency, location, occupation, keyword, title, series number, salary range, and many other specifications. You can find out how federal jobs get filled, learn more about federal hiring processes, and get tips on building your resume, interviewing successfully, and answering a posted position's Knowledge, Skills, and Abilities (KSA) requirements. If you create a free account on the website, you can post your resume online, apply for jobs electronically, and receive automated job alerts for updated listings. USAJOBS also provides a wealth of information on special opportunities available to military veterans, students, disabled persons, and senior workers, as well as job opportunities with international organizations.

Another excellent source of job information is the *Federal Jobs Digest*, a biweekly newspaper that lists thousands of government jobs in the United States and in foreign countries. The newspaper's companion website, www.jobsfed.com, also features thousands of job listings at any one time. The site also offers searches by occupation and state and allows you to set up an "automated search" using location, salary range, occupation, and keywords.

You might also look under "U.S. Government" in the blue pages of your local telephone directory to find the nearest Office of Personnel Management or Federal Job Information Center. By calling this number you may receive automated information pertinent to your own area, or you may be directed to a center where you can get printed materials or conduct a search using a computer touch screen.

State Positions

Every state has its own official website. In most cases, you can reach these sites quickly by using either the naming convention www.state.__.us or www. __.gov, with the two-letter postal code of the state or the state name in place of the blank. For example, if you want to search for job openings with the state of Arizona, you type "www.state.az.us." If you're looking for job openings with the state of Oregon, you type "www.oregon.gov." Note that a few state websites, such as Florida's and Washington's, deviate from this convention.

The following is a list of current web addresses for each state's official site. Keep in mind that these addresses occasionally change and that this may have occurred after this book went to press.

- **Alabama**: www.al.gov
- **Alaska**: www.alaska.gov
- **Arizona**: www.az.gov
- **Arkansas**: www.arkansas.gov
- **California**: www.ca.gov
- **Colorado**: www.colorado.gov
- **Connecticut**: www.ct.gov
- **Delaware**: www.delaware.gov
- **District of Columbia**: www.dc.gov
- **Florida**: www.myflorida.gov
- **Georgia**: www.georgia.gov
- **Hawaii**: www.hawaii.gov
- **Idaho**: www.idaho.gov
- **Illinois**: www.illinois.gov
- **Indiana**: www.in.gov
- **Iowa**: www.iowa.gov
- **Kansas**: www.kansas.gov
- **Kentucky**: www.kentucky.gov
- **Louisiana**: www.louisiana.gov
- **Maine**: www.maine.gov
- **Maryland**: www.maryland.gov
- **Massachusetts**: www.mass.gov
- **Michigan**: www.michigan.gov
- **Minnesota**: www.mn.gov
- **Mississippi**: www.ms.gov
- **Missouri**: www.mo.gov
- **Montana**: www.mt.gov
- **Nebraska**: www.ne.gov
- **Nevada**: www.nv.gov
- **New Hampshire**: www.nh.gov
- **New Jersey**: www.nj.gov
- **New Mexico**: www.newmexico.gov
- **New York**: www.ny.gov
- **North Carolina**: www.ncgov.com
- **North Dakota**: www.nd.gov
- **Ohio**: www.ohio.gov
- **Oklahoma**: www.ok.gov
- **Oregon**: www.oregon.gov
- **Pennsylvania**: www.pa.gov
- **Rhode Island**: www.ri.gov
- **South Carolina**: www.sc.gov
- **South Dakota**: www.sd.gov
- **Tennessee**: www.tn.gov
- **Texas**: www.texas.gov
- **Utah**: www.utah.gov
- **Vermont**: www.vermont.gov
- **Virginia**: www.virginia.gov
- **Washington**: www.access.wa.gov
- **West Virginia**: www.wv.gov
- **Wisconsin**: www.wi.gov
- **Wyoming**: www.wyo.gov

Local Positions

Browse your state's website for city and county job openings. If you live in a metropolitan area, your city may have its own website. Use a popular search engine such as Google. com, Yahoo! Search, or Ask.com to locate other job-related sites. Using search terms such as *jobs, employment, labor, business, help wanted*, and so on and then adding to the term your specific city or state will give you an extensive number of suggested sites. For example, you might enter *"public safety dispatcher" Miami* to find positions available in Miami, Florida.

Be sure to investigate whether your city has a civil service publication that lists upcoming job announcements. In New York City, for example, *The Chief-Leader* is the primary source for learning about the most recent openings for civil service positions. (You can access this publication at www.thechief-leader.com.) You can also find information about state and federal jobs in local newspapers (online and in print) in the Help Wanted section.

The Private Sector

Although public safety dispatcher/911 operator positions do exist in the private sector, you are less likely to find openings because the demand for such work is lower than that of government agencies. However, if you already have experience as a public safety dispatcher/911 operator and want a career change, or you are seeking a job that requires similar skills, your experience will be invaluable in a private-sector job search. After all, what employer wouldn't want to hire a person with experience in handling the day-to-day, moment-to-moment pressure that comes with being a public safety dispatcher?

If you're certain that you want to work in the private sector, consider some of these related jobs:

- **Private ambulance service dispatchers** perform duties that are very similar to those of public safety dispatchers and 911 operators. They relay requests for patient transports to Emergency Medical Technicians (EMTs), handle multiple phone lines, take and route messages, map directions, handle paperwork efficiently and accurately, and have a broad knowledge of medical forms, documents, and procedures. Some of these positions require that candidates have EMT or Emergency Medical Dispatch (EMD) certification.

- **Truck dispatchers** work for local and long-distance trucking companies. They coordinate the movement of trucks and freight between cities, direct pickup and delivery activities of drivers, receive customer requests for freight pickup and delivery, consolidate freight orders into truckloads for specific destinations, assign drivers and trucks, and draw up routes and pickup and delivery schedules.

- **Bus dispatchers** ensure that local and long-distance buses stay on schedule. They handle problems that may disrupt service, and they dispatch other buses or arrange for repairs to restore service and schedules.

- **Train dispatchers** ensure the timely and efficient movement of trains according to orders and schedules. They must be aware of track switch positions, track maintenance areas, and the location of other trains running on the track.

- **Taxicab dispatchers**, or "starters," dispatch taxis in response to requests for service, and they maintain logs on all road service calls.

- **Tow-truck dispatchers** take calls for emergency road service. They relay the nature of the problem to a nearby service station or a tow-truck service and see that the road service is completed.

- **Gas and water service dispatchers** monitor gas lines and water mains, and they send out service trucks and crews to handle emergencies.

All of these are real possibilities for individuals accustomed to communicating with others and managing high-pressure situations.

Employment agencies and job postings are the two most common ways of finding positions in the private sector. Find a local agency and make an appointment to speak with someone about the position you're seeking. Bring two or three copies of your resume with you. Remember that the employment counselor is the first interview of your job search, so dress appropriately and be sure you've prepared for the interview by studying the types of jobs in which you're interested.

Another widely used method of searching for a job is to check postings in print and online newspapers and on career-search websites. In some cases, you'll be directed to an employment agency to apply for a position. In other cases, you'll be able to apply directly with the company offering the position, and it's likely that you'll be able to submit your resume electronically at the same time. Remember that your phone call, cover letter, and resume make an important first impression on those who do the hiring—so be sure that you communicate in a professional manner at all times.

The following list of career-oriented websites is just a sampling of the many job-search resources available online:

- www.careerbuilder.com
- www.simplyhired.com
- www.monster.com
- www.jobsearchusa.com
- www.jobsonline.net
- www.indeed.com
- www.vault.com
- www.wetfeet.com

MASTERING THE INTERVIEW

If you do not need to take an exam and you are called directly to an interview for a public safety dispatcher position, what you wear is very important. Take special care to present a businesslike and professional appearance. A neat and modest dress, slacks and a blouse, or a skirted suit is fine for women; men should wear a suit or slacks, a jacket, and a dress shirt and tie.

If you are contacted for an interview, you are most likely under serious consideration for the position. This doesn't mean that no competition exists for the job—but you are clearly qualified, and your skills and background have appealed to someone in the hiring office. The purpose of the interview is probably to gather information about the following:

- **Your knowledge.** The interviewer wants to know what you know about the area in which you will work. You may be asked questions that probe your knowledge of the agency for which you are interviewing. Make sure you've done your "homework" and educate yourself about the functions and role of the agency.

- **Your judgment.** You may be faced with hypothetical situations (job-related or personal). The interviewer(s) may pose questions that begin with the phrase "What would you do if . . . ?" Think carefully before answering. Be decisive and diplomatic when you reply. There are no "right answers," and the interviewer is aware that you are being put on the spot. How well you handle this type of questioning will indicate how flexible and mature you are.

- **Your personality.** If you are offered the job, you will have to be trained and supervised, and you will be working closely with others. What is your general work attitude? How well do you fit in? The interviewer will make judgments in these areas based on general conversation with you and on your responses to specific lines of questioning. Be pleasant, polite, and open in your responses, but do not volunteer a great deal of extra information. Stick to the subjects introduced by the interviewer. Answer fully, but resist the temptation to ramble.

- **Your attitude toward work conditions.** This is a practical concern. If the job requires frequent travel for extended periods, how do you feel about travel? What is your family's attitude toward your being away from home frequently? The interviewer wants to assess whether you'll be unhappy enough about extensive travel to quit the job—in which case your training will have been a waste of time and money. The interviewer also wants to know how you will react to the prospect of working overtime or irregular shifts.

WHAT TO EXPECT ON THE MEDICAL EXAMINATION

A medical exam is self-explanatory. If there are eyesight or hearing requirements for the position, your eyesight and hearing must be checked against agency standards. If the job requires standing, lifting, or running, you must be medically able to perform all of these activities. Because all government employers afford some sort of health coverage, the hiring agency must be assured of the general health of each employee, or at least have full awareness of current or potential health problems. Drug testing is often included in the medical exam. This is legal if applied routinely and equally to all applicants, and if notice is given to applicants beforehand.

The Physical Examination

Physical performance testing is limited to applicants for physically demanding jobs. Police officers, firefighters, and correction officers, for example, must be able to run, climb, and carry, often under the pressure of personal danger and of the immediate situation. Mail handlers and sanitation workers must be able to lift and carry heavy loads, one after the other. Usually, the physical performance test is a qualifying test—either you can complete it successfully or you cannot. If speed is a crucial aspect of a job, the physical test may be competitively scored and entered into the rating the candidate earns for placement on the certification list.

The Psychological Interview

For a public safety dispatcher/911 operator position, you will undergo a psychological interview. This interview differs from the general information interview or the final hiring and placement interview in that the aim is to evaluate your behavior under stress.

Not all applicants for government jobs are subjected to a psychological interview. It is typically limited to individuals who must carry a weapon, make quick decisions in dangerous situations, or who may find themselves under interrogation by hostile forces. This includes police officers, firefighters, CIA agents, and Drug Enforcement Agency agents, to name a few. This type of position requires that you perform your job without "cracking" emotionally under the strain. Although public safety dispatchers work in far safer conditions, the stressful environment associated with the job usually warrants a psychological interview or test for prospective candidates.

A REWARD FOR PATIENCE

The government hiring process can be lengthy. Officials sort through hundreds of applications to eliminate unqualified applicants. They must weigh education and experience factors of prospective applicants, administer and score exams, conduct interviews, evaluate medical exams and physical performance tests, and verify applicants' references. And after all of this, the government agency must have the funds to fill vacancies. Going through a government job-seeking process may take up to eighteen months from the time you apply until you are hired.

This is the main reason why you should carefully consider whether you want to leave a job that you already have before you receive a formal offer to work as a public safety dispatcher/911 operator. Likewise, don't abandon your search for a government job simply because you've grown tired of waiting to hear about a position. Do not become discouraged by the long process. When you do receive that job offer, the door will open to a good income, many benefits, and great job security.

Public Safety Dispatcher Glossary

ACD: Automatic Call Distributor.

ALI: Automatic Location Identification. In E-911 systems, the caller's billing address is displayed on a screen or console. If the phone number is included, it is called **ANI-ALI**.

ALS: Advanced Life Support.

ANI: Automatic Number Identification. In E-911 systems, the caller's telephone number is displayed on a screen or console. If the address is also included, it is called ANI-**ALI**.

ATF: Shortened acronym denoting the Bureau of Alcohol, Tobacco, Firearms and Explosives, a division of the U.S. Department of Justice. The ATF's mission is to protect communities from violent criminals, criminal organizations, the illegal use and trafficking of firearms, the illegal use and storage of explosives, acts of arson and bombings, acts of terrorism, and the illegal diversion of alcohol and tobacco products.

CAD: Computer Aided Dispatch, a computer system that enables public safety dispatchers to manage 911 calls. The system locates the addresses of 911 callers, maintains status on units available, relays information to officers, and provides various reports.

Call Check: An instant playback recorder used by dispatchers to verify information they receive during calls for assistance. There are two types of call checks: tape and digital memory.

CAP: Civil Air Patrol, also known as the U.S. Air Force Auxiliary. CAP consists of volunteers—some with their own aircraft—who assist in locating downed aircraft and rescuing occupants of the aircraft.

Comm Center: Communications Center.

Consolidated Comm Center: A Communications Center that includes fire, EMS, and/or police all together.

CPS: Child Protective Services, a division of **DSHS** charged with investigating the abuse of minors. CPS places children in foster homes when no parent or guardian is available to care for them.

CTCSS: Continuous Tone Coded Squelch System. Used in public safety radio communications to filter out other users when more than one group is using the same channel.

DEM: Department of Emergency Management or Division of Emergency Management. The part of a city, town, or county government that coordinates disaster planning and resources.

DES: Department of Emergency Services. The part of a city, town, or county government that coordinates disaster planning and resources.

DHS: U.S. Department of Homeland Security, an agency of the U.S. government charged with preventing and deterring terrorist attacks and protecting against and responding to threats and hazards to the nation.

DLS: Dispatch Life Support, the provision of life-supporting advice and directions by telephone to a layperson awaiting the arrival of emergency responders to an out-of-hospital emergency.

DOE: The U.S. Department of Energy, an agency of the U.S. Government charged with overseeing the operation of nuclear reactor facilities and securing radioactive and weapons-grade materials such as plutonium.

DOT: The U.S. Department of Transportation, an agency of the U.S. Government charged with ensuring safe and efficient transportation systems to meet national interests. Agencies that operate under DOT include the Federal Aviation Administration (**FAA**), the National Highway Traffic Safety Administration (**NHTSA**), and the Federal Highway Administration (**FHWA**). Each state also has its own department of transportation, which maintains interstate highways and marine highways. These agencies' responsibilities vary by state.

DSHS: Department of Social and Health Services (in some states called the Department of Health and Human Services or the Department of Public Health and Human Services). A state department responsible for public services such as emergency medical assistance, child protective service, welfare, radiation control, and public health.

EMD: Emergency Medical Dispatch, a practice in which dispatchers provide medical information and instructions by phone to civilians before first responders arrive at the scene of an accident or disaster.

EMS: Emergency Medical Services, a term used to describe a branch of emergency services dedicated to providing out-of-hospital acute medical care and/or transport to definitive care to patients who have an illness or injury that the patient or medical practitioner believes constitutes a medical emergency. EMS may also be known locally as a first aid squad, an emergency or rescue squad, an ambulance squad or corps, or a life squad.

EMT: Emergency Medical Technician. An EMT is an emergency responder trained to provide immediate care for sick or injured people and to transport them to medical facilities.

EMT-P: An **EMT** with paramedic certification.

EOC: Emergency Operations Center, a central command and control facility responsible for carrying out the principles of emergency preparedness and emergency management or disaster management functions at a strategic level in an emergency situation. The EOC ensures the continuity of operation of a company, political subdivision, or other organization.

FAA: Federal Aviation Administration, a division of the U.S. Department of Transportation (**DOT**) charged with providing the safest, most efficient aerospace system possible.

FBI: Federal Bureau of Investigation, a division of the U.S. Department of Justice responsible for investigating federal crimes. The FBI also operates the National Crime Information Center (**NCIC**), which maintains histories of criminals.

FEMA: Federal Emergency Management Agency. An agency of the U.S. Department of Homeland Security (**DHS**) that coordinates nationwide communications, resources, and training for disasters. FEMA also operates the National Fire Academy of the U.S. Fire Administration (**USFA**).

FHWA: The Federal Highway Administration, a division of the U.S. Department of Transportation (**DOT**) that carries out federal highway programs in partnership with state and local agencies to meet the nation's transportation needs.

FPS: Federal Protective Service. A police agency of the U.S. General Services Administration that provides law enforcement and security services to tenants and visitors of all non-military federally owned and leased facilities nationwide.

IACP: International Association of Chiefs of Police.

IAEM: International Association of Emergency Managers.

ICE: U.S. Immigration and Customs Enforcement, an agency of the **DHS.** ICE was established to protect national security and uphold public safety by targeting criminal networks and terrorist organizations seeking to exploit vulnerabilities in the U.S. immigration system, in financial networks, along the nation's borders, and at federal facilities.

IAFC: International Association of Fire Chiefs.

ICS: Incident Command Center.

Logging Recorder: A large reel-to-reel tape recorder with multiple channels used for recording time, date, telephone, and radio traffic. Most tapes for logging recorders can hold 24 hours of data.

MAST: Military Aid to Safety and Traffic. A function of the U.S. Army Aviation Unit, MAST provides helicopter evacuation of injured or sick persons in need of long-distance transportation to a medical facility.

MIS: Management Information System.

Monitor: To listen to a channel before transmitting in an effort to prevent co-channel interference. If receiver is **CTCSS**-equipped, the CTCSS should be disabled so that the user can hear other group exchanges on the channel.

NCIC: National Crime Information Center, a program conducted by the **FBI** consisting of a computerized index of criminal justice information. NCIC is available to federal, state, and local law enforcement and other criminal justice agencies at all times.

NHTSA: National Highway Traffic Safety Administration, a division of the U.S. Department of Transportation (**DOT**) charged with saving lives, preventing injuries, and reducing economic costs that result from road traffic accidents through education, research, the establishment of safety standards, and enforcement activity.

OES: Office of Emergency Services (in some places called the Office of Emergency Management or the Office of Emergency Shelter and Services). The office or department in a city, town, or county that coordinates disaster planning and resources.

Operation Secure. A nationwide communications network of high-frequency radio bands managed by **FEMA**. All state **EOC**s have these radios.

ORI: Originating or issuing agency.

POV: Privately owned vehicle.

PSAP: Public safety answering point; the location where 911 calls are received and dispatched.

REACT: Radio Emergency Action & Coordination Team. A nationwide group of volunteers who monitor citizen band radio channel 9 for emergency communications from motorists who need assistance.

TTD: Telecommunication Device for the Deaf, sometimes called **TTY** (telephone typewriter or teletypewriter), although TTY is also a term used for teletypes in general. An electronic device for text communication via a telephone line, used when one or more of the communicating parties has hearing or speech difficulties.

TTY: See **TTD.**

USFA: U.S. Fire Administration, an entity of the Department of Homeland Security's Federal Emergency Management Agency (**FEMA**). USFA's mission is to foster a solid foundation in prevention, preparedness, and response by providing national leadership to local fire and emergency services.

VoBB: See **VoIP.**

VoIP: Voice over Internet protocol. This is a general term for a family of transmission technologies that deliver voice communications over IP networks, such as the Internet or other packet-switched networks. Other terms that are synonymous with VoIP are IP telephony, Internet telephony, voice over broadband (**VoBB**), broadband telephony, and broadband phone.

400 Frequently Misspelled Words

This list consists of words that have proven troublesome for most test takers and that frequently appear on civil service exam spelling sections. Ask a family member or friend to read this list to you and allow you time to write each word. Then compare your written list with the printed one. Mark with an *X* the words you misspelled and the ones you spelled correctly but guessed on. Now make a list of all the words you marked with an *X*. For each of these words:

1. **Look** at the word carefully.
2. **Pronounce** each syllable clearly.
3. **Picture** the word in your mind.
4. **Write** the word correctly at least three times.

When you feel confident that you have mastered this list, have a friend test you again. Check to see which words you're still having problems spelling. Repeat the study process and see how many you've mastered.

If you are still having trouble with words you are likely to use often, add them to your "spelling devils" list.

A

aberration
abscess
absence
abundance
accessible
accidental
accommodate
accumulation
accurately
achievement
acknowledgment
acquaint
address
adjunct
affectionate
aggravate
aisle
alleged

all right
amateur
amendment
American
ancestor
ancient
anecdote
annoyance
Antarctic
anticipate
apparatus
apparently
arctic
argument
arraignment
arrange
ascertain
asparagus
assessment

assistance
attaché
audience
August
author
available
awkward

B

bankruptcy
barbarian
barren
basically
beautiful
because
beggar
begun
beleaguered
besiege

bewilder
bicycle
breathe
bulletin
bureau
burial

C

cabinet
cafeteria
caffeine
calendar
campaign
capital
capitol
career
ceiling
cemetery
changeable

character
charlatan
chauffeur
chief
chimney
choose
college
column
commitment
committal
committee
community
competitor
confectionery
conscience
conscious
consequence
conquer
consul
continuous
correlation
council
counsel
courageous
criticism
crucial
crystallized
culpable
currency
curtain
customer

D
dairy
deceit
December
decide
deferred
demur
derogatory

descendant
desecrated
desert
desperate
dessert
diary
dictatorship
difficult
dilapidated
diphtheria
disappearance
disappoint
disastrous
disease
dismal
dissatisfied
distinguished
doubt
dying

E
ecstasy
eczema
eight
either
embarrass
eminent
emphasis
emphatically
ephemeral
equipment
essential
exaggerate
exceed
except
exercise
exhaust
exhibition
exhortation
existence

explain
extension
extraordinary

F
familiar
fascinated
February
feudal
fiend
fierce
financier
freight
Friday
friend
forehead
foreign
foreword
forfeit
forward
furniture
further

G
gaseous
gelatin
geography
ghost
gingham
glacier
glandular
gnash
gonorrhea
government
grammar
grandeur
grievous
guarantee
guard
guess
guidance

H
hallelujah
harassed
hearth
heathen
heavily
height
heinous
heretic
heritage
heroes
hieroglyphic
hindrance
hippopotamus
horrify
humorous
hundredth
hygienic
hymn
hypocrisy

I
imaginary
immediate
imminent
impartiality
incongruous
incumbent
independent
indict
inimitable
instantaneous
integrity
intercede
interference
interruption
introduce
irreparably

J

January
jealous
jeopardy
jewelry
journal
judgment
judicial
justice
justification

K

kernel
kindergarten
kiln
kilometer
kilowatt
kitchen
knee
knot
knowledge

L

laboratory
labyrinth
lacquer
leisure
legible
length
lieutenant
lightning
liquidate
literature
loneliness
loose
lose
lovable

M

maintenance

maneuver
marriage
masquerade
materialize
mathematics
matinee
mechanical
medallion
medicine
medieval
memoir
mischievous
misspell
muscle

N

naturally
necessary
negligible
neither
nickel
niece
ninth
noticeable
nucleus

O

obligatory
obsolescence
occasion
occurrence
official
omitted
ordinance
outrageous

P

pamphlet
panicky
parallel

paraphernalia
parliamentary
patient
peculiar
persuade
physician
picnicking
pneumonia
possession
precious
preferred
prejudice
presumptuous
privilege
propaganda
publicity
punctilious
pursuit

Q

quarrel
queue
quiescent
quiet
quite
quotient

R

receipt
recognize
reference
regrettable
rehearsal
relevant
religious
renaissance
repetitious
requirement
resilience

reservoir
resources
restaurant
resurrection
rhetorical
rhythm
ridiculous
routine

S

sacrilegious
scenery
schedule
scissors
secretary
separate
siege
seizure
sophomore
source
sovereign
specialized
specifically
statute
staunch
subversive
succeed
sufficient
surgeon
surgical
surely
stationary
stationery
symmetrical
sympathetic

T

temperamental
temperature
tendency

thorough
through
tomorrow
tragedy
transferred
transient
truculent
Tuesday
typical

U–Z
umbrella
unctuous
undoubtedly
unique
unusual
usage
usual
vacillate
vacuum

valuable
variety
vegetable
veil
vengeance
villain
Wednesday
weight
weird
whether

wholesome
wholly
wield
wouldn't
written
xylophone
yacht
yield
zombie